Black Drama In America
An Anthology

Dr. Darwin T. Turner, 1931–1991

An Anthology Black Drama In America

Second Edition

Edited and with an Introduction by Darwin T. Turner

HOWARD UNIVERSITY PRESS Washington, D. C., 1994

East Baton Rouge Parish Library
Baton Rouge, Louisiana

First published 1971 by Fawcett Publications, Inc., Greenwich, Connecticut

Howard University Press, Washington, D.C., 20017

Copyright © 1994 by Maggie Jean Louis-Turner

All rights reserved

No part of this book may be reproduced or utilized in any form or by any means, electronic or mechanical, including photocopying and recording, or by any information storage and retrieval system, without permission in writing from the publisher. Inquiries should be addressed to Howard University Press, 1240 Randolph Street, N.E., Washington, D.C., 20017.

Manufactured in the United States of America

This book is printed on acid-free paper.

10 9 8 7 6 5 4 3 2 1

Library of Congress Cataloging-in-Publication Data

Black drama in America : an anthology / edited and with an
  introduction by Darwin T. Turner. — 2nd ed.
    p.   cm.
  Includes bibliographical references.
  ISBN 0–88258–062–0 (alk. paper) : $34.95
  1. American drama—Afro-American authors. 2. Afro-
Americans—Drama.   I. Turner, Darwin T., 1931–
PS628.N4B53   1994
812.008′0896073—dc20   92–42322
                                                                        CIP

Cover Illustrations: *Background*—The Howard Players, 1912. *Inset*—The Howard Players, ca. 1949. Both photographs courtesy of the Moorland-Spingarn Research Center, Howard University Archives, Howard University, Washington, D.C.

To the generations of my family:
my continuing past, present, and future

Contents

Foreword ix
Thomas D. Pawley III

Introduction xv
Darwin T. Turner

The Chip Woman's Fortune (1923) 1
    Willis Richardson

Emperor of Haiti (1938; rev. 1963) 19
    Langston Hughes

Our Lan' (1946) 73
    Theodore Ward

Bayou Legend (1946) 147
    Owen Dodson

Take a Giant Step (1953) 225
    Louis Peterson

Trouble in Mind (1955) 291
    Alice Childress

In the Wine Time (1969) 347
   Ed Bullins

Five on the Black Hand Side (1969) 389
   Charlie L. Russell

Great Goodness of Life (A Coon Show) (1970) 441
   Amiri Baraka (LeRoi Jones)

Black Masque: The Passion of Darkie's Bones (1971; rev. 1981) 453
   George Houston Bass

A Soldier's Play (1981) 501
   Charles H. Fuller, Jr.

Ma Rainey's Black Bottom (1984) 553
   August Wilson

Miss Honey's Young'uns (1989) 615
   J. e Franklin

Flyin' West (1992) 667
   Pearl Cleage

Selected Bibliography 725

Foreword

Darwin Turner was a professor of English at North Carolina A & T College when I first met him in Greensboro in 1964 at a party for visiting faculty attending the conference and play festival of the National Association of Dramatic and Speech Arts. Our meeting was casual and perfunctory. My impression was that he was present only because he was head of the division that included drama. The college was experiencing a resurgence of interest in theatre, which I do not recall being present when I last visited the campus during my student days at Virginia State. It hearkened back to the days when Richard B. Harrison (De Lawd of *The Green Pastures*) was a member of the faculty. It was only years later after a sojourn at the University of Michigan and after he had joined the faculty of the Department of English at the University of Iowa that I realized that he had more than a passing interest in theatre—that he was not merely interested in drama as literature.

As chair of Afro-American Studies at Iowa, he sponsored a series of summer institutes focusing on various aspects of African American culture. In the summer of 1974, when the central theme was Afro-American theatre, he assembled a distinguished group of speakers, including Ossie Davis, Ruby Dee, Loften Mitchell, Amiri Baraka, Carlton Molette, Sister Francesca Thompson, Owen Dodson, and others representing a cross section of artists and scholars in the field. It was a momentous occasion that brought together teachers of drama and theatre from all over the country for two to three weeks of intensive study. I participated as a last minute substitute for a speaker who could not attend, somewhat surprised that Dr. Turner knew of my work. The institute was not unlike the one held at the University of California at Santa Barbara in 1968, except that the Iowa institute focused primarily on the history, criticism, and literature of black theatre rather than the production of plays. By then Darwin Turner had published *In a Minor Chord: Three Afro-American Writers and Their Search For Identity, Katharsis, Nathaniel Hawthorne's Scarlet Letter,* and the first edition of the anthology *Black Drama In America,* studies reflecting his diverse critical interests.

A few years later we became colleagues briefly when I returned to the University of Iowa as a visiting professor in the Department of Theatre Arts, an appointment that he strongly endorsed. Two of my courses—History of Black Drama and Theatre and Seminar in Contemporary Black Drama—were cross listed in Afro-American Studies.

It was then that I discovered that he was an advisor to "Black Action Theatre," a black theatre workshop that was producing plays with the full technical support of the Department of Theatre Arts and financial support from the university. The workshop grew out of the student protests of the late 1960s and was presenting the plays of African American playwrights with black directors and actors. One of those workshop participants was Professor Clyde Ruffin, who has since organized similar workshops at Washington University and the University of Missouri at Columbia where he is currently chair of the Department of Theatre.

In 1989, during my tenure as president of the National Conference on African American Theatre, the theme of the annual meeting was "Theatre Criticism By and About African Americans." Dr. Turner delivered the keynote address entitled "Miles M. Jefferson and Black Drama Criticism," a title that does not suggest its scope. His remarks were not limited to the distinguished critic who wrote the annual review in *Phylon,* "The Negro on Broadway," from 1945 to 1957. At least half of the speech was devoted to a review of the history of dramatic criticism by African Americans in which he noted the paucity of criticism, the reasons for it, and proposed remedies. This speech contained a hint (which I must confess I missed at the time and discovered only upon rereading it) of the motivation for the revision of his anthology, namely, "As far as I know, only three anthologies of African American drama are in print. . . . Even if all three are used, supplements are still necessary. *A Black Quartet* (1970), my anthology *Black Drama in America* (1971), Lindsay Patterson's *Black Theatre* (1971), and Ed Bullins's *The New Lafayette Theatre Presents* (1971), to name only a few anthologies published since 1970, have disappeared from print." (There was in fact at least one other in print by two editors named Reardon and Pawley.) In my judgment the address is a significant contribution to the study of African American criticism and deserves a wider reading.

A year later, to my utter surprise, the University of Iowa awarded me its Distinguished Alumnus Award. Knowing that nominations generally proceed from the faculty and that those who had taught me in the 1930s and 1940s had long since passed, I wondered who had offered my name. It was, of course, Darwin Turner. When I thanked him for having done so, he could hardly contain his delight, saying, "You're the first one of my nominees ever to be approved."

At the time of his death, he was the University of Iowa Foundation Distinguished Professor of English, one of the first faculty members to receive this honor. He had joined the faculty at Iowa after resigning from the University of Michigan in anticipation of an administrative appointment which failed to materialize at a historically black university. A prolific writer, he edited some fourteen books and more than seventy-five scholarly articles covering a wide spectrum of subjects. The University of Iowa was a curious anomaly. Located in the heart of the cornbelt, for decades it had sponsored the famous Iowa Writers' Workshop and pioneered in accepting creative writing in lieu of the traditional research for master's theses and doctoral dissertations. As a visiting professor, I found the atmosphere stimulating and infused with a liberality that I never dreamed possible when I first enrolled as a student. Although I am sure he faced obstacles, it was apparently the right atmosphere for Dr. Turner's scholarly interests.

The revised anthology of fourteen plays retains five from the original edition. Playwrights Amiri Baraka and Ed Bullins are represented again, but *The Toilet* and *We Righteous Bombers* have been replaced by *Great Goodness of Life* and *In the Wine Time*. While it is arguable whether the former is more representative of Baraka's work, the latter most assuredly is more typical of the Bullins canon than his version of Camus's *The Just Assassins*. Plays by Alice Childress, Charlie L. Russell, George Bass, J. e. Franklin, Pearl Cleage, and the Pulitzer-Prize winners Charles Fuller and August Wilson create an anthology of both the pioneer playwrights and those who have come to the fore in the post-Vietnam era.

A summary of the history of African American theatre which formed the basis for the introduction to the 1971 edition has been supplemented by an examination of developments over the past two decades, namely the Pulitzer Prize winners, female playwrights, and the Negro Ensemble Company. The original bibliography has been expanded to include published works about African American theatre that have appeared since 1969, thus providing an additional resource for the study of African American theatre.

But why another anthology? In recent years seven have been published. Three of these—those by Margaret Wilkerson, Kathy Perkins, and Elizabeth Brown-Guillory—are devoted exclusively to female playwrights. Errol Hill's excellent compendium is devoted to historical figures. The equally valuable *Roots of African American Drama,* edited by James Hatch and Leo

Hamalian, is a collection of historically significant plays by *early* African American playwrights. *Black Thunder,* edited by William Branch, concentrates on plays of the post–civil rights era. His *Crosswinds* anthologizes playwrights of the black diaspora. This outpouring of collections, with each editor seeking to fill a particular need, is a confirmation of Dr. Turner's judgment that a vacuum exists. *Black Drama in America* was created as an anthology not only for the general public but as a text for both secondary and post-secondary courses emphasizing a comprehensive view of contemporary African American drama. It is a fitting valedictory for an eminent scholar whose writings will continue to stimulate and edify students of African American theatre.

Thomas D. Pawley
Lincoln University
Jefferson City, Missouri

Acknowledgments

The editor and publisher are grateful for permission to reprint the following:

Emperor of Haiti by Langston Hughes. Reprinted by permission of Harold Ober Associates Incorporated. Copyright © 1936 by Langston Hughes, copyright renewed © 1963 by Langston Hughes.

Trouble in Mind by Alice Childress. Copyright © 1970. Renewed 1988 by Alice Childress. Used by permission of Flora Roberts, Inc.

In the Wine Time by Ed Bullins. Copyright © 1968 by Ed Bullins. Reprinted by permission of Helen Merrill, Ltd.

Five on the Black Hand Side by Charlie L. Russell. Copyright © 1969 by Charlie L. Russell. Reprinted by permission of the author.

Great Goodness of Life: A Coon Show by Amiri Baraka (LeRoi Jones). Reprinted by permission of Sterling Lord Literistic, Inc. Copyright © 1970 by LeRoi Jones (Amiri Baraka).

"Song of the Son" reprinted from *Cane* by Jean Toomer with the permission of Liveright Publishing Corporation. Copyright 1923 by Boni & Liveright, renewed 1951 by Jean Toomer.

Black Masque: The Passion of Darkie's Bones by George H. Bass. Copyright © 1981 by George H. Bass. All rights reserved. Reprinted by permission of Ramona W. Bass.

A Soldier's Play by Charles Fuller. Copyright © 1981 by Charles Fuller. Reprinted by permission of Hill and Wang, a division of Farrar, Strauss, and Giroux, Inc.

Ma Rainey's Black Bottom by August Wilson. Copyright © 1985 by August Wilson. Used by permission of Dutton Signet, a division of Penguin Books USA Inc.

Miss Honey's Young'uns by J. e Franklin. Copyright © 1992 by J. e Franklin. Reprinted by permission of the author.

Flyin' West by Pearl Cleage. Copyright © 1992 by Pearl Cleage. Original publication in the second edition of *Black Drama in America* by permission of the author's agent, Howard Rosenstone, Rosenstone/Wender. All inquiries concerning rights to the play should be addressed to Howard Rosenstone, Rosenstone/Wender, 3 East 48th Street, New York, NY 10017. *Flyin' West* was originally commissioned and produced by the Alliance Theatre Company, Atlanta, GA, Kenny Leon, Artistic Director/Edith H. Love, Managing Director. The play was presented as part of AT&T OnStage.

Additionally, the publisher is grateful to the following individuals, whose gracious assistance made this anthology a reality:

Ms. Jacque Roethler, Professor Darwin Turner's former assistant, who helped locate documents and provided other aid critical to the project's completion; Dr. Thomas D. Pawley, III, Curators' Distinguished Professor Emeritus of Speech and Theatre, Lincoln University, Jefferson City, Missouri, who wrote the foreword and provided numerous suggestions for improving the anthology; Dr. Michael S. Weaver, poet, playwright, and Assistant Professor of English, Rutgers University, who wrote the headnotes for Owen Dodson and George Houston Bass; Dr. Kathy A. Perkins, Associate Professor of Theatre, University of Illinois, Urbana, who wrote the headnote for Pearl Cleage; and Mrs. Maggie Jean Lewis-Turner, widow of Professor Darwin Turner, who provided support and encouragement throughout the project.

Introduction

In recent years African Americans have earned recognition and opportunity in the American theatre. These changes are significant in an entertainment medium which, for more than two hundred years, excluded black artists or restricted them to roles conforming to the images that white playwrights cast for them.

During its first one hundred years, the American professional theatre rigidly rejected black performers. As early as 1769, in *The Padlock,* a white dramatist created a role for a black. Despite the continuing availability of such parts, more than one hundred and twenty years passed before an African American was permitted to perform in a professional drama that employed whites. The first, Sam Lucas, played Uncle Tom in *Uncle Tom's Cabin,* a melodrama that had been popular on American stages for more than two decades. Tradition continued even in the production that included Lucas; whites played all the other roles, including that of Topsy.

Black performers fared no better in musical shows. Although white entertainers began to mimic African American song, dance, speech, and manner in the early 1820s and developed "black" minstrel shows in the 1840s, no actual blacks performed in professional minstrelsy until the 1860s. Ironically, for more than one-half century thereafter, many African American minstrels were required to blacken their faces with makeup in order to resemble the black-skinned gargoyle that had become the traditional image of the African American on the American stage.

During the nineteenth century, while most black Americans still suffered in slavery, Ira Aldridge of New York thrilled European audiences with his performances of Othello, Shylock, and Titus Andronicus. Yet Aldridge never was given the opportunity to appear in the leading theatres of his native land.

What is important in this recitation is not the mere fact that discrimination restricted the development of black talent in a particular occupation. More important is the fact that, for almost one and one-half centuries, white audiences saw no real black people on the stage; they saw only the sentimental, melodramatic, or mocking images created by white mimics. Meanwhile, those same audiences were being informed, outside the theatre, that black people lacked artistic talent.

While black performers struggled for roles, black writers experienced even greater difficulty attempting to stage their ideas before white audiences. A play by an African American was produced in New York City as early as 1821. This play, however, probably had little impact on white audiences, for it appeared in the African Grove Theatre, which catered primarily to black audiences. Seventy-five years later, Broadway audiences enjoyed musical shows written by such blacks as Will Marion Cook, Rosamond Johnson, James Weldon Johnson, Paul Laurence Dunbar, and Bob Cole. These shows, however, generally deferred to the prejudices of the audiences by reenforcing the stereotyped images. For example, James Weldon Johnson recalled a producer's fears that audiences would not approve of a love duet between black performers; the producer knew that white audiences did not consider love to be a serious matter among blacks. In 1921 four black artists—Flournoy Miller, Aubrey Lyles, Noble Sissle, and Eubie Blake—collaborated on a musical comedy, *Shuffle Along,* which became a sensation in downtown New York. A departure from the conventional, loosely structured revue, *Shuffle Along* blended story and music into an organic whole in a manner that did not become common in American musical comedies until the late 1940s. Despite these activities by black writers, no serious, nonmusical drama by an African American reached Broadway until 1923, one hundred and fifty-four years after a white playwright had first presented a black character before white American audiences.

During that century and a half, just as white performers had fixed the image of the African American as a "white" mulatto or a thick-lipped, kinky-haired, white-toothed black, so white playwrights also had fixed the stereotyped images of African Americans. The first was the Buffoon, the "Sambo," who elicits laughter because of his ignorance. The role began in *The Padlock,* was popularized in the minstrel shows, continued into the new medium of motion pictures, and remained popular in American theatre through the 1940s.

A second image popularized by white playwrights was the Tragic Mulatto.

The most famous, the prototype perhaps, was Harriet Beecher Stowe's Eliza, heroine of thousands of evenings of flight across slippery ice floes only a half-stage's distance ahead of drooling mongrels posing as bloodhounds. Like "Sambo," the Tragic Mulatto remained popular in the nineteenth and early twentieth centuries, in such dramas as *Neighbor Jackwood* (1857), *The Octoroon* (1859), *The White Slave* (1882), *Captain Herne, USA* (1895), and *The Nigger* (1909). Unlike the Buffoon, the Tragic Mulatto was a sentimental figure, generally female. Noble, virtuous, and attractive, the Tragic Mulatto, with saintly docility, accepted the Fate that shamed her with African blood and, mindful of her manners, she also accepted her alienation from other Americans no fairer, no more attractive, and no more virtuous. Obviously white dramatists did not presume their mulattoes to be representative of African Americans; they sought to evoke pity for white Americans betrayed by Fate.

The Tragic Mulatto did not disappear from the theatre. Changing times, however, altered the theme. In a motion picture such as *Pinky,* the white dramatist warns fair-skinned African Americans of the tragedy that will ensue if they pretend to be white.

As *Uncle Tom's Cabin* furnished the Tragic Mulatto, so it sketched two other types—the devoted Christian Slave and the Carefree Primitive.

Although Harriet Beecher Stowe's Tom is more aggressive than he is assumed to be by people who know him only by report or from stage presentations, Tom is, nevertheless, the prototype of a host of docile black Christians who have shuffled across the stages of the American theatre and through the pages of American fiction for the past century. In theatre his type soon reappeared in Augustus Thomas's *Colonel Carter of Cartersville,* which pictures mutual affection between master and slave. In fiction, Tom spawned Joel Chandler Harris's Uncle Remus and William Faulkner's Dilsey. Another grandchild is Berenice, the cook-confidante in Carson McCullers's *The Member of the Wedding* (1949).

The final prototype from *Uncle Tom's Cabin* is the Carefree Primitive. Like an animal, Topsy "just growed." Like an animal, she lives by instinct, responding only to innate drives. The image of Topsy, a child in age, has been reproduced in numerous older characters who are never to be judged seriously even when they sin; for, like children, they are expected to know no better.

The most vicious stereotype of the African American in American drama is the Black Beast, popularized by Thomas Dixon in *The Leopard's Spots* and in *The Clansman,* which was made into the motion picture *The Birth of a Nation.* The Black Beast actually appeared in two forms. In one, he was the lustful brute, continually dangerous unless restrained. In the other form, he was a fair-skinned mulatto, craftily awaiting opportunity to intermarry with and thus "mongrelize" his benefactor's race.

These were the basic stereotypes familiar to American audiences before black dramatists had the opportunity to present their plays on Broadway—the Buffoon, the Tragic Mulatto, the Christian Slave, the Primitive, and the Black Beast. A few plays, but very few, presented a more realistic picture. Perhaps the best before World War I were Steele MacKay's dramatization of Albion Tourgée's *A Fool's Errand* (1881), the story of an unsuccessful effort by a "carpetbagger" to reform the unreconstructible South; *For a Brother's Wife* (1885), which pictures black refugees in Union Army camps; James A. Herne's *The Reverend Griffith Davenport* (1899), which stresses the cruelties of slavery; and Winston Churchill's *The Crisis* (1902), which dramatizes a slave auction.

Between World War I and World War II, a few white dramatists tried to give more verisimilitude to African American characters, but they succeeded primarily in creating new prototypes. Ridgely Torrence wrote three plays for black actors between 1913 and 1916. The first, *Granny Maumee*, presented in March 1914, depicts a matriarch of royal African blood, embittered because her son was burned to death for a murder committed by a white man, and because she lost her sight in a futile attempt to save her son's life. When her daughter brings home an illegitimate child, Granny Maumee begins to mold the child into an instrument of vengeance against whites until she learns that the child's father is the same white man who lit the fire that destroyed her son. Vengefully she persuades a conjurer to help her trap the man, but she spares him when a vision of her son reminds her of her Christian duty.

Critics justly praised the excellence of Torrence's interpretation of Granny Maumee, for the proud, bitter, vengeful black matriarch was a new figure for the American theatre. But Torrence's emphasis upon Granny Maumee's superstitious beliefs in voodoo and Christianity promoted an idea that had been introduced in William Vaughn Moody's *The Faith Healer* (1909). Superstition became a sine qua non in white playwrights' characterization of blacks for the next decade.

In Eugene O'Neill's *The Dreamy Kid* (1919) the protagonist, a black gangster, endangers his safety by remaining with his grandmother because he fears her curse. In *The Emperor Jones* (1920) Eugene O'Neill postulated that extreme fear would strip the veneer of civilization from a black and leave him at the mercy of his superstition. Mary Wiborg in *Taboo* (1922) and Em Jo Basshe in *Earth* (1927) revealed their fascinations with voodoo. In Paul Green's *The Man Who Died at Twelve O'Clock,* the young protagonist acquires money from a miserly, tyrannical grandfather by playing upon his superstitions; and in Green's *Supper for the Dead,* a conjure woman forces a man to confess that he drowned his child. Of course, the religious superstitions of Marc Connelly's *The Green Pastures* (1930) should be too familiar to require discussion.

In two other plays Ridgely Torrence introduced a prototype and perpetuated a stereotype. *Simon the Cyrenian* (1917) is the story of the slave who carried the cross for Jesus. Torrence idealized the protagonist as a leader of slave insurrections—a man idolized by the slaves and feared by the Roman governors. In *The Rider of Dreams* (1917), a black protagonist wishes to gain wealth without work. The archetype of the character is actually the Indolent Dreamer, long popular in Irish drama, but American dramatists after Torrence represented the figure more often as a black.

Although Eugene O'Neill earned praise for his dramas about African Americans, he seems to stress a fixed opinion that blacks will fail if they attempt to live according to white men's standards. A fugitive from an American chain gang, Brutus Jones (*The Emperor Jones,* 1920) rules despotically as the emperor of a Caribbean island; but, cowed by his own fears, he becomes helpless and is killed by the rebellious natives. Thus, the loot is left, one must surmise, to a white trader, Smithers, who is untouched by the insurrection. In O'Neill's *All God's Chillun Got Wings* (1924), the first attempt by a white dramatist to picture a middle-class black sympathetically, the protagonist seems frustrated in a white man's world. Incapable of passing the bar examinations, he dwindles into being a sexless, paternal protector of his white wife, whose hatred of him and of herself has driven her insane. Ironically, the role of the black whose aspirations surpass his mental ability was played by Paul Robeson, a black Phi Beta Kappa graduate of Rutgers University.

Another major dramatist also envisaged failure for African Americans. In the Pulitzer Prize-winner *In Abraham's Bosom* (1924), Paul Green dramatized Abe McCrannie's failure to educate his people. Although he emphasized the fact that Abe's intense desire to educate his people did not compensate for his own lack of education, Green offered the hope that Abe's young pupils will succeed where Abe failed.

In ten other plays (more than any other white dramatist wrote about blacks), Paul Green sympathetically delineated the black peasants of North Carolina in credible situations. In *In Aunt Mahaly's Cabin* two murderers kill each other while fighting over plunder. *The End of the Row* is based on the theme of miscegenation. In *The Hot Iron* a black wife kills her husband because he mistreats their children. *The Prayer Meeting* focuses on interracial conflict. *Your Fiery Furnace* tells of an ambitious schoolteacher defeated by his son. In *White Dresses,* a black girl who loves a white man learns that they have the same father. In *No 'Count Boy,* Pheeny, a girl who wants adventure, finds romance briefly with an insane youth. *In the Valley* focuses on the conflicts in a triangular affair of a black woman, her husband, and her lover.

Paul Green stressed the fact that his black creations were regional and temporal. Such regional and temporal limitations, however, have not been emphasized in the many productions of DuBose Heyward's *Porgy,* which perceptively revealed many aspects of the life and character of blacks of a particular class in South Carolina but which has been exported in a manner suggesting that it timelessly represents the race as a whole. The libretto of the more famous operetta *Porgy and Bess* was adapted from this drama, which tells of the inhabitants of Catfish Row. The protagonist, Porgy, a crippled street vendor, befriends and falls in love with Bess, mistress of a black "bad man." When Porgy kills the man to protect Bess, Porgy is imprisoned. After his release he learns that Sporting Life has seduced Bess into resuming her drug habit and accompanying him to New York. Hoping to find her, Porgy follows.

In a less well-known work, *Brass Ankles,* Heyward dramatized the melodramatic story of a mulatto wife, passing for white, who gives birth to a dark-skinned child. When she tries to protect her other child by telling her husband that she has had a black lover, the husband kills both the mother and the child.

Ernest H. Culbertson, who also earned a reputation for dramas about African Americans, concentrated on the exotic aspects of their lives. *Rackey* (1920) is the story of the entanglements of an immoral woman. In *Goat Alley,* Sam, a convict, threatens to kill Lucy Belle if she is untrue; she is, and he does.

While the white dramatists' representations of African Americans were dancing across the professional stages of Broadway, black dramatists were finding their outlets only in African American community theatres. In 1917 opportunity was provided at Harlem's Lafayette Theatre. Other theatres followed—the Howard in Washington, the Dunbar in Philadelphia, the Lincoln in Harlem, Karamu House in Cleveland. African Americans formed their own professional groups: the Lafayette Players in New York, the Gilpin Players in Cleveland, the Krigwa Little Theatre movement, which W. E. B. Du Bois organized and developed in several cities. Interest developed rapidly. As Loften Mitchell has pointed out in *Black Drama,* four acting groups developed in Harlem alone during a two-year span near the end of the 1920s. Through these theatres and companies, black writers found performers for their ideas.

The first African American professional dramatists wrote for two audiences—the uptown Harlem audience and the downtown Broadway audience. For the downtown audience they had little choice but to imitate the images already provided by white dramatists and, if possible, to modify those images into more flattering portraits. Willis Richardson, whose one-act play *The Chip Woman's Fortune* (1923) was the first to appear on Broadway, frequently idealized figures comparable to Torrence's Simon.

Richardson emphasized the physical strength, the nobility, and the courage of his heroes. In *The Flight of the Natives* (1927) Mose refuses to permit any man to flog him. When his master, cowed from the attempt, threatens to sell him "down the river," Mose reluctantly decides to escape without his wife, who is physically incapable of withstanding the rigors of flight. As he leaves, however, he swears to rescue her eventually. The heroes of *The Black Horseman* (1929) are tall, athletic Africans eulogized for their bravery. Massinissa, a tall, dark-skinned hero, contrasts with Syphax, his smaller, fairer antagonist.

Massinissa unmasks a Roman spy by torturing him. An African, he argues, would never reveal secrets, no matter how severely he might be tortured. In both works, Richardson glorified qualities which he considered intrinsic virtues of the black man: dignity, nobility, and courage.

In *Little Ham* (1935) Langston Hughes glamorized the Carefree Primitive into a Harlem sporting man. Such blacks of Harlem had become popular in literature but were relatively unknown on the stage except in the roles created by George Walker, the partner of Bert Williams, one of the most famous entertainers in America during the first decades of the twentieth century. Flirtatious, indolent, irresponsible, the Carefree Primitive appeared in his traditional southern setting in *St. Louis Woman* (1946) by Arna Bontemps and Countee Cullen. *St. Louis Woman* is a musical dramatization of Bontemps's novel, *God Sends Sunday* (1931), the story of a black jockey.

Langston Hughes reproduced another familiar stereotype in *Mulatto* (1935), the first play by an African American to enjoy a long run on Broadway. Hughes, however, varied the familiar stereotype of the Tragic Mulatto by substituting militancy for the characteristic docility in a story of a mulatto who wants to be recognized as his white father's son. The play concludes melodramatically with the son's suicide after he has killed his father and with the lynching of a brother who is innocent of any crime. *Mulatto* was the most popular Broadway play written by any African American before Lorraine Hansberry.

Finally, in 1941, Richard Wright and Paul Green dared to present the Black Beast in Bigger Thomas, the protagonist of *Native Son*. Wright, however, modified the stereotype by revealing the hatred and the fear that underlie and motivate Bigger's braggadocio and by charging white America with responsibility for breeding Biggers.

Hired as a chauffeur by the Daltons, white "liberals" who derive part of their fortune from renting slum houses to blacks, Bigger Thomas, having assisted their drunken daughter to her bedroom, is surprised by the girl's blind mother. Fearing that he will be discovered and accused of attempted rape, Bigger accidentally smothers the girl while trying to prevent her from responding to her mother's questions. After a melodramatic chase during which he rapes and kills his black sweetheart, Bigger is caught, tried, and convicted.

Obviously, the one stereotyped character whom African American dramatists avoided was the Contented Slave. When such a character appears, he is most often the villain, or he is a character who must change.

During the 1920s and 1930s African Americans freed themselves from the influence of stereotypes only when they wrote dramas intended for black audiences in community theatres. Here the dramatists presented domestic dramas about ordinary people.

For example, in *The Broken Banjo* (1925) Willis Richardson explored personal emotions and intrafamilial tensions. Having killed a man who broke his banjo, the protagonist is betrayed to the police by an angry brother-in-law who had witnessed the murder. In *Plumes,* Georgia Frank Wilson recreated a traditional triangle as a black youth kills the white who has seduced his black sweetheart.

Despite the economic depression, the 1930s proved to be an active decade for African American playwrights, both in the downtown theatres and in community theatre. In 1933 Augustus Smith's *Louisiana* was staged as a production of the Negro Theatre Guild. To save the morality of an African American girl, two community leaders use the powers of voodoo and Christianity to crush an unsavory tavernkeeper. In the same year, Hall Johnson delighted downtown audiences with *Run, Little Children,* which—part opera, part ballet, part drama—juxtaposed the melodrama of illicit love, the exoticism of pagan ritual, and the realism of Christian church ceremonies.

Both *Louisiana* and *Run, Little Children* suggest the black dramatists' necessity of working with characters and themes popularized by white dramatists. Both emphasize the superstitions of the blacks. Significantly, however, whereas white dramatists emphasized the superstitions of black protagonists, black dramatists identified superstition with minor characters and dramatic antagonists.

In the mid-1930s, Langston Hughes's *Mulatto* also began its run. Written in 1930 but produced in 1935, it broke away from the religious drama of the decade to present a more militant image.

As might be expected, however, greater opportunity for black writers and actors developed in the Federal Theater, especially the Negro Unit at the Lafayette Theatre in Harlem, and in African American community theatres. Among the more interesting efforts of the Federal Theater were William Du Bois's *Haiti,* Frank Wilson's *Walk Together, Children* (1936), and Wilson's adaptation of Rudolph Fisher's novel, *The Conjure Man Dies.* In the opinion of critic Sterling Brown, however, the most artistic production by the Federal Theater was one produced by the Chicago Unit—*Big White Fog* (1938), Theodore Ward's grim, powerful study of poverty, unemployment, prejudice, Garveyism, and communism. Later Ward wrote and secured Broadway production for *Our Lan',* a story of freed slaves who built a future on land promised them with emancipation but who were subsequently driven from the land when the government retracted its promise.

Black community theatres and theatrical groups continued the rapid development that had begun during the 1920s. Randolph Edmonds estimated that more than twenty-five community theatre groups gained special recognition during the 1930s and early 1940s.[1] These successful groups were established in black communities in at least fifteen different states, including

---

[1] Edmonds, "The Negro Little Theatre Movement," *The Negro History Bulletin* (January 1949), p. 84.

such widely separated states as Texas, Connecticut, Ohio, and Maryland. Edmonds has pointed out that many of these groups earned individual importance: the Boston Players performed in the professional production of Paul Green's *Potters' Field*; the Dixwell Players in New Haven regularly won the Baker Drama Tournament; the New Orleans Little Theatre Guild established the longest history of consecutive performances of any black community theatre in the South.[2] The Harlem Suitcase Theater, founded by Langston Hughes and Hilary Philips in the late 1930s, drew upon Hughes's talents for such productions as *Jericho Jim Crow* and *Don't You Want to Be Free?* a pageant history that established a record for a long run of consecutive performances in a Harlem theatre. The Rose McClendon Players, which began at the end of the 1930s, gave distinguished performances of George Norford's *Joy Exceeding Glory,* a story about the religious movement of Father Divine, a black man who claimed to be God, and Abram Hill's *On Strivers' Row,* which satirized the pretensions of middle-class blacks. A promising venture was the Negro Playwright Company founded by Theodore Ward, Powell Lindsay, George Norford, Theodore Browne, and Owen Dodson. The most successful company, however, was the American Negro Theatre founded in 1940 by Abram Hill and Frederick O'Neal. It produced such black-authored plays as Abram Hill's *Walk Hard* and Owen Dodson's *Garden of Time,* but became best-known for a production of *Anna Lucasta,* which originally had been written about a Polish heroine.

A training ground as important as the black community theatre has been the theatres of the more than one hundred historically black colleges of America. Although most of these are integrated to varying degrees today, during the 1930s and 1940s they were segregated institutions housing a community of scholars and students whose opportunity for development was prohibited or restricted in other educational institutions. Consequently, much of the creative talent of the black American community was clustered in the black colleges, located primarily in the South. There, although many directors offered a conventional collegiate repertory, they also had freedom to experiment with plays written by black Americans. Unfortunately, because the American public has not been familiarized with the work of these theatres and because the production records are too incomplete to permit an accurate history, insufficient recognition has been given to this arena.

These theatres have given opportunity to several respected black writers. In the 1920s, Jean Toomer found black college groups receptive to his dramas, which commercial producers felt to be too experimental. More than thirty years later, James Baldwin's first drama was produced in African American college theatre long before commercial producers became interested in Baldwin as a dramatist.

---

[2] *Ibid.*

Even though black college theatres have developed actors, they have been even more important as a training ground for the playwright-directors who have been teachers, and sometimes students, at those institutions. One of the most productive, Randolph Edmonds, wrote about fifty plays and founded two intercollegiate dramatic associations. Others during the 1930s and 1940s were Melvin B. Tolson of Langston University, Owen Dodson of Atlanta and Howard universities, Thomas Poag of Tennessee A and I, and James Butcher of Howard. They were followed in the 1950s and 1960s by such individuals as Clifford Lamb and Waters Turpin of Morgan State College and Carlton Molette II of Spelman College.

In the 1950s African American drama came of age professionally with Louis Peterson's *Take a Giant Step* (1953), a story of a northern youth. Unlike some of the earlier professional productions, its appeal depended neither upon the exoticism or primitivism of its characters nor upon melodramatic denunciations of white oppression. It interested theatregoers primarily as a sympathetic, psychologically credible presentation of the emotional problems of a black youth reared in a predominantly white neighborhood.

The verisimilitude in characterization and incident was continued six years later in Lorraine Hansberry's *A Raisin in the Sun,* the best-known and most popular drama ever written by a black American. Winner of the Drama Critics' Circle Award for 1958–59, taken on tour after an initial run of 530 performances, staged frequently in both college and community theatres, and later made into a motion picture, *A Raisin in the Sun* presented a broad spectrum of African American ideas as it focused on a single family, the Youngers.

Descended from five generations of slaves and sharecroppers, the Youngers have moved North in the hope of realizing their dreams. In the ghetto of Chicago, however, their dreams are dying. Thirty-five-year-old Walter Lee Younger, a chauffeur, cannot support his family. Beneatha, his sister, knows that the family will be financially burdened if she continues with her plans to study medicine. Walter Lee's wife, who is pregnant, suffers with the realization that the family cannot afford another child. Walter Lee's mother desires happiness for her children and a garden for herself; but she sees weariness and sorrow in her children, and in the concrete wasteland of the ghetto she can find space enough only for a window-box plant for herself.

To earn money to support his family, Walter Lee wants to purchase a share of a liquor store with the money his mother has received from the insurance of his father, who died from overwork. Although the mother refuses because she believes the sale of liquor to be immoral, she attempts to develop his self-confidence by entrusting to him the bulk of the money—to be used for Beneatha's education and for his own desires. She holds back only enough to make a down payment on a home, which is in a neighborhood where black people have never lived; exorbitant costs prevent her buying a home in black neighborhoods. After Walter Lee loses the money in a swindle, he considers regaining part of it by selling out to the white residents who offer to buy their home in order to prevent the blacks from moving into the neighborhood. In his despair, however, Walter Lee finally discovers the pride and the courage to inform the representative of the white residents that the Youngers plan to realize at least one dream by moving into their new home.

The play has been judged a comedy because it is amusing, but it is also one of the most perceptive presentations of African Americans in the history of the American professional theatre.

These two plays won the highest plaudits of any during the 1950s. Other plays by black authors, nevertheless, were being produced downtown with a frequency unknown during any previous decade; and the playwrights were developing significantly varied themes and subjects.

Alice Childress wrote *Trouble in Mind,* a satirical exposé of the contrasts between black people and the false but commercially successful images created by whites. An actress, Miss Childress previously had written *Florence* (a one-act play), *Gold through the Trees,* and *Just a Little Simple* (an adaptation based on Langston Hughes's sketches of Jesse B. Semple).

In *A Medal for Willie* (1951), William Branch, in a play produced uptown, voiced sentiments that most Americans failed to hear in black drama until the 1960s. When Mrs. Jackson participates in a hometown ceremony honoring her son Willie, who is to be awarded a medal posthumously for his bravery in Korea, Mrs. Jackson rejects the medal. The southern town, she says, wants to preserve traditions, to keep things as they are; but her Willie had thought that he was fighting to change things so that they would improve for black people. Maybe, she concludes, if Willie had known how little his fighting and death would mean, maybe he would have brought his gun home to fight where the need was greater.

Three years later, downtown producers exhibited Branch's *In Splendid Error,* a historical drama about a critical moment when Frederick Douglass must decide whether to join John Brown's proposed attack on Harpers Ferry.

Langston Hughes, continuously productive, gave Broadway *Simply Heavenly* (1957), a musical adaptation of his book of sketches, *Simple Takes a Wife.* Unfortunately the adaptation for the commercial theatre diminished both the protagonist, Jesse B. Semple, and the material.

In the tales and dialogues of the Semple books, Jesse assumes the dimensions of a folk hero. Even though he drinks, cavorts with women, has difficulty paying rent, and talks ungrammatically and excessively, his foibles never detract from his dignity; for, like the Greek gods and the heroes of various myths, he is larger than life. Reduced to actable dimensions, however, Semple loses his grandeur. In the play he peeks beneath his legs to watch Joyce, his fiancée, change clothes; he turns somersaults; he is thrown from a car to land on his "sit-downer"; he is propped comically in a hospital bed with his legs in traction; sentimentally and pathetically, he tries to reform and to win Joyce.

In short, Semple's reality as the embodied spirit of the black working class is reduced to a caricature of the Harlem barfly; the Chaplinesque comic hero shrinks to a farcical fall guy of the model made familiar by Stan Laurel and Lou Costello.

The second major injury resulting in the adaptation is suffered by the material itself. Even though incidents occur in *Simple Takes a Wife,* they serve merely to generate Semple's philosophizing. Consequently, what is important is not the event itself but the reaction that it stimulates from Semple. For a Broadway show, however, Hughes needed to emphasize action and to minimize Semple's reflections. As a result, undue attention is given to Semple's unsuccessful efforts to seduce Joyce and to flirtations and domestic difficulties.

In the same year Loften Mitchell, in *The Land Beyond the River,* dramatized the experiences of the Reverend Dr. DeLaine of South Carolina, who sued for bus transportation for black children in a rural area. The case developed into an argument for equal schooling. The blacks lost but appealed to the Supreme Court and won in the famous 1954 decision. Threatened and attacked because of his efforts, Reverend Dr. DeLaine was advised by law officials to fight back. After he did, however, he was forced to flee for his life because, as he was told later, he should not have shot at white people regardless of the reason.

Mitchell began the story in the midst of the struggle and carried it through the death of the protagonist's wife to the point at which the decision has been made to go to the Supreme Court. Like *In Splendid Error,* the play occasionally seems to be a documentary; but Mitchell made the drama effective by focusing attention on the psychological tensions of the minister who must decide whether or not to endure almost unbearable pressures to continue a fight in which few people seem interested.

As black drama matured during the 1950s, so it moved toward liberation during the 1960s—liberation of the playwright from some of the stereotypes previously imposed and liberation from thought and aesthetic standards previously prescribed.

The first professional drama of the 1960s, Ossie Davis's *Purlie Victorious* (1961), differed significantly from *A Raisin in the Sun.* Somewhat in the manner of Alice Childress's *Trouble in Mind* but going to an extreme that she had not pursued, Ossie Davis used ridicule as his chief weapon against bigotry and racial oppression. *Purlie Victorious* ridicules all of the conventional myths and all of the conventional stereotypes of southern blacks and whites; optimistically it implies that these relics have finally been removed from the American living room and cast into the garbage can.

Freedom also meant the opportunity for the black dramatist to explore subjects of interest to him according to methods that he chose. Langston Hughes, for example, offered a modernized morality play with music, *Tambourines to Glory* (1963), the story of two women whose efforts to establish a storefront church in Harlem are assisted, and finally controlled, by the Devil. Despite the indifference of many of the critics who reviewed the performance, *Tambourines to Glory,* judged in its frame as a morality play, is an entertaining combination of melodrama, broad comedy, and colloquial poetry.

In quite a different manner, Adrienne Kennedy elicited praise from critics with her Off Broadway production, *Funnyhouse of a Negro* (1963), a nonrepresentational dramatization of the psychoses of a mulatto who hates her black father. Since her first production, Adrienne Kennedy, in such plays as *A Rat's Mass,* has offered nightmarish, surrealistic, intellectual dramas. In 1964 Lorraine Hansberry presented *The Sign in Sidney Brustein's Window,* a drama about the efforts of an idealistic Jewish man to achieve a desirable life.

Despite such diverse efforts as these, African American drama of the 1960s became known especially for militant denunciation of oppression in the manner of James Baldwin and LeRoi Jones (Amiri Baraka). The pattern had been set, perhaps, by *Fly Blackbirds* (1961), a caustic musical show based on the civil rights demonstrations. Two seasons later, however, downtown audiences reeled from the impact of Baldwin's *Blues for Mr. Charlie* and LeRoi Jones's *Dutchman.*

Blues for Mr. Charlie is the story of a black youth who returns to his southern hometown after a drug habit has ended his musical career in the North. Within a brief time he becomes involved in an altercation with a white man who is known to have killed a black man. The black youth is murdered; the white man is tried and acquitted.

The play has been castigated as one that shows only Baldwin's hatred. It is not surprising that some critics and audiences reacted in that manner. Nevertheless, they are mistaken. If Baldwin chose, he could have documented the existence of the characters—the poor white who sustains his ego by abusing blacks; the white man who takes a black's wife as his concubine; the African American who assists the white man in his affairs with black women. Furthermore, the most sympathetic character is not the bitter youth. The man who becomes the most significant is the youth's father, a minister who had dedicated his adult life to helping his race through nonviolent methods. After he learns that "liberal" whites do not prevent injustice based on lies, he decides that he, like the Pilgrim Fathers, must carry his gun to church with him.

While *Blues for Mr. Charlie* was playing in the East, Baldwin's earlier play, *The Amen Corner,* was making its professional debut in the West. Like Baldwin's first novel, *The Amen Corner* explores intraracial experiences within a black church. After she is visited by her dying husband, a minister begins to lose control of her congregation and her son. No longer worshipping her as a sexless saint, jealous leaders of the congregation struggle to dismiss her. Inspired by the presence of his father, the son determines to seek a musical career outside the church. Meanwhile, the minister discovers that she still loves her husband even though she had deserted him. Realizing that she has sacrificed her personal happiness to the church, she fights desperately to maintain her position; but she loses her power to preach. A personal, domestic tragedy, *The Amen Corner* effectively dramatizes a major theme of most of Baldwin's work: man's love for man is more important than his devotion to any cause.

LeRoi Jones gained more notoriety than Baldwin with his first three plays: *Dutchman* (1963), *The Slave* (1964), and *The Toilet* (1964). Each of these plays dramatizes a violent verbal and physical confrontation between blacks and whites.

In *Dutchman* a black youth of Ivy League appearance is riding a subway when he is approached by a white woman who tantalizes him sexually, then taunts him for attempting to be an imitation of a middle-class white man. He defends his way of life, informs her that he understands white people, and warns her to fear the day when he may use that understanding to destroy whites. The white woman kills him and turns her attention to a new black victim. A thought-provoking play that won an Off Broadway award, *Dutchman* suggests the manner in which the white world destroys the black who intellectually has become a threat; simultaneously, it denounces the black who chooses to use his knowledge in sterile pursuits rather than directing it toward the destruction of oppression.

In *The Slave* a black revolutionary returns during a battle to confront his white ex-wife and her husband. After renouncing his former life, fashioned according to European standards, he kills the husband and returns to the battle. Despite the violence of its language and physical confrontation, *The Toilet* suggests that black and white can unite after the black has gained respect by defeating the white.

Regardless of artistic weaknesses that critics may find in these plays, *Blues for Mr. Charlie* and the dramas of Jones may prove to be among the most influential works ever written by black dramatists. Jones has insisted that poems—and plays also, one may assume—are bullets to be used against the enemy. The thesis is valid for many young black people who found in the words of Baldwin and Jones an effective articulation of their bitterness, their frustration, and their hatred. Ignoring psychological weaknesses in the character, black teenagers wildly applauded the bravado with which the young protagonist of *Blues* bellows his defiance of the white establishment. The power of Jones has been even more remarkable. As an artistic and political leader on the East Coast, he has given dramatic form to scenes that show the black man triumphing over a fallen white man. No criticism can minimize the emotional effect of such scenes upon young black people who thrill to seeing, perhaps for the first time in their lives, strong black men triumphing over the white. The significance for them transcends the mere thrill of seeing the "Indians" winning at last. What they are perceiving is that a race stereotyped as cowardly has finally chosen to fight, and is winning. For a suggestive parallel, moviegoers may consider the excitement that they are expected to feel when a Destry, Jr., finally realizing that unaided justice will not triumph, straps on his gun and strides out to face the villain. If these black plays are not bullets for a revolution, they are at least the sinew-strengthening soul food for revolutionaries.

In 1965 black drama began to develop in two directions. With their greater freedom, African American dramatists began to win the plaudits of downtown audiences. Douglas T. Ward, director of the Negro Ensemble Theater, satirized black-white relationships in *Day of Absence* (1965), a story of the frustrations of white southerners who discover that "their" blacks have left them, and *Happy Ending* (1965), a revelation of the manner in which black servants are able to manipulate household affairs for their own advantage. Lonne Elder's *Ceremonies in Dark Old Men* (1968) poignantly dramatized the intrafamilial relationships of black dreamers and their practical sister who serves as breadwinner. Charles Gordone, who numbers Africans and Indians among his ancestors, won a Pulitzer Prize for *No Place to Be Somebody* (1969), an ambiguous drama of a black man defeated in his efforts to seize a position for himself by using the violent methods perfected by white Americans.

Meanwhile, an even more fertile field began to develop in the black community theatres. Perceiving that artistic freedom would be limited as long as the artist had to explain his material to an audience unfamiliar with his culture, black dramatists began to write increasingly for the theatres of the black community. In doing so, they were not seeking dull listeners who would applaud any effort regardless of its ineptness. Instead, they were seeking perceptive audiences who were culturally capable of understanding and evaluating their efforts. This search should not be confused with the white-written, black-acted films of the 1940s that perpetuated the old stereotypes for the entertainment of white audiences. Nor should it be adjudged merely a form of separatism. Instead, it should be seen as an assertion of the fact that black playwrights, like other authors, have the right to create for their own culture. In America the black author's culture is related to, part of, influenced by, but not identical with the culture of middle-class white America. Shakespeare presumed an audience sufficiently conversant with and sympathetic to the principles of monarchy that he would not need to defend his belief in it. Tennessee Williams assumed that he was writing for audiences who understood the myths of the South. Similarly, black playwrights want and need audiences that understand the culture that forms the background of their dramas.

Among the most productive of these black playwrights has been Ed Bullins, whose work was first produced at the New Lafayette Theatre in Harlem. Bullins is known especially for such dramas as *Clara's Ole Man,* in which a middle-class aspirant, seeking an afternoon's romance in the absence of the girl's "old man," discovers that he has stumbled upon a lesbian life in a slum world; *Goin' a Buffalo,* in which a black hustler is betrayed by the man he has befriended and trusted; *The Electronic Nigger,* a satiric presentation of the failure of a writer to hold his own against a pompous, pretentious Negro programmed to defend statistics, surveys, and law and order. The best-known of Bullins's acknowledged plays is *In the Wine Time,* the story of a black youth maturing in a ghetto with only the dreams provided by wine, an uncle-in-law who has been a sailor, and romance with an unattainable woman. Despite his public denials, Bullins is also reputed to be the author of *We Righteous Bombers.*

Many other black dramatists of the community theatre have concentrated on plays designed to educate the masses of blacks to understandings that must characterize their actions. Ed Bullins has labeled such work "black revolutionary agit-prop drama." For students of American drama, "agit-prop" calls to mind the efforts of Clifford Odets and other dramatists of the 1930s to awaken American laborers to awareness of their needs. Actually, however, the ancestry of black revolutionary drama antedates the 1930s by several centuries. In many ways it resembles medieval morality plays, a fact that should not be surprising, since the dramatists wish to teach moral lessons. The characters are allegorical. The black revolutionary represents youth and truth. The white adversary is the Devil. Middle-class blacks are sinners who probably will not reform despite the efforts of the revolutionaries; if they fail to reform, they must be judged and punished. The drama is a contest of good (black) against evil (white) in which good must triumph. A play of negative force—that is, one that ends in failure of the protagonists—has to demonstrate the pitfalls that black people must avoid. Like medieval drama, black revolutionary drama has evolved into black ritual—dramatization of the creed. Unlike most Western drama, however, it is not constructed for the emotional titillation or intellectual enlightenment of passive spectators. Black revolutionary drama aims to involve the audience emotionally, intellectually, verbally, and physically. It succeeds when the spectator becomes the participant.

Amiri Baraka (LeRoi Jones) developed the design for black revolutionary drama and black ritual in his dramas written after 1965. Also significant is Jimmy Garrett, whose drama *And We Own the Night* concludes when a dying revolutionary kills his mother for continuing to view life through the eyes of the white man. Other prominent revolutionary dramatists are Marvin X, Ben Caldwell, Ron Milner, Sonia Sanchez, and Charles Patterson. The New Lafayette Theatre in Harlem and the company of Barbara Ann Teer have guided the way in ritual drama.

* * *

In "The Negro on Stage" (1937), the distinguished literary critic and historian Sterling Brown complained that most of the plays that professional theatre produced about African Americans were written by whites. During the 1970s and 1980s, Brown would no longer have had that concern. Even if one suspects that Broadway theatregoers still favor black theatre that is musical, comic, or sensational, one cannot deny the spectacular increase in the number of African American playwrights whose works have appeared in the professional and semiprofessional theatres of New York City. Certainly, the number is too large to permit the play-by-play analysis I provided for works written up to 1969. Instead, I have chosen to focus on three major aspects of African American theatre since 1970: the Pulitzer-Prize winning plays, black women playwrights, and the work of the Negro Ensemble Company.

One year after Lonne Elder's *Ceremonies in Dark Old Men* was nominated for but failed to earn the 1969 Pulitzer Prize for drama, Charles Gordone's *No Place to Be Somebody* became the first drama by an African American to be so honored (1970). Set in a bar during the present time, *No Place to Be Somebody* reveals the frustrations of a variety of blacks and whites who fantasize that they will achieve happiness and "become somebody" if they can assume different life-styles: a black bar-owner and pimp wants a share of the Mafia's action; his white girlfriend, a prostitute, hopes to relive her first love—for an African American; a fair-skinned African American actor wants American theatre to cast him in black roles; an African American woman seeks a white husband because she believes that such a man will respect and protect her; a white man who has failed to protect his white wife wants to be a black drummer; a naive, liberal young white woman wants to empathize with the suffering of an oppressed American minority. These and others generally experience disillusionment because, in seeking to become someone else, they are betraying themselves.

More than a decade later, in 1982, Charles Fuller became the second black to earn a Pulitzer Prize for drama, for his *A Soldier's Play*. Previously acclaimed for such plays as *The Brownsville Raid* and *Zooman and the Sign*, both based on actual incidents, Fuller set his drama in the World War II period and centered it on the investigation into the murder of Sergeant Vernon Waters, an African American career soldier. Conducted by the first Negro officer whom the African American soldiers and their white commanding officers have ever met, the investigation reveals not only the racism in the armed services but also the tortured psyche of Waters, who is obsessively determined to combat that racism by perfecting his own image and that of each of the soldiers whom he commands.

Five years later, in 1987, August Wilson's second major play earned most of America's coveted theatrical awards—a Tony and a Drama Critics' Circle Award for best play as well as a Pulitzer Prize for drama. Although racism is a dominant issue in *Fences,* the drama is significantly different from *A Soldier's Play*. Set in 1957 in a northern American industrial city (such as Wilson's hometown of Pittsburgh), *Fences* is a domestic drama focused on Troy

Maxson and his family. One of the greatest sluggers in the history of baseball's Negro Leagues, Maxson has been denied national visibility by the unwritten Jim Crow code that barred African Americans from organized baseball during the first half of the twentieth century. Although the barriers have descended and the World Series champion Milwaukee Braves are led by Henry Aaron, who later will break Babe Ruth's record for career home runs, Maxson remains sufficiently embittered and distrustful of whites that he opposes his son's desire to accept a college football scholarship. Baseball and sports, however, are not the major issues of the play. The play instead is about Troy Maxson and others like him who migrated to northern cities. August Wilson describes them in a preface:

. . . They came strong, eager, searching. The city rejected them and they fled and settled along the riverlands and under bridges in shallow, ramshackle houses made of sticks and tarpaper. They collected rags and wood. They sold the use of their muscles and their bodies. They cleaned houses and washed clothes, they shined shoes, and in quiet desperation and vengeful pride, they stole, and lived in pursuit of their own dream: that they could breathe free, finally, and stand to meet life with the force of dignity and whatever eloquence the heart could call upon.

Three years later, in 1990, Wilson earned his second Pulitzer Prize in drama for *The Piano Lesson*. Following the pattern of his three earlier plays—*Ma Rainey's Black Bottom, Fences,* and *Joe Turner's Come and Gone*—*The Piano Lesson* was presented originally at the Eugene O'Neill Theatre Company, premiered in a production at the Yale Repertory Theater, and earned the New York Drama Critics' Circle award as best play of the year. Set in Pittsburgh in 1936, *The Piano Lesson,* like *Fences,* is a domestic drama, which focuses on a piano that is an heirloom in the family of Doaker Charles. Charles's slave grandfather had carved on it portraits of his wife and son who had been traded for the piano. Doaker's brother had lost his life in a successful attempt to gain the piano through theft. At the time of the play, Doaker's nephew wishes to sell the piano to buy the farmland on which his great-grandfather had been a slave, but Doaker's niece, co-owner of the piano, refuses to sell property that her father gave his life to gain. To further complicate the plot, the Charles house seems to be haunted by the ghost of a white man who wants to regain the piano.

In contrast to the rise of black male playwrights in professional theatre in the 1970s and 1980s, African American women playwrights continued to be less visible, despite the fact that during that same period scholars and others focused increased attention on the work of women writers generally. In her bibliography for *Wines in the Wilderness,* Elizabeth Brown-Guillory identified more than one hundred thirty African American women who have written plays that have been produced. Yet if one excludes those such as Barbara Ann Teer and Val Gray Ward who are known especially as directors and playwrights, or those such as Ruby Dee who are known better as performers than as playwrights, or those such as Vinette Carroll who are identified primarily with musical theatre, one is left with relatively few who may be said to have national reputations as playwrights in professional theatre. The fact is somewhat surprising when one contrasts it with the achievement of African American women in other literary paths. Since Gwendolyn Brooks earned a Pulitzer Prize for poetry in 1950, several African American writers have earned Pulitzer Prizes for poetry or fiction. But no African American woman has ever won a Pulitzer Prize for drama.

Barriers remained in place for African American women long after they were lowered for African American men. Whereas plays by black men were produced on Broadway during the early 1920s, no African American woman had a play produced even on Off Broadway until Alice Childress succeeded with *Trouble in Mind* (1955), and four years would pass before Lorraine Hansberry, the first black to win a Drama Critics' Circle Award, stormed and delighted Broadway with *A Raisin in the Sun*. Without a doubt, just as Richard Wright's success with *Native Son* inspired both male and female African Americans to seek opportunity as writers of fiction, so Lorraine Hansberry's critical and popular success with *A Raisin in the Sun* inspired both males and females to hope for achievement as playwrights. But Hansberry provided an additional inspiration for young women. Intelligent, articulate, attractive, proud of her African and African American heritage, outspoken in her support of social and political causes, Lorraine Hansberry provided a highly visible role model.

A generation later, another African American woman achieved high visibility in American professional theatre. With the choreopoem *For Colored Girls Who Have Considered Suicide/When the Rainbow Is Enuf* (1974) Ntozake Shange shocked, delighted, and infuriated her various audiences. Regardless of their reaction, individual theatregoers—both those in the media and the lay public—discussed Shange's dramatic work with particular attention to the voices of women in American life and in American theatre. If Hansberry inspired young women to seek careers as playwrights and social activists, so Shange, fifteen years later, encouraged them to dare to express their feelings about themselves and about their relationships with men.

Although the number of productions and publications of plays by African American women remains less than desirable, evidence suggests that the numbers are increasing. Gaining increased visibility are such talented playwrights as Judi Ann Mason and Pearl Cleage. Among Mason's always powerful works is the haunting *Daughters of the Mock,* which focuses on a woman so embittered by a failed marriage that she forces her daughters to vow to marry and mate only to produce female offspring. (All male children will be destroyed.) Pearl Cleage is best known for *Puppet Play,* in which she explores male-female relationships in a manner evocative of earlier dramatic examinations of black-white relationships. Other recent dramatists of note include Kathleen Collins, Alexis De Veaux, Elaine Jackson, and Sharon Martin. One hopes that the decades that are focused on the literature of African American women will provide success for the playwrights as it has for the novelists.

In recording the history of African American theatre, one must recognize the significance of the Negro Ensemble Company (NEC). Founded in 1967 by Robert Hooks, Douglas Turner Ward, and Gerald Krone and funded initially by a Ford Foundation grant, NEC began as a black-oriented, black-controlled theatre company willing to produce drama by blacks or whites that explored black life and experience. Within a few years after its inception, however, NEC increased its emphasis on training black performers and black playwrights.

Like the American Negro Theatre of the 1940s, NEC has given opportunity to African American actors and actresses. NEC casts have included such well-known performers as Roscoe Lee Browne, Rosalind Cash, Adolph Cesar (who earned distinction as Sergeant Waters in both the stage and film versions of *A Soldier's Play*), Frances Foster, Moses Gunn, Robert Hooks, Jr., Cleavon Little, Stephanie Mills, Denise Nichols, Richard Roundtree, and Douglas Turner Ward. Even more important, NEC has assumed a role practiced but not sustained by the New Lafayette Players of the 1920s and by the American Negro Theatre. It has committed itself to discovering and training young black playwrights and then producing their work. The following is only a partial list of African Americans whose work has been produced by NEC (I have listed one play for each writer): Lennox Brown (*A Ballet Behind the Bridge*), Philip Hayes Dean (*The Sty of the Blind Pig*), Lonne Elder III (*Ceremonies in Dark Old Men*), Charles Fuller (*A Soldier's Play*), Paul Carter Harrison (*The Great McDaddy*), Leslie Lee (*The First Breeze of Summer*), Judi Ann Mason (*Daughters of the Mock*), John Scott (*Ride a Black Horse*), Joseph A. Walker (*The River Niger*), Samm-Art Williams (*Home*), and August Wilson (*Fences*).

Now that NEC has passed its twenty-fifth year of successful operation, there is a need for a carefully researched, analytical history of this important institution.

The plays selected for the second edition of this anthology furnish a representative history of African American drama since 1920. This collection shares with two other anthologies currently in print—*Black Theater*, edited by James Hatch and Ted Shine, and *Wines in the Wilderness*, edited by Elizabeth Brown-Guillory—the conscious effort to reveal the historical development of African American playwrights by including plays written before the current generation. Unlike some of the other anthologies of dramas by African Americans, it does not limit the selections to revolutionary drama or to the dramas best known to Broadway audiences. Focused on "serious" drama, it excludes musical plays even though the work of African Americans in musical theatre is certainly as important as their other work in theatre.

Space limitations have required other difficult choices. For example, in general I have not attempted to include plays published separately through commercial presses—and, thus, relatively accessible to readers. This decision has prompted the exclusion of such meritorious works as Lorraine Hansberry's *A Raisin in the Sun,* Lonne Elder's *Ceremonies in Dark Old Men,* James Baldwin's *Blues for Mr. Charlie,* Joseph Walker's *The River Niger,* Ntozake Shange's *For Colored Girls Who Have Considered Suicide/When the Rainbow Is Enuf,* and August Wilson's Pulitzer-Prize winning *Fences.*

The first play by an African American to be presented on Broadway, Willis Richardson's *The Chip Woman's Fortune* constitutes a beginning for this volume. The prolific Langston Hughes, successful in drama both uptown and downtown, is represented by *Emperor of Haiti,* a historical drama that was published for the first time in the 1971 edition. *Emperor of Haiti* may be Hughes's best dramatic work, even though it is his only play that does not center on blacks born and reared in the United States. A history of African American drama would not be complete without Theodore Ward, whose *Our Lan'* was published for the first time in the 1971 edition. The important world of African American college theatre appears in the romantic and mythic *Bayou Legend* by Owen Dodson, an important contributor to that theatre. Louis Peterson's *Take a Giant Step* reveals the manner in which African American writers of the 1950s emphasized the humanity (the humanness) of the race.

Understandably, it has been more difficult to make selections from the many excellent dramas created since 1953.* I have chosen Alice Childress's *Trouble in Mind* because it effectively satirizes the stereotypical images of African Americans created by white playwrights and directors while it simultaneously explores the difficulties African Americans experience in the theatre both as subjects and as performers. Rather than including the "protest" drama of the 1930s, I have chosen instead to focus on two major aspects of Black Arts dramas. They are represented by Ed Bullins's naturalistic *In the Wine Time* and by Amiri Baraka's allegorical *Great Goodness of Life.* Charlie Russell's *Five on the Black Hand Side* disguises its Black Arts revolutionary formula beneath its emphasis on women's liberation and on humor. George Bass's *Black Masque* provides an example of African American ritual drama. Focusing on adolescents of the 1960s, J. e. Franklin's *Miss Honey's Young'uns* offers a realistic look at internecine racial strife amid the violent climate of the urban South. Charles Fuller's *A Soldier's Play* is one of the four plays by African Americans to win a Pulitzer Prize for drama. Finally, more grimly than *Trouble in Mind, Ma Rainey's Black Bottom* by August Wilson, winner

---

***PUBLISHER'S NOTE:** Following Dr. Turner's death we selected Pearl Cleage's *Flyin' West* (1992), which powerfully depicts the lives of four black women struggling to survive the hardships of homesteader life in Kansas in the late 1800s. Publication in this volume marks its first appearance in print.

INTRODUCTION   xxxv

of two Pulitzer Prizes for drama, recalls difficulties of black performers in theatre.

With no sense of apology but as a statement of fact, I must remind casual readers that good drama is not necessarily great literature. That is, a play that works well on the stage is not necessarily as effective when it is read in the solitude of a study. Furthermore, unlike many contemporary dramatists who have consciously prepared their work for a literary market after the initial run and tour have ended, many African American dramatists have had little cause to hope for book publication. Therefore, one should not expect to find in this anthology a consistent display of the extensive literary directions and interlineations of a James Barrie or a Eugene O'Neill. I must ask the readers, therefore, to imagine themselves in a theatre observing a drama.

To some readers—perhaps especially to some black readers—it may seem that the anthology is too heavily weighted with the tragedy of the failure of black people. Such a weighting, however, implies neither a sense of the inevitability of such failure nor a desire to stimulate a sentimental appraisal of black Americans. If anything, the preponderance of tragedy should suggest a thought: until recent years African American dramatists, like other Western dramatists, expended their energies most significantly in the creation of tragedy.

As editor, I regret the impossibility of an anthology twice this size, one which would include Abram Hill, Lorraine Hansberry, James Baldwin, Adrienne Kennedy, Val Gray Ward, Douglas Turner Ward, Ben Caldwell, Paul Carter Harrison, Barbara Ann Teer, Joseph Walker, Judi Ann Mason, Philip Hayes Dean, Richard Wesley, Ntozake Shange, and the many others who have brought African American drama from minstrelsy, apology, and defense to awareness and assertion.

Finally, I want to express my gratitude to Ms. Jacque Roethler for her invaluable assistance in preparing the manuscript; to Ms. Akiko Ochiai and Ms. Napolita Hopper, my research assistants; and to Mrs. Renée Mayfield, whose excellent and patient editorial supervision has made possible my publications through Howard University Press.

Darwin T. Turner
University of Iowa

Black Drama In America
An Anthology

The Chip Woman's Fortune (1923)

Willis Richardson (1889–1977)

Born in Wilmington, North Carolina, November 5, 1889, Willis Richardson, educated at M Street High School in Washington, D.C., was not the first African American to write a play, but he was the first significantly productive African American playwright. The unfortunate tendency of many people to evaluate the achievements of African Americans according to their successes within the white community is evidenced by the fact that Richardson is best known today as the first African American to have a play produced on Broadway. His contributions to black theatre and to the black community, however, are even more important. Many years before the birth of the generation that is currently affirming the beauty of blackness, Richardson, in his own plays and in those which he anthologized, was teaching the black community to be proud of its character and its history. In several of his more than twenty one-act plays, Richardson recreated black heroes of history—Antonio Maceo, leader of a Cuban rebellion against Spain; Crispus Attucks, the first colonist to die in the Boston Massacre; Massinissa, King of East Numidia; Alexandre Dumas, French playwright and novelist; American slaves who fled from the South; Menelik, emperor of Abyssinia (Ethiopia); and Simon, who carried the cross when Jesus faltered. In addition to teaching pride in heroes, however, Richardson delineated black life realistically in such works as *The Broken Banjo* and *The Chip Woman's Fortune*.

Produced first at the Lafayette Theatre in Harlem on May 7, 1923, *The*

Chip Woman's Fortune eight days later became the first serious play by an African American ever to reach Broadway. Although it evidences some of the supposedly exotic quality of black life that appealed to Broadway audiences during the 1920s, *The Chip Woman's Fortune* seems realistic in characterization and in language.

Selected Plays by Willis Richardson

In *The King's Dilemma and Other Plays for Children* by Willis Richardson. New York: Exposition, 1957.
> *The Dragon's Tooth*
> *The Gypsy's Finger Ring*
> *The King's Dilemma* (1929).
> *Man of Magic*
> *The New Santa Claus*

In *Negro History in Thirteen Plays,* ed. by Willis Richardson. Washington, D.C.: Associated Publishers, 1935.
> *Antonio Maceo* (1935).
> *Attucks, the Martyr*
> *The Elder Dumas*
> *In Menelik's Court*
> *Near Calvary*

In *The New Negro,* ed. by A. Locke. New York: Boni, 1925.
> *Compromise*

In *Plays and Pageants from the Life of the Negro,* ed. by Willis Richardson and May Miller. Washington, D.C.: Associated Publishers, 1930.
> *The Black Horseman*
> *The House of Sham* (1929).

In *Plays of Negro Life,* ed. by A. Locke and M. Gregory. New York: Harper and Brothers, 1927.
> *The Broken Banjo* (1925).
> *The Flight of the Natives*

The Chip Woman's Fortune

CHARACTERS

Silas Green, a store porter
Liza, his wife
Emma, their daughter
Aunt Nancy, the Chip Woman
Jim, her son
Two other men

ACT I
  . . . . . .

The scene is the very plain dining room of a poor colored family. The floor is without covering, and the walls are without pictures. At the center of the floor is a rectangular table with a couple of chairs near it. In the rear wall is a fireplace in which a low fire is burning, and at the left of this sits Liza in a rocker. She is wrapped from the shoulders to ankles in blankets, for she is just up from a spell of sickness. At the right of the fireplace is a window. A door at the right leads through to other rooms and to the back yard. Another door at the left leads to the front of the house. Against the left side near the door stands a Victrola. There is a deep silence as Liza sits gazing into the fire. She looks up at the clock on the mantel, then looks towards the right and calls:

Liza. *(calling)* Emma! Emma!

(Presently Aunt Nancy appears at the right. Every one of us has seen her kind—those old women who go about the streets picking up chips of wood and lumps of coal, or searching in trash cans for whatever they can find. Such is Aunt Nancy. She is old, and her back is bent on account of constant stooping. She is wearing a bonnet which partly hides her black, wrinkled face, and is wearing a shawl over her shoulders.)

Aunt Nancy. You callin' Emma, Miss Liza?
Liza. Yes'm, Aunt Nancy. You seen her?
Aunt Nancy. No'm, Ah ain't seen her.
Liza. Wonder where she is? Ah want her to go to the store for me.
Aunt Nancy. Ah don't know where she is. Ah ain't seen her for the last two hours, but I reckon she'll drop in in a minute or two. How you feelin now?
Liza. Ah'm feelin' pretty good. The medicine you give me last night must be doin' me good.
Aunt Nancy. Ah don't reckon you need no more medicine today.
Liza. Ah reckon not. How you feelin'? Seems like Ah ought to be askin' you that instead of you askin' me.
Aunt Nancy. Ah'm feelin' right sharp for a old woman. To tell you the truth, Ah ain't felt better since the day Ah got married. Ah'm 'spectin' somethin'.
Liza. You 'spectin' somethin'?
Aunt Nancy. Yes'm.
Liza. What you 'spectin'?
Aunt Nancy. Ah can't tell you that, Miss Liza; but maybe you'll find out before the day's gone.

Liza. Is it anythin' good?
Aunt Nancy. Didn' Ah tell you Ah ain't felt better since the day I got married?
Liza. Ah'm glad somethin' good's happenin' to somebody. Ain't nothin' good happenin' to me.
Aunt Nancy. You gettin' better, ain't you?
Liza. Yes'm. Ah'm gettin' better.
Aunt Nancy. That sure is good; and besides, you're young yet; lot o' good things can happen to you before you die.
Liza. Ah hope so.
Aunt Nancy. *(going close to her)* Lemme look in your eyes. *(after looking into her eyes)* Your eyes is startin' to shine. You'll be gettin' all right pretty soon. *(She whispers something into Liza's ear.)*
Liza. *(blushing)* Oh, no'm. Aunt Nancy!
Aunt Nancy. *(laughing)* That's all right, you wait. Ah likes to see a woman's eyes shinin'. It shows she's got some life in her. Ah don't like to see no woman with dead eyes, 'specially a young woman. Ah likes to see 'em pert.
Liza. You ain't by yourself. Everybody likes to see a young woman pert.
Aunt Nancy. Ah was goin' in the woods to dig up some roots, but Ah reckon Ah'll wait 'til tomorrow.
Liza. Tomorrow'll be all right. You don't have to go today.
Aunt Nancy. Ah'll go now and set out on the back steps and think. Ah like to set in the sun and think.
Liza. Think about what?
Aunt Nancy. Ah got somethin' to think about.
Liza. What?
Aunt Nancy. Ah can't tell you everythin'. It ain't good to tell everythin' you think about, you know. 'Spose everybody told all their thoughts?
Liza. That wouldn't never do.
Aunt Nancy. 'Deed it wouldn't never do. Everythin' ud be upside down with other people knowin' what you was thinkin' about. *(She starts out right.)*
Liza. If you see Emma out there send her in to me.
Aunt Nancy. All right, Ah will. *(She looks through the right door.)* Here comes Emma now.

(Emma enters. She is a pretty brown girl of eighteen.)

Emma. You want me, Ma?
Liza. Yes, Ah want you. Where you been?
Emma. Upstairs.
Liza. Upstairs doin' what?
Emma. Combin' ma hair.

Liza. Combin' your hair this time o' day? You combed your hair once this mornin'. What you comb it again for?
Emma. Ah wanted it combed.
Liza. You wasn't always so fond o' combin' your hair. What's comin' off?
Emma. Nothin'.
Liza. *(looking at her more closely)* Come here, gal. *(Emma moves nearer to her.)* Ah believe before God you been puttin' powder on your face. Is you been puttin' powder on your face? *(Emma looks away without answering.)* Where'd you get that powder from?
Emma. Ah bought it.
Liza. Bought it with what? *(as Emma is silent)* Don't you hear me talkin' to you? Bought it with what?
Emma. Bought it with some change Pa gave me.
Liza. Well, wipe it off! Wipe it right off and don't put no more on! Leave it up there and Ah'll use it when Ah get on ma feet. You too young to be powderin'.
Aunt Nancy. *(who still stands near)* Let the gal alone, Liza. You was young like that once and she ain't goin' to be that young but once.
Liza. She don't have to paint herself up like a billboard just because she's young. *(to Emma)* Get the basket. Ah want you to go to the store for me.

(Emma goes out right.)

Aunt Nancy. Ah'll be out on the back steps if you want me.
Liza. All right'm. Ah hope Ah won't need you.

(Aunt Nancy goes out right, and Liza sits rocking until Emma returns. She speaks just as Emma comes in.)

Liza. There's somethin' mighty funny goin' on round here. You primpin' and Aunt Nancy thinkin'. Ah reckon we goin' to have a thunder storm.
Emma. Ain't nothin' funny goin' on.
Liza. What you doin' plasterin' your face up and combin' your hair if somethin' funny ain't goin' on? You know you ain't never combed your hair twice the same day in your life if it wasn't Sunday.
Emma. *(anxious to change the subject)* What did you say to get from the store?
Liza. Get some potatoes and chops and some cakes. Some o' the little ones your Pa likes so much.
Emma. Is that all?
Liza. Yes, that's all. Look a here, tell me this. Did Aunt Nancy take you in the woods and show you how to dig them roots yesterday?
Emma. Yes'm, she showed me, but Ah don't remember much.
Liza. Why don't you? You ain't got your mind on no boy, is you?

Emma. No'm. She says she's goin' to show me all over again so Ah'll know how to find 'em for you when she's gone.
Liza. Aunt Nancy ain't goin' nowhere.
Emma. Ah hope she won't, but if she does Ah'll be sorry. She's so good to me. Ah love her a lot.
Liza. 'Deed she is good. Everybody loves her and they can't help it. Ain't no way in the world to help lovin' somebody that's good to you.
Emma. And Aunt Nancy sure has been good to us.
Liza. Nobody knows that like Ah do.
Emma. *(starting out)* Ah'm goin' now.
Liza. Wait a minute. Start the Victrola off before you go, and go out the back way, it's nearer.
Emma. *(adjusting the needle)* When we goin' to get some new records, Ma?
Liza. New records? You better wait 'til the Victrola gets paid for. You got a plenty o' records.
Emma. But they're all old.
Liza. That's all right, you can keep on usin' 'em. You ought to be glad to get bread to eat and let new records alone.

(Emma starts the machine and goes out right.)

Liza. Don't stay long.
Emma. *(outside the door)* No'm, Ah'll be right back.

(Liza is listening to the Victrola when Silas, her husband, enters from the left. He is a man about forty and is wearing the uniform of a store porter. As he enters Liza looks up at him in surprise.)

Liza. Why, Silas, what you doin' home?
Silas. *(throwing his cap down and moving to the table)* They sent me home.
Liza. Not discharged?
Silas. *(not in the best of spirits)* No, Ah ain't discharged, but it's almost as bad; Ah'm furloughed a couple o' days without pay.
Liza. Furloughed for what?
Silas. *(motioning towards the Victrola)* On account o' that old Victrola. Seems like it's bringin' us more trouble than it's worth.
Liza. What's the Victrola got to do with your job?
Silas. It's just like everything else. When a man's got trouble o' one kind seems like everything goes wrong.
Liza. That ain't tellin' me nothin'.
Silas. Well, you know we ain't paid nothin' on that Victrola since the first payment, don't you?
Liza. Yes, Ah know that. But you been promisin'.
Silas. That's the trouble. Ah been doin' a lot o' promisin' and no payin'.

Liza. *(impatiently)* Well, what else? You just as well tell me all of it at once. Ah don't feel like askin' a million questions.
Silas. The man said he was goin' to send here and get the thing if we didn't pay this month, didn't he?
Liza. Yes.
Silas. Well, you know we ain't been able to pay, so he's goin' to send after it.
Liza. Goin' to take it away?
Silas. Yes.
Liza. So, that's why you got furloughed, is it? 'Cause they goin' to take the Victrola away.
Silas. No, that ain't it exactly.
Liza. Ah see you ain't told me. What is it exactly?
Silas. The manager o' that music place is a friend o' ma boss; and this mornin' while Ah was sweepin' off the front pavement he passed by me goin' in the store. When he seen me he stopped and looked at me hard, then he went in. Ah thought trouble was comin' when Ah seen him look at me so hard. After he came out the boss called me in and told me they was goin' to send after that Victrola; and then he says, "Go home and stay a few days and maybe you'll learn how to pay your debts." So here Ah am.
Liza. Ah'll be mighty sorry to lose that Victrola; but if it can't be helped, it can't be helped.
Silas. No, it can't be helped, but that ain't the worst of it. If Ah don't pay and they take it back, when Ah go back the boss'll always have his eyes on me, and Ah bet it won't be long before Ah'll be losin' ma job.
Liza. What you goin' to do?
Silas. Ah'll do anything to save ma job.
Liza. Ah know you'd like to pay and keep the Victrola; but Ah don't see where you goin' to get the fifty dollars from.
Silas. Ah know one thing.
Liza. What?
Silas. Aunt Nancy's got to start payin' for her room and board.
Liza. *(surprised)* Aunt Nancy!
Silas. Yes. We can't keep her around here as high as everything is.
Liza. *(earnestly)* But look what she done for me. She brought me from flat o' ma back. Ah had one foot in the grave before she come here. And look at me now. Ah'm almost on ma feet.
Silas. Ah can't help it. Ah know she done a whole lot for us, but Ah can't keep things goin' if she don't pay.
Liza. She helps along. She picks up chips and pieces o' coal on the street. That keeps you from havin' to buy 'em.
Silas. Everythin' you sayin' is true, but she's either got to give us some money for stayin' here or she's got to go.

Liza. *(greatly concerned)* If she goes who's goin' to nurse me? Who's goin' in the woods to get the roots to make my medicine?
Silas. If that old woman didn't have money, Ah wouldn't say nothin'.
Liza. *(not understanding)* If she didn't have what?
Silas. If she didn't have money; but Ah know she's got money.
Liza. *(angrily)* Where in the devil would Aunt Nancy get any money from?
Silas. Ain't no use to get mad about it. Ah know what Ah'm sayin'.
Liza. How do you know she's got money?
Silas. Ah know because Ah been watchin' her the last week or so.
Liza. You been watchin' her, is you? Well, what did you find out?
Silas. Ah found out that people passin' in the street give her money every day.
Liza. You ain't talkin' about a cent or two anybody might give a poor old woman, is you?
Silas. No, every day Ah see people givin' her dimes and nickels and quarters. And it ain't no longer than yesterday that Ah seen two rich lookin' men givin' her greenbacks.
Liza. Ah ain't never seen her with no money.
Silas. Ah know you ain't. She hides it.
Liza. Hides it where?
Silas. In the back yard. I know the very place.
Liza. Did you see her hide it there?
Silas. No, Ah didn't see her hide it there, but every time I go out there by that spot she comes right behind me.
Liza. Ah hope you ain't mean enough to try to take her money. Ah mean if she's got any.
Silas. No, Ah ain't been tryin' to take it. Ah just wanted to see what she had there. Ah tried it time and time again, and every time I went close to that spot she come right up.
Liza. Why didn't you wait 'til she went away?
Silas. I done that twice; but every time Ah went out there she come right back just like somethin' drawed her back. Once Ah went out there with a spade and up she comes and stands right on the spot. Ah told her Ah wanted to dig a hole for a post and she said, "Please don't dig it right here, Mr. Silas; Ah got somethin' planted here." You know if somebody has anything planted, they wouldn't go and stand right on the spot.
Liza. *(after a moment's thought)* Well, whether she's got money or not, Ah don't think you ought to put her out after what she's done for us.
Silas. That's the only way I know we can get by.
Liza. That won't make it the right thing to do. A lot o' people get by by doin' the wrong thing. Ah know Emma won't like it.
Silas. It's got to happen just the same if she don't hand out some money. Where's Emma?

Liza. She went after somethin' for dinner.

Silas. When she comes in, tell her what Ah said. 'Course the old woman might get open-hearted and let us have fifty dollars or so; then we won't have no trouble at all and Ah can go back to work tomorrow.

Liza. Maybe she'll let us have that much if she's got it, but Ah don't believe she's got that much.

Silas. *(determined)* Somethin's got to be done. *(as he starts out)* Ah reckon Ah better change these clothes so they'll be clean when Ah do go back.

(He goes out leaving Liza gazing into the fire. Presently Emma returns with the basket on her arm.)

Liza. Ah got a lot o' sad news for you, Emma.

Emma. *(a little frightened at her mother's tone, rests the basket on the table and gazes at her)* What's the matter? Anythin' bad happened?

Liza. They goin' to take the Victrola away.

Emma. The Victrola! Who's goin' to take it away?

Liza. The men from the store's comin' 'cause we ain't been makin' no payments.

Emma. Does Pa know about it?

Liza. Yes, he's the one told me.

Emma. He been here?

Liza. He's here now. They sent him home from work because we ain't been makin' no payments.

Emma. *(fearfully)* He ain't been discharged, is he?

Liza. He ain't been discharged, but he's furloughed and that's just as bad.

Emma. You mean they goin' to let him go back?

Liza. Yes, they'd let him go back today if he could make a good payment on that Victrola; but he reckons he'll have to stay out two or three days as it is.

Emma. Ah'm mighty sorry they put him off, and Ah'm mighty sorry we can't keep that Victrola. Hearin' that thing was about the only pleasure Ah had.

Liza. That ain't the worst yet.

Emma. What, somethin' more? What else is it?

Liza. Your Pa says if Aunt Nancy don't pay some money for stayin' here she's got to go.

Emma. Where's Aunt Nancy goin' to get any money from?

Liza. He says he's been seein' people give her money almost every day, and she's got it buried in the back yard.

Emma. If she's got any money at all, it's just a few cents; but Ah don't believe she's got none.

Silas. *(Entering just in time to hear what Emma says. He is now wearing*

overalls.) Yes, she is got money, too; and she'll either have to pay some or get out.
Emma. *(turning on him)* Ah don't see nothin' fair in that. She picks up chips, she brings home wood and coal, and she nurses Ma. What more do you want?
Silas. *(sitting at the right of the table)* If she'll give me a few dollars or let me borrow a few dollars, maybe Ah can go back to ma job tomorrow.
Emma. If you put her out, Ah believe Ma'll go right back to bed cause there won't be nobody that'll know what to do for her. So Ah don't see nothin' you'll gain by puttin her out.
Silas. If she'll let us have the money—
Emma. If she's got any money it's just a little she's savin' for her son.
Silas. *(surprised)* Her son! Ah didn't know she had no son.
Emma. Yes, seh, she's got a son.
Silas. Where's he? Ah ain't heard nothin' about him.
Emma. He's been in the pen a long time, but Ah reckon he's out now.
Silas. In the pen?
Emma. Yes, seh.
Silas. *(still puzzled)* And she's savin' money for him?
Emma. Ah reckon that's what she's savin' it for if she's got any.
Silas. *(in disgust)* Well, for God's sake! Savin' money for a jailbird!
Emma. She says she wants him to have a few cents to keep him 'til he can get a job.
Silas. Did she tell you all this?
Emma. Yes, seh. Ah wrote a letter for her the other day.
Silas. *(turning to Liza)* Did you know anything about this, Liza?
Liza. No, this is the first time Ah've heard a word about it.
Silas. Why didn't you say somethin' about it?
Emma. You always told me to tend to ma own business. Ah didn't want to be tellin' her business around.
Silas. It's all right to tend to your own business, but it ain't all right to keep secrets from your parents when it concerns 'em. You say her son's out now.
Emma. He was to be out yesterday. She's lookin' for him to come here today.
Silas. What was he sent up for?
Emma. Ah don't know, seh; somethin' about a woman, Ah believe.
Silas. And he means to come here, does he?
Emma. Yes, seh.
Silas. You hear that, Liza?
Liza. Yes, and Ah ain't particular about havin' no jailbird comin' here neither.
Silas. Ah reckon Ah just as well talk to her now as any other time. Was she out there when you come in, Emma?

Emma. Yes, seh, she was sittin' out on the back [steps]; but she got up when Ah came in and started off.

Silas. Well, go tell her to come in here a minute.

Emma. *(as she goes out)* Ah'll have to catch her 'cause Ah reckon she's gone.

Silas. Just go out there and stand by that middle clothes prop and she'll come right in sight. Ah've already tried it a lot o' times myself.

(Emma goes out.)

Silas. Liza, Ah want you to understand Ah'm not actin' this way 'cause Ah mean to be hardhearted. Ah've just got to get out o' this trouble.

Liza. *(discouraged)* Ah'm sorry everything turned out like this, cause I reckon Ah'll have to go back to bed if she goes.

Silas. *(concerned)* Don't say that. The Lord couldn't be that hard on us.

Liza. Ah hope you're right; goodness knows Ah do.

Silas. If Ah can get her to do us this favor before the men come after that Victrola, everything'll be all right. *(There is a pause while they ponder over the situation.)* And even if she will agree to help us, Ah'm tired o' this kind o' life. Ah'm sick o' livin' from hand to mouth.

Liza. Ah reckon we ought to be thankful to be livin' any kind o' way with all the trouble we had. Some people get along better'n we do, but a whole lot o' others don't get along as good. Ah only got one consolation besides believin' in the Lord.

Silas. What's that?

Liza. That things ain't always been like this, and they might not always be like this.

Silas. Ah hope not. *(after he listens)* Here they come.

Liza. Now don't be hard on her, Silas. You know she's been mighty good to us.

Silas. I ain't goin' to be hard on her. Ah'm goin' to be as fair as Ah can.

(Emma enters followed by Aunt Nancy.)

Aunt Nancy. *(moving to the table and speaking to Silas)* You want to see me, seh?

Silas. *(kindly)* Yes'm, Aunt Nancy, Ah want to talk to you. Get 'a chair so she can sit down, Emma.

(Aunt Nancy looks around for a chair; Emma brings her one and she sits above the table.)

Silas. The first thing Ah want to do, Aunt Nancy, is to thank you for all the good things you done for us. And then Ah want to tell you that we're in trouble.

Aunt Nancy. You all in trouble, Mister Silas?

Silas. Yes'm. The men'll be here today after the Victrola, and Ah'm put off from work a few days 'cause Ah didn't pay for it.
Aunt Nancy. Ah'm might sorry for that.
Silas. And you know you been stayin' here with us for six months or more and we ain't been chargin' you a thing.
Aunt Nancy. No, and Ah wouldn't a been able to pay you nothin' no how.
Silas. Now Ah'm askin' if you'll pay us for stayin' or let us borrow a few dollars from you?
Aunt Nancy. *(with a long face)* 'Deed the Lord knows Ah can't pay you nothin', Mister Silas. Ah ain't got nothin' for myself.
Silas. But we know you got money hid out there in the back yard.
Aunt Nancy. Ah got a little money out there, but that ain't for me; that's for ma child.
Silas. *(feigning surprise)* You didn't tell us you had no child.
Aunt Nancy. Ah reckon you'd call him a man, but Ah call him ma child. He's grown.
Silas. Where is he?
Aunt Nancy. Ah reckon he's on his way here now.
Silas. *(still pretending ignorance)* Ah don't see what a old woman like you wants to be savin' money for a grown man for. He ought to be workin' and takin' care o' you. Ain't he workin'?
Aunt Nancy. He's been locked up.
Silas. In jail?
Aunt Nancy. In the pen.
Silas. That's so much the worse. You oughtn't to be savin' money to give to a jailbird.
Aunt Nancy. *(offended)* He ain't no jailbird, Mister Silas; don't call him that. He's ma son.
Silas. He ought to be shamed of hisself for not workin' and takin' care o' you.
Aunt Nancy. That used to be the way when Ah was comin' up. When children used to get grown they used to take care o' the old folks, but now it's different. The old folks has to take care o' the children.
Silas. Ah wouldn't never look out for no grown man.
Aunt Nancy. Ah reckon you wouldn't. Fathers wasn't never like mothers and never will be.
Silas. And 'specially if he went to the pen.
Aunt Nancy. Goin' to the pen ain't nothin'. Some o' the best men in the world's been to the pen. It ain't the goin' to the pen that counts, it's what you go there for. Once it used to be a big disgrace to be locked up; but the people in them days forgot that the Lord was locked up. No, seh, it ain't the bein' locked up, it's what you locked up for. If the Lord had a got locked up for stealin' somethin' or killin' somebody do you think people would be praisin' him like they do?

Silas. I know they wouldn't; but what did your son get locked up for?

Aunt Nancy. He got locked up about a woman, but he done what any other man might a done. He was goin' with a woman what he thought was clean, but she was crooked. He run up on her one night when another man was handlin' her kind o' rough and beat the man up—he beat the man up bad. Then he found out the woman was crooked and he lost his head and beat her up too. That's the worse part of it.

Silas. *(doubtfully)* And they sent him to the pen for that? Just for that?

Aunt Nancy. Yes, seh. The man he beat up was one o' these big fellows what went to church every Sunday, and looked so clean and nice in his biled shirts and white collars and fine clothes all through the week days, but in the night he trailed in the gutter. He used his pull and put up a job on Jim that sent him to the pen.

Silas. Ah don't mean to hurt your feelin's, Aunt Nancy, but your boy can't be much if he beat a woman up.

Liza. 'Deed he can't.

Aunt Nancy. *(hanging her head)* That's the worse part of it. Ah didn't mind him beatin' the man, but Ah never did care much for a man that ud hit a woman—no man but ma own son. *(looking him in the eyes)* And you know a mother can't help that.

Silas. Ah always did think some mothers was too kindhearted.

Aunt Nancy. No, they ain't. Mothers ain't half as kindhearted as God is. If God was hard as some people is, everybody in this world would be farin' mighty bad. You know there ain't no man perfect, and no woman neither.

Silas. I reckon you might be right about that, but the main reason I sent for you was to ask you if you wouldn't let us have a little money. If you can't do it we'll be in a hole sure enough.

Aunt Nancy. Ah wish Ah could. Ah'd be willin' to do anything in the world for you, but he comes first, you know.

Silas. Do you reckon he'll let us have it?

Aunt Nancy. Ah don't know; he's mighty kindhearted. He's takin' a mighty long time to come here too.

(At this time, there is a loud knocking on the outside door.)

Aunt Nancy. *(starting to rise)* Ah reckon that's him now.

Liza. Don't get up, Aunt Nancy; Emma'll let him in.

(Emma goes out.)

Silas. *(to Aunt Nancy)* Why don't you take your bonnet off? You don't want to look like you ain't home.

Aunt Nancy. Never mind. Ah'll keep it on. We won't be here long, Ah reckon.

Emma. *(returning)* It's the men after the Victrola.

(Silas hastens out left.)

Aunt Nancy. *(sighing)* Oh, Lord, Ah thought that was Jim. Ah wonder why he don't come?
Liza. Don't worry, Aunt Nancy, it ain't late.
Emma. Ah reckon he might be lookin' for the place.
Aunt Nancy. But you put this number in the letter, didn' you?
Emma. Yes'm, Ah put it in.
Silas. *(returning)* Ah don't know why Ah done it, but Ah told 'em to wait a few minutes.

(He sits again.)

Aunt Nancy. Ah don't know. Jim might come in a few minutes.

(There is another knock on the door.)

Silas. *(rising)* Ah wonder what they want now?

(He goes out again.)

Aunt Nancy. That might be Jim.
Liza. Ah hope it is.

(Silas returns followed by Jim. When Aunt Nancy sees him she flies towards him. Jim opens his arms and draws her to him.)

Aunt Nancy. *(holding him off and looking at him)* It is you, sure enough? Jim, is it you?
Jim. *(smiling)* Yes'm, it's me.
Aunt Nancy. Come over here.

(She draws him over to the table and we have an opportunity to get a good view of him. He is about thirty, standing over six feet in height and large in proportion. He is wearing a blue shirt with collar attached and a blue suit.)

Aunt Nancy. These is the people Ah been stayin' with all the winter, Jim. *(She names each one in her way of introduction.)* This is Mr. Silas.
Jim. *(smiling as they shake hands)* Glad to meet you, Mr. Silas.
Aunt Nancy. This is Miss Liza.
Jim. *(bowing to Liza)* Glad to meet you Miss Liza.
Aunt Nancy. And this is Emma. *(Jim and Emma bow and smile at each other.)* These people been mighty good to me, Jim.
Jim. *(speaking to all of them)* Ah'm glad to hear that and Ah thank you all for it.
Liza. We ain't been half as good to her as she's been to us.
Emma. Indeed we ain't.

Aunt Nancy. Ah ain't done nothin' that no good woman wouldn't a done. Jim knows me.
Jim. Ah know her well, too.
Aunt Nancy. *(to Jim)* What made you take so long to get here?
Jim. Well, Ah hung around a little while—
Aunt Nancy. Now, Jim, you ain't got no business hangin' 'round when Ah'm waitin' for you.
Jim. And even when Ah got here Ah wasn't sure this was the right place 'cause Ah seen two men hangin' round on the outside and they looked kinder like bootleggers.
Silas. Them's the men that come to take the Victrola away.
Jim. *(turning to Aunt Nancy)* You say these people been good to you, Ma?
Aunt Nancy. Yes, they been mighty good to me.
Jim. *(reaching into his pocket)* Ah got fifteen dollars. You can have that if it'll do you any good. *(He gives it to Silas.)*
Silas. *(taking the money)* Thanks for that. Maybe some o' these days—

(The two men who have been waiting outside enter.)

First Man. Ah'm sorry, but we can't wait all day; we got to get back to the store.
Jim. *(to Silas)* How much do you owe on it?
Silas. Fifty dollars.
Jim. Fifteen dollars won't do much good then, will it?
Silas. Well, it'll help. Ah been tryin' to borrow it from your Ma.
Second Man *(roughly)* Come on, Dan, let's take it; they ain't got nothin'.
Silas. *(as they take hold of the Victrola)* Wait a minute!
Jim. *(turning to his mother)* You got any money, Ma?
Aunt Nancy. Ah got a little Ah been savin' for you.
Jim. How much?
Aunt Nancy. *(who is not very good at figures)* Ah don't know, but Ah reckon it's enough. Ah'll get it. *(She goes out right.)*
Second Man. *(impatiently)* Come on, Dan; this is all a bluff.

(They move the Victrola towards the door.)

Jim. *(getting in the doorway)* There ain't nobody or nothin' goin' out o' here 'til she comes back!

(Jim is such a large man and so nearly fills the doorway that the two men stop and reconsider their plan. They decide to wait.)

Jim. Ah don't mean no harm to nobody and Ah wouldn't hurt a hair in nobody's head; but when Ah say wait, Ah mean wait.
First Man. But you see, mister, we been waitin' a long time already.
Jim. Well, you won't have to wait much longer. She'll be back in a minute.

(Aunt Nancy returns with a rather dirty box which she puts on the table and opens. All gaze into it.)

Aunt Nancy. *(pouring the contents of the box on the table)* This is yours, Jim. Ah been savin' it for you ever since you went away.
Jim. *(staring at the money)* All this for me?
Aunt Nancy. Yes, and you can do anything you want to do with it.
Jim. *(pushing half of the money to Silas).* Here, take this; maybe it'll be enough.

(Judging from the expression on Aunt Nancy's face Jim is giving away too much.)

Silas. *(drawing the money to him)* 'Deed it will be enough. *(After counting the money he hands part of it to one of the men.)* Here's your fifty dollars.

(The first man takes the money and with the aid of the second man pushes the Victrola back to its place. Having done this they start out.)

Jim. *(to Silas)* You better get a receipt for that.
Silas. *(to the men)* Hey, wait a minute. *(The men stop.)* Gimme a receipt for that money. *(The first man writes him a receipt and then they go out.)* That's better. *(after indicating the money left on the table)* Ah reckon you better take the rest of it back, Jim.
Jim. No, you keep it. You all been good to Ma, and ain't nothin' Ah got too good for you.
Liza. She done a whole lot more for us than we could ever do for her.
Aunt Nancy. Ah'd a give you that money before, Mr. Silas, but Ah was savin' it for Jim, and Ah just didn't have the heart to give it away.
Silas. That's all right, Auntie; Ah 'preciated it just as much as if you had give it to me when Ah first ask you.
Aunt Nancy. *(taking up her basket)* Well, Jim, Ah reckon we better be goin'.
Liza. *(quickly, in surprise)* Goin'! Where you goin'?
Aunt Nancy. Goin' to get a place to stay.
Jim. Then Ah'm goin' to look for a job.
Liza. But Ah thought you was goin' to stay here with us.
Aunt Nancy. You ain't got no room for both of us, chile.
Silas. *(shifting the chairs around)* Yes'm, we is. We'll make room.
Jim. No, seh. Ah don't want you to cramp yourself on ma account. It won't take us long to find another place.
Liza. But how'll Ah get along, Aunt Nancy, with you gone?
Aunt Nancy. Ah won't be far away. Ah'll come in and look after you every day.

Liza. Ah'm mighty sorry you goin'; and Ah want to thank you for what you done for us.
Aunt Nancy. *(as she and Jim stand near the door)* Maybe we'll ask you all to do us a favor sometime.
Silas. And we'll be mighty glad to do it.
Aunt Nancy. Well, good day 'til tomorrow.
Silas, Liza & Emma. Good day.
Jim. Good day to all of you.
Silas, Liza & Emma. Good day.

(Aunt Nancy and Jim go out.)

Emma. Ah'm sorry she's gone.
Liza. You might be mighty sorry he's gone too by the way you look at him.
Silas. Deed she must be. She looked at him like her life depended on it.
Liza. To tell the truth, Ah'm mighty sorry she's gone too. She's sure goin' to be a loss to me.
Silas. But she says she's goin' to come around every day to look after you.
Liza. Yes, but that ain't like stayin here.
Silas. Well, there ain't nothin' Ah can do.
Emma. Ah reckon you're mighty glad you didn't put her out.
Silas. Ah am, Ah'm mighty glad.
Liza. She got us out o' trouble, all right.
Emma. Indeed she did.
Silas. Ah got to go and get ma work clothes on and go and see about ma job.
Liza. She saved your job too, Ah'm thinkin'.
Silas. You bet your life she did.

(Curtain)

Emperor of Haiti (1938; rev. 1963)

Langston Hughes (1902–1967)

Born in Missouri, educated at Columbia and Lincoln universities, Langston Hughes, best known as a poet, maintained an interest in drama throughout his forty-six-year career as a professional author. A talented and versatile writer, Hughes also distinguished himself as a writer of fiction and an editor of anthologies presenting diverse aspects of black culture and history.

Even if one considers only his activities in the theatre, Hughes's productivity is significant. He wrote eight full-length plays, three one-act plays, four song plays and a cantata, the librettos for four operas, a screen play, ten scripts for radio and television, and the lyrics for the musical version of Elmer Rice's *Street Scene*. In addition, during the 1930s and 1940s he established three African American dramatic groups—the Suitcase Theatre in Harlem, the Negro Art Theatre in Los Angeles, and the Skyloft Players in Chicago.

His drama frequently suffers from such literary flaws as sentimentalized or farcical situations, melodramatic incidents, and stereotyped characterization. As dramatic entertainment, however, they delighted both the white audiences downtown in New York and the black audiences uptown. *Mulatto* (1935) was the first drama by an African American to have a long run on Broadway—the longest, in fact, of any before Lorraine Hansberry's *A Raisin in the Sun*. Hughes's *Don't You Want to Be Free?*, a one-act historical panorama about

African Americans, set a record in Harlem by lasting for what the author estimated to be almost two hundred performances.

Hughes worked on *Emperor of Haiti* for more than one quarter of a century. He first produced it in 1935 as *Drums of Haiti,* revised it in 1938 under its present title, adapted it into an opera, *Troubled Island* (1949), and completed his revisions of it as a drama in 1963. Located in Haiti at the time of the successful rebellion against the forces of Napoleon Bonaparte, *Emperor of Haiti* focuses on Jean Jacques Dessalines, a black rebel who rose to power as a general and an emperor. The issue of the play, however, is not solely the struggle against the whites but also the manner in which Dessalines becomes corrupted by his sense of power and desire for luxury. Important to his failure was the intraracial rivalry between the blacks and the mulattoes of Haiti. By describing the Haitians' excessive concern about distinctions based on color, class, and culture, Hughes warned African Americans against the destructive divisions which such prejudices can create.

Dramatic Works of Langston Hughes

Full-length Plays
Emperor of Haiti (1938). Three-act tragedy. Produced by Gilpin Players.
Front Porch (1938). Three-act comedy. Produced by Gilpin Players.
Joy to My Soul (1937). Three-act comedy. Produced by Gilpin Players.
Little Ham (1935). Three-act comedy. Produced by Gilpin Players. In *Five Plays by Langston Hughes,* ed. by W. Smalley. Bloomington, Ind.: Indiana University Press, 1963.
Mulatto (1935). Three-act tragedy. Year on Broadway, 1935–36; eight months on the road, produced in various countries. In *Five Plays by Langston Hughes.*
Simply Heavenly (1957). Two-act comedy with music. Produced on Broadway. New York: Dramatists Play Service, 1959. Also in *Five Plays.*
The Sun Do Move (1942). Musical drama. Produced by Skyloft Players.
Tambourines to Glory (1963). Two-act comedy drama with music, adapted from Hughes's novel of the same title. In *Five Plays.*
When the Jack Hollers (1936). In collaboration with A. Bontemps. Produced by Gilpin Players.

One-act Plays
Don't You Want to Be Free? (1936). Historical panorama. Published in *One Act Play Magazine,* October 1938.
The Gold Piece (1921). A play for children.
Soul Gone Home (1937). A fantasy. Published in *One Act Play Magazine,* July 1937.

Operas
The Barrier (1949). Libretto based on *Mulatto.*
Esther (1957).
Port Town (1960).
Troubled Island (1949). Libretto based on *The Emperor of Haiti.* Score by William Grant Still. New York: Leeds Music Corp., 1949.

Song Plays
Black Nativity (1961). A Christmas song play.
Gospel Glow (1962).
Jericho Jim Crow (1964).
The Prodigal Son (1965).

Lyrics for Musicals
Just around the Corner (1951). Book by A. Mann and B. Drew.
Street Scene (1947). Book by E. Rice, New York: Chappell, 1947.

Selected Bibliography about Hughes as Playwright

Emanuel, James A. *Langston Hughes.* New York: Twayne, 1967.
Kaiser, Ernest. "Selected Bibliography of the Published Writings of Langston Hughes," *Freedomways,* VII (Spring 1968), 185–191.
O'Daniel, Therman B. "Langston Hughes: A Selected Classified Bibliography," *CLA Journal,* XI (June 1968), 349–366.
Turner, Darwin T. "Langston Hughes as Playwright," *CLA Journal,* XI (June 1968), 297–309.

Emperor of Haiti

CHARACTERS
(In Order of Appearance)

Josef, a young slave, later Grand Marshal
Azelia, wife of Dessalines
Martel, an elderly slave, later Chief Councillor
Dessalines, slave leader, later Emperor
Congo, a slave, later a Baron
Xavier, a slave
Antoine, a slave, later a Baron
Mars, a one-armed slave, later a Duke
Popo, a slave, later Chief Attendant
Celeste, a slave, later a Lady
Lulu, a slave, later a Lady
Dembu, a slave, later a Major
Pierre, a child, later Chief Bugler
Papaloi, Voodoo Priest
Mamaloi, Voodoo Priestess
Vuval }
Beyard } Free Mullatoes, later Counts
Stenio }
First Old Woman } Servants at the Court
Second Old Woman }
Claire Heureuse, Consort of the Emperor
Lord Bobo, Grand Treasurer

Mango Vendor ⎫
Pepper Vendor ⎪
Cocoanut Vendor ⎪
Melon Vendor ⎪
Thread Vendor ⎬ Market Women on the Quay
Yam Vendor ⎪
Tall Fisherman ⎪
Short Fisherman ⎪
Ragamuffins ⎭
Soldiers
Slaves, Dukes, Duchesses, Courtiers, Servants, Butlers, Pages, Ladies-of-the-Presence, Lady-in-Waiting, A Ragged Boy, A Flower Girl, Dancing Girls, A Male Dancer, Two Children.

CAUTION NOTICE

"Emperor of Haiti" by Langston Hughes. Copyright 1936 by Langston Hughes; renewed © 1963 by Langston Hughes. Reprinted by permission of Harold Ober Associates Incorporated. All inquiries for professional and amateur rights should be addressed to Harold Ober Associates Incorporated, 425 Madison Avenue, New York, N.Y. 10017, Agents for the Estate of Langston Hughes.

SCENES

ACT I

An abandoned sugar mill. Night.

ACT II

Scene 1: A room at Dessalines' palace.
Scene 2: The banquet terrace. Immediately following.

ACT III

A quay in a fishing village. Noon.

Place: The island of Haiti.
Time: The Napoleonic era.

ACT I
• • • • • •

Time: *The year 1791.*

Place: *An abandoned sugar mill in the French colony of Haiti, then officially known as St. Domingue. It is night. Through the broad open door the moon shines. Without, tall coconut palms stand against the stars, and hills rise in the distance.*

At Rise: *Josef, a young black man, stands in the doorway, the curve of a cane knife in his hand. Carefully he inspects the knife. At the noise of footsteps and the breaking of underbrush, his body becomes tense. He listens, then cries in a loud whisper.*

Josef. *(softly, but with great sternness)* Halt! Who's there?

Azelia. *(a woman's voice in the darkness)* Once . . .

Josef. *(to complete a password)* . . . a slave . . .

Azelia. *(continuing the formula)* . . . but soon no more!

Josef. Free?

Azelia. Free! It's me, Azelia, from the Riviere Plantation.

Josef. Come on, then. You gave the password.

Azelia. *(entering, a load of bananas in a flat wicker tray on her head)* Jean Jacques's coming, too, so I run ahead to see if all's safe here.

Josef. *(astonished)* Did Jean Jacques send you?

Azelia. Course not! Jean Jacques fears nothing in Haiti, or anywhere. But he stopped to speak with a guard at the bridge, so I come on. *(putting her burden down on a corner of the cane grinder)* Look, Josef, under these bananas all the arms I could find. *(laughing)* I put this fruit on top to hide what I was carrying, weapons for tonight.

Josef. Did you pass any Frenchmen?

Azelia. Only one old planter on horseback, and he didn't stop us. We kept to the woods mostly. Look! Lift up these bananas.

Josef. *(helping her move the fruit)* Um-umh!

Azelia. Three machetes! See! Two pistols, stolen from the overseer, the butt end of an ax. *(They inspect the weapons.)* Jean Jacques brings a Spanish rifle and a dozen flails.

Josef. We'll need 'em all, I reckon. Do the whites on your plantation smell a rat yet?

Azelia. Don't think so. But the air's full of evil. The overseers drove us like dogs today in the fields.

Josef. On our place, as well.

Azelia. And I'm tired, so tired I can't hardly drag. This "fruit" was heavy.

Josef. I'm tired as hell, too. But this is one night we've got to stay awake. *(turning)* Say, didn't I hear there was a whipping on your place this morning?

Azelia. Yes.
Josef. Who?
Azelia. Jean Jacques was whipped.
Josef. You mean you . . . ?
Azelia. My man.
Josef. Good Lord! For what?
Azelia. Being caught off the place at night without permission. They caught him coming back this morning.
Josef. What'd he tell them?
Azelia. That he'd been to a voodoo meeting.
Josef. Then . . . ?
Azelia. They called all the slaves together to watch him beaten. The foreman gave him fifty lashes, hard. And master and his sons stood around and laughed to see a slave with such a fine name take a lashing.
Josef. What about his name?
Azelia. They said Jean Jacques Dessalines was too much name for a slave to have. Let slaves have just one name, that's what they said.
Josef. Well, after tonight, nobody'll give orders to a slave. I cut my last acre of cane today—if I live or die.
Azelia. And Jean Jacques's took his last beating—if we succeed.
Josef. We'll succeed, or else stay in the hills like the runaway maroons until we're free.

(A noise is heard outside.)

Josef. Be quiet! *(They stop to listen. Josef goes to the door.)* Halt! Who's that?
Martel. *(an old man's voice)* Once . . .
Josef. A slave . . .
Martel. . . . But soon no more.
Josef. Free?
Martel. Free!
Josef. Come in, Martel. We need you wise old men.
Martel. *(entering)* Good evening, Josef, son! Azelia, good evening! Where's Dessalines?
Azelia. Jean Jacques's nearby, Father Martel. I'll tell him you're here.
Martel. Thank you, daughter. But keep to the shadows, the moon is bright.

(Azelia exits.)

Martel. *(to the young man)* Josef, yon moon in sky, mark you how it stares at us?
Josef. Yes, Father Martel.
Martel. A long time that moon's looked down upon Haiti. And tears of dew have fallen from its face in pity upon our troubled island where men are slaves.

Josef. True, Father Martel.
Martel. Even now yon moon looks out across the silver ocean, watching the slave ships sail toward the western world with their woeful burdens. The cries of black men and women, and the clank of chains in the night, rise up against the face of the moon.
Josef. My mother came that way, Martel, in a slave ship. She still remembers Africa.
Martel. Africa! So long, so far away! But tonight the moon weeps tears of joy, son, for Africa. And when in its next passage across the sea, it shines on our sweet motherland, it'll smile and say, "Thy black children in Haiti have thrown off the yoke of bondage, and are men again!" Josef, my children grew up slaves. My grandchildren, too . . . but yours will be free!
Josef. I wait for the beat of the drums to tell me when to lift this knife. *(He raises his machete.)*
Martel. For seventy years I've waited. Now our time is come. When the slave Boukman lays his fingers on the great drum hidden in the cane brake tonight, he'll beat out a signal that'll roll from hill to hill, slave hut to slave hut, across the cane fields, across the mountains, across the bays from island to island, until every drum in Haiti throbs with the call to rise and seek freedom. Then the moon will smile, son.
Josef. And I'll smile, too, Martel.
Martel. But come! I've orders for you, Josef. Time is passing.
Josef. Yes, sir, I'm listening.
Martel. *(motioning to Josef to make a light)* Let us light a lantern. It's safe since sentries now are posted around this mill like the spokes of a wheel. I've just helped Yayou place twenty men who accompanied us from Dondon. So we can have a light. And you need no longer call for the password at the door.
Josef. Then what, sir?
Martel. Go station yourself by the spring and see that no man poisons our water, should there be traitors among us.
Josef. Yes, Father Martel.
Martel. When the drums sound, then come here for instructions from Dessalines.
Josef. From Jean Jacques Dessalines?
Martel. Jean Jacques. Tonight in the name of the slaves the council chose him for our leader.
Josef. I'm glad, for he's strong.
Martel. And to be trusted.
Josef. No one hates the French more than he does.
Martel. And no one's worked harder preparing for this night. Jean Jacques has not slept for weeks. Twice he's been caught coming in at dawn and beaten for it by the overseers. But be about your business, son.

Josef. I'm going now. *(He goes to the door, but pauses there.)* Someone is coming. It's Jean Jacques—*(as he salutes)* Dessalines!

Dessalines. *(entering; a powerful black man in ragged clothing, followed by Azelia)* Hello, Josef. You salute me like a French soldier!

Josef. You're our leader now, Jean Jacques.

Dessalines. *(pleased)* I'm your leader, Josef. *(He returns the salute. Josef exits.)*

Martel. Good evening, son! I'm glad you're early.

Dessalines. I'm glad to find you already here.

(They shake hands and immediately busy themselves with plans.)

Dessalines. You can tell me where the rations are hidden in the hills, can't you, Martel? Twenty miles from the foot of Timber Mountain on the road to Le Trou our first supplies are buried? And the sign is three curved marks on a tree? Is that right?

Martel. Yes, Jean Jacques.

Dessalines. Then forty paces in from the road we'll find a scattering of seashells? And there, dig?

Martel. Yes, that's how 'twas planned. Food's hidden there in the earth, and arms.

Dessalines. *(to Azelia)* Have the women been told to bring cook-pots?

Azelia. We looked out for that. Those little things . . .

Dessalines. Nothing's a little thing now, Zelia.

Azelia. *(jokingly)* How about your pipe, Jean Jacques? *(producing it from her hair)* It's a little thing you're crazy about, but you forgot to bring it.

Dessalines. *(impatiently)* Don't trifle, Azelia. There's too much to do.

Azelia. Forgive me. *(She puts her arm about his shoulder and offers him the pipe.)* Go on with your plans.

Dessalines. *(loudly)* Don't touch me! God! My shoulder's raw as meat!

Azelia. Oh, I'm sorry, Jean Jacques.

Dessalines. *(sarcastically)* We have a kind master, Martel.

Martel. He'll be master no more when the sun rises.

Dessalines. He'll be less than nothing. He'll be dead. Our gentle master will burn in his bed this evening, roasted between his silken sheets.

Azelia. Poor man!

Dessalines. *(turning on her)* Strange you should say *"Poor man,"* Azelia! What's he to you? *(fiercely)* Have you ever been one of his mistresses? Every black woman he's wanted he's had.

Azelia. Not me! No, no! Not me!

Dessalines. Then why cry pity on him? I know you must hate him. But when you say, *"Poor man,"* you make me laugh. The whites never have pity on us. We're just slaves, dogs to them.

Azelia. You're right, Jean Jacques!

Dessalines. They burned Mackandal for trying to be free, didn't they? They had no mercy on him. We'll show no mercy on them now.
Martel. I remember well the burning of Mackandal. Thirty years gone by, 'tis. They made the slaves for miles around witness it, as an example of what happens to any Negro who wants to be free. Burning is a horrible thing, Jean Jacques! I hate to think that we must do it, too.
Dessalines. You're over kind, Martel. I do not love my masters.
Martel. I'd let them live, if they'd leave us free.
Dessalines. They won't, so there's no *if* about it. We have no choice but to kill . . . wipe out the whites in all this island . . . for if the French are left alive to force us back to slavery, we'll never get a chance to rise again. And for us, you and me—Boukman, Christophe, Toussaint, and all our leaders—there'd be only the rack, the wheel, or burning at the stake like Mackandal. Mackandal! *(turning and appealing to the night)* Great Mackandal! Dead leader of rebellious slaves, fight with us now.
Martel. Mackandal is with us, son. His spirit walks the Haitian hills crying the name of freedom.
Dessalines. But the only way to be free is to fight! Or else to die.
Martel. Tonight we fight to live, Jean Jacques.
Dessalines. To live! Men free, alive! Alive! Go, Martel, and tell that to the men on guard without, for some are even yet afraid. I saw it in their eyes. Tell them tonight we strike with all our force, and none must be afraid. There are two ways of being free . . . alive or dead. We'll live! This time, the French will die.
Martel. I'll go, Jean Jacques. *(He exits.)*
Azelia. *(drawing near her husband)* But you and I, Jean Jacques, we must live. *(fiercely)* I will not have you dead.
Dessalines. Why must *we* live any more than the others, Azelia?
Azelia. Because we have loved so little, Jean Jacques, been happy too little. Never a night is mine alone—never just you and me—
Dessalines. That's true, Azelia, but—
Azelia. Every night there's been something to keep you from me. Ever since we've had a hut together, you've been stealing out to crawl through the forest, in the dark, to some secret meeting of the slaves, planning this break for freedom—and I'm left alone. Tonight has taken all our nights, Jean Jacques, the cane field all our days.
Dessalines. But what I've planned—it is good, Azelia?
Azelia. Good, Jean Jacques. But for a woman, love, too, is good.
Dessalines. Yes, yes, I know, but at a time like this, it's foolish. *(He busies himself inspecting a pistol.)*
Azelia. Foolish, I know, but I love you, Jean. *(fearfully)* Listen to me! If we fail, the French will kill you. They'll tear your body on the rack or break you on the wheel.

Dessalines. We will not fail, Azelia. Don't worry.
Azelia. But if we did, I'd share death, too. We've shared so much together. When we were children running wild in the slave quarters, we ate from the same trough where our master fed the dogs. Together we learned to pick the cotton clean. Then in the green cane fields, I watched you swing your knife, big and strong in the sunlight. My man! My Jean Jacques! We tied the cane into bundles, and in the long night learned to stir the bubbling syrup in its copper kettles. But there came a dawn when the kettles boiled, forgotten. That night we knew that love was sweeter than the syrup. Then our little hut together, and I your wife.
Dessalines. Wife? *(laughing)* A word the whites use. We never had a priest, nor papers, either.
Azelia. We had ourselves. You, me! I, you!
Dessalines. *(bitterly)* And neither of us freedom.
Azelia. You always talk of freedom, Jean Jacques! I want to be free, too, but—
Dessalines. But what?
Azelia. I'm afraid. . . .
Dessalines. Afraid? Afraid of what? Don't rile me, Azelia.
Azelia. *(slowly)* Afraid freedom'll take you away from me.
Dessalines. Don't be a fool! Why, when we're free, we can go anywhere and do anything we want to, you and me together.
Azelia. I just want to be together, always with you.
Dessalines. Then don't worry. I'm not going to leave you. I'll even get a paper and marry you like the white folks do, if that's what you want— except that we couldn't read what's on the paper.
Azelia. Are we too old to learn to read now?
Dessalines. I expect we are, Azelia. But not too old to be free. *(rising)* Come on, Azelia, let's look about the mill and see if there're any spies hiding in the rafters, or in that vat yonder, waiting to run back to the white folks with word of our meeting place. *(As Azelia puts out her hands to detain him, he flinches with pain.)* Take care, woman.
Azelia. Forgive me, Jean Jacques, and kiss me just once, for all the years that love has been our chain.
Dessalines. And slavery our master.
Azelia. And freedom your hope.
Dessalines. You're fighting with me, Azelia?
Azelia. Until the end, Jean Jacques.
Dessalines. *(as he kisses her)* Azelia! Azelia! *(turning away)* The crowd'll be here in no time, now. Let's look in this bin and see if it's empty. *(He tries to lift the wooden lid.)* By God, it's heavy! Help me, Zelia.
Congo. *(a deep voice inside the bin)* Hands off, less'n you want a shot through the belly.

Dessalines. *(brandishing his cane knife)* Who's there?
Congo. *(calmly, from within)* Who's out there?
Dessalines. Jean Jacques!
Congo. *(drawling)* Jean Jacques, who?
Dessalines. Jean Jacques Dessalines.
Congo. *(lifting up lid of box and emerging)* Well, tell me something, pal! *(with a half-lazy salute)* Hello, Jean Jacques! Hello, Azelia!
Dessalines. What're you doing, Congo?
Congo. I'm on guard.
Dessalines. On guard?
Congo. On guard—locked in the box, so nobody can bother me—nor the guns, neither, we got stacked in there.
Dessalines. What did you open up for, then, you careless fool?
Congo. Who wouldn't know your voice, boy, as many times as I heard you talking to us slaves around the fire at night—when the white folks thought we was just having a little voodoo dance? You gets around a-plenty, Jean Jacques.
Dessalines. You knowed me by my voice?
Congo. Every black man in North Haiti knows you. We're waiting for you to lead us, if them old slaves in the council ever make up their minds who they gonna pick out.
Dessalines. Then close the box and lock it until I give the word, Congo, for *I am* leader now. *(proudly)* Tonight the council picked me.
Congo. That's good, boy! I'm glad!
Dessalines. Are there two hundred rifles in there, as there should be?
Congo. Two hundred, Jean Jacques.
Dessalines. Then remain on guard! But not inside.
Congo. I got you, chief.
Dessalines. *(laughing)* Chief!
Congo. Like in Africa, Jean Jacques—Chief.
Dessalines. Can you remember Africa, Congo?
Congo. Sure. I was a big boy when that English ship got hold of me. That's why I can do our dances so well. I learnt 'em in Africa.
Dessalines. Well, tomorrow, boy, we'll dance a-plenty. If I can loosen up my back.
Congo. Not whipped again?
Dessalines. Yes, whipped.
Congo. You sure got a mean old master. What kind of whip he use?
Dessalines. A cat-o'-nine tail 'cross my shoulders.
Congo. *(laughing)* Huh! That's nothing! My master uses a tree limb on my head.
Dessalines. *(angrily)* And you laugh and like it?
Congo. *(suddenly sober)* I don't like it; that's why I'm guarding these guns.

Azelia. *(in the doorway)* Listen! I hear a horse down the road, coming fast.
Congo. *(listening)* I hear it, too. There ain't no slaves got horses.
Dessalines. Some free mulatto, perhaps. One of our allies! It's time for everybody to be here, and so far they've only come from Dondon. Where's everyone else? Where's the crowd from Milot, and from Limbe? This is no time to be late!
Azelia. You know how careful everybody's got to be tonight. You warned them yourself not to hurry in case the white folks get to looking out of the corners of their eyes.
Congo. Folks what's been working all day's just naturally slow, anyhow. I know I am.
Dessalines. Not when their life depends on it. *(as the horse's hoofs approach)* Let me go see who's coming there. *(He goes to the door.)*
Congo. It *must* be a mulatto. No Negro's got a horse to ride on. *(muttering)* And I don't trust them mulattoes, myself.
Azelia. Black mother, white father, free.
Congo. Free or not, their white fathers treat 'em almost as bad as us slaves.
Azelia. But they sometimes leave them land and money.
Congo. Then the mulattoes think they're white for sure!
Azelia. And look down on us for being black.
Congo. And for being slaves.
Dessalines. Keep quiet, you. The mulattoes who've joined us hate the whites.
Congo. A little hate ain't enough. If they'd ever been driven to the fields like us, they'd know how to hate a-plenty; I tell you, I don't trust 'em.
Dessalines. Well, they're smart. They've been to school and got an education. We need their heads.
Congo. I'd like to cut their heads off and play ninepins with 'em.
Dessalines. Not those that are with us, Congo. *(going outside the door)* But that's no mulatto on that horse. Even the moon don't brighten up his face. *(calling)* Who's there?
Xavier. *(voice out of breath)* Me, Jean Jacques!
Azelia. It looks like Xavier from Breda Plantation.
Dessalines. It is Xavier. *(as a man comes running toward him)* What's up? A message?
Xavier. *(entering, panting)* Yes, Jean Jacques! A message! Bad news! Some of the white folks done found out.
Dessalines. What? Where?
Congo. How?
Azelia. *(in terror)* Oh!
Xavier. That mulatto, Gautier, we thought was with us, he got cold feet and sent his family into the Cape for safety. The whites on the next plantation, related to him, asked what's up, and he told them they'd better leave for

the Cape, too. Then the white man grabbed him by the throat and made him confess there's trouble in the air.

Dessalines. A yellow dog! What then?

Xavier. The house slaves knew something must be wrong, and old Bajean came out and told me. I gave orders to set fire to the house as soon as I got started on this horse I stole from the stables.

Dessalines. And did they fire the house?

Xavier. I didn't see it burning as I looked back.

Dessalines. It's wise they didn't. T'would alarm the plain for miles about. Everyone had orders not to fire until the drums are beaten. Our plans are to let the whites think they've escaped. Then shoot them down on the road. And the false mulattoes, too! Damn their chicken-hearted souls! Are there many people on the way, Xavier?

Xavier. The roads were empty as I came, but all along in the woods, slaves creep towards here. Soon there'll be a crowd. And all are wondering who is chief?

Dessalines. I am, Xavier.

Xavier. *(stepping forward and shaking hands)* We trust you, Jean Jacques.

Dessalines. Thank you, friend. Now back to your plantation and see if your master's escaped. And if the mulatto who squealed is still living, kill him ere the drums beat.

Xavier. I will, chief. *(He leaves. Horse's hoofs. Sounds of movement and voices without.)*

Congo. You see, I tell you about mulattoes! They're dangerous.

Dessalines. They're not all alike, Congo. Some we can trust. Vuval is one. Stenio's another. These mulattoes are with us. *(looking out)* But say, here come the men we're waiting for. *(calling)* It's time you got here.

(Several enter, including the slaves, Antoine, Mars, Popo, and the women, Celeste and Lulu, with her child, Pierre, a boy of six or seven. Greetings are exchanged.)

Antoine. Greetings, Jean Jacques! We're glad you're leader. *(They shake hands.)*

Lulu. Hello, Azelia! Ain't you proud of your man now?

Azelia. I am that, Lulu. He's chief.

Popo. Hello, Jean Jacques.

Dessalines. Hello, Popo. Congratulate me, boy!

Popo. I knew they'd pick you, Jean Jacques! It couldn't be nobody else. We're sticking with you, partner.

Lulu. Well, it looks like Negroes is getting together at last.

Celeste. It sho do, Lulu!

Dessalines. *(to Celeste)* How about a dance tomorrow night, Celeste, to celebrate our freedom?

Celeste. *(laughing)* Not with Azelia's say-so! I'm scared of you, Jean Jacques. You're a lady-killer.
Dessalines. Not much! Too busy now. *(turning to Mars)* Hello, Mars! Is Dembu, the powder-maker, with you?
Mars. He was right behind us.
Dembu. *(entering)* Here I am, Jean Jacques.
Dessalines. Come aside a moment. I want to talk with you.

(They withdraw into the shadows.)

Congo. *(to the child, Pierre, who has climbed up on the box of guns)* Boy, you better get down off that box, you'll burn your feet.
Pierre. Why, what's in here? *(as he hugs Congo around the neck)*
Congo. You'll see by and by. Stop hugging me! I ain't your pappy.
Lulu. *(to her child)* Pierre, behave yourself. Get down, now, hear?

(The child gets down.)

Antoine. *(to Popo, who is bare from the waist up)* Popo, where's your shirt?
Celeste. Maybe he ain't got none.
Popo. Yes, I got one, but I hid it soaked in oil in my master's storehouse. My girl's to fire it, when the signal's given.
Celeste. *(peering at Popo's breast)* You've sure had a lot of masters, ain't you, Popo? All them brands they done burnt on your breast.
Popo. I been sold four times, but one master was kind, and didn't put his mark on me. Old man Thibault, he said he liked the way I played the drums.
Celeste. You was lucky. When Thibault owned me, he branded me twice. Sure wished I'd learned to play the drums.
Mars. *(a man with one arm)* Talk about drums, we got the biggest drum on the North Plain hidden on our place; Old Lucumi's ready waiting down in the banana grove. He's gonna beat out the freedom signal so's the slaves across the mountains can hear it.
Lulu. Them big old goat drums sure can rock the stars.
Pierre. How far can they sound, mama?
Lulu. Forty kilometres, I reckon, son, or more. Can't they, Mars?
Mars. Farther than that on a clear night.
Pierre. I'd rather have a bugle, that's what I want.
Celeste. For what?
Pierre. A bugle blows pretty. All the white children have 'em.
Celeste. The white children's free.
Mars. Anyhow, a drum can sound twenty times as far as any bugle ever blowed. Bugles don't belong to black folks.
Pierre. That's how come I want one.
Lulu. You can have one, honey, when we's free.

Pierre. Tomorrow?

Lulu. I 'spects tomorrow.

Celeste. Drums is what our gods like, though. Drums is for Legba and Dambala, Nannan and M'bo.

Congo. African gods been knowin' drums a long time. Them tinny bugles just cain't reach they ears.

Antoine. Goat's blood, cock's blood, and drums.

Mars. The drum's a black man's heart a-beatin'. Tonight that beatin's goin' to set the Frenchmen's hair on end.

Congo. This is our night tonight.

Celeste. A mighty night it'll be, too. Bless Legba!

Mars. My one good arm is ready. *(He lifts his single arm.)*

Pierre. Where's your other arm, Monsieur Mars?

Mars. *(bitterly)* The Black Code, son. The French've got it all writ' down that if a slave raise his hand against a white man, they can cut it off. They cut off mine.

Congo. We'll remember that tonight.

Antoine. Let the French dwell a thousand years in hell, they'll never forget this night.

Popo. If there is a hell, I hope I meet no Frenchmen there.

Lulu. Hell's a place for Christians, ain't it? Not for us.

Antoine. That's all. Our voodoo gods ain't mixin' with the white gods.

Celeste. Legba's better.

Popo. White folks must have a special hell, anyhow, for themselves, reserved. They wouldn't go where us black folks goes, would they?

Congo. They'll find out what hell they're headed for mighty soon.

(Sounds of chanting and rattles without. People clear the doorway as a papaloi, in anklets of bone and a high feathered headdress enters, followed by a mamaloi of powerful physique, carrying a live cock. The man has a rattle in one hand and an African drum under his arm.)

Lulu. There's the mamaloi from Lombe.

Celeste. And she carries a live cock to sacrifice on the mountain.

Pierre. The papaloi's got a drum. Lemme go see!

(The women and the child join a crowd that now clusters, chanting, about the high priest and priestess of voodoo, who chatter in an African tongue, calling on the gods.)

Papaloi. Uglumbagolaita! Damballa! Solomini! Keetai!

Mamaloi. Legba! Legba! Legba!

(The women cry and shout.)

Dessalines. *(who is in conference with a group)* Not so loud, there, women. We've plans to make. Call the gods a little softer. Please!

(The group about the priests becomes less noisy. Three mulattoes enter, Vuval, Beyard, and Stenio. They are better dressed than the slaves, and much more polished. They seem out of place.)

Antoine. Who are those mulattoes? Why do they come here?
Mars. Vuval and his friends. They're on our side. They're all right.
Antoine. The smart half-breeds!
Congo. Better we didn't have them with us. They've never been slaves.
Mars. But Vuval's a poor mulatto.
Popo. His French father didn't leave him a thing but books.
Antoine. And half-freedom.
Congo. They're half-men, not black, not white either. Bah!
Mars. *(as the Mulattoes approach)* Hello, Stenio. Evening, Vuval.
Stenio. Gentlemen, good evening.
Vuval. Good evening, comrades. *(indicating Beyard)* My cousin, Beyard.
Beyard. *(rather pompously)* Greetings in the name of liberty.
Popo. *(shortly)* Howdy!

(The mill has gradually begun to fill with slaves standing in groups talking in low voices.)

Vuval. Is it true, the slave council has chosen Dessalines as leader?
Mars. It's true, and good, ain't it?
Beyard. I doubt it's being good. He's ignorant and headstrong.
Vuval. A brave fellow. But he's been nowhere, and he knows nothing.
Congo. He knows the whip well enough to hate it.
Antoine. And he's not afraid.
Popo. He's the finest man in the North Plain. I grew up with him, and worked beside him. He's my friend.
Beyard. Friendship has no judgment, Popo.
Vuval. I thought they might have chosen Stenio, or some one of us as leader who can read and write, as well as speak.
Congo. Speaking's not what we need now, Vuval.
Antoine. We know what the words are—the same as the French use in Paris! Liberty, Equality, Fraternity.
Mars. But Frenchmen keep us slaves in Haiti.
Popo. We want those words in action, here, now, for blacks as well as whites.
Vuval. There are many ways of recreating words, Popo.
Stenio. Oh, don't be literary, Vuval. Slaves can't appreciate it. This is not the poetry club we once had in Cap Français, before the French accused us of being Jacobins.
Beyard. And closed our meetings.

Popo. You mean before you decided to join with us slaves.
Vuval. Yes, we mulattoes didn't always realize you blacks were our natural allies, by force of circumstance.
Popo. And you didn't always think we needed to be free, did you?
Vuval. Perhaps not.
Congo. You were free already, so you didn't give a damn about us, did you, until you needed our help yourselves?
Popo. *(bitterly)* White fathers, yellow skins. You bastards!
Vuval. I don't like that word, *bastard*.
Popo. I don't like you, Vuval.
Vuval. *(stepping forward to strike the Negro)* You dirty slave!
Beyard. *(grabbing Vuval's arm)* Stop!
Popo. Let me at him! The yellow dog!

(But Antoine holds him back.)

Dessalines. *(his voice booming out of the darkness)* Who's starting trouble there? Whoever it is, I'll bust his brains out with my fist!
Antoine. A couple of hot-heads, Jean Jacques! Lost their tempers, nothing more.
Vuval. Somebody lost his tongue.
Dessalines. What's wrong, Popo?
Popo. I'm all right, but this yellow dog's been turning his tongue against you.
Dessalines. *(laughing)* What did he say that could hurt Jean Jacques?
Popo. He said he's fit to lead himself.
Dessalines. That might be true. I'll let him lead with me—what would you think of that, Vuval? I know our need of you.
Vuval. But I don't relish being called a bastard, Jean Jacques.
Dessalines. *(laughing)* Is that all? Why let a word upset you? Only the French have priests and wedding rings. *(to Popo)* Popo, have a little care what names you call our allies.
Azelia. *(as she approaches)* Jean Jacques, the councillors have come. They're ready to begin. Martel's waiting for you.

(Dessalines and Azelia disappear in the crowd about the sugar grinder. The mulattoes withdraw to one side as several old men and women enter. They are the council of slaves. Martel is among them.)

Mars. It must be mighty near midnight!
Antoine. Soon, brother!
Popo. I'm ready!
Congo. There's all the elders.
Antoine. And the old man from Limbe.
Mars. Wise old Martel!
Popo. Sss, you! They're beginning.

(Martel is standing on a box that lifts him slightly above the throng. Around him are several very old slaves, both men and women. The crowd gradually becomes silent as someone knocks three times. Martel begins to speak.)

Martel. Children of slavery, the time is come! For months, in secret and in danger, we've laid our plans. Now we gather here for the final hour. You are the tried and faithful. We old men and women born in slavery and weary with unpaid labor have chosen a leader for you. Not one of ourselves, for our backs are bending. We have chosen a man who's young and strong, wise and brave, to lead the slaves of the north to victory in union with all the blacks of Haiti who answer the call of the drums tonight. Your leader is Dessalines.

Voices. *(in cheers)* Dessalines! Jean Jacques! Dessalines!

(Dessalines' face glows in the lantern light as the old man puts his hand on Dessalines' head in a gesture of blessing. Then Martel steps down and gives him the box.)

Dessalines. *(in a hoarse voice, stirred by emotion)* I don't need to talk, for we're ready.

Voices. Yes, indeed! Ready! Ready!

Dessalines. But I must tell you how full my heart is tonight, and how I keep remembering back to when I was a little naked slave among the slaves. Everyday an old man came to dump a pot of yams into a trough where we ate, and the pigs and the dogs, they ate, too. And we got down alongside 'em, on all fours, and ate—us and the dogs. I thought I, too, was a beast. I didn't know I'd ever grow to be a man. I thought only white folks grew up to be men. The Frenchman drove his sheep to market—just so they drove our parents to the fields when the sun came up. They owned them, too. Overseers with their dogs, whip in hand, always driving Negroes to the fields. And when the white man saw me growing tall, big enough to work, he drove me, too. Slowly I moved, too slow. The overseer lifted high his whip and cut me 'cross the back. And when I turned, he lashed me in the face. I cried out, he struck again. Then I lifted up my head and looked him in the eyes, and I knew I was a man, not a dog! I wanted to be free!

Voices. Free! Free! Want to be free! Free!

Dessalines. Not I alone—thousands of slaves like me wanted to be free! All over Haiti! Now, we're ready. We will not fail! Our time has come!

Voices. Come! Come! It's come!

(Cries of "Legba! Legba! Legba!" from the women, and the chanting of the mamaloi and papaloi grow ever louder as Dessalines continues.)

Dessalines. Our masters on this island are fifty thousand whites to *five* *hundred thousand* Negro slaves. Count on your fingers, black to white—ten to one! Ten Negroes to one white, and yet we're slaves! Shall we go on slaves?

Voices. No! No! No! No!

Dessalines. In France, white men—free men have risen against the king and torn the Bastille down. How much more reason have we, we who are slaves, to rise against our masters! How much more reason to strike back at those who buy and sell us, who beat us with their whips and track us down with their dogs! Why, even the mulattoes are turning against their white fathers and are ready to take our side, too. The poem-writer, Vuval, and his cousins are with us tonight.

Voices. *(murmuring)* Don't want 'em. Can't trust 'em. Put 'em out. Don't need 'em.

Dessalines. We do need them, my friends. We need their help. Make no mistake of that. They can read and write. I've chosen Vuval as my aide. *(to the mulatto)* Come forward, Vuval, show yourself and march with us. *(Vuval takes his place beside Dessalines.)* And now for our plans! Soon the drums of freedom will begin to sound. We'll start for the hills, burning and killing on the way, setting fire to all that's French, their mansions, their barns, their storehouses, their cane fields. Everything from here to Gonaives, Le Mole to Acul, will go up in smoke tonight—tomorrow not a Frenchman must live to tell the tale. In the hills, we'll meet our fellow-slaves from the coast, the slaves from the west and all the leaders. Boukman will be there, Christophe, and Toussaint. Food and arms are buried. There on the mountain top we'll sacrifice a goat to Legba. We'll dance obeah. We'll make powder and bullets, and gather strength until the time is ripe for us to come down to the coast to seize the ports, and claim all Haiti as our own. Then we'll be free!

Voices. *(with a great shout)* Free! Free! Great God-A-Mighty! Free!

Dessalines. Our hills await us. Our hills—where freedom lives, our hills—where the French, with their cannons, can never climb. The French! Bah! How my tongue burns when I say that word! Masters of all this sun-warmed land! Cruel monsters of terror! The French, who broke the bones of Oge on the rack! The French—who tortured Chevannes until his life blood ran down, drop by drop—dead for freedom! The French, who cut their scars upon my back—too deep to ever fade away! Look! *(He rips his shirt wide open, exposing his back covered with great red welts.)* Look what they've done to me! Look at my scars! For these the whites must pay!

Voices. The whites must pay! Make 'em pay! Make 'em pay! Oh, make 'em pay!

(Women begin to sob and moan.)

Dessalines. The sacks of sweet white sugar the French ship off to Paris goes stained with our blood!
Voices. Blood! Blood! Blood!
Dessalines. The soft white cotton the French weave into garments is red with my blood!
Voices. Blood! Blood! Blood!
Dessalines. The coffee our masters sip in the cool of evening on their wide verandas is thick with blood!
Voices. Blood! Blood!
Dessalines. Our masters live on blood!
Voices. Black blood! Black blood! Black blood!
Dessalines. Oh, make them pay! *(pausing)* Make . . . them . . . pay!

(Afar off, a drum begins to beat. The voices rise to a frenzy at its sound.)

Voices. Pay! Pay! Pay! Make 'em pay!

(Instantly, the distant drum-beat multiplies and spreads from plantation to plantation, carrying its signal across the night, until the whole island is throbbing with drum-beats. In the crowded sugar mill there are moans and shouts, hysterical sobs, curses, cries, a crush and swirl of movement. Congo opens the box and begins to distribute guns. Above the tumult, the voice of Dessalines rises in command.)

Dessalines. Revolt! Arise! For Freedom!
Voices. *(echoing his words)* Freedom! Freedom!
Dessalines. Revenge! Revenge! To the hills!
Voices. To the hills!
Dessalines. Free! Kill to be free!
Voices. Free! Free! To be free!
Dessalines. Fire the cane fields! Poison the springs!
Voices. To be free! Free!
Dessalines. Choke the rivers! Ambush the roads!
Voices. Free! Free!
Dessalines. *(raising his cane knife like a sword)* Kill the whites! Kill to be free!
Voices. *(in a mighty shout)* Kill! Kill! Kill!
Celeste. *(a woman's voice, high and clear)* To be free!

(With cane knives and rifles held high, the slaves pour forth into the night. Outside, flames are visible as the cane fields burn. The drums beat louder, ever spreading. Shots are heard. In the distance, harrowing cries, the march of feet. Dessalines stands with his arms uplifted, his back bare. In the lantern light, great red scars gleam like welts of terror across his shoulders. The mamaloi whirls through the crowd, lifting high the sacred cock. The papaloi chants

above his drum, his hands flying, his eyes wild, his feathered head-dress waving. Vuval stands, deathly pale, with his back to the cane-grinder, as if in mortal terror. Above the tumult, Celeste's voice is heard crying in a high, musical cry.)

Celeste. I want to be free! Let me be free! Free!
Azelia. *(lifting her rifle in both hands and calling)* Jean Jacques! Jean Jacques! Jean Jacques!

(He does not hear her. Azelia disappears in the crowd that pours through the door. Voices and drum-beats fill the night.)

(Curtain)

ACT II

SCENE 1

Time: *Several years later.*
Place: *Dessalines' Palace, near Petite Riviere. The Council Chamber; a table against red velvet curtains. A coat-of-arms. A chair, empire style, of plush and gilt with a high back. Two smaller chairs.*
At Rise: *The Emperor, Dessalines, is seated behind the table, many papers before him. He is obviously tired and worried.*
Vuval sits at one end of the table, reading a letter.

Vuval. *(reading)* ". . . forty acres of sugarcane, two hundred plantain trees, an estimated three thousand coffee bushes, seventy pepper trees. Beyond that, I have nothing more to report to the Emperor. Signed: Beyard, Count of Acul."
Dessalines. Is that all?
Vuval. That's all. Every acre of land on his plantation is productive.
Dessalines. And yet he says he cannot pay his tax, and so demands another tribute from the peasants?
Vuval. We have very few markets, sire.
Dessalines. Why doesn't he plant pineapples? There's always a market for them in the States.
Vuval. It takes time.
Dessalines. Time? Time! Always excuses on account of time. We've been free long enough to flourish here. And you mulattoes were always free! Yet Beyard can't make his own plantation pay its tax.

Vuval. He knows how well enough. He can get your money easily by taxation.

Dessalines. I don't want it by taxation. By work I want it. We must produce.

Vuval. *(shrugging)* Perhaps!

Dessalines. If I permit this draining of the peasants, they'll turn on me. Yet if the Empire goes without taxes, how shall we build roads, hire teachers, or run this court? *(commandingly)* Write the Count of Acul I must have from him at once the twenty thousand francs he owes the Treasury.

Vuval. But I thought, perhaps, since Beyard is my cousin. . . .

Dessalines. I have granted you too many favors now, Vuval. I'll give him no reduction, and no further time. *(leaning back)* Read the next communication.

Vuval. It is from General Gedeon's headquarters, signed by Major Longchamps. He wants, post haste, ten burro loads of powder, to be used at the fall maneuvers, and three hundred new winter uniforms for his men, preferably salmon pink with orange trimmings. He writes that he wants his regiment to look as good as Major Loguet's. He also requests a purple plume for his helmet.

Dessalines. *(roaring)* Tell him . . . tell him! *(impatiently)* Damn it, I wish I could write! Tell him to go to hell!

Vuval. Very well, sir; but. . . .

Dessalines. But?

Vuval. He's an important officer.

Dessalines. Well, send the powder. But as for the uniforms, tell him, no! Everybody in Haiti wants to dress like me—and I'm the Emperor.

Vuval. True!

Dessalines. We'd need ten thousand spinning mills to turn out cloth enough to clothe them as they wish.

Vuval. And a million dyes to dye it, if we had sufficient colors.

Dessalines. What next?

Vuval. *(with a gesture of fatigue)* But you haven't forgotten there's a State banquet tonight, have you, Emperor? It's already dusk.

Dessalines. The next letter, Vuval. We must get done with this. *(He wipes his brow.)*

Vuval. *(reading)* "Most High and Mighty King of Haiti, Emperor Jean Jacques Dessalines, Chief General of the army and leader of the blacks, your humble servant begs of you this favor. The peasants of Gros Morne have made bricks and built themselves a school. We are six hundred grown-ups and sixty-seven children. We want to learn to read and write, so will you please send to us a teacher? We have already wrote three times to the Duke of Marmelade, Chief Grande Commissioner of Education, but we never got no answer. We are anxious to learn from books, and put our school to a good use. Please, Emperor of the blacks, if you have time, answer this letter yourself. We send you our humble regards. The love of the liberated people of Gros Morne goes to you. Respectfully yours, Henri Bajean, Blacksmith."

Dessalines. *(sadly, after a painful silence)* I can't read myself. And we have no teachers. *(louder)* Vuval, why did so many mulattoes run away to Paris? We black people need you—you were educated. Now we have no teachers to send to Gros Morne.

Vuval. *(carelessly)* That little village couldn't afford to pay a teacher, anyhow.

Dessalines. Pay? Pay! Pay! Always pay! Does no one know that need fulfilled is pay enough? *(angrily)* Does no one, loving Haiti, find his pay in doing for her? But it's money we need, is it? Then change that letter I ordered you to write—tell Beyard I ask forty thousand francs instead of twenty.

Vuval. *(controlling his anger)* You have given me too many letters today, sire. I cannot write them all.

Dessalines. Write that one now to Beyard and bring it here to me.

(Vuval begins to gather up his papers, as Popo enters.)

Popo. The Councillor Martel's to see you, sire. And I've done laid out your robes of state for the banquet. I put the ruby crown out, too, and polished up the scepter. It shine like a lightening rod.

Dessalines. Let Martel in, Popo. I'll come to dress directly.

(Popo exits.)

Dessalines. *(to Vuval)* Write that letter now, and bring it back and leave it. It must be signed tonight.

Vuval. *(with a note of contempt)* All right, I will.

(Martel enters, very bent and old, but impressive in his simple robes of Court.)

Martel. Jean Jacques, you must be tired. You've been at this all day.

Dessalines. *(as Vuval exits)* If only we had people who would help, Martel. It seems nobody cares. Nobody wants to work.

Martel. That's our problem, son. *(gently)* But do you think it's all the people's fault? When we was slaves, lots of us thought if we was free, we'd never have to work again. And now it seems there's need of harder work than ever. The peasants wonder why.

Dessalines. You and me work night and day, work hard. But what comes of it? It's every arm in Haiti we need. *(wistfully)* I have a dream for Haiti, Martel. I mean to see it true. That's why I made a law that all of us must work all day, and those who own land pay a tax that Haiti may have roads, and docks and harbors fine as any country in the world. The peasants do not understand. They think I'd make them slaves again. And those to whom *I* gave the land, they call me tyrant now. *(puzzled)* How would they have me build, how dam the rivers, how make factories—

Martel. Some have no vision, son.

Dessalines. No use to talk, I've talked till I'm hoarse, talked everywhere. I've told them of this Haiti I would make—where every black man lifts his head in pride, where there'll be schools and palaces, big armies and a fleet of boats, forts strong enough to keep the French forever from our shores. *(confidently)* But I'm their Liberator. The peasants know that. They know 'twas Dessalines alone that drove the whites away.

Martel. But there are still whites in the world, Jean Jacques. And we have need of them, as they once needed us. You've often heard me say, it's time to stop turning our guns against them now.

Dessalines. Why?

Martel. We're free. Let's act like free men, ready to meet others as equals— and no longer speak of *all* white men as enemies. *(sitting down)* Our ports are open now, to English traders. In time, we'll open to the French. The world will drink our coffee. From them we'll buy things in return. We'll need the French.

Dessalines. The French? The French! I never want to hear that word again, Martel. *(slowly)* Even now, although I'm Emperor, my back still aches from the blows they've laid upon it.

Martel. I know. All my years, before our freedom, I, too, never saw the sun rise but to curse it, but now free men can dream a bigger dream than mere revenge.

Dessalines. What dream, Martel?

Martel. A dream of an island where not only blacks are free, but every man who comes to Haitian shores. Jean Jacques, I'm an old man. But in my old age, I dream of a world where no man hurts another. Where *all* know freedom, and black and white alike will share this earth in peace. Of such I dream, Jean Jacques.

Dessalines. Too big a dream, Martel. If I could make Haiti a land where *black* men live in peace, I'd be content.

Martel. Yes, task enough, I know.

(a light knock at the door and a woman's silvery voice calling)

Claire. *(outside)* Jean Jacques, may I come in?

(Without waiting for an answer, Claire Heureuse, consort of the Emperor, enters, arrayed in white, ready for the banquet. She is a lovely mulatto with long black hair. Dessalines rises smiling.)

Dessalines. Claire Heureuse! Come in!

(She runs to him and kisses him lightly.)

Claire. Don't you ever get through work, you two? It's time to play. Hurry, Jean Jacques, get dressed to receive your guests. Father Martel, it's a gorgeous evening. You ought to be in the garden. The sunset is like gold. *(glancing at the table full of papers)* It's hot and musty in here. I'm going to run out, Jean Jacques, and get a flower for my hair. On the way, I'll stop by the banquet terrace and see if our stupid servants overlooked anything. Hurry, darling, and put on your crown. *(She pats him on the cheek as if he were a child, then turns and exits, laughing.)*

Dessalines. Claire, my dear, take care you don't catch cold!

Claire. *(calling back)* Oh, how funny! As hot as it is tonight.

Martel. *(as the door closes)* The Empress is very beautiful, Jean Jacques.

Dessalines. Beautiful, yes. More beautiful than any woman I have ever had.

Martel. The others were slave women. *(coughing)* They told you, I suppose, in the Lord Treasurer's office, that Azelia would not accept the pension you bestowed upon her?

Dessalines. *(as if remembering)* Azelia? Oh, yes! My first wife. They told me so, Martel. Poor, stupid woman! She was good . . . but . . . well, you know! That was before I was an Emperor. *(defensively)* How could I have an empress that can't read or write?

Martel. The Emperor himself. . . .

Dessalines. *(good humoredly)* Can at least sign his name! Vuval has taught me that. But where is Azelia? I loved her—once. *(musingly)* And I remember how she stood by me in those years of battle—nursed my wounds and washed my clothes! Where is she?

Martel. They say she's a vendor of fruit in a village on the coast. . . .

Dessalines. She could have had a job here at Court. At least a servant. . . .

Martel. My son!

Dessalines. Or maybe, Mistress of the Linens. I wonder why she wouldn't take the pension?

Martel. They say she makes her own living—although a poor one—and that she looks much older than she really is.

Dessalines. Well. . . . *(then hesitating, as if loath to say more)* Come, Martel, let's go. The day's been long and hard. I'm tired.

Martel. *(rising)* Tomorrow, son, you must take up that matter of the officers wanting a raise in pay.

Dessalines. Yes, yes—

Martel. And you know there's been no word from General Gerin of late, nor Yayou, either.

Dessalines. Angry, perhaps? I refused to grant them money from the government to go upon a journey.

Martel. Gerin's a dangerous man, Jean Jacques. He'll bear watching. He's been known to talk against you.

Dessalines. I have no fear, Martel. I can take my Palace Guard and wipe up the earth with Gerin. More business for tomorrow?

Martel. Nothing pressing. *(smiling)* Except that Congo has petitioned several times to be raised from the title of Baron to that of Count.

Dessalines. *(as they walk toward the exit)* Damn Congo! He's had all the titles in the book already.

Martel. Yes, but he's about to marry Lady Celeste, and he wants to make her a Countess.

Dessalines. Oh, well, let's make them both Princes and be done with it. Titles are easier to get than money, anyhow.

Martel. They're easy enough, but taxing on the brain to think them up.

Dessalines. The French Napoleon gave himself the name of Emperor. I, too, am Emperor by my own hand. *(He snaps his fingers.)* We might as well get a little glory out of life.

Martel. It's not wise to want too much.

Dessalines. Well, I've got what I want. I built this palace and I've bought myself a crown or two. I am the Emperor, and no one can make me a slave again. What was that Toussaint said about *liberty,* before he left us? How was that, now, Martel?

Martel. Toussaint said, "You can lay low the tree of liberty, but it'll shoot forth again from the roots."

Dessalines. And he was right! Napoleon thought if he imprisoned one of our leaders, there'd be no other. But when Toussaint went down as Governor-General of Haiti, I came up. *(proudly)* I've created the first black Empire in the world, so why shouldn't I glory in it, Martel? I'm a king! I'm on top! I'm the glory of Haiti!

Martel. The glory of Haiti lies in no one man, Jean Jacques.

Dessalines. Where does it lie?

Martel. In the people's love for freedom.

Dessalines. Too much freedom—if they no longer obey me, their Liberator; I'm their freedom—and this Court's their glory.

Martel. Glory is a passing thing, Jean Jacques! Take care!

Dessalines. *(laughing)* This sword takes care of me, Martel. I still can use it!

Martel. Swords won't solve all problems, my son.

Dessalines. No, but they solve a-plenty. Come on, let's dress for the banquet. *(He takes the old man's arm and they exit.)*

(Vuval enters, followed by Stenio, approaching the table with a sheaf of papers. Vuval addresses his friend.)

Vuval. If the Emperor could read, he'd never sign most of the letters I write for him.

Stenio. *(laughing)* A dumb clown! He thinks by letting Claire Heureuse read them over for him, he's safe, not knowing she was on our side before she ever met "His Majesty."

Vuval. A true mulatto, Claire.
Stenio. That's why we brought her back from Paris. I knew he'd fall for her. A mulatto Empress in a black Empire! That's enough to make him the laughing stock of the peasantry.
Vuval. The fool!
Stenio. His Majesty's head is rather thick.
Vuval. But not too thick to be broken. If he knew six garrisons in the South revolted against him this morning, he wouldn't sit so pompously beneath his crown tonight.
Stenio. You've had word from Gerin.
Vuval. Yes, and from General Yayou, too. Port-au-Prince has gone over to the rebels. The mulattoes are in full charge.
Stenio. An end of this black rule at last! Maybe now I can get off to Paris again.
Vuval. Paris! *La Ville Lumiere!* Oh, how I long to see that city of lights, Stenio. It's so damn dark here.
Stenio. In more ways than one, Vuval.
Vuval. But it won't be long now until I'm out of Haiti. Tonight, we'll flee the Court, while His Majesty wears his crown and stuffs himself with food.
Stenio. Good! As for me, that's not soon enough. What are your plans for Claire?
Vuval. She's coming by carriage tomorrow. Her jewels are packed except for a few cheap baubles she'll wear tonight. But it's a ten-hour ride to the coast after dark. You'd better order your men ready to start at once, Stenio. And, you, too, go ahead. I'll catch you. I've a splendid horse.
Stenio. Do you suppose the Black Napoleon will miss me from his banquet table? If not, I'll order the Guard away shortly.
Vuval. I'll say you're ill of fever, if he asks.
Stenio. Yes, the fever of being bored.

(Popo enters. The mulattoes look startled. The Negro stops near the door on seeing them.)

Popo. The Emperor sent me for his letters.
Vuval. *(pushing them across the table)* There they are. I wish the Emperor would learn to write.
Popo. *(seriously)* He will, some day.
Vuval. *(sarcastically)* Perhaps you, too, "Count" Popo.
Stenio. *(lightly)* Don't be absurd, Vuval. Such poetic fancies on your part! My! My! Come, let's drink a bit of champagne in the garden.

(Vuval and Stenio exit, leaving Popo with the letters in his hand. Slowly and

bitterly, Popo begins to tear the letters into bits as his eyes follow the two mulattoes.)

(Curtain)

ACT II
. . . . . .

SCENE 2

Time: *Immediately following Scene 1.*
Place: *A covered terrace, consisting of two levels, whose arched portals are open to the sky. It is early evening. The air is still rosy with sunset. On the upper level, a raised banquet table stretches across the width of the entire terrace, its white linen cloths falling to the floor. At either side, steps to the table. The terrace is not yet lighted, but on the table in silhouette against the evening sky may be seen tall silver candle sticks and great bowls of fruit, pineapples, mangoes, grapes, coconuts, bananas, pomegranates, plums. There are goblets for wine; and china, crystal, and silver.*
At Rise: *Servants move about arranging the table, and two old women in front of the table, on the floor level, are preparing flowers, putting the fruit into bowls, polishing silver.*

First Old Woman. It's getting mighty dark here. How come we can't have no light to work by?
Second Old Woman. You know the Emperor don't believe in wasting candles. He don't believe in wasting nothing.
First Old Woman. Tight-fisted, if you ask me! If I had all the money he's got, I'd fling gold to winds every time I kicked up my heels.
Second Old Woman. At your age, still talking about kicking up your heels!
First Old Woman. Huh! I might be old, but my heart ain't got no wrinkles.
Second Old Woman. Well, I hope the day'll come when we all can have a good time, and nothing else. Look like I work as hard now that I'm free as I did before.
First Old Woman. Well, the Emperor says he want to make Haiti rich—and just as grand as when it belonged to the white folks.
Second Old Woman. Huh! Only thing grand I see around here is that hussy of a new wife he's got and all them diamonds she's a-wearing.
First Old Woman. Shsss! You better stop talking that a-way about the Empress. Lady Celeste'll hear you and out you'll go.
Second Old Woman. Lady my eye! Housekeeper, that's what Celeste is!
First Old Woman. Anyhow, Baron Congo's crazy about her. They about to get married.

Second Old Woman. Congo's a baron, and she's a Lady. If he marry her, what title do that give 'em both?

First Old Woman. What you mean, 'em both? Celeste gonna run him just like she do everything else, and he'll be a Mr. Lady Baron, that's what! *(getting to work)* Hush, here she comes!

(Enter Celeste.)

Celeste. Hurry up, you servants, and put the flowers on the table. We've got to clear things up now. The guests'll soon be arriving.

First Old Woman. We's hurrying.

Second Old Woman. We sure are.

Celeste. *(calling)* Lady Lulu! Oh, Lady Lulu! *(to the servants)* Have any of you-all seen the High Grand Keeper of the Linens? There's no napkins on this table yet.

Servant. *(behind table)* Here she comes, now.

(Enter Lulu, well-gowned, carrying a pile of napkins.)

Lulu. I'll have you know, Lady Celeste, that you don't need to yell for me like as if I were a dog.

Celeste. Why, Lady Lulu, I weren't yelling, were I?

Lulu. *(still peeved)* Well, even if you is engaged to a Baron, I don't have to stand it. My son's a Grand Alimony, hisself.

Celeste. What's that, Lulu? I didn't know Pierre were anything but the Chief Bugle-Blower. I remember, he always wanted a bugle when he were a little slave.

Lulu. *(placing the napkins)* Don't bring up them distasteful epochs, Celeste.

Celeste. Well, we was slaves, once, wasn't we, Lulu?

Lulu. And still half-is! I'm gonna give that Jean Jacques a piece of my mind soon, tired as I is o' working in this palace. I want to take myself a trip to Port-au-Prince and look up a new husband!

Celeste. A husband?

Lulu. Yes, a new husband. These men around here's too banana-bellied to suit my taste.

Celeste. I bet you're sorry you ain't got a man like Congo. He's all right.

Lulu. Huh! I could've had Congo long ago, if I'd-a-wanted him.

Celeste. *(angered)* Lulu, I'll turn that table over getting to you if you don't hush. You know Congo's never even looked at you.

Lulu. *(starting around the table)* Just hold your horses, *Lady* Celeste, till I get down to your level.

First Old Woman. *(warningly)* You better shsss! Here comes the Empress.

Celeste. (flustered) Oh! If you're through your work, you-all just gather up your things and get out of the way. The Empress wants to inspect the table, I guess.

(Claire enters, accompanied by Vuval. The servants exit gradually, scowling. Lulu follows them.)

Claire. This really is a charming terrace, isn't it, Vuval? Such a lush background. Those palm trees and the early evening stars? *(looking around)* But why must these serving women be forever getting things ready? Lady Celeste, you! *(Celeste jumps.)* Can't you manage to prepare a banquet table in less than a week?
Celeste. I-I-I-started this morning, Empress.
Claire. *(sighing)* Oh, well. I suppose I must remember I'm not in Paris where service is an art. *(dismissing her)* Go on, Celeste, I'll look about alone.

(Exit Celeste.)

Vuval. I can hardly wait to see Paris with you, Claire. You've been there so often and know it so well. You can show me everything—the Louvre, the Bois, the Odeon—all the places the great writers write about.
Claire. Of course!
Vuval. Do you suppose I'll ever be a great writer, Claire?
Claire. *(lightly)* If you write enough letters for the Emperor, you might perhaps develop.
Vuval. Don't joke about it, Claire. It's too near my heart. *(passionately)* Darling, there're just two things I want—you, and to write poems as beautiful as Andre Chénier's.
Claire. You have me, dear. Only don't put your hands on my white gown. They may have ink on them. And I have to look nice tonight—for this— am I safe in saying—the last supper at this stupid Palace.
Vuval. No doubt our last, Claire—for the mulattoes have taken over Port-au-Prince, and Gerin the forts to the north! And listen! Should a messenger arrive with news of the uprising for the Emperor, I have given orders to intercept it. Let Dessalines eat, drink and be merry once without being bothered. In the meantime, Stenio can reach the coast.
Claire. Has he gone?
Vuval. Yes, he's well started. And while you entertain your royal husband at the table, I'll slip away from the banquet early and get off, too. On the way, I'll persuade the garrison commanders to side with us. That ought to be easy, for I've been writing the officers vulgar letters lately, calling them all sorts of names, as you know, and the Emperor in his ignorance has signed them—thinking they're what he's dictated.
Claire. Clever, Vuval.
Vuval. Now the generals think Dessalines has turned against them. No wonder they're revolting.
Claire. No wonder!
Vuval. Whereas, on the other hand, the peasants are sure they are going to

starve if they don't get a change of government. *(pleased)* You see, darling, everything's all set. And early tomorrow, you'll come on to the coast with your attendants. We'll have a boat waiting. It's perfectly planned.
Claire. Most cleverly arranged, Vuval. I didn't know you were such a strategist.
Vuval. Will you be glad to get away from Haiti, darling?
Claire. Will I be glad? I hate these ignorant people and their drums. I can't stand those drums every night, beating, beating, back there in the hills.
Vuval. And Jean Jacques?
Claire. That fool, my husband? Vuval, darling, often I can't bear to look at him. He's so common and so—so boorish! And his back! *(with a little cry)* I cannot bear to touch his back! It's all covered with welts! Ugh! Marks of a rebellious slave! And yet he thinks I love him! Bah!
Vuval. You've played your part well, Claire.
Claire. I had to. My people were ruined, as were yours. We had to get back our land, and our money. Now, my brother's put away a half-million francs in a Bordeaux bank.
Vuval. As have my cousin, Beyard and I.
Claire. We'll be safe now, you and I—married in Paris. So you see why I've played my part well! *(laughing)* I've always wanted to be an actress, anyway. Perhaps to be Juliet.
Vuval. And I your Romeo! Sweet Claire! *(remembering something)* But, say, darling, look! With all I've had to do today, I still found time to compose a poem for you.
Claire. Oh, read it to me.
Vuval. *(taking a manuscript from his pocket)* Here it is! Listen! *(reading)*

> TO THE VENUS OF THE ANTILLES,
> CLAIRE HEUREUSE
> Your eyes are twin stars
> In a snow-white face,
> Your lips are two rubies
> Loveliness has traced,
> Your body a flower
> Of marble grace—
> Oh, Venus strayed
> Into a savage palace!

Do you like it, Claire?
Claire. *(laughing)* I like that part about the "savage palace." But it's so short! Is that all you could think to say about me, Vuval?
Vuval. Claire, darling! No pen could write all the lovely things I think of you.

Claire. Dear boy! Give me the poem to keep.
Vuval. Of course! *(handing her the manuscript)* And my heart as well!
Claire. Someone's coming!

(Voices are heard approaching.)

Let us go into the garden a moment, where we can be alone. I've still to get a flower for my hair, my sweet.

(Exit Claire and Vuval, as Martel and Popo enter from the other side.)

Martel. In times like these, if Toussaint l'Ouverture were only here to guide us, Popo! Napoleon's heart must be like stone to trick so great a leader away from his people.
Popo. I wish Toussaint was here. It looks like Jean Jacques don't know how to run things very well. I wish I could help him.
Martel. Jean Jacques is a mighty soldier, Popo, and a brave man. He's not a statesman. But he's our friend, and we love him—so we must help him.
Popo. We must, Father Martel.
Martel. As you protect his body, I'll try to guard his mind. *(despairingly)* But sometimes I don't know, Popo, I don't know. *(looking upward through the open portals)* Haiti, land that should be so happy, grown instead so sad! Land of golden moonlight and silver rain, bright birds, and brighter sun, perfumed breezes and a sea so green, hills of great woods and valleys of sweet earth. Why can't it be a happy land? So many years of struggle, and still vile intrigue binds our wings like spider webs. Oh, most unhappy Haiti! When the drums beat in the hills at night, mournful and heart-breaking, I can feel your sorrow. No wonder the Empress hates your drums! Where is their power now to make the gods smile upon this troubled island?
Popo. Don't you think, Father Martel, Jean Jacques ought to let the Papaloi come back into Court?
Martel. Jean Jacques doesn't believe in voodoo, son. You know that.
Popo. I know, but our people do—and we can't change them overnight. Now, the voodoo doctors are mumbling against the Emperor and stirring up the peasants.
Martel. And the mulattoes are angry because he has designated Haiti officially as the *Black* Empire. They don't like the word *Black*.
Popo. Their mothers were black.
Martel. Yes, it's true! Still, they stand apart and claim their white blood makes them better. But what troubles me most, Popo, is why there's been no news from the coast of late. Two days ago, I sent Xavier to see what's happening. He's due back, but he hasn't come.
Popo. Do you think something's happened to Xavier?
Martel. I don't know. Be alert, son. All's not well, though it would seem so

here at the Palace. *(in a lighter tone)* But come now! Let's look carefully at the table to see if it's properly set. The Emperor is most particular about these occasions of state. And this one must be perfect—for tomorrow I shall warn him that with the treasury in its present state, the Court cannot often afford such lavishness.

Popo. Even if we go back to eating dried fish and yams, I'll stick by him. Jean Jacques has been a friend of mine ever since we were slaves together.

(Enter Celeste and Congo. Congo is carrying a huge pot of flowers.)

Celeste. Put it down right there in the center, so's the air'll smell sweet.

Congo. *(grunting as he stoops)* Huh!

Celeste. And stop grunting! What'd you come up here mooning at me for, anyhow, in my busiest hours?

Congo. *(standing up, resplendent in a nile-green uniform with golden tassels on the shoulders)* I come to show you my new suit, Celeste. This here makes twelve brand new uniforms I bought. How do you like it?

Celeste. *(critically)* I'd like it better if it had more gold on it. *(approaching Martel and Popo)* Good evening, Father Martel. How are you tonight?

Martel. Only fair, daughter, only fair.

Celeste. I hope you got over that little spell of indigestion yesterday so's you can eat this evening well. This is gonna *be* a banquet. And no fooling! We got a dozen roast sheep out there in the ovens, sweet as butter. I wish you could smell 'em.

Congo. *(loosening a buckle)* Um-hum! Lemme loosen up this belt.

(Martel and Popo laugh as they exit.)

Celeste. Lemme go get dressed, as befits a lady. All them Duchesses are gonna be here tonight, so I wants to look grand, too. Come on, Baron.

Congo. Gimme a little kiss first.

Celeste. Can't you wait till we get married?

Congo. Not for just a kiss.

Celeste. *(kissing him)* Here!

Congo. It tastes sweeter'n a honey bee.

Celeste. *(as she starts off)* Wait till you feel the stinger!

Congo. *(running after her)* Um-huh! Gimme another one.

Celeste. Come on, man! The guests are arriving. And the orchestra's playing in the throne room. I want to see the excitement. Besides, I'm saving up one for you tonight—if you're around to get it.

(Celeste exits as the two old women and other servants enter.)

Congo. Aw, come back here and gimme a double kiss now.

Celeste. *(calling off stage)* By and by, baby, by and by.

(Congo exits.)

First Old Woman. The Throne Room's just full o' high falutin' hens and prancin' cocks a-cacklin' and crowin' all over the place.

Second Old Woman. *(as she lights the candles)* Some of 'em's gonna crow their last in a little while, too. Folks is gettin' tired o' seeing some people have everything and the rest of us workin' like dogs. I don't know what the Emperor's thinking about. Why ain't he gived me no velvet dress? I'm human!

First Old Woman. I reckon we can't all be Duchesses, and such.

Second Old Woman. Well, if we can't be Duchesses, we at least ought to be let alone to dance obeah if we wants to, and have our voodoo here in the Court. Legba's gonna curse Dessalines yet, you watch.

First Old Woman. That hussy of a Claire Heureuse went and brought a Catholic priest over from France for herself—and a French one at that.

Second Old Woman. Voodoo was good enough for her mammy. It ought to do for her.

(Softly, in the distance, the music of an orchestra playing European airs is heard.)

First Old Woman. Lawsy! We better hurry up. They done opened the big doors! I reckon the procession's forming to march to the tables. *(to a ragged boy)* Boy, scramble up there and light that big oil lamp, over His Majesty's head. He likes plenty light.

(The boy lights the hanging lantern, and the terrace is flooded with golden light. Noise and music afar—then a bugle call in the distance. The old women leave, as three butlers, in livery, enter and take places, one at each end of the table near the head of the steps, the other behind the tall chair reserved for the Emperor. On the lower terrace, a Flower Girl enters scattering rose leaves. There is a roll of drums; Pierre, a big boy now, and Chief Bugler, enters, crosses the stage, turns with military precision and blows a blast on his horn. The orchestra begins a march. Josef, the Grand Marshal of the Palace, takes his place at the far end of the table. With a long parchment list in hand, he announces, in a loud voice.)

Josef. Hear ye! Hear ye! Hear ye! The Guests of the Emperor bidden to a Banquet of State in honor of His Majesty.

(The band continues, the Grand Marshal reads from his list, and in the order named, the guests enter from the lower terrace, strutting grandly across it to stand in front of the table, waiting there before mounting the steps until the Emperor himself arrives. Their costumes are gorgeously grotesque copies of various European Court styles and periods, but giving in the ensemble an effect of gay and savage splendor. Some of the guests are enjoying themselves immensely, but others are obviously uncomfortable in their regal clothes, while

many are gnarled old peasants, too bent by slavery to even appear at ease in Parisian finery. Josef reads, and in the order called, marching gaily to the music, the Royalty of Haiti enter.)

> The Duke and Duchess of Dondon.
> Count and Countess Claudel de Zouba.
> General Abelard and Madame la Pompeuse.
> Lord and Lady Tountemonde.
> Baron Antoine and the Baroness.
> The Duke of Marmelade and Countess Louise Camille Chaucune Nereide.
> The Chevalier of Gonaives and the Chevalieress.
> The Governor of Milot, Sir Emil Tuce with Madame the Duchess of Limonade.
> Major General Joli-Bois and Lady Fifi Beauregard.
> The Most High Grand Keeper of Records and Seals, Count Vuval.
> Major General Dembu and Lady Lulu Minette.
> The Duke de Savanne-a-Roches and Duchess Coloma Lutetia Floreal.
> Grand Duke Mars and Princess Dianne.
> Baron Congo with Lady Celeste.
> The Grand Chief Treasurer of the Realm, His Highness Lord Bobo Levy.
> Duchess Suzanne Roseide and her husband.

(As the last couple enter the terrace and line up before the table, the music ceases. There is a moment of silence, giggling, and whispering. Several late arrivals sneak in, unannounced.)

Lord Bobo. *(sneezing)* A-choo!
Lulu. Your Highness, Lord Bobo, why don't you use better snuff?
Bobo. It ain't my snuff, Lady Lulu. It's that loud perfume some of you-all ladies uses, done got in my nostrils.
Duke Marmelade. This collar's mighty near choking me to death!
Countess Nereide. But it looks gorgeous, Duke.
Duchess of Limonade. Lawd! *(picking up her feet in pain)* I'm sure gonna take off these shoes soon as I get myself back home. They ain't my size.
Count Claudel. I'm tired of this business, coming here all dressed up every time I turn around.
Celeste. Shsss! Stop all that giggling and talking! You know the Emperor likes silence when he enters.
Lord Bobo. *(after a moment of stillness)* A-choo!

(loud giggling from the women)

Baron Antoine. That were sure good wine they just passed out in the throne room, huh, Baroness?
Baroness Antoine. It were champagne—but I wants to *eat,* now.
Grand Duke Mars. That'll be some time off yet, Baroness. The Emperor serves in courses.
Princess Dianne. A little bit at a time.
Celeste. First course is always just tidbits to give you an appetite.
Duchess Suzanne. I got a appetite already!
Congo. I wants to taste that roast goat.
Lady Fifi. Me, too, Baron.

(The Lady in Waiting to the Empress enters on the upper terrace and proceeds to arrange Her Majesty's seat. The Bugle Boy blows a mighty blast as the drums roll.)

Josef. The Court arrives!

(another roll of the drums)

His Majesty, the Emperor, First Liberator of the blacks and Chief Ruler of Haiti, Jean Jacques Dessalines.

(Preceded by two pages, Dessalines enters on the upper terrace and strides to his chair. He is followed by Martel in his robes of state, and by Popo carrying the royal scepter. Immediately behind comes the Empress Claire Heureuse, accompanied by the Ladies of the Presence. All the guests turn and bow low as they enter. The Emperor and Empress take their seats. An attendant offers the Emperor his crown on a silken cushion; Popo presents the royal scepter. A great cheer arises.)

Voices. *Hail the Emperor! Hail Dessalines! Hail! Hail! Hail!*

(The cymbals clash and the drums roll. The band strikes up a lively march. The guests file around both ends of the table to their respective seats. At a trumpet blast from Pierre, they sit down simultaneously, a glittering row of velvet busts and dark, genial faces behind the banquet table with its crystal and silver.)

Lulu. *(proudly to Congo)* That's my son blowing that bugle! You hear him?
Celeste. Honey, your son ought to learn a new tune! That one hurts my ears.

(As the butlers pass, filling the glasses, the orchestra begins to play a syncopated melody, and a dozen dancing girls whirl across the lower terrace into the empty space before the table. They are wearing anklets of beaten gold; their bushy hair is adorned with precious stones. As they dance before the Court, a weird drum beat becomes audible in the music, gradually louder and more insistent, until finally it drowns out all the other instruments. To the

African rhythm of drums alone, a male dancer enters, feathered and painted like a voodoo god. The girls sink to the floor as the tall, godlike one does his dance of the jungle, fierce, provocative, and horrible. Suddenly, the Empress turns her head, and covers her ears with her hands. She calls to Dessalines.)

Claire. *(appealingly)* Jean Jacques! Jean Jacques!

(Dessalines rises, raising his hand in command.)

Dessalines. *(loudly)* Stop it! Stop! The Empress don't like drums! Stop it, I say!

(The music ceases—but no sooner than the drums on the terrace are silent than another drum, far off in the hills, carries on their beat.)

(Dessalines cries frantically.) Stop them drums, I say. Stop them!
Popo. They are stopped, sire. That drum we hear now's away off in the hills someplace.
Dessalines. I don't care where it is! Order it stopped! My Empress don't like drums! Vuval!
Vuval. *(rising)* I will send someone to see if it can be located.

(He leaves the table and confers with one of the attendants. The attendant exits. But the drum is never silent during the rest of the scene. Its monotonous beat continues, as if calling for one knows not what.)

Dessalines. *(who has remained standing, begins to berate his guest[s])* Drums in the Court! The idea! Suppose we had guests from abroad, what would they think of us? They'd think we were all savages, that's what. Savages! Here I am, trying to build a civilization in Haiti good as any the whites have in their lands. Trying to set up a Court equal to any Court in Europe. And what do I find—voodoo drums in the banquet hall! Who gave orders for that? *(ominously)* Whoever did, will suffer. I'll find out tomorrow. We ought to be done with voodoo drums—all of us! But listen! *(He pauses as the distant drum continues its throbbing beat.)* The peasants, up all nights playing drums! And the fields only half productive. But not only the peasants are to blame. You. You Lords and Ladies, Dukes and Counts, are to blame, too. I give you land, and you neglect to work it. Then when crops are scanty, you try to bully your taxes out of the people, taking back their hard earned money to pay me what the Treasury demands. But that's not what I want. And you're not helping Haiti. The land must produce its own riches. Our peasants must work the land, and make it fertile. Being free frees no man from working. We do have to work. And I'm tired of telling you! I'm tired of sending out orders! I've made up my mind to tell my soldiers to *make* you work from now on!
Voices. What? Do you hear that! Huh! I'm no slave!

Dessalines. *(thunderously)* Silence! Listen to me! We've fought to make Haiti free! I'm going to keep you free—the French'll never return. I'm going to make a great country, trading with all the world—wealthy, and full of plenty to eat. You're going to help me. *(pausing)* Long ago I dreamed a dream that I want to carry through. If you won't help me willingly—then I'll make you. I'm the Emperor! Your Liberator! Jean Jacques Dessalines, who came up from a slave hut to a Palace, to a crown on my head and an ermine cape covering my scars, to this jeweled scepter in my hand. I did it by fighting. The whites called me the Tiger! *(fiercely)* If I have to be a tiger to you, too—I will be! *(pausing—then lifting his glass)* Drink to your Emperor! *(bellowing an imperious command)* Drink!

(The frightened guests leap to their feet, raising their glasses in trembling hands.)

Voices. *(as they drink)* To the Emperor!
Dessalines. *(calmly)* Now, let there be music and dancing—violins, not drums!

(The orchestra plays a minuet as Dessalines resumes his seat. The guests come down from the table and begin to dance with knees still shaking. They are awkward at the minuet, and some pitifully grotesque in their attempts at European graces. Some few of the older folks remain in their places at the table. Vuval disappears. Gradually the dancers dance offstage out of sight at either end of the terrace as the Emperor talks with the Empress.)

Claire, darling, don't you like the wine? And this caviar? I ordered it all the way from Russia especially for you.
Claire. I like you better than wine, Jean Jacques! You're so strong, so wonderful and wise.
Dessalines. Maybe not so wise. *(boastfully)* But nobody'll get the best of me fighting.
Claire. I'm sure they won't, dear.
Dessalines. Why, Napoleon ordered me shot once—all the way from France—but I'm not dead yet! *(He laughs.)*
Claire. Not at all, darling.
Dessalines. But plenty of Napoleon's soldiers are buried right here on Haitian soil, defeated by my troops. Bonaparte rules France—but I rule Haiti!
Claire. And nobly!
Dessalines. Oh, I know I'm nothing much but a fighter, Claire. *(determinedly)* But if fighting's the only way to get things done—then I'll get 'em done!
Claire. You've accomplished such a lot already, dear! And with what ignorant people! Every jewel in that crown's a testimony to your

greatness. Why, your scepter holds a realm of power. *(She rubs her fingers over the scepter, purposely touching his hand.)* What beautiful rings you have on your fingers tonight, darling. Some of them I've never seen before. That emerald! *(lifting his hand)* Oh, how lovely! Why, it's green as the sea at dawn! Please, let me try it on.
Dessalines. *(taking off his huge emerald and slipping it on her finger)* It's too big for you, dear?
Claire. Not much. Let me keep it tonight, darling. I won't let it slip off. It's too lovely!
Dessalines. Women always want to play. *(rising and offering his arm)* Shall we dance?
Claire. Jean Jacques, you know you haven't learned the minuet. You'll step on my slippers.
Dessalines. You're right, darling. *(sitting down again)* I'm clumsy as an ox. Let's just sit here and drink our wine.

(A clatter of horses' hoofs is heard outside.)

What's that? Who could that be riding into the courtyard at this time of night? Popo, go see!

(Popo exits. Martel rises and looks over the edge of the terrace. The distant drum is ever louder in the darkness. Claire toys nervously with the emerald on her finger.)

Claire. Perhaps it's some distant guest arriving tardily.
Dessalines. I hope it's nobody bringing a message. I've had enough to worry my head today. Now, I just want to enjoy you tonight, and this wine, and the cool breeze. I'm tired, honey.
Claire. *(as loud voices are heard without)* Don't worry with anything more this evening, darling, please. Refuse to receive whatever it is.
Dessalines. I hope I can, but it may be something pressing. *(as Popo enters hurriedly)* What is it, Popo?

(Popo, his eyes bulging, whispers to the Emperor. Dessalines leaps up so quickly he overturns his wine. It runs like blood across the banquet cloth.)

Order my horse! Bring him to the terrace. Tell Stenio to report to me at once with my garrison ready to march.

(Popo exits, as Dessalines addresses the Treasurer, Lord Bobo, who sits near by.)

Lord Bob, are you vaults locked?
Lord Bobo. Of course, Your Majesty!
Dessalines. Then give me the keys to the gold.

Lord Bobo. *(rising, trembling)* Of course, Your Majesty. But, but, but— *(He gives Dessalines a huge key fastened to his belt.)*

Dessalines. Martel, remain here! Continue the banquet. I'm going to the coast.

Martel. But what is it, Jean Jacques? What's happened?

Dessalines. Word from Archaie that the peasants have revolted. They're burning the crops, and Yayou's soldiers have joined them. That mulatto Gerin's at the bottom of this. But I'll stop it. Every man will return to his post, or I'll wipe them off the face of the earth!

Martel. Take care, son, take care!

(The remaining guests quickly leave the table and exit hurriedly. Sounds of departing carriages without. The servants, too, have disappeared. Only Pierre, the bugler, remains.)

Popo. *(returning)* Your horse is ready, sire, and mine.

Pierre. *(approaching)* Emperor, I ride with you, too.

Dessalines. You'll have to ride fast, Pierre. *(to Popo)* Popo, take the scepter, and my crown. Bring me my sword. Is the guard forming?

Popo. General Stenio is missing, sire! And the guards are gone.

Dessalines. *(roaring)* What?

Popo. Stenio left word that he precedes you to the Port. Vuval's gone, too.

Dessalines. The insubordinate rascals! Who gave orders for them to leave? I'll bring them back in chains! Quick! My sword! *(Popo exits. Dessalines hangs his ermine cape on the back of a chair. Claire takes it. He addresses Martel.)* Martel, the Tiger rides again.

Martel. Would it not be wise, Jean Jacques, to send some trusted friend ahead to see what conditions are? And would it not be best to pick your soldiers carefully for such a trip?

Dessalines. No soldier can ride as fast as me, Martel. Besides, I'm commander of all the troops in Haiti, and if any have been misled by their rascally commanders, they've but to hear my voice to call me Chief again. I'm going directly to the headquarters of Gerin and take charge. Then I'll subdue the peasants quickly enough. *(to his wife)* Claire, go to your rooms. I'll be back within a day, no doubt. Or certainly by the second dawn.

Claire. *(with a peculiar intonation)* Good luck, Your Majesty. And goodbye.

Dessalines. Not goodbye, darling. Merely goodnight. *(He kisses her. She draws back slightly. As she exits, she wipes his kiss away. Dessalines addresses Martel.)* An Emperor has his troubles, too, same as a slave.

Martel. It's not wise to ever be a master, Jean Jacques.

Dessalines. What do you mean, Martel? A master?

Martel. It's not wise.

Popo. *(entering)* Here, sire, is your hat! Your sword!

Dessalines. *(putting on a plumed helmet and fastening his sword at his belt)* Somebody's got to govern, Martel. The peasants can't rule themselves.
Martel. Some day they can, son.
Dessalines. Until that day comes, then, I'll be their ruler. The French used a whip! *(brandishing his sabre)* I use a sword!

(Exit Dessalines, Popo and Pierre.)

Martel. *(looking after them)* Take care! Take care, Jean Jacques! *(He peers over the terrace as the clatter of horses' hoofs dies down the road.)* Oh, son, beware! Beware!

(The far-off beating of a voodoo drum fills the silence. The old man stands alone, facing the stars. Behind him is the cluttered banquet table where wine has spilled like blood. Slowly, Martel turns and begins to blow out the tapers.)

We might as well save candles, I reckon.

(Curtain)

ACT III

Time: *The following day. Early afternoon.*
Place: *The quay in a little fishing village on the coast. At left, the side of a gray stucco building with a sign hanging from the corner:* HEADQUARTERS, ROYAL HAITIAN ARMY, *Division of the South. On the wall, below, a tattered poster advertising rum. Rear, the low stone wall of an embankment with steps, center, leading up to a seawall, and down on the other side to the beach. Beyond the wall may be seen the tops of sails belonging to fishing boats in the harbor. Hanging from a palm tree, a large fishing net is drying in the sun. At the foot of the wall, on the ground, barefoot market women have spread their wares in the shade of the embankment; mangoes, melons, yams, oranges, limes, sugarcane, cocoanuts, little piles of red peppers. One vendor has thread, thimbles and other trinkets. The women, in bright headcloths, sit with their backs to the wall.*
At Rise: *The market women are laughing and chattering among themselves. Some dip snuff. One smokes a pipe.*

Mango Vendor. It sho' is a fine day.
Pepper Vendor. Yes, indeedy!
Cocoanut Vendor. I likes weather like this myself.
Melon Vendor. You can smell the sea when the breeze blow. Don't it smell good?

Thread Vendor. Sho' do!

(Two fishermen enter.)

Tall Fisherman. Hello, ladies dressed so fine! Who's got a good man on her mind?
Mango Vendor. Where's the good man at?
Tall Fisherman. Right here! Ain't you got a mango for me?
Short Fisherman. *(to the women)* Ask him what he's got for you?
Mango Vendor. *(laughing)* My mangoes are too sweet for men I don't love. *(holding up a pretty one)* But I'll sell you one for a sou.
Tall Fisherman. You'll want one of my fish some of these days. *(mounting the seawall)* My brother's boat's on the horizon now, just loaded down with nice sweet fish.
Cocoanut Vendor. *(tossing her head)* You men always think we womens want something you got. We does very well by ourselves.
Short Fisherman. Until night comes.
Thread Vendor. Huh! If it wasn't for us womens, half the time you mens wouldn't eat. Storm comes, you don't catch nary fish, and we have to feed you.
Tall Fisherman. We supposed to eat! Ain't we worth our board and keep?
Thread Vendor. I gets tired feeding you-all myself. Every time I turn around, looks my husband's asking me for ten sous. Ten sous for this, or for that—tobacco, rum, snuff, always something he wants.
Mango Vendor. Wouldn't be a man if he didn't.
Thread Vendor. Yes, but I gets tired. It looks like all an apron does is work for pants.
Short Fisherman. Suppose you didn't have us men to work for, then what'd you do?
Thread Vendor. Do without.
Short Fisherman. *(strutting)* My woman says she can't do without me.
Cocoanut Vendor. She must be weak.
Mango Vendor. Don't pay no attention to them mens. They's always lying. Here, have a fruit. *(She tosses them each a mango.)* And go on, stop pestering us.
Tall Fisherman. I'll see you later, sweetheart, when my ship comes in.
Mango Vendor. I hope it ain't no row-boat!
Short Fisherman. If I got any nice sea-crabs clawing around in the bottom of the boat, I'll give 'em to you when I come back.
Thread Vendor. I don't like crabs myself. Rather have squids.
Mango Vendor. I'll take the crabs and don't pass me by, neither. I'll be sitting here till sundown.

(The fishermen exit over the seawall toward the water.)

Melon Vendor. Sweet mens! I love 'em! Say, who's still got the same husband they had when they was freed?
Yam Vendor. Lord, chile, I done had me six husbands since then!
Mango Vendor. What's the use of being free if you can't change husbands?
Pepper Vendor. *(a very old woman)* Well, I's still got the man I always had.
Thread Vendor. Aw, Mama Sallie, you know you too old to change.
Pepper Vendor. *(snappily)* I warn't but seventy when the freedom broke out. What's the matter with you?

(Enter two children, who make a purchase of some sticks of sugarcane, then exit, sucking the cane.)

Mango Vendor. A man is like a palm-leaf fan to me. When I feels the need, I picks one up, and when I cools off, I put him down.
Yam Vendor. And me, too.
Cocoanut Vendor. Well, it ain't moral, the priest says.
Mango Vendor. That's right, Zoune, you belongs to them white folks' church, don't you? How long you been in there?
Cocoanut Vendor. *(righteously)* Since before the freedom. My master made all his slaves join the Catholic Church. He said if we didn't, he'd beat the stuffings out of us. I been going to mass mighty near as long as I been colored.
Yam Vendor. That's a long time!
Thread Vendor. Then how come I seed you at the last voodoo dance, just a-calling on Legba?
Cocoanut Vendor. Oh, I believes in voodoo, too. Who says I didn't? Might as well believe in all kinds of gods, then if one fails you, you got another one to kinder help out.
Melon Vendor. Right!

(Enter an old woman, bearing a tray of bananas on her head. As she turns around, one recognizes Azelia.)

Azelia. Bananas! Bananas! Who wants to buy bananas?
Thread Vendor. *(as Azelia stoops wearily and is about to sit down)* Here! You don't pay no taxes for a public stall. Move on!
Yam Vendor. Yes, sister, move on! We pays to have our market by this wall. General Gerin sends an officer out here to collect every morning of the world.
Azelia. All right, I'll move on. Maybe I can sell something to the soldiers in the barracks yonder.
Cocoanut Vendor. Ain't no soldiers. They been gone since sunup.
Yam Vendor. Well, go on, anyhow.

(Azelia tries to lift her basket and fails.)

Cocoanut Vendor. What's the matter? You weak?

Azelia. Tired, awful tired! This basket's mighty heavy. *(brightening)* You-all know, I got weapons in here. It's full of weapons!

Yam Vendor. Huh? What you mean?

Mango Vendor. Shsss! Don't pay her no mind.

Azelia. Don't you see? *(raising up bananas but disclosing nothing beneath)* See there! *(her eyes gleaming)* Machetes! Three machetes, two pistols, the butt end of an axe to fight our way to freedom. And whips! Oh, yes, two whips!

Thread Vendor. *(rising)* Get on! Get on! That's enough of your chatter.

Melon Vendor. Do. Jesus! She's mad as a loon!

Azelia. *(lifting her basket and going on)* That's why I'm tired! So tired! *(as she exits)* This here's a heavy load. Freedom's heavy load.

Mango Vendor. Poor thing! She's crazy.

Yam Vendor. Oh, so that's it?

Thread Vendor. Yes, she's been around here a long time. We know her. Cracked in the head. Always talking about when the slaves rose up against the French.

Mango Vendor. Yes, and even claiming she used to be Dessalines's wife before he got to where he is.

(Everybody laughs.)

Yam Vendor. What Dessalines? Not the Emperor?

Mango Vendor. That's the one.

Cocoanut Vendor. *(still giggling)* Such lies! Such lies!

Yam Vendor. I know she's crazy. What's her name?

Thread Vendor. Azelia, but the soldiers nicknamed her Defilee.

Yam Vendor. Why?

Thread Vendor. I reckon 'cause she runs after them so much. I don't know. She's always following the troops, selling bananas.

Mango Vendor. If she was younger, her basket might not be so heavy. Machetes and pistols! Huh! Don't that take the cake? *(She rises and mounts the steps.)* I'm going up on the wall and see what I can see. Whee! That sun is strong.

Thread Vendor. You just want to see what that old long tall fisherman's doing, I reckon.

Mango Vendor. I ain't studyin' him.

(A band of ragamuffins enters, three or four, pushing and playing with each other, laughing loudly and jabbering in a strange dialect.)

Pepper Vendor. *(to the Ragamuffins)* Get away, you-all! Get away!

(They run to an opposite corner of the stage, laughing.)

Yam Vendor. Old bad boys, just running wild. No manners nor nothing.
Melon Vendor. Ragamuffins right out of the back country, that's what they is! Can't even talk so's you can understand them.
Thread Vendor. They got a dialect all they own, them peoples back yonder in the woods.
Pepper Vendor. They're hungry back there, that's why they come to town.
Cocoanut Vendor. They're just too lazy to work the farms, that's all. The Emperor give 'em land, but they won't work it. They're too free now.
Thread Vendor. Then if somebody makes 'em work, they yell about, "We ain't slaves no more!" That's the way with men! Men is lazy.
Melon Vendor. Lazy, lazy, lazy! If it wasn't fun out riding in a boat on the sea, I don't 'spect they'd even fish.
Yam Vendor. Well, anyhow, to tell the truth, the farmers ain't got no plows to work with. Looks like since we drove the French out, don't no more ships come here bringing tools nor nothing.
Thread Vendor. Things is kinder at a standstill. Haiti's even mighty nigh out of thread and thimbles.
Mango Vendor. *(on the embankment)* Say, look, you-all! I see a strange ship coming. A new one. It's got big red sails!

(The women all rise and peer over the wall, or mount the steps.)

Melon Vendor. It ain't no fishing boat, either, is it?
Thread Vendor. It's a passenger boat, I believe.
Mango Vendor. I seed it once before, at Saint Marc. It belongs to some of the Emperor's officers. Some rich mulatto or 'nother, I reckon.
Thread Vendor. It's sure a big one, all right, 'cause it's anchoring way out in deep water.

(As the women look at the ship, the ragamuffins steal up to the fruit on the ground. One slyly grabs a melon, another a handful of yams, another a mango.)

Mango Vendor. *(turning and seeing them; screaming)* You rascals! Get away from here! Scat!

(The boys scatter.)

Yam Vendor. Curse your rotten hides! Beat it!
Melon Vendor. *(pursuing them)* Put down my melon, you thieves! Gimme back my melon.

(The ragamuffins exit with their fruit, yelling and laughing.)

Thread Vendor. Can't take your eyes off things these days. Thieves is getting awful. Young thieves, too.
Melon Vendor. *(panting)* I wish I could get my hands on them hooligans.

Cocoanut Vendor. We ought to have polices, that's what we needs. Soldiers ain't no good. They steals themselves.
Mango Vendor. They ain't even a soldier around today, nohow.
Yam Vendor. *(going back to the steps and looking toward the shore)* Wonder what that boat's here for?
Cocoanut Vendor. I reckon they getting ready for one of their yachting parties. The spendthrift devils!
Pepper Vendor. And Haiti gone to rack and ruin.
Melon Vendor. 'Way back there in the country where I goes to fetch my melons, the farmers done refused to pay taxes.
Yam Vendor. Yes, and General Gerin took his soldiers away from the barracks today. They say he's put 'em all in that fort ten kilometres down the coast.
Thread Vendor. I hear General Yayou's marching, too.
Melon Vendor. Looks like they getting ready for some more fighting. Look like we'll never be done fighting here in Haiti.
Pepper Vendor. Something's wrong! Something's wrong! And poor Jean Jacques, he don't know what to do.
Thread Vendor. Huh! All the Emperor knows is fight! He's done killed off all the white folks. Now he's looking for somebody else to chop up.
Mango Vendor. He's a brave man, though! You can't say he ain't. And 'cause of him, I'm free.
Pepper Vendor. True, thank God!
Yam Vendor. Well, he ought to chop off some o' these taxes we got to pay every time I turn around. That's why I never has a sou to my name.
Mango Vendor. You got more'n you ever had when you was a slave.
Pepper Vendor. Right! Some of you-all's even got shoes.
Melon Vendor. *(whispering)* But the papaloi says there's gonna be a change soon.
Cocoanut Vendor. That's what the priest said, too.
Thread Vendor. Then you-all's Gods all agree. I 'spects the devil's in it, myself.
Melon Vendor. Somebody's coming! They look like soldiers to me. *(beginning to cry her wares)* Melons! Nice, cool melons!
Yam Vendor. They is soldiers. Yams! Yams! Yams! Mulatto officers, too! Yams! Must be a high class brigade. Yams! Yams!
Mango Vendor. There ain't but a handful, though. We won't sell much to them. Melons! Melons!
Thread Vendor. Every little bit helps. Needles! Thimbles! Thread!

(Enter a squad of soldiers, led by Stenio. Vuval follows. The market women hold out their fruits, calling and beckoning.)

Stenio. Squad halt! *(The soldiers halt.)* Left face! *(The soldiers obey.)* Men, we'll remain here. Clear the square. Get all these old women out. *(commanding)* Break ranks and go ahead.

(loud chatter and protestation among the women)

Melon Vendor. What's this?
Cocoanut Vendor. You gonna clear us out?
Thread Vendor. What officer is he?
Mango Vendor. He don't belong around here.
Yam Vendor. Don't he know we pay for this space?
Stenio. You women'll have to clear out at once! Military orders! So move and move quickly! And shut up! Or else my soldiers will handle you.

(The women begin to gather up their wares in clothes and baskets. Meanwhile Vuval has mounted the seawall. Hurriedly the women exit, left and right, pushed by the soldiers. One soldier grabs a mango and starts to eat it.)

Soldiers. Move on! Get! Step on it!
Stenio. *(to the one who has the mango)* Put that mango down! This is no time to eat. *(to Vuval)* Is the beach clear?
Vuval. Yes, only a few fisherman, and they're several hundred yards down the shore. Our boat's approaching, Stenio. Just arrived, apparently, and has anchored in the bay. *(He waves.)* They're waving at me now. Yes, look, they're beginning to lower the skiff.
Stenio. Good! Claire won't have to wait when she arrives. She ought to be here before long.
Vuval. What did the lookout say about Jean Jacques?
Stenio. The lookout that climbed the palm tree? Oh, he said he could see him clearly crossing the valley without field glasses. He'd passed the Red Bridge, so the Emperor ought to be dashing into the village any moment now.
Vuval. You'd better place the men, then.
Stenio. It's good he can't ride his horse onto the quay here. He'll have to come up those steps on foot. *(to the soldiers)* Squad, attention! *(as they form before him)* Listen carefully, men! A great honor's befallen us, and at the same time a grave patriotic duty! We're chosen by destiny to be the liberators of Haiti! We're to free our country from a power-loving tax-hungry tyrant. It's our privilege and our honor, men, to put an end to the career of a black monster who cares not at all for us, or for Haiti, or for our people, but only for himself. Now his day of reckoning has come. I did not tell you last night why I picked you out so carefully. But I chose you as men loyal to myself and to freedom. Now, we are to strike the blow that will break the shackles of submission forever. We are to put an end to the presumptious Negro who dares call himself "His Majesty."
A Soldier. What?

Second Soldier. You don't mean . . . ?
Third Soldier. Not the Emperor?
Stenio. I mean Dessalines!
Soldier. But what'll happen to us?
Second Soldier. Why, that's treason!
Third Soldier. I don't want to do that.
Fourth Soldier. We'll be done for!
Stenio. You'll be promoted in rank and made commanders. You need have no fear, men. There'll be a Republic and a President. Perhaps myself as President. General Gerin and General Yayou have already begun to take over the forts for the new government. There'll be an end of Emperors, and of tyranny! And we'll be heroes in the eyes of the people! Heroes, men! Heroes!
Soldier. But bullets can't kill Jean Jacques!
Second Soldier. He's got some kind o' magic about him, I heard.
Third Soldier. Yes, he has.
Stenio. Aw, don't be foolish. He's got nothing but arrogance!
Vuval. He's only a man, just like the rest of you.
Stenio. Of course! But he's kept you bluffed too long. We should have done this years ago. But enough talk. That nearby dust cloud makes me think he must be almost here. Men, take the places I'll assign you. At my command, come forth and take them prisoners. *(pointing out hiding places)* You two, there in the doorway of the Army Headquarters. One man behind the embankment wall, near the steps. And the rest of you take the other side.

(The soldiers hide as ordered.)

Vuval, you and I will take our hiding places here where we can see when he dismounts, and be ready to give the command as he approaches. This is a moment I've long awaited, friend.
Vuval. I shall write a poem about this, Stenio. How two young men, believers in liberty, brought down the voracious Tiger, whose jaws devoured the people of Haiti.
Stenio. Write it tomorrow, Vuval. Let's hide now. His horses approach.

(Noise of horses' hooves, then pawing and champing as they are tied nearby. A trumpet blast. Dessalines enters, striding like an angry giant, followed by Popo and Pierre.)

Dessalines. *(looking around)* It's mighty quiet here, and no one comes to greet me. Can't they hear your bugles, Pierre? That villain Gerin must've gone to the hills and taken the whole garrison with him! But where're all the fishermen and the market women?
Popo. Sire, I don't like the feel of things here.

Pierre. Nor do I, my Emperor.
Dessalines. Let's go further.

(As the men advance toward Army Headquarters, Stenio emerges from his hiding place and gives the traitorous orders.)

Stenio. Seize the prisoners!

(The soldiers leap up and seize Popo and Pierre, who struggle with them—but no one dares touch Dessalines. Two soldiers approach him, but back away in awe and terror.)

Dessalines. Who dares put their hands upon a King? *(The soldiers quail. He turns toward those holding his companions.)* Release those men! *(He draws his sword.)*
Stenio. *(also drawing a sword)* You'll give no orders to Stenio's troops, Jean Jacques.
Dessalines. *(turning and seeing Stenio for the first time)* You traitorous dog! Your head'll roll at my feet for this! And now!

(He starts toward him with his sword. Stenio backs away, but Vuval lifts his pistol and fires like a coward from behind. The royal sword clatters to earth. The Emperor staggers, turns, looks at Vuval, and tumbles to the ground, dead.)

Stenio. *(laughing)* Dog! Ha! Ha! Dog, am I? *(He kicks the body of the Emperor.)* Well, you're less than a dog, now. Food for worms, you! *(He turns and barks at the men holding Popo and Pierre.)* Take those prisoners to the barracks. Lock them up without water. We'll court-martial them shortly. *(They exit.)* *(to Vuval, who stands now as if in a daze)* What's the matter with you, man? You've done well. Don't look so woebegone, Vuval. Laugh, poet, laugh! It's not *your* heart that's punctured. You're more than a poet now! Why, you're the new Liberator of Haiti. Your name will go down in history, boy. Put your gun away and come, let's see if we can find a glass of wine. Then you'd better go meet the skiff and prepare for Claire's arrival. Meanwhile, I'll ride south to seek Gerin. Tomorrow we'll set up a Provisional Government at Port-au-Prince in which, no doubt, we'll both have important posts. *(glancing at the body as they move toward the barracks)* Come on! Leave that mess for the scavengers to pick up.

(Vuval, still silent, accompanies his friend toward the Headquarters. In passing, Stenio picks up the Emperor's sword.)

I might keep this trinket as a souvenir. *(They exit.)*

(The fallen ruler lies alone, in the dust, on his back. From either side of the

square come the same ragamuffins who earlier plagued the market women. They steal in awe around the body, then silently creep up and touch it. When they see that the corpse does not move, they cry aloud in their unintelligible dialect, jabbering in wonder at the tassels of gold on his shoulders, the heavy golden cords at his cuffs, his shiny boots. One of the ragamuffins picks up the Emperor's hat with the purple plume and puts it on his head.)

Ragamuffin. *(with the hat)* Ha! Ha! Ha! Ha!

(Two of the boys begin to turn the body over as they unbutton his coat and take it off. While they squabble over the coat, a third removes his silken shirt, the color of wine, and rubs it against his face, groaning voluptuously at the sleekness of the cloth.)

Ragamuffin. *(with the shirt)* Oh! Ah! Th-sssss!

(The body of the Emperor now lies on its face, back bare to the sun. The old welts of his slave days stand out like cords across his shoulders.

Azelia enters with the tray of bananas on her head. Fiercely, she turns on the ragamuffins, chasing them away.)

Azelia. Get away! Get away! That man's sick! Or dead, maybe! And you young fools dancing and laughing, and robbing him out of his clothes. Get away!

(The three ragamuffins exit, running.

Azelia puts away her tray on the wall and goes toward the body, unaware of its identity. She kneels to lift his dusty head in her hands. Suddenly her face is frozen with horror and pain of recognition. Sobbing, she falls across the body.)

Jean Jacques! Jean Jacques!

(For a moment her arms cover the heavy scars on his back. Then she rises slowly to her knees and looks down at the man who was once her husband.)

Oh, my Jean! My dear! *(remembering)* So long together! So much we shared! The cane fields, the slave hut! Freedom! *(bitterly)* Our freedom, Jean Jacques! That took you away from me—to a palace with a throne of gold, and silken pillows for your head, and women fairer than flowers who made you forget how much we'd shared together. Once we slept in a slave corral, together, you and I. But when you slept in a palace, you didn't need Azelia. *(tenderly)* My sweetheart! Oh, my dear! You offered me money, then, too much money for one who loved you. *(Caressingly, she rubs her hands across his body.)* But I still love you, Jean Jacques! I still love you!

(The sound of voices approaching. Two servants cross the steps, carrying a heavy chest, as Vuval appears on the seawall, pale as a ghost.)

Vuval. *(directing the men)* Down the beach, to the skiff.

(The servants exit toward the beach. The others enter with a similar chest and follow the first pair. Then Claire Heureuse comes swiftly across the square, accompanied by her maid. As she passes, in spite of herself, she pauses to glance at the body of the fallen man. Quickly she puts her hands across her eyes and shudders with a memory she can never lose.)

Claire. *(in a whisper)* Those scars! *(As she mounts the steps, Vuval takes her in his arms and they disappear toward the beach. Moaning in crazy monotones, Azelia rocks above her dead. Two fishermen appear on the seawall, carrying strings of silver fish. They pause to look at the strange pair.)*

Tall Fisherman. Who's that laying over there with that crazy old woman?
Short Fisherman. *(coming closer to the body)* He musta been a slave once—from the looks of his back.
Azelia. *(without turning her head)* He was a slave, once . . . *(She gently spreads her shawl over his shoulders.)* . . . then a King!

(The fishermen remove their hats, as

(Curtain)

Our Lan' (1946)

Theodore Ward (1900–1983)

Born in Thibodeaux, Louisiana, Theodore Ward, after a childhood in Louisiana and Missouri, worked at various jobs during his travels from Illinois to Seattle, Washington, before he resumed his education at the University of Utah. While there, he won the Zona Gale Fellowship for Creative Writing, which enabled him to study at the University of Wisconsin. During his lifetime, he was a writer, a teacher, and an actor. One of the organizers of the Negro Playwrights Company, he was better known as the author of two powerful, enthusiastically acclaimed dramas—*Big White Fog* (1938), which critic Sterling Brown described as the most artistic production of the Federal Theater during the 1930s, and *Our Lan'*.

Written in 1941, *Our Lan'* is the story of a group of newly freed blacks. Trusting in the government's promise of "forty acres and a mule" for each Freedman, they struggle to build a new life on an island off the coast of Georgia. After winning a Theatre Guild Award, *Our Lan'* was first produced Off Broadway in the Henry Street Playhouse in 1946. A modified version was produced on Broadway at the Royale Theatre in the fall of the same year. The version published here is that which was produced on Broadway, with one exception. According to the author, when the play was taken to Broadway a decision was made to eliminate the sound of the cannon at the end of the play. It was feared that that final shock might produce panic in an audience already strained to an almost unbearable tension. The author, however, preferred that the ending should be published as it appears in this book.

Our Lan'

CHARACTERS

Negro
Joshuah Tain
Georgana, his daughter
Charlie Setlow
Ellen, his daughter
Gabe Peltier
Tom Taggert
Sarah, his wife
Joe Ross
Patsy, his wife
Edgar Price ⎫
Emanuel Price ⎬ Young Freedmen
Chester ⎭
Lem
Ant Dosia, his mother
Delphine
Roxanna, her young sister
Ollie Webster, a young pre-Civil War Mulatto Freedman
Oliver Webster, his father
Daddy Sykes
James, 13
Beulah, 13
Martha, 12
Ruth, 12
Alice, 6
Fred Douglass, 7

Freedmen

White
Libeth Abarbanel, a school teacher
Captain Bryant } Officers of the Freedmen's Bureau
Captain Stewart
John Burkhardt, a planter
Hank Saunders, his overseer
Rebel Soldier I
Rebel Soldier II
A Cotton Broker
A Sergeant
White Soldier of the Union Army

Acknowledgments are gratefully made to Manuel Gottlieb, from whose "The Land Question in Georgia During Reconstruction" many of the important notes were taken; to Elizabeth Lawson, Wm. Burghardt DuBois and James Allen, whose works were among the major sources consulted.

THE AUTHOR
September 16, 1941

SCENES

ACT I

A cave on the road to Savannah.

ACT II

A forge on the island.

ACT I

SCENE 1

Time: *Evening, January 1865.*
Place: *A cave on the road to Savannah. In silhouette against a fire burning in the Center are three ragged Negroes—Edgar and Emanuel, in their early twenties, and Peltier, aged about thirty-six. They are waiting for a couple of sweet potatoes to bake in the ashes. Down-right, a ledge affords the only entrance and exit.*

Edgar. *(singing in a low voice as he watches the flickering fire)* "Oh, de blind man stood in de way 'n cried: Oh, Lawd, save me—" (*As he ends the slow, plaintive refrain, he rises and goes down to stand at the ledge, looking out, wistful, bewildered, questioning, as he renews the refrain.*) "Oh, de blind man stood in de way 'n he cried: Oh, Lawd, save me—" *(Glancing around, he sees Peltier testing one of the potatoes.)* How dem yams comin', Peltier?
Peltier. *(pushing potato back into ashes with stick)* Dey still hard.
Edgar. Damn! Dey been in de ashes long 'nuff t' be soft ez butter.
Peltier. *(rising)* Ah think Ah git some more brush.
Emanuel. Thas er good idea—we'll need it 'fore de night's gone. *(He straightens out blanket.)*
Edgar. *(as Peltier goes out—seeing Emanuel endangering the blanket)* Look out, Emanuel, 'fore you burn mah blanket!
Emanuel. The Yanks show up, yuh wish Ah had-er burnt it!
Edgar. *(grunting, as he turns back to the ledge)* Phumph!
Emanuel. Anybody steal from de very folks what sot 'em free need thar neck broke!
Edgar. Yank or no Yank, Ah ain't fixin' t' freeze mah behind!
Emanuel. Yuh sing er diffunt story ef Gen'l Sherman ketch yuh.
Edgar. *(ignoring him and singing)* "Oh, de blind man stood in de way 'n cried: Oh, Lawd, save me!" *(scanning the sky, and suddenly amused)* This Januwery wind risin' higher 'n higher—Yes, Sah! *(going on slyly)* Heh! Wouldn't s'prise me if it cut somebody's behind t' er frazzle 'fore mawnin'.
Emanuel. Don't yuh worry 'bout me, Edgar Price.
Edgar. *(joining him)* Who said anything 'bout yuh, Emanuel, Boy?
Emanuel. *(pursuing his own thoughts)* If it wasn't fer de Yanks, whar'd yuh be?—Still in der Quarters, duckin' 'n dodgin' ole Marster!
Edgar. Heh! Thas all yuh know 'bout it.
Emanuel. Yeah—! Yuh de one Cuffee ole Marster ain't never had t' lose er wink of sleep ovah.

Edgar. *(wisely)* A nimble-footed mule keep de skin on his back—but yuh ain't sharp nuff t' catch de scent of that!

Emanuel. *(listening)* Hush! . . . Ah hear somebody.

Edgar. Must be Peltier.

Emanuel. *(rising)* This quick? It can't be . . . *(He goes to ledge and looking out sees newcomers.)* It's a couple of ole folks. Comin up heah—Lawd, Ah wonder if dey got er bite or two?

Edgar. *(joining him with alacrity)* Lawd, Buddyboy, hush your moufe!

Emanuel. *(to newcomers)* Hydy, Folks!

Voice. Hydy!

Emanuel. It's kind-er steep, ain't it?

Ross. *(appearing, puffing—a small black man of sixty-five)* Ah reckon this heah's de tallest hill—*(entering)* in de whole State of Gawgie!

Edgar. *(attempting to assist his companion)* Gimme your hand, Anty, 'n Ah'll pull yuh up!

Patsy. *(in a huff, as she ignores his offer)* Now hold on, Sonny! *(Brushing by him, she turns and admonishes him sharply.)* If yuh want t' git 'long wid me, don't call me "Anty!" *(A huge black woman, she limps to fire.)*

Ross. *(meanwhile—placatingly)* Now, Patsy; de boy didn't mean no harm.

Patsy. *(emphatically)* It's time these youngsters learn we's free—*(parentally, turning to Edgar)* Ah's titled t' a handle on mah name, Sonny—Ahm Miz Patsy Ross, 'n thas mah husband, Mister Joseph Ross.

Ross. Jes call me "Uncle."

Edgar. *(smiling)* Us glad t' meet yuh, Miz Patsy.—Set your carpet sack down 'n catch your breath.—Ahm Edgar Price 'n this nomannered rapscallion heah's Emanuel.

Patsy. *(her good nature rising)* Yuh all brothers, hunh?

Edgar. No'm. Us ain't no kin. Us jes goes by de name of ole Marster.—*(emphatically)* But us goin' change that.

Ross. This heah's er mighty nice cave yuh all got.

Patsy. De Lawd will provide, hunh, Son.—But lemme set down 'fore this leg slays me! It's worse'n er prickly pear—*(sitting)* Too much trampin' for mah weight Ah speck.

Emanuel. Whar yuh all come from, Uncle?

Ross. Ah reckon us kivvered evvy road in de State of Gawgie, Sonny. But us used t' blong t' Jeb Winters, down in Ware County—few miles jes this side of Waycross, 'case yuh know whar dat.

Peltier. *(reentering with armful of brushwood)* How de yams?

Edgar. *(stooping to fire quickly)* Damn! Ah bet dey burnt t' er cinder! *(He sighs with relief as he rakes potatoes from fire.)* Dey all right.

Peltier. Den les have 'em.

Edgar. Drop your wood 'n meet Miz Patsy 'n her husband, Mr. Ross.—*(to*

latter) This ouah new partner whut jes joined up wid us de udderday.— He named Gabe Peltier.
Peltier. Hydy!
Ross. Us glad t' meet yuh.
Emanuel. *(to Patsy)* Yuh all et supper?
Ross. *(interposing)* Supper? Sonny, Ahs still waitin' fer breakfust.
Patsy. *(admonishingly)* Now, Mister Ross!
Emanuel. *(to his buddies)* Yuh speck us could let 'em have tha lil one?
Edgar. 'Cose. (Picking up potato, he finds it too hot to handle.) Doggone!
Emanuel. *(pushing the potato with stick)* Here yuh is, Miz Patsy.—Us ain't got but two or we'd give yuh all more.
Patsy. Gawd bless yuh, Son.—It's er shame for us t' take it.
Edgar. Go long, Mam. Us glad t' split wid yuh. *(dividing other potato)* Here, Peltier.
Peltier. *(forlornly, to Ross)* Don't look much like Freedom, do it?
Ross. Sure don't.—But tell me sompen, yuh all—Yuh heayd anything 'bout Gen'l Sherman givin' all de Freedmens rations?
Peltier. Whar yuh heah dat?
Ross. Us met er man this mawnin' say das whut dey tell him.
Edgar. Ah bet mah freedom 'gainst er lead nickel: anybody git rations from de Yanks goin' sweat for 'em.
Patsy. *(shocked)* Whut—?
Emanuel. *(explanatorily)* Edgar de kind got t' have de whole shoat or nuffin.
Edgar. Pay yuh best t' bank tha fire.
Emanuel. Oh, sure—Cuz yuh done run outer chips.
Edgar. Heh! But Ah reckon yuh never will learn no sense, Emanuel, boy. Yuh can't see de Yanks ain't all candy-sweets 'n gravy!
Ross. Ah think Ah git what yuh mean, Sonny. We can't git nowhar wukin' for board. Here tiz de year of Ouah Lawd 1865. Us been free two whole years. But Ah got mah first time t' make er dollar.
Peltier. Dem Yanks don't mean us nogood, nowhar.—Ah wuz t' Missippi—
Emanuel. Missippi—Yuh been t' Missippi?
Peltier. *(nodding)* Hit's wuss thar!
Edgar. How yuh mean?
Voice. *(below—calling)* Hallo!
Edgar. *(crossing to ledge)* More comany for de Big House—*(calling down)* Hallo!
Voice. Mind if we come up?
Edgar. Naw, Sah! Us got plenty good room!
Ross. Evvywhar yuh turn somebody trampin'!
Patsy. Ah speck de Lawd must-er got us mixed up wid de Israelites. Looks like we got evvything goes wid de wilderness but de pillar of clouds by day 'n fiah by night.

Setlow. *(Entering. He is a wiry mulatto, quite gnarled and forty. Behind him are his children, Ellen, a good looking mulatto of twenty, and James, a lad of thirteen.)* How yuh all come on?

Ross. Jes poorly—How's yourself?

Setlow. Ahm still lookin' up.—But lemme make yuh all's 'quaintance. Mah name Charlie Setlow, 'n thas Ellen, mah oldest, 'n James.

Ross. Us right glad t' meet yuh.

Edgar. *(smiling)* Set your carpet sack down, Miss Ellen, 'n draw up t' de fiah.

Ellen. Us ain't cold, thanky.

James. Pappy, mah belly feel like er empty croakersack.

Setlow. Ellen, Ah speck yuh better stir up dem turnips—*(to others)* They's frost bitten 'n Ah's mighty skeered they won't do.

Ellen. Ah don't think they'll hurt nobody—*(getting out turnips)* Only us ain't got er pinch of salt!

Edgar. Us had some salt. Emanuel whut yuh do with tha salt?

Emanuel. Yuh de las one had it.

Edgar. *(discovering salt)* Oh, heah yuh is, Miss Ellen. *(Joining her, he's arrested by her delicate hands, or pretends to be.)* Bless mah soul! *(teasingly)* Whar yuh git dem lil ole hands? In de Big House, Ah bet!

Ellen. *(pleased)* Now hold your buzzin', Mister Bumblebee.

Edgar. Fingers ain't big ez er goose quill; skinny's honeysuckle stems—Blessed me!

James. Pappy, Ellen ain't cookin'; she's sparkin'!

Ellen. *(reaching for him)* Ahma crucify yuh!

(James scurries beyond reach. Edgar laughing, sits near her.)

Edgar. Gimme de water jug, Pappy.

(Setlow hands jug, and she begins preparation of her turnips.)

Ross. Brer Setlow, which way yuh all bound?

Setlow. *(hesitatingly)* Well . . . Ah tryin' t' make it t' Sawanny.

Ross. *(interested)* Yuh got some prospects dar?

Setlow. Well, t' tell yuh de truth, Ah heard Gen'l Sherman fixin' t' give way de lan'.

Ross. *(excited)* 'N yuh do say!

Setlow. That's what dey tell me.

Peltier. *(sharply)* It's talk, Man. Nuttin' but talk.

Setlow. How yuh know?

Peltier. Year 'fore las, dey said Gen'l Grant was gwine do de same. 'N me, de big fool: Ah tramped clean cross Alabama 'n Missippi t' Vicksburg.—But Ah wish yuh could seed what Ah found!

Edgar. What, Peltier?

Peltier. Dem Yanks wuz herdin' everybody like cattle in de camp—Ole folks, women 'n chillun; some sick, some half-naked, with sores from head t' foot . . . Some dyin' by de cart loads.
Patsy. Do, Jesus!
Peltier. But wait. Yuh ain't heard de wuss yit. *(bitterly)* All dem, like me 'n yuh, able t' wuk. Phey! Dey turn dem ovah t' de planters!
Ross. Oh, go long!
Peltier. *(quietly)* Leasin', dey called hit—Jes er-nother name for slavery!
Setlow. *(after a moment)* Well, Ah kin see tain't no use gwine t' Sawanny.
Patsy. *(quietly)* Sometimes Ah wonder if dese white folks got good sense.
Ross. Me, too. Dey set er man free wid no job 'n no lan', 'n tell him t' go farge for hissef.—But how's he gwine farge?
Edgar. Dey figger us like de birds, Ah guess.
James. Thas what Mammy said, Christmas.
Setlow. Whut Ah tell yuh 'bout buttin' in ole folks' conversation?
Patsy. Chillun de same evvy generation.—But whar yuh leave your wife, Brer Setlow?
Setlow. *(quietly)* Ah had bad luck 'bout her, Mam.
Patsy. Oh, yuh don't say.
Setlow. All this trablin' round 'n fust one thing 'n er-nother.—Us bury her side de road New Year's Day.
Patsy. Lawdy, jes two weeks ago!

(Ellen hides her brimming tears.)

Setlow. *(taking out Bible)* Yes'm.
Patsy. Blessed Jesus!
Emanuel. *(seeing Bible)* Is yuh er preacher, Mr. Setlow?
Setlow. *(sadly)* Ahm jes er man of Gawd, Son—*(reading by firelight)* "Then Job arose 'n rent his mantle 'n shaved his head 'n fell down upon de ground 'n worshipped 'n said: Naked came Ah out of mah mother's womb, 'n naked shall Ah return thither; de Lawd gave 'n de Lawd hath taken away; Blessed be de name of de Lawd."
Patsy. *(after a moment)* Well, yuh kin be thankful yuh still got your chillun. Me 'n Mister Ross loss ouahs 'fore de war.
Ross. Yes, Suh. Saw em sold t' one stinkin' trader aftuh er-nother till de last wuz gone—God knows whar.
Setlow. They sold two of mine.

(silence)

Ellen. *(drying her eyes, she sees James going to ledge.)* Come back here, James.
James. Ah hear singin'.
Emanuel. *(joining him)* Ah bleve so, too!

(They listen. Wind is heard.)

Ross. Heah anything?
Emanuel. Naw, Sah. *(turning back)* Ah guess we's been hearin' things.
James. But Ah heard singing.
Patsy. Ah speck it's de wind, rollin' cross dese barren hills.
Ross. Barren is de name for 'em. *(preoccupied)* Maybe if us jes had somebody us could send t' see Father Abraham, us could show him what er fix us is in. Thus us could axe him, if he ain't plannin' t' gin us de lan', if he wouldn't sell it t' us, 'n let us pay in er year or two.

(They appear to dwell on the wisdom of his words, and all is silence.)

James. *(springing up and rushing to ledge)* There tiz ergain!
Edgar. Ah believe yuh right. *(He also goes to ledge.)*
Patsy. *(catching sound)* Somebody singin' all right.
James. *(looking out, excitedly)* There they come!
Edgar. *(looking)* It's er whole drove of folks comin' round de upper bend.
Ross. *(scrambling up)* 'N yuh do say!
Setlow. *(listening)* Them's ouah folks, too!

(sound of singing)

Ross. *(looking out)* Did yuh ever see such er passel in de moonlight?
Setlow. Lawdy, it's same's de year of Jubilee!
Ellen. *(eagerly)* Pappy, yuh spose they mighter heayd 'bout de lan'?
Setlow. Praise Gawd, Ellen—they jes might!
Voices. *(led by a powerful baritone, growing rapidly louder)* "Ah lookd ovuh Jordan 'n what did Ah see: Coming fer t' carry me home—A band of angels comin' after me: Comin' fer t' carry me home . . ."
Ellen. Lawdy, thar's somebody thar sure kin sing!
Patsy. Yes, Lawd. They could use him in de Heabenly Choir.
Ross. He got er baritone won't behave!
Emanuel. *(excited)* Ahma go down dar 'n meet em.

(Exit Emanuel.)

Setlow. *(shouting after him)* See if yuh kin find out if they gwine t' Sawanny!
Voice. *(singing nearby)*
  "Ahm trampin'
  Trampin'
  Trampin'
  Tryin' t' make Heaben mah home—Hallelujah!"
Ellen. *(carried away)* Pappy, us oughter take in behime em!

Voices. *(singing rollickingly—as the horde of passersby ostensibly move on)*
"Now if yuh git to Haebem
Before Ah do
Tell all mah friends
Ahm comin too!

(fading)

Trampin'
Trampin'
Tryin' t' make Heabem mah home!"

Emanuel. *(below, shouting)* Edgar, come on yuh all. They givin' way lan'!

Setlow. Great Gawd A'mighty; hit's true!

Peltier. Can't be!

Edgar. *(simultaneously)* Whar, Emanuel?

Ellen. *(interposing)* Lawd, Pappy; les go!

Setlow. Hush, Gal!

Emanuel. *(simultaneously)* In Sawanny—Gen'l Sherman givin' everybody lan'!

Setlow. Lawd er mercy—Come on, Chillun! *(He is struggling to gather his belongings.)*

Peltier. Yuh goin'?

Setlow. Ah ain't gwine stay!

Emanuel. *(appearing, excited)* Come on, yuh all. They say yuh got t' be there in de mawnin', if yuh want t' git yor share!

Setlow. Ellen, will yuh hep me git these things!

Edgar. *(grabbing up blanket)* Damn if Ah ain't gwine be thar!

Ross. *(seeing Patsy getting her bundle)* Whut yuh fixin' t' do, woman?

Patsy. Go!—What yuh think?

Ross. *(amazed)* But your leg!

Patsy. *(shouting)* Don't stand thar talkin', Mister Ross! Git on out-er heah down tha road!

James. *(anxiously, as Setlow starts out)* What 'bout de grub, Pappy?

Patsy. *(pushing Ross)* Git on, Mister Ross!

James. *(frantically)* Pappy, yuh leavin' de grub!

Setlow. Git on—Ah'll git de pot!

Edgar. *(catching James, as others crowd out)* Come on, Boy. Us gwine t' Sawanny; git ouah fawty acres 'n ouah mule! *(Yelling, he disappears.)* Whaaaaaaaaaaaaaaaaaaawhooooo!

(exit)

Setlow. *(following with pot and bundles)* De Yanks done blowed de horn! Whoopeeeee!

Peltier. *(unable to resist)* Dey might be right 'n dey might be wrong—But make way for me, Cuffees, cuz ahm coming long!—Yahoo!

(exit)

(Blackout)

ACT I

SCENE 2

Time: *Afternoon, two days later.*
Place: *The forge on an island off the coast of Georgia. The lights pick out Daddy Sykes, a rusty-black old fellow of seventy, who is sitting on the steps of the Cottonhouse, scratching his crinkled gray head in an attitude of surprise and amazement, as he listens to the sound of voices singing, some little distance off left.*

In a moment, as the light increases, the whole scene becomes visible and the spectator notices that an old storehouse is down left, its porch about a foot above the ground. Beyond it, an old oak with overhanging moss and a circular seat about its roots. A path behind the oak curves off up left. Here a bit of weedy field and open sky. On the other side, the forge juts, enclosing the rear and revealing the firebox set in a niche in the wall, blackened with soot and age. A pathway separates the forge from the Cottonhouse on the right, as the latter protrudes into the scene in a state of near decay. The steps to the latter are further forward, leading up to a narrow porch. A rain barrel, with an angle iron suspended above it with a rod for striking attached to a cord, are on the upper side of the steps. Remnants of old farm equipment, an overturned anvil, and several tufts of weeds are scattered like dumb witnesses remarking the vanished prosperity of this former slave kingdom in the sea.

Voices. *(singing, joyfully)* "Roll Jordan roll—Roll Jordan roll . . . (etc.)."
Sykes. *(puzzled)* What de debil! *(seeing a good-looking girl of sixteen appear, suddenly on porch behind him)* Roxanna, whut yuh reckon tiz?
Roxanna. *(excitedly)* Ah donno, Daddy Sykes—*(running down and off up left)* But Ahm sure goin' see!
Voices. *(in an outburst of frenzied shouting)* Whooooooopeeeeeeeeeeeee! Here we is, Folks!

(Delphine enters. She is an extremely attractive, brown, young woman of

twenty-three wearing a woolen shawl about her shoulders, and clutching it above her full bosom.)

Sykes. *(seeing her)* Will yuh listen t' dem fools!
Voices. *(frenzied)* Done crossed ole Jordan at last! Bless Gawd! Bless Gawd!
Delphine. *(amazed)* Goodness gracious me!
Voices. *(in religious frenzy)* Bless Gawd! Bless Gawd!
Another. *(calling)* Beulah! Yuh Beulah! Come back heah!
Sykes. Ole Marster ain't goin' like this!

(A group of children run in wildly, only to disappear off up right.)

Delphine. *(attempting to intercept one)* Little Girl, wait! Wait! *(The children laugh merrily in the distance.)*
Peltier. *(entering with Taggert)* Hi, Folks—Kin we git through t' de Quarters dis way?
Delphine. Yes, Sah. But who yuh all?
Peltier. De new owners—
Delphine. *(amazed)* What yuh mean?
Taggert. *(going off right with Peltier)* Tell yuh later, Daughter.

(exit)

Voices. *(singing merrily, as group approaches)*
"Oh, dem golden slippers
Oh, dem golden slippers . . . (etc.)."

(Dancing and prancing, a crowd of men and women enter, filling the area with the rich spectacle of their antics and colorful garments, which, for all their bedraggled condition, affords an atmosphere of pageantry. Roxanna, in complete rapport, dances on the arm of Lem.)

Delphine. *(attempting to catch Roxanna)* Roxanna, you come here to me! *(Roxanna evades her.)* All right, Miss! You wait!
Ross. *(Prancing, he waves a ticket above his head, and addresses Delphine.)* Shake your foot, Daughter.—Us got tickets for the lan'! *(singing in parody)* "Oh, de golden ticket! Oh, de golden ticket!"

*(Cutting a step he disappears in crowd.
Ollie Webster, an aristocratic mulatto, immaculate in the apparel of a gentleman of the times, crosses to stand aside on porch of storehouse.
Edgar, Emanuel, and Chester are in crowd wearing Union Army uniforms and carrying rifles.
Joshuah Tain, a leader of the band, stands protectingly as all swirl about him, his lips puckered slightly in his habitually winning smile. One senses his sincerity and warmheartedness, which seem to bind him to the others in*

deep, sympathetic accord. Indeed, he is an expression or symbol, if you will, of the best traits of his people. There is a sure sense of dignity about him and his very physical strength bespeaks something of the relentlessness and courage which characterized the bulk of the vilified black men of the period—a people conditioned by the terrors of ruthless oppression who communicated their spirit from generation to generation; not by precept but by example—now graphic, now more or less obscure; not passive, not insurrectionary, but always passed on: the son emulating the inarticulate father; the daughter fashioning her life on the pattern offered by her mute but undaunted mother. In a word, one senses that here is a man.)

Joshuah. *(as they swirl to a halt)* What er ilun'! What er ilun'!

Ross. It's de lan' of Canaan!

Dosia. *(a rawboned woman of fifty, in grip of religious ecstasy)* True, Jesus—True, Oh Lovely Lamb!

Joshuah. *(fervidly)* Ah no sooner spied her, 'fore she commence t' seep into mah bones, 'n Ah said t' myself: Joshuah, look yonder; dar's yor home. At last, yuh 'n yor people got er home!

(Delphine gazes upon him and is enraptured.)

Dosia. *(wildly)* 'N it's all on account of yuh, Joshuah!

Ross. Us got t' gib him er big honor!

Patsy. How 'bout makin' him Gubner?

Dosia. Yeah. Das just what!

Joshuah. *(lifting his arms)* Hold on, yuh all. Hold on. *(indicating forge)* Gimme er fiah yonder, 'n er hammer 'n er pair of tongs, 'n Ah'll make yuh anythin' from er spike t' er two-wheel driver. But don't axe me t' be no Gubner!

Ross. But, Joshuah, us got t' hab er gubment—?

Joshuah. *(noticing Delphine)* Ah know. But we'll settle dat later.—Set up er Council or sompen—*(crossing to Delphine)* How do?

Delphine. *(bashfully)* Fine, Suh.

Joshuah. Mah name's Joshuah Tain. What might be yor's?

Delphine. Delphine.

Joshuah. *(smiling)* Delphine. Thas sure is er pretty name. But Ah reckon yuh kin wear it!

Delphine. *(pleased)* Ah speck t'wouldn't do t' try to 'spute yor word.

Joshuah. *(laughing)* Take a blind judge not t' back me up.

Ollie. *(joining them)* I agree with you perfectly, Mr. Tain!

Joshuah. This is Mr. Ollie Webster—

Ollie. *(to Delphine)* Had I known you were here, I would've visited this island sooner.

Joshuah. *(laughing)* Who wouldn't? *(to all)* But Ah didn't git chance to tell yuh all. His papa was one of de main men what talked Gen'l Sherman into lettin' us have de lan'.

Ross. 'N yuh do say!

Joshuah. But not only that. Ah speck through his Papa's goodness, we goin' have er teacher!

Patsy. Lawdy, a teacher!

Joshuah. Yes, Mam. This mawnin' he sot down 'n writ us er letter t' de Abolitionists up Norf 'n axed 'em t' send somebody.—Now ain't that sompen?

Ollie. Oh, it was nothing, Mr. Tain. We free men are proud to do all we can to help you climb.

Joshuah. 'N yuh kin depend on it; we won't let yuh down!—But, Delphine, who heah sides yuh?

Delphine. Jes mah lil sister, Roxanna, there, 'n Daddy Sykes, here.

Joshuah. *(pointedly)* 'N de white folks—?

Delphine. They's away—Cept'n for de overseer, Mister Hank. Marse Burkhardt 'n Master Luther, they gone t' war; 'n Miss Burkhardt, she is in Paris. She left me t' take care of de house.

Joshuah. Whar this overseer?

Delphine. He live in Savannah, 'n only comes over now 'n then t' keep his eyes on things. But what yuh all mean by callin' this yor home?

Joshuah. Gen'l Sherman done gin us de whole Ilun'—

Delphine. Yuh don't say!

Joshuah. That's 'bout de Alpha 'n de Omega of it.

Sykes. De Alpha 'n de Omega, hunh?—Delphine, yuh better tell these crazy Cuffees sompen.

Patsy. *(sharply)* What's de matter wid this ole man?

Delphine. Daddy Sykes, Ah think yuh better hush!

Sykes. But what 'bout Mister Hank? What he gwine say?

Delphine. Ah don't know, and what's more, I don't care!

Ross. *(approvingly)* Thas tellin' him, Daughter!

Sarah. *(outside, calling)* Joshuah!

(The group turns up left.)

Delphine. *(to Patsy—sotto voce)* Is you all's leader married?

Patsy. No, chile—Why?

Delphine. *(stepping off embarrassedly)* I jes asked.

Sarah. *(Entering, angrily—bearing a bundle. Behind her is Setlow rolling a barrel of flour.)* Joshuah! Do you know them Yanks ain't gin us er speck of meat?

Crowd. What! No!

Joshuah. Dar wuzzn't no meat t' be had, Sarah.

Sarah. Den, Joshuah, how us goin' live?

Joshuah. We gwine draw on de Commissary of de Almighty!
Dosia. Joshuah, what kind of blasphemin' talk is this?
Joshuah. *(indicating sea—off left)* Ant Dosia, yuh see tha ocean yonder?
Dosia. 'Cose Ah see it.
Joshuah. Well, what yuh think de Lawd put de fish 'n shrimp 'n 'is sister in tha water for?
Sarah. *(appeased—laughing)* Lawd, Joshua, leave it t' yuh!

(rumble of voices off right)

Joshuah. What now? *(turning up, as Peltier and Taggert enter, angrily)* Yuh come in like de whirlwind.
Peltier. *(furiously)* Ah wish yuh could see them huts!
Taggert. They ain't fitten fer er dawg t' sleep in!
Joshuah. Is tha so?
Peltier. They ain't nothin' but er nest of spiders 'n lizards 'n thousand-legs—
Taggert. Not only tha. You ought t' see de roofs.
Joshuah. *(easily)* Well, if they ain't right, we'll jes have t' fix em.
Peltier. Take er month t' fix dem roofs.—Meanwhile, whar we goin' live?
Taggert. Yeah. 'N de nights still frosty, too!
Ross. De Big House empty ober dar.
Dosia. Das right. De white folks gone!
Joshuah. Tha don't cut no figure. We can't use it.
Taggert. How come we can't?
Joshuah. Cuz it don't blong t' us.
Sarah. *(sharply)* What yuh care? Mah chillun got t' hab er dry place t' stay.
Taggert. 'N she don't mean *maybe!*
Joshuah. *(gently)* Gen'l Sherman gin us de lan', Tagg. He didn't say a mumblin' word 'bout de Big House.
Taggert. Damn dat.
Joshuah. All right. Ah tell yuh what. We'll let de chillun sleep in de Big House til we fix dem huts. Will dat suit you?
Sarah. It's more like it.
Ross. Yuh all worried 'bout de huts—but what 'bout de mules? How come us ain't got no mules?
Joshuah. *(pained)* We ain't got none, Brer Ross, cuz de Army ain't had none t' spare!
Peltier. 'Fore Gawd, Joshuah! Keep on dis way goin' be de same here like twuz t' Missippi. How in the world we goin' raise er crop wid no mules?
Joshuah. *(sharply)* Now listen, everybody. There's sompen we got t' git straight right now. We didn't come heah t' have no barbecue. Just yistiddy we had 'bout ez much chance ez er housefly in de winter time. But today you kickin'. Yuh got lan'. Yuh got de chance t' look forward

t' yor own bale of cotton, yor own ca'iage 'n span. 'N yet yuh kickin'! Whut yuh think this is? A lil ole measly patch of ground? This is er whole ilun'!

Setlow. Thus saith de Lawd God of Israel. Ah brought yuh up from Egypt, 'n brought yuh forth out of the house of bondage. And Ah delivered yuh out of de hand of de 'Gyptians 'n out of de hand of all dat oppressed yuh, 'n drobe dem out befo' yuh 'n gave yuh their lan'!

Dosia. Amen! Amen!

Joshuah. Yuh ready wid your "Amen." But how many yuh see we got de chance t' turn dis ilun' into de prettiest 'n most bountiful spot in de ocean? Jes bloomin' wid flowers 'n bumper crops? Lawd, Ah tell yuh, it's like er barrel of heabenly waters! *(quickly)* Only dar's er few tadpoles in it got t' be fished out 'fore we kin drink. Cuz dem tadpoles like *(pointing off right)* dat frozen ground 'n all dem weeds yuh see stretchin' yonder. They's dem broken down huts yuh don't want to live in. But when a man's in de hot sun 'n famished for water, he don't go thirsty just cause de waterboy bring him er bucket wid er few tadpoles in it, do he?

Setlow. Deed he don't!

Ollie. *(stepping forward)* Mr. Tain, it just occurs to me; I may be able to help you with respect to the huts.

Joshuah. Is that so? How?

Ollie. I think I can arrange fer you to get lumber.

Edgar. Not so us can build?

Ollie. Yes.

Edgar. *(elated)* Hot ziggedy damn!

Ollie. My father owns a half interest in a sawmill—just outside of Savannah. It has been closed since the outbreak of the war. I think I can persuade him to let you use the steam-donkey and bandsaw.

Joshuah. That'd be a Godsend, Mr. Webster.

Ross. Yes, Lawd! Wid all tha timber yonder, us could build us er town!

Joshuah. You speak t' him, Mr. Webster. Tell him we'll come git it, 'n pay him fer his trouble in de bargain.

Ross. Yeah, Suh. 'N ef he don't care t' wait, maybe us git him one of dem mortages yuh heah tell of.

Ollie. *(going—laughing)* Well nevermind the mortgage. I'm sure he'll be glad to do what he can. But I must get aboard. I'll see you again in a day or two.

(exit)

Joshuah. Thanks er lot fer yor pains, 'n tell yor Pa we all say de same!

(whistle of steam scow, shrilling above ad libs of farewell)

Joshuah. *(to Edgar)* That's de whistle blowin' for yuh, boys!
Ellen. *(suddenly regretful)* Oh, no! No!
Edgar. It's all right, Sugar Tit. It's all right.
Ellen. But, Edgar—Oh, they'll kill yuh!
Edgar. *(embracing her)* Kill me! Shucks, Sugar Tit. De Reb ain't born kin settle mah hash!
Ellen. You don't know, Honey!
Patsy. Shame on yuh, Ellen. Them boys goin' way t' fight for ouah freedom. Yuh ought t' be proud to see em go.
Sarah. Tiz er shame though—'n dey jes got married!
Edgar. She all right. Yuh all, jes look after her, 'n don't forget t' save mah fawty! *(to Ellen—going)* Come on, Honey. 'N cheer up. Them Rebs ain't goin' have no more chance wid me then er hen-house full er chickens wid er weasel!

(exit, as Emanuel and Chester also break away and go out, the crowd ad libbing)

Ross. *(shouting after them)* Eberytime yuh spy er Reb, don't stop t' spit. Jes let him hab it!
Joshuah. Remember, this is yor chance t' gain de glory! *(turning to others)* But come on, everybody. Let's see what kin be done 'bout dem cabins. *(going)* Tell dem bats t' git dar carpet sacks 'n move on over t' de Big House cuz de new tenants heah 'n they takin' over. Yes, Suh, 'n ain't got no room t' spare!

(exit, others following)

Delphine. *(arresting Roxanna)* Yuh wait!

(Lem halts also.)

Roxanna. But, Delphine. Ah want t' go with them.
Delphine. You've seen them huts before—*(to Lem)* 'Scuse us, young man. There's sompen I want t' say private.
Lem. *(going)* Sure, sure!
Delphine. Now, listen, Roxanna. You's started sompen I ain't goin' have. That boy ain't been here a minute, but already yuh's let him get out of place.
Roxanna. Lawd, Delphine. I ain't did nothing with tha boy but just dance with him.
Delphine. And you don't even know his name—
Roxanna. I was just trying to be nice.
Delphine. That ain't what I'm talking 'bout. I got no objection to yuh tryin' t' be nice. But yuh don't be nice to people by getting out of place with em, or lettin' them git outer place with you. Tha boy ain't in your

class. One look should-er told you he ain't nothin' but er field hand. And from now on I want you t' remember that. You understand?

Roxanna. So I ain't sposed t' even speak t' him, hunh?

Delphine. Of course you speak t' him. But yuh let him stay his distance. I promised Mammy I was goin' raise you right. 'N Ah mean to do it. If yuh make a mistake, it ain't goin' be my fault. I want yuh t' be somebody. 'N if you listen t' me, yuh will. Someday you'll run cross a man of quality—one like that Mister Ollie was just here.

Sykes. *(entering excitedly)* Now us gwine see sompen sho nuff!

Delphine. What're you talking about?

Sykes. *(pointing off left)* Yuh see de Gypsy Belle easin' t' de wharf yonder, don't yuh?

Delphine. *(tensing)* Mister Hank! Roxanna, run warn 'em. Quick. Catch 'em 'n tell de leader—

(exit, Roxanna, running)

Sykes. Ah knowed us wuz gwine run into sompen. Ah seed de *sign!* Bat bumped square into me last night.

Delphine. It did? What's de meanin' of that?

Sykes. Somebody round heah in fer bad luck.

Delphine. Is yuh sure?

Sykes. De sign say: tarrible luck!

Delphine. Oh, Daddy Sykes, yuh jes tryin' t' put bad mouth on 'em. Tha sign could mean anything.

Sykes. Hab it yor way. Go right ahead.

Delphine. Yuh don't reckon he got his gun?

Sykes. Mister Hank always carry tha forty-four! *(Delphine whirls and runs off.)* Whar yuh goin'?

Delphine. Ahma warn de leader! *(exit)*

Sykes. *(quickly taking seat)* Ah ain't gwine hab nuffin' t' do wid it mahsef!

Delphine. *(reentering at once with Joshuah and others)* He's mean 'n sneaky as de devil. Yuh got t' watch every move he make.

Joshuah. Ah understand. *(to others)* Spread out, yuh all. 'N jes leave everything t' me.

Ross. *(sotto voce)* Heah he come.

Saunders. *(entering—a wiry, leathern-faced white man of perhaps forty)* By Golly, what's goin' on heah? *(coming down)* What de dickens yuh Cuffees doin' on this island? What yuh call this?

Joshuah. Well, Ah reckon, Suh, yuh might say we's jes gettin' settled.

Saunders. *(shocked)* Well, Suh! So yuh walk on the place and make yourselves t' home, eh? *(kicks barrel)* What's this?

Joshuah. Flour.

Saunders. Yuh sure come t' settle all right. *(to Joshuah)* But tell me. Whose land do yuh think this is?
Joshuah. Ouahs.
Saunders. *(shocked)* What?
Joshuah. Gen'l Sherman told us t' come heah 'n stake out fawty acres er piece, 'n he give us tickets for it.
Saunders. *(laughing)* He did, eh?
Ross. He did dat. *(exhibiting ticket)* Heah's mine right heah. Good fer *fawty* any part of this ilun'.
Saunders. *(curious)* Let's see it. *(Ross exhibits it beyond his reach.)* Hand it here.
Ross. Yuh kin see it from heah, can't yuh?
Saunders. *(authoritatively)* Gin it to me!
Ross. *(evading him)* What fer?
Saunders. *(laughing)* What's the mattuh, yuh fraid Ah'll keep it?
Ross. *(restoring ticket to pocket)* Gen'l Sherman told me t' take good care of mah ticket!
Saunders. Well, Ah suppose the Gen'l must have his little joke. *(turning to Joshuah)* But don't yuh know yuh must have a deed to own land?
Joshuah. We git deeds. Gen'l Sherman say atter de war. He told us t' jes go head 'n raise a crop.
Saunders. And how do you expect to raise a crop without stock?
Patsy. Ah kin plow lan' same as er mule. With these hands Ah raise cotton dis year; buy two mules!
Saunders. By Golly, yuh Cuffees take de cake! *(Looking around, he scratches his head in a quandary.)* Yuh make me feel Ah ought t' trust yuh—'n by Golly, thas just what Ahm goin' do. Ah was plannin' t' drive yuh off de place. But Ahm not goin' do it. Ahma let yuh go t' work 'n start earnin' your own livin'.
Joshuah. We ain't wukin' fer no white man!
Setlow. No, Bless Gawd!
Saunders. Where yuh goin' t' find work if not from a white man?
Joshuah. *(sharply)* We goin' wuk. We goin' wuk all right. We goin' wuk right heah on de lan' what blongs t' us!
Peltier. Yeah! 'N Ah'd like t' see any man put me off this lan'!
Saunders. Mind yor tongue, nigger!
Peltier. *(quietly)* Spose yuh make me!
Saunders. *(reaching for gun)* Why, confound yor black hide!
Joshuah. *(simultaneously with two others crowding him, pinning him in a vise between them)* Now jes er minute, Suh! Pay yuh best not t' start nothin' here!
Saunders. *(indecisively)* Ah see yuh all lookin' fer trouble!
Joshuah. Naw, Suh. We's peaceful folks.

Saunders. Yuh call it peaceful seizing other people's property!
Joshuah. Been any seizin' done, Suh, yuh must see de 'spute's 'tween yuh 'n Gen'l Sherman 'n his Army.
Saunders. *(relaxing)* This land belongs to John Burkhardt, and there ain't a Yankee living who can turn it over t' you. Why, confound it, there ain't a white man South of the Mason-Dixon line who would'n rather be dead than live under such topsyturvy conditions. By Gawd, it's the same as makin' us slaves and yuh masters. But perhaps, that is what yuh want?
Joshuah. You couldn't pay me t' be nobody's stinkin' master. 'N furthermore, Ah'd advise you t' git on way from heah 'n leave us erlone.
Saunders. Ah see yuh one of these smart alecks. But never mind. *(going)* You jes stay heah. *(laughing)* Yuh'll learn! *(exit)*
Dosia. *(after a moment)* That ain't no good laugh.
Peltier. Tha scoundrel lucky somebody didn't bust his brains out!
Ross. *(ominously)* If yuh ask me, this ain't de last of him.
Patsy. De Lawd delivered Daniel!
Joshuah. *(after a moment)* We's in ouah rights. This country don't blong t' his kind no more. *(suddenly going, cheerfully)* But come. Let's git de grub divided up 'n see what we kin do 'bout tryin' t' git settled 'fore de night comes down. *(raising song)* "Didn't my Lawd deliver Daniel . . ."
Others. *(singing)*
"Daniel!
Daniel!"

(Their voices soaring over the island, they all follow Joshuah out in courage and hope.)

(Blackout)

ACT I
· · · · · ·

SCENE 3

Time: *April, 1865, or three months later.*
Place: *The same. The former atmosphere of complete dilapidation has changed to one of thriving improvement. There are no tufts of weeds, and in the rear several furrows of upturned soil show that the land is being plowed, while the presence of a Donkey steam engine indicates that the Freedmen are planning to build new homes as soon as the crop shall have been planted.*

>*Outside, nearby, the men are singing a work song, which they humorously compose as they bend their backs to the arduous task of breaking the soil without the assistance of an animal.*

Voice. *(male chorus singing)*

> "Ole Marster sot in de shade 'n he cried:
> Hoe, Boy, hoe!
> Ole Marster sot in de shade 'n he cried:
> Hoe, Boy, hoe!
> Ole Marster sot in de shade 'n he cried:
> Git all dem weeds 'fore Ah tan yor hide!
> Hoe, Boy, hoe!
> Hoe, Boy, hoe!
> Hoe, Boy, hoe!"

(Emerging in pairs, a team of Freedmen drawing a plow to which they've harnessed themselves by means of a rope. They are sweat drenched. Entering they cross, describing an arc to reverse the plow before disappearing again, as continuing to sing, they strike a new furrow.)

> "Now Ah know ole Marster goin' be good 'n sore
> Hoe, Boy, hoe!
> Ah know ole Marster goin' be good 'n sore
> Hoe, Boy, hoe!
> Ah know ole Marster goin' be good 'n sore
> Cuz we wuk for ousefs or don't wuk no more!
> Hoe, Boy, hoe!
> Hoe, Boy, hoe!
> Hoe, Boy, hoe!"

(As their voices fade, Delphine saunters in. For a moment she halts to gaze at their retreating figures—her mood one of deep preoccupation.

Ellen appears up left. Halting, she sizes up the situation, then exclaims in confirmation of her suspicions.)

Ellen. Ahanh! haaaaaaaaahanh! *(seeing Delphine turn with a guilty flush)* No wonder you can't spend no time at de net!
Delphine. Why—What yuh mean?
Ellen. *(laughing)* Nevermind. Yuh ketch on!
Delphine. *(lamely)* Why—Ahm on mah way t' de net right this minute.
Ellen. *(teasingly)* Shame, shame on yuh!
Delphine. *(embarrassed, knowing the drift of Ellen's insinuations)* But Ah don't understand. What's Ah got t' be shame 'bout?

Ellen. *(laughing)* Ah's had my eye on yuh all winter, Girl. Yuh ain't hangin' round dis forge for nothin'.
Delphine. Lawd, a pusson can't even walk out de house widout bein' 'cused of bein' up to sompen!
Ellen. Yuh needn't try t' throw me off, Girl. Yuh got yor cap set on Joshuah, er mah name ain't Ellen.
Delphine. Yuh so smart!
Ellen. *(disarmingly)* Now ain't no use rufflin' up yor feathers, Delphine, 'specially not wid me. Ahm wid yuh, Honey!
Delphine. *(surprised)* Yuh wid me?
Ellen. 'Cose. But tell me—Ahm jes dyin' t' know how yuh makin' out?
Delphine. But ain't nothin tween me 'n Joshuah.
Ellen. *(coaxingly)* Oh, come on, Honey. Why be like tha? Yuh kin tell me!
Delphine. But ain't nothin t' tell.
Ellen. *(matter-of-fact-ly)* Oh, there must be sompen!
Delphine. Ahm *tellin'* yuh now.
Ellen. *(seriously)* Wid all de looks tween yuh 'n him these last three months. *(convincingly)* Yuh can't tell me that. *(laughing)* Yuh all sweet on one ernother, 'n Ah know it.
Delphine. *(seriously)* Oh, Ah ain't sayin' Ah don't like him. But Joshuah can't see me, dear.
Ellen. Aw, go on, Girl.
Delphine. All dem smiles yuh see, don't mean a thing.
Ellen. Ah don't believe tha. How's he talk?
Delphine. He don't. He ain't never said nothin' t' me.
Ellen. *(amazed)* No?
Delphine. No.
Ellen. *(puzzled)* Maybe yuh ain't give him de right chance—?
Delphine. *(tittering)* Ah think he's skeered.
Ellen. Skeered how?
Delphine. Cuz Ahm so young.
Ellen. What?
Delphine. Ah think he think Ah ain't ole enuff.
Ellen. *(thoughtfully)* Tha could be, him being ouah leader 'n all that. Still, must be sompen wrong wid you. Maybe you too slow, girl?
Delphine. Ah can't put mahself on him.
Ellen. Shucks, Girl. Yuh green! Yuh get what yuh want, yuh better copy from Delilah.
Delphine. In de Bible?
Ellen. Sure. Yuh know how she got way wid Sampson.
Delphine. *(laughing)* Lawdy! But yuh don't mean tha.
Ellen. Ah don't? Yuh know how long it took me t' git mah husband, Edgar?

Delphine. No. How long?
Ellen. *(laughing)* Ah met him like this evenin'; 'n next mawnin' Ah had him at de alter!
Delphine. Oh, go long, Ellen!
Ellen. Yuh don't bleve me, yuh axe Miss Patsy. *(turning)* Ah got t' go— *(laughing)* Ah don't bleve in walkin' when there's a rig for hire! Not this chile. *(seeing Ollie off left)* Umph! Here's Ollie. *(exit—up right)*
Ollie. *(Entering, he tosses gear on ground beside forge, and sees Delphine.)* Well, good morning, Beautiful!
Delphine. Hello, Ollie. How're yuh?
Ollie. Surprised.
Delphine. Surprised 'bout what?
Ollie. *(coming down)* Finding you sitting out here all by your pretty self.
Delphine. *(flattered)* Oh, go on, Ollie.
Ollie. *(joining her)* Anyone would think you've something against me.
Delphine. What do you mean? Why?
Ollie. You make it your business to evade me, you little heart breaker.
Delphine. *(uneasily)* Lawd, Ollie. What's got into yuh?
Ollie. *(catching her)* Come here to me, you little peach!
Delphine. Ollie, is yuh crazy?
Ollie. The sweetest little peach in Georgia!
Delphine. *(evading his lips as he embraces her)* Oh, Ollie! Ollie, stop! Don't yuh see de men in de field!
Ollie. Kiss me!
Delphine. No!
Ollie. Oh, you're going to be kissed!
Delphine. No, Ollie! Don't—doooon—*(He smothers the word with his lips. She struggles feebly, and succumbing wilts in sheer physical response. But in a moment, flushing with shame and anger, she breaks away and slaps him.)* Oh, yuh—!
Ollie. *(rubbing his cheek)* Now was that nice?
Delphine. *(glancing anxiously off right)* Yuh had no right t' put yor hands on me!
Ollie. *(laughing)* You little temptress. How could I help it?
Delphine. *(sharply)* Yuh sposed t' be a gentleman, ain't yuh? Did Ah ever git out of mah place wid you? Did Ah ever give yuh de least cause to be so free wid me?
Ollie. Oh, come now. It wasn't that bad. Why I felt you let yourself go!
Delphine. *(shocked)* Oh, Ah hate you!
Ollie. Well, I see I shall have to speak to Daddy Sykes.
Delphine. What yuh mean?
Ollie. You understand very well what I mean.
Delphine. *(worried)* The ole man better not fool wid me!

Ollie. *(amused)* Oh, no? You make me desperate, and I'll have you *fixed*—I'll get some of Daddy Sykes' love powder.

Delphine. Tha ole man can't do nothin' t' nobody. Daddy Sykes jes ignant. He full of talk. He jes try t' make folks think he knows somepen 'bout *signs* 'n *Voodoo*.

Ollie. You believe in him all right—though you needn't fear my ever being so weak as to resort to him for help. I admit I'm crazy about you, and I've wanted to tell you so for some time. But that isn't what worries me. What I'm really concerned about is your future.

Delphine. My future?

Ollie. Yes. You haven't given it a thought, have you?

Delphine. Ah ain't had no cause t'—not lately.

Ollie. No.—Why not?

Delphine. Oh, lots of reasons.

Ollie. Like what? You're not going to tell me you're perfectly satisfied being lost over here on this God-forsaken island?

Delphine. No. But still, for one thing; the place ain't like it used to be. There's folks heah now, 'n we all gittin' long so fine. Someday Ah 'spose it's goin' be real nice.

Ollie. I thought you were smart, a beautiful girl like you. Has it never occurred to you what you might make of yourself in Savannah—among the up-to-date? Among people of class and distinction?

Delphine. *(laughing)* Shucks! When Joshuah git through wid this islan', Ah reckon yuh city 'ristocrats goin' be wantin' t' move ovah heah.

Ollie. That's rich! Joshuah—Prospero disguised as a clodhopper. He waves his magic wand, and, presto, he transforms the whole island! But, after all, you're not to be blamed. You've no way of knowing what life is like in Savannah—for people of my standing and culture—free men, who've never known what it is to call another "Master," who for generations have been educated abroad—in the best schools on the Continent—as I was. Otherwise, you'd appreciate your chances and make an effort to get above this, this living like a common field hand!

Delphine. Ollie, yuh know very well ain't nothin' for a girl like me in Savannah.

Ollie. You underestimate yourself. Why with the proper clothes and my support—a beauty like you. Why you'd be the envy of Savannah society.

Delphine. *(laughing)* Ollie, Ah do bleve yuh's tryin' t' turn mah head.

Ollie. You belong, Baby. You're not only good looking, but you've a head on your shoulders. Why, you could even teach school.

Delphine. Now Ah know yuh tryin' t' make a fool of me.

Ollie. You think I'm joking? Why, after the war the Freedmen's Bureau is going to open schools all over the South. They're going to need teachers, thousands of them.

Delphine. *(impressed)* But, Ollie, yuh know Ah can't even read 'n write.
Ollie. That's no serious handicap. I could teach you as much in a month or two, and if you were willing to listen to me, in two years I guarantee, you will have prepared yourself to take one of the schools.
Delphine. Oh, Ah'd give most anything if Ah thought Ah could rise that high!
Ollie. You can, I tell you. If you're willing to study.
Delphine. *(enthralled)* Oh, Ah'll study, Ollie. Ah'll study night 'n day.
Ollie. Good. I'll arrange a place for you and your sister to stay—
Delphine. You don't mean in Savannah?
Ollie. Yes. Only it must be understood that this is a matter strictly between us.
Delphine. I don't git this.
Ollie. If I'm to help you, there mustn't be any talk, neither here nor in town. I can't afford to have Papa get the wrong idea. I need his help too badly.
Delphine. Wrong idea about what? 'N why is somebody goin' talk?
Ollie. Oh, you should understand how people gossip. I've never mentioned this before. But you see, well, when we get the vote, I'm going to the legislature. That is, if Papa backs me. So I have to be careful. He's the big cheese in the state.
Delphine. Ah heard yor Papa run er barbershop.
Ollie. He does. *(Hearing men approaching from the field, he crosses up to look—Meanwhile.)* That's where he got his influence. *(turning back, resolved to leave)* But come. Walk down to the landing with me.
Delphine. Ain't yuh goin' wait 'n see Joshuah?
Ollie. *(escorting her out, down left)* No. Tell him I left the gear on the anvil. *(exit together)*
Taggert. *(entering and going to the water barrel, but seeing children off right as he crosses path between cottonhouse and forge)* Lawd, yonder go them chillun on de way t' de woods. *(Cupping his hands, he calls, as the other men file in wearily.)* Beulah! Didn't Ah tell yuh not to go in dem woods! Come on back from thar!
Setlow. Knowin' tha boy of mine, 't'wouldn't sprize me if he put 'em up t' it.
Taggert. Ahma have t' skin 'em yet. First thing Ah know one of 'em'll be pickin' up er thorn er gittin' snake-bit!
Joshuah. When Ah wuz dar aige de skin on de bottom of mah feet wuz thick'n er bullhide. *(He hands a dipper of water to Taggert, who drinks before dropping to stretch out wearily.)*
Setlow. *(meanwhile)* Us git this crop in, thar'll be no more feet on de ground as far as mine's consarned. His barefoot days gone foreber— *(shaking his head wistfully)* But he'll never know.

Joshuah. *(joining them)* No. None of this comin' generation. But it won't be long now. With Gen'l Sherman chasin' Johnson 'n Bragg through Calina, 'n Grant hot behind Lee as er fiah in de pineys, this war 'n all ouah troubles goin' be over 'fore yuh know it. *(going up to harness)* But what yuh all say, we git this section done 'fore de sun gits too hot!
Lem. *(hesitantly—as others bestir themselves)* Mister Joshuah. . . .
Joshuah. What is it, Lem?
Lem. How bout gittin' Daddy Sykes t' take mah place fer a day or so?
Peltier. *(laughing)* It'll never happen! Daddy Sykes say he wuked sixty years for nothin' 'fore freedom, 'n now he bound to use his wits!
Ross. *(laughing)* Tha ole rascle. Tha sounds jes like him.
Lem. *(bitterly)* Tha ole man jes livin' off us like er tick!
Joshuah. *(placatingly)* Daddy Sykes ole 'n feeble, Lem. He doin' 'bout much as anybody kin speck.
Lem. Not t' me he ain't. Ah's sick of it. Ah got t' have er rest.
Ross. Shucks, Lem. Us jes on the varge of treein' de coon!
Joshuah. Sure. Three more days 'n we'll be through plowin'. Then, 'cept for de timber for de houses, we kin set back 'n take it easy.
Lem. But Ah tell yuh, Mister Joshuah; Ah's come t' de end of mah tether. Mah shoulder's killin' me!
Peltier. So's mine.
Setlow. Yuh better say all de rest of us!
Joshuah. Sure. Jes grit yor teeth, Lem, 'n come on.
Lem. But Ah been grittin' mah teeth, Ah tell yuh!
Joshuah. *(soberly)* So yuh jes goin' walk off 'n leave us in de lurch, hunh?
Lem. *(desperately)* Ah can't hep it!
Joshuah. *(sharply)* Any man say *can't* don't blong on this ilun'! But Ah been watchin' yuh for de las week. 'N thar's one thing clear: yuh ain't got Ant Dosia's blood. Yuh's de youngest in de gang. Yor muscles hard as er hickry jint. But from sun up t' sundown heah lately, all yuh been doin' is stallin'. *(harshly)* What yuh miss is de bullwhip! Yuh's free 'n yuh got yor own patch o lan'. But in yor heart yuh still ain't nothin' but er triflin' slave. Now if yuh want-er go, git!
Lem. *(hurt)* Yuh kin hurt mah feelings, Mr. Joshuah. Thas all right. *(to others)* But Ah want yuh all t', Ah want yuh all t' take er look at this. *(He exposes his fleshless collarbone.)* Jes take er look!
Ross. *(looking)* Great Gawd A'mighty! Why de bone's bare!
Setlow. *(dumbfounded)* It's er wonder yuh ain't cotched de lockjaw, Son.
Joshuah. Ah axe your humble pardon, Lem; Ah didn't have de least idea.
Setlow. Couldn't nobody know.
Peltier. *(to Lem)* Yuh should-er spoke up 'fore now!
Joshuah. *(to Lem)* Yuh go on t' de Quarters. This ebenin' we'll git yuh cross t' Savannah t' Cap'n Bryant. See if he can't git one of de Army

doctors t' do somepen fer yuh. In de meantime, Ah hope yuh try t' fergit what Ah said.
Lem. *(going)* Thas all right, Mr. Joshuah. Ah ain't paid yuh no mind.

(exit right)

James. *(dashing across up right)* Pappy, heah's Cap'n Bryant! *(Lem reenters.)*

(exit left)

Beulah. *(following him with other children, shouting gleefully)* Cap'n Bryant! Hi, Cap'n Bryant!

(exit left)

Lem. *(looking off left)* He bringin' er lady!
Peltier. *(as he and others move up, obviously as excited and anxious to welcome the visiting Captain as the children)* Er lady!
Taggert. *(calling off right)* Sarah! Hey, Sarah! Run heah, yuh all. Heah's Cap'n Bryant!
Joshuah. Ah wuz hopin' we'd be done plowin' 'fore this.
Peltier. Why yuh say tha, Joshuah?
Setlow. Still, we done beat de deadline.
Joshuah. Ah know. But we ought t' be ready t' plant.
Peltier. What yuh all make of de lady?
Ross. Speck she 'bout one of de 'ristocrats.
Joshuah. *(greeting the newcomer)* Well, well, Cap'n Bryant, if this ain't er Jack-in-de-box!
Bryant. *(entering—up left with woman)* In the army, Joshuah, the first lesson you learn is: Take them by surprise!
Joshuah. *(laughing, as the young Union officer—who is perhaps thirty-five—and his companion come down)* Well, Suh, yuh sure is got it down pat! *(Delphine and several other of the older girls, together with the children, crowd in behind Libeth, who is a good-looking young white woman in her twenties and dressed in a plain bustle of good material.)* But what's up?
Bryant. *(smiling)* It's a big occasion.
Joshuah. Tha so—How come?
Bryant. *(smiling)* Who do you suppose this lady is?
Joshuah. Now, Cap'n Bryant, don't tell me yuh done got married!

(The girls titter.)

Bryant. *(embarrassed)* This lady, Joshuah, is Miss Libeth Arbarbanel, of Hartford, Connecticut, the teacher you sent for.

Delphine. *(Exclaiming—she rushes to wipe bench with her apron.)* De teacher!
Ross. Now Ah's seed er miracle!
Libeth. *(to Joshuah, extending her hand)* How do you do, Mister Tain?
Joshuah. *(wiping his hand on his trousers)* Lawd, Mam—this is too much for me!
Bryant. *(to Libeth)* I warned you, you'd create a sensation.
Libeth. Captain, please!
Delphine. Won't yuh sit down, Mam.
Libeth. *(taking a seat on the bench)* Thank you, dear.
Joshuah. *(as the women enter)* What yuh all reckon, Folks. It's de teacher!
Women. *(surprised)* De teacher! Lawdy! Gawd bless her soul! She done come sure nuff!
Sarah. *(seeing the children swarming over Libeth)* Beulah, what yuh chillun goin' do? Git back 'n stop swarmin' ovah de lady like hivin' bees.
Patsy. *(warmly)* Yuh can't blame de bees, Sarah, whar thar's honey!

(laughter)

Joshuah. Quiet, everybody! *(turns to Bryant)* Cap'n Bryant, will yuh—er—?
Bryant. No, no, You're the officer of the day.
Joshuah. *(feeling inadequate)* Ah thot yuh might care t' say er word—t' sort of make us all acquainted?
Bryant. Later, perhaps.
Joshuah. *(embarrassed—to Libeth)* Ah speck Ah ain't quite got yor name straight yit, Mam.
Libeth. *(nervously)* It is awful. But it's Libeth Abarbanel.
Joshuah. Well, Miss Libeth . . . *(carefully—feeling his way, but with gravity)* Low me, Mam, t' bid yuh welcome. Ah donno jes what Ah kin say, cept'n deep down in de hearts of ebery one of us, as Ah speck yuh kin see, there's er well of gladness 'n pride t' see yuh heah 'mongst us. Ah reckon there ain't but one way to put it. Yuh's like Father Abraham, de way we see yuh. He done broke ouah bonds 'n sot us free. 'N yuh's come t' hep us break de chains of ignance.
Libeth. *(moved)* Mr. Tain, you make me feel very proud and very much ashamed. When I accepted your invitation, I did so thinking it was the only charitable thing a God-fearing woman could do. But you give me a new sense of my responsibility. Since listening to you, I know now, I should've gone down on my knees and offered thanks for the opportunity you were giving me. I say this in spite of any hardships which we may be called upon to undergo. All I ask is that you will trust me, and be diligent; for, for my part, I shall consider it my God-given

privilege to do all in my power to help you, as you've so wisely said, break the chains of ignorance.

Bryant. Hear! Hear!

Joshuah. Thank yuh, Mam. Yuh's er great woman, 'n Ah promise yuh, if we kin git haf de fairness yuh's showed in them few words, we gwine prove ouahsefs in de eyes of de world!

Bryant. I can bear witness to that. I've just returned from a trip of inspection. And General Sherman is going to be a proud soldier when he hears of it.

Joshuah. *(glancing around)* Yuh all heah tha?

Bryant. To put it bluntly, you're going to justify your emancipation in the eyes of all!

Setlow. Glory to Gawd!

Joshuah. Cap'n yuh make us feel mighty proud!

Bryant. I intend that you should. You deserve to be congratulated. But while I'm about it, let me also give you a word of advice. In a few months you're going to have a crop—*(seeing a Corporal enter to halt and salute smartly)* What is it, Corporal?

Corporal. Message for you, Sir. Major Cotton ordered it brought at once!

Bryant. *(taking the telegram)* Thank you, Corporal. *(Opening it he reads, then exclaims.)* Good Lord!

Joshuah. *(breathlessly)* What is it, Cap'n?

Bryant. *(moved)* It's all over!

Joshuah. What, Cap'n—Not de war?

Peltier. *(fearfully)* We ain't loss?

Bryant. Lost! *(ecstatically)* We've won! Lee has surrendered his sword to General Grant. Victory has fallen to the Union! Long live the Union!

(The Freedmen are stunned.)

Taggert. *(his voice low but ringing with profound fervor)* Surely, this is de hand of Gawd!

Dosia. *(dropping to her knees, in tears)* We thank yuh, Jesus!

Sarah. *(clutching Beulah, with tears of joy)* Mah darlin'. There be no auction block fer yuh!

Patsy. No, Jesus! *(The memory of her own offspring like a vision before her mind's eye, she addresses them in apostrophe.)* No more chains! No more scorn! Yuh free, Chillun—Free t' walk de earth like every natural man!

Setlow. *(like a clarion, caught in the grip of intense emotion)* Thus saith de Lawd God of Israel: Behold, I will open de way!

Joshuah. *(lifting the magnificent old spiritual, triumphantly)*
"Go down Moses,
Way down in Egypt lan'!
Tell ole Pharaoh . . . (etc.)."

(All the sufferings and pent up joy surging up, after all the bitter generations of oppression, in one prolonged note of certitude, overflowing through the vehicle of the glorious song, their voices ring out and their tears flow unashamedly . . .)

(Dimout)

ACT I
. . . . . .

SCENE 4

Time: *April 14, 1865, or a week later.*
Place: *The same. It is afternoon. Shortly, the laughter of happy children, playing at recess.*

James. *(entering to perch on circle-seat of oak, agilely—and shout excitedly)* Hey, Miss Libeth. Ah tell yuh what!
Libeth. *(entering up right)* Yes, James.

(The other children follow.)

James. Les' play "Underground railroad!"
Fred. *(gleefully)* Oh, goody—goody!
Libeth. Is there such a game?
Beulah. Oh, yes Mam!
James. It's a good game. It's a lot of fun! You'll see!
Libeth. It certainly sounds interesting. But do we have time?
Beulah. *(anxiously)* It don't take but er minute. We'll be through before recess is over.
Libeth. All right, go on and play it. I think I should like to see your underground railroad.
Fred. *(pleading)* James, can I be the poor slave—hanh, James?—Can I?
James. You know you too little, Fred!
Fred. Miss Libeth, can't I be the poor slave? They don't ever let me be the poor slave!
James. He's too little, Miss Libeth.
Fred. I ain't neither.
James. Get away, boy—go on!
Libeth. Now, one moment, James. Let's be fair. If Fred doesn't suit the part, perhaps there's another he can play?
James. He'll be er run-away. He knows that. Beulah, you be the Paddyroller!

Ruth. And I'll be Moses.* I ain't never been Moses!

James. Well, go on, Ruth. You're Moses. *(Ruth goes up to forge with others behind her.)* Go on with Moses. *(mapping out area)* Play like this is the road with the woods on both sides. Beulah, you hide behind the tree. And, Miss Libeth, you get out the way. *(He joins Ruth, as latter hides behind corner of forge.)*

Ruth. *(Playing game—she peeps out, then waves an admonishing hand to those behind her.)* Hush, Chillun! Hush Ah say. Sounds like a Paddyroller!† *(creeping out alone)* There's a Paddyroller out there or my name ain't Moses—*(halting, and turning to others)* Who'll go out there and see? Who'll go scout the way?

Fred. *(appearing gleefully)* That ain't the way it goes. You left out the "path to the Promise Land!"

Ruth. Tain't no skin off your nose—

Fred. If you're going to play it, play it right!

Ruth. Miss Libeth, make Fred hush!

Libeth. Fred, it's not nice of you to criticize Ruth.

Fred. She ain't playing it right!

Libeth. Nevertheless, she has a right to try her way.

Ruth. *(sticks her tongue out at Fred and continues game)* Don't worry, chillun. I'll get you to the land of Canaan. I ain't never failed yet. But I ask you, who'll volunteer to go scout the way?

James. *(emerging)* I'll go, Moses. Send me!

Ruth. Well, go poor slave, and may the Lawd Gawd go with you!

James. *(Stooping, he peers around cautiously, then, creeping forward, he begins talking, fishing cunningly, baiting the suspected unseen enemy.)* I expect I'm going to have to get a new pair of ears—*(raising his voice)* because looks like I can't catch up with them lowdown run-away rascals to save my life—

Beulah. *(springing out, triumphantly, as he comes down, passing tree)* Ah haaaaaaaaaaaaaaahannah!

James. *(feigning fear)* Oh, look out there, Massa. You like to scared this poor slave almost to death. Whyn't you holler or something?

Beulah. *(gruffly, shaking switch at him)* Cuffee, what youh doing out here this time of night?

James. Lawdy, Massa—What I'm doing? Don't you know?

Beulah. *(sharply)* You dad burn tootin' I know. You're running away, you rascal!

---

*The slaves' nickname for Harriet Tubman, a slave who, after escaping, returned to the South many times to lead others to freedom.

†A white patroller, guarding the road to prevent escapes.

James. Lawd, Massa, you never was so wrong in all your born days. I'm a trusted slave!

Beulah. Then what you doing out here at Midnight?

James. Marster sont me to catch them scoundrels trying to run off to Canada.

Beulah. You's a liar, Cuffee. And I'm-a cut your hide to a frazzle!

James. *(cringing)* Oh, Lawdy, Massa. You got me wrong. My white folks quality folks. Where I come from, the Big House is lit up every night, and lil Misses and the gay blades don't do nothing but just spoon beneath the Dixie Moon and dance till day in the mornin'. Lawdy, you couldn't pay me to run away. I wouldn't be here this minute, if it wasn't for ole Marster sont me to get a line on this devilish *underground* somewhere round here somewhere.

Beulah. *(puzzled)* Is you trying to fool me, Cuffee?

James. No, Sah, Massa. I ain't that crazy!

Beulah. Lemme see your *pass!*

James. *(edging away, as he raises his voice, sounding the alarm to the others)* Lawdy, Massa—*Somebody* better come here and tell you sompen! *(Ruth and others creep rapidly forward.)*

Beulah. *(unaware of their approach)* Stop your hollering. I can hear you.

James. *(stalling, as Ruth and others creep up behind Beulah)* I'm just surprised to see you ain't know me—Asking me for sompen like that. Everybody knows ain't none of Marster John's slaves ever have to tote no pass.

Ruth. *(pouncing on Beulah)* Here's your pass, you devil! *(She and others bear Beulah to the ground, and pummel her.)* I reckon from now on, he'll know better'n to cross the path of Moses. *(going triumphantly, waving the others to follow)* Come on, Chillun! On to Canaan! *(Laughing merrily, they disappear with Libeth in their wake.)* Hi, Mister Joshuah!

....

(Alternate opening of Scene 4, for use where children cannot be cast. At Curtain, Libeth seen reading to children beneath a tree.)

Libeth. *(reading)*
"It was two by the village clock,
When he came to the bridge in Concord town.
He heard the bleating of the flock,
And the twitter of birds among the trees,
And felt the breath of the morning breeze
Blowing over the meadows brown.
And one was safe and asleep in his bed

>   Who at the bridge would be first to fall,
>   Who that day would be lying dead,
>   Pierced by a British musket-ball. . . ."

(to children) That was Crispus Attucks. I want you to remember and be proud of the name, for he is one of our country's greatest heroes. The poet doesn't say anymore about him. But there are other books that tell the whole story, and from them we know who he was and how he, a Negro citizen of Concord, was the first to shed his blood for *liberty and freedom for all* in our native land. *(glancing at watch and rising)* But, we must get back to class—

Ruth. Oh, Miss Libeth, you didn't finish!

Libeth. *(going)* We must keep to our schedule—

James. But, Miss Libeth, that ain't fair!

Libeth. *(turning)* Ain't—?

James. Isn't.

Libeth. That's better. *(going)* Since there are only two more stanzas, perhaps we may finish it inside—

Beulah. Oh, Goody! Goody!

James. *(going, and meeting leader)* Hi, Mister Joshuah!

. . . .

Joshuah. How're you, Sonny? *(entering, up right)* Good morning, Mam.

Libeth. Good morning, Joshuah—what about my class?

Joshuah. *(laughing)* Well, Mam. You know how tiz with ole folks. They still scratchin' their heads. But don't worry. Ah speck everybody'll be there tonight.

Libeth. *(going)* Well, they'd better. I insist upon it. And you tell them I said so.

(exit)

Joshuah. *(Smiling, he goes down left to retrieve wagon wheel beside porch of storehouse, and singing, rolls it up to forge.)*
>   "Oh, some go t' church for t' sing 'n shout,
>   Way in de middle of de air . . .
>   Fore six months dey's all turned out,
>   Way in de middle of de air . . .
>   Oh, Zekiel saw de wheel . . .

Delphine. *(emerging on porch of cottonhouse, and picking up refrain)*
>   "Yes, Lawd!"

Joshuah. *(Hearing her, he drops wheel by forge and comes down, singing.)*
>   "Zekiel saw de wheel . . ."

Delphine. *(singing above her smile)*
>   "Yes, Lawd!"

(together)

> "Zekiel saw de wheel
> Way in de middle of de air!"

(They conclude with a burst of warmhearted laughter.)

Delphine. *(solicitously)* Oh, yuh too warm—look how yuh sweatin'!
Joshuah. *(pleased)* When Ah get t' wukin' 'n singin' I can't help sweatin'.
Delphine. *(pressing him onto steps)* Here, sit down 'n lemme wipe yo forehead.
Joshuah. *(embarrassed)* Yuh goin' git yor hankcher dirty.
Delphine. *(laughing nervously)* What if Ah do? Ah can always wash it, can't Ah?
Joshuah. Yuh know; yuh's a mighty fine gal t' be runnin' round loose.
Delphine. *(slyly)* Who'd want me?
Joshuah. *(laughing)* Shucks, Ah bet yuh like de greasy pig. Yuh been t' a hund'd County Fairs, but ain't nobody cotched yuh yit!
Delphine. No. Mister Joshuah; yuh know yuh spoofin'!
Joshuah. Some might call it spoofin'. But Ah call it good common sense. A gal like yuh get any man she want!
Delphine. *(probing)* Any man maybe but de right one.
Joshuah. *(probing)* Ah wonder if yuh'd know him, if he popped up now?
Delphine. A woman's heart don't fool her, Mister Joshuah. She take one glance at de *man for her,* and right away she say to herself: "Thas him!"
Joshuah. *(soberly)* Anybody can be carried away at first sight. But that don't mean they can't make a big mistake.
Delphine. Oh, thas jes a chance yuh have t' take.
Joshuah. Not if yuh use good common sense.
Delphine. What's a person's heart care 'bout common sense? If yuh love somebody, yuh love 'em.
Joshuah. *(slowly)* It looks tha way when yuh young. But when yuh git older 'n wiser, yor heart might sway yuh, but yuh listen t' yor head.
Delphine. Yuh think tha makes anybody any happier?
Joshuah. Ah wouldn't say that. But at least it keeps 'em from gittin' hurt.
Delphine. But what makes yuh think they got t' get hurt?
Joshuah. How can they help it, if they git somebody don't really love em?
Delphine. But you can't see inside of people! All you can go by is de way yuh feel toward 'em—forget about your fears, 'n live in hope.
Joshuah. Yuh pretty deep, Delphine. Pretty deep. Yuh speak about hope, but Ah wonder?
Delphine. Ah see yuh don't think Ah bleve what Ah say.
Joshuah. Tain't tha, Delphine. But les look at it like this. Take a man my

aige, say: Spose he fell in love wid somebody no older 'n you. Common sense'd tell yuh, It wouldn't do him no good t' hope, now would it?

Delphine. *(laughing nervously)* Thas accordin'.

Joshuah. *(catching her as she goes behind him)* Accordin' t' what?

Delphine. Well, for instance—

Joshuah. *(hopefully)* What—?

Delphine. Well, spose tha somebody was really like yuh: Good-hearted 'n strong—er regular Moses t' his people? Ah reckon most women 'd be proud to have him. Ah reckon for most women it'd be like de story of de Mountain 'n de Sea.

Joshuah. Proud, eh? Phumph!

Delphine. Why de grunt?

Joshuah. Pride without love is like er body widout er soul. But love—that's ernother story. It's like er flower stragglin', tryin' t' bloom in de middle of de woods. But what's this 'bout de mountain 'n de sea?

Delphine. *(disappointed)* It's jes er story.

Joshuah. Ah don't spect Ah ever heard that one. How's it go?

Delphine. Oh, it don't matter.

Joshuah. But it do. Ah'd like very much t' hear it. How's it go?

Delphine. Well— *(her modesty driving her to cross behind him)* De Mountain was big 'n de Sea was free. But no matter how she'd roll, 'n no matter how she'd pitch; every trail she make t' reach de Mountain ended right back in de ditch!

Joshuah. *(suddenly rising)* Thas er powerful story.

Delphine. But—?

Joshuah. *(driving his fist into the palm of his hand)* It just goes t' bear me out.

Delphine. Ah don't see how.

Joshuah. *(thoughtfully)* This mountain of yors is sot in his ways. Nothin' pleases him more'n stayin put—

Delphine. Ah see Ah picked de wrong story.

Joshuah. No. Hit's er timely parable. There's some like de mountain, 'n some like de sea, jes got t' go rovin', jes bound t' be restless, specially when they young. Take yuh, if yuh got er good chance t' leave heah now, you'd be gone. But wid me—Well, this ilun' 'n mah Fawty. Well, they jes bout sum up mah heart's desire. Ah can't hardly wait t' git de gear fixed on tha Donkey yonder, cuz Ahm itchin' t' git de mill started. Ah want t' build me er house, Delphine. Ah want t' build it *(pointing off right)* yonder, mongst dem oaks, facin' de sea. Ah want t' build it low 'n ramblin', wid oak logs two feet thick 'n well seasoned, so it'll last. Kin yuh understand that?

Delphine. *(impressed)* Like de Rock of Ages, hunh?

Joshuah. Thas it. Like de Rock of Ages. Ah want t' build it wid er fireplace, where Ah kin sit through de long winter nights 'n watch de logs burnin'; maybe catch de sound of de sighin' winds. Den, for summer, Ah wan't t' build me er porch, where Ah kin rair back, prop mah feet up, 'n look cross de water t' Savannah yonder, 'n watch de twinklin' lights.

Delphine. *(thoughtfully)* An thas all—?

Joshuah. *(landing)* Well, cose er man can't have much of er home widout er woman—Only—

Delphine. Ahm listenin'—?

Joshuah. *(grimly)* She got t' be de kind goin' walk cross de doorsil 'n say wid me: "Heah, Lawd, at last is mah refuge!"

Delphine. *(shocked)* Refuge! Ah can't see her! Ain't no woman want nothin' like that!

Joshuah. No? Why not?

Delphine. *(earnestly)* Er woman want t' look forward t' havin er lil life!

Joshuah. *(upset)* Now yuh show your aige! Anybody git life got t' plant it.

Delphine. In er tomb—?

Joshuah. *(pained)* Tomb—Phumph! But it's jes like Ah been sayin'.

Delphine. *(defensively)* But don't yuh see, Mr. Joshuah. Yor house is too gloomy. *(earnestly)* Er house ought t' be like er weddin' feast, bright 'n cheery; wid friends comin' 'n goin'. *(carried away by her deepest instinct and hopes)* It ought t' have chillun, runnin' everybody crazy, rompin' 'n squealin' from mornin' till night! Don't yuh gree wid me?

Joshuah. *(moved and smiling)* Well, Ah admit hit's er pretty picture—specialy de part bout de chillun. *(sobering)* But Ah still say, first we got t' git out de rain 'n try t' stay out. Once we git set, hit'll be time nuff t' set out de jug in friendship—whole-'n-hearty!

Sarah. *(rushing in)* Joshuah!

Joshuah. *(annoyed)* Jes er minute, Sarah.

Sarah. But, Joshuah!

Joshuah. Nevermind. Lemme finish—

Sarah. Ah jes want t—

Joshuah. *(to Delphine, as Sarah stands aside with a look of consternation)* De pint Ah want yuh t' see: We got de lan' 'n we kin build on it. But we got t' feel ouah way—like tryin' t' build er road through er vargin swamp. We got t' hack way, 'n keep one eye on de sun—*(turning)* Now what is it, Sarah?

Sarah. Ah come heah t' axe yuh ef yuh got er minute t' spare t' go yonder 'n see 'bout de pig done fell in de well!

Joshuah. Good Gawd! 'n yuh wait all this time t' tell me!

Sarah. *(accusingly)* Yuh tole me t' shut up. Ah tried t' tell yuh!

Joshuah. *(running up to forge to pick up rope)* Lawd, if yuh all ain't er pester t' mah soul! *(running out)* Owen! Tom! Run heah! De pig's in de well!

Sarah. *(to Delphine)* All this time! Ah speck we goin have pork chops fer supper!

(They burst into laughter.)

(Blackout)

ACT I

SCENE 5

Time: *That evening.*

Place: *The same. Prior to visibility it is clear that something in the nature of a catastrophe has struck the life of the Freedmen.*

Patsy is heard leading them in the "Crucifixion," her rich contralto voice leadened with a note of profound sorrow.

Around her and dimly limned against the surrounding shadows, the Freedmen are massed in clusters, their heads and bodies bent beneath the weight of the overwhelming disaster which characterized the shock of President Lincoln's assassination throughout the nation.

The wealthy Negro Freedman, Oliver Webster Sr., is alone under the oak.

Patsy. *(singing)*
"They crucified mah Lawd,
'n he never said er mumblin' word. . . ."

Chorus.
"Not er word,
Not er word. . . ."

Patsy.
"They nailed him t' de tree
'n he never said er mumblin' word. . . (etc.)"

Joshuah. *(after a moment, entering with Libeth and Emanuel)* What's this 'bout Father Abraham?

Crowd. *(wailingly)* He gone, Joshuah!
They done shot President Lincoln—
They done laid him low!
Ouah best friend gone, Joshuah. He gone!

(The women moan.)

Joshuah. *(joining Webster)* Is this er fact, Mister Webster?

Webster. Yes, my friend. President Lincoln was shot in cold blood last night.
Joshuah. Mah Gawd from Heabem—Ah can't bleve it!
Libeth. How did it happen?
Webster. He was shot in the back of the head, as he sat in his box at the theatre. This morning he died just before day.
Libeth. How dreadful!
Joshuah. Who did it? Who could 'er?
Webster. An actor by the name of Booth, according to the news. But I think he was hired for the job. I think the planters are in it up to their necks, and I fear we're in for bloody times!
Dosia. Oh, Jesus, no!
Ross. *(to Webster)* Yuh think dey after *us?*
Taggert. Who else, Man?
Sarah. Joshuah, what us goin' do?
Joshuah. This is a hard 'n bitter blow. But les don't be skeered. Remember, we still got friends—folks like Gen'l Sherman 'n General Grant. Folks like Miss Libeth heah.
Taggert. Yeah. But what 'bout de lan'?
Peltier. De lan'?
Lem. Brer Tom, what yuh mean?
Taggert. What Ah want t' know—what we goin' to do 'bout it now dis happen?
Joshuah. We goin' er-head 'n raise er crop, thas whut.
Taggert. Us never git this lan' now!
Joshuah. Tom what kind of talk is this?
Taggert. Ah ain't goin' make no fool of mahsef!
Lem. Ah say de same. Ain't no use wukin' for nothin'!
Taggert. No!
Lem. What yuh say, Brer Ross?
Ross. Ain't much sense tryin' t' kill er bear less'n yuh big nuff t' skin him!

(silence)

Joshuah. Well, is yuh all through talkin' like chillun?
Peltier. *(quietly)* Them skunks game nuff t' shoot de President; they must have sompen up thar sleeves!
Taggert. What yuh think, Mister Webster?
Webster. I can only repeat. It looks very bad!
Taggert. *(victoriously)* Ah told yuh all so!
Joshuah. Tha can't be you talkin', Mister Webster.
Webster. *(embarrassed)* I'm only trying to be honest, Mister Tain.
Joshuah. What yuh think kin be gained by sech talk?
Webster. The people have to know the truth!

Joshuah. *(sharply)* Mr. Webster, we got this lan'!

Webster. Mr. Tain, I happen to be one of those who waited on General Sherman and induced him to settle you on the land. But I'd be less than a friend if I failed to admit it's a question as to how long you can expect to keep it!

Joshuah. Mister Webster, is yuh fergettin' de Yanks?

Webster. *(coldly)* The Yanks have shaken hands with treason and said: "Let us forget!"

Joshuah. *(pained)* Ah don't bleve it. It don't make sense!

Webster. We're treading in deep waters, Sir. The assassination is proof of it!

Taggert. 'Cose!

Joshuah. This murder ain't nothin' but er case of de pot of hate simmerin' down t' er mess of tryin' t' git even.

Webster. If only it were that simple.

Joshuah. Yuh got no grounds for sayin' it ain't.

Webster. The facts speak for themselves. President Lincoln was the planters' friend.

Joshuah. *(shocked)* What—!

Webster. *(relentlessly)* His policy toward them was always "forgive and forget"!

Joshuah. *(bitterly)* Mister Webster, if Father Abraham's dead, he died cuz of us!

Dosia. Oh, pity de sweet soul! *(She moans.)*

Patsy. Yes, Lawd. Give him de full cup ob mercy. He done laid down his life for dem dat was lowly and bad oppressed.

Ross. He was our friend, and now he's gone. He won't be back no more—

Patsy. Oh, shed de briney tear.

Ross. *(going on)* 'N we's left at de mercy of de den of thieves!

Setlow. *(pointedly)* He promised he'd never see de righteous forsaken, nor his seed beggin' bread. But de brigand done laid in wait for his life, and dem what should moan his loss look down on de byre wid scorn!

Webster. *(getting the point)* He stood against slavery and for that—well, you've a right to revere him!

Joshuah. Den les do dat, 'n say to ouahsefs: He done sot ouah feet on de right road, 'n we goin' tread hit wid courage.

Webster. I agree with you in that, my friend. But I would remind you, courage is bereft without wisdom.

Joshuah. Nothin' could be wiser than stickin' to our aims.

Webster. Yes. But we must be flexible. We must go ahead. But with open eyes, and a readiness to anticipate our enemies and shift accordingly. If the planters are responsible, and I believe they are, then, there must be a plot, and in my opinion, they shot Mr. Lincoln in spite of his friendliness because they want to frighten the North into making an agreement.

Joshuah. Like what?

Webster. Ask yourself. What do the planters want most? They want a full pardon for their rebellion and the restoration of their lands.

Peltier. It makes sense.

Joshuah. They can't get way wid it!

Webster. That's not the point.

Joshuah. Meaning?

Webster. What overall and long-range plan can we make to defeat them? That is the big question before the race. Either we look far ahead with wisdom, or the future of every Freedman in the South is doomed!

(silence)

Setlow. Is yuh got some idea for er plan?

Webster. We must win the ballot.

Joshuah. De ballot?

Webster. Exactly. The whole country will support us.

Joshuah. *(darkly)* So thas yor idea—

Webster. It's not mine only. Just last week I met with several of our leaders in Charleston, and they all felt it's the wisest course we can take. The assassination of President Lincoln makes it only clearer.

Joshuah. 'N de meantime, yuh plan t' fergit 'bout de lan', is tha it? Is tha what yuh call *far-seein?*

Webster. The question is too dangerous to handle right now. We must work for political power.

Joshuah. 'N yet yuh call yorself er educated man!

Webster. *(annoyed)* We cannot afford, Mr. Tain, to appear before the whole country as being selfish.

Joshuah. *(exploding)* Selfish or no selfish. We got this lan' n' anybody who speck t' be er leader round heah got t' fight for ouah right t' hang on t' it!

Libeth. But, Mister Tain. Perhaps he's right. You can't afford to be partisan.

Webster. It would be fatal. As it is the planters are preparing to fight like cornered rats for the land.

Joshuah. Ah say let 'em!

Webster. But that will mean war all over again.

Joshuah. Den let it be war den!

Libeth. But are you sure that's what you want?

Joshuah. Ah'd sooner hab war den see mah people slip back in de mire.

Webster. The trouble with you, Mister Tain, is you don't understand the importance of the ballot. All over the world it is prized as the people's most precious possession.

Libeth. Indeed! That's very true.

Joshuah. *(aroused to the depths)* It's easy fur anybody t' prize sompen they ain't got. Ah remember tha 'bout Freedom. But votin'—this much Ah know 'bout tha. Votin' ain't much. Ah's seed it all mah life, here in Gawgie 'n down in Lusana too. De man what holds de lan' holds de office. Look at de poor white folks. They vote. But what do they git out-er it? A gallon or two of corn likker come 'lection day, 'n atter tha, nothin but de same ole struggle 'n de same ole shack full of raw-boned babies. Ah sayd it once 'n Ah say it ergain; let dem what have de ears t' hear, let 'em hear: We got this lan', 'n votin' or no votin', we tend t' keep it! We's lost Father Abraham. But we ain't goin' let tha discourage us. We goin' moan his loss. But we goin' do it in sorrow, 'n not in despair. Ah say tha cuz despair 'n hope don't mix, 'n hope was de first big thing he give us. The planters might skeer some. But not us—not us, who's felt de lash; who know what tiz t' see er brother's brains dashed out, er father shot down in de middle of de field, 'n er mother hanged for liftin' her hand 'gainst de Overseer. No! They don't skeer us, cuz we was brought up in de house of horror! *(Suddenly pausing, he looks over the group and his eyes soften and a note of tenderness marks his tone.)* Now t' git back t' Father Abraham. He's lyin' up yonder in Washington. Soon, they'll be puttin' him in de cold, cold grave.

Dosia. *(moaning)* Lawd, Lawd!

Patsy. Wrap him in your arms, Sweet Jesus!

Joshuah. *(sadly)* To some folks thas goin' be de end of him. But not t' me 'n yuh—

Dosia. No, Lawd!

Joshuah. For us, he's like er evergreen tree wid de roots planted deep in ouah hearts—

Setlow. Amen!

Joshuah. So long as we live, he live; 'n Ah think thas goin' be for ouah chillun, 'n their chillun's chillun, on 'n on till de end of time. *(The women sob.)*

Setlow. Amen! Amen!

Joshuah. Thas all Ah know t' say, 'n Ah think thas all tha needs t' be sayd. But if any of yuh all want t' add er word, say it. Den, Ah think it would be mighty nice if us took de night off 'n sing some songs t' his memory.

Delphine. *(After a moment broken only by the stifled sobbing, she lifts her voice in a note of ineffable sadness.)*

"Steal away, steal away
Steal away home t' Jesus
Steal away, steal away
Steal away home
Ah ain't got long t' stay here. . . ."

(Gradually the entire group joins in, and their voices ring tenderly over the island.)

"My Lawd calls me; he calls me by
The thunder
He calls me by
The lightnin'
The trumpet sounds with-a mah soul
Ah ain't got long t' stay here. . . ."

(Slowly the Curtain is lowered.)

(Curtain)

ACT II

SCENE 1

Time: *A week later.*
Place: *The same. A storm is brewing. But now there is no wind, and only an overcast sky.*
From the distance comes the ring of the Freedmen's axes, felling timber for the houses they hope to build.
Daddy Sykes is seated on the porch of the cottonhouse, his feet on the top step, smoking his pipe.
He appears oblivious of Edgar, who approaches, singing.

Edgar. *(singing off right)* "Oh de blind man stood in de way 'n he cried: Oh, Lawd, save me!" *(Entering—wearing his Union Army uniform—he sees Sykes.)* Seen mah wife?
Sykes. Ellen? She down t' de wharf.
Edgar. Howcome yuh ain't in de woods wid de gang?
Sykes. What Ah need wid er house?

(thunder far off)

Edgar. Ah never thot of tha. *(hearing thunder)* Ah bleve it's goin' storm sure nuff.

Sykes. Yuh see eny fightin'.

Edgar. Ah ain't seed nothin' but er lot of boxes 'n crates!

Sykes. Made yuh wuk, hunh?

Edgar. *(going)* Yeah. Ah never did get t' smell no powder.

Sykes. Speck yuh lucky—dem Rebs is er tarble people.

Edgar. *(turning)* Ah don't bar nothin' on two feet mahsef, ole man. Cuz Ahm like de briar patch; step on me 'n Ahm bound t' snag yuh! *(seeing others as he goes out up left)* Good mawnin', Folks!

Ollie. *(entering with Delphine)* What does an ignorant field hand like Joshuah know about it? *(joining Sykes)* Daddy Sykes, go tell Mr. Tain I said I must see him right away. Tell him it's about the sawmill.

Sykes. *(rising annoyed)* Mah mind tole me not t' set heah!

(exit right)

Ollie. *(to Delphine)* My father says the whole scheme is doomed. These people will never get the land, now that Lincoln is dead. Didn't you hear him when he was over here last week?

Delphine. *(worried)* Yeah. But—

Ollie. Then you should see. The best Joshuah can hope for is a job on somebody's plantation. But perhaps you wouldn't mind spending your life with him in a filthy hut—with a dirt floor to walk on—Where the only way you can prepare a meal is by stooping in front of a smoky fireplace?

Delphine. Ah didn't say Joshuah wanted to marry me.

Ollie. Then you'll remain a housemaid.

Delphine. Ahm through being er housemaid.

Ollie. You won't be able to avoid it. You've no education.

Delphine. Ahma git one. Ahma teach too—if it's de las thing Ah do on this earf! Miss Libeth already teachin' me.

Ollie. What're you going to do when your former master returns and breaks everything up?

Delphine. Marse Burkhardt might be dead, for all anybody know.

Ollie. But can't you see. Even if he is, there's his family to take over. You've no chance, unless you listen to me. Say the word, and I'll be back for you tomorrow night, and take you and Roxanna both to Savannah with me.

Delphine. Sure, in the dark! Behime everybody's back!

Ollie. You don't trust me. You think nothing of my friendship—

Delphine. Ah didn't say tha.

Ollie. But you show it, when you refuse to listen. You'd rather think of these clodhoppers.

Delphine. Maybe Ah ain't ez proud as yuh, Ollie. Ah can't jes jump up 'n leave behind their back—run er-way like I got sompen t' hide in de dead of night.

Ollie. There's no other way. But, of course, if you think nothing of your little sister's welfare—

Delphine. Why can't Ah jes tell Joshuah? You can trust him.

Ollie. Not after today.

Delphine. Why not?

Ollie. *(going up to look off right)* You'll see in a minute.

Delphine. *(watching him)* What yuh fixin' t' do?

Ollie. *(turning back, and indicating donkey and bandsaw off left)* Take that donkey and bandsaw back.

Delphine. *(amazed, as he rejoins her)* But, Ollie, how come?

Ollie. We have to get them out of Burkhardt's reach.

Delphine. But you know they all plannin' on buildin' homes!

Ollie. We have to be practical. In times like these, you have to look out for yourself, or be dragged under. It's like I've been trying to get you to understand. For your own good, you'd better get wise, and make up your mind. I may not be free to come here anymore, after today.

Delphine. Yuh jes have t' give me more time!

Ollie. But I tell you they may bar me away from the island.

Delphine. Ah know Joshuah. He wouldn't do nothin' like tha. He's de biggest person yuh ever seed.

Ollie. Look, Delphine. You're not concerned whether Joshuah or any of the others know about our plans. You're just afraid. You don't trust me. Yet you're scared to lose my friendship because you know I can do more for you in a minute than that big yokel can do for you in a year. Isn't that it, or the way it stands?

Delphine. Joshuah respect me. Ah say tha much for *him!*

Ollie. You can't live on respect, my dear.

Patsy. *(shouting in the distance)* Hey, yuh mens! Whar yuh all runnin' off t' in sech er hurry?

Ollie. Damn it, they're coming. *(to Delphine)* I'm offering you everything, Honey. I'd ask you to be my wife, if I could. But I can help you. If only you'll let me, I'll give you an education and tomorrow when I'm independent we'll—

Patsy. *(shouting)* Mister Ross! Don't yuh heah me? Whar yuh all goin'?

(thunder)

Joshuah. *(entering with men)* Hello, Ollie—*(He comes down, his hollow greeting as ominous as the approaching storm.)* What's this 'bout de sawmill?

Ollie. *(hesitantly)* Well, it's probably going to prove a shock to you. But my father thinks the mill parts are no longer safe here. He's asked me to tell you he's sorry. But as long as the situation is as uncertain and as critical as it is, it's best that you return them.

Crowd. *(muttering)* Thar now! Well, well! Phumph! Phumph! Phumph!

Joshuah. Yuh don't mean sompen' else done come up?

Ollie. He's only trying to protect himself. That donkey, you know, cost a fortune. We can't risk losing it or having it damaged. Mr. Venerable, his partner, and he have talked it over, and they figure it's the wisest course to take at the moment.

Joshuah. *(quietly)* Ah kin see things might look dark, Ollie. But they can't be so bad anybody got t' be skeered.

Ollie. You don't realize how things are going. You're isolated, cut off here on the island.

Sarah. *(leading women in)* What's the matter?

Taggert. Ollie goin' take de sawmill 'way.

Ross. He jes goin' throw us back.

Sarah. But, Ollie, how come?

Taggert. Ah thot us wuz goin' have all summer t' git lumber ready.

Ross. Yeah. Now us gwine hab t' put up log cabins wid er axe?

Ollie. You don't have to build now.

Joshuah. But tiz goin' throw us back, Ollie. 'N less'n there's sompen yuh ain't tellin' us, it's hard t' see how yuh all kin act like this.

Ollie. You've no idea how high feeling is running on the mainland. Washington is a bedlam, and no one knows what the new President, Johnson, is going to do. He's a Southerner, you know—from Tennessee.

Joshuah. *(quietly)* All threatenin' storms don't break, Ollie.

Ollie. Those who are sensible take cover, nevertheless, when they see clouds gathering. The planters are returning daily. Suppose this man Burkhardt comes back and find the mill operating on his property? Why he might take an axe or crowbar and smash that Donkey to pieces!

Joshuah. Oh, no he won't. In de fust plact, what's t' stop us from puttin' er guard over it?

Peltier. Yeah. We protect it, Ollie. We protect it wid blood!

Ollie. You can't protect it from the law.

Joshuah. What law?

Ollie. We've no legal right to set up a mill on another man's property. Burkhardt may go to Court and claim the mill and get it.

Joshuah. He never git way wid it. De Jedge Advocate wid us!

Ollie. Yes. With *you.* You're Freedmen. It's the business of the Bureau to look out for *you.*

(lightning)

Joshuah. 'N dey'll look out for you all too. Cap'n Bryant stick up for anybody on ouah side.

Ollie. That's a matter of conjecture, Mr. Tain.

Joshuah. Meanin'—?

Ollie. Simply, he may or he may not.

Joshuah. Well, look, Ollie. Spose Ah go back wid yuh 'n talk t' yor Pa?

Ollie. It's impossible. He's out of town. He left yesterday for Charleston.

Setlow. Well, what 'bout his partner?

Ollie. You'd never get anywhere with him. He's dead set against it.

Joshuah. But Ah can try!

Ollie. But I tell you it'd only be a waste of time. He was opposed from the start. Now he's blaming Papa and me for jeopardizing his whole future. It's no pleasure to me to come here and disappoint everyone. But I've no responsibility whatsoever in the matter.

Taggert. *(sharply)* Den if thas de case; yuh had no bizness bringin' em heah!

Ollie. *(stung)* I was only trying to be of help to you, and you ought to be ashamed to make a remark like that.

Patsy. *(bitterly)* Yuh de one ought t' be shame, Mister Ollie—gittin' folks' heart set on sompen', den go snatch it way.

(The sky begins to darken.)

Ollie. Oh, be reasonable, Miss Patsy. You're not out doors. You know you can get along in your huts for the time being.

Sarah. *(pained)* Yuh kin say tha, Ollie. But yuh 'n yor Pappy 'n his partner, yuh all ain't never had t' spend de night in er leaky hut. Ain't none of yuh ever had t' go through sech misery as we did last winter. Yuh don't know what tiz t' see yor chillun suffer. Yuh ain't never had to lay through de night listenin' t' em whimper, wid de rain'n snowy-wind sweepin' in from every corner of de sea, 'n all yuh got t' keep em warm is er quilt of dry grass for kivver—if yuh had, Ollie. *(bursting into tears)* Yuh all'd have some pity. Yes, yuh would!

Ross. *(bitterly)* They thot us pay in er year or two. They think t' darsefs: dem Cuffees got lan'. Pretty soon dey hab money. Now dey think us don't git lan', us ain't goin' hab money. So dey pull dar freight!

Patsy. Thas de Gawd's trufe. Dey jes desertin' us!

Edgar. Yeah! 'N dey de ones wuz goin' do so much t' hep us climb!

Ross. Sure! So proud t' hep us—whar all tha pride now, Ollie?

Setlow. Ah came unto mine own 'n dey received me not!

Peltier. *(angrily)* Us jez been fools. Us oughter knowed better'n t' speck anythin' from "'ristocrat mulattahs!"

Ollie. Mr. Tain, why do you stand there and be silent?

(There is a terrific flash of lightning, followed by thunder.)

Joshuah. *(glances at sky, then going)* Come on some of yuh, gimmer er hand.

(exit up right)

Ross. But Joshuah—de storm!
Edgar. Looks more like er hurricane!
Peltier. Damn if Ahm goin' out dar.

(The wind rises rapidly to fury.)

Setlow. *(above the wind to Ollie)* Yuh can't git cross tha water now! Yuh better figger on stayin' de night!

(The sudden deafening crash of lightning and thunder starts them all stampeding.)

Patsy. *(running out)* Hab mercy, Lawd!
Ollie. *(catching Delphine)* Can you put me up for the night?
Delphine. *(in wind)* What yuh say?
Ollie. Can you pick me up in the Big House for the night?
Delphine. Ah guess ah have t'.

(Exit all.)

(Blackout)

ACT II

SCENE 2

Time: *It is a bright sunny morning, six weeks later.*
Place: *The scene is the same and unchanged, except that growing cotton plants may be seen at the edge of the field by the forge. Nearby the women are singing.*

Women. *(singing off right)*
    "Oh, sometimes Ahm tosst'd 'n driven
    Sometimes Ah don't know whar t' roam.
    Ah's heard of a city called Heabem
    Ahm tryin' t' make it mah home. . . ."

(The women bearing hoes and with their skirts tucked around the waist, enter to cross and go off up left—still singing.)

"True believer, Ahm strivin' t' make it mah home. . ." (etc.).

(Joshuah emerges from the cottonhouse to come down and go up to the forge to get his sledge hammer, as the singing dies in the distance.)

Ellen. *(entering and greeting him)* Hello, Joshuah. Looks like we're in fer another hot one. *(She picks out a light-weight hoe.)*

Joshuah. Ah reckon yuh can't git way from it this time of year. *(returning to cottonhouse)* Dis is June, yuh know. But if we kin jes scape er drought, everything goin' be fine 'n dandy.

(exit within)

Georgana. *(entering up left with Roxanna, bearing a big basket between them)* Good mawnin, Miss Ellen. How's yuh today?

Ellen. Ahm jes fine. How de catch?

Georgana. We got one whopper. *(displays fish)* Jes look at him.

Ellen. Lawd, he's big as er hoss. But, Roxanna, how's Delphine this mawnin'?

Roxanna. She ain't got no more fever, 'n she been settin' up de last couple of days. But she still can't keep er thing on her stomach.

Georgana. Miz Patsy say, she think unbeknownst t'her, Delphine bout swallowed er fly!

Ellen. Er upset stomach is er terrible thing. *(going)* But if she settin' up, it means she gettin' better, n' das de main thing!

(exit)

Roxanna. If Ah wasn't skeered it was goin' git too hot, Ah speck Ah'd try t' pick me some berries today.

Georgana. Yuh come on, gal, 'fore these fishes all spile.

Roxanna. *(getting basket)* Oh me! *(seeing Lem off right)* Yonder go Lem. Lookin' like somebody in de hands of de slave trader.

(Exit together, up right.
In a moment, Delphine enters, singing sadly, and her movements show the results of her long illness.)

Delphine. *(singing as she drags herself down to sit beneath oak)*
  "Sometimes Ah feel like er motherless chile
  Oh sometimes Ah feel like er motherless chile
  Sometimes Ah feel like er motherless chile
  A long way from home!"

(Joshuah emerges on the porch to halt there gazing upon her sympathetically, but she does not see him.)

  "A long way from home!
  A long way from home!"

(She flicks a tear from her eye.)

Joshuah. *(coming down, hesitantly)* Delphine. *(Startling her, he joins her quickly.)* Lawd, Delphine, forgive me for mah bad jedgment. Don't git up. Ah heard yuh singin' 'n Ah was so glad t' know yuh back on yor feet, Ah didn't stop to think. But lemme look at yuh! *(admiringly)* De same lil ole Delphine. Cept for them tears yuh ain't changed er lick! Lawd, how Ah do rejoice t' see yuh. *(going up to forge to get box)* But wait. *(returning)* Here, put yor feet on this box. Yuh oughter have er pillow. Reckon Ah could git yuh one from de Big House?
Delphine. No, thank yuh, Joshuah. Ahm all right.
Joshuah. Den rair back cuz Ah got sompen t' tell yuh can't wait.
Delphine. *(starting up)* No, please!
Joshuah. Oh, yes. Ah been holdin' back too long already!
Delphine. *(rising and crossing right)* No! No!
Joshuah. *(following her)* As Gawd is my jedge, Delphine. Ah love yuh pass al understandin'. 'N Ah want t' take yuh for mah lovin' wife!
Delphine. *(sinking on bench by porch, despairingly)* Oh, Joshuah!
Joshuah. Ah know yuh think Ah don't trust yuh, Delphine. But bleve me; if yuh seed me drawin' back, it wuzzn't for no lack of faith in yuh as er woman. Ah wuz jes skeered t' try t' run gainst nature. Ah figured yuh wuz 'titled t' a man yor own aige. But ever since yuh been sick, there ain't been a night passed Ah ain't been under yor window, hopin' 'n prayin' for yuh 'n lookin' de facks in de face. There ain't many men livin' got mah strength. Theys few'n far between got more *git up* erbout 'em. De ladder jes ain't been built Ah can't climb—All Ah axe yuh is jes put yor trust in me 'n say "Yes." Will yuh?
Delphine. *(regretfully)* It's too late, Joshuah. De boat we might-er caught done come 'n gone!
Joshuah. *(puzzled)* Ah don't understand? Yuh mean yuh love somebody else?
Delphine. *(whispering)* No, Joshuah.
Joshuah. Den what yuh talkin' 'bout?
Delphine. *(in tears)* Don't ask me, Joshuah. Just forget everything. *(She sobs.)*
Joshuah. Here here—don't cry like tha. 'N don't try t' gimme no answer now. Yuh been er very sick woman. *(cheerfully)* In er-nother week or so yuh goin' be yor old sef ergain!
Delphine. *(firmly)* Joshuah, soon's Ah git better Ahm goin' erway.
Joshuah. *(shocked)* Lawd, Delphine! Now Ah know yuh need t' git back in bed.
Delphine. Ah's got t' go, Joshuah.
Joshuah. But whar? Oh this don't make sense! Whar yuh go?

Delphine. "Whar" don't matter.
Joshuah. *(floundering)* But, Delphine; is Ahm someway t' blame?
Delphine. Yuh ain't got nothin' t' do wid it, Joshuah.
Joshuah. Den' tell me.
Delphine. Don't ask me, Joshuah. Just forget everything.
Joshuah. Ah got t' know!
Delphine. Yuh make it hard for me, Joshuah. Yuh force me.
Joshuah. But Ah's titled t' some idea!
Delphine. All right, Joshuah. Yuh want t' know. Well . . . Ahma have er . . . baby.
Joshuah. *(stunned)* Great Gawd, no!
Delphine. Ah knowed Ah wuz goin' hurt yuh.
Joshuah. *(sick)* Phumph! Phumph! Phumph! *(silence)* It can't be so. It can't be, Delphine.
Delphine. It's de truth, jes de same.
Joshuah. *(after a moment)* Yuh mind tellin' me who de Daddy?
Delphine. No.
Joshuah. Den who?
Delphine. Ollie.
Joshuah. *(stabbed)* Phumph! But Ah might er knowed it. . . . *(He shakes his head, sadly.)* When this happen?
Delphine. De night of de storm.
Joshuah. *(raging inwardly)* Ah oughter kill him. Ah oughter take him in these hands 'n crush every bone in his yaller body!
Delphine. *(quietly)* Tha wouldn't set nothin t' rights.
Joshuah. Tell me. What he say 'bout it?
Delphine. *(quietly)* He donno.
Joshuah. *(incredulously)* Yuh ain't told him?
Delphine. *(coldly)* Ah'd rather depart 'n go t' hell!
Joshuah. Den yuh don't want him?
Delphine. Ah wouldn't have him now if Ah loved him!
Joshuah. Yuh don't have t' lie t' me, Delphine.
Delphine. Ah ain't.
Joshuah. *(cynically)* Phey!
Delphine. It's de truth. He come in mah room—
Joshuah. *(sarcastically)* 'N cose he jes overpowered yuh!
Delphine. *(preoccupiedly)* Ah reckon Ah was jes weak 'n skeered—all mixed up at de moment. Strong az Ah know mahsef, Ah think someway he 'bout gin me er dose of love powder.
Joshuah. *(snorting)* Yuh *must* think Ahma fool!
Delphine. *(sincerely)* Ahm jes tellin' yuh like it happened.
Joshuah. *(sharply)* Don't Ah know yuh could er screamed!
Delphine. *(pained)* Oh, Joshuah, can't yuh understand. *(Her anguish rises to a wail.)* Ah didn't know what t' do!

Joshuah. *(bitterly)* Eh, hey! *(silence)* But Ah never did have no chance wid yuh.
Delphine. Yuh hate me now, don't yuh? Yuh despise me!
Joshuah. *(preoccupiedly)* Ah was right from de first. BUT Ah ain't de first ole man sot his heart on er young woman. Every snaggled toothed dog ever lived t' run cross er bone he couldn't chaw, come up ergainst de same thing!
Delphine. Ah's hurt yuh t' yor soul!
Joshuah. *(bitterly)* How else yuh speck me t' be? Ah thot yuh was sompen. But yuh had t' throw yorsef erway on er man who, Ah bet mah life, think he's too good for yuh t' even wash his drawers! Yuh, who everybody been braggin' on as er woman of cha'cter! Yuh who was so busy tryin' t' raise yor sister up right! *(sharply)* Er fine example yuh's turned out t' be. Yuh! Nothin' but er wanton woman!
Delphine. *(angrily)* Now jes er minute, Joshuah. Yuh may think yuh got cause t' be hurt. But that don't give yuh de right t' try t' spit in mah face. Maybe Ah am wanton-hearted, 'n it twarn't no love powder—though Gawd knows sompen made me sick enough t' die! But yuh ain't neither kith nor kin t' me. Furthermore, yuh had yor chance, 'n yuh can't deny Ah had er right t' be skeered when nobody don't know what's goin' happen today or tomorrow, 'n me wid Roxanna t' depend on me. Anyway, like it stand, whatever mistake Ah made is tween me 'n Gawd, 'n it's none of yor bizness!
Joshuah. *(crushed)* Ah guess yuh right. Tain't none of mah bizness.
Delphine. Now Ahm goin' back t' de house. But Ah jes want t' remind yuh. Ah told yuh Ah plan t' leave here, soon's Ahm strong enough. So yuh can set yor mind at rest fars de danger of mah settin er bad example is concerned. *(softening)* On de other hand, Ah want yuh t' know Ah ain't got no hard feelin's gainst yuh for what yuh said. Ah know how Ah'd feel . . . *(her eyes brimming)* if things had been de other way round . . . *(clutching his arm and leaning against his shoulder, as he stands like a rock braving the storm)* Ah want yuh t' know, too. Ah still think yuh's de finest man Ah's ever known! *(Turning, she goes out up right, and he eases himself down to sit focused in pain and regret.)*

(Curtain)

ACT II
· · · · · ·

SCENE 3

Time: *October.*
Place: *The scene is the same, only now the soft tone of fall lends a warmth*

and rich sense of harvest. The Freedmen are ginning their cotton, baling it, and setting it outside for shipment to the mainland. Through earth and industry they have reaped a bountiful crop, and an unsuppressible joy bespeaks their realization that they have in their hands now, complete and undeniable, the economic means which can guarantee their new life.

Edgar. *(with others at step of cottonhouse)* Yuh all know what Ahm-a do soon's we sell de cotton?

Emanuel. Ah bet Ah can guess!

Edgar. *(enthusiastically)* Ahm gwine t' Sawanny 'n buy Ellen er dress, 'n Ahm-a git me er new suit of clothes. For once in mah life Ahm-a see whut er new suit feels like.

Lem. *(excitedly)* Ah jes want t' git t' Sawanny 'n see de sights!

Ross. So some of dem tricksters kin git yor money, huh?

Joshuah. *(within cottonhouse)* Hey, men. Here she comes!

Ross. *(as a bale of cotton plummets unto the porch, and the men jockey it off and into line with other bales)* How many more, Joshuah?

Joshuah. *(emerging on the porch, and wiping sweat from his brow)* Thas de las of 'em. How they look t' yuh all?

Ross. Jes like pure white gold!

Lem. *(up center, as they set bale alongside others there)* Hey, everybody. Yonder Brer Setlow 'n Owens—dey got Ollie wid 'em!

Edgar. Ollie?

Joshuah. De stinkin' rat. It can't be.

Lem. *(as Joshuah joins them)* No? Look yonder.

Peltier. *(to Joshuah)* Why yuh call him tha, Joshuah?

Joshuah. *(coming down)* Oh, don't pay me no mind.

Setlow. *(outside, approaching, triumphantly)* "Lift up yor head, O ye Gates! Be ye lift up, ye everlastin' doors, 'n de Kin of Glory shall come in!"

Lem. *(excitedly)* They got good news!

Setlow. *(entering with Ollie—going on joyfully)* "Oh bless ouah Gawd, ye people, 'n make de voice of His praise t' be heard!"

Lem. What's de good news? 'N whar de cotton agent?

Setlow. *(ignoring him)* "For Thou O Gawd has proved us: Thou has tried us as silver is tried—"

Joshuah. *(impatiently)* Deed. But speak!

(Ollie looks on amused.)

Setlow. *(undauntedly)* "Thou has caused men t' ride ovah ouah heads; we went through fiah 'n water, but Thou broughtest us into a wealthy place!"

Edgar. *(boiling)* Ollie, what is this?

Ollie. The land is yours.
All. No!
Setlow. "Yea, de sparrow has found a house, 'n de swallow a nest for herself where she may lay her young!"
Ross. Great Gawd from Whom all blessing flow! It can't be true!
Ollie. But it is. Congress has passed the Civil Rights Bill with the Stevens' Amendment, which gives you the land!
Edgar. *(waltzing with Lem)* Shout hallelujah!
Lem. *(breaking away)* Ahm gwine carry de news! *(running off with a shout)* Hy, Delphine—Miz Sarah! We got de lan'. We got de lan'!
Joshuah. *(gazing across the field)* Ouah lan'! Gawd bless yuh, Thad Stevens!
Taggert. Joshuah, this calls for er celebration.
Peltier. Yeah, Joshuah. How ['bout] er barbecue wid music from town?
Joshuah. Ah reckon we'll have t' do sompen. *(suddenly remembering)* By de way, Brer Setlow, what 'bout de Cotton Agent?
Setlow. Us couldn't git none.
Edgar. All de agents in Sawanny, 'n yuh couldn't git *one*?
Setlow. They say they ain't buyin' less de Yanks say so.
Ross. *(puzzled)* Ollie, what yuh make of this?
Ollie. The agents claim all Freedmen must have a permit to sell.
Edgar. Well, Ah'll be damn!
Joshuah. *(to Setlow, avoiding Ollie like the plague)* Did yuh check wid Cap'n Bryant?
Setlow. *(uneasily)* Cap'n Bryant ain't here no more.
Joshuah. No—?
Setlow. Yes, Suh.
Ollie. *(volunteering)* Captain Bryant has been removed.
Ross. Ah don't like this.
Joshuah. *(to Setlow)* But why?
Setlow. Gawd knows.
Taggert. *(angrily)* Ah bet mah head 'gainst anybody's rope, this heah's some of dis President Johnson's doins!
Edgar. Yeah! Tha Tennessee hillbilly settin' in de saddle ridin' high!
Taggert. Sure. Every time dey call er Reb's name, it's "pardoned," sezee!
Emanuel. *(up center looking off)* Joshuah, look yonder! Soldiers!
Joshuah. Soldiers? *(They all plunge up to look.)*
Setlow. Dis don't make sense . . .
Peltier. *(looking off left)* Joshuah, Ah don't like de looks of this.
Joshuah. *(He gauges the situation outside for a moment, then in sudden decision, going.)* Come on. Git yor guns!

(Swiftly they disappear. Shortly there's the sound and then the appearance of a group of white Union soldiers.)

Sergeant. *(commandingly, as they march in, bringing them to a halt near the forge)* Squads, halt! At ease. *(He salutes Captain Stewart, as the latter, Burkhardt and Saunders pass through the ranks.)* Any further orders, Sir?
Stewart. *(coming down)* Summon the Freedmen.
Burkhardt. Nevermind, Captain. *(He goes to angle iron.)* This will bring them. *(He strikes iron, then turning indicates cotton.)* Just look at that cotton! By rights every pound of it is mine!
Stewart. *(pointedly)* There, Mr. Burkhardt, you put it in the nutshell!
Burkhardt. I don't think I quite understand you, Captain Stewart.
Stewart. How do you planters expect me to cooperate with you, when you persist in such an attitude?
Burkhardt. *(Laughing, he turns to inspect his property.)* Oh, don't pay any attention to my remark, Captain. It's not easy to adjust overnight, you know.
Stewart. But you're not even trying to adjust. That's what's making my task so hard. The Freedmen sense it. That's why they're so intractable.
Burkhardt. Oh, I wouldn't worry about the niggers. We know how to handle them.
Stewart. *(dryly)* As slaves perhaps.
Burkhardt. *(kicking the side of the cottonhouse support)* You don't change an ear of corn by removing the shucks.
Stewart. But you can change a man by removing his chains.
Burkhardt. *(easily)* That, Captain Stewart, is debatable.
Stewart. You may think so. But I think you're in for a big awakening.
Burkhardt. *(hardening)* Just how do you mean that?
Stewart. *(critically)* Your entire policy is shortsighted. Take this cabal you've formed yourselves into, for example: This business of fixing the Freedmen's wages at five dollars per month. It's foolhardy to think you will be able to get them to work for it.
Burkhardt. I see the niggers have been lying to you, Captain.
Stewart. The Bureau has sufficient proof. On the mainland you're offering them six cents per day. That's peonage!
Burkhardt. *(annoyed)* I've no idea what you're talking about. But I'll say this. Knowing how lazy and shiftless the niggers are, he'll be a lucky planter who can break even at the rate.
Stewart. I can see that by that crop over there, which you were praising a moment ago.
Burkhardt. That crop's an accident.
Stewart. Perhaps. However, it seems a good indication of the value of sound policy.
Burkhardt. *(darkly)* Such as confiscation?
Stewart. I hold, Mr. Burkhardt, with your Alex Stevens: Your conduct

toward the Freedmen should be kind, magnanimous, just! Then you may hope to organize them into a class of trustworthy laborers.

Burkhardt. Alex's a dreamer.

Stewart. He recognizes the urgency of cooperating with the Bureau.

Burkhardt. *(coolly)* Your Freedmen's Bureau, Captain Stewart—if I may be permitted a moment of plain speaking—is nothing but a devilish device to control and humiliate us before our former slaves. It's frankly, an alien power!

(Joshuah and others enter—the men bearing arms.)

Stewart. *(seeing them)* Who's Joshuah?

Joshuah. Me, Suh.

Stewart. I'm Captain Stewart of the Bureau, and this is Mr. John Burkhardt, owner of the island. *(attempting to flatter him)* He was just remarking how well you've done this year.

(rest of the women crowd in)

Burkhardt. *(suavely)* I don't see how you did it—and all by yourselves! But I can see we're going to get along. *(drawing batch of papers from his breast pocket)* I've called you so you can sign these contracts.

Joshuah. *(hostilely)* Contracts—for what?

Burkhardt. *(easily)* For you and your people to work the land.

Joshuah. *(glancing at his people)* This heah's de first time Ah ever heard of folks needin' er contract t' work thar own lan'!

Saunders. *(smugly)* Ah tole yuh, Cuffee, this wasn't yor land.

Joshuah. Yuh hush, Man. We don't keer nothin' 'bout what yuh tole nobody. This is ouah lan'.

Crowd. Yeah. By Gawd! Yuh damn tootin'!

Joshuah. *(to Saunders, indirectly)* 'N if yuh know what's good fur yuh, yuh better git on off this ilun 'n don't come back disturbin' us in ouah homes no more.

Saunders. By Gawd, Captain, are you goin stand thar 'n let this nigger insult me—a white man!

Stewart. I advised you gentlemen to let me handle things.

Burkhardt. All right, Captain. You explain to them.

(Ollie enters.)

Peltier. We don't need no splainin'!

Edgar. *(vehemently)* They think we don't know de Gubment done passed de Stevens Bill—Heh!

Setlow. Answer not a fool accordin to his folly.

Stewart. *(sharply)* Silence. And you, Elder, save your sermon for Sunday.

(shifting) It's true there was such a bill. But not any more. The President has vetoed it. He has thrown it out.

Edgar. *(sarcastically)* Heah yuh tell it, Gawd done put de fish out in hell!

Stewart. *(Glancing sharply at him, he turns to others.)* The President felt the bill was a mistake. I'm not here to lie to you. General Howard sent me here to represent your interest. He is my superior, and the President told him to make arrangements to restore the land to its former owners. I know you expected the Government to give you the land. But that is not to be. It's not my duty to question why. All I can do is tell you, if you want to remain here, you must come to an agreement with Mr. Burkhardt, the rightful owner. Those contracts in his hand were drawn up by General Howard himself to safeguard your interest. You've already shown yourselves to be wise and industrious people. Under the term of the contracts, if you remain the same, in three years you will be privileged to purchase your own forty acres if you so desire. Do you understand? Is it clear to all of you?

Joshuah. We already got this lan'!

Peltier. Yeah! *(banging the butt of his gun down)* By Gawd!

Patsy. He ain't talkin' t' me!

Edgar. 'N nobody else. He got t' tell a taller tale den dat t' buck mah eyes!

Ollie. *(stepping forward)* Just a moment, Folks. I think you're making a mistake—

Joshuah. *(ominously)* Yuh keep out of this!

Ollie. But if President Johnson has vetoed the bill—

Joshuah. *(menacingly)* Ah say mind yor own bizness!

Ollie. *(ignoring him to appeal to others)* It's your welfare, Folks. You can't just take the land—

Joshuah. *(grappling him from behind)* Damn your stinkin' soul!

Ollie. *(in pain)* Look out! You're breaking my back!

Setlow. Brer Joshuah! Brer Joshuah! You'll kill him.

Ollie. *(desperately)* Help!

Ross. Joshuah! Turn him loose.

Joshuah. *(easing up)* Ahma turn yuh loose. But if yuh ever put yor foot on this ilun' ergin, Ahma mash yuh t'er yaller pulp! *(shoving him)* Now git—'fore Ah change mah mind!

Setlow. *(as Ollie reels off up left)* Yuh too hard on him, Joshuah.

Joshuah. Tha buzzard! He don't mean us no good. Take mah word for it. *(turning to Stewart)* Ez Ah wuz sayin t' yuh, Suh. Gen'l Sherman give us his word; de Gubment wuz goin' give us er clear title t' this lan. We donno nothin' 'bout yuh 'n this Gen'l Howard bizness, 'n we ain't goin' sign no contracts.

Stewart. *(coldly)* You've just demonstrated what sort of man you are. No one can reason with you. But I warn you, violence won't get you anywhere in this case!

Joshuah. Ahm bankin' on mah rights, 'n so's mah people!

Stewart. *(sharply)* You're misleading your people! The Government is not going to give you the land. It is not going to do so because the planters have lost so heavily in life and property during the rebellion, while you have gained so much in your emancipation!

Edgar. So us don't git nothin' cept wuk? Well, damn such freedom ez that!

Joshuah. *(angrily)* We'll still be slaves till every man can raise his own bale of cotton 'n say: "This is mine!"

Ross. *(as silence ensues)* Ah thot all de Yanks wuz wid us.

Patsy. *(shrewdly)* Tha ain't no Yank. Thas jes some Reb dey done dressed up in Blue 'n brought here t' lie t' us!

Stewart. *(sharply)* You know better!

Joshuah. Cap'n yuh say yuh's er Yank. In yor heart who yuh think is de real owners of this lan'. Dem who been placed here by de Gubment, or de planters who been fightin' 'gainst de Gubment?

Stewart. *(angrily)* Bad soldiers must have misled you!

Patsy. Yuh better not let Gen'l Sherman heah yuh say tha!

Stewart. *(shouting)* Enough! *(catching himself)* Either sign those contracts or get off the island!

Joshuah. *(ominously)* 'N spose we tell yuh, us ain't goin' do neither one?

Stewart. You'll sign all right. *(warningly)* And if you commit any outrage, the Bureau will punish you with the utmost severity!

Joshuah. *(quietly)* Well, yuh might ez well git it straight. We ain't goin' sign!

Stewart. *(feeling it a personal affront)* You defy my authority?

Joshuah. *(quietly)* We're free. Yuh got no 'thority over us.

Stewart. *(after a moment)* Have you finished?

Joshuah. *(quietly)* Ez far ez *words* is consarned!

Stewart. *(ignoring challenge)* Mr. Burkhardt. Use the lid on that barrel for them to sign. *(to others)* And you, Freedmen. Form a line up there. *(seeing no man move)* I command you to line up there!

Setlow. *(breaking ominous pause, repeating with quiet resolution)* "Gawd is ouah refuge 'n strength, a very present hep in de time of trouble—"

Stewart. *(interposing, sharply)* I command you to fall in line!

Setlow. "Therefore will not we fear, though de earf be removed, though de mountains be carried into de midsts of de sea!"

Stewart. *(turning to soldiers)* Attention!

(The women break for cover, along with Burkhardt and Saunders, as the soldiers obey.) Port Arms!

Joshuah. *(meanwhile)* Fall in Guards!

(In a flash the Freedmen square off for battle. Grimly the two groups stand

at bay. Stewart seems to be searching for a sign of weakness. Joshuah resolute and alert, with a sense of come what may.)

Stewart. *(in a quandary, but finally capitulating, commands his men)* Fall back!
Joshuah. *(as the soldiers back off left; Stewart covering their retreat, his back toward them protectingly)* Steady, men. Hold yor fiah! *(His revolver in one hand and the other outstretched, he wards off the danger of an unwitting blast on their part.)*

(Exit soldiers.)

Lem. *(in a moment)* Dey runnin' for de boat!
Edgar. Joshuah, must we crack down?
Joshuah. No. Let 'em go.
Setlow. Yeah. 'N let de will of Gawd prevail!

(Blackout)

ACT II

SCENE 4

Time: *A week ensues.*
Place: *The Freedmen, facing inactivity and their own sense of powerlessness to affect their bitter situation, have begun to exemplify a sense of high dudgeon. Although it is never quite successful in transcending their basic capacity for patience, it emerges, expressing itself in sharp, explosive outbursts and attempts to fix the blame for the adverse turn of affairs. Beyond this mood, the only noticeable change is the presence of a barricade, which they have erected by using the bales of cotton.*

Edgar. *(armed as others around him, indignantly exploding)* All dis settin' round like er yard full of chickens wid de pip! *(barking)* Daddy Setlow, how long we got t' wait?
Lem. Thas what Ah wanter know!
Setlow. Who can tell de ways of Gawd? Be patient, Boy!
Edgar. Damn patience. Damn hit t' hell 'n back!
Peltier. Ah blame dis Peoria Bradley.
Taggert. Thas whar yuh wrong. Peoria Bradley's de only real man we got 'mongst de Colored in Sawanny.
Edgar. He done had er whole week. 'N heah we is wid cotton nuff t' fill up anybody's warehouse.

Lem. Yeah. Look like he could-er done found *one* agent.
Webster. *(outside, calling)* Hello, in there. How do you get in?
Peltier. *(at barricade)* Come round de end thar.
Lem. Das Webster, ain't it?
Taggert. Yeah. He 'bout come see 'bout what Joshuah done t' Ollie.
Edgar. If he know like Ah know, he better git on back cross tha water!
Webster. *(entering)* Where's Mister Tain?
Peltier. Joshuah? He be here in er minute.
Webster. Perhaps one of you can inform me. Why is it, in spite of all I've done for you folks, you allowed my son to be assaulted?
Edgar. He spoke up for de white folks, thas why.

(Joshuah enters up right.)

Webster. Isn't it true Mister Tain was jealous over some girl here?
Lem. *(vehemently)* Jealous. Thar now!
Joshuah. *(coming down)* Ah'll answer tha mahsef, Suh.
Webster. Well?
Joshuah. *(going)* Come on wid me. Ah'll splain things.
Webster. *(arresting him)* Explain here. If my son is wrong, speak right out. I'm not interested in having anything hidden.
Joshuah. *(eyeing him)* Yuh seem t' be sure of yorsef ez er Jersey Bull.
Webster. *(pointedly)* Aren't you?
Joshuah. *(coolly)* Ah's seed too many of em fall in de hands of de butcher!
Webster. If you think you can bluff me, Mister Tain—
Joshuah. *(catching his arm)* Awh, come on, Man. Quit actin' like er fool!
Webster. *(resisting)* Why can't you answer me here?
Joshuah. *(forcing him)* Ah sed come on!
Webster. *(sputtering some protest is drawn off up left)*
Edgar. *(laughing)* Heh! Ah thot that was goin' be hell here t'reckly!
Sarah. *(sharply)* Tha Ollie is er snake. 'N if Ah was Joshuah, Ah'd told his Pappy so right for everybody. Ah'd er took him down er peg or two!
Taggert. How yuh know so much old lady?
Sarah. *(indignant)* Ollie ain't no earfly good. Ah know what Ahm talkin' 'bout, ain't Ah, Ant Dosia?
Dosia. *(sharply)* Ah ain't in tha mess. So just leave me out.
Sarah. But yuh know Ah know what Ahm talkin' 'bout.
Ellen. *(sensing undercurrent)* What is this, Miss Sarah?
Patsy. Dey got sompen up thar sleeve.
Ellen. What is it, Miss Sarah. Come on 'n tell us?
Sarah. *(amused)* Ask Ant Dosia.
Dosia. *(sharply)* Ah told yuh Ah wuzzn't in this.
Lem. *(like the others, deeply intrigued)* Oh, Mammy, go on 'n tell it!

Setlow. *(warningly)* If yuh all do know sompen, Ah'd advise yuh t' keep it t' yorsefs.

Sarah. *(darkly)* De truth goin' out jes de same. Mother Nature goin' see t' tha.

Patsy. Sarah, yuh can't mean what Ahm thinkin'?

Sarah. Ah do if what Ant Dosia say is true.

Dosia. *(exclaiming, though she too is secretly enjoying the drama)* Yuh all hear this woman. Yuh witness!

Sarah. Yuh mean t' sit thar, Ant Dosia, 'n deny what yuh told me t' mah face?

Dosia. Ah ain't denyin' nothin'!

Sarah. Yuh act like it.

Dosia. All Ah know de gal told me somebody tricked her. 'N thas all Ah told yuh! But yuh had no bizness openin' yor leaky mouf!

Sarah. Ah ain't hidin' no skunk!

Patsy. *(dumbfounded, but piqued by the scandal)* Jesus me! Yuh all can't mean what yuh sayin'.

Sarah. If it's er lie, Ant Dosia told it.

Dosia. *(coolly)* De gal knittin' feet for sox all right.

Patsy. Go long!

Dosia. *(nodding)* So hep me! But who de cause, Ah donno no more 'n yuh. It coulder been tha Ollie, but thas more'n Ah know.

Lem. Lawdy—the nasty rascal!

(Roxanna bursts into tears and runs out, up right.)

Sarah. *(contritely)* Lawd, us forgot all bout tha chile.

(All are silent.)

Ellen. But yuh know. Ah thought she had her cap set on Joshuah.

Sarah. Tha Big House pizened hussey—Joshuah wasn't good nuff for her.

Georgana. Yuh all wrong. Pappy ain't wanted her. Pappy ain't care nuffin' 'bout her.

Lem. *(ruefully)* Ain't nobody had no chance wid the high-yaller rascal!

Ellen. This done took all de run out er me.

Patsy. Yuh said it, Chile. Anybody had er told me Delphine would come wid her *leg broke,* Ah wouldn't er bleved it!

Dosia. *(sympathetically)* De gal say whoever twuz must-er gin her dose of love powder.

Ellen. Love Powder!

Patsy. Den tha mean Daddy Sykes!

Sykes. *(indignantly)* Ah been settin' heah speckin' sompen like dis. Ah knowed twan't be long for yuh all dragged me in it.

Sarah. Awh go on, yuh ole spider-cookin' hellion! Yuh mixed up in it all right.

Joshuah. *(reentering with Webster, the cotton agent, and two ragged Confederate soldiers—the latter barefooted)* Heah's de Agent, Folks, what Peoria Bradley done sent us.

Setlow. *(relieved)* Thank God.

Broker. *(examining cotton)* You seem t' have a pretty good crop.

Joshuah. *(proudly)* Us raised fifty-two bales—fawty of 'em long staple. *(He follows the broker up beyond earshot, and they begin bargaining.)*

Reb I. *(indicating barricade)* By Gawd, Ah see yuh all really mean t' shed white blood!

Edgar. *(as he and others tense)* So what 'bout it?

Reb I. What yuh gittin' riled erbout? We ain't got nothin' ergin yuh Cuffees.

Edgar. *(suspiciously)* Yuh talk like yuh wid de planters?

Reb I. Hell! For mah part yuh can kill all de planters in de Gawd damn South!

Ross. We ain't atter killin' nobody, Reb. We jes goin' keep dis lan'.

Reb I. 'N Ah don't blame yuh. De Yanks ain't got no right t' go kickin' yuh off de place. They oughter be heppin' yuh.

Reb II. *(agreeing bitterly)* Sure Gawd oughter. Like Ah was tellin' mah wife: "They should er took de lan' 'n gin it t' yuh niggers 'n us." De damn planters got everything, 'n er poor son-of-a-bitch of a white man like me 'n yuh, Hill—why, hell, we can't even light in de swamp!

Webster. *(conciliatorily, following Broker down)* I think Mr. Tain understands the difficulty of your position, Sir. But why not consider it from the long-range point of view?

Broker. How's that?

Webster. It can hardly be to your advantage to let them crush these people. The Freedmen are going to be the main source of your business tomorrow.

Broker. If Ah didn't know that, Ah wouldn't be here, running the risk of becoming a marked man to the planters. But at the same time, Ah've got to recognize the fact, if Ahm caught with that cotton, they'll confiscate it.

Joshuah. *(sharply)* Tha crop's worth seven thousand 'n eight hund'd dollars!

Broker. But Ah've no permit! What do you want me t' do—pay yuh market prices for cotton Ah have t' smuggle?

Joshuah. But, Suh. Yuh can pay more 'n seventeen cents! Cotton sellin' for Thirty!

Broker. *(adamant)* It's your cotton. Ah'll give you seventeen for the lot.

Joshuah. We can't do it.

Broker. *(going)* Then the deal's off. *(To rebs)* Come on, Boys.
Taggert. *(to Joshuah)* What 'bout de chillun—?
Joshuah. *(arresting Broker)* Wait, Mister. *(as the Broker rejoins him)* How 'bout takin' part of de crop—say, ten bales?
Broker. *(thoughtfully)* It won't hardly pay. But, waal, just t'make a load, Ah'll give you fifteen for five.
Joshuah. *(pained)* Yuh jes said seventeen.
Broker. For the lot.
Setlow. Thas jes givin' it way!
Taggert. De chillun got t' eat!
Joshuah. *(to Broker)* Make it sixteen?
Broker. Look, Ahm only tryin' t' do you a favor. Is it a deal or ain't it?
Joshuah. *(coldly)* It's a deal.
Webster. *(as Broker counts out money)* I'm sorry, Mr. Tain. I have to go now. But about that son of mine—well, I hope you won't let the matter come between us, or fail to let me know if there's anything I can do in the future.

(exit)

Joshuah. *(Nods, as he counts money, and the Broker and his men go up to begin taking cotton.)*
Ross. Looks like everywhar we turn de white folks want t' give us de worst of it.
Patsy. Ah wouldn't feel too bad 'bout it. We ain't never had more 'n jes 'bout nuff t' keep body 'n soul together. 'N when yuh come t' think 'bout it, we still got plenty cotton left.
Peltier. *(bitterly)* Ah'd jes ez soon see it all sot on fiah ez t' swallow this!
Edgar. Nevermind. De baddest dog meet his match some day!
Joshuah. Patsy is right. We got no cause t' give up heart. All we got t' do is hold on. *(Marshalling them out, he attempts to cheer them up by raising song.)*
    "Hold on!
    Hold on!"

(Gradually the Freedmen pick up song.)
    "Keep yor hand on de plow
    Hold on!"

(Dimout)

ACT II

· · · · · ·

SCENE 5

Time: *It is the following afternoon.*
Place: *The scene is unchanged, and Setlow is guarding a batch of supplies which he and others have apparently just brought from the mainland—a huge basket with smoked hams, etc., a barrel of flour, and large bags of beans, around which the women hover.*

Setlow. *(sharply)* Get back yuh all. Sarah, Ah mean it now! Get way n' let de vittals be. Ah wouldn't fool wid nothin' till Joshuah comes!
Sarah. Ah was jes lookin' t' see if yuh all brung a lil sompen for de chillun. Dey 'bout t' run Miz Libeth crazy, shut up yonder in de Big House.
Taggert. *(guiltily)* Here's a lil stick of Mint Ah was goin' give Alice.
Sarah. *(taking it)* This'll never do. But, heah, Minnie. Take dis candy t' Miz Libeth.
Georgana. Lawd, peppermint! *(drooling as Minnie takes candy)* Gimme jes' er lick, Minnie.
Sarah. No, Minnie! Go on t' de Big House.

(Exit Minnie.)

Ellen. *(Up right, sitting on a bale, she sees Delphine in distance.)* Heah come Miss Love Powder!
Patsy. Shame on yuh, Ellen. Shame!
Ellen. *(saucily)* Oh, Miz Patsy, don't be fogey! *(suddenly inspired by diabolical idea)* Ah jes thot of sompen. *(Springing down she comes forward.)* Pappy!
Setlow. What daughter?
Ellen. Ah betcha thar's one thing yuh all forgot t' bring.
Setlow. What?
Ellen. *(as Delphine enters—pointedly)* Betcha didn't git no diapers!
Setlow. Diapers for what?
Ellen. *(innocently)* Can yuh all beat this. Dey done gone all de way t' Savannah n' ain't come back heah wid *diaper one!*
Sarah. *(catching her drift)* Lawdy! 'N no rattle neither, Ah bet.
Ellen. Too early for de rattle! But now diapers—*(stabbingly)* 'n talcum— who was it tellin' me 'bout tha new brand of baby talcum. *(innocently)* Wuz it yuh, Delphine?
Delphine. *(in the dark)* Baby talcum—when?
Ellen. *(casually)* Somebody wus tellin' me 'bout some new brand they say don't chafe. Oh, yeah, love powder. Thas what they call it.
Sarah. *(laughing)* Shucks, gal. Yuh want t' know de latest, yuh oughter see Daddy Sykes!

Ellen. Daddy Sykes? *(innocently)* Lawd, Daddy Sykes, whyn't yuh tell somebody yuh wuz in de love powder bizness?

(There is an outburst of laughter, and Delphine trembles. Her eyes swim, and for a moment she is transfixed with indecision.)

Joshuah. *(entering)* What's so funny?

(The laughter ceases suddenly.)

Delphine. Ah guess de joke's on me. *(She turns to go.)*
Joshuah. *(arresting her, as he senses situation)* On yuh? *(to others)* What is this? *(suddenly feigning laughter)* But Ah bet Ah know. Yuh done smoked us out, ain't yuh? Well, it's 'bout time. We been puttin' it off till after de harvest. But's de truth; we's goin' git married.
Georgana. *(shocked)* Pappy, yuh don't mean it?
Patsy. *(impulsively embracing Delphine)* Gawd bless yuh, Honey chile!
Ross. Yuh all sure fooled everybody!
Setlow. *(shaking hands with Joshuah)* Deed yuh all did!
Ellen. Oh, how kin you ever forgive me, Delphine? But Ah didn't know!
Sarah. *(joining them)* Move, Ellen—Delphine, Honey, yuh must forgive me—*(whirling, to attack)* But, Ant Dosia, this is your fault!
Dosia. *(angrily)* Don't yuh tell tha lie!
Joshuah. *(interposing)* Now hold on!
Sarah. *(to Dosia)* Yuh told me, didn't yuh?
Dosia. *(defensively)* 'N she tole me!
Joshuah. *(attempting to arrest the developing storm; sharply)* What diffunce do it make who told who what? Now yuh know. *(His outburst brings a momentary silence.)* Yuh all, take this stuff t' de Quarters 'n divide it 'tween yuh.
Dosia. *(angrily)* Ah jes want t' git it straight!
Lem. *(getting bag of beans)* Oh, Mammy, come on 'n hush!
Dosia. Don't yuh tell me t' hush!
Lem. Den come on!
Dosia. *(going, belligerently)* Ah don't bite mah tongue for nobody! *(exit)*
Edgar. Ellen, grab hold de other end of dis basket.

(She complies, and they follow the others out, leaving Delphine and Joshuah alone.)

Joshuah. Did yuh say sompen t' Ant Dosia?
Delphine. Yeah.
Joshuah. What yuh do tha for?
Delphine. Ah thot she might be able to help me—in mah condition.
Joshuah. You shouldn't er said nothin'.
Delphine. Ah don't mind em knowin'—though twas mighty fine of yuh t' try t' cover up for me.

Joshuah. Ah meant what Ah said. If yuh can ever git over mah actin' sech er fool last summer.
Delphine. Joshuah, yuh jes erbout de biggest man Gawd ever made.
Joshuah. Ahm jes in love wid yuh, 'n soon's we git straight wid this Burkhardt—
Delphine. *(crossing)* No, Joshuah. Yuh know tha can never be.
Joshuah. *(joining her)* Yuh need me, Delphine, 'n it's be good for yuh.
Delphine. *(sitting on bench)* It won't work.
Joshuah. Yuh still thinkin' bout de bitter words Ah said?
Delphine. *(thoughtfully)* Ah jes know, for one thing, after this, you'll never trust me.
Joshuah. *(quietly, gazing inwardly)* Dey say er burnt chile dreads fiah. Thas true. *(turning to her)* But if Ah bear de mark where Ah been singed, what must Ah think 'bout de scar on yuh?
Delphine. Ah's learned mah lesson, all right. But yuh forget there's one sharp stone goin' always stick in your craw.
Joshuah. *(after a moment)* Yuh mean de chile? *(She nods.)* Yuh wrong, Delphine. Ah admit Ah thot er lot 'bout it. But de chile goin' need er father. 'N when er man means right by er woman, what's hers is his'n. Nothin' else don't matter.
Delphine. Yuh's changed.
Joshuah. Ah jes been thinkin'.
Delphine. 'N yuh'll go on thinkin'.
Joshuah. No. This ain't nothin' new. *(quietly)* As er people we's always been up against it.
Delphine. Ah don't catch yuh.
Joshuah. *(explaining)* De chile ain't mine. Thas so. But look back er ways, 'n what yuh see?
Delphine. Ah don't follow yuh.
Joshuah. *(gazing into the distant past)* Take yor Mammy 'n mine—'n Ah reckon pretty near everybody else's Mammy. Ain't none of em ever had no *sayso* 'bout de father of thar chillun. *(turning to her gently)* So whether it's er case of er high-yaller wid love powder, or ole Marster's whip, it's all de same in de end. *(Her eyes swimming in response to his humanity, she creeps into his arms. For a moment they are silent, as he strokes her hair.)* Yuh feel better? *(She nods.)* Den Ahm glad. Mighty glad. Holdin' yuh like this's jes like de blossoms on er cherry tree. It's like Lusana magnolias round sundown.
Delphine. Oh, Joshuah, yuh's like er warm wool blanket t' mah soul.
Joshuah. Yuh's er comfort t' me too, Darlin'. Yuh's what mah heart been wantin', 'n wid de hep of Gawd, yuh what Ahm goin' keep for de rest of mah life. Come what may.
Delphine. Yuh don't have t' tell me, Joshuah. Ah's knowed it ever since de

day yuh all come heah. But like de story Ah told yuh 'bout de mountain 'n de sea, Ah couldn't bleve it'd happen t' me. *(Profoundly moved, she smothers her face in his bosom.)*

Joshuah. Mah darlin'. Mah lil Delphine!

Delphine. *(whispering)* My Joshuah. *(Silence reigns between them. But in a moment a shot sounds.)*

Joshuah. *(Snapping erect, tense and listening, he is propelled to his feet as two more shots follow in rapid succession—yelling.)* Fall in Guards! *(taking her and momentarily embracing her)* Run hep Miz Libeth! Keep de chillun in de house. Better take 'em t' de attic. Hurry now!

Delphine. Oh, Gawd.

Joshuah. *(sending her away)* Hurry, hurry. Thar may be shootin'!

Delphine. *(She clutches him to her then breaking away.)* Be careful, won't yuh, Joshuah. *(Taking a long look at him, she turns and runs off up right.)*

(exit)

Emanuel. *(running in up left)* Dey comin', Mister Joshuah.

Joshuah. How many of 'em?

Emanuel. Dey got five boat loads.

(The other Freedmen pour in.)

Joshuah. Everybody heah? Good.

Edgar. *(up left at barricade)* Ah see Burkhardt wid 'em.

Joshuah. Phumph! Burkhardt, eh? Ah reckon they goin' want t' parley ergain. But lissen, Men. Don't none of yuh all let tha fool yuh. Thar must be thirty men out there. Yuh know what tha means. Ah want yuh t' go t' yor posts, 'n jes remember: Ain't nobody ever got nothin' worthwhile for nothin'. Some of ouah leaders don't understand tha. They's turnin' one Convention after ernother into de graveyard of all ouah hopes. Thar ain't er single one of 'em voted yet, 'cording t' Mister Webster, t' give us de lan'. It's got to be up t' us. We ain't many. 'N it's hard t' stand yor ground when yuh know deep down in your heart de best yuh can do is serve as er lesson. Remember John Brown. Him 'n his lil handful stood up for ouah freedom 'n they sot de whole country on fiah! Git t' yor post now, 'n hold your fiah till yuh heah from me.

(Owens, Peltier, Ross, and Emanuel enter the storehouse, left, while Setlow and others take position at the barricade.)

Lem. *(panting, as he runs in)* Ah thot they was gwine pick me off.

Joshuah. Yuh go wid dem in de storehouse.

(Exit Lem down left.)

Edgar. *(at barricade)* Heah dey come!

Joshuah. *(joins him to peep over barricade, then command)* Halt! War yuh is, Yanks!

Stewart. *(outside shouting)* I've something to say to you.

Joshuah. Well, git yor men back 'n den come on!

Edgar. *(in a moment)* He bringin' Burkhardt.

Joshuah. *(going down right)* Let em through.

Libeth. *(entering, excitedly)* Mr. Tain, what's going to happen?

Joshuah. Ah donno, Mam. But this ain't no place for yuh. Yuh got t' git back t' de Big House.

(Stewart and Burkhardt enter.)

Libeth. Perhaps I can help.

Stewart. Who're you, Madam—the teacher?

Libeth. Yes, Sir.

Stewart. *(joining Joshuah)* You don't think very much of her to expose her in this manner.

Libeth. I came of my own accord, Captain.

Stewart. Well, please retire to a place of safety!

Libeth. *(courageously)* I'm sure there can be no necessity for that, Sir.

Stewart. It's my duty to warn you, Madam. *(turning to Joshuah)* I see you've erected a barricade. What're you trying to do, bluff the Army? *(Joshuah is silent.)* You do not reply!

Joshuah. Yuh go head, Cap'n. We listenin'.

Stewart. Well, be sure you get this straight. I've two platoons out there. But I've no desire to shed your blood. So what's the answer?

Joshuah. Yuh already know how we feel, Cap'n. *(quietly)* This is ouah lan', 'n we tend t' stay heah like anybody else wid er just claim.

Stewart. *(snorting)* Now it's a *just claim!* *(glances at Burkhardt)* I see I've encouraged you by remaining away all week. Well, contrary to what you may think, I delayed my return because I was determined to be fair to you. Last week after I left here, I wired Headquarters explaining your case. In spite of my orders I did that. I even went so far as to wire General Howard himself. I've yet to receive a reply. But do you know what I *have* learned? General Howard himself has gone to Edisto Island, up the coast, to do exactly what I'm supposed to do here. You can see for yourselves, if General Howard has gone to Edisto Island to see to it personally that the Freedmen there sign the agreements, you must do so also. You must either sign or vacate the island. It must be one way or the other. So make up your minds.

Joshuah. What yuh say 'bout Gen'l Howard 'n this 'Disto Ilun' might be true. But dis ain't 'Disto Ilun'. We done made up ouah minds 'bout dem contracts.

Stewart. You intend to defy the United States Government?
Libeth. Mr. Tain. Think! What chance have you?
Joshuah. Miz Libeth, Ah told yuh t' git back in de house whar yuh blong!
Libeth. But, Mister Tain—
Joshuah. *(firmly)* Yuh been too good t' us fer me t' hurt your feelings, Mam. Git back in de house 'n stay in er woman's place!

(With a gesture of despair, she goes out up right.)

Burkhardt. *(to Joshuah)* I wonder if you realize the leading niggers of the country are against this mad idea of confiscation?
Joshuah. This is Gawgie. We ain't had no Convention yit.
Burkhardt. But you can see which way the wind is blowing. The most influential men of your race understand this question.
Joshuah. Dey's ignant.
Burkhardt. Ignorant to you, and I suspect you can neither read nor write. *(turning to others)* What about you, Boys? Are you going to let this fellow lead you to your deaths? Have you thought about your families—your women and children? What's going to happen to them if you get yourselves killed off?
Setlow. What Joshuah say goes for all of us—
Stewart. *(sharply)* Speak for yourself! *(to others)* What've you men to say? *(as they are silent)* You leave me no alternative. *(to Joshuah)* We're going to retire.
Joshuah. Jes er minute, Cap'n. *(under the weight of his responsibility)* Yuh say if we sign dem contracts, in three years we kin buy lan'?
Stewart. *(eagerly)* That's right.
Joshuah. *(turning)* Den, Mr. Burkhardt. We got er lil money. Nuff t' pay yuh part down—
Burkhardt. *(quickly)* Hold on. I didn't say I wanted to sell.
Edgar. *(vehemently)* Ah haaaaaaannnh!
Burkhardt. If I sold, I'd have nowhere to go myself.
Joshuah. *(glancing at Stewart)* Den, how 'bout part of de ilun'?
Burkhardt. I'm afraid I wouldn't be interested.
Joshuah. *(swallowing)* Jes er few acres?
Burkhardt. *(angry at being so exposed)* But I'm not interested.
Joshuah. Ah see yuh ain't mean t' be fair. *(bitterly)* Yuh think yuh got de ups on us. But don't let tha fool yuh. 'N don't let what happen heah today fool yuh neither. *(looking off, his eyes sharp with inner pain)* Cuz neither yuh nor all de rest of de planters put together goin' ever kill de thing we's after. We know what's what. Yuh think if we ain't got no lan', we have t' wuk for nothin'. But yuh never git way wid it. This is ouah lan'. We done wukked 'n paid for it. Not only here, but all ovah this cruel South. De graves *(pointing off right)* ovah yonder is mah

witness. De slaves sleepin' in 'em declare Ahm right 'fore Gawd. It was us what first did de tillin' t' make it give up de sweet sustenance of life, 'n yuh kin mark mah word: Though yuh won't even sell now, tha same sun yuh see yonder goin' yit rise 'n find dem what does de tillin' gatherin' in de harvest. Yuh kin go, Cap'n. We'll hold ouah fiah till yuh git back t' yor men. *(Burkhardt goes out.)*

Stewart. You're a bitter man, Tain. Think it ovah a little longer. I'll give you fifteen minutes if you wish.

Joshuah. *(quietly)* We's holdin' ouah fire, Cap'n, till yuh git back t' your men!

Stewart. So be it.

(exit)

Joshuah. *(covering his retreat)* Hold it men. Hold it!
Patsy. *(entering, shattering the ominous silence)* Gimme er gun somebody!
Joshuah. *(sharply)* Ah told yuh womens t' stay out de way!
Patsy. Gimme er gun. Ahm in this fight.

(A bugle blares)

Joshuah. *(as shot sounds)* Fiah men! Fiah! Let em have it!

(His voice is drowned in the crack of rifle fire.)

(Blackout)

(The stage remains in darkness and there is no sound. But shortly as the lights come up we note that it is now late afternoon and, among the Freedmen, Patsy is distinguished on an improvised stretcher, as [s]he is borne off.)

Ross. *(emerging from the storehouse)* Joshuah!
Joshuah. What, Brer Ross?
Setlow. *(at barricade)* Here come de boat back!
Joshuah. Did they get more men?
Setlow. Ah don't see none.
Joshuah. Thas funny. *(seeing Peltier emerge from storehouse)* How yuh all farin'?
Peltier. *(quietly)* Yuh lookin' at what's left.
Joshuah. *(stunned by realization of his losses)* Lawd.
Ross. *(hesitating)* Ah hate t' say it, Joshuah. But there ain't no hope for us.
Joshuah. Yuh done lost Patsy—
Ross. Tain't tha, Joshuah. But soon's dark fall, they git us. Dey surround us!

Setlow. *(at barricade)* Heah's Stewart ergin.
Joshuah. *(goes up)* Come on in, Cap'n.
Stewart. *(Entering he surveys scene.)* I've a cannon being put ashore! *(pausing apparently to permit news to sink in)* I can blow you all to hell with one round. However . . . I've come to offer you your last chance. I want to appeal to you as one man to another. You've lost men and so have I. It's senseless bloodshed. I know how you feel. I know Mr. Burkhardt has refused to meet you halfway. But it's his land, and in the judgment of the government, you must give over. *(glances at sun)* I'm going to give you until sundown. That should be in about ten minutes. But take my solemn advice. The moment the sun disappears beneath the horizon, I shall order the gunners to touch off the cannon. And then, unless you shall have changed your minds, may God be with you and have mercy on your souls!
Joshuah. *(quietly)* Thank yuh, Suh, for your kindness. But 'fore yuh go, there's sompen Ah wan t' axe yuh. Ah might have er couple of men who might want t' accept your offer. If they do, what yuh goin' do t' em?
Stewart. *(quietly, after a moment)* They will be free to leave the island.
Joshuah. Thank you ergin, Suh.

(Exit Stewart.)

(turning to others) Well, yuh all heard him, men. Tomorrow ouah folks goin' be homeless ergin. They goin' need yuh?
Setlow. Who can understand de ways of Gawd!
Joshuah. Meanin'?
Setlow. Ah shall not be moved.
Joshuah. Peltier, yuh see mah pint, don't yuh?
Peltier. *(bitterly)* Ah come in this thing wid mah eyes wide open, Joshuah. Ah admit, Ah didn't think de Gubment would give us sech er raw deal, though Ah seed how dey treated eberbody in Missippi. But Ah guess Ah had de idea all de time, dey was gwine think twice 'bout forcin' us. But I still think you're right, and if yuh can stay, Ah can too!
Joshuah. Well, yuh'n Brer Setlow go hold de storehouse. Brer Ross, Ah won't axe yuh. *(takes out roll of bills)* Here, take dis money. Do de best yuh kin by de womens 'n chillun. Yuh better try t' send Miz Libeth back home. *(seeing Delphine run in)* Go back, Delphine. *(She throws herself in his arms.)* Here, Brer Ross. Take her long.
Delphine. They fixin' t' blow yuh t' smithereens wid er cannon, Joshuah!
Joshuah. Ah know. Thas jes Yankee bluff. Yuh go hep wid de chillun.
Delphine. Ah ain't gwine without yuh.
Joshuah. But yuh ain't in no condition t' be heah. Think of de chile!
Delphine. If yuh really thinkin' 'bout de chile, then yuh come on wid me!

Joshuah. Yuh know Ah can't. *(desperately)* Why don't yuh hep me by doin' what Ah tell yuh?

Delphine. Ah want t' hep yuh, Joshuah. Ah do! Ah do!

Joshuah. Den go!

Delphine. *(breaking)* Oh, Joshuah, you don't know mah heart. Don't try t' send me way. If yuh won't come wid me, lemme stay here. Don't try t' send me way. Lemme stay here whar Ah blong, whether Ahm livin' or dead!

Joshuah. Lawd, what Ahma do? *(He tries to hand her to Ross, but she eludes him and drops to the ground like a child reluctant to be moved.)* Get up, Delphine!

Ross. Pick her up, Joshuah. De sun almost down!

Joshuah. Get up, Delphine—please!

Delphine. Ah rether be dead.

Ross. Pick her up, Joshuah! *(seeing him in helpless dismay)* De sun sinkin' fast, Joshuah. Dey fiah, dey kill her sure. Do sompen!

Joshuah. Ah reckon ain't nothin' Ah kin do. Yuh go on, Brer Ross.

Ross. 'N leave her?

Joshuah. Yeah. She is mah woman. If she wanter stay heah, Ah ain't got no right t' drive her way. Yuh git on.

Ross. *(going in dismay)* Gawd have mercy!

(Exit.)

Joshuah. Git up, Honey.

Delphine. *(Rising she dusts her skirt, then turns to him softly.)* Yuh mad wid me?

Joshuah. No . . . Ahm proud of yuh! *(For a moment he holds her close to his bosom. Then, leading her to seat beneath oak.)* But yuh better sit.

Delphine. Ah want t' see what dey doin' out there.

Joshuah. No. It's best not t' think 'bout em. Sit down 'n les talk.

Delphine. *(sitting)* All right. 'Bout what?

Joshuah. *(For a moment he stands watching outside, while she gazes upon ground at her feet, her arms wrapped about her knees.)* Tell me 'bout de time when yuh wuz a lil girl heah on de ilun'? *(sits)*

Delphine. No. Yuh tell me how come yuh t' be sold down de river, like dey say.

Joshuah. Ah made some pikeheads, 'n one of ole Marster's boys found 'em.

Delphine. What's er pikehead?

Joshuah. It's er piece of sharp iron yuh fix t' er pole so yuh can stick de enemy.

Delphine. Oh. So yuh wuz plannin' er risin' gainst de Masters?

Joshuah. Yeah. We had de day all set. Us didn't need but er few more pikeheads. But one day, Joel, de youngest of de boys found 'em where Ah had 'em planted in de well. They couldn't prove nothin' zactly. But dey figgered couldn't nobody made dem pikeheads but me, so dey sold me down t' Lusana.

Delphine. *(She draws her shawl about her shoulders.)* But Georgana says your wife wuz killed.

Joshuah. She wuz. Poor Hannah. She throwed her life away tryin' t' save me. De High Sheriff come t' git me, 'n Ah broke 'n run. Hannah, she seed he was goin' shoot, so she jumped in de way, 'n he killed her stone dead.

Delphine. She must er been er fine woman.

Joshuah. *(Rising he peeps out.)* Yuh'n her very much de same. *(turning back to join her)* Yuh got de same sort of soft eyes 'n brown skin. Yuh got hips like her, 'n yuh carry yorself like yuh mount t' sompen in de world!

Delphine. *(after a moment)* Ah reckon if things had er been diffunt, maybe me 'n yuh'd both been somebody, wouldn't us?

Joshuah. *(glancing at sun)* Yeah. Ah speck so.

Delphine. *(drawing her shawl about her)* Ahm gittin er lil chilly.

Joshuah. *(putting his arms around her)* Dis fall, yuh know, Winter jes er-round de corner.

Delphine. *(wistfully)* Yeah. Pretty soon de nights goin' be frosty. Yuh git up in de mawnin' 'n find de ground all covered wid white. *(shivering)* Sing sompen, Joshuah.

Joshuah. Lawd, Honey, how can Ah sing?

Delphine. *(swallowing)* Yuh kin try—

Joshuah. It's funny. Ah can't seem t' think of nothin'.

Delphine. Sing "Deep River."

Joshuah. All right, if de words can git through mah dry throat. *(He struggles for a moment, then lifts song.)* "Deep river . . . (etc.)."

(The lights begin to fade.)

Delphine. *(As he concludes stanza, she continues the song in tender requiem.)* "Oh, deep river . . . (etc.)."

(In the distance, scarcely audible, the chorus joins her. In a moment their voices soar up—but Delphine, unable to bear the strain any longer, breaks with a sob and throws herself on Joshuah's breast as the curtain begins to fall slowly.

The chorus soars, as the lights dim out, and the couple are left in darkness, and all is ineffable sadness.

Just as the curtain closes completely, there is the sound of a cannon being fired.)

(Curtain)

Bayou Legend (1946)

Owen Dodson (1914–1983)

Born and reared in Brooklyn, New York, Owen Dodson had excellent models for achievement in his parents. Dodson was the ninth child of Nathaniel Barnett Dodson, a free-lance writer for the African American press, and Sarah Elizabeth Goode Dodson, who was a social worker and church volunteer. In 1936, Owen Dodson received his B.A. from Bates College in Lewiston, Maine. In 1939, he received his M.F.A. from the Yale Drama School, which he entered on a fellowship. His teaching career began at Spelman College in Atlanta immediately after he received his M.F.A. In 1947, he began teaching at Howard University, where he remained for twenty-three years, after which he retired to New York to concentrate on his poetry. After a medical discharge from the navy for asthma in 1943, Dodson received a Rosenwald Fellowship. Subsequently, he wrote and directed a Negro-history pageant, *New World A-Coming,* which played with overwhelming success at Madison Square Garden in New York. As a result, Dodson was appointed executive secretary of the Committee for Mass Education in Race Relations at the American Film Center, a new organization.

Dodson's long and distinguished career as a writer includes his work in drama, poetry, and fiction. His voice is singular among African American writers. He was too young for the Harlem Renaissance. He mastered the English sonnet, as did Countee Cullen, and he dressed European forms in the embellishing attire of black vernacular and gospel rhythms. Yet he did not write folk literature like Langston Hughes, nor was he erudite in the manner of Melvin Tolson. Dodson's voice is unique in its originality.

In 1946, his first collection of poems, *Powerful Long Ladder,* was published. His first and best novel, *Boy at the Window,* published in 1951, is semiautobiographical. In it Coin Foreman, a sensitive nine-year-old boy, grows to puberty. Dodson's poetic sensibility imbibes the narrative with rich imagery and metaphor. In 1952, he received a Guggenheim Fellowship to write a sequel to *Boy at the Window,* which he entitled *Come Home Early, Child* and completed in Ischia, Italy. In 1970, his book of poems, *The Confession Stone: Song Cycles,* was published. He considered this to be his masterpiece. A series of monologues concerning the life of Jesus, this work has been often performed at Easter services. He collaborated with the visual artist Camille Billops and the Harlem photographer James Van Der Zee for a book of images and poems entitled *The Harlem Book of the Dead.* Owen Dodson's fiction and drama have been anthologized in more than sixty texts and translated into Japanese, German, Dutch, Italian, and Czech. Upon invitation, he read his work on two occasions at the Library of Congress.

At the beginning of his tenure at Howard University, Dodson achieved his first success there with the production of *Bayou Legend,* an adaptation of Henrik Ibsen's *Peer Gynt* (1867) set in a Louisiana bayou. Again Dodson's poetic sensibility renders his work with the enriching complexities of his poetic powers, which were themselves full of the African American folk sensibility. The characters traverse a world thick with references to folk belief, to Catholicism and the Vodun related to it, and to legend, all of it rigged along the frame of the African American storytelling tradition.

Selected Published Plays by Owen Dodson

Divine Comedy, in *Black Theatre, USA.* ed. James V. Hatch and Ted Shine. New York: Free Press, 1974.
The Shining Town, in *Roots of Black Drama.* ed. Leo Hammalian and James V. Hatch. Detroit: Wayne State University Press, 1989.

Books Published by Owen Dodson

Poetry
Powerful Long Ladder. New York: Farrar, Straus, 1946.
The Confession Stone. Ontario, Canada: Leeds Music, 1968. Revised and enlarged as *The Confession Stone: Song Cycles.* London: Breman, 1970.
The Harlem Book of the Dead. Owen Dodson, James Van Der Zee, and Camille Billops. New York: Morgan & Morgan, 1978.

Fiction

Boy at the Window. New York: Farrar, Straus & Young, 1951. Republished as *When Trees Were Green.* New York: Popular Library, 1967.
Come Home Early, Child. New York: Popular Library, 1977.

Biographies on the Life of Owen Dodson

Sorrow Is the Only Faithful One: The Life of Owen Dodson. James V. Hatch. Champaign: University of Illinois Press, 1993.

• •

Bayou Legend

For Wilson Lehr

CHARACTERS

Maud Grant
Naomi, a friend
Mrs. Candymame, a gossip
Bettysue Candymame, her daughter
Apocalypse, a blacksmith
Yancey, a young man
Troy, another young man
Reve Grant, Maud's son, a dreamer
Bijou, a young woman
Willie Silvers, betrothed to Bijou
Ulysses, a tavern owner
Bijou's Father
Bijou's Mother
Sophie-Louise Grave
Charlotte Grave, her young sister
Mr. Grave, their father
A Girl
Clove ⎫
Oleander ⎬ Three shrimp maidens
Tulip ⎭
Hethabella, daughter of Loup Garou
Loup Garou, a king of the sea
1st Councillor
2nd Councillor
3rd Councillor
A Talking Bird
A Child, son of Reve and Hethabella
Fernand Ballon, a Frenchman

Josiah Cheever, a New England sea captain
Jason Weatherdrift, a contractor
Zempoaltepec, a Spanish Indian
Princess Teaka, a voluptuous Indian
Inca Priest, also a Stranger and the Toy Moulder
White Female Ape
Inventor Ape
White Male Ape
Perdido
A Priest

SCENES

ACT I

Maud Grant's house beside a bayou

A road

Palmetto Farm

An island

The Court of King Loup Garou beneath the waters of Bayou Goula

Maud's house

ACT II

A beach in Panama, about 1850

Palmetto Farm

ACT I

The footlights go up on a bright curtain. We hear music that has three themes: one of imaginative playfulness, one of universal sadness and romantic death, one of the driving insistence of love. As the curtain opens, there is Maud Grant's little house beside a bayou in 1837 Louisiana. It is a picture of realism with a fairy tale quality, of the beautiful hanging gloom of the gray moss and the flashy gaiety of peasant costume together with the easy dilapidation of the poor.

Out of the unseen bayou waters at back rise cypress trees hung with Spanish moss. On either side are live oaks also with Spanish moss. Late afternoon sunlight comes through the trees onto the house downstage left. It is simply constructed, well proportioned, made of mud mixed with moss and sticks plastered between supporting timbers, the slanting roof is covered with palmetto branches. A mound beneath one side of the roof is covered with bright flowers. Stalks of deep purple sugar cane are stacked against the house and a large, drying fishnet hangs. The stage slopes up toward the back. Maud Grant, a small lean woman, is hulling rice in the hollow of a tree trunk with a thick pounder while her friend, Naomi, is shelling shrimp on the step to the house door.

Naomi. Someone sure gonna be surprised out of his breeches to have shrimp and rice tonight.
Maud. Oh, sure!
Naomi. Don't be crossways, Maud. He'll be home soon smiling and talking big as a Mardi Gras in New Orleans.
Maud. He better not be in nobody's New Orleans. I'll hull him to a pulp.
Naomi. You'll worry the soul case out of yourself fretting; and then when he come, you'll be just as nice.
Maud. Go on away from here.
Naomi. Well, I ain't known you for twenty years not to shut my mouth when you hull that rice so anxious.
Maud. Go on humming that song.
Naomi. It is a nice song. *(humming)*
Maud. Humph. *(Naomi hums and Maud hulls quietly until—)*
Voice. *(offstage)* If you don't stop walking so slow, Bettysue, you'll be sorrier than Reve Grant down at Ulysses!
Naomi. Aw, aw—here comes Mrs. Candymayme. *(urgently)* No fussing now, Maud. I'll take care of her.
Maud. When I ever fuss with that big, flapping-mouth hypocrite.

(Naomi hums louder. Mrs. Candymayme and her little daughter, Bettysue,

come in stage right. Mrs. Candymayme has a gossip smile and the tongue of an adder puffing to inject poison into somebody's business.)

Mrs. Candymayme. Good evening, Naomi. Pleasant evening for the guests invited to the wedding.

(Maud keeps hulling.)

Naomi. My rheumatism been just itching for rain. That's funny now.
Mrs. Candymayme. Good evening, Mrs. Grant, I just dropped by cause Bettysue here just love to pass this house. *(silence from Maud and Naomi)* Don't you, darling?
Bettysue. Uh huh.
Mrs. Candymayme. *(to Bettysue)* Well, if you feels that way, say hello to Mrs. Grant and Mrs. er . . . Naomi. Forgot your final name.

(Naomi doesn't say a thing.)

Bettysue. *(shyly)* Good evening, Mrs. Grant.
Maud. *(because she likes children)* Good evening, child.
Mrs. Candymayme. *(to Bettysue)* Well, we ain't so popular around here as we is in town. If you wants to take it that way.
Maud. *(hulling)* Humph.
Mrs. Candymayme. We just seen somebody, ain't we, Bettysue, be of sure interest here?
Bettysue. *(shyly)* Yes, Mama.
Mrs. Candymayme. Now who was it we saw . . . let me think . . .
Bettysue. Reve Grant, mama?
Mrs. Candymayme. That's right, we did see him. You just so smart.
Maud. Well, so did I. Yes, I did. *(sharply)* Now go about your frigging business.
Naomi. *(placating)* Mrs. Grant's not feeling so well.
Maud. *(to Naomi)* Keep your big mouth out of it. I'm feeling fine as Christmas. *(to Mrs. Candymayme)* Now get out of here before I plop you over the head with this hulling club. *(She moves toward her.)*
Mrs. Candymayme. *(retreating a step or two)* Come on here, Bettysue. We don't want to be associated with no common trash, 'specially where we ain't wanted.
Maud. *(moving toward her)* I'll crack her head like a pecan nut.
Mrs. Candymayme. *(retreating further)* Bettysue we gonna be late for Miss Bijou's wedding. We gotta get dressed in our new finery. *(louder)* Some folks ain't, you know.
Maud. We been invited to the best of places. Now get on out of here before I'm sorry I mashed you to a pulp.
Naomi. *(grabbing Maud by the shoulders)* Now, Maud, Maud . . .

Mrs. Candymayme. *(to Bettysue—loftily)* She do take after her son.
Maud. *(struggling out of Naomi's grasp and starting for Mrs. Candymayme)* Oh—Oh—you low gossiping, nasty, dirty . . .
Mrs. Candymayme. *(retreating but careful to keep Bettysue between herself and Maud, and talking to Bettysue all the while)* Wonder she don't know her son lying on the floor at Ulysses' place with his breeches split. *(a little nasty laugh)* He resembles something called for and couldn't come. Say Apocalypse just mashed* his *head in. (She runs out yanking her daughter. Maud runs out after her but comes back almost immediately.)*
Maud. I declare. Oh, I declare, I'm so mad.
Apocalypse. *(offstage in his big blacksmith voice)* Where he slip to do you think?
Yancey. *(offstage)* I reckon he's hiding in the bushes.
Troy. Like a snake in the grass.

(laughter)

Apocalypse. *(Entering with a small group of young people. He is a large blunt fellow in speech and physique.)* I hope you brought that sazerac, son?
Yancey. Plenty and to spare. Ulysses can't see like he used to.
Apocalypse. I bet that boy wish he had some.
Troy. Probably swallow the whole bottle.
Apocalypse. Who, Ulysses?
Yancey. You know who. *(nodding in Maud's direction)*
Apocalypse. Can I help you pound that rice, Mrs. Grant? *(Troy can hardly contain himself. He begins to choke on his un-let-out laughter.)* Some man ought to be helping with all that pounding you got to do, Mrs. Grant.
Naomi. *(to Maud)* Hull that rice and don't you stop.
Yancey. Nice fine weather, Mrs. Grant.

(Troy just hangs onto Yancey, holding his laughter in, stamping his foot.)

Apocalypse. For a wedding you mean, Yancey? *(with elaborate innocence)* Mrs. Grant, is Reve at home?
Maud. *(Ready to take her huller and beat their heads in, but Naomi holds her hands and they hull together. Maud manages to answer with strained dignity.)* My son's out earning his living for me.
Apocalypse. Well, since he's earning *(winking to his friend)* tell him to drop on in at my place. We got something to settle up.
Yancey. *(winking at Troy and Apocalypse)* Look like that's settled already. Reckon you got some clean rags and ointment, Mrs. Grant. Somebody gonna need fixing up.

(Troy bursts out with his laughter, dancing.)

Apocalypse. *(very mock serious)* You boys oughtn't talk like that. That particular person you speaking of only got one rib broke, and just a little old bit of blood from his leg. He don't need no serious fixing up.
Troy. He just got a sore . . . *(He pats his behind; they all laugh except Apocalypse.)*
Apocalypse. *(mock serious)* You can cut the biggest fool. Now you all go on and get all fixed up for the wedding. *(They hesitate.)* Go on now. *(They scamper off nasty now and swaggering.)* You won't forget to tell him, Mrs. Grant.
Maud. *(holding her temper, managing a dignity also)* I'll—I'll tell my son.

(Apocalypse swaggers out.)

(going into house and exiting immediately with shawl) I'll find Reve and when I do I'll mash his brains in. Making a showcase out of himself and me.
Naomi. Maud, stay right here. He'll be home.
Maud. *(snatching away)* Humph. Let me loose.

(She goes off. People, dressed for the wedding with gifts brightly wrapped and baskets, dainty parasols, elaborate bonnets, pass by. They chatter gaily but as they pass the Grant house they stop talking; as they are almost off, they begin to chatter again. Naomi takes her dish of shrimp into the house, comes out with her shawl and goes in the direction Maud went. A small group is just ready to go off when they hear a scream and stop where they are downstage. Reve scampers in with Maud in his arms. She is protesting. Their words shoot back and forth. Maud's charging, Reve's teasing. To the crowd this is a big moment.)

Reve, you're lying!
Reve. Who says so?
Maud. I do and I know where of I speak. Will you swear to your poor old mother that it's the God's truth.
Reve. Humph.
Maud. *(making a big queer sound)* See. You're afraid to swear. You telling a package of lies.
Reve. Every word is true as true can be.
Maud. Lies. I know that, yes I do.
Reve. The truth!
Maud. Lies!!
Reve. The truth!!!
Maud. I been hearing from . . . *(Reve thrusts a stick of sugar cane in her mouth and dances about her gaily. Maud taking it out and spitting bits from her mouth during her next speech. But before she continues she notices the small group looking at them. She runs down quickly and cries*

"shoo;" *they run off. She returns to Reve, talking as she does so.)* How can you look me straight in the eye. You go on off when the work's piled up, leaving me to slave. You jump from island to island in the bayou looking for some buried treasure or other. Wonder you don't get drowned. *(pauses)* Did you see some of them spirits? *(suspiciously)* Where you get a boat anyway?

Reve. I walk the water on hyacinth leaves.

Maud. Ha! You go off hunting dirty alligators and then have the grit to come on back with your breeches in rags and your shirt torn nigh off. Oh, I know where you been all right—down to Ulysses' place. Yes you were—fighting.

Reve. Ha!*(Reve begins whistling.)*

Maud. Stop that whistling! Where'd you find this galloping alligator you been telling me about?

Reve. Bayou Goula.

Maud. *(Scornful laugh. She begins hulling rice again.)* Lord help us.

Reve. I was walking bayou waters on hyacinth leaves and I bent down to pick a flower, and lo and behold the leaves commenced moving.

Maud. *(imitating him)* "The leaves commenced moving"—Ulysses' sazerac commence working, you mean.

Reve. I liked to died. I went on over behind a cypress tree to see what was moving. I wanted to run but I couldn't, I wanted to holler but I couldn't. And guess what? A mean old alligator with slanty eyes reared his mean head from under the hyacinths. He said: "Go on away Reve Grant, if you duly know what's good for you."

Maud. Humph. I can hardly hold my temper. *(She pounds harder, but on his next speech she hulls less and less. Then she becomes entirely engrossed.)*

Reve. *(grabbing a stalk of cane to use as a gun)* Then I come to and I said: "Ha, ha, ha," in answer. "And I'll get even with you if it's the last thing I do." Alligator fell plop into the water, disappeared for a while and then swam on up again thrashing his big tail and opening and closing his big mouth trying to belittle me. I waded on over there and took out my hunting knife to see that he was sure enough dead. When I raised my hand, when I held my knife high ready to strike him his last, when my knife came down on his back—it broke.

Maud. Oh sweet Savior. Are you all right, Reve?

Reve. Have you ever been by Bayou Goula when twilight's about to settle and the Loup Garous gurgle underneath in their kingdom of slime?

Maud. Oh—what come next?

Reve. Have you ever been up to your knees in living mud?

Maud. Once, once—oh—

Reve. Have the black vultures ever followed you?

Maud. Oh Lord. Nobody's black vultures gonna gobble on me.

Reve. Have you ever been mounted on a crazy alligator with a red face and hands like a man?

Maud. My heart can't bear it, Reve.

Reve. *(quickly, acting it out)* He rushed through the swamp water, his tail was a whip on my back. I looked behind and the water was red from his blood. It stank like rotted shrimp, yes it did. The vultures was following us making the flapping sound. And a big green-colored bear was growling on the shore as we swam past. All of a sudden big flamingos flew up before us and that alligator got up and again went faster like he was going to spread wings . . .

Maud. Oh suffering Job, Lord have mercy . . .

Reve. . . . and follow them laughing birds. Mama, the dying sun was resting on the eyes of other alligators and they shone from under the water like lighted stones. And all along the way I could smell the yellow jasmine and silverbell, the redbud and the trumpet vine, I smelled the irises and I shouted out so loud the water bubbled: "No alligator with big sharp teeth and a hard back going to have me, even if he can talk back." I shouted: "Reve ain't going to die this way." And then—oh—

Maud. What? *(breathlessly)* What, son?

Reve. I can't tell this part . . .

Maud. Go on, go on.

Reve. When I shouted, that alligator, he dive down under the water and there I am clinging to his knots and scales. We shot by every kind of fish till we came to a place that was so green I kept blinking my eyes. And Mama—guess what was there for people. Whoooo Whee. Saw somebody with a body like a frog, yes I did . . .

Maud. You didn't . . .

Reve. . . . and the head of a man. Saw somebody with a head like a snake and body like a man, little tiny snake head, and guess what . . .

Maud. Oh Lord . . .

Reve. . . . saw a two-headed man in the underwater. One head just like a pelican and one like a snake and he talk out of both side his faces. Man like a shrimp and legs like a girl with pretty garters made of butterflies—I liked to died. They was uttering sounds that was all mixed up and laughing green and red laughter.

Maud. And what else?

Reve. Oh every which thing. I was scared to death but I kept on holding on.

Maud. I bet you did.

Reve. Nobody going to outdo Reve, so I hold on and steered that alligator on up again. He was just thrashing with his tail and talking about what he was going to do. I steered him up like I was driving a buggy up a slippery hill, and when we got up again I went straight for the quicksand bed and did he commence to wrestle, whoo, he just thrashed about but he was bleeding and his blood was stinking and the vultures was hollering and clapping their wings like thunder. Now here comes the queer part . . .

Maud. Go on.

Reve. Little old tiny insect flash in my eye and I blinked and when I open my eyes again . . . that alligator had disappeared and I was holding the skin in my hand. Just the skin. The old water bubble and steamed and I waded on out and come on home.

Maud. Where's the skin now, Reve?

Reve. Somewhere. *(snaps a piece of sugar cane and begins to suck it)* If you find it, sell it and live like a queen.

Maud. *(inspecting him)* Your hands and the flesh he took from your leg. Reve, how's that broken up rib? Praise my Lord for this miracle. My son is saved. Don't worry about them torn breeches, son, or your shirt. *(She looks up at him. He is smiling and he sucks his cane. She grabs the cane from his mouth. Smacking him.)* You snake-mouth you. Every other word you utter got a poison lie in it to sting your Mama. That's the tale of the Lord Garou and the wandering boy. I heard it from my Mama's knee. And you been telling me, I been listening . . .

Reve. *(peering over rice huller)* What happened once can happen again.

Maud. *(sitting on step)* You always lying—conjuring up the unseen to be seen. You got a devil in you. You spin out your stories like a warm robe for me to walk in and then you rip it off and I'm ashamed and mad and mean that I been taken in. Most times I don't know what's true and what's the air and swamp water of your lying.

Reve. I ought to smack you; I never lie.

Maud. *(in tears)* Lord I wish I was dead, dead and buried in this sour ground because nothing's going to help you, son. I could cry and pray all night, yes I could, but you're good for nothing, Reve, just good for nothing.

Reve. *(kneeling by her)* Mama, you're talking the truth so don't fret. Just be happy.

Maud. *(in his arms now)* Be happy. How in God's name can I be happy? Deep down in my bones I'm ashamed. Yes, ashamed when I think of all we had—once, long ago. Where's the money now? Where's the possum and the crabs? The turkeys and the wine? Where's my fine house and my horse and buggy?

Reve. *(standing)* Where's last night's dinner?

Maud. You shut up when I'm talking. Your father, yes he did, he drank up every last cent gouging and entertaining a bunch of folks from as far as New Orleans.

Reve. Aw—

Maud. *(worked up now)* Look at this place. Every other window busted in, and the fence broken; every time I turn around some bill collector's rapping on the door.

Reve. All right. All right. I know the story by heart. Every time we in a hole we climb out, don't we?

Maud. There's no place to climb to now. *(looking at him sucking cane)* Great suffering Job, have you ever seen such a puffed up, proud, blowing toad as I have for a son?

Reve. Humph.

Maud. No one hardly ever comes any more since your father was peddling his wares like a monkey in the streets. Naomi comes . . .

Reve. Oh Naomi . . .

Maud. Yes, Naomi . . . she's kinder than you, you big toad. You should be helping me instead of galavanting around, scaring all the town girls half to death, fighting every which ragamuffin.

Reve. There you go getting it wrong; just like a woman. Who you been gossiping with?

Maud. Every which person heard you yelling.

Reve. That was him!

Maud. Him!

Reve. I hit him within an inch of his life.

Maud. He didn't beat you like they said?

Reve. Who said? Why I gave him such a lam with this fist.

Maud. You are good for nothing. You'll be the death of me yet. Fighting this one, lamming that one. Just supposed you'da killed him—poor little Apocalypse.

Reve. Little Apocalypse! *(He winks at her laughing and rubs himself. She smiles even if she is mad. He goes to her again and tweaks her nose.)* Ha—you sweet old lady bee—honey Maud. You ugly thing. Just you wait—everybody will be bowing and scraping to you again. I'll do something wonderful.

Maud. *(contemptuously)* You! *(laughs)*

Reve. You just wait.

Maud. *(stops laughing and moves from him)* If you ever sewed a patch in your rotten breeches that's all I could expect.

Reve. I'll be a Senator, President, King, Emperor. Yes I will.

Maud. Great God and little fishes he's going straight out of his mind.

Reve. Wait. You just wait.

Maud. I could live to be a Methuselah, and you'd still have torn breeches.

Reve. Just you wait. I'll show old Maud.

Maud. Stop. Reve.

Reve. I will be great.

Maud. *(earnestly)* Stop it this minute, you're crazy as a bessie bug, but sometimes I think you might have amounted to something if you didn't lie so. Look at Bijou. She thought the sun rose and set with my Reve. You could have had her—bed, farm and everything, if you'd set your mind to it.

Reve. *(with mock surprise)* Is that right?

Maud. Her daddy worship her. He'd eat bird seed right out from her hand. He'd hem and haw but Bijou would have him eating bird seed out of her hand. *(quietly)* Besides her daddy got a mortgage on this place. *(tears again)* They been free folks just like us but no squandering there. You could be dressed just as fine . . .

Reve. *(interrupting)* Put on your shawl. Let's journey.

Maud. Where?

Reve. To Palmetto Farm.

Maud. No, Reve, No.

Reve. I can still marry . . .

Maud. Not this time. No you can't.

Reve. Any time I please . . .

Maud. When you were riding that alligator in the water—I heard that . . . well, anyway, Willie Silvers snatched that girl.

Reve. Not him. Folks laugh at him like he was a billy goat.

Maud. Just the same he snatched that pretty girl . . .

Reve. *(ignoring)* I'm commencing to leave.

Maud. . . . and that pretty farm.

Reve. I'm still going.

Maud. The wedding's tonight.

Reve. I'll be there tonight.

Maud. My sweet Savior, there he goes again, putting his big foot in it.

Reve. Everything's going to be sweet and dandy. *(shouting and laughing)* Yes, they will be. *(He lifts her off her feet.)*

Maud. Let me down.

Reve. We're going if I have to tote you there. *(He moves toward bayou at back.)*

Maud. Help! Help! Jesus, tell this fool to turn me loose. Reve, we'll drown. *(He steps down.)*

Reve. No we won't. I wasn't born to die no common way.

Maud. *(sarcastic)* You'll die beside a bayou spitting blood if you don't set me down.

Reve. Ah—here we are. It's nice and slick here. Now will you be still. I might slip any minute.

Maud. You are a toad's belly!

Reve. Whee—curse me, lam me. That won't touch me. Now we're going down—easy, easy . . .

Maud. Don't you let me fall.
Reve. *(tossing her a little)* Whee—whoops—let's play riding the alligator. I'm the alligator and you're me.
Maud. I feel like nothing a-tall lessen it's a big fool.
Reve. Here we are. It's smooth as a floor here. *(wades back to bank)* Kiss alligator a fine kiss to pay him for the fine ride.
Maud. *(smacking him)* Here's your kiss.
Reve. That's not worth a red cent.
Maud. Nor was the ride. Now set me down.
Reve. Not till we get to that wedding. Since you brought it all up. Talk to that billy goat Willie Silvers and tell to his face that he's one.
Maud. Let me down.
Reve. And tell him what I'm made of.
Maud. I'll tell him what a devil you are, what a liar.
Reve. Go on.
Maud. *(kicking him)* I'll preach a sermon, yes I will, till they run you off the place.
Reve. You will! Then I reckon I'll just go on by myself.
Maud. And I'll follow right behind.
Reve. You can't walk that far.
Maud. I could walk to New Orleans I'm so mad. Set me down.
Reve. Promise then.
Maud. I promise to tell the God's truth.
Reve. No you won't.
Maud. Ha! How you going to make me stay behind.
Reve. *(holding her very high like an offering over his head; his arms straight up)* Now let me see. Hmmm. I think—I think I'll set . . . I'll set . . . you right. *(He lifts her to the roof.)*
Maud. *(screaming)* Let me down.
Reve. *(capering)* Preach a sermon from that mount. *(laughing)* Now. *(He stands off inspecting her there then puts his hands to his lips calling.)* Old lady, what in the world are you doing up in that pulpit?
Maud. *(Reaching in her pocket for some rice. She throws it at him.)* I hope some gets in your eyes and blinds you.
Reve. Don't fall off.
Maud. *(fuming)* I hope all the voodoo gods curse you . . .
Reve. Is that so?
Maud. . . . and you turn into a Loup Garou.
Reve. Oh, oh, oh . . .
Maud. I didn't mean that, son. I didn't mean no curse, no I didn't. Bye now. *(Reve runs into the house and comes out with his guitar. He starts a taunting song and then goes off at back singing and playing.)*
Maud. Come back here, you snake-mouth you. *(Mrs. Candymayme and*

Bettysue have entered and watch unseen by Maud.) Come back here, you liar. He's gone. Oh, that boy will kill me yet. *(screaming)* Help! Help!

Mrs. Candymayme. *(to Bettysue)* Look yonder at Mrs. High and Mighty. Now how do you expect she got up there. Climbing at her age. Did you ever see the like?

Bettysue. No Mama.

Maud. Fetch me a ladder to fetch me down.

Mrs. Candymayme. Asking favors now, Bettysue, when everybody's mighty peeved with her boy.

Maud. When I get down from here, I'll put you in that rice huller and hull you to pieces.

Mrs. Candymayme. Whoo-oo-oo.

Voice. What's up?

Mrs. Candymayme. Reve done set his mother on her own roof. That is if you want to take it that way. *(She goes off laughing. Maud is fretting in desperation.)*

(Reve's song rises up and to that tune the house slides off left and a fence slides on downstage right.* Reve comes in singing and playing. It is getting toward twilight. His song over, he hits a big final defiant chord. He looks over the landscape as he walks the upper spokes of the fence balancing himself with his guitar. He points off right.)

Reve. Palmetto Farm. It sure is pretty lying there like a big strawberry in a plate. *(jumping down)* I wonder if Bijou is sitting there all alone. *(shading his eyes)* Whoo Whee. I should say not. Folks crowding in there—almost look like midgets from here. I'm going back home. They'll be grinning behind my back, I know that, be whispering, be tucking pins in my name. *(He moves downstage strumming absently.)* Wish I had a drink. Maybe I could slip in the back way, maybe. Wish I had me some sazerac. Then if they talked about me till doomsday it wouldn't hurt me, not one bit. *(He snaps his fingers.)* Not one bit. *(He hears talking and moves downstage behind a clump of bushes. Mrs. Candymayme and Bettysue come in. Mrs. Candymayme has seen Reve.)*

Mrs. Candymayme. *(to Bettysue)* No wonder he turned out to be the backside of nothing with a drunken daddy and that mother, have mercy.

Bettysue. I like him.

Mrs. Candymayme. If I ever see you talking to him, have mercy.

Reve. *(snapping his fingers)* Let her talk till her sharp tongue get long enough to cut her own throat. *(He strums his guitar, but tires of that. He lies on his back and picks a handful of phlox and stargrass. He holds*

---

*The road is upstage parallel to fence.

them high in the air and throws them higher and they flutter down. He lies back. Then sits up leaning on one elbow. Music from the farm gently fills the air. Reve looks up and points.) Look at that funny cloud. Looks just like a flying horse all fixed up: saddle and bridle and all. And look at that rider; that's me. *(laughs)* There's Maud following on a broomstick: "You blowed up toad, you Reve. Come on back here, you. Stop yourself riding that horse. Everybody'll think you're crazy." Poor Mama, scared. Scared. I ain't scared. She's afraid to be left lonesome. *(pause)* Look at me dressed like a prince in silver and gold and everybody following me. *(stands)* I'm going to glory like the brightest cloud. "Maud's son is sure something." And: "Ain't Reve something." And: "He can get him any girl he want, you hear me."

(Apocalypse appears at back and leans on the fence listening.)

Apocalypse. Having a good time talking to yourself. *(turning to others unseen but who soon crowd about him)* Guess who's here? Reve Grant, the drunken bayou boy.
Reve. You better get back to work, Blacksmith. I just seen a horse that wanted his shoes mended.
Apocalypse. He's already forgotten the fighting down at Ulysses!
Reve. You just leave me be.
Apocalypse. What you been doing since I made you kiss the floor? *(laughter from the crowd)*
Reve. What I been doing? Something wonderful. Make you scratch your head in wonder.
Apocalypse. Coming down to Palmetto Farm. Thought your heart was thumping for Bijou. *(puts his hand in his shirt and moves it in and out; laughter)*
Reve. You're an alligator's spit.
Yancey. Goodbye—we'll kiss the bride for you. *(They stroll off, laughing.)*
Reve. Bijou can marry that old billy goat Willie Silvers. Won't do me no harm. *(looks at himself)* I sure look a sight. If I had me a new shirt, and some doeskin breeches, I'd show them all. *(takes up his guitar; turns as he thinks he hears something)* Thought I heard some laughing. Well, they can laugh and laugh. I'm going on home. *(Far off the sound of a fiddle is heard and faint clapping. Reve goes toward the fence and looks toward the farm. He begins tapping his foot in time.)* Look at that dancing. All those girls. I'm going, yes I am, I gotta go. *(He begins to dance using his guitar as a partner.)* See you later, Mama.

(The sun has begun to set over the swamp, and the live oaks move off right and left leaving only the view of the great swamps and the bright blooming flowers. Reve dances down the hill and wildly vaults over the fence. The sun

goes down slowly as he dances, leaving him a dancing silhouette in the twilight. The music has flared up. Reve disappears and it is dark. Stars come out. When the light comes on again, it comes from lanterns on poles and where the oaks were are the buildings of Palmetto Farm looking like posters. Two barns at stage right and the small picturesque front of the farmhouse and porch are at stage left. The side porch has a long table filled with good things to eat and drink. Right center is a small platform with a fiddler and others about him playing various instruments. The dancing is at a height. All the people are brightly dressed and little children are dancing by themselves to the side. Serving girls are passing food and drink down right in a circle of older folks who are gossiping with Mrs. Candymayme and their leader. They are dancing the carabine. A graceful man takes a girl by the hand and makes her turn around very rapidly. The woman waves a red handkerchief over his head and everyone sings at once.

As they dance, the bride, Bijou, in her bridal outfit, runs across the stage from the farmhouse, downstage and then upstage and across to the back of the farmhouse and disappears. A few boys who aren't dancing call after her and Yancey runs behind her as she is downstage calling.)

Yancey. Kiss the bride. Gimme a kiss, Bijou. Gimme a kiss, Bijou.

(A girl pulls Yancey's hand and they join the other dancers. As this dance comes to an end, the couples scatter two by two to finish a drink or get another, panting happily. A woman whispers something to Mrs. Candymayme.)

Mrs. Candymayme. Now ain't it funny, in all this carrying on the bride is all by herself crying.
A Woman. *(by Mrs. Candymayme)* She's so happy, bless her heart.
Mrs. Candymayme. *(significantly)* If you wants to take it that way. *(Ulysses passes her and she takes a glass from his tray.)* Mmmmmm. Tasty. But strong. Well *(slapping woman next to her on the thigh)*, we don't get married every day, do we?
Woman. No, we don't.
Mrs. Candymayme. Some don't get married at all. *(She laughs at her joke.)*
Bettysue. *(pointing to drink)* Mama, can I have some of that?
Mrs. Candymayme. Ever see a billy goat go to the barber? Ever hear a cat ask to have his whiskers cut off? Ever see a fish walking on dry land?
Bettysue. No, mama.
Mrs. Candymayme. Then go away and don't ask for what little girls ain't supposed to have. Go on now and romp. *(Bettysue goes off slowly.)*
Ulysses. *(Circulating near gossiping group again. Mrs. Candymayme takes another glass.)* There's plenty and to spare.

Yancey. *(yelling across to Ulysses)* Keep it going, Ulysses. We going to dance till we drop and the stars go out. We going to need all you got. *(Ulysses crosses to Yancey.)*

Troy. *(to fiddler and players)* Saw a tune out. *(The musicians strike up their music and Troy begins a solo dance. The young folks gather around him.)*

Yancey. *(beginning clapping)* Make them hear it up in New Orleans.

Girl. Empty that fiddle.

Another. Get that music out.

Girl. *(watching Troy)* Ohoooo, can't he swing his feet! I'm gonna get him to whirl me around when he's through.

Yancey. *(grabbing her)* Lemme show you exactly how it's done.

(The dancing begins generally again but upstage, and the musicians' backs are to the audience facing the dancers. The bridegroom, Willie Silvers, comes whimpering to the gossip group where Bijou's father and mother are.)

Willie Silvers. *(to Bijou's father, stuttering)* She says she's not going to do it even if we are married. *(Mrs. Candymayme stops talking.)*

Bijou's Father. What are you talking about? Speak up like you got a tongue in your mouth!

Willie. She shut herself up in her room. She won't even talk to me through the door.

Father. Well go on then and get the key and fetch your bride.

Willie. Where's the key?

Father. *(noticing Mrs. Candymayme's listening)* If you don't get away from here like you got some good sense. . . .

(Willie Silvers crosses stage. Mrs. Candymayme whispering to the woman next to her. The whole gossip corner starts buzzing.)

Troy. *(coming in)* Now we going to have some real fun. Reve Grant's on his way.

Apocalypse. Who told him to come?

Ulysses. Nobody.

Apocalypse. *(to the girls)* Don't even give him a howdy-do. *(The girls giggle.)*

Girl. We won't even look at him.

(The young people are facing stage right; but, as Reve enters, they turn their backs on him. Reve looks as if he had run all the way. He puts down his guitar by the fiddlers' platform.)

Reve. *(to Group)* Who's the best dancer amongst all you pretty girls?

Girl. *(nearest to him)* I don't reckon I can even dance. *(She giggles.)*

Another. *(to the girl beside her)* I've danced so much tonight my feet are worn down to the marrow bone.
Another. Every dance I got been promised.
Reve. *(to another girl)* Will you dance with me?
Girl. *(hesitating)* Well, I . . .
Apocalypse. *(pulling her to him)* You know I got this next one.
Reve. *(to another)* You?
Girl. I was just about ready to set out for home. *(She moves off. An old man meets her.)*
Reve. *(to another)* May I dance with you?
Girl. I don't believe we been introduced. *(Little Bettysue who has been watching goes up to Reve and looks at him admiringly.)*
Bettysue. Will you dance with me, Reve Grant? *(Reve turns and gives her a big smile and holds out his arm. As she is about to reach for it, Mrs. Candymame's voice cuts through the music.)*
Mrs. Candymayme. If you don't come over here, Bettysue, I'll whip you to an early grave. *(She rises indignantly and yanks Bettysue, leaving Reve in the center of the stage alone. The crowd laughs and turns to what they were doing. Reve is subdued now. He glances shyly at the group of young people. He goes downstage right and sits on a bench. From down right a group enters. Sophie-Louise, her young sister, Charlotte, and her father, Grave. Charlotte holds a bean-bag, tossing it up and down.)*
Mrs. Candymayme. *(seeing the new group)* Those there folks just moved down beside the Giddens. Very religious.
Woman. *(beside Mrs. Candymayme)* They seem real nice.
Mrs. Candymayme. If you wants to take them that way. *(As Reve looks at Sophie-Louise his face changes from its former aggressive quality to one of softness and compassion. He approaches Grave.)*
Reve. May I dance with your daughter?
Grave. *(with French accent)* After we've said good evening to the host.

(The family moves toward the farmhouse. Once Sophie-Louise looks back and Reve is looking at her. Their eyes meet. It is enough. As they move into the farmhouse, Reve smooths his hair and brushes his torn breeches and then starts toward the farmhouse. Apocalypse, coming out of the door.)

Apocalypse. Where you going?
Reve. None of your business.
Apocalypse. Seem to be going the wrong way. *(He stands in front of Reve who looks at him eye for eye.)*
Yancey. *(snottily)* You ain't scared of Apocalypse are you, Reve?
Reve. I ain't scared of nothing.
Troy. Remember what happened at Ulysses'.

(The dancing begins again quietly in the background. Sophie-Louise comes to the door.)

Sophie-Louise. *(French accent)* Are you the boy who wanted to dance with me?
Reve. You bet. Don't you remember? *(gently)* Come on.
Sophie-Louise. I can't go far. Mama said not to.
Reve. Mama. You tied to your mama.
Sophie-Louise. Don't laugh at me. Please don't.
Reve. Are you sure you grown?
Sophie-Louise. I'll be confirmed soon.
Reve. You're Catholic. All Saint's Day and everything.
Sophie-Louise. Yes.
Reve. What's your name?
Sophie-Louise. Sophie-Louise Grave.
Reve. My name's Reve Grant.
Sophie-Louise. *(withdrawing her hands)* Oh.
Reve. What's the matter?
Sophie-Louise. I—I—forgot something. I must go inside to fetch it.
Reve. Please come back, please. *(She runs into the farmhouse. A group of the young folks titter. Reve picks up his guitar and starts off.)*
Willie Silvers. *(approaching Bijou's mother who is at the Candymayme group)* She's just sitting. I saw through the keyhole.
Bijou's Mother. She who?
Willie Silvers. Bijou won't unlock the door and let me in.
Bijou's Father. *(low and angry)* My great God. Go on away from here. What a son-in-law I have.
Bijou's Mother. He'll be all right. Don't go making a mountain out of a mole hill.
Bijou's Father. *(looking at Willie Silvers)* A mole hill is right.

(Yancey saunters over to the exiting Reve.)

Yancey. Want some sazerac, Reve?
Reve. NO!
Yancey. Just a swallow.
Reve. Not a swallow.
Yancey. *(pulling out a bottle and drinking)* Mmmmmmmmmm.
Reve. *(quickly)* Gimme some. *(grabs the bottle and drinks)*
Troy. Have another Reve. It's free.
Reve. Nope.
Yancey. Afraid your mama going to catch you? *(holds out bottle to Reve who takes a long one)*
Girl. *(to Yancey)* Come on, Yancey. Let's go.

Reve. *(to girl)* Are you afraid of me?
Yancey. *(egging him on)* You showed us what you could do down at Ulysses'.
Reve. Just get me started. Then you'll really see.
Yancey. Here we go! *(The young people have formed a semi-circle about Reve.)* Come on, Reve.
Troy. Tell us what you can do so spectacular.
Girl. We itching to hear.
Reve. *(offhand)* Some other time.
Crowd. Tell us now.
Reve. I can conjure the devil and put him in his place.
Troy. That ain't nothing much.
Reve. *(ignoring Troy)* Once I conjured the devil through a wormhole in a pecan nut, right straight into that nut.
Yancey. You got to do better than that.
Reve. That devil swore and then he wept, he promised, he got down on his knees, he offered me his platinum pitchfork, he took off one horn of gold and rubies and waved it before me, trying to tempt me. He did every which thing, but in the end. . . .
Girl. Uh Huh—
Reve. Tears was running down his old cheeks like pearls, but he had to crawl on in and then I stopped up the hole. You should have heard the noise he made in there, a-buzzing and a-rumbling and calling names. Tears was just running down his face cause that pecan nut was just sweating. He cried so it was a living shame.
Girl. Ohooooo. Have you still got him in there, Reve?
Reve. He's right here in my pocket.
Troy. Let us see.
Reve. I promised him I'd let him out when I found somebody wickeder than him. I think I'll let him out.
Yancey. Who's that, Reve?
Reve. Apocalypse. *(The crowd roars.)*
Yancey. *(leaving)* Apocalypse ought to hear this.
Reve. *(over them on the fiddlers' platform)* And . . . I can ride a horse through the clouds . . . *(laughter)* . . . and an alligator under the bayou.
Girl. I'm crazy about any man that can do all that.
Reve. One day I'll ride high over all and let the devil out over everything. *(He says this with such intensity and fierceness that the crowd quiets down and senses something evil.)*
Bijou's Father. Now you're talking like you haven't got any sense a-tall.
Reve. Don't be so frigging smart. You'll see. Just wait.
Troy. Just wait till Apocalypse come and punch your teeth out. *(laughter again)*

Mrs. Candymayme. I can see him dancing from a rope in the town square eating air for breakfast. *(The sordid realistic touch of Mrs. Candymayme calms the crowd down and as music begins they disperse leaving Reve alone.)*
Willie Silvers. *(who has been on the edge of the crowd listening)* Reve, is it really true that you can ride through the clouds?
Reve. I can do anything.
Willie Silvers. Can you open up locks?
Reve. Anything you name, Willie.

(Reve turns from Willie Silvers as Sophie-Louise crosses stage with Charlotte who is tossing her bean-bag. Reve goes to them leaving Willie Silvers by himself. Bettysue approaches Charlotte and looks intently at the bag. Charlotte solemnly tosses it to her and they begin tossing it back and forth. They continue to do so until Sophie-Louise leaves.)

Reve. *(to Sophie-Louise)* I'm glad you came back. Will you dance with me now?
Sophie-Louise. No.
Reve. Why?
Sophie-Louise. *(confused)* You—you look so wild.
Reve. Summer's coming. Everything's wild. Come on, Sophie. Come on, dance with me.
Sophie-Louise. No. You've been drinking. *(She moves away toward the little girls and, still aware of Reve, joins their tossing game.)*
Willie Silvers. *(seeing Reve free again)* Reve, please help me get Bijou out of her room.
Reve. *(watching Sophie-Louise)* Leave me alone. *(goes to Sophie-Louise who continues to toss while he speaks)* Will you dance with me, Sophie-Louise? I—I know I look like a ragamuffin but I don't always. You're ashamed of me. *(She continues tossing.)*
Sophie-Louise. I can't.
Reve. Why—?
Sophie-Louise. Mama and Papa. Papa. . . .
Reve. Papa. He's a pillar of the church I bet. Dance with me?
Sophie-Louise. *(stops tossing and catching; faces him)* Go home. Please go home.
Reve. *(Low and hurt and vicious and mad. He'll shock her into paying attention. He's let his pride go and pleads.)* I'll call up voodoo Gods Damballa be Rouge. We'll steal your soul away. We'll dress your sister in a dress of flames and she'll dance till she's a crisp of bone. *(Sophie-Louise grasps Charlotte's hand and backs away but Reve is wound up.)* I'll turn myself into a Loup Garou and in the night when you're asleep,

I'll drink your blood and rob your soul and you won't have no rosary to call on God. I'll . . . *(breaks off and quickly, tenderly)* Dance with me?

Sophie-Louise. *(running off into house; drops her rosary)* You are the devil! *(Reve picks it up and holds it a second before he puts it in his pocket. Bettysue is alone with the bean bag. Mrs. Candymayme comes out of the house, sniffs past Reve, takes the bean bag from Bettysue, smells it, hands it back, grabs her hand, and bustles back into the farmhouse.)*

Willie Silvers. *(coming to Reve again)* Reve, I'll give you my pirogue if you help me.

Reve. Keep still, Willie.

Willie Silvers. It's tied to a tree right by the bayou. You can have it now and paddle home.

Reve. Come on, stuttering boy. *(They exit behind the farmhouse. A few scattered couples are dancing. A crowd appears in the doorway, Apocalypse leading them.)*

Ulysses. *(to Apocalypse)* Keep your big mouth shut Apocalypse.

Apocalypse. Where's that lying, low down Reve Grant?

Yancey. Said you were worse than the devil.

Apocalypse. I'll beat him till his teeth bleed.

Yancey. Settle it here and now. *(Sophie-Louise, Charlotte and Grave enter.)*

Troy. Let them talk it out.

Apocalypse. *(rolling up his sleeves)* No more talking.

Yancey. Find Reve Grant.

Charlotte. Don't let them fight.

Bettysue. Mama, is Reve Grant gonna get hurt? *(Mrs. Candymayme just laughs.)*

Crowd. Find Reve Grant! Find Reve Grant!

Apocalypse. I'll beat him till his teeth bleed.

Grave. *(to Sophie-Louise)* You see now. *(She doesn't answer.)*

Crowd. Find Reve Grant! Find Reve Grant! Find Reve Grant!

Maud. *(Maud comes in with the pounder from the rice huller in her hand.)* Where's Reve? I'll give him such a beating he won't be able to sit down.

Apocalypse. You too little to fight him. Let me do it.

Yancey. Let Apocalypse tend to him.

Troy. Yes, let him do it.

One. Beat him up.

Another. Lam him.

Troy. *(doubled over in laughter)* Tear him limb from limb.

Apocalypse. Hang him.

Maud. Hang who? Reve! You just try. I'll take this bony fist and . . . Where is Reve *(calling)* Reve! Reve!

Willie Silvers. *(running in, stuttering)* Oh Lord, Lord. . . .
Bijou's Father. Great God, pull yourself together. What's the matter?
Willie Silvers. Reve, Reve, he just . . .
Maud. *(going up to him)* Have you killed my son?
Willie Silvers. No, No! *(He runs up the slope.)* Look, look at him. *(More run up and focus off stage up right.)*
Some. Look at them.
Yancey. He's got Bijou!
Another. He's carrying her away in the pirogue.
Willie Silvers. Right down the bayou.
Maud. Watch out, Reve, watch out.
Troy. He's got his guitar too. Sure didn't forget that guitar.
Bijou's Father. *(coming downstage)* He'll pay for this. My God, he'll pay with his good-for-nothing life.
Maud. *(turning on him)* I won't let you harm one hair on his head. Do you hear, not one hair. No you won't.

(There is a roll of thunder as Bijou's father and men start toward upstage right after Reve. They retreat.)

Troy. Plenty of thunder makes more sugar in the cane.
Maud. *(running upstage)* Reve, a storm's coming up. Reve don't get lost in the storm. Reve, Reve, Reve.

(Sophie-Louise and Grave go to Maud and try to get her to come down. The thunder is rolling away. Men come out of the house putting on raincoats. They move upstage again.)

Maud. *(limp and quiet, whispering to them as they pass)* Don't go hurt my son. Don't lay no traps like he was a muskrat. *(We hear the bark of hound dogs.)* Don't do that. *(The men go silently by. As the lights dim and storm music rises, Maud is being led downstage by Sophie-Louise and Grave.)* We gotta get there first and warn Reve. Only I don't know where that boy's gonna hide, no I don't.

(The thunder is only in the music now and that becomes lower allowing a gay, risqué song to rise above it. The voice is accompanied by a guitar. When the lights come up the sky is sullen gray. We are on an island. There is one cypress tree down right with Spanish moss. Only the area about the tree is lit. Reve is sitting on a stump near the tree playing his guitar unconcerned about the low thunder of Bijou. There is a thin mist rising. Bijou in her bridal gown, her hair falling down, her whole appearance torn and pathetic, is tugging at one of Reve's sleeves.)

Reve. *(still playing)* Stop that.

Bijou. *(crying)* I gave up everything for you. Where shall I go now? What shall I do?

Reve. *(still playing)* Go any which way. *(He continues to sing and she continues to cry.)*

Bijou. Oh, oh, what can I do now!

Reve. *(finally)* Oh shut up. Shut! You go your way, I go mine. Now leave me alone. *(He continues his song on his guitar. Bijou stops crying. She paces back and forth upstage from Reve. She works herself into a ripe anger. Suddenly she rushes down and before Reve can prevent it she has broken all the strings on his guitar with one swift jerk.)*

(starting to strike her but thinking better of it) What a piddling mean thing to do. Just like a woman. Every last one. *(afterthought)* Except Sophie-Louise.

Bijou. Who?

Reve. Who, who, who. Not you, that's who. Go on back to your papa.

Bijou. *(changing tactics)* Reve, honey. I'm sorry about the guitar but I was so mad.

Reve. Take your hands off me.

Bijou. You ruined my life—tore it to little pieces.

Reve. What can I do with you now?

Bijou. Palmetto Farm. That could be yours, Reve.

Reve. Where's your rosary? Where's your flowing hair? Where's your little sister holding your hand?

Bijou. *(crying again on her knees by the stump)* Oh, Reve.

Reve. *(driving it in)* Are you going to be confirmed?

Bijou. You've gone out of your head.

Reve. Who feels like praying when you pass by? Tell me that. *(Reve has been hugging his guitar.)*

Bijou. I'm sorry I broke the guitar.

Reve. *(quietly, thinking of Sophie-Louise)* It's not the guitar. What else can you give me, Bijou? *(He moves away from her.)*

Bijou. *(after him, defiant)* You can't jump out of this so easy. They'll take everything your mother got and hunt you down. *(pause)* Marry me, Reve. Marry me. *(He shakes her off in disgust.)* Why did you do it?

Reve. Willie Silvers told me to come and get you. So I did. Nobody's sorry.

Bijou. I couldn't help it.

Reve. *(contemptuously)* You couldn't help it.

Bijou. I couldn't marry no Willie Silvers.

Reve. Go on away.

Bijou. I hate you, Reve. I'll call them all out to hunt you down.

Reve. Call Apocalypse. Call all Palmetto Farm.

Bijou. Are you so set?

Reve. Like a tombstone rock.

Bijou. I'll row that boat back and I'll row you to hell. *(She runs out.)*
Reve. *(pausing, then calling)* I don't want to see another woman as long as I live.
Bijou. *(calling back)* All but her.
Reve. *(after a second with his broken-string guitar still in his hand; tenderly)* Yes, Bijou, all but Sophie-Louise.

(The distant voices become clearer now and the sound of the dogs' echo. Reve dashes upstage and is lost in the mist that rises. There is the faint roll of thunder and out of it Maud's voice comes, a lost and tired voice.)

Maud. *(Mist about her clears so that we see her moving restlessly and Sophie-Louise's calm figure.)* Blood hounds and voices after him. Who's going to help? My God-forsaken Jesus, who? If Reve calls, the thunder rolls the call away or the echo calls the hunters. If he finds the path, the steaming mist will set him off it, yes it will. And then there's the quicksand all around to gobble him up, alligators with red heads and black rattle snakes and giraffes . . .
Sophie-Louise. There are no giraffes around here.
Maud. Reve said there was. Oh Lord, Lord, Lord. Folks just yelling, just spiteful, wanting to kill my Reve. They ain't a-going to do it. No, they're not. Even if the devil trying to lead him astray, no one going to lay one finger on my boy.
Sophie-Louise. Here's a place to sit down. *(leading her gently to the stump)* Sit down now, Mrs. Grant.
Grave. *(voice calling)* Sophie-Louise! *(echo)* Sophie-Louise!
Maud. Is that Reve? Child, that's Reve. *(calls)* Reve—
Sophie-Louise. It's only my Father. *(calls back)* Father, here we are. *(echo)* Father, here we are.
Maud. I thought that was Reve. I don't know what I woulda done if you hadn't come, no I don't.
Sophie-Louise. I couldn't let you come alone.
Maud. You so clean in heart.
Sophie-Louise. *(simply)* I wanted to come.
Maud. *(starting to cry)* It's all my fault. Yes, it is—everything. But I done the best I knew how. My husband just leave us alone and he drink, drink and left us all by ourselves. I told Reve stories—all kinds of stories, yes I did, to make him happy. *(forgetting her tears as she goes on)* Told him about the slaves in chains wailing in the ghost house and Madame La Laurie, about Loup Garous that half-human and half-animal; they change when they get the desire and they get it all the time, so I hear. *(warming)* Yes, and I made up stories of flying horses and alligators that talk and about the voodoo: Marie Lavlan, who's the queen, and I said about magic fire that flame up high enough to meet

the stars. Oh, I just carried on. I said about brides stole away on they wedding night. *(pause)* He were such a blessed little boy, spry like a rabbit, but just as still when I made the stories. Oh he was. Annie Christmas got a mustache like a man and she hauled a river boat clear up the Mississippi from New Orleans to Natchez and wasn't even out of breath. I said about the sweating jungles of Africa where my mama was born. Oh, Sophie-Louise, I'm just prattling.

Sophie-Louise. Go on. Please.

Maud. *(laughing)* You would have thought we was crazy as bessie bugs when we played the kingdom game. That were a game! A place we fashioned out of our head never seen in nobody's air or water or on the earth. Child, this were a secret meeting place under the bayou Goula with all kinds of crazy shapes. Reve said: "They should have two heads or three heads." "As many as you like, my boy," I said. He was no bigger than a gnat but he love them stories. . . . *(There is a sound.)* Great God. *(She runs upstage and is lost in the mist.)* Reve, Reve. . . . *(She returns pulling her shawl about her shoulders.)* It's nothing and nobody.

(Grave enters.)

Grave. He can't find his way.
Maud. He—can't—find—his—way.
Grave. I think he's lost.
Maud. No, he ain't. Reve's smart as a whip. He can do anything.
Grave. I meant his soul.
Maud. God won't forsake him.
Grave. Has he prayed?
Maud. Reve can ride a flying horse through the air.
Grave. Pray for him. We must save his soul.
Maud. Save his body. Drag the bayous, search the islands and if he been conjured, ring the church bell. Sophie-Louise, go ring that bell.

(Grave has wandered into the mist.)

Grave. *(calling)* Here's a footprint.
Maud. Jesus Lord. *(She moves upstage.)* If you find him I'll work my fingers to the bone and pay you back.
Grave. It's my Christian duty.
Maud. *(loud and laughing through tears)* Everybody that ain't here helping is a heathen.
Grave. Here's another footprint. Another.
Maud. Then that's the way we'll go.
Grave. I'll go this way. You two go home. I'll find him. *(He goes into the mist.)*

Maud. I should go with him. *(stumbles)* Your papa's a fine man, one of the finest men I know.
Sophie-Louise. *(walking with her downstage)* Tell me more.
Maud. About Reve?
Sophie-Louise. Yes. Tell me everything.
Maud. Everything. *(smiling up at Sophie-Louise)* You'd get real worn out listening to an old lady's prattling.
Sophie-Louise. I could listen all day and all night.

(As Maud and Sophie-Louise start off the thunder comes up and lightning begins to zig-zag and the sound of a voice rushing down over all.)

Maud. *(letting out a cry)* Oh my son, my son. He'll get wet to the bone. *(Rushing back on stage into the direction Grave went, Sophie-Louise catches her.)*
Sophie-Louise. *(firmly)* You're going home. In the storm is no place for Reve Grant's mama.
Maud. Go on home without Reve?
Sophie-Louise. There's nothing else to do.
Maud. Yes. You're right, child. I'll go on home and wait till he comes back. Reve's some place talking to himself, that's where he is.
Sophie-Louise. *(taking her offstage)* I know he'll be back.

(They are off and the storm bangs and clamors. Reve comes rushing in with his broken guitar. He looks about, puts his guitar at the foot of the tree.)

Reve. *(noticing it is the same place he was before)* Going in full circles, back where Bijou broke my guitar strings. But I still got my guitar. I'm free as a bird whipping through the air. *(He jumps up and takes hold of a jutting branch of the tree and swings.)* I could rip this branch off. I could push this little old island down into the Gulf of Mexico like Annie Christmas. Bijou and her papa can go straight to hell! Rain and thunder, *(There is bright other worldly laughter.)* eagle birds flying through the rain *(laughter)* and lightning—you reckoned my strength from the time I was born on Maud's lap. That was nothing—I wouldn't give a pelican for that. You wait, *(exulting with his feet on the branch now and one hand on the main trunk, the other lifted)* and see what Reve Grant's going to be. *(The biggest laughter of all. Reve hears it now. The thunder has stopped, the lightning doesn't zig-zag, the rain is gone. An aquamarine color fills the sky. Reve jumps down and stands looking at the strange air. Repeats his last line with some wonder.)* You wait and see what Reve Grant's going to be. *(The laughter is near now.)* That ain't nothing to laugh about.

(Three girls, Tulip, Oleander and Clove, come running in with orange, red and lemon tights underneath the flying film of pale green gauzes.)

Girls. *(surrounding Reve)* Oh, isn't it?
Reve. Where'd you come from?
Girls. Over yonder.
Reve. Over yonder's a lot of places.
Tulip. Not our over yonder. *(They all laugh.)*
Reve. *(laughing too)* Pretty girls like you should be with strong muscled men.
Oleander. Our men left us.
Reve. Nobody with his right senses would leave pretty girls like you. *(They all laugh and get closer to him.)* Now tell me just where are your men?
Tulip. *(giggling)* Mine turned himself into a plow and just now he's plowing up the farm.
Oleander. *(giggling)* Mine's gone to see what Annie Christmas got that I ain't got.
Clove. Mine turned himself into a star and does nothing all night but twinkle on and twinkle off.
Reve. *(putting his arms about them)* Well now that's too bad for them cause I'm just the boy for you.
Clove. Sure you can do it?
Reve. I've got the power.
Oleander. *(looking up at him)* Mmmmmmm.
Tulip. I don't know so much about that.
Reve. *(trying to grasp them tighter)* You'll see what I've got.

(Girls laughing squirm away and run laughing. Reve chases them.)

Oleander. You'll get your belly full.
Tulip. He's got the power, he says.
Clove. He'll need it. *(They just scream with laughter.)*
Reve. *(running in and out)* I'm just the boy for you.
Tulip. We're thirsty.
Oleander. Give us a drink.
Clove. Then see what we can do.
Reve. You'll have all the sazerac you can drink.
Tulip. That's not what we want.
Clove. *(as the girls gather together)* Come on with us.
Reve. Where you going?
Oleander. We going to jump in Bayou Goula.
Reve. You'll drown and I couldn't stand that.
Tulip. Come on and see. *(They start running off with Reve after them.)*
Reve. *(halting)* Wait till I get my guitar and then I'll play you girls some music later on.

(The girls giggle. As Reve reaches for the guitar a sound comes from the

trees. A strange gargling sound, Ahhhhhhh, followed by a laugh. The girls who have been giggling while Reve went for his guitar look at each other and then silently flee. Reve stops in the position of bending for the instrument. Stars begin to glow in the sky. The tree seems to have stars in its branches too. Night birds begin to sing, not so much like the birds as the artificial sounds from an old music box. Then we hear a woman laughing high and sensuous. Reve reaches for his guitar with his left hand. A voice stops him.)

Voice. So you're left-handed, too. Now ain't that something.
Reve. *(looking up)* Well, I'll be.
Voice. Say a left-handed boy owes the devil a day's work. But I reckon you done paid with many a day's work. *(laughter again)* Now how did you think you could play that old guitar right with a left-handed stroke and all the strings busted in two?
Reve. Tell me who you are.
Voice. Think I'll just fetch it up here for myself.

(Reve reaches for it again but it goes up like magic into the tree.)

Reve. *(not too bold)* You give me my guitar back or I'll lam you.

(A strange light begins to glitter in the tree and two golden hands part the Spanish moss and we see her. She is dressed in green splashed with sequins and over her shoulders a film of gauze. Her hair is full of sequins. Her skin is honey colored and her eyes—deep violet. Her lips are bright carnival red. She has begun to play the guitar and sing an enticing song and look teasingly down at Reve.)

The strings—the strings were broke.
Hethabella. Were they? Well ain't that funny I didn't notice.
Reve. They were broke. *(gazing up at her)* Tell me your name.
Hethabella. You're so smart, I bet you could guess it.
Reve. I'll—I'll give you everything.
Hethabella. Everything's so large. I couldn't begin to see it. What do you reckon everything is?
Reve. You can see me all right. *(She laughs.)* My name's Reve Grant.
Hethabella. Mmmmmmmmmmm . . .
Reve. You've heard of me, I guess.
Hethabella. Mmmmmmmmmmmm.
Reve. What's your name?
Hethabella. Hethabella and I'm the baddest woman that ever walked.
Reve. My, but you're pretty. *(through her laughter)* I can be like nothing you ever had before . . .
Hethabella. Mmmmmmmmmm.
Reve. . . . you wouldn't have to mess up them pretty hands doing nothing but playing my guitar.

Hethabella. You wouldn't beat me?
Reve. A king's son never does nothing like that.
Hethabella. A king's son!
Reve. Uh Huh.
Hethabella. Well, my papa's a king too. *(The guitar just glides down through the air to where it was.)* What else would you do?
Reve. Plenty to eat and drink.
Hethabella. I'll have the drink. *(Reve laughs. She utters the Ahhhhh sound.)* My papa's got a castle that's a secret right under Bayou Goula waters.
Reve. My mama's got a great big castle that's no secret setting right on top of dry land.
Hethabella. I'll take you down there if you got something to drink and we can carry on.
Reve. Mmmmm.
Hethabella. Want to know my papa's name? King Loup.
Reve. Want to know my mama's name? *(laughing)* Queen Maud.
Hethabella. When my papa gets his temper up, he froth at the mouth and that's what makes a flood.
Reve. When my mama gets a temper up, the whole town know it.
Hethabella. My papa eat golden fishes and silver snakes and can he drink!
Reve. My mama can ride through the air on a horse.
Hethabella. *(laughing)* If your queen mama's so smart, why you wear them torn breeches?
Reve. *(evasively)* You should just watch me in my dancing clothes.
Hethabella. On special nights and days I usually wear dresses of platinum cloth and slippers with rubies and in each hand I carry a diamond big as mockturtle eggs.
Reve. What do you do with them diamonds?
Hethabella. They just for show.
Reve. What's that you got on now? It's real pretty with no skirt a-tall.
Hethabella. *(laughing)* That remind me. Where I live everything's like nothing you ever seen before. Now don't fret when you enter my papa's castle if you think everything you gazing on look like a lot of cast away stuff and all mixed up.
Reve. Now that's a coincidence. In my mama's castle everything looks like it's falling to pieces.
Hethabella. Black look like white and ugly just as fine.
Reve. The little look big and the dirty just as clean.
Hethabella. *(flying down from the tree)* I can see we going to get along just fine.
Reve. *(taking her in his arms)* Like the strips to the brake cane and the stars to your hair.

Hethabella. *(feeling his arm muscle)* My, but you're strong.
Reve. I reckon you should just stay right here with me.
Hethabella. I need something to drink.
Reve. Don't worry about that now.
Hethabella. Wouldn't do much harm if I return home after a while.
Reve. You and me can scamper and play.
Hethabella. *(laughing)* And I was just feeling so low I could have gnawed the crab grass. Never can tell what's going to happen. *(sinking to the ground)*
Reve. You sure can't. *(beside her)*
Hethabella. Then after a time we'll see my papa's place.
Reve. *(as he bends to kiss her)* We can see him any old time.

(She begins to laugh, but he shuts her laughter off with a big kiss and all the stars and the lighted sky go out. Sensuous scarlet music rises out of the darkness and when the lights go up again we are under the waters of Bayou Goula in the domain of King Loup Garou and the music picks up his raucously fantastic theme. The atmosphere is aquamarine. Roots from the water hyacinth above hang down delicate and weblike, contrasting with the bottom huge trunks of water cypress that seem like columns built rather than grown. They give the stage a mazelike appearance. Aquamarine colored water flowers grow up from the floor of the bayou, thick and rubbery, as if their substance were green blood and their odor poisonous. Between two of the cypress trunks is stretched the skin of a dead animal not unlike a purple octopus. Liquid can be milked out of the long tentacle fingers. Between two other trunks is a throne resembling a green toadstool. The whole place impresses with its dilapidated fantastic otherworldliness. The creatures that inhabit this place are strange combinations of the physical characteristics of men, birds, and undersea creatures. For instance, one may have the body of a frog and the head of a man; another the head of a snake and the body of a man with little snake-heads for toes and fingers; another the shell of a turtle and the feet and hands of a muskrat, or the body of a man and the webbed feet of some strange bird; some may have two heads not necessarily identical—one of an egret, one of a pelican. The King who is standing on his throne has the head and hands and feet of a man but the body of an alligator, the voice of a feminine creature with an evil tone like a worm is continually wiggling in his throat. About him are three of his chief councillors all talking at the top of their weird voices. The King stamps his feet and scratches the thick knots and scales of his body. His movements are almost a dance as are those of the others in this scene except Reve. Although King Loup acts like a petulant child at the beginning, you sense his force and his compelling fantastic evil.)

King Loup. *(over their voices utters a phlegmy gargling sound)*
Ohhhhhhhhhh. My knots and scales are duly itching for my daily pint.

First Councillor. *(bullfrog body, head of a man)* What do you think my belly's doing?
Second Councillor. *(shrimp body and head of a man, feminine legs with fancy garters with water butterflies on them)* My color's gone. What do you think I need?
Third Councillor. *(body of a man with two heads, one of a pelican, one of a snake)* My heads are so hungry they've begun to debate.
King Loup. *(whimpering)* I'm the King. I duly want my pint.
First. We do all the work. What about us?
Other Two. All of us!
King Loup. *(letting out the phlegmy gargle sound)* Ohhhhhhhhhh. *(The Councillors quickly go into a huddle.)*
First. We have a plan, Your Majesty.
King Loup. *(no whimpering now)* I knew you'd duly get a plan if I caused a stink. You'd better not try any of that change back stuff with me. You duly can't unless I give the word. And I'm not giving it. *(businesslike)* What's your plan?
Second. *(in his shrimp sly voice pointing to the skin between the trees)* There's some left. A pint or two. Before the others come let's divide it.
King Loup. You are wise councillors—almost as wise as your king. *(pointing to the Third Councillor)* Divide it and bring it here. Leave a cup or so in just in case. *(The Third Councillor goes to the skin and begins to milk a tentacle, then another and then another with frantic urgency. He holds four seaweed bowls on a tray or can while King Loup chatters away watching him with sly quick glances.)* It's getting duly scarcer and scarcer and what we do get is thinner and thinner. Too much water in it. I sent Hethabella up to see what she could do. What have you thought up?
First. I can't think until I've drunk.

(The Third Councillor passes the steaming bowls—the last he keeps for himself.)

King Loup. *(crafty)* Are they even? *(He inspects each bowl. Seeing that the Third Councillor has more.)* Ahhhhhhh—I knew you'd cheat. *(quickly grabbing the bowl)* Gimme that.
Third. You know I have two mouths to feed.
First. But my stomach's the biggest.
Second. I've got to get my color back.
King Loup. I'll set my daughter on you and then you'll see. *(pouring a little more in each cup)* She'll be back soon and you'll duly see.
Second. She's been gone a long time.
King Loup. But she duly sent me a message by a spider.

(They wait for more about Hethabella.)

First. Is Princess Hethabella . . . ?
King Loup. Drink up and shut up. *(They all begin to sip and make grunting or shrill noises. There is a great beating of wings and a large fantastic bird runs in so swiftly they drop their cups and in their greed curse and get down on all fours to lick up the spilled stuff, ignoring the Talking Bird.)*
Talking Bird. King Loup Garou, King Loup Garou. *(He pecks at them till they stop.)*
King Loup. Never bother me at meal time.
First. We'll pluck your feathers out.
King Loup. One by one.
First. What do you want?
King Loup. All right. What have you to say? Duly say it, or I'll pluck your feathers out.
Talking Bird. *(insolent)* Your daughter's been plucked.
King Loup. Princess Hethabella?
Talking Bird. Yes, Your Majesty.
King Loup. Where is she?
Talking Bird. On her way down here with the Christian boy.
King Loup. What denomination?
Talking Bird. Baptist, I think.
First. This will never do.
Third. Better not mess up with no Christian.
First. He'll break up our kingdom.
Third. He'll dissolve us. Prayers and bells will ruin us.
Second. *(shyly)* But he has drink. Probably fresh, Loup.
King Loup. *(irritated)* Use my full title when addressing me.
First. We can't stand on protocol at a time like this.
King Loup. We'll stand on our throne. *(He does so. They are all in attitudes of thought except the bird, who's busy at the spilled liquid.)* Ahhhhhhhhhhhhhhhhhhh—*(They all become alert again.)* So that's what Hethabella meant. Have the Christian boy brought here, that is, if he's arrived.
First. No.
Third. No, no!
First. No, no, no!
Second. Yes. *(They all look up at the Second Councillor.)* He has—drink.
King Loup. Yes he probably has; Hethabella's no empty brain, I guess. *(He beckons them all with a finger. They move to him and he leans over them whispering gibberish. They nod seriously and then they all smile and then laugh. The bird begins to sing.)*

King Loup. *(over the noise)* Summon my daughter. Bring my crown and sceptre of power. And scamper. *(They scamper off.)* My knots and scales are duly better.

(He begins to sing and caper a song about how clever Hethabella is. The crown and sceptre are brought back by attendants with the Councillors officiously following. They begin to deck him out to music that is discordant like early Stravinsky. The Court assembles from all directions in all shapes and guises like a masque. They chatter away with [. . .] various stinging sound[s]. The King struts among his Loup Garous. Hethabella enters and the Court is more silent. They bow and she gives them the warm shoulder. The shrimp maidens: Tulip, Oleander and Clove as they pass the half masculine, half feminine Second Councillor, giggle.)

Clove, Oleander and Tulip. *(bowing and giggling)* Good evening Mama and Papa.
King Loup. *(as Hethabella passes him bowing with a clever smirk)* I told you you'd duly get something changing into that shape and dressing up instead of hobbling along with broken teeth and rags.

(She laughs and wriggles away and goes among her shrimp maidens again. He takes his sceptre, dips it into the skin, waves it over the chattering, shrieking throng. They stop at once in whatever attitude they were in. He struts back to his throne. Reve is silently brought in by the three Councillors and stood before King Loup Garou, who carelessly waves his sceptre and they assume their normal attitudes. The Shrimp Maidens wiggle and wave to Reve showing their legs in unison like trained chorus girls. King Loup gives them a look; they stop. He is sitting on his throne and looking at Reve from head to toe. The whole throng follows him.)

Can you repeat your catechism?
Reve. Never learned one word of it.

(The Councillors smile approval.)

King Loup. What church do you duly enter every Sunday?
Reve. *(smiling)* I ride alligators each and every Sunday.
King Loup. *(remembering)* Ahhhhhhhhhh. *(The Court repeats his sound.)* You want my daughter?
Reve. I've already had her.

(The Court is shocked and sets up an uproar, but King Loup waves his sceptre as they are ready to pounce on Reve. Hethabella and the Shrimp Maidens smile broadly, trying to be virgins in appearance.)

King Loup. *(to all)* Your time will duly come. *(to Reve)* Will you marry her?

Reve. If she's got all the money and power she says she has.

(Hethabella giggles among her Shrimp Maidens.)

King Loup. *(slyly)* I have the power, but I could divide it. Half for you while I'm alive and all when I'm dead.
Reve. When will you die?
King Loup. Ahhhhhhhhhhhhh. Huh. Well, now that's a question, but there are just a few little things you've got to approve ahead of time. *(He looks at the Councillors. They beam. He turns back to Reve.)* Once you're in here, you can't want to live anywhere else. You can't even go out or see the sky again or breathe fresh air.
Reve. That's easy if I have the power here. What's next?
First. *(pompous bullfrog voice)* Who's better, Loup Garous or men?
Reve. *(glancing at Hethabella)* They're just about the same the way I'm looking.
King Loup. *(slyly)* Except we don't need anything except what we need to keep us alive!
Reve. And what is that?
King Loup. *(rising again; comes to[ward] Reve a step and gurgles not without a slimy cruelty)* Ahhhhhhhhhhhhhhh. Drink.

(The whole Court stirs.)

Reve. Sazerac? Brandy? Whiskey? That's easy.
King Loup. Blood.
Reve. Blood. What kind of blood?
King Loup. The blood of anyone who wants power.
Reve. *(angry)* Do you take me for a downright fool?
King Loup. Your blood.

(The Court sighs low like wind under water.)

Court. Your blood.
Reve. NO!
King Loup. *(almost hypnotically)* Power, Power, Reve Grant.
Reve. You know my name?
King Loup. Power, Reve Grant. You must give something for power.
Reve. How did you know my name?
King Loup. I offer him power, he asks how I know his name.
Reve. *(angry)* How *do* you know my name!!
King Loup. You rode an alligator through Bayou Goula.
Reve. *(swaggering now)* Yes, I did, why we're old friends. Now can I go—
King Loup. Blood, Reve, blood for power.
Reve. *(deciding on another approach)* I said no. *(The whole Court is*

focused on him; he pauses then.) Well now—just to talk it over every which way. Um—what kind of power. I just want to know.

King Loup. Look at the power. *(He holds his sceptre and walks over to the skin.)*

Reve. I can see that. But what I'm itching to know is . . . after . . . after . . . what's going to be left of me.

Court. Ahhhhhhhhhhhhhh.

Reve. *(He is a little scared.)* Will I be dead, will I be alive? Will I be forever and ever?

King Loup. Forever and ever, dead alive? What does that duly mean? Nothing here. Look at my subjects, look how they smile.

Reve. I want to know about me, yes I do.

King Loup. Don't you trust me, Reve Grant?

Reve. *(lying)* Oh, I trust you all right.

King Loup. Then gamble—

Court. Heads or tails.

King Loup. Toss the coin for your life. Gamble for power. Gamble and be with us.

Reve. I want to know for sure.

King Loup. You gain and you give up; You climb and you descend; You climb into power, You climb into blood. Blood is power, Reve. Blood for power, friend, Look . . . *(He dips the sceptre in the skin and holds it high over the Court.)* Dance . . . Dance . . . *(Music begins like wind, bubbling under water. The Court starts to dance quick and frantic. King Loup holds the sceptre lower and the dance gets faster. Higher and the dance is faster still. He holds it very low and the dance is slow motion.)* All this for you, for your blood. Well, Reve Grant? *(Reve shakes his head, no. Sly)* I already know your blood, hot thick, rich. I bit your thigh when we rode the waters.

Reve. *(snaps fingers)* I made up that story out of my head.

King Loup. Did you, Reve? Did you? What about sweet, innocent Hethabella? Doesn't she have a part of you? *(hissing)* Gamble, Gamble, Reve.

Reve. *(starting out)* I'm going . . .

King Loup. *(With his sceptre in hand he blocks Reve's way and very quietly.)* Why don't you try it, my friend, Reve?

(He puts the sceptre in Reve's hand. Reve is fascinated and can't decide. Suddenly he grips it hard and waves it high over Hethabella and the Shrimp Girls. They take the stage dancing a sexy dance with the Court dancing a stiff counterpoint. King Loup takes the sceptre after he noticed Reve's fascination with the power. He then stops the dance with one swift gesture. The Court move back to their normal positions.)

King Loup. Will you have it, Reve Grant? Not for a minute, for as long as you live.
Councillors. Will you have it?

(Reve panting as Hethabella walks toward him with a kind of evil love in her movements and he looks at the sceptre in King Loup's hand. The crowd leans forward for his decision.)

King Loup. Will you have the power, Reve, in exchange—?
Councillors. In exchange.
Court. For blood!
Reve. *(suddenly seizing the sceptre from the King runs to the skin of blood)* Yes! *(laughing as he dips it in)* Yes!! Yes!!!

(He takes it out of the skin and waves it over the crowd. Nothing happens. He dips it again and waves again. Nothing happens.)

King Loup. *(sly)* There's no blood left. None at all. Not a single drop.
Second. He tried to trick us.

(Reve is looking frantically for a way out as the Court begins to close in.)

First. *(low hiss)* You tried to get power without paying for it.
Third. *(lower hiss)* You tried to cheat us.
King Loup. We duly win.
Hethabella. *(running to King)* No, please. If he'll stay with me, save him.
King Loup. Have your baby brat. I curse it before it's born. I loved you once, my daughter, but you have duly betrayed me.
Hethabella. Please don't hurt him. *(to Court)* Please!
King Loup. *(to Hethabella)* I'll duly turn you back and you'll look like yourself again. *(to Reve)* But you, Reve Grant—you'll go round and about searching for power. You are mine now. Ours. One of us. Once you taste my kind of power and once I taste your blood, you are dead inside, dead to the roots of your heart.
Reve. *(calling)* Open that prayer book, Sophie-Louise. Ring the bells, Mama. Help me, Mama, I'm dying. *(They are closing in and a dark music impels them.)* Sophie-Louise, Sophie-Louise, pray for me.

(At the sound of Sophie-Louise [praying] for Reve, Hethabella, who has been sobbing on the toadstool throne, joins the crowd to avenge herself instead of to save Reve. Reve is center. They begin to stalk him in a dance movement. The aquamarine light is everywhere now like a living force.)

King Loup. Ahhhhhhhhhhhhhhh.

(As if that sound is the signal the crowd descends on Reve, dancing about him until we don't see him at all; only his cries rise up. As the dance is at its

height, bells begin to ring and a chant rises up. The dancers begin to wail as if they had been struck and King Loup utters his sound. Everyone runs now as the church bells and prayers rise up. Reve is left alone in a pool of light. He is panting, holding up the rosary of Sophie-Louise. The one he picked up at the wedding. The lights go out altogether and Sophie-Louise's theme swells up.

The front has been taken off Maud's house. We see inside. Garlic is hanging from the ceiling; there is a small bed by the window and a rough chest near it. Little else is left in the room besides a chair and a stool. Clothes are strewn about and some bric-a-brac. It is the next morning and sun up. Reve comes running in from upstage right but stops behind a tree as he hears singing. The song is not a happy one. Sophie-Louise is in the house putting wet clothes in a basket. She comes out and starts hanging them on a line which is on the stage left side of the house. Charlotte comes running in from downstage right carrying a small package.)

Charlotte. Sophie-Louise, Sophie-Louise . . .
Sophie-Louise. What's the matter, Charlotte? Stop running. You look like you've seen a ghost rising out of Bayou Goula.
Charlotte. *(breathlessly)* I . . . I just saw Reve Grant.
Sophie-Louise. *(stopping her work)* Are you sure?
Charlotte. I . . . I think I did. He was talking to himself.
Sophie-Louise. You're frightened.
Charlotte. *(starting to cry)* I'm all right now.
Sophie-Louise. Be a good girl and bring the food into the house. Did Mama give you everything?
Charlotte. Yes.
Sophie-Louise. Mrs. Grant will need all of it. Take it into the house and set it on the table. *(She continues her work but is obviously thinking of Reve Grant. Charlotte comes from the side of the house and is about to enter when Reve who has come from behind the tree tiptoes quietly to her.)*
Reve. *(whispering)* Charlotte, where are you going with that basket of food. I haven't eaten since yesterday, no I haven't. *(Charlotte stands still, too frightened to call or speak.)* I won't hurt you. Who were you talking to back there—my Mama?
Charlotte. Sophie-Louise.
Sophie-Louise. What do you want, Charlotte?
Charlotte. It's Reve Grant.
Sophie-Louise. Go away, Reve, I'll run away.
Reve. I've come back safe and whole.
Sophie-Louise. Go away, Reve. Please.
Reve. *(laughing)* Still afraid to dance?

Sophie-Louise. Your mama's gone to sell most of her things to keep herself together and you've come again to cause more trouble.
Reve. Do you know where I was last night? Under Bayou Goula with the King's daughter.
Sophie-Louise. *(not believing)* It was a good thing then that we rang the bells. Now please go away.
Reve. They won't catch me. *(suddenly very tender)* Sophie-Louise, dance with me?
Sophie-Louise. *(crying and putting her work down)* Oh, Reve. *(She runs off.)*
Reve. Well, aren't you going to say yes.
Charlotte. *(breaking away from Reve)* She's gone and left me.
Reve. So she's gone, yes, she has. Charlotte—are—look, Charlotte, give this to Sophie-Louise. It's her rosary. It's here. *(putting rosary in her hand)*
Charlotte. Let me go.
Reve. Take it to her.
Charlotte. Let me go!
Reve. *(gripping her arm tighter)* Don't try anything with me, you little brat.
Charlotte. I'm scared of you. I'm scared. Let me go.
Reve. Scared of me? *(taking something else from his pocket)* Look—here's a silver toy I moulded. Don't you want it?
Charlotte. *(sobbing)* No.
Reve. *(quietly now)* I'll let you go but Charlotte—give her the rosary. *(He lets her go and she runs off still holding the basket. Reve calls after her.)* Be sure you give it to her. *(He kicks some stones.)* Now I've got to hide in the swamps again while they hunt me down like a muskrat. *(with irony)* Muskrat Reve. No Maud to bring you your dinner. Get your own dinner, build your own house. Hide, Reve, hide for a long time in a lonesome place.

(Voices are heard and footsteps. He looks about rapidly and then goes quickly out. The sun begins to rise slowly. Maud and Naomi enter downstage right.)

Maud. Well, I sold just about everything. I didn't get much, but I sold it.
Naomi. I wish you hadn't.
Maud. The way they all just looked at me while I was haggling and bargaining. The silver teapot I never used—that's gone, Naomi. *(They are in the house now. Maud begins to look for something. Naomi tries to put things in order.)* Now where's that dratted thing?
Naomi. What you looking for?
Maud. Huh. What am I looking for? You know, Naomi—the—the . . . what am I looking for? Oh—the key to this here chest.

Naomi. It's right in the keyhole where we left it.

Maud. Now ain't that funny? Yes it is. *(She starts to open the chest but sits on it wearily.)* Oh—oh. That Bijou's papa wants the mortgage money. Where I'm going to get that much money? I hardly got a rag to my name. Nobody to help and no Reve to argue with.

Naomi. Bijou's father going to let you stay in the house.

Maud. Never thought I'd come to charity.

Naomi. *(still tidying up)* Lord, have mercy, Reve sure been a trial to you.

Maud. *(her voice alive now)* Reve. You gone clear out of your senses. It's the devil's work. He did it all, yes, he did. He just beckoned Reve along. *(picking up a coat on the chest)* Well, bless my soul, here's the coat of Reve's. I didn't sell this. Get me my sewing kit, Naomi, and bring me them old stockings. They make a fine patch.

Naomi. We threw them stockings out.

Maud. No, we didn't. *(She begins looking about.)* I can find them even if you can't. *(sees something)* Look what's here. Reve's old toy-casting ladle. He used to make out like he was molding toys with this. He'd say: "Now I melt this piece of tin, now I shape it, now I stamp my toy." And once, Naomi, once when company come, Reve come on in and ask his papa for a piece of tin to mold. And his papa say: "Don't use no tin, son, here's a piece of silver." Silver. "Now melt that!" He was showing off giving him silver. Reve melt it too. *(Starting to thread a needle. Her hand trembles. Suddenly.)* I wonder what dying is like. I reckon it's black. Some folks declare it's white as hominy grits, some folks say it's gold. I reckon it's black.

Naomi. *(going to her)* Go to bed now. I'll just sit here and do all the mending and fixing.

Maud. Everything's coming toward me like in a big swing. Coming so close—and then just fading away. *(Naomi helps her to the brass bed.)* You know Naomi, I sold Reve's breeches to that old blacksmith Apocalypse and when his back was turned I stole them back again. Reve needs them breeches.

Naomi. You shouldn't have done that. That's a high sin.

Maud. *(still with humor)* The Bible says God forgive every sin. Yes it does. Every one. *(Naomi is putting her to bed when a Gimmie bird begins to sing outside. They both turn.)* *(simply)* That's a Gimmie bird singing and you know what that means, Naomi.

Naomi. You're going to get well, Maud.

(The bird's song becomes high and compassionate. Maud's house slides off and a crudely built hut glides in on the other side. The roof is covered with Spanish moss. Reve is fixing the door.)

Reve. I've got to make me a fat bolt to keep away those pestering Loup

Garous and Bijou and her crabbish papa. If I don't I'll never hear the end of it. They'll be sneaking around about dark and crying: "Open up that door, Reve; you know we like the quicksilver, we like your dreams." And they'll be crawling about every which way. "We at the chimney, Reve, we the chimney smoke" and "We in this here crack. You didn't think no stingy old cabin could keep us out." So I'm going to make me this bolt.

(There are footsteps and Reve moves toward her as if she were unreal.)

Sophie-Louise. It's Sophie-Louise—it's me, Reve.

Reve. Sophie-Louise! *(Suddenly he is very shy.)* Did you get the rosary beads? *(Sophie opens her hand and they dangle.)* I can't believe my own eyes, no I can't. And you didn't just pass by on your way somewhere? You came here to see me after all I've done. *(She nods.)* Every day I said to myself talking out loud to all the bayous, talking to birds and the stargrass: "Sophie-Louise is coming this very day," and the echo would echo back: "Sophie-Louise is coming this very day." Night came and shadows and no Sophie-Louise.

Sophie-Louise. It's almost night now.

Reve. And you're here.

Sophie-Louise. *(sitting on the stump)* Oh, Reve. Charlotte didn't tell me. I heard your voice in the wind, even in silences I heard. *(quietly)* Your mama told me all about you too.

Reve. She shouldn't have said nothing.

Sophie-Louise. Every day was no sunlight, nothing. Night was no sleep, nothing. I couldn't cry or laugh. I had to come here.

Reve. To dance with me.

Sophie-Louise. To love you.

Reve. *(apprehensive)* But your father—and Charlotte.

Sophie-Louise. I've left them behind forever, Reve, and ever.

Reve. For me. *(He gets down on his knees and wipes her tears with his hands.)* You know I can't go back. I'm nothing.

Sophie-Louise. I came for you, Reve. I didn't care what you'd done or what you could do.

Reve. *(They sit in silence for a moment. Suddenly Reve rises and moves away.)* If I leave here, they'll smack me in jail. I'm like a robber, Sophie-Louise, like the moss on these trees, good for near nothing.

Sophie-Louise. When I was coming here, folks I met asked me where I was going, I must have looked so helpless. I said: "I'm going home." That's all and they left me alone.

Reve. *(coming back to her in one leap)* Then I don't need no puny locks against the devil or anything living or dead, in my head or in the air, if you come into my house. Sophie, you're the stargrass, the silverbell, the redbud and . . . everything. *(With one large sweep he lifts her in his arms.)* You're all the flowers every one, yes you are, and the deer and the sweet singing of all the sweet birds. Come into my house—it's a mean old house, ain't fit . . .

Sophie-Louise. It's your house, Reve. It's a palace. *(He carries her to the door and pauses there.)*

Reve. I'll put you down if you want to change your mind because this means forever.

Sophie-Louise. And ever and ever.

Reve. Thank you, honey. *(He kicks the door open and they enter. He comes out calling.)* I'll get some wood and make a fire. *(He leaps joyously away.)*

Sophie-Louise. *(calling)* All right. *(After a moment we hear her singing.)*

Reve. Now my palace is going to rise up like a pine to . . . *(He looks up and sees the first star.)* to touch that star, the first one. *(He looks toward the house and repeats.)* That star. *(With vigor he turns away and gets his axe and starts off to chop the wood. An old woman in a torn and filthy green dress comes hobbling in, leading an ugly, limping child, who has a dirty bottle in his hand.)*

Hethabella. Evening, Reve, Mr. Longgone!

Reve. Who's that?

Hethabella. Why an old friend. I live hardly a stone's throw from here. I'm your neighbor.

Reve. I don't know nothing about that.

Hethabella. While you was heaving and chopping and fixing your fine palace here, why mine just naturally grew up beside it.

Reve. *(uneasy)* I got things to do.

Hethabella. You always did, but I'm here now.

Reve. You're crazy as a bessie bug.

Hethabella. Once I were. On that day you promised me everything just for an example.

Reve. I never promised you that. *(snaps his fingers)*

Hethabella. Not so fast—recall that night you made me dance at my papa's. *(The sky turns the strange aquamarine color.)*

Reve. I recall no such frigging thing. I never clapped eyes on you or your papa, if you ever had one.

Hethabella. *(to the Child)* Give your papa a drink, he's always been mighty thirsty.

Reve. Papa—you mean that nasty brat.

Hethabella. Why Reve—he's the spitting image of you. Look at that dried up limping leg, it favor your limping mind.

Reve. Get on away.

Hethabella. Ahhhhhhhhhhhh.

Reve. That big hellion.

Hethabella. He grew up like a weed. Nothing we could do about it.

Reve. *(starting to strike her)* You chewed up, snotty old hag, don't come around here saying you know me.

Hethabella. That's exactly what I'm saying and I see you just as bad mannered as ever. What did you expect me to be? Fine and fair. I lost my bright eyes, lost my pretty hair birthing your brat. But Reve Grant, all you got to do is to turn her *(pointing to house)* out of doors, shake her out of your mind and I'll be like I was. Do that, Reve Grant.

Reve. Get away, you snotrag.

Hethabella. I'll cling like poison in a rattling snake.

Reve. *(furious, lifting his axe)* You . . .

Hethabella. *(defiant, yelling harshly)* Go on. Go on. *(Reve lowers his axe.)*

(Sophie-Louise's song rises up and they are both still for a moment. Hethabella starts for the house but Reve pulls her away.)

Hethabella. *(whispering fiercely)* You got to do more than that to shut me up. I'll be back every day, every which hour. I'll be at the windows and the cracks watching you and her. When you sit together, I'll be between you knocking at your knees. When you're lying together, I'll squirm on in between. I'll spit a rotten tooth in your mouth. I hope you live happy, left-handed Reve.

Reve. You stinking, conjuring devil!

Hethabella. Take your son; he's just as nice. Come here, spider, sting your papa. *(Boy goes up and spits right on Reve.)*

Hethabella. *(kissing him as she pulls him to her)* Ain't he smart? When you get big, you're sure going to be something.

Reve. For her, for Sophie-Louise, it's not her fault, go on away.

Hethabella. *(nasty)* For Sophie-Louise, for Sophie-Louise . . . and I got to carry this angry, ugly face and this lumpy body . . .

Reve. She's not to blame.

Hethabella. She ain't to blame. *(to the boy)* Ain't that true, son?

(The boy giggles and when they are almost off, tosses his bottle at Reve. Reve ducks. The aquamarine color fades at their exit.)

Reve. *(taking up the axe and rings it hard into a log)* How can I walk straight into her arms when all my sins will be peeking in the window panes at me? I could put Hethabella out of my mind, I could drown her in Bayou Goula, but Bijou would rise up weeping out of the waters and the Loup Garous would laugh out of the fire I built to warm myself. If I touched Sophie-Louise she'd feel blood on her skin, she'd smell my sins, she'd catch my evil and she'd die in my arms holding her rosary, too

weak to make the sign of her cross. I got to get away—I got to run free of all the evil before I come again. However I do it, I got to do it.
Sophie-Louise. *(Sophie-Louise comes to the door.)* Are you coming in, Reve?
Reve. Honey, wait inside—it's damp and you'll catch cold. It's getting dark and I've got a burden to carry.
Sophie-Louise. Can't I help you carry it?
Reve. Stay there quiet. I'll bear this burden alone.
Sophie-Louise. Come back soon, Reve.
Reve. Just you be patient. I may be a little while and then again it might take longer. But wait. Will you do that?
Sophie-Louise. Of course, Reve. I'll wait.

(Sophie-Louise stands in the doorway with light surrounding her. Reve is out of sight but she waves. She stands there looking, then closes the door. All is black on stage but presently we hear her singing.)

(Evening in Maud's little house. Through the window near her bed you can see the sun in its last glow. Beyond, the reflections in the swamp make the world outside a dark golden color. There's a fire in the fireplace but it's very dim and hardly needed; a cat is lying on a stool below the foot of the bed. Maud on the bed seems small and pathetic. She is picking at the sheets and putting her hand to her mouth as if she were eating earth.)

Maud. I'm gonna die and Reve ain't about, no he ain't. I been so lonely in the nights, so lonely in the days. I got nobody, nobody—to stretch a hand to and say: Tell Reve, honey, tell Reve I'm real sick—I'm—that Maud's dying, his mama, tell that to my springtime-singing Reve. I wanted to tell him a heap of things more. Now he'll never know I loved him so much even when I scolded—and whipped him—never. And I'm going away while the sun falls down—without Reve, yes I am.
Reve. *(enters; stands by the door and says like an actor charmingly, sweeping off an imaginary cap)* Evening, M'am.
Maud. Evening, Sir. *(turns and sees it's Reve)* I thought—thought—no, Maud, close your eyes again and dream he's here . . . dream.
Reve. Mama.
Maud. *(knowing now he's really here)* Oh Reve, honey, my boy, bless you for coming. Oh Reve, Reve. *(urgently)* No—you shouldn't a come—no—no—they'll catch you, they'll put you in jail, kill you. Go on away. *(She turns her head from him.)*
Reve. I had to come—I don't care a penny for them, Mama, I don't care about dying—I'm here with you—old Maud, mean and hateful as a rattling snake.

(Maud laughs hoarsely and Reve laughs.)

Maud. Naomi said: "He ain't coming, don't wait for no Reve." That's what she said. She's a liar. Ain't she a liar, Reve? I am so happy now she's a liar.

Reve. You're repeating yourself like a crazy old little baby. No. You're not stirring out of here.

Maud. Reve, I'm dying. Dying fast. Nobody can stop that.

Reve. *(to himself)* I was running away from hurt and sorrow. I wanted to be free and I run right into hurt and sorrow. *(turning to Maud)* Mama, tell me can I help you? Can I get a blanket to keep you warm? Can I fix the fire, can I fetch . . .

Maud. *(Something in her voice stops him.)* Reve. Yes—when I close my eyes in peace, when my open eyes don't know the light, close my eyes, son, and bury me in a fine casket, fine as any . . . *(She chokes on an ironic laugh.)* A fine casket. We ain't got nothing fine left—no fine money, no fine friends—nothing.

Reve. Shh. Shh. Mama. Don't bother about that now.

Maud. Look, Reve, what they left—nothing. Didn't matter to them. Oh the robbers—if I had my strength . . .

Reve. *(angry)* Shut up. Shut!

Maud. *(angry too)* Drink. That drink. That did it to you. Yes, it did and the Lord knows that. You didn't know what was what when you was setting on that drunken alligator drunk and flying away with a girl in your arms . . . that other time.

Reve. Don't talk all that now. It's useless as a cottonweed. Let's talk something light and sparkling—anything, anything except this present moaning, this hurt and sorrow. *(changing tone)* Look there at that pussycat. I thought he was dead a long time ago.

Maud. In the night he sing his fear sickness on the fence and singing like that mean—you know what it mean.

Reve. Shhh. Shhhh. You keep quiet, Mama, just keep quiet. *(quickly)* Anything happen while I was away?

Maud. Word circling round about a pretty girl pining her heart away for a delta home.

Reve. *(hastily)* How's Willie Silvers doing?

Maud. Say she close her ears when the old folks pray, when they unfasten their hearts and tears roll down. Go on, see her, Reve, son, go and maybe patch things up . . .

Reve. That old, loud-talking blacksmith, Apocalypse, how's he doing?

Maud. I don't give a hoot in the swamp for the blacksmith. Her name, say her name, Reve. Let's talk about her pretty name.

Reve. We're gonna forget everything that got a thorn in it. I'll cut some sugarcane, yes I will. You always liked the sweetness. Look at that bed—almost too small for Maud. When I was a little old boy I wouldn't go to sleep—in this very bed here, I'd cough and toss and turn. And then you'd come on along and pull the bedclothes to, singing songs with a joke in the midst of them. I'd go to sleep laughing or dreaming of a fine carriage pulled by fine horses—one was always like your hair now, smooth to touch . . . *(strokes her hair)*

Maud. *(taking his hand)* Like my gray hair . . . *(perking up)* We'd ride together in that carriage, yes we did. The whole floor would be our pathway.

Reve. . . . and the window open . . .

Maud. *(laughing)* Naomi's cat was the horses.

Reve. We put her on a stool.

Maud. Her tail was wagging.

Reve. Yes.

Maud. The moon was a hot color.

Reve. A switch from a live oak . . .

Maud. Was the whip . . .

Reve. A wonderful whip.

Maud. And we'd ride, my Reve and I . . .

Reve. Out of the window down oak lane with the moss tickling our faces, and we'd ride past the biggest white house and then the horses grew wings, big wings like eagle birds, over the swamp, over islands, the smell of the bayous in your hair, up—up we'd go . . .

Maud. I really drove them horses.

Reve. With one hand—you put the other around me like a shawl to keep me warm. It was cold in the sky.

Maud. *(a little sob)* It sure was cold.

Reve. *(keeps it going)* You always kept me warm, God bless you, you mean old Mama. *(pause)* What's the matter?

Maud. My back, I been lying here so long. It's them bed sores. Go on, Reve—"What a wind . . ."

Reve. Sit up—I'll help you. *(helping her)* Now there, now there, ain't that better?

Maud. I want to ride away, Reve.

Reve. Ride? We're riding.

Maud. That's just fine. *(significantly)* I'm riding away. Ain't that good?

Reve. You sure can mess up the bedclothes. Let me fix them smooth. How about a song—the one about the bear who jumped rope with the lion.

Maud. You know very well *(loudly)* there's no lions round here. You know that, Reve. There's bears but no lions. *(pause)* Get me my Bible, son. Read me a scripture to ease my mind.

Reve. We're riding past the moon to a castle between the moon and near heaven. They're having a picnic there. Such food! We're going there! I'll drive this time. What a picnic they're having.

Maud. Am I invited, Reve?
Reve. Of course and I'm even invited too. *(He throws a cord around the back of the chair where the coat is, takes a switch and sits at the foot of the bed.)* Giddiup! Come on, Ouachita. Want another quilt, Mama? That's right. Zip—now we're on again. Giddiup, Sabine, giddiup.
Maud. I hear something ringing.
Reve. The horses! Bells ringing . . .
Maud. They don't sound natural.
Reve. We're over the swamp now. Wheee, wheee, wheeeeee.
Maud. I'm afraid. There's a sighing, moaning, wildness in the night. I hear it.
Reve. It's the live oaks blowing in the wind, talking, laughing. Shhhh.
Maud. What's all that light over yonder sparkling to my eyes?
Reve. The castle is lit up—there's music and laughter and dancing.
Maud. Is that right?
Reve. And outside is a welcoming committee with St. Peter out in front.
Maud. Am I welcome? Tell me that, son.
Reve. Welcome as a queen. St. Peter has a bowl of wine.
Maud. And what else?
Reve. Little sweet hot cakes.
Maud. And what else?
Reve. Coffee—served by the Preacher's wife . . .
Maud. You don't say so.
Reve. Yes I do. And she's holding all that out to Maud.
Maud. Oh Reve, Oh . . .
Reve. And corn on the cob.
Maud. What a picnic you're taking an old lady to.
Reve. Giddiup . . . Ouachita . . . come on there, Sabine . . .
Maud. Sure you know the way?
Reve. I've been a thousand times.
Maud. I'm tired out—wearied out.
Reve. We're almost there.
Maud. Let me close my eyes and you'll take me there.
Reve. Giddiup—show how fine you can ride. Look at that castle. See that prancing and carrying on? Folks just crowding in. *(stands, acting)* Here we are. How do you fare tonight St. Peter, sir? I hope you fare well. What, you won't let Maud in? She's a pillar of the church. There's nobody that deserves your welcome more. It don't matter about me. I can go around the back. I'm not nothing much. I'm a liar. I didn't treat my mother very good. But everything's gonna be different from now on. Take her in, sir, set her a good place. She's a pillar—nobody deserves a welcome more. *(pause)* Look, look over there in that cloud. It's the Lord. Now you'll see, St. Peter, sir, you'll see. *(listening)* He says my

mother's welcome here—that's what the Lord says. *(He laughs and turns to Maud.)* I knew you'd be welcome, Mama. *(His voice is anxious.)* Don't stare like that, Mama. What's the matter? Don't stare like that . . . *(goes to her)* . . . it's Reve. We're there, Mama. *(He feels her forehead and hands. He throws the cord away.)* Mama. Rest yourself, Sabine. We're there—the trip's over, over. *(shuts her eyes and bends over her)* Thanks for everything, Maud, everything, Mama, the scolding and the songs. You thank me too—I drove you to your rest and peace. *(kisses her)* That's the driver's pay.

(Naomi comes in.)

Naomi. You came, Reve. I didn't expect you'd come. That musta made her real happy. My, she's sleeping sound. Maud . . ?

Reve. She's dead. *(Naomi weeps. Reve walks about. He stops by the bed.)* Bury her good, Naomi. As fine as you can. I've got to get away, you know.

(Naomi nods.)

Naomi. Where you going?
Reve. Right straight down to the Gulf of Mexico.
Naomi. As far as that?
Reve. I'm going farther than that, Naomi, yes I am. *(He goes out.)*

(Curtain)

ACT II

The music before the curtain rises is tropical with some hint of the percussion sounds of the Incas that give sharpness and point to the sensuous theme. There is another theme that runs inexorably through all of this prelude: Something bitter and hard is in it. The scene is a beach in Panama about 1850: lush, tropical. There are palm trees and thick bright underbrush at back. The late afternoon sun surrounds a colorful, striped tent from which a canopy extends. Under it is an oblong table with the remains of a meal. Fernand Ballon, Josiah Cheever, Jason Weatherdrift are standing at the back of the table leaning over Lares Zempoaltepec who is seated. They are all concentrating on a map that is spread out before them. They are dressed in tropical suits. Zempoaltepec is a fierce looking Spanish Indian from Yucatan, with high cheek bones, copper-colored skin and an angry scar on his forehead; a large sombrero on his back, strings about the neck hold it; Ballon is a roly poly Frenchman with a shrewd glint in his eyes; Josiah

Cheever is a thin-lipped New England sea captain; Jason Weatherdrift is a small, quiet contractor not without a certain softness in his face.

Zempoaltepec. *(tapping a spot on the map)* At this point, Señors, the land makes a sharp drop. In that palisade is copper. Below, four miles east, land of endless gold begins. We have made tests. There is no doubt in my mind.

Cheever. Aye, but if the revolution fails?

Zempoaltepec. He will join us. The prize is too large. He respects prizes.

Cheever. Aye, I hope so. Two of my ships have dropped anchor ten miles up the coast with guns and ammunition the last six months.

Ballon. Six months! We will be in possession of the Panama in two months, Monsieur, perhaps one. *C'est possible.*

Zempoaltepec. *(tapping another spot on the map)* Cheever, when the signal is given your ships will land here and unload. This is the important spot. Drive a wedge here and the revolution is over, Señors. *(turning to Weatherdrift)* The extension to the railroad will run from here to here, where it is needed most. Will you have enough workers when the time comes?

Weatherdrift. They die quickly from cholera and malaria . . .

Ballon. Let them die, Monsieur Weatherdrift. There will be others to take their places.

Weatherdrift. Sometimes coolies sit on the beaches at high tide smoking their opium pipes watching the tide rise higher and higher until they are washed out to sea. They are in bloody despair. Often, too often.

Ballon. In that case, Monsieur, I must add opium to my list of imports.

Weatherdrift. *(sarcastically)* Yes, add opium. In Cheapside I saw the same look in men's eyes, only they sat in garbage instead of sand.

Zempoaltepec. I repeat, with Señor Grant's aid we will conclude this revolution and Panama will *(laying his hands flat on the map)* be ours.

Cheever. Aye. But with his aid.

Zempoaltepec. We will have that.

Ballon. Suppose he will not join us. *C'est possible.* Perhaps he has not the physical stamina—to me he does not look right around the eyes. If he is ill, all our troubles are over. *(laughs)*

Zempoaltepec. *(low, glancing toward tent)* Shhhh . . . I don't think so. He has a golden nugget for a brain, iron in his constitution, and magnets for hands and tin for a heart.

Cheever. *(ignoring them)* Ballon is right, aye. We want no barnacles on our vessel. We've sailed too far for that. *(whispering)* Aye, but let us say he will not join us.

Zempoaltepec. Then, Señors, we will have another plan perhaps, eh?

Weatherdrift. I say put the proposition to him fairly.

Cheever. *(bitterly)* Fair, aye, fair. That's all that counts. I've invested in arms. Fair or otherwise we must not lose.
Zempoaltepec. Señor Grant will invest his money our way or . . .
Ballon. We'll invest it for him, *enfin*.
Weatherdrift. *(hotly)* What do you mean by that?
Zempoaltepec. Control your voice.
Ballon. You'll never have your fine house in London if you let your temper burn it down before it's built.
Zempoaltepec. *(rapping)* Señors, his schooner is anchored within our reach. *(low)* If he refuses—
Cheever. Yes?
Zempoaltepec. *(lightly)* We will man his schooner . . .
Cheever. . . . and his wealth.
Zempoaltepec. . . . and leave him here.
Weatherdrift. We're not bandits.
Zempoaltepec. *(directly)* Do you want to build your railroads and bridges?
Weatherdrift. Well I . . . Yes. Yes, I do.
Zempoaltepec. Then let us proceed. I have thought of the alternate plan in case Señor Grant . . .
Ballon. By all means, Monsieur, tell us.
Cheever. Aye. Aye.
Weatherdrift. What is it?
Zempoaltepec. You shall see. You know the grove of palms.
Cheever. Aye—
Zempoaltepec. A princess waits there for my call.
Weatherdrift. A princess?
Zempoaltepec. Princess Teaka *(smiles)*—well, she is not royal—except in—er—body but she will serve to—er—*(He makes shape of feminine body.)* in case Señor Grant objects to our proposition.
Ballon. *(laughing)* I see. *(laughing)* I see.
Cheever. Mermaids for stubborn kingfishes.
Ballon. Can she be trusted, Monsieur, with a task of such delicacy?
Zempoaltepec. She could make the Red Sea part if she knew a trinket was at the bottom of it. *(takes a little highpitched flute from his pocket and plays a short tune)*
Weatherdrift. *(normal voice)* I don't see how she fits in.
Zempoaltepec. *(low)* Señor, your voice! You will.
Ballon. *(to Zempoaltepec)* Your talents are amazing—flutes, princess girls, schemes by the dozen—la, la, la.

(Teaka, a shapely, dark Indian girl with a long rope about her middle and little else on, undulates in and, going immediately to Zempoaltepec, kneels.)

Ballon. *(noticing the entrance, follows her with his eyes)* La, la, lala— *(reaches for the bowl of grapes and bites into one still watching Teaka)*

Zempoaltepec. *(low)* Just listen, my dear. Our Señor Grant—you have seen him—*(She nods.)* may be here any minute. Wait out there. *(pointing to direction from which she came)* When I toss this hat in the air, you know what to do. Ha? *(She nods, yes.)* He has rings and pearls as large as your bright eyes and in that tent . . . and a box of quinine you can sell for a pretty penny. *(She nods gleefully and greedily, yes, yes.)* They are yours if you do your *(waves his hand)* work well. *(She nods again. A whistled tune comes from the tent. Zempoaltepec glances quickly toward the sound.)* Now be off, Teaka. *(Ballon throws her a grape and she scampers off as he laughs. Normal tone.)* As I was saying, Gentlemen, you would be astounded if you knew the real resources here waiting for us . . .

(Reve enters from tent bringing a tray with a decanter, glasses, and cigars. He sets it on the table. He is a handsome, middle-aged man now, dressed in a traveling suit of the period.)

Reve. Sorry I had to leave you before the meal was over, gentlemen, but I was looking for this vintage. *(holding up the decanter)* The best Napoleon could offer. . . .

Ballon. Ah, Napolean brandy . . . However, we missed you, Monsieur Grant.

Zempoaltepec. It is always a pleasure to be in your presence.

Reve. . . . made me neglect my guests. And the last few days I've had slight dizzy spells. But I have my store of quinine inside.

Ballon. You cannot afford to be ill, Monsieur and you are a host of hosts, *mon frère,* Grant; nevertheless, I recognize your fine taste—your exquisite *ton,* we could not do without you.

Cheever. *(standing; moving to shake Reve's hand)* Aye.

Zempoaltepec. Your taste has width, Señor. It has wit for the delicate; robustness for er . . . er . . . the robust. You are cosmopolitan. We feel uplifted even in these surroundings. That is what Señor Ballon meant.

Reve. Thank you, gentlemen. Thank you.

Zempoaltepec. While you were gone, we were discussing the proposition . . .

Ballon. Which is excellent.

Zempoaltepec. If you will allow me to show you. *(moving toward the map)* On this map I have drawn . . .

Reve. *(interrupting)* Gentlemen, gentlemen—first let us finish our party. I read somewhere that business is best digested when the warmth of good wine and a cigar tingles the mind; yes, I have. *(Reve passes out cigars while the men help themselves to brandy.)*

Zempoaltepec. *(reluctant to turn from business but determined to put Reve in an amiable frame of mind)* I have prospected for precious metals a good deal in my Yucatan, in Honduras—you dig layer by layer into the earth until one day it is revealed. Let us search you, Señor Grant, for that precious metal that gives off such light and wisdom. Er—er—how did you grow into what you are? That is a large question, I know, but it would help us to realize your philosophy.

Reve. *(leaning back with his cigar and drink)* I have not allowed that precious metal, as you so neatly put it, to become tarnished by responsibility to anyone but myself. I have refined it, polished it, kept it for myself alone. That's man's first duty. I have taken every opportunity, examined it and said right out loud: "This will profit me or this will hinder me." That is my only philosophy. Don't bear others on your back. Let them bear you.

Ballon. It is not easy to keep such a principle, Monsieur.

Zempoaltepec. Oh, but, Señor Grant is an extraordinary man.

Reve. You are right, Zempoaltepec. But even I had to fight to keep this philosophy. Once I nearly lost it. When I was a boy: wild and handsome, a girl with royal blood tried to change me—make me over so that I would see the world through her father's eyes, yes she did, but I stuck to my principles. *(Reve's voice falters; he sways slightly; they make as if to help.)* Please, gentlemen, it is nothing, really, please. Now where was I? Oh, yes, principles . . .

Cheever. Aye, you are a man of principles.

Ballon. More than that, he is a poet.

Zempoaltepec. Tell me, Señor Grant—this has puzzled me—you say you have never had an education and yet your knowledge seems boundless as our enterprise.

Reve. I taught myself everything I know. I've picked up seeds here and there and let them grow within me. I've dipped into every subject—even religion.

Zempoaltepec. The holy Bible, Monsieur?

Weatherdrift. You have had time for that?

Reve. When evil days fall upon thee—then thou will be able to rest in the Lord. The quotation is not exact, but the thought is there.

Cheever. Aye, you are a practical man.

Reve. I believe in what is useful.

Cheever. You will never fall upon evil days, Monsieur. You are too clever.

Reve. So was Lucifer. Nevertheless, I am prepared, yes, I am. And there is no need to offend the greatest power of all.

Zempoaltepec. *(laughing)* You do not let an opportunity slip by.

Reve. That's how I became what I am now.

Cheever. Aye, seize every opportunity.

Zempoaltepec. Here is opportunity on this map, Señor, in the jungles behind us and the hills beyond them. An opportunity that seldom comes to any man, has come to us here.

(The men nod. Reve fills his glass.)

Reve. *(twinkling)* In those jungles beyond, I was told the San Blas Indians—keep their women hidden . . . *(Ballon chuckles but Zempoaltepec gives him a hard look.)*
Zempoaltepec. *(pointedly)* . . . just as this rich earth hides precious metals.
Reve. *(drinking)* All day long the women are shut up in the caves, but when night comes down . . . *(laughs sensuously and gestures with his hands, nudges Ballon)* Eh, Ballon? *(Ballon twinkles.)*
Zempoaltepec. *(laughing also)* Night comes down suddenly in Panama.
Reve. I have noticed that.
Zempoaltepec. The sun is setting now. Before night comes, Señor, look at this map. *(He hands the map to Reve.)*
Ballon. If *we* stop the revolution the way to great wealth is open to all of us.
Zempoaltepec. Panama is rich, Señor Grant—in gold and copper. Everything is here—for us.
Ballon. Rum trading, Monsieur, opium . . .
Cheever. Slaves . . .
Weatherdrift. Railroads, industry. . . . An opportunity to lift these people out of poverty, a chance beyond wealth, a chance to shape destiny—here.
Reve. *(quietly sipping)* What is your proposition?
Zempoaltepec. As long as the revolution lasts we can do nothing, but if one faction wins by our aid, Panama will be ours.
Cheever. Aye, we have ships loaded with ammunition ready to land.
Weatherdrift. With your aid. *(urgently)* Join us.
Ballon. It is late, Monsieur. We must decide soon.
Reve. *(turning his glass in his hand)* Gentlemen, I've worked hard, yes I have, to gain the wealth stored *(pointing off)* in that schooner. I won't put that money in any scheme unless I am certain of one thing.
Zempoaltepec. The profit is limitless—a whole country.
Ballon. Yes, Monsieur, a whole rich wilderness.
Reve. *(pouring himself a drink and pausing while they wait for his decision)* Gentlemen, let me tell you a story.
Ballon. *(put out)* By all means, Monsieur. *(They breathe deeply and lean back to listen.)*
Reve. When I was nothing but a boy I was stepped on, laughed at, humiliated. So I left home to see the world. I had nothing but dirty breeches and a light in my head when I shipped for Frisco. On the way I worked till my knees bled and my hands ached. *(sipping brandy)* I thought I'd die once or twice. But life is always good no matter how terrible it becomes. Death is bitter as rotten shrimp. I held on to life

with all my strength and *(piously)* God watched over me. *(taking a ring off his finger and tossing it in the air)* This ring contains the first piece of gold I ever had. I, too, prospected for gold, Zempoaltepec, but in the frozen hills of Frisco. One day I stumbled across a dead man frozen in the snow, hugging a great bag of gold. Naturally I couldn't leave the gold there for any which person to find or a snow storm to cover. *(sipping brandy)* Then I came to the Spanish Main. With that gold I set myself up in the smuggling business—operated in island after island. *(Reve extracts from a box near his seat a large chain with manacles.)* I carry this to remind me of those days.

Weatherdrift. You never were caught?

Reve. Caught! I always worked behind the scenes. No one ever knew that I was the hand, gentlemen, behind thousands of slaves who entered Charleston from Trinidad, St. Kitts, Guadeloupe, Haiti—from any which island where there were black . . .

Weatherdrift. Slaves! *(pause)* Black slaves? You, Mr. Grant? Many men would say that was evil work . . .

Reve. *(turning to Weatherdrift)* You think it was evil?

Zempoaltepec. *(appeasing)* Señor, he means many *foolish* men might think so.

Weatherdrift. I just meant—his own people.

Reve. He's right, Zempoaltepec. After a few years my conscience did begin to kick me. I knew that one day I'd have to account for my actions. So each and every Spring I shipped idols to the West Indies *(picks a long thin idol out of a bag)* like this one, gentlemen. And every Autumn I sent missionaries with every which thing needed for conversion: rum, Bibles. *(He takes a Bible from the bag and lays it on the table.)*

Cheever. Aye. How did the exchange work out?

Reve. Better than I expected. While the natives worshipped the idols I sold, the missionaries were busy converting them from the idols. You can't get into trouble when you balance evil with good. *(drinking)*

Ballon. Clever, Monsieur, extremely clever.

Reve. I tell you this because every hour since I was a boy I have dreamed that some day, somehow, I would have a world I dreamed of hard and real between my hands. That's why I have done what I have done. I have my wealth.

Zempoaltepec. Señor, your dream can become hard and real now.

Reve. Now . . .

Ballon. Yes, Monsieur.

Cheever. Hoist your sails with ours.

Reve. *(evasive)* You want an answer to your proposition. First, what do I receive in return for my money?

Zempoaltepec. We are prepared to share all with you.

Reve. *(gulping a drink)* Share.
Zempoaltepec. Shares in the copper and gold mines.
Ballon. In rum and opium imports.
Weatherdrift. The railroads.
Zempoaltepec. In every enterprise.
Reve. That is generous, yes it is. *(The men exchange glances and smile.)*
Zempoaltepec. Let us drink a toast to Señor Grant and our whole enterprise. *(They take up glasses.)*
Ballon. Monsieur Grant, I misjudged you altogether.
Cheever. Aye, forgive me.
Zempoaltepec. Drink, Señors.
Reve. Just a moment. I *only* said your offer was generous.
Ballon. But we understood that . . .
Reve. Have *you* understood *my* terms entirely?
Zempoaltepec. State them.
Reve. *(to each in turn)* I'm not interested in shares in rum and opium, Ballon, or in your railroads, Weatherdrift, or in copper mines. I've already experienced those adventures. I have my wealth. *(pointing out to schooner)* I have my souvenirs. *(pointing to Bible, chain, idol)*
Ballon. Then you want nothing in return?
Reve. I didn't say that.
Zempoaltepec. What do you want?
Reve. Power—power to rule men.
Cheever. But these people fight to rule themselves in their country, not to be ruled.
Zempoaltepec. He is right, Señor.
Reve. You're falling back on puny phrases. I know what all your interests are. *(sarcastically)* Fighting to rule themselves while you prepare to squeeze them dry as this coral. I won't risk one dollar in your scheme unless you meet my terms. Listen, I was a black boy in a white world. I always had to look up. Now I'll look down. I must rule. The people will bow to me. I want power; I want a title—King, Emperor, Sultan, Lord of my Universe. Once I met a man with a box of toys. He made them act at his bidding.
Ballon. Yes, Reve Grant . . . so?
Reve. I want to be that man. If I adopt your plan, remember I give the order, yes, I do, I decide, I shape, I mold. You'll be my cabinet or what you'll call yourselves. *(laughs)*
Ballon. Well, well, Reve Grant—I don't know what to say. This is impossible.
Cheever. *(significantly)* Not impossible, Ballon.
Zempoaltepec. Let us say—it comes as a surprise.
Reve. Surprise or not, I won't change my mind.

Weatherdrift. I beg you, Sir.
Ballon. Perhaps we will change ours.
Reve. I sail at dawn; you have 'til then.
Zempoaltepec. Is that your decision, Señor?
Reve. Gentlemen, take your time; talk it over among yourselves. I'll stroll down to the schooner. You'll find me there. *(He puts on his topee, starts down right.)*
Weatherdrift. Mr. Grant?
Reve. *(without turning)* Yes, Weatherdrift—

(Zempoaltepec grips Weatherdrift's arm.)

Weatherdrift. The brandy was excellent.
Reve. I thought you'd like it, yes I did. Always a pleasure, gentlemen.

(He is off—the men gather together. Zempoaltepec tosses his hat in the air with a flourish and the men rush out of sight up back to watch. Teaka runs in from down right and collapses sensually near the hat just as Reve reenters.)

Reve. What is the matter, girl?
Teaka. Oh, oh, oh . . .
Reve. Perhaps some brandy.
Teaka. *(clinging to his thighs)* No, don't leave me.
Reve. I certainly won't, not as long as you cling to me like that. Mmmmmmmmmmm.
Teaka. Something terrible was chasing me. *(begins sobbing)*
Reve. *(looking about)* There is nothing to be afraid of here.
Teaka. No more?
Reve. No more.
Teaka. *(She lies flat, her breasts moving rhythmically.)* I hear something.
Reve. My what a shape, such legs!
Teaka. *(sitting up)* Something is out there. *(points down left)*
Reve. *(looking)* Nothing. You just lie here.
Teaka. You are so good to protect me.
Reve. Ah, ha, ha, for a pretty little Eve like you. . . . What is your name?
Teaka. Teaka.
Reve. I'm Reve Grant.
Teaka. Yes, yes, Grant.
Reve. *(laughs)* Grant, eh. *(She rises. Zempoaltepec can be seen peering from behind a tree. Reve's back is to him. Teaka gives a little shimmy. Reve looks up and sees her.)* I can see you're not afraid now.
Teaka. Not with the strong Granti. *(She shimmies a little more.)*
Reve. My, you're a performer too. *(She giggles.)* I know a tune you could dance to. *(He sits cross-legged and begins whistling, holds out his hands to her.)*

BAYOU LEGEND

Teaka. Pretty ring.

Reve. You like that ring, eh? Dance, Teaka and you shall have it. *(She shimmies her midriff.)* Dance, Teaka. *(She continues to shimmy. Giving her the ring.)* There now, dance.

Teaka. More.

Reve. Later. *(laughing and stroking her thigh)* Dance, girl. *(He begins to whistle.)*

Teaka. In the tent—more?

Reve. *(winking)* After you dance for me, eh?

Teaka. Stand up.

Reve. *(rising)* All right.

Teaka. Take rope. *(He takes one end of rope she has about her middle. He giggles as she touches him.)*

Reve. Ah, oh, ha, he. *(He kisses her. The men come cautiously from behind the trees. Teaka holds Reve in close embrace until men are off, unseen by him. Then with Reve holding one end of rope she begins to dance while he whistles—now she is the rope's length away from him. Strange instruments offstage make a background. She darts lusciously about him while he laughs. She binds him in the rope, dancing all the while.)* What grace you have—What legs, Ah, ha, ha, ha. *(She laughs too—loud, insinuating.)* What kind of dance do you call this?

Teaka. I tie you up so I can dance for you. *(She secures knots and begins dancing again. Reve wiggles, laughs, pants.)* Without being afraid of your hands.

Reve. What a joke. Ha. Ha! *(She just leaps.)* You're not really afraid of your Granti, are you?

Teaka. *(She leaps into the tent.)* No, No, No—no more.

Reve. Come where I can see you, Teaka . . . Teaka . . . Oh Evie, Adam is waiting for you. *(Suddenly she appears from the tent laden with [scarves] and jewels on her wrists and fingers. The moon comes out.)* You found all that, oh. Well, you can have the scarfs but the jewels—Teaka, Teaka . . . Come here, Teaka. Teaka—that box, that box, you have no need for that quinine—it's only quinine, it's only quinine. *(She begins laughing, the music has stopped, darkness has fallen, she runs off and her laughing comes back echoing and cold.)* Oh you—you witch. Teaka, Hethabella? Hethabella! Where am I? *(pauses, staggers)* My head aches. Weatherdrift, Ballon, Cheever—*(gazes out suddenly)* The lanterns on my schooner are lit—Zempoaltepec! Rip loose this rope. I see it now. A trick. A goddamned trick. The bastards. They'll sail away and steal everything. No they can't. Lord, I've done nothing to deserve this—in a little while they'll be out to sea. By morning they'll be miles away. I want my money back. Lord, help me, listen: I sent missionaries to spread your word. I've helped you. You know that, yes you do. Help me, now. Don't let them have my wealth. I worked too hard to get it. I won't be tied here like a puppet. I won't, no I won't. Help me. Somebody, anybody. I feel hot, cold . . . *(silence)* I must really be ill. Malaria—don't let me die here! Maud, ring the bells . . . ring the bells again. So—Sophie-Louise *(quietly, ironically)* Sophie-Louise. I wish you were here now. I wish it, oh, I wish. Night came and shadows—but no Sophie-Louise. I had almost forgotten you. *(The wind blows faintly.)* Why did I leave you? My dreams have tied my hands. *(The wind blows louder.)* Sophie-Louise help me!!!

Voice of Sophie-Louise. Reve, Reve. It's nearly dawn, my Reve.

Reve. *(almost in a trance, straining)* What's that? Only the wind.

Voice of Sophie-Louise. My Reve—

Reve. It's a dream, just a dream, yes, it is. I'll never be free again, I know it. Help me again. Don't let me die here.

Voice of Sophie-Louise. Rrrreeevveee . . .

Reve. Even the wind is against me.

Voice of Sophie-Louise. *(Reve starts again.)* Oh, Reve—I heard your voice in the wind, even in the silences I heard . . .

Reve. It is you, Sophie-Louise, it is. Free me, honey. *(realistic again)* No, I can't go back. I left everything and I can't hold it again.

Voice of Sophie-Louise. I left everything behind forever, Reve, everything except you.

Reve. *(tense again)* It is you Sophie—the stargrass, you're the silverbell and . . .

Voice of Sophie-Louise. Are you coming, Reve?

Reve. I'd come if I were free—I'd run home and love you as if the years hadn't passed, yes I would, only free me.

Voice of Sophie-Louise. I'll wait—wait Reve. *(fading as wind blows)* Rrrreeevvveeeee. . . .

Reve. *(Reve's whole body struggles in the direction of the voice. He seems in a trance.)* Speak again—Sophie-Louise, honey, free me, Sophie-Louise, Sophie-Louise, Sophie . . . speak, set me free, honey, do that—

Old Priest. *(It's almost like a chant. From down left an old Inca priest has been watching. He is in rags and has a cape made of long dried grasses. Quietly.)* Can I help you? *(Reve doesn't hear. He is chanting Sophie's name.)* Can I help you?

Reve. *(in direction of Sophie's gone voice)* I'll come back and you'll forget I was lost. Sophie-Louise, Sophie-Louise. I don't want a kingdom or my money, I don't want Teaka or any other thing but your face, your goodness . . . untie me—loose me. *(The Priest begins untying Reve who doesn't turn. All his concentration is on Sophie.)* Everything's turned to ashes but you. Free me, Honey. . . . *(Suddenly he feels that the ropes have loosened. He abstractly unwinds them but his face is still* *concentrated in the direction of Sophie. Humbly.)* I am free; you've set me free to return and love you again.

Reve. *(The wind. Suddenly Reve turns as if something pointed had touched him. He is face to face with the Priest.)* I thought . . .

Old Priest. You were wrong. I untied you.

Reve. But I am free, yes I am, to go home.

Old Priest. Where is that?

Reve. *(points in the direction from which Sophie's voice came)* That way.

Old Priest. You have lost your way, I'm afraid.

Reve. No, for the first time I know it.

Old Priest. *(quietly)* Can you go back to a voice?

Reve. It was more than a voice. My life, hope . . .

Old Priest. You look like a man that has destroyed himself—but didn't you set out to prove something to yourself?

Reve. How did you know that?

Old Priest. We all set out . . .

Reve. *(more to himself)* For a minute I thought you knew me.

Old Priest. Perhaps I do. So you are going back without accomplishing what you set out to do.

Reve. I'm going to someone I never should have left. I'm sick, I'm dying.

Old Priest. Will she love you still when you come with none of your fine dreams made true?

Reve. How do you know my dreams?

Old Priest. *(shrugs)* Don't they still mean something to you?

Reve. Only that voice I heard means—anything. Good-bye old man. *(starts off and staggers against a stool and falls)*

Old Priest. *(helping him up)* I know where there's a kingdom for the taking.

Reve. I don't believe it.

Old Priest. Neither did I until I saw the place.

Reve. Where?

Old Priest. Come with me and I will show you what you have sought, face to face.

Reve. My road is clear now. I know it.

Old Priest. *(smiling)* You thought that voice freed you too. You were wrong. Why journey over half the world to an uncertainty?

Reve. *(Reve turns. Undecided.)* You only freed my hands, my body, yes you did. But that voice freed . . .

Old Priest. Your heart.

Reve. Yes—that's what it did.

Old Priest. Your ambition too?

Reve. Who are you really? Just answer that.

Old Priest. I'm an old Priest who knows of a kingdom that needs a king.

Reve. You said that.
Old Priest. That needs you.
Reve. Me?
Old Priest. You have experience *(lets this soak in)*, determination, knowledge, you have followed only the path that added to your ambition.
Reve. Good-bye.
Old Priest. *(softly)* All right, Reve Grant.
Reve. Reve Grant. How do you know my name?
Old Priest. Our paths have crossed many times.
Reve. I don't remember . . .
Old Priest. Who would notice an old man in rags.
Reve. I can't think. Am I dying?
Old Priest. You will die . . . sometime . . sometime . . .
Reve. *(staggering)* Help . . . me . . . home.
Old Priest. *(Taking Reve's arm. They begin to walk. The first row of jungle trees part and they move off up left. We hear the Old Priest's voice.)* The temple is on a mountain only a short walk and we'll be out of the jungle climbing to a kingdom you'll never forget. At dawn the bells ring in the new day. You hear them for miles. *(Bells ring clear and cool. Reve and the Priest have disappeared. Appearing with Reve.)* The Temple of the Sun: Ynti.

(The last row of trees part and reveal the exterior of the Temple of the Sun at Cuzco. It is on high ground and has a broad base that pyramids up. We don't see the top. The facade is decorated with strange stone carvings and weird gargoyle faces. It is early morning. The whole effect in the light is one of decay from mold, erosion, misuse. There is a pagan quality too and the broken statues seem to grin directly at Reve who is surprised and his first impulse is to run away but the Priest takes up a long staff that leans against the facade. It is encrusted with jewels. He turns and looks at the staff and then to the Old Priest.)

Reve. Well, I never dreamed anything like this—no, I never did. Not even when I was dreaming, frisky boy. *(looking at facade faces)* You know these faces can't scare me. They have a secret and I'll get it out of them, yes I will.
Old Priest. We offer you what you've searched for all your life.
Reve. I might be tricked.
Old Priest. In that case you can go back by our own road to your voice. *(looking at the temple and at the staff)* This is here—concrete centuries. Power and glory, all you want. A kingdom surpassing dreams.
Reve. Perhaps you're right. *(Old Priest twists the staff so that it catches the light. Reve looks at it.)* And you say there is power—and a crown?

Old Priest. *(pausing)* Are you ready? *(The strange bells again. The Old Priest stands aside for Reve to enter a thick encrusted door which he has opened. The music rises. Suddenly it is dark and we see Reve at the entrance to a room framed by the door, against the brilliant rectangular light. It is a large stony room with grinning carved faces on the walls.)* We'll take over. *(The Priest takes a resonator whistle out of his pocket and blows. Three doors open and suddenly a great clatter is heard. Swinging from ropes and rushing through the doors come white apes screaming and clattering. The Old Priest locks the door with a big key. Reve is bewildered at the clattering throng that surrounds him.)*

Old Priest. *(whispering)* Absolute reason died last night. They thought I was crazy.

Reve. Crazy?

Old Priest. *(whispering)* That was before last night.

Reve. These white apes . . .

Old Priest. They were apes. I've made them flesh of my flesh. *(He raps a gong. The apes straighten up. Their arms now hang humanly; their heads straighten.)*

Reve. I . . . I . . . see.

(The Priest raps his staff and the apes walk to their places, some daintily, some archly, some with dignity, some aggressively. They imitate men and women. They sit about the room.)

Old Priest. And you, my dear friend, are their King.

Reve. The honor is too great, yes it is.

Old Priest. Nothing is too great for Reve Grant.

Reve. My time is short. I have appointments. *(angrily)* I've been tricked.

Old Priest. I promised you a kingdom.

Reve. *(trying to get out without ruffling the Old Priest)* I really must go.

Old Priest. *(laying a hand on Reve's arm)* Where? To your voice?

Reve. What voice?

Old Priest. Have you forgotten already? *(pause)* We have been practicing secretly for you. We knew you would come to us someday. Now the hour has come to show you.

Reve. I appreciate everything, but . . .

Old Priest. *(draws up stool for Reve; bids him sit; raps with staff)* The hour has come. *(The chamber begins to echo.)* Reason died last night. Long live Reve Grant in the reward prepared for him. Come meet your King.

Reve. No! No! I'm not their kind. This is not the kingdom I dreamed of.

Old Priest. Isn't it?

Reve. I'm not worthy.

Old Priest. Yes, you are.

Reve. I'm not fit.

Old Priest. You have prepared for many years by following your own path. That is their creed. They will be themselves entirely with you to teach them so much.

Reve. Let me out of here.

Old Priest. *(ignoring him)* Do you have the key? Let us proceed then. *(The apes go into more animated activity as Priest raps staff. They then gather in groups and go about their own business.)* Now I'll show you what deep concentrated lives *we* live. *(He moves from Reve and then turns and beckons him to follow. Reve does so. They pause before a group that sit eating. One eats daintily, another gouging the food into his mouth. But they all eat continuously.)* Nothing else satisfies them. Day in and day out they stuff themselves.

One Eater. *(looking up grinning, then stands and runs hand over her fat shape)* The more I eat, the skinnier I get. *(to Reve directly)* Isn't that so?

Reve. Well . . . ?

Eater. The more I eat the skinnier I get. *(Eater begins to shake from side to side. Then she sits again and eats. The other eaters follow.)*

Reve. *(to Priest)* They talk English?

Old Priest. They are learned men.

Reve. Yes. *(pause as Priest looks him in the face)* Yes, they are.

Female Ape. *(The Old Priest and Reve move on. A clatter is heard overhead. Reve looks up. A female ape is calling from her swing. She looks down at Reve and beckons flirtingly.)* Wanna come up here? Wanna come up here?

Old Priest. Every man she sees she wants. She gets them, too.

Reve. *(moving away)* She won't get me.

Female Ape. *(still beckoning)* Wanna come up here? Wanna come up here?

Old Priest. *(to female ape, winking)* There's time for that—later.

Reve. *(taking some coins from his vest)* Perhaps she'd like to play with these.

Old Priest. *(whispering)* Put your money away, Reve Grant, she doesn't require it. *(They move to one ape lying on his belly drawing on a large paper.)* He invents all day long. *(to inventor)* What are you working on today?

Inventor. A secret war. All men will die.

Reve. Everybody knows that.

Inventor. You're a liar. *(over his drawing again)* A secret war. All men will die.

Female Ape. Wanna come up here? Wanna come up here?

Eater. The more I eat the skinnier I get.

Old Priest. *(raising his voice but not paying attention to the phrases that* *background what he says; moving with Reve to another group that has begun to play music on strange sounding pan pipes, Tinyas, five-string guitars, and thin and thick drums)* They play their music all day, perfecting their technique.

Reve. Doesn't it annoy the others?
Old Priest. The others are concentrating on themselves.
Reve. It could drive a man mad.
Old Priest. There is only sanity here. Reason died last night. Everything is upside down, outside.
Reve. Don't they have any senses?
Old Priest. No. They are men, only animals have feeling. *(rapping his staff)* Your King is here!
Female Ape. Wanna come up here? Wanna come up here? *(The eaters begin to shimmy.)*
Inventor. All men will die tomorrow.

(The music plays louder. A group of apes near the musicians begin dancing. The place is in an uproar. The female ape glides down and rushes toward a male ape holding him in a tight embrace.)

The Male Ape. I'll die in love. I'll die in love.
Female Ape. Wanna come up here?
Reve. *(pointing to the lovers)* She'll hug him to death!
Old Priest. She wants love.
Inventor. A secret war. Everyone will die.

(The music becomes maddening, the dancers dance harder. Reve puts his hand over his ears.)

Reve. Tell them to stop.
Old Priest. You are their King. You tell them.
Eater. Skinnier I get. Skinnier I get.
Reve. Am I going crazy? All right. All right. All right. I'm one of you. Stop. Only stop. *(Nobody stops. To Old Priest.)* Help me! Help me! I can't think any longer. I don't even know my name.
Female Ape. Wanna come up here?
Reve. *(in frenzy to Old Priest)* What is my name?
Old Priest. King Reve. King Reve.
Apes. King Reve. King Reve.

(Reve screams and sinks down. The Old Priest takes a crown of old grass and straw from his garments, rips off his old cloak, and puts them on Reve. The apes lift Reve high and place him on the swing and he swings back and forth.)

Old Priest. He's a King now. *(The apes prostrate themselves. In a terrible* *voice, low and piercing.)* You've seen me before, Reve Grant. You knew you had to come to me at last.

(The music gets louder and the apes rise and scream gesticulating up at Reve crowned in the swing. With his hair dishevelled and the rags with the crown of straw, he looks like some old King Lear. Hanging only by his two hands, he falls in a heap to the floor. Every ape has disappeared. The Old Priest is no longer old. He stands upright. In one hand he has a molding ladle. He is dressed in a dark cassock and he stands over Reve.)

Reve. *(Limp with agony, coming to. Even his voice seems old and cracked.)* Where am I? Who am I?
The Stranger. Reve Grant.
Reve. I'm Reve Grant. Now I remember—I think I do. Give me my crown! I was promised a crown.
The Stranger. *(picking up a crown of dried grass)* It's on your head.
Reve. I was promised a sceptre. *(The Stranger hands him the bottle of brandy.)* Tricked. I was tricked. *(He tries to stand but cannot.)* I wanted freedom, glory. *(The Stranger hands him the chains.)*
The Stranger. You had your choice. You should have selected more wisely. You chose the kingdom of compromise, of nothing, of mediocrity.
Reve. How is a man to know? How is a man to know?
The Stranger. Ask his heart.
Reve. Where is mine?
The Stranger. *(holding up the ladle)* Do you know what this is, Reve Grant? *(Reve crawls away frightened.)* Do you know?
Reve. Let me go home.
The Stranger. That's only putting it off.
Reve. Let me go home.
The Stranger. I'll find you wherever you go.
Reve. Let me go home.
The Stranger. Remember, Reve. *(He puts robe of rags around Reve.)* You've forgotten your royal robe. *(He is lost in darkness and only a small light is on Reve. He feels at his crown, rips it off and begins to whimper.)*
Reve. Let me go home, let me go. *(He staggers off. There is no answer and the light goes out.)*

(When the music dies away we see that Palmetto Farm has run down. There is the platform where the fiddlers played before and on either side of it two poles which hold a sign saying: HALLOWEEN AUCTION SALE OF INSTRUMENTS AND RARE BELONGINGS OF SPIRITS, GHOSTS AND OTHERS. *Crowd of boys, girls, and adults are downstage near the porch. Everyone wears a little costume mask. Perdido is in the middle of the platform. Near him is a large*

box. It is Halloween night. Some children are dressed up in old clothes or costumes, many have balloons. They are singing softly and dancing around the platform informally. Reve is lying in the same place on stage where we left him last scene.)

Willie Silvers. *(old man now)* Hurry up, hurry up, you all, or we won't be near enough ready when the priest come for All Saints.

(All gather round the platform.)

Perdido. First I'm gonna show you what we got, then you can make your bids. Make sure your mask's tied mighty tight or else the spirit of Annie Christmas or Reve Grant or somebody will leap outta the bayou and there ain't no telling then what will happen. *(A little girl screams and the crowd laughs.)* Now this here . . . *(He holds up something that looks like dried thick leaves on a string.)* This here is the string of ears Annie Christmas wore about her neck. Ears of all the men she killed. *(A make-believe shudder goes through the crowd. A girl comes up and Perdido puts the necklace around her neck. She stands up to his left.)* And here is the old toy molder Reve Grant used to make leaden toys out of and cast them into the bayou for the evil folks to play with. *(A child takes the molder and stands beside the necklace girl. Perdido holds up a terrifying mask of a black cat with a skin attached to it like an apron with admiration.)* Here's the black cat Reve Grant skinned with his own teeth when he went to the Voodoos and crawled like a snake. *(A boy runs up and puts on the mask and skin and stands beside the other two behind Perdido.)*

Perdido. I hate to take this one out—it give me the ice chill in my spine.
Crowd. Come on! Let us see it! That's what I'm gonna bid on!
Perdido. This one probably gonna be the most expensive of all.
Crowd. Show it to us.
Perdido. *(taking out an alligator mask and hanging body)* Reve rode the bayous and under the water on this alligator—he saw ever kinda thing and it were never seen before. *(A young boy puts it on and stands by the other three. Quickly Perdido pulls out and puts on himself a long cloak.)* This here's the cloak Reve Grant stole Bijou away in on her wedding night.
Reve. Some sazerac!! I need a drink. *(Someone hands him one.)* Then I'll auction off more rubbish. All my own—every last thing.
A Boy. What have you got?
Reve. A palace. Set beside a Bayou Desire and built of cedar wood.
Boy. A penny.
Reve. A penny with a drink and it's yours. *(He is handed a drink which he puts on the table beside him.)*

Perdido. *(He leads the crowd over to Reve. The masked ones gather behind Reve in a semicircle.)* We'll have that old man dancing the carabine.

Reve. Sabine, my shining horse. What do you bid for him?

One. Show him to us.

Reve. He's near the sunset, boys, waiting for night to gallop to the moon. He races as fast as your Reve Grant could fashion a lie.

Perdido. What else have you got, old man?

Reve. A dream of a prayer book. You can have it for a plate of shrimp.

Perdido. Eat 'em yourself. *(laughter)*

Reve. I have an empire, too. Here it is. *(He throws his hands out as if he were tossing gold with a magnificent gesture.)* Run for it.

Boy. Where's your crown?

Reve. A crown. Yes, a crown of Spanish moss that will fit anyone. *(pointing to his hair and his beard and eyes successively)* Here's the white hair of a man crazy as a bessie bug. Here's the beard of a prophet whose prophecy never came true. Here's a pair of eyes that have seen more glories than Solomon and women sweeter than Sheba, all of it you can have if you point out to me a sign telling me which way to go home.

Perdido. You mean the crazy house most likely.

Reve. Now that might be. *(Crowd laughs.)* Tell me one thing before I go. *(He turns to the masked figures.)* Who was Reve Grant? *(The masked faces go from side to side. They jump up and down. They begin to dance about Reve. Cries.)* Who was he? *(The dancing continues.)* Who was Reve Grant? *(He runs in and out of the dancers. He grasps Perdido's arm. The dancers stop.)* Who was he?

Perdido. He could tell the tallest tales; all about how he did this and that wonderful doing. I think he did them too.

Reve. Where's that crackerjack Reve Grant now?

Perdido. He went out past the Gulf of Mexico. He tipped a great big island into the sea and made the earth quake. I felt it too. When he spoke he spit fire and burned his mama's hair; oh, he did everything. And they tell me he poisoned children what played with golden toys, just to get them toys.

Reve. *(bowing)* Now thank you. Thank you all. *(Pathetically. As he leans old and decrepit against the table sweeping some of the refreshments off, an uneasy silence falls over the crowd that was mocking before. Then a church bell begins to ring softly. The children with the masks of Reve's exploits take them off and leave them around Reve. Nearby, but offstage, we hear a Priest's voice intoning an All Saints Day service. The two boys with tapers light the candles the crowd already had. The crowd responds in a chant to the Priest's leadership. Now the Priest enters with acolytes and a cross. The crowd kneels, the Priest blesses them briefly. He takes up the chant again and leads the procession. They move off. A little apart* *from the last person is Sophie-Louise with a candle and a rosary, saying her beads. She moves across stage and as she is almost off Reve recognizes her. Reve tries to stand but he can't make it. He is alone now with only a light from the farmhouse to show him. He turns in the direction Sophie-Louise went. A ghostly music comes from the direction of the platform where the fiddlers played on Bijou's wedding night—it plays the same song as when Reve first asked Sophie-Louise to dance. Reve's body sways to the music. He stops—leans in the direction Sophie-Louise went and whispers.)* Dance with me, Sophie-Louise. *(He moves off to follow the procession.)*

(All is dark and silent except the chanting of the Priest and the response of the people, and then stars come out and shine through the live oaks that have slid in. We see tombstones and vaults with flowers and candles that are still-flamed in the moonlight. On one vault stone down left we recognize the name Maud Grant. Before this vault Sophie-Louise is kneeling. A few from the procession are leaving now. Willie Silvers moves from darkness toward Sophie-Louise. The chanting has almost faded.)

Willie. *(as Sophie-Louise finishes her beads and starts to rise)* Good evening, m'am.
Sophie-Louise. *(looking up)* I did not see you here. I thought it was a shadow.
Willie. I-I am a-a shadow, Sophie-Louise.
Sophie-Louise. That is nice that you know my name.
Willie. I've s-seen you often. The first time was at Bijou's wedding.
Sophie-Louise. I can't see your face. I am almost blind, but Bijou's wedding. I remember that. Oh, yes, I remember. *(pause)* I was saying prayers for an old friend, Maud Grant.
Willie. I remember her.
Sophie-Louise. My whole family is buried here.
Willie. I-I know . . .
Sophie-Louise. Tonight there is something different. Something in the air. Somebody.
Willie. Nobody new been buried in the past three months.
Sophie-Louise. Not dead, *mon ami,* not dead. Something is here and I should recognize it. I feel it but do not know . . . *(trails off)*
Willie. *(uneasy)* Everybody's gone home. Can I help you home?
Sophie-Louise. No, merci. I do not want to leave yet. Goodnight, M'sieu'.
Willie. May the L-L-Lord bless you. *(He leaves.)*
Sophie-Louise. *(not realizing that he has gone)* Yes. And may Le Bon Dieu bless all of us. *(She stands for a moment and then takes her stick that leans against the vault. She starts off down left. Reve enters up right and moves in and out of tombstones toward her. She is off and Reve is about*

to follow when a figure stands before him. Reve is determined to get to Sophie-Louise and tries to get by. The figure lays a hand on Reve.)
Reve. I must go after her. Turn me loose. I say turn me loose. *(They tussle. A strong wind rises blowing most of the candles out. The figure has disappeared and Reve is grappling with himself, panting now. He brushes off his coat and starts out again.)*
Stranger's Voice. *(from up right says quietly)* Now where are you going so fast?
Reve. None of your business.
Stranger. *(appearing from shadows)* I'd advise you not to try that wrestling again. You might get hurt—or—
Reve. Or?
Stranger. Or something worse.
Reve. Who are you?
Stranger. I've been waiting to see you again since our first meeting.
Reve. I never clapped eyes on you. Say your say, I'm in a hurry.
Stranger. *(holding up an odd instrument)* I'm a toy molder. That's all. It's very simple. Last time I saw you, you were being crowned. But your memory is short.
Reve. I never was crowned anything. I don't want to buy toys.
Molder. I'm not a peddler, Reve Grant.
Reve. What do you want with me?
Molder. You'd make an interesting toy. I want to melt you down. *(holds up instrument)*
Reve. Melt? Take that dirty old thing away from here. It smells like rubbish.
Molder. Oh, my ladle's clean, clean as can be considering what's been in it. Are you coming? *(Reve makes a gesture of disgust and starts off. The Molder stands before him again.)* I've ordered a good coffin for you and reserved a vault. My Master wants your soul . . . *(sternly)* . . . now!
Reve. *(disturbed now)* I do remember you—an Old Priest.
Molder. That's correct. Now your soul, if you please.
Reve. I don't please.
Molder. You must.
Reve. *(sensing what might be in store for him)* I must. *(pause)* I—I can't think now. Yes—yes, you are . . .
Molder. I told you. A molder of toys. Leaden toys, Reve. *(Reve laughs.)* It's not a joke.
Reve. *(ironically)* Now I meet you, now. When I was knee high to a grasshopper my mama told me if I was good, if I helped gather the crop, if I fed the chickens—I'd meet the molder of toys. *(snaps out of his confusion)* Well, I've met you, so I must've been good. It's logic— I've done nothing wrong.

Molder. *(quiet, but so serious even Reve becomes alarmed)* Not so fast. You can't wipe away your deeds that way. Yes, you have sinned, not deeply—you walked all around the fire of evil and every once in a while you stuck your finger in. You were like a child fascinated by the brightness but afraid to go further. Something always held you back and whispered "No."

Reve. Sure. That's it, yes it is. I never did nothing much bad, as you said just now. *(He starts to move away.)* Then I can go, just like I came.

Molder. No you can't. You'll be in my ladle with the rest of the rubbish to be melted down. What toy would you like to be?

Reve. The rest of the rubbish . . .

Molder. Yes. Your soul is good for nothing else.

Reve. *(after a moment's hesitation)* You're a man of intellect, I can see that just as plain. Why do you want to fool around with toys? Child's play—why man you're above that. Yes, you are.

Molder. *(firmly)* I want your soul.

Reve. You won't get it. No, you won't. Why you said I wasn't evil, well then I was good.

Molder. You're not going to Heaven, you know. You could never get there even if the population decreased a good deal and angels were needed desperately.

Reve. Who wants Heaven. I never mentioned Heaven . . .

Molder. And you weren't evil enough for Hell. So . . . I get you for my ladle. I get all the rubbish, the in-betweens, the souls that compromised.

Reve. Now look here . . . I have some money.

Molder. Reve Grant!

Reve. Well then—I lied. I—I said I never did any evil. I was evil as Hell, let me tell you. I was a hellion, yes I was.

Molder. Prove it.

Reve. I will too.

Molder. My Master won't be impressed.

Reve. When I get through with proving, he'll wish he'd never sent for me. *(The Molder looks him straight in the eye.)* I *am* fit for Hell, but you think I'll stand here and say Reve was rubbish, just rubbish, well you . . .

Molder. What?

Reve. Give me this chance. It's only natural for me to want a chance to prove what I know is true.

Molder. All right. You'll have a chance.

Reve. *(swaggering again)* You just go on and peddle those toys you mold so fast. *(He starts off.)*

Molder. Prove it here.

Reve. Among the dead? Tombstones can't testify.

Molder. The living or the dead, the answer will be the same. *(Reve tries to think of a way out.)*

Reve. Now the dead are dead. Isn't that true?

Molder. That's true.

Reve. Well then how can . . .

Molder. *(final)* Prove it here. *(Reve doesn't know what to do.)* What real evil, Reve?

Reve. Well now—well—I—well there was Bijou. Why I beat that girl within an inch of her hide. I ruined her life, yes I did. She died because of me. She hated me in the end. There! I stole her away on her wedding night.

Molder. You did all that out of spite, not evil.

Reve. Just the same she hated me.

Molder. Did she?

Reve. The devil with her. Let her burn for all I care; burn her kiss. *(He takes the flowers Willie put on her vault and throws them away.)*

Molder. I thought you wanted a chance.

Reve. Yes I do. But you want to bring up the dead. Is that fair? Why don't you let me talk to someone who's walking and talking and breathing? I couldn't even answer her back.

Molder. Whatever you say. Only I haven't much longer.

Reve. I suppose you're going to stand around and watch.

Molder. I'll stay out of sight. I saw someone coming this way. Maybe he's your salvation.

Reve. Who? I can find my own proof. There's enough of it.

Molder. He may know you.

Reve. *(looking off downstage)* Don't try to trick me again. *(He turns but the Molder is gone. Reve looks down again and hides behind the first tombstone, peeking out every once in a while to see how near the one coming is. An old man looking like a picked bird enters puffing and blowing. Reve peeks out and pulls his head in again.)*

Old Man. *(whining)* Everybody's duly run on. I walked so fast, too. I'll just sit down here and get me some rest. *(He sits on the nearest tombstone fanning himself with both his hands. Reve starts to crawl from behind the stone where he had hidden without being noticed, but the Old Man spies him. Old Man unafraid, whistles at him. Reve turns and stands up as if he wasn't doing anything.)*

Reve. Thought I had lost something around here.

Old Man. Let me help you. Mighta been a piece of money. *(suddenly)* How about a penny for a poor old man?

Reve. I don't have one red cent.

Old Man. You know, your voice sounds mighty familiar to me. I know you from somewhere.

Reve. Well, yours doesn't to me. *(starting off)* I'm in a hurry. Important business doesn't wait for nobody, no it doesn't.
Old Man. *(standing and bowing)* Prince Reve.
Reve. Prince Re . . . I never saw you before.
Old Man. *(going up to him)* Under the bayous setting on the floating roots of cedar trees.
Reve. *(moving away)* Go on from here.
Old Man. Ahhhhhhhh.
Reve. *(going up to him)* Hethabella's Papa. King Loup, yes you are. *(The sky turns that aquamarine color.)*
King Loup. My crown, my scepter all gone.
Reve. I can see that.
King Loup. That's duly right. I'm begging my daily bread these days.
Reve. *(expanding)* I was looking for someone like you.
King Loup. Everything's different. Hethabella's turned out to be a big mess but that boy of yours—he's got frisking little babies in every parish and then . . .
Reve. I want to ask you something.
King Loup. Yes, your highness.
Reve. Stop calling me that.
King Loup. I always admired you, Reve.
Reve. Then will you do something for me?
King Loup. Will you give me something to eat?
Reve. Anything you want.
King Loup. *(quickly)* What do you want me to do?
Reve. Swear that I was evil, doing your daughter so bad and deserting my own son, your grandson, too. And tricking you.
King Loup. Who me? You didn't trick me.
Reve. *(lowering his voice)* Don't talk so loud.
King Loup. *(whispering)* I got to decline, hungry as I am, fallen from grace as I duly am. I can't swear nothing like that.
Reve. *(whispering)* You're out of your head.
King Loup. I duly remember you wouldn't no more plunge yourself into being a Loup Garou cause you was scared of the evil—blood drinking and all. You wouldn't go all the way.
Reve. *(whispering)* Sh—sh. Don't talk so loud.
King Loup. *(whispering)* I'm just trying to duly answer your question.
Reve. *(whispering)* Not so loud. Go on to a hospital. You're sick or crazy—one.
King Loup. *(whispering)* Have you got any bread?
Reve. *(trying to push him out)* Go on to a hospital.
King Loup. *(whispering)* Can't get into a hospital. Nobody believes King Loup is living any more. I'm supposed to be a legend. I'm just a story, Reve.

Reve. *(disgusted)* Goody-bye.

King Loup. I'm like the chimney smoke. I'm something in the wind. *(He has gone off mumbling and the aquamarine color goes too. Reve starts off up left. The Molder steps out from behind a tombstone.)*

Molder. Were you going to look for me?

Reve. *(lying)* Yes, I was.

Molder. Your proof?

Reve. More than you could bear. Why that old man was a friend of mine in crime. We'd tempt people into the Bayou Goula and drain their blood. He still recalls all that, yes he does. *(starting off)* Good-evening, Mr. Molder.

Molder. You're saved?

Reve. I told you so. *(starts walking)*

Molder. I'll just call him back to put his testimony in writing. We keep an accurate file. *(moves away to call, putting his hands to his lips)*

Reve. I don't think you'd better do that. He was mighty hungry. I believe he must have dropped by the wayside. Probably too weak to talk.

Molder. Your time's up, Reve. Come on. You know I heard everything. That whispering didn't fool me.

Reve. *(afraid now)* One more chance. One—only one. *(talking fast)* Now listen to this: In Panama I was ready to take over the whole country and beat the people down so I could stand up over them. I didn't care about their freedom or nothing.

Molder. I'm talking about the things you did. We'll erase what you were supposed to have done. You know, Reve, you never could separate what is real and what you dream up.

Reve. But I would have done all that evil.

Molder. It's almost dawn, Reve.

Reve. I ruined Sophie-Louise.

Molder. You were ashamed of her goodness.

Reve. Hethabella?

Molder. You were afraid to plunge into her evil. So you chose rubbish instead. You wouldn't do one thing or the other.

Reve. The slaves I smuggled. Maud—call them up.

Molder. Do you really want me to do it?

Reve. *(desperate)* Yes. Yes.

Molder. Let the slaves rest, they're tired.

Reve. You told me you could call them up.

Molder. *(a little tired)* Slaves for St. Kitts, Trinidad, Haiti, missionaries to the same place. I know all about it.

Reve. Then Maud, she had a mouth on her. She'll tell you.

Molder. I thought you didn't want testimony from the dead.

Reve. Well, it's different now.

Molder. All right. It's your trial. *(coming down before Maud's vault, calling softly)* Maud. *(The sky becomes dim. The stars go out.)* Just for a short while, Maud. *(From behind the low vault Maud rises and all the moonlight seems to gather about her.)* Maud, I wanted to ask you about Reve.

Reve. *(desperate)* Mama save me. Please tell him how I treated you, how you slaved and slaved and I left you, yes, I did, to crawl around. Tell him how mean I was.

(Maud keeps looking at the Molder.)

Molder. Tell me about your son.
Maud. About Reve?
Molder. Yes.
Maud. Great suffering Job. That snake-mouth. He dumped me in the brake cane like a package of garbage where any old thing could bite me to death, any old thing . . . but oh the party he took me to at St. Peter's . . . it was a hallelujah to me, yes it was.
Molder. You'd better get your rest now, Maud. Dawn will be up soon. Good morning.
Maud. *(curtseying)* Good evening, sir. *(She disappears.)*
Reve. Mama, you come back here. *(no response)* Damn you, God damn you for lying on me. *(to Molder)* I cursed at my mama. That's evil.
Molder. Only words, Reve, only words. It's time.
Reve. *(dully)* Time.
Molder. *(starting out up left)* We go this way, Reve Grant.
Reve. I have until dawn. Until then. It's not dawn yet.
Molder. There are no more witnesses for you to call.
Reve. I know that, yes I do.
Molder. It will be over soon.
Reve. *(almost dazed)* Until dawn. I want to sit by myself till dawn . . . dawn.
Molder. You know I'll find you.
Reve. I won't be far away.
Molder. No tricks?
Reve. None. I've played them all.

(The Molder goes off. Reve moves down right. As he does the tombstones and vaults move off. There is low music. Reve sits wearily on the ground. Calling, his back to the audience.)

Reve. Who's here in the whole land . . .

(echo)

    Who's in Heaven . . .

(echo)

    Who's in Hell . . .

(echo; standing)

    To save Reve Grant.

(echo)

    Tell me that?

(no echo this time; putting his head in his hands)

    I'm alone and poor as crab grass. *(He coughs, then gives a low chuckle.)*
    I'll die by a bayou spitting blood. *(He begins to whimper.)*
    I don't want to die before I'm dead.

(A song sung by a woman rises up. Reve listens. Murmuring.)

    Sophie-Louise.

(louder)

    Sophie-Louise.

(louder)

    Sophie-Louise.

(He runs off. And now as the song continues, it is that dark hour before dawn. When light comes up again it is faint. The orchestra has taken up the song. We recognize the hut Reve built among live oaks. There is a light in the window. Now Reve is moving behind the trees. He comes out panting as if he had run to this song from the open space. The singing stops but the music continues.)

Reve. *(calling)* Sophie-Louise! Sophie-Louise! *(Sophie-Louise comes to the door.)*
Sophie-Louise. Who called me? Tell me who you are and what can I do to help you, M'sieu.
Reve. *(coming out of the shadows)* I'm a sinner, tell me I'm a sinner, save me.
Sophie-Louise. Who are you?
Reve. I don't know.
Sophie-Louise. *(carried away)* Your voice. It's your voice.
Reve. Oh Sophie-Louise. Sophie-Louise! *(She gropes to find him.)* Tell him how I sinned against you!
Sophie-Louise. Tell who? There is no one here. Oh, Reve, Reve, Reve, Reve. It's Reve.

Reve. Tell my crimes against you.

Sophie-Louise. Crimes? No crimes or sins. None at all.

Molder's Voice. Reve Grant.

Reve. *(anguish)* Hurry. Shout them out.

Sophie-Louise. *(Sits on the step. Reve moves to her.)* There is nothing to shout, my dear. The church bells will ring. That is all.

Reve. I'm lost unless you tell my crimes.

Sophie-Louise. *(taking his head in her lap)* Rest. Rest quietly, my Reve.

Reve. Where have I been since I held you in my arms between the live oaks and the cabin?

Sophie-Louise. In my faith, in my hope, and love. *(as dawn is washing the sky with pink and gray and blue)* No crying, my boy.

(She rocks him gently and then begins to softly sing a lullaby. Her song rises and the orchestra takes it up. The sun comes in rays between the live oaks and some fall on Reve and Sophie-Louise. Way downstage in shadows the Molder stands, motionless, waiting, but Sophie-Louise doesn't know that and continues to sing and rock Reve in her lap and stroke his hair as the curtain falls.)

(Curtain)

Take a Giant Step (1953)

Louis Peterson (b. 1922–)

Born and reared in Hartford, Connecticut, Louis Peterson, after earning a bachelor of arts degree in English from Morehouse College in Atlanta, studied at the Yale School of Drama and earned a master's degree in drama from New York University. Since then, he has studied drama briefly in a playwriting class taught by Clifford Odets, has acted professionally (Ward's *Our Lan'* provided one of his roles), and has written for motion pictures and for television.

Peterson gained prominence with the first Broadway production of *Take a Giant Step* during the season of 1953–54. A sensitively written, supposedly semi-autobiographical drama, *Take a Giant Step* explores the emotional frustration of a middle-class African American youth reared in a predominantly white neighborhood. In its emphasis the drama reflects a major thrust of such writers as Gwendolyn Brooks, Robert Hayden, Ralph Ellison, James Baldwin, and Lorraine Hansberry, who, during the late 1940s and the 1950s, attempted to educate white audiences to awareness both of the humanity of African Americans and the manner in which—despite some cultural differences—African Americans resemble their American neighbors in virtues and aspirations. Many of the problems of Spencer Scott, the protagonist, are the problems of a male American adolescent seeking to define his manhood. *Take a Giant Step,* however, demonstrates further significance as one of the first plays to dramatize realistically rather than melodramatically the racial problems that middle-class northern African Americans experience in schools, neighborhoods, and occupations where they are the minority. Like life itself, the play reveals ambiguity. By the end, Spencer Scott believes that he has identified the path to manhood, but readers may wonder whether his adult life will be any less frustrating than that of his father.

Selected Plays by Louis Peterson

Count Me for a Stranger (n.d.).
Entertain a Ghost (1962).

Take a Giant Step

CHARACTERS

Spencer Scott
Grandmother
Tony
Iggie
Frank
Man
Violet
Poppy
Rose
Carol
Lem Scott
May Scott
Christine
Gussie
Johnny Reynolds
Bobby Reynolds

SCENES

ACT I

Scene 1: The home of the Scotts. Late afternoon.
Scene 2: A bar in the Negro section. A few hours later.
Scene 3: Violet's room. Immediately following.

ACT II

Scene 1: Same as Scene 1, Act I. Later the same evening.
Scene 2: Spencer's bedroom. Two weeks later—early afternoon.
Scene 3: Same as Scene 1, Act I. The following day.

Note: It is essential to the mood of the play that the settings be simple and suggestive rather than elaborately realistic.

ACT I

SCENE 1

If you walked down a rather shady, middle-class street in a New England town, you would probably find a house very similar to the one in which the Scotts live. It was a rather ordinary house when it was built and it is a rather ordinary house now, but it has been well cared for, devotedly watched and cared for, and it gives off an aura of good health and happiness if houses can ever know such things. The house has been cut away to expose to view to the audience the back entrance hall, a kitchen up left, a dining room left, a living room and a hall right in which there is a front door and a staircase leading to the upstairs. At the very top of the stairs, there is a little chair almost like a child's chair. If the house has any character at all it should resemble a fat old lady who has all the necessary equipment of living about her person.

If you walked down a rather shady, middle-class street in a New England town you would probably hear the same sounds that you are hearing when the Curtain rises. The sounds of boys playing baseball in the lot across the street. Spencer Scott enters from right into his own yard. He is a Negro boy of seventeen years. He has a croquet stake in one hand that he has pulled up out of the ground, and books in his other hand. He is hitting the side of his leg with the stake. The time is the present—Fall—late October. It is a fine day—a golden warm day which is typical of New England at this time of year. After a moment Spence, still carrying the stake, walks into the hall. He slams the front door. On the door slam offstage noises stop. Grandma immediately calls offstage:

Grandma. *(in bedroom upstairs)* Spence. Spence. Is that you?
Spence. Yes, it's me, Gram. Who the hell does she think it is—Moses? *(jacket and books on sofa)*
Grandma. Where have you been?
Spence. No place.
Grandma. Well, why are you so late coming home?
Spence. No reason in particular, Gram. I just took my time. You know how that is—don't you, Gram—when you just want to take your time coming home? *(sits on sofa; takes off shoes)*
Grandma. Just a minute—I can't hear you. I'll be right down.
Spence. If you do—I'll tell Mom that you've been horsing around again today.
Grandma. Just you be quiet and come up and help me.
Spence. *(gets up, goes upstairs)* You know you haven't got any business

coming downstairs. Mom told you to stay up. Not only am I going to tell Mom, but when the doctor comes, I'm going to tell him too.

Grandma. *(appears at door)* Tell him. You think I care. Now come up and help me.

Spence. *(goes all the way upstairs and helps her)* Just lean on me, and hold tight to the railing, and I think we'll make it.

Grandma. *(comes downstairs)* I don't know why I can't come downstairs if I want to. *(pauses as she labors down the stairs)* And you keep your mouth shut about it, too.

Spence. *(coming downstairs)* I've already told you what I'm going to do. I'm going to spill the beans all over the house.

Grandma. You do and I'll tell your mother you were late coming home from school and that you haven't practiced yet.

Spence. You'd better put all your concentration on getting down the steps, Gram, or you're gonna fall and break your behind.

Grandma. Now you stop that kind of talk—you hear me?

Spence. Now be careful, Gram—and don't get excited.

Grandma. Well then—you stop it—you hear me?

Spence. All right, Gram. All right. Just stop hopping around like a sparrow.

Grandma. I never thought I'd live to see the day when my own daughter's child was cursing like a trooper.

Spence. Haven't said anything yet, Gram. All I said was if you weren't careful you'd fall down and break your behind. And you will, too.

Grandma. Take your hands off me. I can do the rest myself. *(Crosses downstage toward kitchen. She notices the stake.)* What are you doing with that dirty thing in the house?

Spence. I wanted it. Something to bang around.

Grandma. You're banging dirt all over the rug. *(She is going into the kitchen. Spence is going toward the living room.)* Where are you going?

Spence. I'm going in and practice. *(crosses to piano)*

Grandma. Wouldn't you like something to eat first?

Spence. No, I wouldn't. You think you can trick me—don't you? *(crosses down center to Grandma; crosses to piano)* I'm going in and practice and then you won't have a thing to tell Mom when she gets home.

Grandma. Suit yourself. *(She sits on sofa. He sits down and begins practicing scales. There is a pause.)* Spencer, would you get me a glass of water? I'm so out of breath.

Spence. *(still practicing)* You mooched down all those stairs without batting an eye. You can get your own water. *(piano starts)*

Grandma. You're a mean little beggar.

Spence. I know it.

Grandma. Well, come out and talk to me. I won't tell her.

Spence. You're sure?

Grandma. You don't take my word?

Spence. I took your word the day before yesterday, and as a result I had to practice two hours in the morning.

Grandma. Well go get it and stop that racket.

Spence. *(gets up, crosses to bookcase for book)* You know, sometimes Gram, I think that you're uncultured and have no respect for art. *(crosses to sofa with book)* Put your right hand on this. Now repeat after me.

Grandma. I'll do no such thing.

Spence. *(taking the book)* O.K. then—don't. *(moves right)*

Grandma. What do you want me to say?

Spence. *(coming back, sits on sofa)* I swear and promise that—no matter what happens—I will not tell anybody that Spencer Scott did not practice this afternoon—and if asked I will lie and say that he did.

Grandma. I swear and promise that—no matter what happens—I will not tell anybody that Spencer Scott did not practice this afternoon—and if asked I will lie and say that he did.

Spence. Telling also includes writing notes to said parties.

Grandma. Telling also includes writing notes to said parties.

Spence. I swear and promise under fear of death.

Grandma. I swear and promise under fear of death.

Spence. Amen.

Grandma. *(starts to answer, changes her mind)* No—I'm not—*(He puts her hand on book.)* Amen.

Spence. Kiss the book.

Grandma. I'll do no such thing. It's dirty.

Spence. Just one more time, Gram. Kiss the book.

Grandma. *(She kisses and notices.)* This isn't the Bible.

Spence. *(gets up; puts book on TV)* It's "Crime and Punishment." Don't try welching. *(crosses toward kitchen)* What do you want to eat?

Grandma. Anything will do.

Spence. We'll have some crackers and cheese. *(gets cheese out of refrigerator)* Gram—now there's just one more thing. I won't tell Mom about your coming downstairs if you'll—

Grandma. *(crossing for shoes at window right)* No—I'm not going to do it. I'll be a party to no such thing.

Spence. O.K., Gram. It's your funeral. You don't even know what kind of a bargain I was going to strike up with you.

Grandma. Yes, I do. You want a bottle of your father's beer.

Spence. *(closes refrigerator)* All right, Gram. Fine. When you're taking twice as many of those ugly, nasty tasting pills—don't say I didn't try to be a good sport.

Grandma. *(gets shoes at window)* One glass.
Spence. *(opens refrigerator)* It's a deal. One glass. *(to kitchen)* What shall I do with the rest of the bottle? *(Grandma crosses left.)* If he sees half a bottle he'll know right away.
Grandma. Pour it down the sink. *(crosses to right of table)*
Spence. Good idea. *(He opens the bottle and pours a glass.)*
Grandma. *(as he starts to pour the rest out)* How much is left?
Spence. Not much.
Grandma. Well bring it here. Shame to let it go to waste.
Spence. *(as he brings another glass over to the table)* You know, Gram. You ought to be in politics. You sure strike a hard bargain. *(sits left of table)*
Grandma. *(sits right of table)* If I didn't you'd walk all over me. *(pouring beer)* This is nice—isn't it?
Spence. Sure is. *(He picks up the stake again and starts hitting his leg.)*
Grandma. Put that dirty thing down. Stop hitting yourself with it. Where have you been?
Spence. *(still hitting himself)* Well I suppose I might as well tell you. Mom's probably going to hear it coming up the street.
Grandma. Well—what is it?
Spence. What could you possibly imagine as being just about the worst thing that could happen to me?
Grandma. You haven't gotten any little girls in trouble—have you?
Spence. Nothing like that, Gram. Worse.
Grandma. What have you done? Will you stop hitting yourself with that thing.
Spence. Well, Gram, I just went and got my ass kicked out of school today.
Grandma. Spencer Scott! What were you doing?
Spence. Nothing much. Just smoking in the john.
Grandma. Smoking! Where?
Spence. In the john—the can, Gram. The Men's Room.
Grandma. Well that's a pretty nasty place to be smoking if you ask me. What were you smoking?
Spence. A cigar.
Grandma. A cigar. Cigarettes are not dirty enough, I suppose. You have to start smoking cigars.
Spence. What are you getting so excited for? I took one of Pop's.
Grandma. Well you ought to be ashamed of yourself. Disgracing yourself in school.
Spence. *(gets up, crossing right)* Well I sure loused myself up proper this time.
Grandma. Where are you going?
Spence. To see if there's any mail. *(at piano; takes mail)*
Grandma. There's none for you.

Spence. Well you don't mind my looking anyhow, do you? *(He goes through the mail.)*

Grandma. You come right back here. I want to know more about this.

Spence. Just a second, Gram. Be patient—will you? *(pause)* I sure think that's a crummy way to behave. *(crosses down)* I've written him three letters now—the least he could do is answer one of them. *(puts letters on TV)*

Grandma. Who are you talking about now?

Spence. Mack—I'm talking about Mack.

Grandma. Your brother's probably busy with his lessons. You know what college is like.

Spence. No, I don't know what college is like. He's probably busy with the broads. The last letter I wrote him was about some damn important problems I got. He'll answer soon enough when he finds out they've shoved me into some loony bin. *(crosses back to left of table, hitting himself with stake)*

Grandma. What's the matter with you, Spence?

Spence. Aw! I don't know, Gram.

Grandma. Stop hitting yourself with that thing.

Spence. Will you leave me alone? Don't you understand that when a guy's upset he's got to hit himself with something? You gotta do something like that.

Grandma. *(softly)* What's the matter, Spence?

Spence. Aw, Gram. Cut out the sympathy please. Go on and finish your beer and get back upstairs before Mom catches you.

Grandma. Tell me about it, Spence?

Spence. *(pause)* There's nothing to tell. What's there to it. *(pause)* If you're gonna sit there and look at me that way I'm gonna start feeling sorry for myself and then I'm gonna start bawling—and then you'll start bawling and we won't get anywhere.

Grandma. What do you want me to do?

Spence. Keep eating.

Grandma. All right. I'm eating.

Spence. *(pause)* Well—from the very beginning of school I could've told you that that Miss Crowley and I weren't going to see eye to eye.

Grandma. Who's Miss Crowley?

Spence. The history teacher, Gram. The one that thinks she's cute. She's always giving the guys a preview of the latest fashions in underwear.

Grandma. Nasty little hussy.

Spence. That's the one. Well, today they started talking about the Civil War and one of the smart little skirts at the back of the room wanted to know why the Negroes in the South didn't rebel against slavery. Why did they wait for the Northerners to come down and help them? And this Miss Crowley went on to explain how they were stupid and didn't have sense enough to help themselves. *(crosses chair left of table; sits)* Well, anyway, Gram, when she got through talking they sounded like the worst morons that ever lived and I began to wonder how they'd managed to live a few thousand years all by themselves in Africa with nobody's help. I would have let it pass—see—except that the whole class was whispering and giggling and turning around and looking at me—so I got up and just stood next to my desk looking at her. She looked at me for a couple of minutes and asked me if perhaps I had something to say in the discussion. I said I might have a lot of things to say if I didn't have to say them in the company of such dumb jerks. Then I asked her frankly what college she went to.

Grandma. What did she say?

Spence. She told me I was being impudent. I told her it was not my intention to be impudent but I would honestly like to know. So she puts one hand on her hip—kinda throwing the other hip out of joint at the same time—and like she wants to spit on me she says "Scoville." Then I says, "And they didn't teach you nothing about the *up*rising of the slaves during the Civil War—or Frederick Douglass?" She says, "No—they didn't." "In that case," I said, "I don't want to be in your crummy history class." And I walk out of the room. When I get out in the hall, Gram, I'm shaking, I'm so mad—and I had this cigar I was going to sell for a sundae. I knew I couldn't eat a sundae now 'cause it would just make me sick so—I just had to do something so I went into the Men's Room and smoked the cigar. I just had about two drags on the thing when in comes the janitor and hauls me down to old Hasbrook's office—and when I get down there—there's Miss Crowley and old Hasbrook talking me over in low tones—and in five short minutes he'd thrown me out of school.

Grandma. I should've thought he would've given you another chance.

Spence. He's given me many other chances, Gram. I guess I'm just a chronic offender.

Grandma. How long are you out for?

Spence. It would've been one week, but since we have a week's vacation next week, he made it two weeks. Then I'm supposed to come back dragging Pop behind me like a tail. Is he going to be burned! *(pause)* Do you suppose Mom will go for the story, Gram?

Grandma. I'm not sure.

Spence. You mean she's not going to go for it at all.

Grandma. I'm afraid that you're going to get what you rightfully deserve.

Spence. That's a nasty thing to say—considering the fact that I was justified.

Grandma. There are ways and ways of being justified.

Spence. You mean that I shouldn't have gotten sassy with the fruit cake.
Grandma. Spencer, I'm not going to say one more word to you if you don't stop using language like that—and put that stick down.
Spence. *(gets up, throwing the stake on the floor)* God—you're getting to be a crumb—just like the rest of the whole crummy world.
Grandma. Where are you going?
Spence. No place. Where in hell is there to go?
Grandma. You ought to be thrashed with a stick for using that kind of language to me.
Spence. Listen—are you my friend or not? *(crosses back to Grandma)*
Grandma. No—I'm not—not when you talk like that.
Spence. *(closer to Grandma)* Well—thanks for that. Thanks. You're a real good Joe. You're a psalm singer—just like the rest of them, Gram. Love me when I'm good—hate me when I'm bad. Thanks. *(crosses right)*
Grandma. Don't mention it.
Spence. You're welcome. *(sits in armchair right)*
Grandma. The pleasure was all mine.
Spence. For an old lady—you can sure be plenty sarcastic when you want to be.

(pause)

Grandma. These will be exactly the last words I will say to you today, Master Scott.

(From outside a Voice begins calling Spence. Softly at first, and then more loudly.)

Tony. Spence.
Grandma. Who's that calling you?
Spence. Tony.
Tony. Hey—Spence!
Grandma. Well—what does he want?
Spence. I don't know, Gram. I haven't asked him yet.
Tony. Spencer!
Grandma. Well, why don't you answer him?
Spence. Let him wait—let him wait—it won't hurt him. He likes to holler like that anyway—he has to use his voice some place. No one could ever accuse him of speaking up while he's in school. *(rises)*
Tony. Spencer!
Grandma. *(gets up)* Spencer Scott—if you don't answer him—I will.
Spence. All right, all right. *(He starts for the door and opens it.)* What're you doing there? *(Tony bounces in. He is a young Italian boy.)*

Rehearsing for the Metropolitan or something? Come on in. *(crosses to Grandma left)*

Tony. *(crosses to center)* Hi, Spence. Hello, Mrs. Scott.

Grandma. Tony—since the first day you could talk—*(sits)* I've told you that I'm not Mrs. Scott. I'm Mrs. Martin. How long are you going to keep doing that?

Tony. I forget, Mrs. Martin. *(front of sofa)*

Spence. You forget lots of things—don't you, pal. *(pause; back of chair)* Well—you got a week's vacation so it certainly can't be because you want me to help you with your algebra—besides I won't be doing algebra for a while. I got the heave-ho as you well know.

Tony. Thrown out?

Spence. Yep.

Tony. For how long? *(crosses to right)*

Spence. Not counting vacation—for a week.

Tony. Gee!

Spence. Well—you said it. Thanks, pal. *(pause; sits left of table)* Well, Tony—what little favor can I do you?

Tony. Gee, Spence. I'm sure sorry. All the guys were talking about it on the way home from school.

Spence. Yeh! Yeh! I know. I caught their sympathy when Miss Crowley was bitching me out.

Grandma. I'm going to tell your mother.

Spence. *(looking at Grandma)* Gram.

Tony. That's not the way it was at all. *(pause)* What could we say?

Spence. Exactly what you did. It was fine. What'd I call you when you came in—a pal? That's what you all were. *(Grandma goes into kitchen.)* Two hundred carat, solid gold plate pals. *(to piano; sits)*

Tony. *(crosses right)* Geez—Spence—I'm sorry you feel that way about it.

Spence. *(gets up)* Ah! You're scratching my back with a rake, Tony. Remember the time the cop had you for stealing apples down at Markman's?

Tony. Sure I remember.

Spence. Did I or did I not shoot him with my slingshot? Remember the time Mrs. Donahue comes out of her house and calls you a dirty wop?

Tony. Well, hell, this was in school.

(Grandma crosses to sink with glass.)

Spence. Did I stand there and let her get away with it? I did not. That night, as nice as you please, I throw a nest of caterpillars through her window.

Tony. *(to center)* Yeah! And when she found out who did it—I cut your telephone wires for three nights running so she couldn't get to your mother.

Grandma. *(enters room)* I think I should warn you both now—that everything you're saying is going to be used against you—because I'm going to tell all of it.

Spence. *(crossing to Grandma)* Oh! No, you won't. If you so much as open your craw, Gram, I'll spill everything—and I'll really spill. I'm desperate. *(crosses to Tony)* So there's a big difference about whether it's in school or not. Has that ever made any difference to me?

Tony. Naw!

Spence. Naw! Is that all you've got to say?

Tony. No—it isn't.

Spence. You're a crumb, Tony—just like the rest of them. *(crosses to right)* And another thing— I dunno—maybe I'm getting deaf and need a hearing aid or something, but I don't hear you guys calling me for school any more in the morning.

Tony. *(crosses to Spence)* Ah, Spence—how many times do I have to tell you. I'm taking Marguerite to school in the morning.

Spence. And where are you taking her at night when you mozey past the house with her curled around your arm like a snake?

Tony. We're doing our home work together.

Spence. It's a little dark up in the park for home work.

Tony. Spence—cut it out—your grandmother.

Spence. My grandmother knows what the score is. She's been knowing it an awful long time now. She's going on eighty-three years old. You can talk freely in front of her.

Tony. Lay off—will you?

Spence. I'll lay off, Tony. I'll lay off plenty. You and that Marguerite Wandalowski. Two crumbs together. That don't even make a damn saltine.

Tony. *(close to Spence)* It's not her fault. I told you before. *(Spence crosses to center.)* She likes you. She thinks you're a nice kid. *(crosses; sits on ottoman)* It's her father—he—well he just doesn't like colored people. I'm sorry, Mrs. Martin. But that's the damn truth. Spence—he just doesn't like them.

(Spence goes to the piano.)

Grandma. Well, I don't like Polish people either. Never have—never will. They come over here—haven't been over, mind you, long enough to know "and" from "but"—and that's the first thing they learn. Sometimes I think Hitler was right—

Spence. *(down two steps)* You're talking off the top of your head, Gram. You know he wasn't right. What've you got to say that for?

Grandma. I don't care— I don't like them. Never have—never will.
Spence. *(crosses to Grandma)* You say "them" as though it was some kind of bug or something. *Will* you do me a favor like a real pal, Gram? Quit trying to mix in things that you don't understand. *(to Tony)* O.K., Friend—you've said your piece—what did you come over for? *(crosses down to Tony)*
Tony. Nothing— I didn't want nothing.
Spence. Aw—cut the bull, Tony. You must've come over here for something. You just don't come here for nothing any more. What do you *want*? *(Tony crosses to TV set. Spence crosses to above chair right.)* You feel uncultured—you want to hear a little Bach or something? You want to see a little television—borrow a book? I just read a good one—all about the causes and preventions of syphilis.
Grandma. Spencer Scott!
Spence. *(turns to Grandma)* That's what the book said, Gram. Bring it out in the open—so I'm bringing it out.
Grandma. I'm going to tell your mother about that.
Spence. *(crosses left)* I'll betcha I'll tell her about it before you do. *(to Tony)* So what'd you come over for? *(no answer)* Maybe I can guess. You're playing baseball over in the lot. You haven't got enough equipment. You thought maybe I'd be willing to lend some of mine. Right, Tony?
Tony. The guys asked me. I didn't want to.
Spence. Aw!—why didn't you want to? You're my friend, aren't you? Just because I'm sore at you? Damn sore at you?
Tony. Cut it out now, Spence, I did the best I could.
Spence. There's no doubt—and I'm a bum to be mad at you— *(crosses to kitchen)* So I'll tell you what I'm going to do. *(He goes out into the back hall off kitchen and comes back with a baseball glove.)* Who's the pitcher?
Tony. Gussie.
Spence. *(back to Tony; throws glove)* Give this to Gussie with my regards. *(crosses to kitchen)*
Tony. Give it to him?
Spence. *(crossing back to living room with mask and mitts)* As a gift—you know what I mean—like Christmas—give it to him. And here's a catcher's mitt and mask for you. *(crosses to kitchen)*
Grandma. What on earth are you doing? Are you drunk, Spencer?
Spence. They're mine—aren't they—well, I don't want them any more. *(crosses to Tony)* And here's a bat I'm contributing to the game. I think that's just about everything.
Tony. *(picks up stuff)* You're sure you won't be wanting these back?
Spence. Geez—the things you can't understand. I'm giving them to you because you've been such good friends to me—one and all.

Tony. *(starts to pick up equipment; starting to go)* Well thanks, Spence—thanks.

Spence. Think nothing of it. But there's just one more thing I want you to know. If I couldn't do any better than Marguerite Wandalaowski and her old man I'd cram my head into a bucket of horse manure.

Grandma. Now see here—

Tony. *(crosses to Spence)* See—that's the way you are. You can't do one nice thing without a dirty dig at the end. I ought to throw these things in your puss—

Spence. You won't though—will you?

Grandma. *(gets up)* Take 'em back, Spence. Take them right back.

Tony. Somebody—some day is going to take a poke at you.

Grandma. *(takes swing)* If he hits you, Spence—hit him right back.

Spence. *(crosses up)* He's not going to hit anyone, Gram. He's just talking to be sure he hasn't lost his mouth some damned place. *(throws Tony to door)* Now scram the hell out of my house before I beat you and your whole team over the head. Get out! *(Tony exits quickly.)* Well I sure went and milked myself in public that time. *(sits on chair right)*

Grandma. What are you talking about now?

Spence. Aw, Gram— I just went and did it again. You think I wanted that crumb to know how he hurt me?

Grandma. *(crosses to Spence)* Come on, Spence, let's you and I go watch television.

Spence. Sometimes, Gram—you get the most disgusting ideas.

Grandma. Well, then I'm going back upstairs. I don't understand what's wrong with you. You're just no fun to be with any more—cussing and ripping and tearing. Won't even watch a little television with me.

Spence. *(gets up, crosses to ottoman)* Go on in and watch it by yourself then—go on. Spend the rest of life with your head stuck in front of an old light bulb. *(sits)*

Grandma. What on earth is wrong with you, Spencer?

Spence. *(rises)* Gram—you've been sitting down here listening all afternoon. Don't you see that I'm an outcast? *(sits on ottoman)*

Grandma. How?

Spence. They don't want me around any more, Gram. I cramp their style with the broads.

Grandma. Why?

Spence. Why! That's a stupid question. Because I'm black—that's why.

Grandma. Well, it's a good thing if they don't want you around. *(turns right to window)* I told your mother years and years ago, "May—stay out of the South End, cause mark my words there's nothing down there, nothing—*(Spence crosses to kitchen.)* but Wops and Germans and Lord knows what else they'll get in the future." And what did they get—more Wops and Germans and a few Polacks thrown in for good measure and not one self-respecting colored family in the whole lot.

Spence. *(crosses to sofa)* Cut out that kind of talk. Sometimes, Gram—you're no help at all. I tell you my troubles and you tell me how we shouldn't have moved here in the first place. *(sits on sofa)* But we're here, Gram—right here—and I was born here—and they're all the friends I've got—and it makes me damned unhappy, Gram.

Grandma. *(crosses close to Spence)* Now—now—don't cry. Don't cry, Spencer. Everything's going to be all right.

Spence. I had it all planned how I was going to make Tony feel like two cents the next time I saw him—and I had to go and get mad.

Grandma. Your father is going to get you a new bicycle.

Spence. Shove the bicycle.

Grandma. Now why would you want to do that? The best thing to do, I should think, would be to get on it and ride it. *(crosses to ottoman with pillow)* Go and get the hair brush, Spencer. Your hair's a mess.

Spence. I don't want you messing around with my hair. That's sissy.

Grandma. Suit yourself. *(sits on ottoman)*

Spence. *(rises, crosses to kitchen)* If I get the hair brush you've got to promise to help me.

Grandma. All right. *(He exits left in kitchen for the hair brush.)* Spence, you don't suppose you could go back up to school and tell them you were eating one of those chocolate cigars, could you?

Spence. *(returns; sits down at Grandma's feet; gives her brush)* I got a feeling that those things don't light too well, Gram. *(pause)* What am I going to do, Gram?

Grandma. *(brushing his hair)* Well, now—I'm not sure—but one thing I am sure of. I don't know why you gave that boy all of your things. I think that's silly—damn silly if I might say so.

Spence. Do you suppose this happens to everyone, Gram?

Grandma. I suppose so. *(pause)* We haven't done this in a long time—have we?

Spence. What?

Grandma. Don't you remember when you were a little boy I used to do this every day. You'd stand—you were much shorter than you are now—and I'd brush and comb your hair. I used to do that for all my boys. They'd sit and tell me all their troubles while I combed and brushed their hair.

Spence. One dumb crummy girl at school the other day asked me if we had to comb and brush our hair.

Grandma. What did you tell her?

Spence. I told her we very seldom bothered until the bugs got so fierce they started falling into food and things like that—then it was an absolute necessity.

Grandma. Spencer—you didn't?

Spence. I would've if I'd thought of it in time. *(pause)* Gram—if you take the bus down at the corner and stay on it when it gets to Main Street—it will take you right out to the colored section, won't it?

Grandma. Well, it used to. I don't know if it still does or not. Why?

Spence. I was just wondering. It's getting late, Gram. Mom will be home in about a half hour. You'd better get back upstairs.

Grandma. *(putting down the brush)* Yes—hurry—come on and help me. *(gets up, crosses to stairs)*

Spence. *(stays seated)* Gram— I don't suppose you could lend me five dollars, could you?

Grandma. *(at foot of stairs)* What on earth do you need that much money for?

Spence. Well, Gram—you and I know that an hour from now I'm going to be about the smallest thing crawling on two legs. The Old Lady is sure going to give me hell.

Grandma. You shouldn't talk about your mother that way.

Spence. *(rises, crosses to stairs)* I know, Gram—I know. It's easy for you to say—but it's true. And then I'm going to get cussed out. Pop is going to say that I'm no good and I'm no son of his. In short—he's going to call me a bastard.

Grandma. That isn't what he means.

Spence. *(helping Grandma upstairs)* It's sure the hell what it sounds like. In other words, Gram—if you'd lend me five dollars— I could go out and get some flowers for Mom and some cigars for Pop and begin by telling them how sorry I am, and it might take the edge off what is going to be at best a hell of an evening. *(Grandma on landing)* What do you say, Gram?

Grandma. Well—all right. You go back downstairs and I'll get it for you.

(Spence helps her off. Pause. Then he runs to kitchen, gets suitcase and clothes. Doorbell rings.)

Spence. Dear, dear God—if that's my mother, just kill me as I open the door. *(Crosses to door. He hides suitcase left of piano. Opens door.)* Hi! Iggie—did you give me a scare!

Iggie. Hiya, Spence.

Spence. I'm in a terrible hurry, Iggie. What do you want?

Iggie. I just came over to see if you have any stamps to trade.

Spence. *(crosses left, gets shoes)* I haven't got much time. Come on in—but you can't stay long. I've got to go somewhere.

Iggie. *(comes in)* Where are you going?

Spence. No place. *(pause)* You sure you came over to trade stamps?

Iggie. *(at sofa)* Sure—that's what I came over for. I finished my home work early—and so I thought I might—

Spence. *(sits in chair left of table)* You know, Iggie—you're going to be out of school for a week. You didn't have to get your home work done so soon. That's the most disgusting thing I ever heard.

Iggie. *(crosses to table)* Now look, if I want to get my home work done—that's my business. I don't tell you it's disgusting when you don't get yours done at all, do I?

Spence. *(crosses back to sofa)* O.K.— O.K., Iggie. I only thought you came over because you heard I got kicked out of school.

Iggie. No, Spence— I hadn't heard.

Spence. You're sure?

Iggie. I told you I hadn't heard, didn't I? *(sits right of table)*

Spence. *(crosses right to close door)* That kind of news has a way of getting around. *(looking at him)* Well, what are you thinking about? *(crosses back to sofa)*

Iggie. Nothing. I was thinking that if I got kicked out of school, I guess I'd just as soon I dropped dead right there on the floor in the principal's office.

Spence. O.K., Iggie. You don't need to rub it in. I get the picture. *(looks upstairs)*

Iggie. I'm sorry, Spence. Is there anything I can do?

Spence. Now, Iggie—pardon me for being so damn polite—but what in the hell could you do about it?

Iggie. I only want to help, Spence.

Spence. *(crosses left to below table)* Well, you can't—so let's drop it, shall we?

Iggie. I didn't mean that business about dropping dead. I probably wouldn't drop dead anyway. There's nothing wrong with my heart.

Spence. *(sits on sofa)* Iggie—will you please cut it out.

Iggie. Anything you say. I didn't mean to offend you.

Spence. You didn't offend me, Iggie. You just talk too much—that's all.

Iggie. I'll try to do better in the future.

Spence. Look, Iggie— I've gone and hurt your feelings—haven't I? Hell— I'm sorry. I've always liked you, Iggie. You're a good kid. I'm apologizing, Iggie.

Iggie. It's O.K., Spence. I know you're upset.

Spence. *(crosses down left)* I know how sensitive you are and all that and I just mow into you like crazy. I wish someone would tell me to shut my mouth. *(He walks to the stairs.)* Gram—hurry up with that dough, will you. Iggie—look—I'll tell you what I'm going to do for you. *(He goes over to the piano and comes back with his stamp album.)* Here—Iggie—it's yours. I want you to have it—because you're my friend.

Iggie. Your album! But don't you want it, Spence?
Spence. No, Iggie, I don't want it.
Iggie. But why? I think you must be crazy. *(stands)*
Spence. Hell, Iggie—because I'm growing up. I'm becoming a man, Iggie. And since I'm going out in just a few minutes with my girl friend—you know it's time for me to quit fooling around with stuff like that.
Iggie. Have you got a girl friend?
Spence. Yeh! Yes— I have—as a matter of fact I might get married soon. Forget all about school and all.
Iggie. Really. Who is the girl, Spence?
Spence. Just a girl—that's all. And if everything works out O.K., I won't be coming back. You know, I'll have to get a job and stuff like that. Now you've got to go, Iggie, cause I've got to finish packing and get dressed. *(leads Iggie center)*
Iggie. Where are you going, Spence?
Spence. I can't tell you, Iggie.
Iggie. Are you sure you're feeling all right?
Spence. Yes, Iggie, I'm feeling all right.
Iggie. *(crossing to door)* Thank you for the gift. I appreciate it.
Spence. Forget it.
Iggie. It's a beautiful album.
Spence. It certainly is.
Iggie. *(crosses to center)* Hey, I was just thinking—maybe I could go up and talk to old Hasbrook. It might do some good.
Spence. *(crosses to door)* I don't care about that any more, Iggie. I'm pretty sure I won't be coming back to school.
Iggie. Are you sure you want me to have this, Spence?
Spence. Yes, Iggie, I want you to have it.
Iggie. *(crossing to door)* Well— I hope I'll see you soon. *(He is opening the door.)*
Spence. *(at door)* Hey, Iggie! You won't mind if just once in a while— I come over and see how you're doing with it?
Iggie. I hope you will. Goodbye. *(exits)*
Spence. Geez— I don't know what's wrong with me. I think maybe my brains are molding or something. *(gets suitcase, shoves clothes inside and runs upstairs)* Hey, Gram—will you hurry up with that five bucks so I can get the hell out of here before I really do something desperate!

(Curtain)

ACT I

SCENE 2

The Curtain rises on a bar and restaurant. It is a very small bar with very few bottles. The bottles that are there are mostly of blended whiskey and rum. A Woman stands at the telephone which is on the right wall. There is one table and a booth at left; a table and chairs down center, table up center; juke box left. The bartender, Frank, stands behind the bar, getting it ready for the evening. Rose and Poppy are seated at the center table, and Carol sits at the table in the left corner. Violet, the woman at the telephone, is speaking. Frank and a Man are arguing loudly at the bar.

Violet. *(at phone)* Hello. Hello. Is Lonny there? What's that you say? Hey, Frank, I can't hear a god damned thing.
Frank. Aw, shut up.
Violet. What's that you said to me?
Frank. I said "Aw, shut up." Now shut up.
Violet. Listen, Frank, don't you be jumping salty with me.
Poppy. *(at center table)* Hey Violet—cut the crap, will you, and get back on the phone.
Frank. Comes in here, spends the whole damn afternoon, and buys two bottles of ginger ale. Cheap— *(He smothers the last word under his breath.)*
Rose. *(gets up)* What's that you called us?
Frank. You didn't hear it, did you?
Rose. It's just as well I didn't—cause if I'd heard it— *(sits)*
Violet. Hey! All of you—shut up. I can't hear a word. *(returns to the phone)* I said is Lonny there? He's not. Well, Sugar, could you tell me when you expect him? What? Would you mind telling me for how long? What in hell did he do? Lonny did that? Well, ain't that something. Well, if you happen to see him on visiting days—just tell him Violet called. Violet—roses are red—you know. That's right—thank you. *(hangs up)* Well, Poppy, you can scratch Lonny's name out of the book. *(sits on stool, faces right)*
Poppy. Hell, Violet—by the time we're through today—you're going to have more scratched-out names than anything else in this book. What happened to him?
Violet. *(faces center)* You remember reading the paper about that girl—in the three paper bags at the railroad station—in the locker?
Poppy. *(nods)* Yeh.
Violet. Lonny!

Rose. Girl—are you kidding?
Violet. *(crosses to table, sits back of it)* Frank, bring us another bottle of ginger ale.
Frank. What do you want in it?
Violet. We still have whiskey of our own—thank you.
Frank. Then it'll be fifteen cents a bottle.

(Man crosses to right of juke box. Spence enters down right. He is carrying some books. He stands by the door looking left at Carol at the corner table.)

Rose. Fifteen cents?
Frank. Either put your money where your mouth is or shut up.
Violet. Well—give us the bottle and some ice.
Frank. The ice will cost you a dime. *(crosses to Carol with drink)*
Poppy. Damn—let's get the hell out of here before he begins charging for sitting down.
Violet. It's all right, Poppy. Pay the man.
Poppy. *(to Frank)* Well, bring it on over—you chinchy skunk.
Frank. Call me names like that—you can come over and get it yourselves. *(Frank notices Spence at bar.)* Can I help you, pal? *Spence doesn't hear at first. Everyone turns around.)* Hey! You—over there.
Spence. You talking to me?
Frank. Yeh. What do you want?
Spence. Nothing. It's kind of warm outside—and I kind of came in here to get cool.
Frank. Out.
Spence. *(with great discomfort)* I'm cool now. So—I'll be going. *(Looks at Carol. He hovers about door back of bar and finally exits.)*

(Frank crosses back to bar.)

Poppy. *(after a pause)* Well—do we get our stuff or don't we?
Frank. I told you—get it yourselves.
Rose. *(rising)* Let's get the hell out of this dump.
Violet. It's all right— I'll get it. *(goes to bar and picks up the bottle of ginger ale and the ice)* And here's a quarter tip for you, Frank, for being so gracious.
Poppy. All right, Violet—don't be going crazy over there now. Every little bit helps, and if we don't raise the money for the rent, we'll be out in the street tomorrow.
Violet. *(ignoring her)* Thank you, Frank. You're a real gentleman. I'm going to tell all my friends to come over and trade with you. *(crosses to table with glasses and ice)*
Frank. You can tell those whores that I don't want them in my place.
Poppy. Aw man—shut up.—Who else is left in that book of yours, Violet?

Violet. I don't know—let me see. Well, there's Sidney. We haven't called Sidney.
Poppy. What's his number? *(gets up)*
Violet. Two—eight nine two seven. Whose turn is it?
Poppy. *(crosses to phone)* Mine. Why in hell you think I'm getting up?
Frank. And don't be coming in here with food. This ain't no lousy picnic grove.
Violet. Well, it's lousy.
Poppy. Shh.
Frank. *(throws rag at her)* You heard what I said. Just be sure you clean up that mess before you leave.
Violet. *(throws rag back)* I ain't no janitor.
Poppy. *(on phone)* Hello, Sidney. This is Poppy. One and the same. Haven't seen you lately. Well that's too bad. *(pause)* Sugar, we're in a bad spot 'cause tomorrow the rent man is coming around, an— *(Violet crosses to phone.)* Well now, Sugar, Violet is sitting right here and she's upset about the rent too. Do you remember the time you took Violet down to New York and registered in that hotel as Mr. and Mrs.? *(Rose crosses to bar above Poppy.)* Well now—Honey—to get down to New York, you had to cross a state line. Now have you ever heard of the Mann Act? Well, Violet has. Well— I don't know all the details of it, but it seems you can get into about ten or fifteen years worth of trouble for carrying girls over state lines for the kind of purposes you had in mind.*(Man crosses to bar.)* Now all Violet is asking for is about ten dollars—that roughly comes out to seventy-five cents a year, and she wants it tonight—at Carter's drug store—or else the F.B.I. Now have you got all that, Sugar? Fine—we'll be looking for you, hear? *(She hangs up, crosses back to her chair.)* Well, Sidney suddenly decided he had ten loose dollars around some place. We're supposed to meet him in Carter's in fifteen minutes. *(sits in her chair)*

(Violet follows, sits above table.)

Rose. *(crosses back to her chair, sits)* Girl! I ain't never seen anything like you in my whole life.
Poppy. How much more we got to raise, Violet?
Violet. Let's see—that's Sidney—ten dollars! *(gets up, crosses up to rear table)* All we need is fifteen more.
Frank. Coming in here—blackmailing people on my telephone.
Poppy. We ain't blackmailing anybody. We're just keeping ourselves available. There's no telling—next week sometime—one of those boys might be glad that we're still here.
Man. *(at the bar)* I can't see why.
Rose. Why don't you shut up?

Man. This is a place of business. Man comes in here to have a quiet drink. If it ain't a bunch of whores, it's a television set.
Poppy. Mister—don't you be calling us whores, hear—or I'm liable to come over there and knock you breathless.
Rose. Come on, Poppy. Don't pay no attention to him.
Violet. Coming in here for a quiet drink—he calls it. I seen you lamping the little girl over in the corner. You ought to be ashamed of yourself. *(crosses to Carol)* Baby, if he bothers you—just come over and tell me and I'll knock his brains out. Hear?

(Carol says nothing. Violet returns to center table. Spence appears down right, outside door; carries books.)

Rose. Violet—come on and get your book out. We ain't got all night.
Poppy. I don't know why in hell we ain't got all night. We haven't got anything else to do. *(They look at her.)* Well—have we?
Violet. No—we haven't, stupid. *(Spence enters, sits on stool below bar, puts books on bar.)* But you don't have to say it in here—do you? Hell—you have to keep up some pretenses, Poppy. *(crosses up stage; sits in chair)*
Spence. *(knocking on the bar)* How about a little service here—sport?

(Rose crosses to Violet.)

Frank. *(eyeing him)* What do you want now?
Spence. A glass of beer. *(Frank laughs, still eyes him.)* I said a glass of beer.
Frank. How old are you?
Spence. *(pointing at the Man)* Did you ask him how old he was?
Frank. No— I didn't.
Spence. Then why in hell are you asking me?
Frank. I know him. He comes in here all the time.

(Man crosses left to juke box.)

Spence. Well, my name is Spencer Scott—so now you know me. Give me a glass of beer.
Frank. What're you—just coming from school with all those books? The teacher didn't keep you after school all this time, did she? *(He laughs. He reaches for a book.)* What's this? *(reading the title)* The Interpretation of Dreams by Sigmund— *(Spence gets up, grabs book.)* You don't believe in that stuff, do you?
Spence. Hey—do you run a quiz show or something? You know there are other joints on this street that probably got colder beer than you got anyway. *(pause)* I've been to the library, see. And inside this book is my library card. They have pink cards for children and yellow cards for adults. This is a yellow card. Now as to more personal things— I've

been walking a hell of a long way and I've got a headache—now will you please give me a glass of beer. I've got money for it—see— I can pay for it. I'm not drunk already. What do you say?

Frank. How old are you?

Spence. Twenty-one.

Frank. When were you born?

Spence. *(without batting an eye)* January 20, 1932.

Frank. *(getting a piece of paper)* Let's see. Yep. *(figuring it out)* That makes you—twenty-one.

Spence. That's what I said.

Frank. You look mighty young to be twenty-one.

Spence. Beer— Hah? A nice tall one.

Frank. We got a special on whiskey today.

Spence. You know—hot shot—you got remarkable powers of persuasion there. But I asked you for a beer.

Poppy. That's right, Sugar—don't drink none of that man's whiskey. He ferments it himself.

Violet. You sure are right, Frank—that whiskey is special. Specially awful.

(Three Flowers laugh uproariously.)

Frank. Quiet over there. I'm minding my business.

Poppy. Say, Sugar—did I hear you say something about a dream book?

Spence. Yeh— I found it in the library. *(Man blows smoke at Carol.)* It's supposed to be pretty sexy.

Violet. Come on over and sit down with us.

Spence. Sure. *(crosses to center table)*

Poppy. Does that book say anything about umbrellas? I keep having the damndest dreams with umbrellas in them.

Spence. I don't know. I've just glanced through it. *(sits left in chair)*

Poppy. Do you mind if I take a look?

(Rose crosses down, sits center.)

Spence. Help yourself. *(looks at Carol)* You girls hang around here a lot?

Rose. No, this isn't one of our usual hangouts. We come here about once a month to take care of a financial transaction. Do you live around here?

Spence. Yeh—around here. *(pause)* Say—do any of you know the girl over in the corner?

(Man crosses to bar.)

Rose. No—we don't know her at all. Mousey little thing—ain't she?

Spence. No, I don't think she's mousey at all.

Poppy. Hell, I can't find a thing about umbrellas in this book. This is the damndest dream book I ever saw.

Spence. Give it to me— Here I'll find it for you. *(He takes the book.)*
Violet. *(gets up, crosses to Rose; looking at her book)* Whose turn is it next?
Rose. Mine. *(gets up, starts for phone)*
Violet. You call Homer. The number is two—five eight seven six.
Rose. Two—five eight—
Violet. Seven six—and here's the dime.

(Both cross to phone. Rose dials. Violet at bar.)

Spence. Did you say a cane or an umbrella?
Poppy. An umbrella, Sugar. *(moves to center chair)* Hell—there ain't much difference between canes and umbrellas, is there? What does it say about canes?

(Violet turns to center.)

Spence. It doesn't say much. It just says that a woman dreams about a man carrying a cane. It must mean you're plenty batty because they got her whole case history written up here.
Poppy. Well, I didn't say I dreamed of canes, did I? Don't be trying to push her dreams off on me. Look for umbrellas—and don't be looking in those crazy people's dreams either. Look for some nice person that dreams of umbrellas.
Rose. Nobody answers.
Violet. Well, keep ringing—his mother is always home.
Rose. Well, what will I say if his mother answers?
Violet. Just ask for Homer, stupid.
Rose. *(in phone)* Hello, Homer? This is Rose. Well, I know an awful lot of Homers, too, and I know which one you are. Rose Thompson. How you been? Haven't seen you in a month of Sundays.
Spence. Wouldn't that be a hell of a thing—a month with only Sundays in it? You'd spend your whole life in church.
Violet. Ssh.
Poppy. Shut up.
Rose. *(in phone)* Well, Sugar, I was calling you because we are kind of in a jam. Violet—Poppy and me. That's right—the three flowers. We need money for the rent. I don't know— I guess everyone is trying to save money what with Christmas coming and all and they must be cutting down on the little luxuries. Oh! Homer—you say the most terrible things. *(putting her hand over the mouthpiece)* The son of a bitch. *(She takes her hand off.)* Well, how about it? Well, I guess we'll just have to talk to your wife, Sugar. No, I don't think I want to talk to her tonight. You'd never. Well, just thanks for nothing, Homer. The same to you quartetted. *(hangs up and sits on stool)* Can you beat that? He said he

TAKE A GIANT STEP   249

didn't give a damn whether his wife knew or not. There's something terrible immoral about that.

Poppy. You're damn right. It's getting to the point where no one has any respect for marriage these days. I just wish somebody would ask me to marry them. I'd split their heads wide open.

Spence. *(putting down the book)* Hey! Pardon me, are you girls prostitutes or something?

(All turn to him.)

Poppy. Honey—we try to be.

Spence. You know—I've never met any real prostitutes before. You wouldn't mind if I asked you a couple of questions—would you?

Violet. Well, Honey—right now we're in a little hot water—and we also got to go out and pick up a little something down at Carter's drug store. *(at table down center)* But as soon as we come back we'll answer all your questions. Why don't you go over and talk to the little girl over there until we come back? *(crosses back to table up center)*

Spence. Are you sure she wouldn't mind my bargin' over there like that?

Poppy. What if she does? You can sit anywhere you want in this place. Go over there and sit down. *(gets up)*

Violet. *(crossing down to table)* Let's go, girls.

Rose. I don't see why all of us have to go to get a little ten dollars from Sidney.

Poppy. Because in union there is strength. *(crosses to Rose)* Now get the hell off that stool and let's go. I assume that none of us have any more names in our books? *(exits up right)*

Violet. Your assumption is absolutely correct.

(Violet and Rose exit up right. Frank crosses table center, gets bottles, cleans table, returns to bar.)

Spence. *(who has been going over to the left table very slowly—has just arrived—and is standing undecided right of booth)* Do you mind if I sit down? *(Carol shakes her head. Spence sits down. He sits looking at her for a time.)* You're sure I'm not bothering you or anything, 'cause if I am, I can get the hell up and go someplace else.

Carol. These tables aren't reserved. You can sit anywhere you please. If you bother me I can get up and get the hell out of here, that's all.

Spence. *(rises, crosses right)* I'm sorry.

Carol. Where are you going?

Spence. I guess—

Carol. Sit down, kid. I didn't mean to scare you away.

Spence. *(looks at Man)* I suppose a nice girl does have to be careful about

who she talks to in a joint like this. *(crosses back to booth)* You don't need to be afraid of me, though.
Carol. What makes you think that I'm such a nice girl?
Spence. *(sits right in booth)* You can just tell—that's all.
Carol. What makes you think that I'm not like Violet, Rose, and Poppy?
Spence. Aw! Quit your kidding.
Carol. Well, thanks for thinking that I'm different from Violet, Rose, and Poppy.
Spence. Well, you are—aren't you?
Carol. Yeh—in one or two respects I guess I am.
Spence. *(relieved)* I thought you were. *(pause; gets closer—hand out)* My name's Spencer Scott. Everybody calls me Spence.
Carol. *(takes hand)* I know. I heard you when you came in.
Spence. Yeh. That's because I've got such a damn big mouth. I've got a theory as to why I talk so loud. I think it's because of my youth. I guess as I get older like Mack maybe—I won't talk so loud. *(pause)* Mack is my brother. *(pause)* He used to talk loud when he was a kid.
Carol. You're not really twenty-one, are you?
Spence. I was lying then. See, I've got to lie about my age until I get to be twenty-one. Since I lie about that, as you can guess, I lie about other things too. But as soon as I get to be twenty-one not another goddamn lie is going to pass my lips.
Carol. That's very sweet.
Spence. I really honestly mean it.
Carol. I really honestly believe you. *(She takes a sip of her drink and then nervously bangs the drink down on the table. Looks at Man.)* Damn it. Who in the hell does he think he's looking at?
Spence. Who?
Carol. That guy over there. He keeps staring at me.
Spence. You want me to go over and speak to him?
Carol. *(restraining him)* No! No! Don't bother.

(Pause. Man sits at chair up stage, reads paper. Frank has fallen asleep, his head on the bar.)

Spence. Well, now that we know each other—would you mind telling me your name?
Carol. My name's Carol—Carol Pearson.
Spence. Is that Carol spelt with an "e" or with the "e" left off?
Carol. That's Carol with the "e" left off.
Spence. I never knew a Carol with the "e" left off before except in a book I used to read as a kid. It was called "The Birds' Christmas Carol." Did you ever read it?
Carol. No, I don't think I ever did.

Spence. I know you'd never believe it to look at me—but I read that book around ninety times I guess. That book used to make me cry like a baby. It was about a little girl named Carol who was doomed to die—and finally at the end, she dies—on the same day she was born—Christmas Day. Well, the last time I read that book I expected to cry again. I grabbed the old box of Kleenex and opened the book, and as I was reading, it was like me and the author had a big fight. She was trying to make me cry and I was damned if I was going to do her the favor. The whole book, believe it or not, was set up to make you cry. I gave the book to Iggie the next day.

Carol. *(after a pause)* So—what about it?

Spence. Iggie's a friend of mine. He's kind of hard to talk to because he's real shy. You know what I mean? But he knows I like him and I think he's getting a lot better. I got a theory about that. Would you like to hear it?

Carol. I can hardly wait.

Spence. Well—it's this. My theory is that everybody needs somebody else. What do you think about that?

Carol. I think you've got something.

Spence. I kind of thought that you'd think so. *(pause)* I need somebody too, I guess. I know you wouldn't believe it to look at me but you're looking at one of the most friendless persons in the whole United States.

Carol. Aw! Come on—

Spence. Well, I guess that that wasn't exactly the truth—because you see there's my Gram. She's the only pal I got left—I guess.

Carol. *(pulling out a cigarette)* Have you got a match, kid? *(Spence pulls out matches. Carol takes them.)* Thanks. So your Mom and Pop don't trust you, is that it?

Spence. They'd like to—but I sure as hell think they're not so sure that I'm not going to turn out the family skeleton.

Carol. So what makes you think that you're so friendless? *(crosses to juke box)*

Spence. Well, that's a story and a half. You see I live—I mean used to live down at the South End. *(turns right)* There aren't many colored families down there; in fact, there are about two. So Mack and I grew up with the white kids who lived on our street. We had lots of good times together—and it wasn't until the kids started getting interested in sex that my troubles began.

Carol. How do you mean?

Spence. Well, actually it started happening last summer. For weeks they wouldn't call me. To be frank with you—I thought it was because my personality wasn't so hot maybe. You see— I'm a real guy. *(Carol has* *put nickel in juke box which doesn't work. She gives up and returns to booth. Sits.)* I play the piano—but not enough for the guys to think I'm a sissy. I'm a little thin but I got a build that would knock you out to be perfectly honest with you—but I still thought that something was wrong with me—

Carol. That's an old, old story, kid.

Spence. What do you mean?

Carol. I can finish it for you. You're pretty fed up with the whole business, aren't you? You don't know what the hell to do because you're lonely. It's a hell of a feeling. So you start smoking, drinking beer. You want to be a real grown up guy before your time. The only thing you know is that this kid stuff is for the birds—so you're going to run away from it—get to be an adult because maybe being an adult will bring a couple of things with it. Happiness—a nice girl—maybe—

Spence. Yes, I guess that's it. But all the kids my age are interested in the broads now. So I was passing by here—saw you in the window—and decided to give it a whirl.

Carol. *(laughs)* Thanks—for seeing me in the window.

Spence. I know you think it sounds pretty silly because I know how girls are about going around with boys that are younger than they are—but have you ever gotten a really good look at the Kinsey report?

Carol. No, I'm afraid I don't read much.

Spence. Well—I'm honestly not one to boast—but it says in that book that boys my age are usually pretty sexy. In fact, they're sexier at my age than they ever will be again in their whole goddamn lives. And what with my other qualifications that I have told you about, I should be a pretty good boy friend to have.

Carol. You know—I'd almost bet that that was the truth.

Spence. Well, what do you say? I know I started off all wrong. I should have started off by shooting you the old bull about how lovely you are and all that stuff, but I figured that if I asked you to be my girl friend you'd know that I thought you were pretty and all that because I really couldn't be interested in a lemon. I also want you to know that if everything goes right between me and you and we decide that we love each other, I'm perfectly willing to get married. *(Carol moves down stage on bench.)* My father wants me to go to college but I'd be perfectly willing to forego that if everything works out okay. How about it?

Carol. Spence, you're a sweet kid and that was about the sweetest proposal I've ever had. *(She watches Spence who has pressed glass to forehead.)* Is there something wrong?

Spence. Naw—just a headache. Too much beer, I guess.

Carol. *(taking glass from him)* You know what you ought to do? Go on home and let your grandmother give you a great big kiss and tuck you in.

Spence. Don't you understand? I won't be going home. I've got to look for a job. What do you say?

Carol. I've already told you what I say. Go on home. I don't want to hear any more of your troubles. I've got troubles of my own. You talk about getting a job. What in hell could you do? You couldn't do any better than my husband.

Spence. Your husband?

Carol. Yes. He works all day and he works all night and we've still got nothing. He's what is commonly known as unskilled labor. I guess you know what that means. *(pause)* I'm sorry, kid.

Spence. You should have told me you were married in the first place. I feel like a great big can of garbage. *(turns away)*

Carol. You didn't hear a word I said, did you, kid? *(Gathers her purse. Man crosses bar.)* I've got to go now.

Spence. Where are you going?

Carol. You see that guy in the corner of the bar? Well, he's been staring at me all night. I hope he has some money. I hope he has a car—a nice car with a top that goes down. I can go for a drive in the country and for maybe two hours I can have some fun.

Spence. I think that's terrible.

Carol. So do I—there's two of us. *(finishes drink)* And if my husband ever finds out, he'd kill me, so I guess there's three of us. But I'm going anyway because I've got to. I can't go home to that lousy one-room flat and wait all night. It's too quiet there. There's nobody to talk to. It's just no fun—that's all.

Spence. *(pause)* If you're going—why don't you go?

Carol. It's funny how when you're young you can be so selfish about your feelings, isn't it? Thank you for the proposal. *(rises, crosses right of table)* Please don't be sore. I tried to help you, Spence. There's a nursery rhyme I used to know. It goes,

"Merry have we met, and merry have we been,
Merry let us part, and merry meet again."

Let's not part angrily. *(He doesn't answer.)* Spence! *(She walks over and kisses him squarely on the mouth.)* Good luck, kid.

(She walks over to the Man at the bar. He pays for her, and they leave together up right. The Three Flowers reenter up right. Violet enters first.)

Violet. *(offstage)* I don't care what you say, it's a stinking way to behave. *(sees money Man has left on bar, picks it up, crosses to center table, sits)* Standing us up like that.

Poppy. Every little bit helps.

Rose. *(crosses to juke box, puts nickel in)* And then not answering the phone is the rudest thing I ever heard of.
Poppy. *(crosses to right of table, sits)* I told you to stop worrying about it. Tomorrow morning, on his way to work, I'll get him. And he'll either cough up that ten bucks or I'll snatch him baldheaded. That ten-spot is as good as got—so stop worrying about it.

(Juke box starts playing.)

Violet. Hey! Spence. We're through with our business. You can come over now if you want to.

(Spence doesn't move.)

Rose. *(crossing to center table, sits left)* Well as far as I can see we might as well be dead. We might just as well amble on over to the graveyard and lie down.

(Spence sits for one more moment, with his head hidden from them, and then he rises, crosses in.)

Spence. Hey! Violet—is there any lipstick on my mouth to speak of?
Violet. There sure is, Honey.
Poppy. What're you doing smearing lipstick all over your mouth like that? You queer or something?
Spence. Cut the comedy. Did you see that girl over there in the corner?
Rose. You mean she kissed you?
Spence. Yeh. I guess I'm what you call a pretty fast worker, huh?
Violet. How would you like to come with me? *(gets up)*
Spence. Where are we going?
Violet. You said you wanted to talk to me, didn't you? I just thought we could go some place where we could be alone—a quieter place.
Spence. Sure—that's okay with me.
Violet. Let's go, Sugar— I know just the place. *(Spence leans against booth.)* What's the matter, Honey?
Spence. Nothing. Been drinking too much, I guess.
Violet. Well, come on, Sugar—You got enough money to buy me a sandwich or something?
Spence. *(as he exits up right, Violet following)* Sure—I got two dollars and thirty-nine cents.
Violet. *(coming back to table down center)* That sounds like the price of something in a fire sale—doesn't it? Well, Hell—*(exits up right)*

(Curtain)

ACT I

SCENE 3

Violet's room. Violet is turning the key in the lock as the curtain rises. Spence is behind her. When they enter there is the distinct sound of muffled voices.

Spence. What's that?
Violet. *(sits chair right, takes off shoes)* The two men next door. Don't worry about them—they're deaf.
Spence. *(standing center)* It sounded like they were in the next room.
Violet. They are. The walls are very thin.
Spence. Thin is hardly the word. You might say they were put together with spitballs. You been away or something?
Violet. (crossing left to drapes) No, why?
Spence. Nothing except that it looks like you've put everything to bed for the night.
Violet. *(crosses to bed, takes off cover, folds it, puts it behind curtain)* Oh. Those are my covers. It keeps things neat and clean.
Spence. Say, I thought you wanted to go to another restaurant where we could talk?
Violet. It's much more comfy to talk here. We can have something sent in if we want it. Don't you want to take your jacket off? It's pretty warm in here. *(turns on light above bureau)*
Spence. *(crossing chair right)* Thanks— I guess I will. You wouldn't happen to have something to eat hanging around, would you? *(Violet crosses behind drapes.)* I'm feeling pretty groggy. I think perhaps it's because I haven't had any supper.
Violet. There's some crackers up there. (She points to the bureau. Crosses to bureau—then behind drapes.)
Spence. Thanks. *(crosses to bureau, gets crackers and starts eating them)* What kind of radio is this?
Violet. It's a short wave radio. It gets the police calls. *(takes clothes off line, crosses behind drapes)*
Spence. Why would anyone want the crumby police calls?
Violet. For a number of reasons.
Spence. What ever happens in this crumby town that should interest anybody?
Violet. *(crossing to him)* Sugar—that radio is like a husband to me. Now why don't you stop worrying about the radio and take off your tie and get comfortable so we can talk.

Spence. *(at bureau)* I can talk with my tie on. That's never been one of my difficulties.
Violet. Would you like to hear a little music?
Spence. That would be nice.
Violet. *(turns on the radio; crosses back of drapes)* You wouldn't mind if I changed into something a little more comfortable, would you?
Spence. Not at all.
Violet. I won't be a minute.
Spence. You wouldn't have a little cheese to go with these crackers, would you?

(Radio plays Chopin Sonata in B flat minor. Opus 35. Funeral March.)

Violet. Look around and see.
Spence. Any place in particular? *(looks in sink)*
Violet. Just look around. I seem to remember seeing some cheese around here a couple of days ago. What's that they're playing?
Spence. It's Chopin.
Violet. Is he playing or being played?
Spence. He's being played. Chopin's dead.
Violet. Recently?
Spence. *(crossing right)* Not too recently. Over a hundred years ago.
Violet. Isn't that sad?
Spence. *(looking on bed table and under bed)* I guess it was when it happened. Well— I don't seem to find any cheese around here at all.
Violet. I guess Poppy must've taken it for the trap. *(reenters)* Now—how do I look? *(She has emerged in a bronze satin negligee with marabou around the collar and down the front.)*
Spence. Do you honestly feel more comfortable in that?
Violet. Oh! Much much more. *(She moves over to the bed, sits.)* Now come on and let's sit down over here so we can talk.
Spence. *(sits in chair right)* I should think that it would tickle the back of your neck something awful. What shall we talk about?
Violet. Why I thought you wanted to talk to me. *(pause)* Do you have to listen to that?
Spence. Not necessarily. *(rises and switches radio off)* These crackers don't seem to be doing a damn bit of good.
Violet. Come on back.
Spence. Sure. *(He sits back down on the chair right.)*
Violet. Come on closer.
Spence. What for? I can hear you from here.
Violet. *(crawling over bed)* Aw! Come on, Sugar. Stop being so bashful.
Spence. I'm not being bashful. *(She pulls Spence by the hand.)* All right, I'll come. You don't have to pull me. *(He sits on bed.)*

Violet. *(puts her arms around his neck)* Now tell Violet all about it.
Spence. All about what?
Violet. What's troubling you.
Spence. Nothing's troubling me.
Violet. Supposing you give Violet a little kiss. That might make you feel better.
Spence. I honestly don't see how a kiss is going to do anything for my hunger.
Violet. Well, try it, baby, and see. *(Spence gives her an experimental peck on the cheek.)* Oh! Come on, Sugar. You can do better than that. *(She grabs Spence, pulls him back on the bed and kisses him.)*
Spence. *(after some time, breaks away, crosses right)* God damn it.
Violet. What's the matter?
Spence. *(gets the jacket from chair and starts to put it on)* I left my books over in the bar.
Violet. Well—what about it?
Spence. They're library books. If they were my books I wouldn't care.
Violet. *(gets up, stands left of bed)* Say—what's the matter with you anyway?
Spence. I told you. My books are over there.
Violet. So let them stay there. No one's going to run away with them.
Spence. How can you be so sure of that?
Violet. Listen, Sugar—no one that ever goes in Frank's ever reads nothing. Take my word for it.
Spence. I'd better go.
Violet. *(jumps onto bed, runs over it, and holds door)* Hey! Are you trying to run out on me?
Spence. Why would I do a thing like that?
Violet. *(still standing on bed)* Well that's sure as hell what it looks like. *(pause)* What happened to all those questions you had to ask me? What happened to all that big talk you were throwing around in the bar?
Spence. Nothing happened to it. I got a headache and I'm hungry—at least I think I'm hungry.
Violet. I think you're just plain scared.
Spence. Scared of who?
Violet. Scared of me—that's who. *(a thought dawning on her, gets down from bed)* Hey! How old are you anyway?
Spence. I told you—twenty-one.
Violet. *(sits on bed)* If you're twenty-one, I'm sweet sixteen. Come over here. *(Spence sits in chair.)* You've never been in a place like this before—have you? You're kind of scared, aren't you?
Spence. Well—to be perfectly honest with you, I guess I am kind of scared. I guess I just want to go and get my books—if you don't mind. *(crosses to door)*

Violet. *(crossing to door)* Look, kid— I most certainly do mind. *(Spence sits in chair.)* Let me tell you how this mess works. You've taken me out of circulation for roughly fifteen minutes now—fifteen minutes in which anything could happen—and if you think that you're just going to put your coat on and walk out of here—you've got another thought coming. I want my two dollars and thirty-nine cents.
Spence. But that's all the money I have.
Violet. I know it's all the money you have. You think if you had more I'd be asking for two dollars and thirty-nine cents? What do you take me for anyway? It ain't that I don't understand, Sugar, it's just that business is business.
Spence. *(reaching into his pocket)* Is it all right if I keep a half dollar for supper?
Violet. You can take the crackers as you leave. I want my two thirty-nine. *(taking it, crossing to bureau, puts money away)* Thank you. And another thing—if you ever tell anybody that all you paid me was two thirty-nine I'll have your head on a platter. You hear me? *(sits on bed, leans back)*
Spence. I understand. Is it all right if I go now?
Violet. Suit yourself. *(Puts key on bed table. Spence starts to go, then stops.)* What's the matter—did you lose something?
Spence. I was just thinking.
Violet. Thinking what?
Spence. Well—if I go back to that bar— Poppy and Rose are still there— aren't they?
Violet. They'd better be.
Spence. Well— I was just thinking—if I go back over there in such a short time they'll know that—
Violet. You was a bust? They sure will.
Spence. I was just wondering—if you'd mind terribly if I stayed about fifteen minutes more.
Violet. Help yourself.
Spence. *(goes over and sits stiffly in down right chair)* You wouldn't tell them—would you?
Violet. Tell them what?
Spence. That I was such a—bust?
Violet. If you can keep my secret I can keep yours. *(They sit in silence for some time.)* You know—if you're going to sit there— I'm afraid that you're going to have to say something. If there's one thing I can't stand it's silence.
Spence. What do you want me to say?
Violet. I don't want you to say anything that you don't want to say. Just talk. *(gets pillow and doll from behind drapes)*

Spence. What time is it?
Violet. The fifteen minutes ain't passed yet. You know the old saying about a watched pot never boiling. *(sits back on bed, arranges doll's dress)*
Spence. Would you like me to read to you for a while?
Violet. Do I look like an old lady to you?
Spence. No.
Violet. Well I can see to read to myself, thank you very much.
Spence. I'm sorry. I'm—
Violet. Forget it. Just forget it.
Spence. I wonder—if you'd do me a favor?
Violet. As long as there's no money involved—yes.
Spence. Well—there is. I was wondering if you'd loan me a dime for bus fare. I want to go home.
Violet. Well, can't you walk?
Spence. It's down at the South End.
Violet. Well that's what I get for playing around with kids. Just reach in and take a dime—and only a dime. *(Spence walks over to the bureau and opens it and takes a dime. Violet watches carefully, lying on her stomach, head down stage. He closes it and then stops and leans on it.)* What's the matter with you, anyway?
Spence. Nothing— I just don't feel good. *(starts for the door)* Thanks for the dime.
Violet. Don't bother thanking me. It hurts me to give it to you.
Spence. *(at door)* Well—thanks anyway. But there's one thing I want you to know.
Violet. What's that?
Spence. I think that's one of the ugliest bath robes I've ever seen in my life! *(He walks out the door as—)*

(Curtain)

ACT II

SCENE 1

As the Curtain rises on Spence's home—there is one light on—the light over Lem Scott's chair. He is in it. He is asleep with a newspaper in his lap. The rest of the house is quiet—superficially at least. It is later the same evening. Someone passes in the street outside,—they are whistling. It wakes Lem.

Lem. *(half-asleep)* May—we got to— *(rises, crosses to center below stairs)* Well, I'll be damned. May! May!

May. *(upstairs)* What do you want?
Lem. What time is it?
May. Five minutes have passed since you asked me that the last time. It's ten minutes after ten.
Lem. *(yawns)* Well—where the hell is he?
May. Daddy— I don't know. I've told you that over and over again. I haven't got one idea left.
Lem. Well, how can you be up there asleep—when for all you know he could be dead some place? *(crosses down right)*
May. If he's dead, Daddy—there's nothing we can do about it until we know. I'm not asleep.
Lem. Is that mother of yours asleep?
May. I don't see how she could be.
Lem. *(picks up more newspapers)* I think she knows more than she's letting on.
May. Well, there's a five hundred watt light downstairs in the pantry. Why don't you bring it up along with your rubber hose and give her the third degree?
Lem. Why don't you cut out being so smart. That's the trouble with your whole family—they think they're smart. *(kicks stool)*
May. *(appears at head of stairs)* Why don't you just go back to your paper, Daddy—or watch the television for a while?
Lem. When I get my hands on that little bastard I'll break every bone in his body.
May. *(coming down the stairs to left side of sofa, sits)* Now that's no way to talk, Daddy.
Grandma. *(offstage)* It most certainly is not. It's disgraceful.
May. Mama—will you please keep out of it? *(turns on lamp by sofa)*
Grandma. The truth is the truth and should be spoken at all times.
May. Mother, please!
Grandma. *(enters, sits on landing)* Don't please Mother me. The truth is the truth. It's disgraceful. If there are any bastards around—it's you who've sired them. My May is a good girl.
Lem. Would you please tell her to stay out of it?
May. Mother, please.
Grandma. Well, speak up to him. Don't let him get away with talk like that. Just speak up.
May. I'd speak up, Mama, if you'd give me half a chance.
Grandma. Calling your husband "Daddy" all the time. If that isn't the silliest thing I ever heard.
May. Mother, if you don't keep out of this, I'll come upstairs and give you a pill and shut your door.
Grandma. And I'll spit out the pill and open the door. So there.

Lem. *(gets up—crosses to foot of stairs)* Will you two stop that bickering and let's get down to the point at hand. *(calling up to Grandma)* Do you know where he is? *(no answer)* Hey! Old lady— I'm talking to you.

Grandma. If you're talking to me—my name is Mrs. Martin, and I'd thank you to remember that. No—I don't know where he is, and if I did I wouldn't tell you.

(Lem turns away.)

May. Would you tell me, Mama?

Grandma. Tell you?—After your telling me to shut up? I wouldn't tell you a thing.

May. I didn't tell you to shut up, Mama.

Grandma. Well, you said "Mother please," which is the same thing.

Lem. There's no use talking to her. *(sits in his chair, takes up paper)*

Grandma. Calling your son a bastard—the very idea. No wonder he uses such terrible language. No wonder he's in trouble down there at— *(She stops.)*

Lem. Where is he in trouble?

(no answer)

May. Mama—what trouble is Spence in?

Grandma. *(rising)* I'm a little tired. If you don't mind I think I'll go to bed now. *(from arch)* Good night.

Lem. *(rises, crosses to stairs; on stairs)* I'm gonna—

May. We'll sit here and wait for him—that's all. *(Lem crosses right to chair.)* I'm a little worried now, Lem.

Lem. It's about time.

May. Oh, don't be silly. I was worried before. You don't suppose we should call the police, Lem?

Lem. What for? We haven't done anything—have we?

May. They'd help us find him.

Lem. There'll be no police in this house—ever—for any reason.

May. Now you're being silly.

Lem. You heard what I said. I don't want any police in this.

May. *(rises; crosses right to window)* Ssh! He's coming up the steps—and he's carrying a bag, Lem.

Lem. *(crosses to center)* A bag? Well, I'll be damned!

May. Now don't holler at him until we find out what's wrong.

Lem. Don't worry. I'll handle this. You just stay out of it.

(Spence enters right. Lem lights cigar.)

Grandma. *(as Spence shuts door)* Spence—is that you?

Spence. *(takes off coat; crosses to foot of stairs)* Yes, it's me, Gram.

Grandma. Would you come right upstairs, please. I've dropped my glasses and can't seem to find them.

Spence. I'll be right up, Gram.

Lem. You'll come in this house and sit down, young man. I want to talk to you.

Spence. It'll just take a second, Pop.

Lem. A second too long. Sit down now. The traitor upstairs can wait for her glasses. She can't read in the dark, anyhow.

(Spence sits on stool.)

May. *(crosses to left of Spence)* Spence—you don't look well. Where have you been?

Spence. To the library.

Grandma. Spence— I haven't told them a thing. If they say I have they're lying.

Lem. *(crossing down to Spence)* Will you shut her up?

May. *(to center)* Mother, please.

Grandma. Oh! Shut up, yourself. Mother please— Mother please. Why don't you tell me to shut up and be done with it?

Lem. *(over Grandma's last sentence)* I can't even think with her carrying on up there. So—you were at the library and you brought a suitcase to carry home a couple of books.

(May crosses to Spence.)

Spence. Well— I had a tough time finding the books.

Lem. I get it. You knew you were going to have a tough time finding the books so you just packed an overnight bag in case you had to spend the night.

May. Have you had anything to eat, Spence?

Spence. As a matter of fact I haven't.

Lem. Will you please stop interrupting?

May. I'll go and heat up something. *(goes into the kitchen, turns on kitchen light)*

Lem. Do you think I'm crazy, Spence?

Spence. I honestly don't think you're crazy, Pop.

Lem. Well, you must think something like that. Don't you think I know what time the library closes?

Spence. What time does the library close, Pop?

Lem. *(a pause)* May! *(crosses to arch up left center)*

May. Yes?

Lem. You'd better come in here and talk to this little bastard before I break his neck.

Grandma. There he goes again. It's disgraceful.

(May comes in with saucepan and ladle. Lem crosses up right.)

May. *(to Grandma)* All right now. Spence, where have you been?
Spence. I told you—to the library. I got the books to prove it.
May. I think it's been pretty well settled, Spence—that you did go to the library. The point is, where did you go after that? *(He doesn't answer.)* It isn't like you, Spence, not to answer. *(They wait. May puts pan on dining table, crosses to Spence.)* Very well, Spence. When you came in I smelled beer on your breath. Have you been drinking beer?
Spence. Yes.
Lem. Well, I'll be damned.
May. Daddy—please.
Grandma. Don't be calling that man "Daddy." He's no husband of mine.
May. Who have you been drinking beer with, Spence?
Spence. I'd rather not say.
May. Why not, Spence?
Spence. *(gets up, crosses to TV)* Well, Mom, to be frank with you, I don't honestly think that you'd know any of them.
May. I'd still like to know.
Spence. Mom, I'm trying to be honest with you. If you keep asking me I'm going to lie about it—and I'd rather not lie about it, Mom.
May. *(crosses to Spence)* Very well, Spence—we'll let that pass for now. A few minutes ago your Grandmother said that you were in some kind of trouble.
Grandma. I didn't quite hear that. What's that you said I said?
May. Are you in trouble, Spence?
Spence. I sure am.
May. What happened?
Spence. I—got kicked out of school.
Lem. *(crosses to left)* Well I'll be good and goddamned.
May. Do you know what you did that was wrong?
Lem. *(crossing to right)* The little genius gets kicked out of school.
Spence. I don't think that I honestly did anything that was wrong.
Lem. That clinches it. He gets kicked out of school for doing nothing.
Spence. I didn't mean that, Pop. I didn't mean that I didn't do anything. I just felt that I was justified.
May. What happened, Spence?
Spence. Look, Mom— I don't want to go through all that again. I don't feel like it. *(crosses to ottoman down stage of May)* The teacher, Miss Crowley, that is, said something about Negroes. I was sitting there. I told her she was wrong. She got mad— I got mad. I walked out of her room and went into the Men's Room. I was mad so I smoked a cigar. *(sits on ottoman)* They caught me and brought me down to the

principal. They threw me out of school for a week. That's all there was to it.

Lem. *(moves to Spence)* What are you talking about—that's all there was to it? We got a genius on our hands, May. He knows more than the teacher. What do you think of that? *(turning on Spence)* Where did you get that cigar?

Spence. Out of your box.

Lem. *(to May)* There you are!

May. In other words you stole cigars from your father?

Spence. I wouldn't exactly call it that.

Lem. Well, that's damn well what I'd call it. *(crosses to above chair right)*

May. You and I will go back to school Monday, Spence, and you will apologize to Miss Crowley and be reinstated in school.

Spence. There's a week's vacation.

May. Then we will go up on the following Monday.

Spence. I don't think I can see my way clear to doing that, Mom.

May. *(crosses sofa table for knitting)* There will be no more discussion about it, Spence. A week from Monday—and it's settled.

Spence. I'm not going to school with you, Mom. I'm going to stay out for the week. I won't go back to school and apologize to anyone.

May. You want to disobey both your father and me?

Spence. I don't want to disobey either of you. I kind of felt that you'd be on my side.

Lem. You'll do what you're told. *(comes down stage)*

Spence. I suppose you can make me go up there with you—but I won't apologize to anyone.

Lem. Stop talking back to your mother.

Spence. I'm not talking back to her. I just want her to understand how I feel.

(May is above Spence.)

Lem. *(crossing to Spence)* We don't care how you feel. Now, what do you think of that? You talk about what you'll do and what you won't do. We do things we don't like to do every day of our lives. I hear those crumbs at the bank talking about niggers and making jokes about niggers every day—and I stay on—because I need the job—so that you can have the things that you need. And what do you do? You get your silly little behind kicked out of school. And now you're too proud to go back. *(crosses up right)*

Grandma. Will you listen to him running his big mouth.

May. *(crossing down)* Mama. We've given you boys everything that you could possibly want. You've never been deprived of anything, Spence. I don't need to tell you how hard we both work, and the fact that I'm in pain now doesn't seem to make any difference to you. I have arthritis in my wrist now, so badly that I can barely stand it, and it certainly doesn't help it any to hear you talk like this.

Spence. I'm sorry your wrist hurts, Mom.

(Lem is at piano.)

May. *(crosses right)* You're not sorry at all. If you were, you'd do something about it. We've bent every effort to see that you were raised in a decent neighborhood and wouldn't have to live in slums because we always wanted the best for you. But now I'm not so sure we haven't made a terrible mistake—because you seem not to realize what you are. You're a little colored boy—that's what you are—and you have no business talking back to white women, no matter what they say or what they do. If you were in the South you could be lynched for that and your father and I couldn't do anything about it. So from now on my advice to you is to try and remember your place.

Spence. You'll pardon me for saying so—but that's the biggest hunk of bull I've ever heard in my whole life.

Lem. *(crossing down to him)* What's that you said?

Spence. *(rises)* You both ought to be ashamed to talk to me that way.

Lem. *(walks over and slaps him full across the face)* Now go upstairs and don't come down until you can apologize to both of us. Go on.

Spence. *(Crosses to foot of stairs, stops second step. May crosses down right.)* I'll go upstairs, Pop, because you're my father and I still have to do what you tell me. But I'm still ashamed of you and I want you both to know it. *(He is walking upstairs.)*

Lem. *(crossing to foot of stairs)* That smart mouth of yours is going to get you into more trouble if you don't watch out. *(Spence has disappeared. Lem crosses down right.)* It's those damn books you've been reading—that's the trouble with you.

May. I don't think you should have slapped him, Lem.

Lem. What was I supposed to do? Let the little skunk stand there and cuss us both out? *(going over to the stairs)* And be sure you go straight upstairs. Don't be stopping in the traitor's room.

Grandma. He can stop in my room if he wants to. Who's to stop him. I'd like to know?

Lem. *(starts upstairs, holding paper)* I will.

Grandma. If you come into my room with your nasty mouth I'll bat you on the head with my cane.

Lem. *(returns to room, waves paper)* It's a fine thing when a man can't get a little respect in his own house.

Grandma. What have either of you done to get respect, I'd like to know? Nothing but bully the boy.

May. All right, Mother—now you keep out of it.
Grandma. *(on stairs)* I'll not keep out of it. When I've got something to say, I say it, and you know it, so don't try to hush me up.
May. *(crossing to foot of stairs)* Mother, if you come down those stairs I'm going to tell the doctor.
Grandma. *(Comes downstairs. May crosses to piano.)* Oh! Tell him, smell him, knock him down and sell him. What you think I care? All this slapping and going on.
Lem. Where did Spence go? *(sits on his chair)*
Grandma. *(at bannister, crossing to sofa)* He went to his room. Where do you suppose he would go? He still does what you tell him, though why I'll never know.
May. Mother—please.
Lem. Oh! Let her go ahead and run herself down. It won't take long.
Grandma. That's where you're wrong. I have no intention of running down. I've got a few things to say and I'm going to say them. *(picks papers off sofa, throws them at Lem)*
Lem. Well, hurry up and say them and let's get it over with.
Grandma. I will. Don't you worry your head about that. I'm going to sit down first. *(Grandma sits on sofa. May crosses to piano.)* Now in the first place—that nasty little hussy that's teaching history in that school deserves exactly what she got—and the only thing that I think is that Spence didn't tell her enough.
May. He can't go around talking to people like that.
Grandma. That's a lot of twaddle and you know it. *(May crosses left to kitchen arch.)* Now, in the second place—when you moved down here, did you ever stop to take into consideration that something like this was bound to happen sooner or later, and that the most important thing might be just having your love and company? You did not. You kept right on working—and instead of your company, they got a book or a bicycle or an electric train. Mercy—the stuff that came in this house was ridiculous.
Lem. *(gets up, crosses to piano)* That's none of you—
Grandma. Will you let me finish? Well, I don't agree with that kind of raising one bit—and allow me to be the first to tell you both. You got away with it with Mack because Mack had Spence. But do you know that that boy is absolutely alone? He hasn't a friend in the world. You didn't know, did you, that all his little pals around here have taken to the girls and the little girls' mothers don't want their little daughters going around with a colored boy. Did you know that there was a dance up at school last week and Spence couldn't go because he didn't have anybody to take? Well, whether you know it or not, he's alone. And now you want to desert him completely by not backing him up. You

moved him out of a slum and taught him to think of himself as something to be respected—and now you get mad when he does the things that you made it possible for him to do. That bull—as he called it about staying in his place. I'm ashamed of you both and I want you to know it. I've said what I came down here to say—now help me out of this sofa. Well, don't just stand there like a dumb ox—help me up.

(Lem moves over, helps her.)

May. You hadn't ought to come downstairs, Mother. You know that.
Grandma. I'll come downstairs when I want to. Now—what do you think of that? *(shoves Lem away)* The trouble with you two is that you're too careful. I'm an old lady and I haven't got much longer to live one way or the other. I'll come downstairs when I want to. *(crosses to stairs)*
May. Did Spence tell you all this? *(crosses right)*
Grandma. Well, I certainly didn't find it out by talking to the neighbors.
Lem. *(crosses to sofa, sits)* Well—why in hell didn't he say so when we were talking to him?
Grandma. How could he? You attacked him like a rattlesnake the minute he came in the door.
Lem. I did not.
Grandma. You laid in wait and attacked him just like a rattlesnake. I heard you. *(She is staring up the stairs.)* I'm going to send him downstairs. *(She is slowly mounting the stairs.)* Talk to him. Be nice to him. *(on landing)* Don't be crumbs all your lives. *(She disappears.)*
May. *(starting to go to kitchen)* I'd better go and put the food on again.
Lem. *(gets up, follows her)* You'll stay right here.
May. He's hungry, Lem.
Lem. You can do all of that when we're through. You're not going to leave me here by myself. What will I say to him?
May. I don't know.
Lem. Why didn't you tell me all this was going on anyway?
May. Because I didn't know, Daddy.
Lem. It's a mother's place to know what's happening to her son—isn't it?
May. *(crossing to Lem)* You know— I didn't know how it was going to take place, but somehow I knew it would turn out to be my fault.
Lem. *(moves right)* I didn't say—
May. Oh! Shut up.
Lem. *(turns to her)* What did you say to me?
May. *(moves right)* I said "Shut up." I told you not to hop on him the minute he came into the house. Maybe if you'd asked him questions instead of calling him names you would've found all this out and you wouldn't have to stand here looking so foolish now.
Lem. You were just as bad as I was.

May. I'm going out in the kitchen. You can talk to him by yourself.

(She starts to exit as Spence starts down the stairs.)

Lem. *(sotto voce)* You stay in here.
May. I will not. So there. *(She exits into kitchen.)*
Lem. *(his back to stairway, pretends not to notice Spence; gets up his nerve and then)* Come on down, Spence. *(Spence starts down again. Lem crosses right.)* We're going to have a little talk. *(Spence comes into the room.)* Sit down—Son.
Spence. *(walking over to the chair right)* Thanks, Pop. *(sits on stool)*
Lem. Are you comfortable?
Spence. Yes, Pop.
Lem. *(at right of Spence)* How do you feel?
Spence. I feel all right, Pop. I'm a little groggy, but I guess that's from the— *(He pauses.)* stuff I've been drinking.
Lem. *(moves close to Spence)* Serves you right. Now you gotta stop going around doing things like that. You hear? And another thing—You've got to stop talking back to me. If there's one thing that makes me good and damned mad it's talking back. I can't stand it and I won't stand it. *(crossing left)* It doesn't show the proper respect. You got that?
Spence. Yes, Pop.
Lem. *(after a glance into the kitchen)* You heard from Mack lately?
Spence. No, I haven't, Pop.
Lem. *(crossing right)* Well, I guess he's busy. You know how it is when you go to college.
Spence. Yes, I guess he is busy.
Lem. And that's what you've got to start thinking about—because you'll be busy, too, when you get to college. And you're going to college—you know that, don't you?
Spence. Yes, Pop—I do.
Lem. Well—just to be sure. Now you go on and forget these little bastards around here. Don't pay any attention to them. *(crosses chair right)* You've got bigger things to think about—and if they won't play with you—you just tell them to go to hell—because you're better than any ten of them put together. All right. Now—you got your books and you've got your music—and if there's anything you want—you just tell me about it and I'll get it for you. Understand? *(Lem sits.)*
Spence. Yes, Pop.
Lem. *(rises, crosses up)* And don't mind what those lousy teachers say either. The big thing is for you to graduate and get the hell out of that lousy school. And if they say anything you don't like—just forget it—'cause you're going to college—and you can't afford to get your butt thrown out of school too often. You understand?

Spence. Yes, Pop.
Lem. All right then. *(crosses to his chair, sits)* It's all settled. Now you just forget the whole business. And if anything else happens—you just come to us and we'll take care of it. Understand?
Spence. Yes, Pop.
Lem. All right then. *(Lem returns to paper. Pause.)* Your mother's fixing you something to eat. You'd better go out and get it.
Spence. If you don't mind, Pop, I don't feel like eating. I think I'll just go to bed now.
Lem. Now—that's what I'm talking about. It's silly to go around moping.
Spence. *(rising, crosses to stairs)* I know it's silly, Pop. I know that. I'm going to try to do what you told me, but I want to go to bed now—that's all. *(He is on the stairs.)* Goodnight, Pop. *(He turns.)* And thanks for helping me, Pop. *(starts up)*
Lem. It's all right. *(He is sitting down with the paper.)*

(From upstairs a voice—muffled and rather terrified, cries.)

Grandma. Spence! Spence!

(Spence pauses for a moment and then rushes upstairs.)

Lem. *(jumping from the chair and running upstairs)* May! Come up here.
May. *(from the kitchen)* What? What's the matter? *(She comes out.)* Where are you?
Lem. Up here—come up here quickly. *(May runs up the stairs. There is the sound of Lem's voice.)* Now that's right—up here on the bed. There. Go down and call the doctor; tell him to get here as soon as he can. The number is on the pad.
May. Mama! Mama!
Lem. Get out of the way, May.
Spence. *(Rushes downstairs, goes to the telephone and dials the number. He waits.)* Hello! Is Doctor Sloane there? This is Dr. Sloane? This is Spencer Scott. You've got to come over as soon as you can. It's my Grandmother. I don't know what's the matter with her. You've got to come—
May. *(enters from the top of the stairs)* Spence! *(Spence puts his hand over the mouthpiece and waits.)* Tell him he doesn't have to hurry. She's dead. *(Spence hangs up the phone without telling him. May keeps coming down the stairs and down right; sits in chair.)* She didn't have to suffer, Spence, and she died quickly. We can thank God for that.

(Spence starts for the stairs as Lem starts down. He meets his father, who holds him.)

Lem. Where are you going?

Spence. Let me go— Pop, I said let me go. Damn it, Pop—take your hands off me.
May. *(rising)* Let him go, Lem.

(Lem releases him. Spence goes off as Lem comes down the stairs. May sits down and Lem stands silent, above her. Spence comes down the stairs again and goes into the kitchen. He doesn't notice his father or mother and goes quickly to get his coat, off left in kitchen.)

Lem. Where are you going Spence?
Spence. *(putting on coat)* Out—outside for a while.
Lem. *(crossing to center)* I think you'd better stay here with your mother, Spence. She needs you.
Spence. I can't. She's got you anyway.
Lem. I don't think you'd better go out now.
Spence. Leave me alone! Will you?
Lem. How can you be so selfish? Your mother needs you. *(He starts right. Lem holds him.)* What's the matter with you anyway? You've got a fever. You'd better go to bed.
Spence. I'm not going to bed. I want to go out for a few minutes. That's all. I want to be by myself for a few minutes.
May. You don't have to go outside to cry, Spence. You don't have to be ashamed before us. *(Spence begins to sob incoherently, his head on Lem's shoulder; breaks away from his father and runs out of the house. Lem starts after him.)* Let him go, Lem.
Lem. *(stopping at front door)* But he's got a fever. He can't—
May. Let him alone, Lem.
Lem. *(crosses down right to her)* I'll call the doctor. You go and rest. He can have a look at Spence while he's here.
May. You'd better call Mack too, Lem. He's so far away. I don't think he'll be able to come home.
Lem. I'll call him.
May. What's Spence doing, Lem?
Lem. He's standing over in the lot—that's all.

(Curtain)

ACT II

SCENE 2

At the Curtain's rise, Spence's room is in semi-darkness because the shades are drawn. The door is shut. On the chair by Spence's bed stands a tray of *food. On the bureau is a decanter of water, a bottle of pills and medicine. Spence is in bed—asleep to all obvious intents. A Woman appears climbing the stairs outside of the room and enters. She is carrying a clean pillow slip, which she places on the chair right. She glances over at the bed and then begins to pull the shades. Sun springs into the room as she does so. She is a woman perhaps in her late twenties, good-looking and trim. It is two weeks later—early afternoon.*

Christine. You know, I've met many a mulish critter in my day, but you're the worst mule I've ever met. Now you ain't asleep because I heard you tipping around up here not ten minutes ago. Now open your eyes and eat your lunch.

Spence. I don't want it.

Christine. *(crosses with tray to bureau)* You know you don't have to eat it? You know that, don't you? But don't blame anyone but yourself when your bones are rattling around inside of your skin like two castanets hit together—you understand? I suppose you don't want your medicine either. *(crosses up of bed)* Boy, you sure do beat all. You're the stubbornest cuss I ever met. I'll ask you one more time. Are you going to take this medicine or aren't you? Speak up, 'cause I don't have all day.

Spence. No.

Christine. I didn't quite catch that. Don't be mumbling at me, boy. Was it "Yes" or "No" that you said?

Spence. I said "No."

Christine. Boy, you know you're going to make some girl a pretty miserable husband one of these days. 'Course, you know, I don't believe you're not eating. *(crosses to bureau)* I think you sneak downstairs after I leave and eat everything in sight. *(pause)* Did you hear me? *(no answer; crosses to bed)* Spence, won't you please sit up and eat something? Anything? Crust of bread? You know it kills me when folks don't eat. *(no answer)* I never knew anybody who could pick out just the right way to worry somebody. Won't you eat just a little bit?

Spence. *(head up in bed)* I said "No."

Christine. *(crosses to chair for pillow slip, returns)* Well, I guess that settles it—don't it? Then you can get out of bed so I can make it.

Spence. You don't need to make it today.

Christine. The devil you say. I've taken enough from you today already. Now just get out of that bed before I pick you up and throw you out of it. You're not supposed to stay in bed all day anyway. The doctor said to get up and walk around and to get some air if you felt like it.

Spence. Don't you get sick of repeating yourself?

Christine. *(crosses to bureau, returns with decanter)* You've got 'til I count three. One—two—three—*(throws water)*

Spence. *(throwing the covers off and laughing in spite of himself)* All right—all right. I'm getting up now. *(He goes right and sits in chair.)* You make me sick.

Christine. The feeling is oh so mutual. *(She begins to make the bed—stands above it.)* I've seen a mess of mourning in my day, but if the mourning you do don't beat anything I've ever seen yet, I don't want a nickel. But at the rate you're going you're not going to have much longer to mourn. You're going to be joining them that you're mournin' for if you don't watch your step.

Spence. What do you say to my making a little bargain with you?

Christine. What is it?

Spence. I'll eat that slop that you brought up here if as soon as that bed is made you get the hell out of here and leave me alone.

Christine. *(takes food tray from chair to bureau)* There ain't no call to be rude and nasty. All I'm saying is that you look like a bag of bones and you do.

Spence. I've always been skinny.

Christine. *(pours medicine in soup)* It's humanly impossible for somebody to be as skinny as you are and live. Consumption is chasing you in one direction and pneumonia is chasing you in the other—and when they meet with you in the middle, it's sure going to be a mess.

Spence. Why don't you shut up?

Christine. *(moves to above bed, continues making it)* Why don't you eat your lunch instead of sitting up there looking like death warmed over?

Spence. *(gets out of the chair and viciously picks up the tray from the bureau; brings it back, sits down with it and begins to eat)* Now will you let me alone?

Christine. *(crosses to bureau, gets out socks)* Who's bothering you?

Spence. You are.

Christine. *(crosses to him, puts wrapper around shoulders)* Aw! Go on, boy. You know you love it.

Spence. *(tasting the soup)* What kind of soup is this?

Christine. *(putting on left sock)* What'd you say?

Spence. I said, "What kind of soup is this?"

Christine. Chicken.

Spence. Well, it tastes damn peculiar. *(tasting it again)* What's in it?

Christine. Nothing.

Spence. What's in this soup? *(pause)* You put the medicine in the soup.

Christine. Does it taste awful?

Spence. It tastes just like hell. You sure are a lousy cook. No wonder you can't keep a husband.

Christine. I'll have you know that I've only had one husband—and he died.

Spence. I'm not surprised.
Christine. *(throws socks down, rises, crosses to bed, works on sheet)* I'm not speaking to you again today. And that's final.
Spence. You're not really mad, are you, Christine? *(pause)* Christine, I was just kidding. *(pause)* Aw! Come on, Christine. You know I don't really think that you killed your husband.
Christine. *(laughing; crosses to Spence)* Boy, you sure are a mess. *(They look at one another.)* You feel better now—don't you?
Spence. I guess so.
Christine. *(puts on right sock)* You're getting some color in your cheeks.
Spence. Don't you think that you're hurrying things a little, Christine? I haven't finished eating yet.
Christine. If there's one thing I can't stand it's skinny men around me. Never could stand skinny men since I can first remember. You wouldn't be a bad-looking boy if you just weren't so skinny.
Spence. Thanks, Christine. Thanks. You're a real tin pitcher full of complaints today. You're as generous with the old complaints as Gram. *(He stops eating.)*
Christine. *(rises, stands over Spence left of him)* Now what's the matter? What've you stopped eating for?
Spence. You know what's the matter.
Christine. *(fixes something on tray)* Now there isn't any point in thinking about that now.
Spence. I know there isn't, but I can't help it.
Christine. Just don't think about it.
Spence. That's a very stupid thing to say. You can't just stop thinking about someone because they're dead, can you?
Christine. Yes, yes you can if you want to. You just don't open the door and let yourself in, that's all.
Spence. What are you talking about?
Christine. Nothing. Now eat your lunch. *(to above bed)*
Spence. *(begins eating again)* You know, it's funny. I got expelled from school—Gram died—and I got sick—and so I couldn't go to school anyway—even if they hadn't kicked me out. Funny the way things turn out.
Christine. Yes, it is—isn't it? *(She stops work, listens.)*
Spence. You know, Christine, I was just thinking. 'Course last week was the funeral and I figure maybe the guys didn't want to come and see me then. But I've been home all this week. *(Christine crosses to him, gets tray.)* Wouldn't you have thought that one of them would have come over to see me by now?
Christine. *(putting tray on bureau)* Nothing surprises me any more.
Spence. What do you mean by that?

Christine. Nothing. *(feels his head)* I don't think you have any more fever. You want to take your temperature?
Spence. Naw! *(pause)* Your hands are very warm, Christine.
Christine. Warm hands—warm heart.
Spence. That would be fine except that that's not the way it goes.
Christine. *(crossing to bed)* It goes that way for me and that's what matters.
Spence. *(rises, crosses to right of bureau)* Were you born here, Christine?
Christine. No. I was born in Alabama. Birmingham, Alabama, in Ensley, near the steel mills.
Spence. I'll bet you didn't like it much down there, did you?
Christine. No, I didn't like it much down there.
Spence. Is your family still there?
Christine. *(crosses down to front of bed; changes pillow slip)* My father was killed in the mills when I was a little girl. My Ma died a couple of years ago. I had two brothers and two sisters. I don't know where they are now.
Spence. *(crosses to bed, sits)* What made you come way the hell up here by yourself?
Christine. *(laughing)* I wanted something better, I guess. I decided I was coming up North to try my luck. I worked for a whole year before I'd saved the money, and the day I had what I thought was enough, I went down to the railroad station. *(stops work)* Boy was that some day! The sun was shining and I felt real good like you feel maybe once or twice in your whole life. When I got to the ticket window, the big man had a calendar, and it had an advertisement for a big insurance company on it. So I looked at the name of the town and then I told him that that's where I wanted my ticket to take me. Then I went home and packed my mama's cardboard suitcase, and that same night I caught the train. And that's the last I ever saw of my mother and my brothers and sisters and Rusty.
Spence. Who the hell was Rusty?
Christine. *(Sits at the head of bed. Spence sits in middle.)* Rusty was my dog. Well, I didn't go to work for the insurance company. I went into service for a while and then I got married. And that's what I meant when I was telling you about the doors. See, my husband died about two years after that and about two months after he died, I had a baby and he was born dead.
Spence. Christine!
Christine. Well, I tell you for a while I felt like all I wanted to do was die myself. Then I realized that you just can't go on like that. It's like your mind is divided into little rooms and each time you go back into one of those rooms your heart likes to break in two. So all you do is shut the

doors—and lock them—to those little rooms in your mind and never let yourself in them again. So I've got two little locked rooms in my mind. One for Bert, my husband, and one for my baby that never had a name. Do you want some more to eat?

Spence. No, Christine, I don't think so. You sure do make me feel crumby, Christine.

Christine. Why?

Spence. Well, I've been giving you a pretty hard time about what's been happening to me. *(pause)* I'm sorry, Christine.

Christine. That's all right, boy. You're just unhappy—that's all. But you'll get used to that. Pretty soon you'll be able to laugh a little bit and make jokes, even while you're unhappy. It won't be this bad forever. *(rises)* Well, the bed's made, the house is clean, and you've had your lunch. So—

Spence. Don't go, Christine. Stay with me.

Christine. *(crossing to bureau for tray)* I've got another cleaning job, Boy.

Spence. Just for a little while longer. *(pause)* If you have to go, well then I guess you have to, but if you could stay just a little while longer it would mean a lot to me. It isn't that I'm afraid of anything, but I get to thinking about all the things I've got to do.

Christine. What have you got to do?

Spence. Well, I've got to really get well—first of all. I'll take the medicine and I'll take a hell of a lot of vitamins and I figure that'll fix me up all right.

Christine. *(crossing to him with pills)* There's no time like the present to begin.

Spence. Honest, Christine.

Christine. A little water? *(She gets water glass from the tray.)*

Spence. *(takes the pill)* I know what you're going to say. "You're beginning to look fatter already." *(She laughs merrily and hugs him.)* You're going to make me spill the water.

Christine. *(releases him; takes glass and puts it on tray)* What else?

Spence. Well, I'm going to cut out the damn smoking and drinking and that ought to fix up the old body. *(rises, crosses right)* Then I've got to go up to school and make peace with old Hasbrook and Crowley. But the other things are going to be a hell of a lot harder to do.

Christine. What are they?

Spence. *(sits in chair right)* I've got to do something about the guys and my Gram, Christine. I'm going to be honest with you about Gram—it's going to be hard. I miss her a hell of a lot. But she's dead, Christine. She's dead—and you can tell yourself that and you can accept it, and maybe I'm a little selfish about it, but you know that no other living soul is talking with her or having fun with her. She didn't ditch you. She died. But the guys are different, Christine. They're not dead. They're over in the lot playing baseball. They're still horsing around up in the park. I don't suppose they can really help what's happened because that's the way it is. I've said some pretty lousy things to them, Christine, and I don't want it to be that way. *(He pauses. He is near tears.)* God damn it—I hate being black, Christine. I hate it. I hate it. I hate the hell out of it.

Christine. *(crosses to him, holds him)* Ssh!
Spence. I'm sorry I said that, Christine.
Christine. It's all right, Spence. You don't have to explain to me. *(She releases him, but still holds his hand)*
Spence. And I've got to cut out this goddamn crying. Everything makes me cry. I don't understand it. I was watching television the other day—a damn soap opera—and started crying like a baby. That's damn peculiar.
Christine. It's not so peculiar as you think.
Spence. There's just one more thing, Christine.
Christine. What is it?
Spence. I don't know whether I should tell you or not.
Christine. Sure you can tell me.
Spence. How are you so sure? You don't even know what it is yet.
Christine. I'll take the risk.
Spence. You promise you won't say anything about it to anybody?
Christine. I won't mention it to a soul.
Spence. No matter what it is?
Christine. I've already said I won't tell it, haven't I?
Spence. Well. I want to sleep with a girl, Christine. *(Christine turns away laughing.)* What's the matter with you?
Christine. Nothing. I just swallowed wrong.
Spence. Yeh!
Christine. *(turns to him)* Yeh! And many more of them right back at you. Who's the lucky girl?
Spence. Aw! Christine. You know I haven't got any girl in mind. I think about it quite often, but I can't think of anybody. I suppose you think that sounds pretty horny to be thinking of it all the time?
Christine. *(turns away)* No, I wouldn't say that.
Spence. You wouldn't?
Christine. No, I wouldn't.
Spence. You know, Christine. You're a funny Joe. To look at you no one would think that somebody could talk to you like this.
Christine. *(quite dryly, turns to him)* Thanks.
Spence. Have you had much experience, Christine?
Christine. Enough.
Spence. Off hand—how much experience would you say you've had?

Christine. Now that's the kind of question it's every woman's right to leave unanswered.
Spence. You think that's a pretty nosey question?
Christine. I not only think it's a nosey question. I know it is.
Spence. O.K. *(Rises. Crosses to below bed. Christine sits chair right. Pause.)* Would you say, off hand, that I was trying to rush things, Christine?
Christine. How do you mean?
Spence. *(crossing down right)* You'd just as soon we talked about something else, wouldn't you?
Christine. I just didn't understand what you meant, that's all.
Spence. *(crossing to center)* Well, I mean about my age and all. Do you realize that I'm going on eighteen and have never slept with a girl?
Christine. That's terrible—isn't it? *(turns away)*
Spence. It sure as hell is. Hell, I'm practically a virgin. And you know I was thinking when I was sick, supposing I died. Supposing I just passed out now and died. *(indicates imaginary body on floor)* Why, I'd regret that I hadn't slept with anybody for the rest of my life practically.
Christine. I guess that would be pretty terrible—wouldn't it?
Spence. I think that you're having a hell of a good time laughing at me.
Christine. I most certainly am not.
Spence. You sure as hell are. You've got a sneaky laugh line around your whole mouth.
Christine. *(turns to him)* Spence— I'm not laughing. I wouldn't laugh at you when you're telling me things like this. If I'm doing anything I'm remembering, and I might be just smiling a little bit at the memory, but I'm not laughing at you.
Spence. You really honestly don't think that it's peculiar or anything?
Christine. How could anything so natural be peculiar?
Spence. That's a funny thing for you to say.
Christine. Why is it so funny, might I ask?
Spence. *(sits on foot of bed)* Well, I'm pretty sure, although I've never asked her, that Mom would give me a swat for my pains if—
Christine. *(rises, crosses to him)* And what makes you think that your mother and I should have the same ideas?
Spence. Well—you're both older than I am.
Christine. Well, I'm not anywhere near as old as your mother. I might be a widow, but I'm a young widow, and I'm not through yet by a long shot.
Spence. I didn't mean—
Christine. I know exactly what you mean. Just remember you're no Tiny Tim yourself.
Spence. I didn't mean what you thought I meant at all. I just meant that you seem to understand a lot of things. Aw! Hell— I don't mean that. I mean you seem to understand me—and I'm grateful. That's all.

Christine. *(crosses to chair left; after a pause)* Well, we've done enough talking for one afternoon. I've got to go.
Spence. Christine!
Christine. *(turning around)* What is it now?
Spence. *(pause)* Nothing.
Christine. *(crossing to center)* Nothing is what you ask for, nothing is what you'll get.
Spence. *(rises)* Christine!— *(She stops.)* I'd appreciate it if you didn't turn around.
Christine. Why?
Spence. *(standing behind her)* Because I'm going to ask you something and if you're going to laugh at me I'd just as soon you weren't laughing in my face.
Christine. I won't laugh.
Spence. Well, would you mind not turning around just the same?
Christine. All right.
Spence. Well— I don't know quite how to say it. *(pause)* Do you like me, Christine?
Christine. I certainly do.
Spence. No kidding?
Christine. No kidding.
Spence. I was sure hoping you weren't. Because I like you too, Christine.
Christine. Thank you.
Spence. Well, I know that liking doesn't mean loving—but I kind of thought—that since—well—you're lonely, aren't you, Christine?
Christine. I've been lonely for a long time now, Boy.
Spence. Well—in case you didn't know, I'm lonely too, Christine—and I know that you're older than I am and I know it makes a lot of difference.
Christine. I have to go, Spence.
Spence. But what I'm lacking in age, Christine, I sure make up for in loneliness and so we do have that much in common. Don't we, Christine?
Christine. Yes.
Spence. So maybe—if you stayed, Christine—since things are like I said they were—we might find a little happiness together. I don't mean for forever or anything like that—but could you call and say that you couldn't make it?
Christine. You know you're very young, Spence, and you could be very foolish too. You know that—don't you?
Spence. Yes, Christine, I know.
Christine. And I could be very foolish to listen to you.
Spence. I know, Christine.

Christine. *(turns to him)* It's funny. I have to look at you, because I can't believe that you said what you just said. You said, that since we were both lonely maybe—just for an afternoon—we could find happiness together. You know that so soon?
Spence. Yes, Christine.
Christine. You see, I didn't laugh. I ain't laughing at all. I'll try to come back. I'll try. *(She gets the tray from the bureau and goes to the door.)*
Spence. You know where the phone is. If you can't come back, Christine, you don't need to come up and tell me. Just go. But if you can, there's a bell downstairs on the table that Mother uses to call us to meals. Would you ring it—if you can?
Christine. I'll try. *(She exits.)*
Spence. *(crossing down right, then to door; listens)* Why in hell is she taking so long?

(Sound of hand bell off right. Spence crosses slowly to window, pulls shade down as lights fade.)

(Curtain)

ACT II

SCENE 3

The scene is the same as Scene 1. As the Curtain rises, May is coming out of the kitchen. She walks over to the piano and rings the bell. It is the following afternoon—Saturday.

May. Spence! Spence! Are you asleep?
Spence. *(upstairs)* No.
May. Well, suppose you come downstairs and get lunch. Hurry up now. I have a lot of work to do, and you're holding me up.
Spence. What's the big hurry?
May. *(crosses to dining room, gets fruit salad and milk from refrigerator)* Never mind. Just come downstairs and don't ask so many silly questions.
Spence. *(appears at head of stairs)* O.K. So I'm coming. You sure do get yourself upset about nothing at all. Why don't you take it easy? *(makes basketball throw with sweater from stairs onto armchair right)*
May. Have you gotten your clothes together yet?
Spence. *(coming downstairs, crossing to dining table)* What clothes?

May. *(counting groceries on shelf)* Your school clothes. I told you to get them ready and I'd have them pressed this afternoon.
Spence. *(sits right of table, starts eating)* They're all right.
May. I'm not going to have you going to school looking like a tramp.
Spence. You sure got peculiar notions of what a tramp looks like.
May. Never mind the sass. Did you get them ready?
Spence. They're hanging up in the closet—just waiting to be taken off the hangers and brought down to the tailor's. How much more ready could they be?
May. I told you to bring them down. You know you could cooperate a little bit more. Now I suppose I'm going to have to climb upstairs and bring them down. I told you my knee—
Spence. All right. All right. I'll get them— *(gets up, crosses to stairs)*
May. You're hollering at me, Spencer. *(pause)* You can't get them now. Just sit down and eat your lunch.
Spence. *(crosses back to chair)* You know, Mom, I got to give it to you. You sure do know how to fix a guy's stomach for this lunch. *(pause as he sits again)* You know, I could wear my Sunday suit to school Monday and Chris could take these clothes. I don't want you to strain your knee any more than you have to. Or I could take them down myself?
May. *(turns to shelf)* Chris? Christine won't be back Monday or any other day.
Spence. *(pushes chair back)* What are you talking about?
May. Christine will not be back. You're no longer ill. There's no need for Christine any longer.
Spence. *(rises, crosses to May)* But I thought you said—
May. I changed my mind. I called her and told her this morning.
Spence. What did you tell her?
May. I told her that her services were no longer needed by me. I decided that there was no need to spend that money since I could do the things myself. I've been doing them myself anyway.
Spence. But you said you were too tired when you got home.
May. Well, I've changed my mind. Why all this interest in Christine?
Spence. *(crossing back to table)* Nothing. I just thought—
May. I know what you just thought, young man, and don't think I don't.
Spence. Now what are you talking about?
May. You know my eyes weren't put on—
Spence. The way they were put on for nothing. I know.
May. All that pampering and coddling she did with you makes me sick to my stomach.
Spence. *(crossing to her)* Will you please explain what you mean by that?
May. I don't know. What should I mean by that? Maybe you can tell me. Well, I've heard those stories about maids being left alone in houses

with boys before. I'm not saying it's gone that far yet. But an ounce of prevention is worth a pound of anybody's cure.
Spence. *(crossing down)* You know, you sure have got a dirty mind.
May. Don't be so sure that it's I that have a dirty mind. And if you say that to me again you'll get a good slap for your pains.
Spence. How in hell—
May. Don't use that kind of language before me.
Spence. All I did was come down to eat lunch and then you start on me about a suit of clothes. *(crosses right)* I'll take the suit down to the tailor myself. I wouldn't have you strain yourself. As far as Christine is concerned, if she pampered and coddled me—then I'm grateful to her. And you promised her a job after I was sick and I think you're damned dirty—
May. Spencer!
Spence. *(crossing to table)* Yes, I think you're damned dirty to get rid of her. Now—that's all I've got to say and you can take this food away now because I can't eat it. *(crosses right)*
May. *(taking glass away)* Suit yourself. No one is going to beg you to eat, young man.
Spence. Mom—no one had to beg me to eat. All I wanted was a little peace to eat. I was perfectly willing to eat. *(crosses to stairs)*
May. Where are you going?
Spence. *(climbing stairs)* To the tailor. Where did you think I was going?
May. You haven't got time.
Spence. What do you mean I haven't got time? All in hell—
May. *(crosses to living room)* Be careful.
Spence. All in hell I got left in the world is time—time for everything. If there's any little thing you want done from now on—just let me know.
May. *(crosses to table, takes plate away)* You haven't got time to go to the tailor's now.
Spence. *(on landing)* Why not?
May. Because I asked some of your friends over this afternoon.
Spence. You did what?
May. *(turning to shelf)* I asked some of your friends over for ice cream and cake this afternoon.
Spence. *(coming downstairs)* Are you kidding?
May. I'm perfectly serious.
Spence. *(in center)* Why didn't you make a little pink punch to go with it?
May. I did.
Spence. Well, you can call them the hell back up and tell them to stay home.
May. *(turns, crosses to him)* Spence—don't you dare.
Spence. You heard what I said. You can call them up and tell them to stay

home. *(May crosses left. Spence follows her.)* What right did you have to do that? It's none of your business. It's my business and you stay out of it. I'm not bribing those kids with ice cream, cake or pink punch. I'm never going to bribe anyone to be my friend.

May. You'll do what you're told and you'll stop being so fresh. Do you understand that? *(Spence crosses to below table.)* And I don't want to hear another word out of you about what you'll do and what you won't do. When you start talking like that it's about time you went out and got a job of your own and bought a house of your own— *(Spence tucks in shirt-tails.)* but as long as you're under this roof, you will do what you're told. *(Spence turns to go to front door.)* Where are you going?

Spence. I'm going to get the hell out of here. That's where I'm going.

May. *(following him)* Go ahead—and see how far you get acting the way you act. *(both at front door)* Your father's right about you. You're too proud. You think you can go through life being proud, don't you? Well, you're wrong. You're a little black boy—and you don't seem to understand it. But that's what you are. You think this is bad; well, it'll be worse. You'll serve them pink punch and ice cream—and you'll do a lot worse. You'll smile when you feel like crying. *(She begins to cry.)* You'll laugh at them when you could put knives right into their backs without giving it a second thought—and you'll never do what you've done and let them know that they've hurt you. They never forgive you for that. So go on out and learn the lesson. Now get out of here. Get out of here and don't ever come back. *(May crosses to sofa, sits. Pause.)* You think it's easy for me to tell my son to crawl when I know he can walk and walk well? I'm sorry I ever had children. I'm sorry you didn't die when you were a baby. Do you hear that? I'm sorry you didn't die. *(She is completely overcome.)*

Spence. *(crossing down)* Don't cry, Mom. I'm sorry. I'm sorry I've made it so difficult. I didn't mean to hurt you, Mom. *(pause)* What time did you tell them to be here?

May. Around one.

Spence. Well, they'll be here any minute. Is everything ready?

May. It's in the pantry. The ice cream is in the refrigerator.

(Tony and Gussie enter outside the door.)

Spence. Don't cry, Mom. I'm sorry. It seems to me that for the past two weeks all I've done is apologize to people. I seem to be apologizing for trying to be a human being. *(The bell rings.)* That must be some of them now.

May. Do you want me to stay?

Spence. No. You can go out if you want to.

May. *(crosses to stairs, starts up)* I have some shopping to do. *(stops on landing, turns)* Spence, don't be rude to them.

(Spence opens the door.)

Gussie. Hi, Spence!
Spence. Hi, Gussie! Hi, Tony! *(Tony and Gussie enter. Gussie first. He crosses to right of sofa.)* What's the matter, Tony? You're not speaking or something?
Tony. Hi, Spence! I'm sorry about your grandmother. *(crosses to below armchair right)*
Spence. Thanks. Where are the rest of the guys?
Gussie. They'll be around. *(pause)* You going back to school Monday?
Spence. Yeh! I'm going back Monday. It's kind of creepy having a party for no reason—isn't it? See—I've been sick—you probably didn't know— my Mom thought it would be a big surprise if the gang came in today. That's all. Sit down.
Tony. *(sits on stool)* We didn't see you around. We wondered what was wrong.
Gussie. *(sits on right arm of sofa)* You're better now—ain't you?
Spence. Yeh! I'm better now. *(pause)* What you guys been doing?
Gussie. Knocking around. That's all.

(pause)

Spence. You been playing baseball lately?
Tony. Not much— No. We've had too much homework lately.
Spence. *(crosses left)* Oh! I thought I heard you guys a couple of times but it was probably somebody else.
Gussie. Yeh! It must've been somebody else.
Spence. Would you like some ice cream or anything?

(May appears at head of stairs. They rise.)

May. *(coming downstairs)* Don't get up. It's nice seeing all of you again.
Tony and Gussie. How do you do, Mrs. Scott!
May. Just stay where you are. I'm going down to the grocer's. Haven't seen you in a long time, Tony.
Tony. I've been pretty busy lately.
May. Well, don't be such a stranger. We miss you.
Spence. *(crosses to kitchen)* I'll get the ice cream.
Gussie. Yeah. We've been pretty busy.

(Iggie enters right, crosses to door, followed by Johnny and Bobby Reynolds.)

May. Well, any time you want to come over and watch television—come. Spence will be very glad to see you. *(Bell rings.)* I'll get it.
Spence. *(puts ice cream, plates and spoons on table as May opens door)* Well, here you are. Help yourselves.

(Tony crosses to table, sits left of it. Gussie crosses to left of table.)

May. Hello, boys. Come on in.
Iggie. Hello, Mrs. Scott. *(crosses left)*
Johnny. Hello, Mrs. Scott. *(May is at door. Iggie crosses left to table. Johnny is right of Bobby.)* My brother and I were very sad to hear of your recent—
Bobby. —death in your family.
May. Thank you, boys. I have to go now. Spence will entertain you. I'll be back in a little while. *(exits)*

(Bobby and Johnny cross left.)

Spence. *(crosses to them)* Well, if it isn't the Reynolds boys. Come on in.
Iggie. *(above table, his rear in Tony's ice cream)* Hey, Spence. I didn't come to see you, because I thought maybe you wouldn't want any visitors, but I kept asking your mother about you.
Spence. *(crossing to Iggie)* Well—thanks, Iggie. Thanks.
Tony. Hey, Iggie, will you get your ass out of my ice cream?
Iggie. I'm sorry. *(crosses to ottoman, sits)*

(Spence is just about to tell Tony off.)

Tony. Nothing to be sorry about. Just get out of it is all.
Gussie. *(interrupting impending fight between Tony and Spence, crosses in; nervously)* This is fun—ain't it, Spence?
Spence. Yeah! *(crosses Reynold Boys in living room)* Come on, you guys. Get yours while the getting is good.

(Bobby and Johnny cross to table. Gussie crosses right.)

Gussie. Hey! Spence. This is fun. We ain't had so much fun since we made that party that time—stealing off Mr. Markman. Remember that?

(Iggie rises, crosses to dining room shelf for cake.)

Spence. I sure do. I was responsible for getting dill pickles. What did you have to get?
Gussie. The ice cream. I had to get the ice cream.
Johnny. *(crosses to ottoman, sits)* How did you do it?
Gussie. *(to center)* Gee, you guys are new around here. Well, Tony here— was the onliest one of us that had any money. He had a lousy dime—a lousy dime—so we all goes into Sam Markman's store big as you please

and tells him we want a ten-cent guinea grinder. *(puts ice cream on sofa)* Can you imagine—that fat Jew bastard—with a damn Jew store making guinea grinders.
Tony. *(crosses right to Gussie, then to stool, sits)* For Christ's sake. Will you cut it out? Iggie's here.
Gussie. *(turns left)* Who? Oh! Iggie— I didn't even see you, Iggie. Geez— I'm sorry. No offense meant, Iggie.
Iggie. *(by refrigerator)* It's all right.
Gussie. *(with rising intensity)* Yeh! Well, there we all were. So while he's cutting the damn bread in two. I'm practically falling into his ice cream freezer. I'm pulling the pints of ice cream out as fast as a son of a bitch and throwing them out the door. Tony is behind the candy counter stuffing his pocket with chocolate bars. *(Iggie crosses to center.)* And old Spence is in the barrel with the pickles. They're way down at the bottom, see, and he can't reach them—so there he is practically swimming in the pickle juice when Old Markman turns around and sees him. So he pulls his arm out, and he's got a pickle in his hand, and he says without blinking an eyelash, "Looks like you'd better be ordering some more pickles, Mr. Markman. They're getting pretty damn hard to reach." Remember that, Spence? *(sits on right end of sofa)*
Spence. Sure—I remember. You want some more cake, Iggie?
Iggie. No thanks, Spencer. *(sits on left end of sofa)*
Spence. Well, if you want more just reach for it. *(sits on piano chair)*
Bobby. What happened after that, Gussie?
Gussie. *(rises, crosses down)* What do you mean what happened? We goes up to the park with a guinea grinder, six quarts of ice cream, twelve chocolate bars, and a big loaf of cake that Spence finally got under his sweater. Geez—did he look funny. He looked like he had eight babies in there. *(sits on sofa)* Boy, did we have fun. *(Johnny crosses to table.)* Got any more of the cake, Spence? Goddamit, your mother sure does make good cake.
Spence. Sure! *(He takes the plate. Crosses to shelf for cake.)*
Gussie. Gee, I don't know why we been staying away from here so long. I've been missing that good stuff your Mom dishes out.

(pause)

Spence. *(at shelf)* That was the day Tony broke his arm, remember?
Gussie. *(taking the cake)* Geez, that's right.
Johnny. *(crosses to ottoman, sits)* How did that happen?
Gussie. Geez, you guys are new around here, ain't you? *(rises, crosses to Johnny)* Well, after we'd stuffed [ourselves] with all that food, we decided to play Tarzan. So, you know that big oak tree over near the golf course? We decides to play in that. We're all leaping for the

branches and making the ape call— *(He imitates it.)* then it gets to be Tony's turn—so Tony makes with the ape call and jumps for the branch, and the next thing you know he's falling right through the goddamn tree, hitting his head on one branch, his can on the next, and finally *VOOM* he hits the ground with the damndest noise I've ever heard. I'm convinced that he's dead. We're both honestly convinced that he's dead, he's so still. We're both scared to go near him so we keep calling from a distance—*(calling to Tony who sits on stool right)* "Tony! Tony!" Finally we notice his stomach moving, so we goes over, and son of a bitch if there ain't a big piece of bone sticking right through his damn shirt. What the hell did they call that, Tony?

Tony. A compound fracture.

Gussie. Yeh! That's right. We sure did have fun that summer. *(sits on sofa)* Remember, Spence?

(Tony crosses to table, sits.)

Spence. Yeh! I remember.

Gussie. Those sure were the good old days. *(pause)* Hey! As a matter of fact we're going up to the park tonight. We're going on a hay ride. You're all better, ain't you, Spence?

Spence. Yes.

Gussie. Well, why in hell don't you come along?

Tony. *(Puts down his plate sharply on the table, rises. Everybody reacts to the slip.)* You did say you were coming back to school Monday, didn't you, Spence?

Spence. Yes, Tony. Monday I'm coming back to school.

Tony. *(crosses to living room)* Well, I guess we gotta be going. *(Bobby rises.)* Why don't we call you for school on Monday?

Spence. *(rises)* Well, as a matter of fact my father is going to be driving me up to school on Monday. He's got to come with me—so we'll go up together.

Tony. Yeh! Well, Gus and me gotta be going.

(Gussie rises.)

Spence. *(crosses down right)* As a matter of fact, you know, I said when you first came in there was no damn reason for this party. Well, actually there is.

Tony. *(crosses down right to Spence)* Yeh! What? It ain't your birthday. I know when your birthday is.

Spence. Well, you know, I've been doing a hell of a lot of fooling around and I've been neglecting my lessons, not practicing, and all manner of things like that. And if you're going to college you got to be a little

more serious about things than I've been. So from now on I've got to buckle down to the old books and concentrate on things of the mind.
Gussie. Yeh! I guess you're right.
Spence. So I've got a little schedule made out for myself. In the morning before school I've got to practice. And in the afternoon after school I've got my home work to do. So you see I'm going to be pretty busy.
Gussie. Geez, Spence. You sure do play the piano damn good. You know that? Are you going to be a musician or something?
Spence. I don't know. Maybe. I haven't given it too much thought. So I had all you guys over to kind of say goodbye and all 'cause I don't think I'm going to have much time for playing around. 'Course, it's going to be a little hard at first 'cause I'm not used to it, so all you guys could help me if you just kind of let me alone and let me get my work done.
Tony. Sure, we'll do that, Spence.
Gussie. Sure. Sure, Spence.

(Gussie crosses to left of piano.)

Spence. Thank you—you're real pals.
Tony. Thanks for the ice cream. *(He exits front door.)*
Spence. It's O.K. It was fun.
Johnny. *(on exit)* Sure. Geeze, you guys sound like you must've been pretty crazy in those days. See you, Spence.

(Iggie rises also.)

Spence. Stay a second, Iggie. I want to talk to you.
Bobby. *(on exit)* Thanks for the party, Spence.
Gussie. *(crosses down to Spence)* Hey, Spence! Geez, I can't get over that summer. We really did have a hell of a lot of fun, didn't we?
Spence. *(with a hand on Gussie's shoulder)* Yeh! We sure did. It was the best summer I ever had.
Gussie. Goodbye, Spence.

(They shake hands. General ad libs from boys off right.)

Spence. *(crosses left to Iggie)* Hey! Iggie, I'm sorry for what happened— I mean Gussie's talking that way. He's just dumb and he needs a good paste in the jaw for his pains, but I couldn't do it. I'm sorry, Iggie.
Iggie. I understand.
Spence. Then O.K., Iggie. That's all I wanted to talk to you about. Thanks for coming to my party. *(crosses to ottoman, sits)*
Iggie. Sure. *(starts to go, stops)* Did you really mean it, Spencer, about going to college?
Spence. Yeh! Yeh, I did. That is something, isn't it?

(Live ad libs blend into recorded baseball game.)

Iggie. You don't know which one?
Spence. No, no, not yet.
Iggie. Well. *(pause)* I'd better be going. *(He starts for the door.)*
Spence. Iggie! *(Iggie turns.)* Look. I know you're busy and all that but would you mind if I came over and looked at the old stamp collection?
Iggie. Do you want it back, Spencer?
Spence. No, I don't want it back. I'd just like to see what you've added to it—that's all.
Iggie. Come over any time.
Spence. Thanks, Iggie. Thanks.
Iggie. *(on exit)* Goodbye, Spence.

(Pause. Iggie has exited, leaving front door open.)

Spence. Goodbye, Iggie.

(Spence rises, crosses to table to get plates as May enters up left, crosses to kitchen door and enters. She carries a full shopping bag.)

May. Where is everyone?
Spence. Gone.
May. They didn't stay long.
Spence. No, they didn't.
May. *(puts bag on dining table)* What happened?
Spence. *(center; stopping)* Nothing—nothing. I just told them that I didn't want to see them anymore. That's all. I just said it to them before they said it to me.
May. You'll never learn, will you?
Spence. Mom, you've just got to believe that I'm trying to learn. I'm trying as hard as I know how. I might be wrong, but if I am, I think I'd like to find that out for myself.
May. What are you going to do?
Spence. I don't know, Mom. I don't know.
May. *(crosses in)* Spence, look at me— You're not running away, are you?
Spence. No, Mom, I'm not running away—and if you don't mind, Mom, let's not talk about it anymore—I did the right thing. So let's just both try to forget it happened and go on to something else. Okay? *(He walks to piano, starts to sit, then walks to front door and closes it, shutting out the baseball sounds. He sits at piano and starts to play "Praeludium.")*
May. *(after a few bars)* Spence.—I love you very much.

(May picks up bag, crosses to kitchen. Spence watches her, surprised, then turns back to the piano. As he resumes playing, May crosses to dining table and starts collecting dishes.)

(Slow Curtain)

Trouble in Mind (1955)

Alice Childress (b. 1920–)

Born in Charleston, South Carolina, but reared and educated in Harlem, Alice Childress has earned recognition not only in theatre but in the world of letters in general. She has written two novels for adolescents—*A Hero Ain't Nothin but a Sandwich* (1973) and *Rainbow Jordan* (1981)—and one novel for adults—*A Short Walk* (1979). Her most widely known work, *A Hero Ain't Nothin' but a Sandwich,* examines the life and attitudes of a thirteen-year-old drug addict from his perspective and from the perspectives of those who know him. As a literary work, it won the 1975 Jane Addams Award for a novel for young adults. As a film, it was selected as the best screenplay of 1977 at the Virgin Islands Film Festival, and it earned her an award for outstanding contribution to the performing arts from the Black Filmmakers' Hall of Fame. The too-little-known novel *A Short Walk* is a powerful presentation of the maturing of an African American woman who searches for identity and independence. In fiction, Childress is also known for an early work, *Like One of the Family . . . Conversations from a Domestic's Life* (1956).

Alice Childress's career in theatre has been even more extensive. Beginning as an actress with the American Negro Theatre in 1940, she subsequently assumed greater responsibility with that organization as play director and as a member of the board of directors. While working with the American Negro Theatre, she produced her first drama, *Florence* (1949), a one-act play culminating in an African American domestic's decision to encourage her daughter not to give up but to continue to strive for success as an actress. Childress's best-known dramas are *Trouble in Mind* (1955); *Wedding Band* (1966), the story of an interracial romance; and *Wine in the Wilderness* (1969), in which a black woman teaches reality to an African American painter seeking to depict the essence of black women. Childress has also written plays for children—*When the Rattlesnake Sounds* (1975) and *Let's Hear It for the Queen* (1976).

More thoroughly than any other literary work, *Trouble in Mind*, which earned an Obie (Off Broadway) Award, adumbrates the problems that African Americans experience in theatre both as subjects and performers. Plays about "the problem" address only subjects considered safe in the ultraconservative world of American theatre, but white writers and directors applaud their own daring for presenting such safe plays on outworn issues. Unlike white performers, blacks have limited opportunities because roles are scarce. The few roles that exist require stereotypic displays of ignorance, docility, dependence, sexlessness, and impotence. And the African American performers are doomed if they demonstrate formal training or independent thought.

Selected Published Plays by Alice Childress

Let's Hear It for the Queen. New York: Coward, McCann, & Geoghegan, 1976.
Mojo and String: Two Plays. New York: Dramatists Play Service, 1971.
Trouble in Mind. In *Black Theater,* ed. Lindsay Patterson. New York: New American Library, 1971.
Wedding Band: A Love/Hate Story in Black and White. New York: French, 1973.
When the Rattlesnake Sounds. New York: Coward, McCann & Geoghegan, 1975.
Wine in the Wilderness: A Comedy-Drama. New York: Dramatists Play Service, 1969.

• • • • • • • • • • • • • • • • • • • •

Trouble in Mind
A Comedy-Drama in Two Acts

Trouble in Mind was first presented at the Greenwich Mews Theater, New York City, November 4, 1955.

CHARACTERS

Wiletta Mayer
Henry
John Nevins
Millie Davis
Sheldon Forrester
Judy Sears
Al Manners
Eddie Fenton
Bill O'Wray

ACT I

Time: *Ten o'clock Monday morning, fall, 1957.*
Place: *A Broadway theater in New York City. Blues music in—out after lights up.*
Scene: *The stage of the theater. Stage Left leads to the outside entrance, Stage Right to upstairs dressing rooms. There are many props and leftovers from the last show: a plaster fountain with a cupid perched atop, garden furniture, tables, benches, a trellis, two white armchairs trimmed with gold gilt. Before the curtain rises we hear banging sounds from offstage left, the banging grows louder and louder. Curtain rises. Wiletta Mayer, a middle-aged actress, appears. She is attractive and expansive in personality. She carries a purse and a script. At the moment, she is in quite a huff.*

Wiletta. My Lord, I like to have wore my arm off bangin' on that door! What you got it locked for?

(lights up brighter)

Had me standin' out there in the cold, catchin' my death of pneumonia!

(Henry, the elderly doorman, enters.)

Henry. I didn't hear a thing . . . I didn't know . . .
Wiletta. *(Is suddenly moved by the sight of the theater. She holds up her hand for silence, looks out and up at the balcony. She loves the theater. She turns back to Henry.)* A theater always makes me feel that way . . . gotta get still for a second.
Henry. *(welcomes an old memory)* You . . . you are Wiletta Mayer . . . more than twenty years ago, in the old Galy Theater. . . .

(is pleased to be remembered)

You was singin' a number, with the lights changin' color all around you. . . . What was the name of that show?
Wiletta. *Brownskin Melody.*
Henry. That's it . . . and the lights . . .
Wiletta. Was a doggone rainbow.
Henry. And you looked so pretty and sounded so fine, there's no denyin' it.
Wiletta. Thank you, but I . . . I . . . *(hates to admit she doesn't remember him)*
Henry. I'm Henry.
Wiletta. Mmmmm, you don't say.

Henry. I was the electrician. Rigged up all those lights and never missed a cue. I'm the doorman here now. I've been in show business over fifty years. I'm the doorman . . . Henry.
Wiletta. That's a nice name. I . . . I sure remember those lights.
Henry. Bet you can't guess how old I am, I'll betcha.
Wiletta. *(would rather not guess)* Well . . . you're sure lookin' good.
Henry. Go ahead, take a guess.
Wiletta. *(being very kind)* Ohhhhh, I'd say you're in your . . . late fifties.
Henry. *(laughs proudly)* I fool 'em all! I'm seventy-eight years old! How's that?
Wiletta. Ohhhh, don't be tellin' it.

(She places her script and purse on the table, removes her coat.
Henry takes coat and hangs it on a rack.)

Henry. You singin' in this new show?
Wiletta. No, I'm actin'. I play the mother.
Henry. *(is hard of hearing)* How's that?
Wiletta. I'm the mother!
Henry. Could I run next door and get you some coffee? I'm goin' anyway, no bother.
Wiletta. No, thank you just the same.
Henry. If you open here, don't let 'em give you dressin' room "C." It's small and it's got no "john" in it . . . excuse me, I mean . . . no commode . . . Miss Mayer.
Wiletta. *(feeling like the star he's made her)* Thank you, I'll watch out for that.
Henry. *(reaches for a small chair, changes his mind and draws the gilt armchair to the table)* Make yourself comfortable. The old Galy. Yessir, I'm seventy-eight years old.
Wiletta. Well, I'm not gonna tell you my age. A woman that'll tell her age will tell anything.
Henry. *(laughs)* Oh, that's a good one! I'll remember that! A woman that'll tell her age . . . what else?
Wiletta. Will tell anything.
Henry. *Will* tell. Well, I'll see you a little later. *(He exits stage left.)*
Wiletta. *(saying goodbye to the kind of gentle treatment she seldom receives)* So long. *(rises and walks downstage, strikes a pose from the "old Galy" and sings a snatch of an old song)*
   Oh, honey babe
   Oh, honey baby . . .
(She pushes the memory aside.) Yes indeed!

(John Nevins, a young Negro actor, enters. He tries to look self-assured but

it's obvious that he is new to the theater and fighting hard to control his enthusiasm.)

Good morning. Another early bird! I'm glad they hired you, you read so nice er . . . ah . . .
John. John, John Nevins.
Wiletta. This is new for you, ain't it?
John. Yes, ma'am.
Wiletta. Yes, ma'am? I know you're not a New Yorker, where's your home?
John. Newport News, that's in Virginia.
Wiletta. HOT DOG. I shoulda known anyone as handsome and mannerly as you had to come from my home. Newport News! Think of that! Last name?
John. Nevins, John Nevins.
Wiletta. Wait a minute . . . do you know Estelle Nevins, used to live out on Prairie Road . . . fine built woman?
John. Guess I do, that's my mother.
Wiletta. *(very touched)* No, she ain't!
John. *(afraid of oncoming sentiment)* yes . . . ah . . . yes she is.
Wiletta. What a day! I went to school with Estelle! She married a fella named Clarence! Used to play baseball. Last time I hit home she had a little baby in the carriage. How many children she got?
John. I'm the only one.
Wiletta. You can't be that little baby in the carriage! Stand up, let me look at you! Brings all of yesterday back to my mind! Tell me, John, is the drugstore still on the corner? Used to be run by a tall, strappin' fella . . . got wavy, black hair . . . and, well, he's kind of devilish . . . Eddie Bentley!
John. Oh, yes, Mr. Bentley is still there . . .
Wiletta. Fresh and sassy and . . .
John. But he's gray-haired and very stern and businesslike.
Wiletta. *(very conscious of her age)* You don't say. Why you want to act? Why don't you make somethin' outta yourself?
John. *(is amazed at this)* What? Well, I . . .
Wiletta. You look bright enough to be a doctor or even a lawyer maybe. . . . You don't have to take what I've been through . . . don't have to take it off 'em.
John. I think the theater is the grandest place in the world, and I plan to go right to the top.
Wiletta. *(with good humor)* Uh-huh, and where do you think I was plannin' to go?
John. *(feeling slightly superior because he thinks he knows more about the craft than Wiletta)* Ohhh, well . . .

Wiletta. *(quick to sense his feeling)* Oh, well, what?

John. *(feels a bit chastised)* Nothing. I know what I want to do, I'm set, decided, and that's that. You're in it, aren't you proud to be a part of it all?

Wiletta. Of what all?

John. Theater.

Wiletta. *Show business,* it's just a business. Colored folks ain't in no theater. You ever do a professional show before?

John. Yes, some off-Broadway . . . and I've taken classes.

Wiletta. Don't let the man know that. They don't like us to go to school.

John. Oh, now.

Wiletta. They want us to be naturals . . . you know, just born with the gift. 'Course they want you to be experienced too. Tell em' you was in the last revival of *Porgy and Bess.*

John. I'm a little young for that.

Wiletta. They don't know the difference. You were one of the children.

John. I need this job but . . . must I lie?

Wiletta. Yes. Management hates folks who *need* jobs. They get the least money, the least respect, and most times they don't get the job.

John. *(laughs)* Got it. I'm always doing great.

Wiletta. But don't get too cocky. They don't like that either. You have to cater to these fools too. . . .

John. I'm afraid I don't know how to do that.

Wiletta. Laugh! Laugh at everything they say, makes 'em feel superior.

John. Why do they have to feel superior?

Wiletta. You gonna sit there and pretend you don't know why?

John. I . . . I'd feel silly laughing at everything.

Wiletta. You don't. Sometimes they laugh, you're supposed to look serious, other times they serious, you supposed to laugh.

John. *(in polite disagreement)* Sounds too complicated.

Wiletta. *(warming to her subject)* Nothin' to it. Suppose the director walks in, looks around and says . . . *(She mimics Manners.)* "Well, if the dust around here doesn't choke us to death, we'll be able to freeze in comfort."

John. Yes?

Wiletta. We laugh and dispute him. *(She illustrates.)* "Oh, now, Mr. Manners, it ain't that bad!" . . . White folks can't stand unhappy Negroes . . . so laugh, laugh when it ain't funny at all.

John. Sounds kind of Uncle Tommish.

Wiletta. You callin' me a "Tom"?

John. No, ma'am.

Wiletta. Stop sayin' ma'am, it sounds countrified.

John. Yes.

Wiletta. It is Tommish . . . but they do it more than we do. They call it bein' a "yes man." You either do it and stay or don't do it and get out. I can let you in on things that school never heard of . . . 'cause I know what's out here and they don't.

John. Thank you. I guess I'll learn the ropes as I go along.

Wiletta. I'm tellin' you, now! Oh, you so lucky! Nobody told me, had to learn it for myself.

(John is trying to hide the fact that he does not relish her instructions.)

Another thing, he's gonna ask your honest opinion about the play. Don't tell him, he don't mean it . . . just say you're crazy about it . . . butter him up.

John. *(This remark really bothers him.)* What *do* you think of our play?

Wiletta. Oh, honey, it stinks, ain't nothin' atall. Course, if I hear that again, I'll swear you lyin'.

John. Why are you doing it? A flop can't make you but so rich.

Wiletta. Who said it's gonna flop? I said it ain't nothin', but things that aggravate me always *run* for a long time . . . cause what bugs me is what sends somebody else, if you know what I mean.

John. *(defensively)* I studied it thoroughly and . . .

Wiletta. Honey, don't study it, just learn it.

John. I wouldn't, couldn't play anything I didn't believe in . . . I couldn't.

Wiletta. *(understands he's a bit upstage now)* Oh, well, you just a lost ball in the high grass.

(Millie Davis, an actress about thirty-five years old, enters. She breezes in, beautifully dressed in a mink coat, pastel wool dress and hat, suede shoes and bag.)

Millie. Hi!

Wiletta. Walk, girl! Don't she look good?

Millie. Don't look too hard, it's not paid for. *(models the coat for Wiletta as she talks to John)* You got the job! Good for you.

(Wiletta picks up Millie's newspaper.)

John. And congratulations to you.

Millie. *(taking off her coat and hanging it up)* I don't care one way or the other 'cause my husband doesn't want me workin' anyway.

Wiletta. Is he still a dining-car waiter?

Millie. I wanted to read for your part but Mr. Manners said I was too young. They always say too young . . . too young.

Wiletta. Hear they're lookin' for a little girl to play Goldilocks, maybe you should try for that.

Millie. Oh, funny.

Wiletta. *(commenting on the headlines)* Look at 'em! Throwin' stones at little children, got to call out the militia to go to school.
John. That's terrible.
Millie. *(quite proud of her contribution to Little Rock.)* A woman pushed me on the subway this mornin' and I was ready for her! Called her everything but a child of God. She turned purple! Oh, I fixed her!

(Judith Sears, a young actress, is heard offstage with Sheldon Forrester, an elderly character man.)

Judy. This way. . . .
Sheldon. Yes, ma'am. Don't hurt yourself.

(Sheldon and Judy enter, Judy first.)

Judy. Good morning.

(Others respond in unison.)

John. Hello again, glad you made it.
Millie. Hi! I'm Millie, that's John, Wiletta, and you're?
Judy. Judith, just call me Judy.
Sheldon. *(bundled in heavy overcoat, two scarves, one outer, one inner)* And call me Shel!
Wiletta. Sheldon Forrester! So glad to see you! Heard you was sick.
Millie. I heard he was dead.
Sheldon. Yeah! Some fool wrote a piece in that *Medium Brown Magazine* 'bout me bein' dead. You can see he was lyin'. But I lost a lotta work on accounta that. Doctor says that with plenty of rest and fresh air, I oughta outlive him.
Wiletta. Bet you will, too.
Sheldon. Mr. Manners was lookin' all over for me, said nobody could play this part but me.
Millie. Not another soul can do what you're gonna do to it.
Sheldon. Thank you.

(John starts over to Judy but Sheldon stops him.)

Didn't you play in er . . . ah . . . er . . .
Wiletta. He was in the last revival of *Porgy and Bess*. Was one of the children. *(She watches John's reaction to this.)*
Sheldon. Yeah, I know I remembered you. He ain't changed much, just bigger. Nice little actor.
John. *(embarrassed)* Thank you, sir.
Wiletta. Sheldon got a good memory.
Millie. *(to Judy)* What're you doing?
Sheldon. She's *Miss* Renard, the Southerner's daughter. Fights her father 'bout the way he's treatin' us.

Millie. What I want is a part where I get to fight him.
Wiletta. Ha! That'll be the day!
Sheldon. Bill O'Wray is the father, he's awful nice.
Millie. Also wish I'd get to wear some decent clothes sometime. Only chance I get to dress up is offstage. I'll wear them baggy cotton dresses but damn if I'll wear another bandanna.
Sheldon. That's how country people do! But go on the beach today, what do you see? Bandannas. White folks wear 'em! They stylish!
Millie. That's a lot of crap!
Sheldon. There you go! You holler when there's no work, when the man give you some, you holler just as loud. Ain't no pleasin' you!

(John starts toward Judy again; this time Millie stops him.)

Millie. Last show I was in, I wouldn't even tell my relatives. All I did was shout "Lord, have mercy!" for almost two hours every night.
Wiletta. Yes, but you did it, so hush! She's played every flower in the garden. Let's see, what was your name in that T.V. mess?
Millie. Never mind.
Wiletta. Gardenia! She was Gardenia! 'Nother thing . . . she was Magnolia, Chrysanthemum was another. . . .
Millie. And you've done the jewels . . . Crystal, Pearl, Opal! *(Millie laughs.)*
John. *(weak, self-conscious laughter)* Oh, now . . .

(Judy has retreated to one side, is trying to hide herself behind a book.)

Sheldon. Do, Lord, let's keep peace. Last thing I was in, the folks fought and argued so, the man said he'd never do a colored show again . . . and he didn't!
Wiletta. I always say it's the man's play, the man's money and the man's theater, so what you gonna do? *(to Millie)* You ain't got a pot nor a window. Now, when you get your own . . .

(Sheldon clears his throat to remind them that Judy is listening.)

Honey, er . . . what you say your name was?
Judy. Judy.
Wiletta. *(sweeps over to Judy and tries to cover the past argument)* I know I've seen you in pictures, didn't you make some pictures?
Judy. No, this is my first job.
John. *(joshing Wiletta)* Oh, you mustn't tell that because . . .
Wiletta. *(cutting him off)* You're just as cute as a new penny.
Sheldon. Sure is.

(a brief moment of silence while they wait for Judy to say something)

Judy. *(starts hesitantly but picks up momentum as she goes along)* Thank you, and er . . . er . . . I hope I can do a good job and that people learn something from this play.
Millie. Like what?
Judy. That people are the same, that people are . . . are . . . well, you know . . . that people are people.
Sheldon. There you go . . . brotherhood of man stuff! Sure!
Wiletta. Yes, indeed. I don't like to think of theater as just a business. Oh, it's the art . . . ain't art a wonderful thing?
Millie. *(bald, flat statement to no one in particular)* People aren't the same.
Judy. I read twice for the part and there were so many others before me and after me . . . and I was so scared that my voice came out all funny. . . . I stumbled on the rug when I went in . . . everything was terrible.
Millie. *(another bald, flat statement)* But you got the job.
Judy. *(uneasy about Millie's attitude)* Yes.
John. *(to the rescue)* And all the proud relatives will cheer you on opening night!
Judy. *(Nothing can drown her spirits for long.)* Yes! My mother and father . . . they live in Bridgeport . . . they really don't want me here at all. They keep expecting something *terrible* to happen to me . . . like being murdered or something! But they're awfully sweet and they'll be so happy. *(abrupt change of subject)* What do you think of the play?
Wiletta. Oh, I never had anything affect me so much in all my life. It's so sad, ain't it sad?
Judy. Oh, there's some humor.
Wiletta. I'm tellin' you, I almost busted my sides laughin'.

(Sheldon is busy looking in the script.)

John. It has a social theme and something to say.
Judy. Yes.
Wiletta. Art! Art is a great thing!
Millie. It's all right except for a few words here and there . . . and those Gawd-awful clothes. . . .
John. Words, clothes. What about the very meaning?
Sheldon. *(Startles everyone by reading out loud. His finger runs down the page; he skips his cues and reads his lines.)* Mr. Renard, sir, everything is just fine. . . . Yes, sir. . . . Thank you, sir. . . . Yes, sirreee, I sure will . . . I know. . . . Yes, sir. . . . But iffen, iffen . . . *(He pauses to question the word.)* Iffen? *(Now he understands.)* Iffen you don't mind, we'd like to use the barn.
Millie. Iffen.

Sheldon. Hush, Millie, so I can get these lines, I'm not a good reader, you know.
Millie. Iffen you forget one, just keep shakin' your head.

(Offstage we hear a door slam. Al Manners, the director [white], is giving Eddie Fenton, the stage manager [white], a friendly chastising.)

Manners. *(offstage)* Eddie, why? Why do you do it?
Eddie. *(offstage)* I didn't know.
Sheldon. *(assumes a very studious air and begins to study his script earnestly)* Mr. Manners.

(Eddie and Manners enter, followed by Henry. Eddie is eager and quick. He carries a portfolio and a stack of scripts. Manners is in his early forties, hatless, well-tweeded product of Hollywood. He is a bundle of energy, considerate and understanding after his own fashion; selfish and tactless after ours. Henry is following him around, ready to write out a coffee order.)

Eddie. *(with a smile)* You asked my opinion.
Manners. That, my friend, was a mistake.
Eddie. *(laughing while cast smiles in anticipation of Manners' words)* Okay, I admit you were right, you were.
Manners. *(enjoying himself)* Of course I was. *(to company)* All of his taste is in his mouth!

(burst of company laughter, especially from Sheldon and Wiletta)

Eddie. *(playfully correcting Manners)* All right, Al, play fair . . . uncle . . . a truce.
Manners. *(to company)* Greetings to New York's finest.
All. Good morning. . . . Flatterer. . . . Hello. . . . Good Morning.
Manners. *(to Henry)* Coffee all around the room and count yourself in. *(hands him a bill)* Rolls? Cake? No . . . how about Danish . . . all right?
All. Yes. . . . Sure. . . . Anything. . . . O.K.
Sheldon. I like doughnuts, those jelly doughnuts.
Manners. Jelly doughnuts! What a horrible thought. Get Danish . . . all right?
All. Sure. . . . Anything. . . . That's fine.
Manners. *(after Henry exits)* If you were looking for that type, you could never find it! A real character.
John. One of the old forty-niners.
Manners. No, no . . . not quite that. . . . *(turns off that faucet and quickly switches to another)* Everyone on speaking terms?
All. Of course. . . . Old friends. . . . Oh, yes. . . . Sure.

Manners. *(opens the portfolio with a flourish)* Best scenic design you've ever laid eyes on.

(All gasp and sigh as they gather around him. They are quite impressed with the sketch. Judy is very close and Manners looks down at her hair and neck which is perched right under his nostrils. Judy can feel his breath on her neck. She turns suddenly and Manners backs away a trifle.)

You er . . . wear a beautiful dress in the third act and I wanted to see if you have nice shoulders.

(Judy backs away slightly.)

I wasn't planning to attack you.

(Cast laughs.)

Millie. I got nice shoulders. You got one of those dresses for me?
Sheldon. *(determined to enjoy everything)* Ha! He wasn't gonna attack her!
Manners. *(suddenly changes faucets again)* Oh, I'm so weary.
Eddie. *(running interference)* He was with Melton on this sketch until four a.m.
Manners. Four thirty.
Eddie. Four thirty.
Manners. *(swoops down on Wiletta)* Ahhhhh, this is my sweetheart!
Wiletta. (with mock severity) Go on! Go 'way! Ain't speakin' to you! He won't eat, he won't sleep, he's just terrible! I'm mad with you.
Sheldon. Gonna ruin your health like that!
Wiletta. Gonna kill himself!
Manners. Bawl me out, I deserve it.
Eddie. Melton is so stubborn, won't change a line.
Manners. But he did.
Eddie. Yes, but so stubborn.
Manners. A genius should be stubborn. *(points index finger at Sheldon)* Right?
Sheldon. *(snaps his finger and points back)* There you go!

(Cast laughs.)

Manners. *(to Wiletta)* You'd better speak to me. This is my girl, we did a picture together.
Cast. *(ad lib)* Really? How nice. She sure did. That's right.
Manners. *(as though it's been centuries)* Ohhhhhh, years and years ago. She and I worked together, too.
Millie. *(to Wiletta)* Remember that?
Sheldon. *(proudly)* I was helpin' the Confederate Army.

Manners. And what a chestnut, guns, cannons, drums, Indians, slaves, hearts and flowers, sex and Civil War . . . on wide screen!
Sheldon. Oh, just horrible.
Manners. *(touchy about outside criticism)* But it had something, wasn't the worst. . . . I twisted myself out of shape to build this guy's part. It was really a sympathetic character.
Sheldon. Sure, everybody was sorry for me.
Manners. *(to John)* Hear you went to college. You're so modest you need a press agent.
Sheldon. He was one of the children in the last revival of *Porgy and Bess*.
Manners. Ohhhh, yes . . . nice clean job.
Judy. I'm not modest. I finished the Yale drama course. Girls . . . girls . . . can go to the Yale drama. . . .
Manners. Yale. I'm impressed.
Judy. You're teasing.
Manners. No, you are. Well, where are we? Bill O'Wray is out until tomorrow, he's in a rehearsal for a TV show tonight.

(proper sighs of regret from the cast)

Wiletta. Oh, I was lookin' forward to seein' him today.
Sheldon. Yeah, yeah, nice fella.
Manners. Works all the time.

(now some attention for Millie)

You look gorgeous. This gal has such a flair for clothes. How do you do it?

(Millie is pleased. Manners changes the subject.)

Ted Bronson is one of our finest writers.
Wiletta. Knows art, knows it.
Eddie. He was up for an award.
Manners. Really, Eddie, I wish you'd let me tell it.
Eddie. I'm sorry.
Manners. Ted's been out on the coast batting out commercial stuff . . . meat grinder . . . he's in Europe now . . . Italy . . . about a week before he can get back . . . he did this "Chaos in Belleville" a while back. Producers gave him nothing but howls. . . . "It's ahead of the times!" "Why stick your neck out?" "Why You?"
Sheldon. *(raises his hand, speaks after Manners gives him a nod)* Who is chaos?
Eddie. Oh, no.
John. *Who?*

Manners. *(holds up his hand for silence)* Chaos means er . . . ah, confusion. Confusion in Belleville, confusion in a small town.
Sheldon. Ohhhhhh.
Manners. I was casually talking to Ted about the er . . . er, race situation, kicking a few things around . . . dynamic subject, hard to come to grips with on the screen, TV, anywhere . . . explosive subject. Suddenly he reaches to the bottom shelf and comes up with "Chaos." I flipped a few pages . . . when I read it bells rang. This is *now,* we're living this, who's in the headlines these days?

(eloquent pause)

Sheldon. How 'bout that Montgomery, Alabama? Made the bus company lose one, cold, cash, billion dollars!
John. Not a billion.
Manners. Here was a contribution to the elimination of . . .
Sheldon. I know what I read!
Manners. A story of Negro rights that . . .
Sheldon. How 'bout them busses!
Judy. And they're absolutely right.
Millie. Who's right?
Manners. A contribution that really . . .
Judy. The colored people.
Manners. Leads to a clearer understanding . . .
Millie. Oh. I thought you meant the other people.
Manners. A clearer understanding.
Judy. I didn't mean that.
Manners. Yale, please!

(all silent)

I placed an option on this script so fast. . . .

(Sheldon raises his hand.)

I tied it up, Sheldon, so that no one else could get hold of it. When I showed it to Hoskins . . .
Wiletta. *(to Sheldon)* The producer. Another nice man.
Manners. Well, the rest is history. This is my first Broadway show. . . .

(applause from cast)

But I definitely know what I want and however unorthodox my methods, I promise never to bore you.
Sheldon. *(popping his fingers rapidly)* He's like that.
Manners. I bring to this a burning desire above and beyond anything I've . . . well, I'm ready to sweat blood. I want to see you kids drawing pay envelopes for a long time to come and . . .

(Sheldon applauds; the others join him. Sheldon aims his remark at Millie.)

Sheldon. Listen to the man! Listen.

Manners. *(holds up his hand for silence)* At ease. *(mainly for John and Judy)* I ask this, please forget your old methods of work and go along with me. I'll probably confuse the hell out of you for the first few days but after that . . . well, I hope we'll be swingin'. Now, you're all familiar with the story. . . .

Wiletta. Oh, I never had anything affect me so much in all my life.

All. *(ad lib)* There was one part. . . . I have a question. . . . Uh-huh. . . . A question. . . .

Manners. We will *not* discuss the parts.

(John groans in mock agony.)

Judy. One little thing.

Manners. We will not discuss the parts.

(Eddie smiles knowingly.)

We will not read the play down from beginning to end.

Sheldon. *(popping his fingers)* There he goes!

Manners. We will *not* delve into character backgrounds . . . not now. Turn to act one, scene two, page fifteen.

(Actors scramble madly for places in scripts.)

Top of the page. Eddie, you read for O'Wray. Judy! Stand up!

(Judy stands hesitantly while Manners toys with a sheet of paper.)

Walk downstage!

(Judy is startled and nervous, she walks upstage. The others are eager to correct her but Manners will not tolerate cast interference. He crumbles the paper, throws it to the floor, takes Judy by the shoulders and speedily leads her around the stage.)

Downstage! Center stage! Left Center! Right Center! Up Right! Up Left, Down Center, Down Right, Down Left, Upstage . . . DOWNSTAGE!

Judy. I know, I forgot. . . .

Manners. Don't forget again. Take downstage. *(notices the paper he threw on the floor)* A trashy stage is most distracting.

(Judy starts to pick up the paper.)

Hold your position! Wiletta, pick up the paper!

(John and Sheldon start for the paper.)

I asked Wiletta! *(catches Wiletta's eye)* Well?

Wiletta. *(shocked into a quick flare of temper)* Well, hell! I ain't the damn janitor! *(trying to check her temper)* I . . . well, I . . . shucks . . . I . . . damn.

Manners. *(Even though he was trying to catch them off-guard, he didn't expect this.)* Cut! Cut! It's all over.

(Everyone is surprised again.)

What you have just seen is . . . is . . . is fine acting. *(He is quite shaken and embarrassed from Wiletta's action.)* Actors struggle for weeks to do what you have done perfectly . . . the first time. You gave me anger, frustration, movement, er . . . excitement. Your faces were alive! Why? You did what came naturally, you believed. . . . That is the quality I want in your work . . . the firm texture of truth.

Judy. Oh, you tricked us.

Millie. I didn't know what to think.

John. Tension all over the place.

Wiletta. *(Still having a hard time getting herself under control. She fans herself with a pocket handkerchief and tries to muster a weak laugh.)* Yes indeed.

Manners. *(gingerly touches Wiletta and shivers in mock fear)* She plays rough. "Well, hell!" Honey, I love you, believe me.

Sheldon. Oh, she cut up!

Wiletta. *(Tries to laugh along with them but it's hard going. From this point on, she watches Manners with a sharp eye, always cautious and on the look-out.)* Yes . . . well, let's don't play that no more.

Manners. Top of the page. Judy, you're appealing to your father to allow some of his tenant farmers . . . *(He glances at script to find the next direction. Sheldon leans over and whispers to Wiletta.)*

Wiletta. Sharecroppers.

Sheldon. Oh.

Manners. . . . hold a barn dance. Now! Some of them have been talking about voting.

Sheldon. Trouble.

Manners. *(points first to Millie, then Wiletta)* Petunia and Ruby are in your father's study . . . er . . . er . . . *(consults script again)*

Sheldon. *(without consulting script)* Cleanin' up. Sure, that's what they're doin'.

Manners. Tidying up. Your father is going over his account books, you're there . . .

Sheldon. *(with admiration)* Lookin' pretty.

Manners. There's an awful echo coming from our assistant director.

Sheldon. *(laughs)* 'Sistant director! This man breaks me up all the time!

Manners. *(liking the salve)* What, what did you say?
Sheldon. Say you tickle me to death.
Wiletta. Tickles me too.
Manners. Take it!
Judy. *(reading)* Papa, it's a good year, isn't it?
Eddie. *(with a too-broad Southern accent)* I'd say fair, fair to middlin'.

(Cast snickers.)

Manners. All right, Barrymore, just read it.
Judy. Papa, it's Petunia's birthday today.
Eddie. That so? Happy birthday, Petunia.
Millie. *(wearily)* Thank you, sir.
Manners. *(correcting the reading)* You feel good, full of ginger . . . your birthday!
Millie. *(remembers the old, standard formula; gives the line with a chuckle and extra warmth)* Thank you, sir.
Judy. It would be nice if they could have a stomp in the barn.
Millie. *(Her attitude suggests that Judy thought up the line.)* Hmmph.
Eddie. No need to have any barn stomp until this election business is over.
Millie. What the hell is a stomp?
Judy. I can't see why.
Manners. A barn dance. You know that, Millie.
Eddie. Ruby, you think y'all oughta use the barn?
Wiletta. *(pleasantly)* Lord, have mercy, Mr. Renard, don't ask me 'cause I don't know nothin'.
Eddie. Well, better forget about it.
Judy. Oh, papa, let the . . . let the . . .
Millie. *(for Judy's benefit)* Mmmmmmmmmmph. Why didn't they *call* it a barn dance?
Judy. . . . let the . . . *(stops reading)* Oh, must I say that word?
Manners. What word?
Millie. *Darkies.* That's the word. It says, "Papa, let the darkies have their fun."
Manners. *What* do you want to say?
Millie. She could say . . . "Let *them* have their fun."
Manners. But that's Carrie. *(to Sheldon)* Do you object?
Sheldon. Well, no, not if that's how they spoke in them days.
Manners. The time is now, down south in some remote little county, they say those things . . . now. Can you object in an artistic sense?
Sheldon. No, but you better ask him, he's more artistic than I am.
John. No, I don't object. I don't like the word but it is used, it's a slice of life. Let's face it, Judy wouldn't use it, Mr. Manners wouldn't . . .

Manners. *(very pleased with John's answer)* Call me Al, everybody. Al's good enough, Johnny.
John. Al wouldn't say it but Carrie would.

(Manners gives Wiletta an inquiring look.)

Wiletta. Lord, have mercy, don't ask me 'cause I don't know. . . . *(She stops short as she realizes she is repeating words from the script. She's disturbed that she's repeating the exact line the author indicated.)*
Manners. *(gives Judy a light tap on the head)* Yale! Proceed.
Eddie. *(reads)* Ruby and Petunia leave the room and wait on the porch.
Judy. Please, papa, I gave my word. I ask one little thing and . . .
Eddie. All right! Before you know it, them niggers will be runnin' me!
Judy. Please don't use that word!
Manners. Oh, stop it!
Wiletta. That's her line in the play, Mr. Manners, Carrie says . . .
All. Please, don't use that word.

(Manners signals Eddie to carry on.)

Eddie. *(reads)* Carrie runs out to the porch.
Judy. You can use the barn!
Millie. Lord, have mercy . . .
Eddie. *(intones)* Wrong line.
Millie. *(quickly corrects line)* Er . . . er, somethin' seems to trouble my spirit, a troublous feelin' is in old Petunia's breast. *(stops reading)* Old Petunia?
Wiletta. Yes, *old* Petunia!
Judy. *(reads)* I'm going upstairs to lay out my white organdy dress.
Wiletta. No, you ain't, I'm gonna do that for you.
Judy. Then I'll take a nap.
Millie. No, you ain't, I'm gonna do that for you.
Eddie. Wrong line.
Millie. Sorry. *(corrects line)* Yes, child, you rest yourself, you had a terrible, hard day. Bless your soul, you just one of God's golden-haired angels.
Manners. *(Frantically searching for that certain quality. He thinks everything will open once they hit the right chord.)* Cut! Top of page three, act one, as it's written. Ruby is shelling beans on the back porch as her son Job approaches.
John. If I can read over . . .
Manners. Do as I ask, do it. Take it, Wiletta.
Sheldon. *(popping his fingers)* He's just like that.
Wiletta. *(reads)* Boy, where you goin'?
John. Down to Turner's Corner.

Wiletta. You ain't lost nothin' down there. Turner and his brother is talkin' 'bout votin', I know.
John. They only talkin', I'm goin'.
Sheldon. Mr. Renard say to stay outta that.
John. I got a letter from the President 'bout goin' in the army, Turner says when that happen's, a man's sposed to vote and things.

(Millie and Judy are very pleased about this line.)

Sheldon. Letter ain't from no President, it come from the crackers on the draft board.
John. It *say* from the President.
Wiletta. Pa say you don't go.

(Manners is jotting down a flood of notes.)

John. Sorry, but I say I'd be there.
Sheldon. I don't know who that boy take after.
Eddie. Ruby dashes from the porch and Sam follows her. Carrie comes outside and Renard follows her. *(Eddie reads Renard.)* You pamper them rascals too much, see how they do? None of 'em's worth their weight in salt, that boy would steal the egg out of a cake.
Judy. *(Tries to laugh while Millie watches coldly. Manners is amazed at the facial distortion.)* It says laugh.
Manners. Well?
Judy. *(laughs and continues reading)* But I can't help feeling sorry for them, they didn't ask to be born.
Millie. *(just loud enough for Judy's ears)* Hmmmmmph.
Judy. I keep thinking, there but for the grace of God go I. If we're superior we should prove it by our actions.
Sheldon. *(commenting on the line)* There you go, prove it!

(Manners is taking more notes. Judy is disturbed by the reactions to her reading. She hesitates. Manners looks up. The phone rings. Eddie goes off to answer.)

Judy. She *is* their friend, right? It's just that I feel reactions and . . .
Manners. What reactions?
Millie. I was reacting.
Manners. Ohhhhh, who pays Millie any attention, that's her way.
Millie. There you go.
Sheldon. Sure is.
Judy. *(tries again but she's very uncomfortable)* I . . . I keep thinking . . . there but for the grace of God . . .
Manners. Are you planning to cry?
Judy. No, but . . . no. *(She's fighting to hold back the tears.)*

Sheldon. Millie's pickin' on her.
Manners. Utter nonsense!
Judy. My part seems . . . she seems so smug.
Millie. *(to Sheldon)* Keep my name out of your mouth.
Wiletta. *(to Sheldon)* Mind your business, your own affairs.
Manners. This is fantastic. What in the hell is smug?

(Henry enters with a cardboard box full of coffee containers and a large paper bag.)

Cut! Coffee break! *(to Judy)* Especially you.
Henry. Told the waiter feller to fix up everything nice.
Manners. *(looks in bag)* What's this?
Henry. That's what you said. I heard you. "Jelly doughnuts!" you said.

(Sheldon gets a container of coffee for Judy and one for himself.)

Manners. I won't eat it!
Henry. But I heard you.
Manners. Take your coffee and leave.

(Henry starts to leave without the coffee.)

Don't play games, take it with you.

(Henry snatches a container and leaves in a quiet huff. Sheldon hands coffee to Judy but Millie snatches it from his hand.)

Millie. I know you brought that for me.
Manners. Where do they find these characters? All right, he's old but it's an imposition . . . he's probably ninety, you know.
Wiletta. *(laughs and then suddenly stops)* We all get old sometimes.
Eddie. *(hurries onstage; looks worried)* It's Mrs. Manners . . . she . . . she says it's urgent. She has to talk to you *now* . . . immediately.
Manners. Oh, you stupid jerk. Why did you say I was here? You and your big, stupid mouth. Couldn't you say "He isn't here now, I'll give him your message"?
Eddie. I'm sorry. She was so . . . so. . . . Well, she said right off "I *know* he's there." If I had any idea that she would . . .
Manners. I don't expect you to have *ideas!* Only common sense, just a little common sense. Where do you find a stage manager these days?
Eddie. I can tell her you can't be disturbed now.
Manners. No, numbskull, don't do another thing, you've done enough. *(with wry humor)* Alimony is not enough, every time I make three extra dollars she takes me to court to get two-thirds of it. If I don't talk to her I'll have a subpoena. You're stupid. *(He exits to the telephone. During the brief silence which follows, Eddie is miserably self-conscious.)*

Wiletta. *(tries to save the day)* Well, . . . I'm glad it's getting a little like winter now. We sure had a hot summer. Did you have a nice summer?
Eddie. *(choking back his suppressed anger)* I worked in stock . . . summer theater. It was O.K.
Wiletta. That's nice. What did you do?
Eddie. *(relaxing more)* Kind of Jack of all trades . . . understudied some, stage managed, made sets. . . .
Millie. And did three people out of a job.
Judy. I spent the summer with my folks. Soon as we open, I want everyone to come up to Bridgeport and have a glorious day!

(Manners returns, looks up briefly.)

Daddy makes the yummiest barbecue, you'll love it.
Wiletta. You better discuss it with your folks first.
Judy. Why?
Millie. 'Cause we wouldn't want it discussed after we got there.
Sheldon. No, thank you, ma'am. I'm plannin' to be busy all winter lookin' for an apartment, I sure hate roomin'.
Eddie. I have my own apartment. It's only a cold-water walk-up but I have it fixed real nice like the magazines show you . . . whitewashed brick and mobiles hanging in the kitchen and living room. I painted the floors black and spattered them with red and white paint . . . I learned that in stock . . . then I shellacked over it and waxed it . . . and I scraped all of the furniture down to the natural wood. . . .
Millie. Oh, hush, you're making me tired. Cold-water flat!
Eddie. It gives a cheery effect. . . .
Millie. And it'll give you double pneumonia.
Sheldon. Yeah, that's the stuff you got to watch.
Eddie. Well, it's only thirty dollars a month.
Sheldon. They got any colored livin' in that buildin'?
Eddie. I . . . I . . . I don't know. I haven't seen any.
Sheldon. Well, there's none there then.
Eddie. *(slightly ill at ease)* Sheldon, I'll gladly ask.
Sheldon. *(in great alarm)* Oh, no, no, no! I don't want to be the first.
Millie. Damn cold-water flats! I like ease, comfort, furs, cars, big, thick steaks. I want everything.
Eddie. *(trying to change the subject)* Aren't there a lot of new shows this season?
Judy. My mother says . . . gosh, every time I open my mouth it's something about my parents. It's not stylish to love your parents . . . you either have a mother-complex or a father-fixation!

(She laughs and Manners looks up again. He doesn't care for her remarks.)

But I'm crazy about my parents, but then maybe that's abnormal. I probably have a mother-father-fixation.

Wiletta. What did your mother say?

Judy. "Never have limitations on your horizon, reach for infinity!" She also feels that everyone has a right to an equal education and not separate either.

John. She sounds like a wonderful woman who . . .

Judy. *(raising her voice)* Oh, I get so mad about this prejudice nonsense! It's a wonder colored people don't go out and *kill* somebody, I mean actually, really do it . . . bloody murder, you know?

Sheldon. There's lotsa folks worse off than we are, Millie.

Millie. Well, all I hope is that they don't like it, dontcha know.

Manners. *(boastful about his trials and troubles)* The seven-year-old kid, the seven-year-old kid . . . to hear her tell it, our son is ragged, barefoot, hungry . . . and his teeth are lousy. The orthodontist says he needs braces . . . they wanta remake his mouth. The kid is falling to pieces. When I go for visitation . . . he looks in my pockets before he says hello. Can you imagine? Seven years old. The orthodontist and the psychiatrist . . . the story of my life. But he's a bright kid . . . smart as a whip . . . you can't fool him. *(a big sigh)* Oh, well, let's go. Suppose you were all strangers, had never heard anything about this story except the snatches you heard today. What would you know?

Millie. It's my birthday.

(Wiletta is following him closely; she doesn't care to be caught off-guard again.)

John. Carrie's father has tenant farmers working for him.

Manners. Yes and . . .

Judy. They want to hold a barn dance and he's against it because . . .

John. Some of the Negroes are planning to vote for the first time and there's opposition . . .

Sheldon. His ma and pa don't want him mixed in it 'cause they smell trouble.

Judy. And my father overheard that John is in it.

Sheldon. And *he don't like it,* that's another thing.

Wiletta. *(amazed that they have learned so much)* Mmmmmm, all of that.

John. But Job is determined.

Judy. And he's been notified by the draft board.

Sheldon. And the paper, the paper!

Manners. Paper?

Wiletta. You know, upstage, downstage and doin' what comes natural.

Manners. Not bad for an hour's work.

Eddie. Amazing.

Sheldon. *(popping his fingers)* Man is on the ball. Fast.
Manners. Now we can see how we're heading for the lynching.
Sheldon. *(starts to peep at back page of script)* Lynchin'?
Manners. We're dealing with an antilynch theme. I want it uncluttered, clear in your mind, you must see the skeleton framework within which we're working. Wiletta, turn to the last page of act one.
Eddie. Fifty.
Manners. Wiletta, dear heart . . . the end of the act finds you alone on the porch, worried, heartsick . . .
Wiletta. And singin' a song, sittin', worryin', and singin'.
Manners. It's not simply a song, it's a summing up. You're thinking of Renard, the threats, the people and your son. . . .

(Wiletta is tensely listening, trying to follow him. Manners stands behind her and gently shakes her shoulders.)

Loosen up, let the thoughts flood over you. I know you have to read. . . .
Wiletta. Oh, I know the song, learned it when I was a child.
Manners. Hold a thought, close your eyes and think aloud . . . get a good start and then sing . . . speak your mind and then sing.
Wiletta. *(not for thinking out loud)* I know exactly what you want.
Manners. Blurt out the first thing that enters your mind.
Wiletta. *(sings a mournful dirge of despair)* Come and go with me to that land, come and go with me to that land . . .
Manners. Gosh, that guy can write.
Wiletta.
   Come and go with me to that land where I'm bound
   No confusion in that land, no confusion in that land
   No confusion in that land where I'm bound . . .
Millie. *(wipes her eyes)* A heartbreaker.
Eddie. Oh, Wiletta, it's so . . . so . . . gosh.
John. Leaves you weak.
Manners. Beautiful. What were you thinking?
Wiletta. *(ready to move on to something else)* Thank you.
Manners. What were you thinking?
Wiletta. I thought . . . I . . . er, er . . . I don't know, whatever you said.
Manners. Tell me. You're not a vacuum, you thought something.
John. Your motivation. What motivated . . .
Manners. *(waving John out of it)* You thought *something*, right?
Wiletta. Uh-huh.
Manners. And out of the thought came song.
Wiletta. Yeah.
Manners. What did you think?

Wiletta. I thought that's what you wanted. *(She realizes she is the center of attention and finds it uncomfortable.)*
Manners. It won't do. You must know why you do a thing, that way you're true to me, to the part and yourself. . . .
Wiletta. Didn't you like it?
Manners. Very much but . . . I'm sure you've never worked this way before, but you're not carrying a tray or answering doorbells, this is substance, meat. I demand that you *know* what you're doing and *why*, at all times. I will accept nothing less.
Wiletta. *(to John and Judy)* I know, you have to justify.
Sheldon. *(worried and trying to help Wiletta)* You was thinkin' how sad it was, wasn't you?
Wiletta. Uh-huh.
Manners. It's new to you but it must be done. Let go, think aloud and when you are moved to do so . . . sing.

(Wiletta looks blank.)

Start anywhere.
Wiletta. Ah, er . . . it's so sad that folks can't vote . . . it's also sad that er, er . . .
Manners. No. *(picks up newspaper)* We'll try word association. I'll give you a word, then you say what comes to your mind and keep on going . . . one word brings on another. . . . Montgomery!
Wiletta. Alabama.
Manners. Montgomery!
Wiletta. Alabama.
Manners. Montgomery!
Wiletta. Reverend King is speakin' on Sunday.
Manners. Colored.
Wiletta. Lights changin' colors all around me.
Manners. Colored.
Wiletta. They . . . they . . .
Manners. Colored.
Wiletta. "They got any colored in that buildin'?"
Manners. Children, little children.
Wiletta. Children . . . children. . . . "Pick up that paper!" Oh, my . . .
Manners. Lynching.
Wiletta. Killin'! Killin'!
Manners. Killing.
Wiletta. It's the man's theater, the man's money, so what you gonna do?
Manners. Oh, Wiletta . . . I don't know! *Darkness!*
Wiletta. A star! Oh, I can't, I don't like it. . . .
Manners. Sing.

Wiletta. *(sings a song of strength and anger)*
   Come and go with me to that land

(The song is overpowering; we see a woman who could fight the world.)

   Come and go with me to that land
   Come and go with me to that land—
   where I'm bound.
Judy. Bravo! Magnificent!
Manners. Wiletta, if you dare! You will undo us! Are you out of your senses? When you didn't know what you were doing . . . perfection on the nose. I'll grant you the first interpretation was right, without motivating. All right, I'll settle for that.
Wiletta. *(feeling very lost)* I said I *knew* what you wanted.
Manners. Judy! I . . . I want to talk to you about . . . about Carrie. *(He rises and starts for the dressing room.)* Eddie, will you dash out and get me a piece of Danish? Okay, at ease.

(Eddie quickly exits. Manners and Judy exit stage right toward dressing rooms.)

Millie. *(to John)* Look, don't get too close to her.
Sheldon. Mind your own business.
John. What have I done?
Millie. You're too friendly with her.
Wiletta. Justify. Ain't enough to do it, you got to justify.
John. I've only been civil.
Millie. That's too friendly.
Wiletta. Got a splittin' headache.
Sheldon. *(to Wiletta)* I wish I had a aspirin for you.
Millie. *(to John)* All set to run up and see her folks. Didn't you hear her say they expect something terrible to happen to her? Well, you're one of the terrible things they have in mind!
Sheldon. Mind your business.
Millie. It is my business. When they start raisin' a fund for his defense, they're gonna come and ask me for money and I'll have to be writin' the President and signin' petitions . . . so it's my business.
Sheldon. I tell you, son, I'm friendly with white folks in a distant sorta way but I don't get too close. Take Egypt, Russia, all these countries, why they kickin' up their heels? 'Cause of white folks. I wouldn't trust one of 'em sittin' in front of me on a merry-go-round, wouldn't trust 'em if they was laid up in bed with lockjaw and the mumps both at the same time.
John. Last time I heard from you, you said it was the colored who made all the trouble.

Sheldon. They do, they're the worst ones. There's two kinda people that's got the world messed up for good, that's the colored and the white, and I got no use for either one of 'em.
Millie. I'm going to stop trying to help people.
John. Hell, I'm through with it. Oh, I'm learning the ropes!
Sheldon. *That's* why they don't do more colored shows . . . trouble makers, pot boilers, spoon stirrers . . . and sharper than a serpent's tooth! Colored women wake up in the mornin' with their fists ball up . . . ready to fight.
Wiletta. What in the devil is all this justifyin'? Ain't necessary.
Millie. *(to Sheldon)* And you crawlin' all over me to hand her coffee! Damn "Tom."
Sheldon. You talkin' 'bout your relatives, ain't talkin' 'bout me, if I'm a "Tom," you a "Jemima."
John. I need out, I need air. *(He exits stage left.)*
Sheldon. White folks is stickin' together, stickin' together, stickin' together . . . we fightin'.
Wiletta. Hush, I got a headache.
Millie. I need a breath of air, too, before I slap the taste out of somebody's mouth. *(Millie grabs her coat and exits stage left.)*
Sheldon. I hope the wind blows her away. They gonna kick us until we all out in the street . . . unemployed . . . get all the air you want then. Sometimes I take low, yes, gotta take low. Man says somethin' to me, I say . . . "Yes, sure, certainly." You 'n' me know how to do. That ain't *tommin'*, that's common sense. You and me . . . we don't mind takin' low because we tryin' to accomplish somethin'. . . .
Wiletta. I mind . . . I do mind . . . I mind . . . I mind. . . .
Sheldon. Well, yeah, we all mind . . . but you got to swaller what you mind. What you mind won't buy beans. I mean you gotta take what you mind to survive . . . to eat to breathe. . . .
Wiletta. *(tensely)* I mind. Leave me alone.

(Sheldon exits with a sigh.)

Henry. *(Enters carrying a lunch box. Wiletta turns; she looks so distressed.)* They've all flown the coop?
Wiletta. Yes.
Henry. What's the matter? Somebody hurt your feelin's?
Wiletta. Yes.
Henry. Don't fret, it's too nice a day. I believe in treatin' folks right. When you're just about through with this life, that's the time when you know how to live. Seems like yesterday I was forty years old and the day before that I wasn't but nineteen. . . . Think of it.
Wiletta. I don't like to think . . . makes me fightin' mad.

Henry. *(giving vent to his pent-up feelings)* Don't I know it? When he yelled about jelly doughnuts, I started to land one on him! Oh, I almost did it!

Wiletta. I know it!

Henry. But . . . "Hold your temper!" I says. I have a most ferocious temper.

Wiletta. Me too. I take and take, then watch out!

Henry. Have to hold my temper, I don't want to kill the man.

Wiletta. Yeah, makes you feel like fightin'.

Henry *(joining in the spirit of the discussion)* Sure I'm a fighter and I come from a fightin' people.

Wiletta. You from Ireland?

Henry. A fightin' people! Didn't we fight for the home rule?

Wiletta. Uh-huh, now you see there.

(Wiletta doesn't worry about making sense out of Henry's speech on Ireland; it's the feeling behind it that counts.)

Henry. O, a history of great men, fightin' men!

Wiletta. *(Rallying to the call, she answers as though sitting on an amen bench at a revival meeting.)* Yes, carry on.

Henry. Ah, yes, we was fightin' for the home rule! Ah, there was some great men!

Wiletta. I know it.

Henry. There was Parnell! Charles Stewart Parnell!

Wiletta. All right!

Henry. A figure of a man! The highest! Fightin' hard for the home rule! A parlimentarian! And they clapped him in the blasted jailhouse for six months!

Wiletta. Yes, my Lord!

Henry. And Gladstone introduced the bill . . . and later on you had Dillon and John Redmond . . . and then when the home rule was almost put through, what do you think happened? World War One! That killed the whole business!

Wiletta. *(very indignant)* Oh, if it ain't one thing, it's another!

Henry. I'm descended from a great line! And then the likes of him with his jelly doughnuts! Jelly doughnuts, indeed, is it? What does he know? Tramplin' upon a man's dignity! Me father was the greatest, most dignified man you've ever seen . . . and he played vaudeville! Oh, the bearin' of him! *(angrily demonstrating his father's dignity)* Doin' the little soft-shoe step . . . and it's take your hat off to the ladies . . . and step along there. . . .

Wiletta. Henry, I want to be an actress, I've always wanted to be an actress and they ain't gonna do me the way they did the home rule! I want to be an actress 'cause one day you're nineteen and then forty and so on . . . I want to be an actress! Henry, they stone us when we try to go to school, the world's crazy.

Henry. It's a shame, a shame. . . .

Wiletta. Where the hell do I come in? Every damn body pushin' me off the face of the earth! I want to be an actress . . . hell, I'm gonna be one, you hear me? *(She pounds the table.)*

Henry. Sure, and why not, I'd like to know!

Wiletta. *(quietly)* Yes, dammit . . . and why not? Why in the hell not?

(blues record in; woman singer)

(Curtain)

ACT II

Time: *Ten o'clock Thursday morning.*
Place: *Same as Act I. (blues music—in—up and out)*
Scene: *Same as Act I, except furniture has been changed around; some of the old set removed. Bill O'Wray, a character actor (white) stands upstage on a makeshift platform. He radiates strength and power as he addresses an imaginary audience. Manners stands stage left, tie loosened, hair ruffled. He is hepped up with nervous energy, can barely stand still. Eddie is stage right, in charge of the script and a tape recorder; he follows the script and turns up the tape recorder on cue from Manners. O'Wray is delivering a "masterful" rendition of Renard's speech on "tolerance." Manners is elated one moment, deflated the next. Eddie is obviously nervous, drawn and lacking the easy-going attitude of Act I.*

Bill. *(intones speech with vigor and heartfelt passion)* My friends, if all the world were just, there would be no need for valor. . . . And those of us who are of a moderate mind . . . I would say the majority . . .

(light applause from tape recorder)

. . . we are anything but light-hearted. But the moving finger writes and having writ moves *on*. No, you can't wash out a word of it. Heretofore we've gotten along with our Nigra population . . . but times change.

(applause from tape recorder)

I do not argue with any man who believes in segregation. I, of all people, will not, cannot question that belief. We all believe in the words of Henry Clay—"Sir, I would rather be right than be president."

(Eddie sleeps his cue.)
Manners. Dammit! Eddie!

(Eddie suddenly switches to loud applause.)

Bill. But difficulties are things that show what men are, and necessity is still the mother of invention. As Emerson so aptly pointed out—"The true test of civilization is not the—census, nor the size of cities, nor the crops—but the kind of man the country turns out." Oh, my friends, let every man look before he leaps, let us consider submitting to the present evil lest a greater one befall us—say to yourself, my honor is dearer to me than my life.

(very light applause)

I say moderation—for these are the times that try men's souls! In these terrible days we must realize—how oft the darkest hour of ill breaks brightest into dawn. Moderation, yes.

(very light applause)

Even the misguided, infamous Adolph Hitler said—"One should guard against believing the great masses to be more stupid than they actually are!"

(applause)

Oh, friends, moderation. Let us weigh our answer very carefully when the darkskinned Oliver Twist approaches our common pot and says: "Please, sir, I want some more." When we say "no," remember that a soft answer turneth away wrath. Ohhh, we shall come out of the darkness, and sweet is pleasure after pain. If we are superior, let us show our superiority!

(Manners directs Eddie to take applause up high and then out.)

Moderation. With wisdom and moderation, these terrible days will pass. I am reminded of the immortal words of Longfellow. "And the night shall be filled with music and the cares that infest the day shall fold their tents like the Arabs and silently steal away."

(terrific applause)

Manners. *(slaps Bill on back; dashes to Eddie and turns the applause up and down)* Is this such a Herculean task? All you have to do is listen! Inattention—aggravates the hell out of me!

Bill. *(When Bill drops out of character we see that he is very different from the strong Renard. He appears to be worried at all times. He has a habit of negatively shaking his head even though nothing is wrong. Bill O'Wray is but a shadow of a man—but by some miracle he turns into a dynamic*

figure as Renard. As Bill—he sees dragons in every corner and worries about each one.) I don't know, I don't know. . . .
Manners. (*fears the worst for the show as he watches Bill*) What? What is it?
Bill. (*half dismissing the thought*) Oh, well . . . I guess. . . .

(*Eddie is toying with the machine and turns the applause up by accident.*)

Manners. Hello, Eddie, a little consideration! Why do you do it? Damned childish!

(*Eddie turns off machine.*)

What's bothering you?
Bill. Well, you never can tell . . . but I don't know. . . .
Manners. Bill, cut it out, come on.
Bill. That *Arab* stuff . . . you know, quietly folding his tent . . . you're gonna get a laugh . . . and then on the other hand you might offend somebody . . . well, we'll see. . . .
Manners. Eddie, make a note of that. Arab folding his tent. I'll take it up with Bronson.

(*Eddie is making notes.*)

Bill. I'm tellin' you, you don't need it . . . wouldn't lose a thing . . . the Longfellow quote . . . I don't know, maybe I'm wrong but . . .
Manners. You act like you've lost your last friend! I'm the one holding the blasted bag.
Bill. (*taking "Show Business" out of his coat pocket*) Well, maybe I shouldn't have said . . .
Manners. I'm out of my mind! When I think of the money borrowed, and for what! Oh, I'm just talking. This always happens when the ship leaves port. The union's making me take three extra stage hands. (*laughs*) . . . they hate us! *Coproduce*, filthy word! You know who I had to put the bite on for an extra ten thousand? My ex-wife's present boyfriend. Enough to emasculate a man for the rest of his life!
Bill. How is Fay? Sweet kid. I was sure surprised when you two broke it off. Oh, well, that's the way. . . .
Manners. She's fine and we're good friends. Thank God for civilization.
Bill. That's nice. Ten thousand? She must have connected up with a big wheel, huh?
Manners. I've known you long enough to ask a favor.
Bill. All depends.
Manners. Will you stop running off at lunch hour? It looks bad.
Bill. Now, wait a minute. . . .
Eddie. I eat with them all the time.
Manners. Drop it, Eddie. Unity in *this* company is very important. Hell, I

don't care, but it looks like you don't want to eat with the colored members of the cast.
Bill. I don't.
Eddie. I guess you heard him.
Manners. Bill, this is fantastic. I never credited you with this kind of . . . silly, childlike . . .
Bill. There's not a prejudiced bone in my body. It is important that I eat my lunch. I used to have an ulcer. I have nothing against anybody but I can't eat my damn lunch . . . people *stare*. They sit there glaring and staring.
Manners. Nonsense.
Bill. Tuesday I lunched with Millie because I bumped into her on the street. That restaurant . . . people straining and looking at me as if I were an old lecher! God knows what they're thinking. I've got to eat my lunch. After all . . . I can't stand that . . .
Manners. *(laughs)* All right but mix a little . . . it's the show . . . do it for the show.
Bill. Every time I open my mouth somebody is telling me don't say this or that . . . Millie doesn't want to be called "gal" . . . I call *all* women "gal" . . . I don't know . . . I'm not going into analysis about this . . . I'm not. How do you think my character is shaping up?
Manners. Great, no complaints . . . fine.

(Wiletta drags in, tired and worn.)

'Morning, sweetie.
Eddie. Good morning.
Wiletta. *(indicating script)* I been readin' this back and forth and over again.
Manners. *(automatic sympathy)* Honey, don't . . .
Wiletta. My neighbor, Miss Green, she come up and held the book and I sat there justifyin' like you said. . . .
Manners. Darling, don't think. You're great until you start thinking. I don't expect you to. . . .
Wiletta. *(weak laugh)* I've been in this business a long time, more than twenty-five years and . . .
Manners. Don't tell it, you're beautiful.
Wiletta. Guess I can do like the others. We was justifyin' and Miss Green says to me . . .
Bill. *(gets in his good deed)* Wiletta, you look wonderful, you really do.
Wiletta. Huh?
Bill. You . . . you're looking well.
Wiletta. Thank you, Miss Green says . . .
Manners. *(wearily)* Oh, a plague on Miss Green. Darling, it's too early to

listen to outside criticism, it can be dangerous if the person doesn't understand . . .

Wiletta. Miss Green puts on shows at the church . . . and she had an uncle that was a sharecropper, so she says the first act . . .

Manners. *(flips the script to Act III)* We're hitting the third today.

Wiletta. Miss Green also conducts the church choir . . .

Manners. Wiletta, don't complicate my life. *(to Bill and Eddie)* Isn't she wonderful? *(to Wiletta)* Dear heart, I adore you.

Wiletta. *(feels like a fool as she limply trails on)* She . . . she did the Messiah . . . Handel's Messiah . . . last Easter . . . and folks come from downtown to hear it . . . all kinds of folks . . . white folks too.

Manners. Eddie! Did I leave the schedule at home?

Eddie. *(hands him the schedule)* I have a copy.

Wiletta. Miss Green says, now . . . she said it . . . she says the third act doesn't justify with the first . . . no, wait . . . her exact words was, "The third act is not the natural outcome of the first." I thought, I thought she might be right.

Manners. *(teasing)* Make me a solemn promise, don't start thinking.

Sheldon. *(enters in a rush and hastily begins to remove scarves, coat etc.)* Good mornin', there ain't no justice.

(Bill O'Wray glances at "Show Business" from time to time.)

Eddie. What a greeting.

Sheldon. I dreamed six, twelve, six, one, two . . . just like that. You know what come out yesterday? Six, one, three. What you gonna do?

Manners. Save your money.

Bill. Hey, what do you know?

Manners. Did we make the press?

Sheldon. *(to Wiletta)* Friend of mine died yesterday, went to see about his apartment . . . gone! Just like that!

Bill. Gary Brewer's going into rehearsal on *Lost and Lonely*.

Manners. Been a long time.

Bill. He was in that Hollywood investigation some years ago.

Sheldon. *(to Eddie)* They musta applied whilst the man was dyin'.

Manners. He wasn't really in it, someone named him I think.

Bill. You knew him well, didn't you?

Manners. Me? I don't know him. I've worked with him a couple of times but I don't really know him.

Bill. A very strange story reached me once, some fellow was planning to name me, can you imagine?

(Millie enters wearing a breathtaking black suit. She is radiant.)

Eddie. That's ridiculous.

Bill. Nothing ever happened, but that's the story. Naming *me*.

Manners. *(as he studies schedule)* Talking about the coast, I could be out there now on a honey of a deal . . . but this I had to do, that's all.
Sheldon. Y'all ever hear any stories 'bout people namin' me?
Manners. What?
Bill. Oh, Shel!
Sheldon. *(This is a burden he has carried for quite some time.)* I sang on a program once with Millie, to help some boy that was in trouble . . . but later on I heard they was tryin' to overthrow the gov'ment.

(Manners, Eddie and Bill are embarrassed by this.)

Millie. Oh, hush! Your mouth runs like a race horse!
Sheldon. Well, ain't nothin' wrong with singin' is there? We just sang.
Millie. *(as she removes her hat)* A big fool.
Manners. *(making peace)* Oh, now. . . . we're all good Americans.
Bill. *(to ease the tension)* I . . . I . . . er, didn't know you went in for singing, Sheldon.
Sheldon. Sure, I even wrote me a coupla tunes. Can make a lotta money like that but you gotta know somebody, I ain't got no pull.
Wiletta. *(to Millie)* He talks too much, talks too much.
Manners. Ah, we have a composer, popular stuff?
Sheldon. *(stands and mechanically rocks to and fro in a rock and roll beat as he sings)*
    You-oo-hoo-oo are my hon-honey
    Ooo-oo-ooo-oo, you smile is su-hu-hunny
    My hu-hu-hunny, Bay-hay-hay-bee-e-e-e
. . . and it goes like that.
Manners. Well!
Sheldon. Thank you.
Bill. I don't know why you haven't sold it, that's all you hear.

(Sheldon is pleased with Bill's compliment but also a little worried.)

Millie. Hmmmmmph.
Eddie. Really a tune.
Sheldon. *(to Bill)* My song . . . it . . . it's copyrighted.
Bill. Oh?
Sheldon. I got papers.
Millie. *(extends her wrist to Wiletta)* Look. My husband is in off the road.
Wiletta. What's the matter?
Millie. A new watch, and I got my suit out . . . brought me this watch. We looked at a freezer this morning . . . food freezer . . . what's best, a chest freezer or an upright? I don't know.
Judy. *(She enters dressed a little older than Act I; her hair is set with more precision. She is reaching for a sophistication that can never go deeper than the surface. She often makes graceful, studied postures and tries*

new attitudes, but very often she forgets.) Greets and salutations. Sheldon, how are you dear?
Sheldon. Thank you.
Judy. *(as Millie displays her wrist for inspection)* Millie, darling, how lovely, ohhhhh, exquisite . . .
Wiletta. *(really trying to join in)* Mmmmm, ain't it divine.

(Henry and John enter together. Henry carries a container of coffee and a piece of Danish for Manners. Henry is exact, precise, all business. He carries the container to Manners' table, places pastry, taps Eddie on the shoulder, points to Manners, points to container, nods to Manners and company, turns and leaves, all while dialogue continues.)

John. *(Enters on a cloud. He is drifting more and more toward the heady heights of opportunism. He sees himself on the brink of escaping Wiletta, Millie and Sheldon. It's becoming very easy to conform to Manners' pattern.)* I'm walking in my sleep. I was up all hours last night.
Manners. At Sardi's no doubt.
John. No!
Judy. Exposed! We've found you out.

(General laughter from Millie, Judy, Bill, Eddie and Manners. Judy is enjoying the intangible joke to the utmost but as she turns to Wiletta her laughter dies . . . but Wiletta quickly picks it up.)

Wiletta. Oh, my, yes indeed!
John. I struggled with the third act. I think I won.

(Millie sticks out her wrist for John's inspection.)

Exquisite, Millie, beautiful. You deserve it.

(During the following the conversation tumbles criss-cross in all directions and the only clear things are underscored.)

Manners. Tell him what I told you this morning.
Bill. Why should I swell his head?
Manners. *(arm around John's shoulder)* Hollywood's going to grab you so fast! I won't drop names but our opening night is going to be the end.
Millie. *(to Wiletta)* Barbara died!
Judy. *(to Manners)* Oh, you terrify me!
Millie. *Died alone in her apartment.* Sudden-like!
John. I've got to catch Katherine's performance, I hear it's terrific!
Bill. She's great, only great.
Millie. *I wouldn't live alone!*
Manners. She's going to get the award, no doubt about it!
Judy. Marion Hatterly is good.

Manners. Marion is as *old as the hills!* I mean, she's so old it's embarrassing.
John. But she has a quality.
Sheldon. *(to Millie and Wiletta)* People dyin' like they got nothin' else to do!
Judy. She has, John, a real quality.
Sheldon. *I ain't gonna die,* can't afford to do it.
Manners. You have to respect her.
Eddie. Can name her own ticket.
John. Imperishable talent.
Millie. *Funeral is Monday.*
Wiletta. *(weakly, to no one in particular)* Mmmmm, fascinatin'. . . .
Manners. Picnic is over! Third Act!
Sheldon. I know my lines.
Bill. Don't worry about lines yet.
Manners. No, let him worry . . . I mean it's okay. Beginning of third!
Wiletta. *(Feels dizzy from past conversation. She rises and walks in a half-circle, then half-circles back again. She is suddenly the center of attraction.)* It . . . it's night time and I'm ironin' clothes.
Manners. Right. We wander through it. Here's the ironing board, door, window . . . you iron. Carrie is over there crying.
Judy. Oh, poor, dear, Carrie, crying again.
Manners. Petunia is near the window, looking out for Job. Everyone is worried, worried, worried like crazy. Have the lynchers caught Job? Sam is seated in the corner, whittling a stick.
Sheldon. *(flat statement)* Whittlin' a stick.
Manners. Excitement. Everyone knows that a mob is gathering.
Sheldon. *(seated and busy running one index finger over the other)* I'm whittlin' a stick.
Manners. *(drumming up excitement)* The hounds can be heard baying in the distance.

(Sheldon bays to fill in the dog bit. Manners silences him with a gesture.)

Everyone *listens!* They are thinking—has Job been killed? Ruby begins to sing.
Wiletta. *(begins to sing with a little too much power but Manner directs her down)* Lord, have mercy, Lord have mercy . . . *(hums)*
Millie. *(in abject, big-eyed fear)* Listen to them dogs in the night.

(Manners warns Sheldon not to provide sound effects.)

Wiletta. *(trying to lose herself in the part)* Child, you better go now.

(Bill whispers to Eddie.)

Eddie. *Line. Miss Carrie,* you better go now.

Manners. Oh, bother! Don't do that!

(Eddie feels resentful toward Bill as Bill acts as though he had nothing to do with the correction.)

Wiletta. This ain't no place for you to be.
Judy. *(Now plays Carrie in a different way from Act I. There is a reserved kindliness, rather than real involvement.)* I don't want to leave you alone, Ruby.
Sheldon. Thassa mistake, Mr. Manners. She can't be alone if me and Millie is there with her.
Manners. Don't interrupt!
Sheldon. Sorry.

(Bill shakes his fist at Sheldon in playful pantomime.)

Wiletta. Man that is born of woman is but a few days and full of trouble.
Judy. I'm going to drive over to the next county and get my father and Judge Willis.
Millie. No, you ain't. Mr. Renard would never forgive me if somethin' was to happen to you.

(Sheldon is very touched and sorry for all concerned as he whittles his stick.)

Judy. I feel so helpless.
Sheldon. *(interrupts out of sheer frustration)* Am I still whittlin' the stick?
Wiletta. Dammit, yes.
Manners. *(paces to control his annoyance)* Shel.
Sheldon. I thought I lost my place.
Wiletta. *(picks up Manners' signal)* Nothin' to do now but pray!
Sheldon. *(recognizes his cue)* Oh, yeah, that's me. *(knows his lines almost perfectly)* Lord, once and again and one more time . . .

(Millie moans in the background. Wiletta's mind seems a thousand miles away. Manners snaps his fingers and she begins to moan background for Sheldon's prayer.)

Your humble servant calls on your everlastin' mercy . . .
Millie. Yes, Lord!
Sheldon. . . . to beseech, to beseech thy help for all your children this evenin'. . . .
Millie. This evenin', Lord.

(Manners is busy talking to John.)

Sheldon. But most of all we ask, we pray . . . that you help your son and servant Job. . . .
Wiletta. Help him, Lord!

Sheldon. *(doing a grand job of the prayer)* Walk with Job! Talk with Job! Ohhhhh, be with Job!
Judy. Yes!

(Manners and Bill give Judy disapproving looks and she clasps her hand over her mouth.)

Wiletta. *(starts to sing and is joined by Sheldon and Millie)* Death ain't nothin' but a robber, cantcha see, cantcha see . . .
Manners. *(is in a real tizzy, watching to catch Bill's reaction to the scene, and trying with his whole body to keep the scene up and going)* Eddie! Direction!
Eddie. The door opens and Job enters!
Wiletta. Job, why you come here?

(Manners doesn't like her reading. It is too direct and thoughtful.)

Millie. *(lashing out)* They after you! They told you 'bout mixin' in with Turner and that votin'!
Manners. Oh, good girl!
Wiletta. I'm the one to talk to my boy!
John. *(a frightened, shivering figure)* If somebody could get me a wagon, I'll take the low road around Simpkin's Hollow and catch a train goin' away from here.
Wiletta. Shoulda gone 'fore you started this misery.

(Manners indicates that she should get rougher; she tries.)

   Screamin' 'bout your rights! You got none! You got none!
John. I'm askin' for help, I gotta leave.
Manners. *(to John)* Appeal, remember it's an appeal.
John. *(as though a light has dawned)* Ah, you're so right. *(reads with tender appeal)* I gotta leave.
Manners. Right.
Wiletta. You tryin' to tell me that you runnin' away?
Sheldon. *(worried about Job's escape and getting caught up outside of the scene)* Sure! That's what he said in the line right there!

(Manners silences Sheldon with a gesture.)

Wiletta. You say you ain't done nothin' wrong?

(Manners looks at Eddie and Bill with despair.)

John. I ain't lyin' . . .
Wiletta. Then there's no need to be runnin'. Ain't you got no faith?
Sheldon. *(sings in a shaky voice as he raps out time)*
   Oh, wella, time of trouble is a lonesome time
   Time of trouble is a lonesome time . . .

(joined by Millie)

    Feel like I could die, feel like I could die . . .
Wiletta. Tell 'em you sorry, tell 'em you done wrong!
Manners. Relate, Wiletta. Relate to what's going on around you!

(to John)

    Go on.
John. I wasn't even votin' for a black man, votin' for somebody white same as they. *(aside to Manners)* Too much? Too little? I fell off.

(Manners indicates that he's on the beam.)

Wiletta. I ain't never voted!
Sheldon. No, Lord!
Wiletta. I don't care who get in! Don't make no nevermind to us!
Millie. The truth!
John. *(all afire)* When a man got a decent word to say for us down here, I gonna vote for him.
Wiletta. A decent word! And that's all you ever gonna get outta him. Dammit! He ain't gonna win nohow! They done said he ain't and they gonna see to it! and you gonna be dead . . . for a decent word!
John. I ain't gonna wait to be killed.
Wiletta. There's only one right thing to do!

(Everyone turns page in unison.)

    You got to go and give yourself up.
John. But I ain't done nothin'.
Sheldon. *(starts to sing again)* Wella, trouble is a lonesome thing . . . lonesome . . . lonesome . . .
Manners. *(The song even grates on him.)* Cut it, it's too much.
Judy. My father will have you put in the county jail where you'll be safe.
John. But I ain't done nothin'!
Judy. I'm thinking of Ruby and the others, even if you aren't. I don't want murder in this community.
Wiletta. *(screams)* Boy, get down on your knees.
Manners. *(to Eddie)* Muscular tension.

(Eddie makes a note.)

Wiletta. Oh, Lord, touch this boy's heart!
Sheldon. Mmmmmm, Hmmmmmmmm. Hmmmmmm . . .
Wiletta. Reach him tonight! Take the fear and hatred out of his soul!
Millie. Mercy, Lord!
John. Stop, I can't stand no more. Whatever you say, anything you say.

Sheldon. Praise the Lord!
Eddie. Renard enters.
Bill. Carrie, you shouldn't be here.
Wiletta. I told her. I'm beggin' you to help my boy, sir. . . . *(She drops script and picks it up.)*
John. Ohhh, I can't sustain.
Manners. Don't try. We're breaking everything down to the simplest components . . . I want simple reactions to given circumstances in order to highlight the outstanding phases.

(Wiletta finds her place.)

Okay, let it roll.
Wiletta. I'm beggin' you to help my boy.
Bill. Boy, you're a mighty little fella to fly in the face of things people live by 'round here. I'll do what I can, what little I can.
Wiletta. Thank you, sir.
Judy. Have Judge Willis put him in jail where he'll be safe.
Bill. Guess it wasn't his fault.
Wiletta. He don' know nothin'.
Bill. There are all kinds of white men in the world.
Sheldon. The truth.
Bill. This bird Akins got to sayin' the kind of things that was bound to stir you folks up.
Millie. I ain't paid him no mind myself.
Bill. Well, anything you want to take to the jailhouse with you? Like a washcloth and . . . well, whatever you might need.
John. I don't know, don't know what I'm doin'.
Bill. Think you learned a lesson from all this?
Millie. You hear Mr. Renard?
Sheldon. He wanna know if you learned your lesson.
John. I believed I was right.
Sheldon. Now you know you wasn't.
Bill. If anything happens, you tell the men Mr. Akins put notions in your head, understand?
Sheldon. He wanna know if you understand.
Bill. Come along, we'll put you in the jailhouse. Reckon I owe your ma and pa that much.
John. I'm afraid, I so afraid. . . .
Millie. Just go, 'fore they get here.
Eddie. Job turns and looks at his father.

(Sheldon places one finger to his lips and throws up his arms to show that he has no line.)

Finally he looks to his mother, she goes back to her ironing.
Bill. Petunia, see that Miss Carrie gets home safe.
Millie. Yes sir.
Eddie. Job follows Renard out into the night as Ruby starts to sing.
Wiletta. *(sings)*
> Keep me from sinkin' down
> O, Lord, O, my Lord
> Keep me from sinkin' down. . . .

Manners. Cut, relax, at ease!
Millie. *(brushes lint from her skirt)* I'll have to bring work clothes.
Sheldon. *(to Millie)* I almost hit the number yesterday.
Millie. I'm glad you didn't.

(Bill crosses to Manners; we hear snatches of their conversation as the others cross-talk.)

Judy. *(to John)* Did you finish my book?

(John claps his hand to his forehead in a typical Manners gesture.)

Bill. *(a light conference on Wiletta)* A line of physical action might . . .
Sheldon. *(to Millie)* I almost got an apartment.
Manners. Limited emotional capacity.
Millie. *(to Sheldon)* Almost don't mean a thing.
Manners. Well, it's coming. Sheldon, I like what's happening.
Sheldon. Thank you, does he give himself up to Judge Willis and get saved?
Manners. *(flabbergasted, as are John, Judy, Bill and Eddie)* Shel, haven't you read it? Haven't you heard us read it?
Sheldon. No, I just go over and over my own lines, I ain't in the last of the third act.
Judy. Are my motivations coming through?
Manners. Yeah, forget it. Sit down, Sheldon . . . just for you . . . Renard drives him toward jail, deputies stop them on the way, someone shoots and kills Job as he tries to escape, afterward they find out he was innocent, Renard makes everyone feel like a dog . . . they realize they were wrong and so forth.
Sheldon. And so forth.
Manners. He makes them realize that lynching is wrong. *(He refers to his notes.)*
Sheldon. *(to Wiletta)* What was he innocent of?
Wiletta. I don't know.
John. About the voting.
Sheldon. Uh-uh, he was guilty of that 'cause he done confessed.
Manners. Innocent of wrong-doing, Sheldon.

Sheldon. Uh-huh, oh, yeah.
Manners. Yale, you're on the right track. John, what can I say? You're great. Millie, you're growing, gaining command . . . I begin to feel an inner as well as the outer rendering.
John. If we could run the sequence without interruption.
Sheldon. Yeah, then we could motorate and all that.
Manners. *(to Wiletta)* Dear heart, I've got to tell you . . .
Wiletta. I ain't so hot.
Manners. Don't be sensitive, let me help you, will you?
Wiletta. *(trying to handle matters in the same way as John and Judy)* I know my relations and motivations may not be just so . . .
Sheldon. *(wisely)* Uh-huh, *motivation,* that's the thing.
Wiletta. They not right and I think I know why . . .
Manners. Darling, that's my department, will you listen?

(John is self-conscious about Wiletta and Sheldon. He is ashamed of them and has reached the point where he exchanges knowing looks with Bill, Eddie and Manners.)

Wiletta. You don't ever listen to me. You hear the others but not me. And it's 'cause of the school. 'Cause they know 'bout justifyin' and the . . . antagonist . . . I never studied that, so you don't want to hear me, that's all right.
Judy. *(stricken to the heart)* Oh, don't say that.
Sheldon. He listen to me, and I ain't had it.
John. *(starts to put his arm around Wiletta)* Oh, Wiletta . . .
Wiletta. *(moving away from him)* Oh, go on.
Manners. Wiletta, dear, I'm sorry if I've complicated things. I'll make it as clear as I can. You are pretending to act and I can see through your pretense. I want truth. What is truth? Truth is simply whatever you can bring yourself to believe, that is all. You must have integrity about your work . . . a sense of . . . well, sense.
Wiletta. I'm tryin' to lose myself like you say but . . .
John. *(wants to help but afraid to interrupt)* Oh, no . . .
Manners. *(sternly)* You can't lose yourself, you are you . . . and you can't get away. You, Wiletta, must relate.
Sheldon. That's what I do.
Wiletta. I don't see why the boy couldn't get away . . . it's the killin' that . . . something's wrong. I may be in fast company but I got as much integrity as any. I didn't start workin' no yesterday.
Manners. No, Wiletta, no self-pity. Look, he can't escape this death. We want audience sympathy. We have a very subtle point to make, very subtle. . . .

Bill. I hate the kind of play that bangs you over the head with the message. Keep it subtle.
Manners. *(getting very basic)* We don't want to antagonize the audience.
Wiletta. It'll make 'em mad if he gets away?
Manners. This is a simple, sweet, lovable guy. Sheldon, does it offend you that he gives himself up to Judge Willis?
Sheldon. No, not if that's how they do.
Manners. We're making one beautiful, clear point . . . violence is wrong.
Wiletta. My friend, Miss Green, say she don't see why they act like this.
John. *(Thinks he knows how to handle Wiletta. He is about to burst with an idea. Manners decides to let John wade in.)* Look, think of the intellectual level here . . . they're under-privileged, uneducated. . . .
Wiletta. *(letting John know he's treading on thin ice)* Look out, you ain't so smart.
John. *(showing so much of Manners)* They've probably never seen a movie or television . . . never used a telephone. They . . . they're not like us. They're good, kind, folksy people . . . but they're ignorant, they just don't know.
Wiletta. You ain't the director.
Sheldon. *(to John)* You better hush.
Manners. We're dealing with simple, backward people but they're human beings.
Wiletta. 'Cause they colored, you tellin' me they're human bein's. . . . I *know* I'm a human bein'. . . . Listen here . . .
Manners. I will not listen! It does not matter to me that they're Negroes. Black, white, green or purple, I maintain there is only one race . . . the human race.

(Sheldon bursts into applause.)

Millie. That's true.
Manners. Don't think "Negro," think "people."
Sheldon. Let's stop segregatin' ourselves.
John. *(to Wiletta)* I didn't mean any harm, you don't understand. . . .
Bill. *(To Millie as he looks heavenward and acts out his weariness)* Oh, honey child!
Millie. Don't call me no damn honey child!
Bill. Well, is my face red.
Millie. Yea, and on you it looks good.
Manners. What's going on?
Millie. Honey child.
Wiletta. *(mumbling as all dialogue falls pell-mell)* Justify.
Bill. *(with great resignation)* Trying to be friendly.
Wiletta. Justify.

Millie. Get friendly with someone else.
Manners. May we have order!
Sheldon. *(in a terrible flash of temper)* That's why they don't do more colored shows! Always fightin'! Everybody hush, let this man direct! He don't even have to be here! Right now he could be out in Hollywood in the middle of a big investigation!
Eddie. The word is production!
Sheldon. That's what I said, production.
Eddie. No, you didn't.
Sheldon. What'd I say?
Manners. *(bangs table)* I will not countenance another outbreak of this nature. I say to each and everyone of you . . . I am in charge and I'll thank you to remember it. I've been much too lax, too informal. Well, it doesn't work. There's going to be order.
Wiletta. I was only sayin' . . .
Manners. I said *everyone!* My patience is at an end. I demand your concentrated attention. It's as simple as A, B, C, if you will apply yourselves. The threat of this horrible violence throws you into cold, stark fear. It's a perfectly human emotion, anyone would feel it. I'm not asking you to dream up some fantastic horror . . . it's a lynching. We've never actually seen such a thing, thank God . . . but allow your imagination to soar, to take hold of it . . . think.
Sheldon. I seen one.
Manners. *(can't believe he heard right)* What?
Bill. What did you see?
Sheldon. A lynchin', when I was a little boy 'bout nine years old.
Judy. Oh, no.
Wiletta. How did it happen? Tell me, Sheldon did you really?
Manners. Would it help you to know, Wiletta?
Wiletta. I . . . guess . . . I don't know.
Bill. *(not eager to hear about it)* Will it bother you, Sheldon? It could be wrong for him . . . I don't know. . . .

(Eddie gives Manners a doubtful look.)

Millie. That must be something to see.
Manners. *(with a sigh)* Go on, Sheldon.

(Manners watches cast reactions.)

Sheldon. I think it was on a Saturday, yeah, it had to be or elsewise I woulda been in the field with my ma and pa.
Wiletta. What field?
Sheldon. The cotton field. My ma said I was too little to go every day but

some of 'em younger'n me was out there all the time. My grandma was home with me. . . . *(thinks of grandma and almost forgets his story)*
Wiletta. What about the lynchin'?
Sheldon. It was Saturday and rainin' a sort of sifty rain. I was standin' at the window watchin' the lilac bush wavin' in the wind. A sound come to my ears like bees hummin' . . . was voices comin' closer and closer, screamin' and cursin'. My granny tried to pull me from the window. "Come on, chile." She said, "They gonna kill us all . . . hide!" But I was fightin' to keep from goin' with her, scared to go in the dark closet.

(Judy places her hands over her ears and bows her head.)

The screamin' comin' closer and closer . . . and the screamin' was laughin'. . . . Lord, how they was laughin' . . . louder and louder. *(Sheldon rises and puts in his best performance to date. He raises one hand and creates a stillness . . . everyone is spellbound.)* Hush! Then I hear wagon wheels bumpin' over the wet, stony road, chains clankin'. Man drivin' the wagon, beatin' the horse . . . Ahhhhhhhh! Ahhhhhhhh! Horse just pullin' along . . . and then I saw it! Chained to the back of the wagon, draggin' and bumpin' along. . . . *(He opens his arms wide.)* The arms of it stretched out . . . a burnt, naked thing . . . a burnt, naked thing that once was a man . . . and I started to scream but no sound come out . . . just a screamin' but no sound. . . . *(He lowers his arms and brings the company back to the present.)* That was Mr. Morris that they killed. Mr. Morris. I remember one time he come to our house and was laughin' and talkin' and everything . . . and he give us a fruit cake that his wife made. Folks said he was crazy . . . you know, 'bout talkin' back . . . quick to speak his mind. I left there when I was seventeen. I don't want to live in no place like that.
Manners. When I hear of barbarism . . . I feel so wretched, so guilty.
Sheldon. Don't feel that way. You wouldn't kill nobody and do 'em like that . . . would you?
Manners. *(hurt by the question)* No, Sheldon.
Sheldon. That's what I know.

(Bill crosses and rests his hand on Sheldon's shoulder. Sheldon flinches because he hadn't noticed Bill's approach.)

Oh! I didn't see you. Did I help y'all by tellin' that story?
Manners. It was quite an experience. I'm shot. Break for lunch, we'll pick up in an hour, have a good afternoon session.
Millie. Makes me feel like goin' out in the street and crackin' heads.
Judy. *(shocked)* Oh!
Eddie. Makes my blood boil . . . but what can you do?
Manners. We're doing a play.

Millie. *(to Judy)* I'm starved. You promised to show us that Italian place.
Judy. *(surprised that Millie no longer feels violent)* Why . . . sure, I'd love to. Let's have a festive lunch, with wine!
Sheldon. Yeah, that wine that comes in a straw bottle.
Judy. Imported wine.
Millie. And chicken cacciatore . . . let's live!
Wiletta. *(crosses to Manners while others are getting coats; she has hit on a scheme to make Manners see her point)* Look here, I ain't gonna let you get mad with me. You supposed to be my buddy.
John. Let's go!
Manners. *(opens his arms to Wiletta)* I'm glad you said that. You're my sweetheart.
Millie. Bill, how about you?
Bill. *(places his hand on his stomach)* The Italian place. Okay, count me in.
Eddie. *(stacking scripts)* I want a kingsize dish of clams . . . raw ones.
Wiletta. Wouldn't it be nice if the mother could say, "Son, you right! I don't want to send you outta here but I don't know what to do. . . ."
Manners. Darling, darling . . . no.
Millie. Wiletta, get a move on.
Wiletta. Or else she says "Run for it, Job!", and then they catch him like that . . . he's dead *anyway,* see?
Manners. *(trying to cover his annoyance)* It's not the script, it's *you.* Bronson does the writing, you do the acting, it's that simple.
Sheldon. One race, the human race. I like that.
Judy. Veal Parmesan with oodles and oodles of cheese!
Wiletta. I was just thinkin' if I could . . .
Manners. *(indicating script)* Address yourself to this.
Judy. *(to John)* Bring my book tomorrow.
John. Cross my heart.
Wiletta. I just wanted to talk about . . .
Manners. You are going to get a spanking. *(He leaves with Eddie and others.)*
Millie. Wiletta, come on!
Wiletta. *(abruptly)* I . . . I'll be there later.
Millie. *(miffed by the short answer)* Suit yourself.
Judy. *(to Wiletta)* It's on the corner of Sixth Avenue on this side of the street.
John. Correction. Correction, Avenue of the Americas.

(laughter from Manners, Millie, Sheldon and Bill offstage)

Judy. *(posturing in her best theatrical style)* But no one, absolutely no one, ever says it. He's impossible, absolutely impossible!
Wiletta. Oh, ain't he though.

John. *(bows to Judy and indicates that she goes first)* Dear Gaston, Alphonse will follow.

Wiletta. John, I told you everything wrong 'cause I didn't know better, that's the size of it. No fool like an old fool. You right, don't make sense to be bowin' and scrapin' and tommin'. . . . No, don't pay no attention to what I said.

John. *(completely Manners)* Wiletta, my dear, you're my sweetheart, I love you madly and I think you're wonderfully magnificent!

Judy. *(Judy suddenly notices his posturing and hers; she feels silly. She laughs, laughter bordering on tears.)* John, you're a puppet with strings attached and so am I. Everyone's a stranger and I'm the strangest of all. *(She quickly leaves.)*

John. Wiletta, don't forget to come over! *(He follows Judy.)*

Wiletta. *(paces up and down, tries doing her lines aloud)* Only one thing to do, give yourself up! Give yourself up . . . give up . . . give up . . . give up . . . give up . . . give up.

(Lights whirl and flicker. Blues record comes in loud—then down—lights flicker to indicate passage of time. Wiletta is gone. Stage is empty.

Bill enters, removing his coat. He has a slight attack of indigestion and belches his disapproval of pizza pie. Others can be heard laughing and talking offstage.)

Bill. Ohhhhhh, Ahhhhh. . . .

Manners. *(Enters with Eddie. Eddie proceeds to the table and script. Manners is just getting over the effects of a good laugh . . . but his mirth suddenly fades as he crosses to Bill.)* I am sorry you felt compelled to tell that joke about the colored minister and the stolen chicken.

Bill. Trying to be friendly . . . I don't know . . . I even ate pizza.

Eddie. I always *think* . . . think first, is this the right thing to say, would I want anyone to say this to me?

(burst of laughter from offstage)

Bill. Oh, you're so noble, you give me a pain in the ass. Love thy neighbor as thyself, now I ask you, is that a reasonable request?

Manners. *(for fear the others will hear)* All right. Knock it off.

Bill. Okay, I said I was sorry, but for what . . . I'll never know.

(Sheldon, Millie, Judy and John enter in a hilarious mood. Judy is definitely feeling the wine. Sheldon is supplying the fun.)

Sheldon. Sure, I was workin' my hind parts off . . . Superintendent of the buildin' . . .

John. But the tenants, Shel! That's a riot!

Sheldon. One day a man came along and offered me fifty dollars a week just to walk across the stage real slow. *(mimics his acting role)* Sure, I took it! Hard as I worked I was glad to slow down!

(Others laugh.)

Judy. *(holds her head)* Ohhhhhh, that wine.
Millie. Wasn't it good? I wanna get a whole *case* of it for the holidays. All that I have to do! My liquors, wreathes, presents, cards . . . I'm gonna buy my husband a tape recorder.
Judy. *(to John)* I'm sorry I hurt your feelings but you are a little puppet, and I'm a little puppet, and all the world. . . . *(She impresses the lesson by tapping John on his chest.)*
Manners. Judy, I want to go over something with you. . . .
Judy. No, you don't . . . you're afraid I'm going to . . . hic. 'Fraid I'll go overboard on the friendship deal and *com*plicate matters . . . complications. . . .
Manners. Two or three glasses of wine, she's delirious. Do you want some black coffee?
Judy. No, no, I only have hiccups.
Millie. *(to John)* Which would you rather have, a tape recorder or a camera?
John. I don't know.
Sheldon. I'd rather have some money, make mine cash.
Manners. *(to Judy)* Why don't you sit down and get yourself together? *(She sits.)*
John. *(to Manners)* I . . . I think I have some questions about Wiletta and the third act.
Manners. It's settled, don't worry, John, she's got it straight.
John. I know but it seems . . .
Manners. Hoskins sat out front yesterday afternoon. He's mad about you. First thing he says, "Somebody's going to try and steal that boy from us."
John. *(very pleased)* I'm glad I didn't know he was there.
Manners. Eddie, call it, will you? Okay, attention!
Eddie. Beginning of the third.

(Company quiets down, opens scripts. Wiletta enters.)

Manners. You're late.
Wiletta. I know it. *(to Millie)* I had a bowl of soup and was able to relate to it and justify, no trouble at all. *(to Manners)* I'm not gonna take up your time now but I wanta see you at the end of the afternoon.
Manners. Well . . . I . . . I'll let you know . . . we'll see.
Wiletta. It's important.

Manners. *(ignoring her and addressing entire company)* Attention, I want to touch on a corner of what we did this morning and then we'll highlight the rest of three!

(Actors rise and start for places.)

John, top of page four.

John. When a man has a decent word to say for us down here, I gonna vote for him.
Wiletta. *(with real force; she is lecturing him rather than scolding)* A decent word? And that's all you ever gonna get out of him. Dammit, he ain't gonna win nohow. They done said he ain't and they gonna see to it! And you gonna be dead for a decent word.
Manners. *(to Eddie)* This is deliberate.
John. I gotta go, I ain't gonna wait to be killed.
Wiletta. There's only one right thing to do. You got to go and give yourself up.
John. I ain't done nothin'.
Judy. My father will have Judge Willis put you in the County Jail where you'll be safe.

(Manners is quite disheartened.)

Wiletta. Job, she's tryin' to help us.
Judy. I'm thinking of the others even if you aren't. I don't want murder in this community.
Wiletta. Boy, get down on your knees.

(John falls to his knees.)

Oh, Lord, touch this boy's heart. Reach him tonight, take the fear and hatred out of his soul!
Sheldon. Hmmmmmm, mmmmmmm, mmmmmmmm. . . .
Millie. Mercy, Lord.
John. Stop, I can't stand anymore. . . .

(Wiletta tries to raise John.)

Manners. No, keep him on his knees.
John. I can't stand anymore . . . whatever you say. . . .

(Again Wiletta tries to raise him.)

Sheldon. *(to Wiletta)* He say keep him on his knees.
Wiletta. Aw, get up off the floor, wallowin' around like that.

(Everyone is shocked.)

Manners. Wiletta, this is not the time or place to . . .

Wiletta. All that crawlin' and goin' on before me . . . hell, I ain't the one tryin' to lynch him. This ain't sayin' nothin', don't make sense. Talkin' 'bout the truth is anything I can believe . . . well, I don't believe this.
Manners. I will not allow you to interrupt in this disorganized manner.
Wiletta. You been askin' me what I think and where things come from and how come I thought it and all that. Where is this comin' from?

(company murmuring in the background)

Tell me, why this boy's people turned against him? Why we sendin' him out into the teeth of a lynch mob? I'm his mother and I'm sendin' him to his death. This is a lie.
John. But his mother doesn't understand . . .
Wiletta. Everything people do is counta their mother . . . well, maybe so.
John. There have been cases of men dragged from their homes . . . for voting and asking others to vote.
Wiletta. But they was *dragged* . . . they come with guns and dragged 'em out. They weren't sent to be killed by their mama. The writer wants the damn white man to be the hero—and I'm the villain.
Millie. I think we're all tired.
Sheldon. Outta order, outta order, you outta order. This ain't the time.
Manners. Quiet please. She's confused and I'd just as soon have everything made clear.
Wiletta. Would you do this to a son of yours?
Manners. She places him in the hands of Judge Willis and . . .
Wiletta. And I tell you she knows better.
Bill. It's only because she trusts and believes. Couldn't you trust and believe in Al?
Manners. Bill, please.
Wiletta. No, I wouldn't trust him with my son's life.
Manners. Thank you.
Sheldon. She don't mean it.
Wiletta. Judge Willis! Why don't his people help him?
Manners. The story goes a certain way and . . .
Wiletta. It oughta go another way.
Entire Company. *(in unison)* Talk about it later. We're all tired. Yes. We need a rest. Sometime your own won't help you.
Manners. Leave her alone! *(Manners is on fire now. He loves the challenge of this conflict and is determined to win the battle. He must win.)* Why this great fear of death? Christ died for something and . . .
Wiletta. Sure, they came and got him and hauled him off to jail. His mother didn't turn him in, in fact, the one who did it was one of them so-called friends.
Manners. His death proved something. Job's death brings him the lesson.

Wiletta. That they should stop lynchin' *innocent* men! Fine thing! Lynch the guilty, is that the idea? The dark-skinned Oliver Twist. *(points to John)* That's you. Yeah, I mean, you got to go to school to justify this!

Manners. Wiletta, I've listened, I've heard you out . . .

Wiletta. *(to Sheldon)* And you echoin' every damn word he says—"Keep him on his knees."

Manners. I've heard you out and even though you think you know more than the author . . .

Wiletta. You don't want to hear. You are a prejudiced man, a prejudiced racist.

(gasp from company)

Manners. *(caught off-guard)* I will not accept that from you or anyone else.

Wiletta. I told this boy to laugh and grin at everything you said, well . . . I ain't laughin'.

Manners. While you give me hell-up-the-river, I'm supposed to stand here and take it with a tolerance beyond human endurance. I'm white! You think it's so wonderful to be white? I've got troubles up to here! But I don't expect anyone to hand me anything and it's high time you got rid of that notion. No, I never worked in a cotton field, I didn't. I was raised in a nice, comfortable, nine-room house in the mid-West . . . and I learned to say nigger, kike, sheeny, spick, dago, wop and chink . . . I hear 'em plenty! I was raised by a sweet, dear, kind old aunt, who spent her time gathering funds for missionaries . . . but she almost turned our town upside down when Mexicans moved in on our block. I know about troubles . . . my own! I've never been *handed* any gifts. Oh, it's so grand to be white! I had to crawl and knuckle under step by step. What I want and what I believe, indeed! I directed blood, guts, fist-fights, bedroom farces and the lowest kind of dirtied-up sex until I earned the respect of this business.

Wiletta. But would you send your son out to . . .

Manners. I proclaim this National Truth Week! Whites! You think we belong to one great, grand fraternity? They stole and snatched from me for years, and I'm a club member! Ever hear of an idea man? They picked my brains! They stripped me! They threw me cash and I let the credit go! My brains milked, while somebody else climbed on my back to take bows. But I didn't beg for mercy . . . why waste your breath? I learned one thing that's the only damned truth worth knowing . . . you get nothin' for nothin', but nothin'! No favors, no dreams served up on silver platters. Now . . . finally I get something for all of us . . . but it's not enough for you! I'm prejudiced! Get wise, there's damned few of us interested in putting on a colored show at all, much less one that's going to say anything. It's rough out here, it's a hard world! Do you think I can stick my neck out by telling the truth about you? There are billions of things that *can't be said* . . . do you follow me, billions! Where the hell do you think I can raise a hundred thousand dollars to tell the unvarnished truth? *(picks up the script and waves it)* So, maybe it's a lie . . . but it's one of the finest lies you'll come across for a damned long time! Here's bitter news, since you're livin' off truth. . . . The American public is not ready to see you the way you want to be seen because, one, they don't believe it, two, they don't want to believe it, and three, they're convinced they're superior—and that, my friend, is why Carrie and Renard have to carry the ball! Get it? Now you wise up and aim for the soft spot in that American heart, let 'em pity you, make 'em weep buckets, be helpless, make 'em feel so damned sorry for you that they'll lend a hand in easing up the pressure. You've got a free ride. Coast, baby, coast.

Wiletta. Would you send your son out to be murdered?

Manners. *(So wound up, he answers without thinking.)* Don't compare yourself to me! What goes for my son doesn't necessarily go for yours! Don't compare him *(points to John)* . . . with three strikes against him, don't compare him with my son, they've got nothing in common . . . not a Goddamn thing! *(He realizes what he has said, also that he has lost company sympathy. He is utterly confused and embarrassed by his own statement.)* I tried to make it clear.

John. It is clear.

(Manners quickly exits to dressing room. Eddie follows him. Judy has an impulse to follow.)

Bill. No, leave him alone.

John. *(to Wiletta)* I feel like a fool. . . . Hmmph, "Don't think Negro, think *people*."

Sheldon. *(to Bill)* You think he means we're fired?

Bill. I don't know . . . I don't know. . . .

Millie. Wiletta, this should have been discussed with everyone first.

Sheldon. Done talked yourself out of a job.

Bill. Shel, you don't know that.

Sheldon. *(During the following scene, Sheldon is more active and dynamic than ever before.)* Well, he didn't go out there to bake her no birthday cake.

(Judy is quietly crying.)

Millie. We got all the truth we bargained for and then some.

Wiletta. Yes, I spoke my mind and he spoke his.

Bill. We have a company representative, Sheldon is the deputy. Any complaints we have should be handled in an orderly manner. Equity has rules, the rule book says . . .

Sheldon. I left my rule book home. Furthermore, I don't think I want to be the deputy.

Millie. He was dead right about some things but I didn't appreciate that *last* remark.

Sheldon. *(to Wiletta)* You can't spit in somebody's eye and tell 'em you was washin' it out.

Bill. Sheldon, now is not the time to resign.

Sheldon. *(taking charge)* All right, I'm tryin' to lead 'em, tryin' to play peace-maker. Shame on y'all! Look at the U.N.!

Millie. The U.N.?

Sheldon. Yes, the United Nations. You think they run their business by blabbin' everything they think? No! They talk sweet and polite 'til they can outslick the next feller. Wisdom! The greatest gift in the world, they got it! *(to Wiletta)* Way you talked, I thought you had the 'tomic bomb.

Wiletta. I'm sick of people signifyin' we got no sense.

Sheldon. I know. I'm the only man in the house and what am I doin'? Whittlin' a doggone stick. But I whittled it, didn't I? I can't write a play and I got no money to put one on. . . . Yes! I'm gonna whittle my stick! *(stamps his foot to emphasize the point)*

John. *(very noble and very worried)* How do you go about putting in a notice?

Sheldon. *(to John)* Hold on 'til I get to you. *(to Wiletta)* Now, when he gets back here, you be sure and tell him.

Wiletta. Tell him what?

Sheldon. Damn, tell him you *sorry*.

Bill. Oh, he doesn't want that.

Wiletta. Shame on him if he does.

Millie. I don't want to spend the rest of the day wondering why he walked out.

Wiletta. I'm playin' a leadin' part and I want this script changed or else.

Sheldon. Hush up, before the man hears you.

Millie. Just make sure you're not the one to tell him. You're a great one for runnin' to management and telling your guts.

Sheldon. I never told management nothin', anybody say I did is lyin'.

Judy. Let's ask for a *quiet* talk to straighten things out.

Bill. No. This is between Wiletta and Manners and I'm sure they can . . .

John. We all ought to show some integrity.

Sheldon. Integrity . . . got us in a big mess.

Millie. *(to John)* You can't put in your notice until after opening night. You've got to follow Equity rules. . . .

Sheldon. Yeah, he's trying to defy the union.

Wiletta. *(thumping the script)* This is a damn lie.
Millie. But you can't tell people what to write, that's censorship.
Sheldon. *(to Wiletta)* And that's another point in your disfavor.
John. They can write what they want but we don't have to do it.
Sheldon. You outta order!
Bill. *(to John)* Oh, don't keep stirring it up, heaping on coals . . .
Judy. Wiletta, maybe if we appeal to Mr. Hoskins or Mr. Bronson . . .
Sheldon. The producer and the author ain't gonna listen to her, after all . . . they white same as Manners.
Judy. I resent that!
Bill. I do too, Shel.
Judy. I've had an awful lot of digs thrown at me . . . remarks about white, white . . . and I do resent it.
John. *(To Judy. He means what can you expect from Sheldon.)* Sheldon.
Bill. *(to Judy)* I'm glad you said that.
Sheldon. I'm sorry, I won't say nothin' 'bout white. *(to Wiletta)* Look here, Hoskins, Manners, and Bronson . . . they got things in . . . er . . . common, you know what I mean?
Wiletta. Leave me alone . . . and suit yourselves.
Millie. I know what's right but I need this job.
Sheldon. There you go . . . talk.
Wiletta. Thought your husband doesn't want you to work.
Millie. He doesn't but I have to anyway.
Judy. But you'll still be in New York. If this falls through I'll have to go back to Bridgeport . . . before I even get started.
John. Maybe I'll never get another job.
Millie. Like Al Manners says, there's more to this life than the truth. *(to Judy)* You'll have to go to Bridgeport. Oh, how I wish I had a Bridgeport.
Bill. Okay, enough, *I'm* the villain. I get plenty of work, forgive me.
Judy. Life scares me, honestly it does.
Sheldon. When you kick up a disturbance, the man's in his rights to call the cops . . . police car will come rollin' up here, next thing you know . . . you'll be servin' time.
Millie. Don't threaten her!
John. Why don't you call a cop *for* him . . . try it.

(Henry enters carrying a paper bag.)

Henry. I got Mr. Manners some nice Danish, cheese and prune.
Millie. He can't eat it right now . . . leave it there.

(Eddie enters with a shaken but stern attitude.)

Eddie. Attention company. You are all dismissed for the day. I'll telephone you about tomorrow's rehearsal.

Sheldon. Tell Mr. Manners I'm gonna memorize my first act.

(Eddie exits and Sheldon talks to company.)

I still owe the doctor money . . . and I can't lift no heavy boxes or be scrubbin' no floors. If I was a drinkin' man I'd get drunk.

Millie. Tomorrow is another day. Maybe everybody will be in better condition to . . . talk . . . just talk it all out. Let's go to the corner for coffee and a calm chat. *(suddenly solicitous with Judy)* How about you, honey, wouldn't you like to relax and look over the situation? Bill?

Bill. I have to study for my soap opera . . . but thanks.

Judy. Yes, let's go talk.

Millie. John? Wiletta, honey, let's go for coffee.

Wiletta. I'll be there after a while. Go on.

John. We couldn't go without you.

Sheldon. We don't want to leave you by yourself in this old theater.

Wiletta. There are times when you got to be alone. *This is mine.*

(John indicates that they should leave. Millie, Sheldon, Judy, John and Bill exit.)

Henry. Are you cryin'?

Wiletta. Yes.

Henry. Ah, don't do that. It's too nice a day. *(sits near tape recorder)* I started to throw coffee at him that time when he kicked up a fuss, but you got to take a lotta things in this life.

Wiletta. Divide and conquer . . . that's the way they get the upper hand. A telephone call for tomorrow's rehearsal . . . they won't call me. . . . But I'm gonna show up any damn way. The next move is his. He'll have to fire me.

Henry. Whatcha say?

Wiletta. We have to go further and do better.

Henry. That's a good one. I'll remember that. What's on this, music?

Wiletta. *(Turns the machine on and down. The applause plays.)* Canned applause. When you need a bit of instant praise . . . you turn it on . . . and there you are.

(He tries it.)

Henry. Canned applause. They got everything these days. Time flies. I bet you can't guess how old I am.

Wiletta. Not more than sixty.

Henry. I'm seventy-eight.

Wiletta. Imagine that. A fine-lookin' man like you.

(sound of police siren in street)

Henry. What's that?

Wiletta. Police siren.

Henry. They got a fire engine house next to where I live. God-in-heaven, you never heard such a noise . . . and I'm kinda deaf. . . . Didn't know that, did you?

Wiletta. No, I didn't. Some live by what they call great truths. Henry, I've always wanted to do somethin' real grand . . . in the theater . . . to stand forth at my best . . . to stand up here and do anything I want. . . .

Henry. Like my father . . . he was in vaudeville . . . doin' the softshoe and tippin' his hat to the ladies. . . .

Wiletta. Yes, somethin' grand.

Henry. *(adjusting the tape recorder to play applause)* Do it . . . do it. I'm the audience.

Wiletta. I don't remember anything grand . . . I can't recall.

Henry. Say somethin' from the Bible . . . like the twenty-third psalm.

Wiletta. Oh, I know. *(She comes downstage and recites beautifully from Psalm 133.)* Behold how good and how pleasant it is for brethren to dwell together in unity. It is like the precious ointment upon the head, that ran down upon the beard, even Aaron's beard; that went down to the skirts of his garment; as the dew of Hermon, and as the dew that descended upon the mountains of Zion; for there the Lord commanded the blessing, even life forevermore.

(Henry turns on applause as Wiletta stands tall for the Curtain.)

(Curtain)

In the Wine Time (1969)

Ed Bullins (b. 1935–)

One of the most talented and prolific dramatists identified with the Black Arts movement of the 1960s and 1970s, Ed Bullins was born and reared in Philadelphia. In the late 1950s, he moved to California, where he continued his education at Los Angeles City College and at San Francisco State University. Winner of numerous grants and awards, Bullins earned the Vernon Rice Drama Desk Award for 1968 (for *Three Plays by Ed Bullins*—"The Electronic Nigger," "A Son, Come Home," "Clara's Ole Man"). Three years later, he received the Black Arts Alliance Award (for *In New England Winter*) and the first of three Obie (Off Broadway) awards (for *The Fabulous Miss Marie*). In 1975, he was honored with the New York Drama Critics' Circle Award (for *The Taking of Miss Janie*).

Although his dramas display both nonrepresentational and representational techniques and reflect European as well as African American influence, Bullins is most frequently identified with black cultural nationalism and with the Black Arts drama that he created and promoted. Bullins has articulated and demonstrated his ideas in periodicals and anthologies that he edited and in works that he produced through Black Arts West (which he founded in 1965) and the New Lafayette Theatre (for which he served as playwright-in-residence and associate director from 1967 to 1972). Although he promoted the "agit prop" significance of the kind of drama that he identified as "black revolutionary drama" (see the headnote to *Great Goodness of Life* in this volume), most of Bullins's Black Arts dramas would be placed in the category that he identified as "Theatre of Black Experience." Rather than attempting to teach an African American audience a political lesson through didactic directness, Bullins more often attempts to require such an audience to infer the lesson to be learned. In order to educate the audience to awareness of the need to improve the black community, Bullins shows the audience the ugliness, the treachery, the disunity of the present community.

In the Wine Time was Bullins's first full-length drama and the first of his Twentieth Century Cycle (a proposed series of twenty plays). It depicts a sordid world in which dreams fade almost before they focus, a world in which love does not exist or can be expressed only through violence, a world in which only the naive fail to expect betrayal. Nevertheless, in this play, Bullins suggests a ray of optimism missing from most of his later work: Even though his own dreams have failed, Cliff Dawson encourages his nephew Ray to continue to seek his own dreams.

Selected Published Plays and Collections by Ed Bullins

The Duplex: A Black Love Fable in Four Movements. New York: Morrow, 1971.
Five Plays. Indianapolis: Bobbs-Merrill, 1969.
Four Dynamite Plays. New York: Morrow, 1972.
The Gentleman Caller. In *A Black Quartet: Four New Black Plays.* New York: New American Library, 1970.
How Do You Do: A Nonsense Drama. Mill Valley, CA: Illuminations Press, 1967.
In the Wine Time. In *Black Theatre,* ed. Lindsay Patterson. New York: New American Library, 1971.
The Taking of Miss Janie. In *Famous American Plays of the 1970s,* ed. Ted Hoffman. New York: Dell, 1981.
The Theme Is Blackness: The Corner and Other Plays. New York: Morrow, 1973.

Selected Edited Works by Ed Bullins

Black Theatre. 6 issues (1969–72). [A periodical].
The Drama Review. Black Theatre Issue, 12 (Summer 1968).
The New Lafayette Theatre Presents the Complete Plays and Aesthetic Comments by Six Black Playwrights. Garden City: Doubleday, 1974. Includes *The Fabulous Miss Marie* by Bullins.
New Plays from the Black Theatre. New York: Bantam, 1969. Includes *In New England Winter* by Bullins.

• •

In the Wine Time

In the Wine Time was first produced at the New Lafayette Theatre on December 10, 1968. The production was directed by Robert Macbeth. Sets were designed by Roberta Raysor, lighting by Ernest Baxter and Richard Macbeth. The cast was as follows:

CHARACTERS

Cliff Dawson	*Sonny Jim*
Lou Dawson, Cliff's wife	*Bette Jean Howard*
Ray, Lou's nephew	*Gary Bolling*
Miss Minny Garrison	*Rosanna Carter*
Bunny Gillette	*Helen Ellis*
Mrs. Krump	*Voice of V. Rachman Cyrille*
Eddie Krump	*Voice of Leopoldo Mandeville*
Beatrice	*Roberta Raysor*
Tiny	*Yvette Hawkins*
Silly Willy Clark	*Whitman Mayo*
Red	*Kris Keiser*
Bama	*George Miles*
Doris	*Peggy A. Kirkpatrick*
A Policeman	*Bill Lathan*

In this production the characters of Mr. Krump, the girl, and some Derby Street residents were omitted.

CAUTION NOTE

Professionals and amateurs are hereby warned that *In the Wine Time* is fully protected under the Copyright Laws of the United States of America, the British Commonwealth, including the Dominion of Canada, and all other countries of the International Copyright Union and Universal Copyright Convention, and are subject to royalty. All rights, including professional, amateur, motion picture, recitation, lecturing, public reading, radio and television broadcasting and the rights of translation into foreign languages are strictly reserved. Particular emphasis is laid on the question of readings, permission for which must be secured from the author's agent in writing.

All inquiries concerning the amateur and professional production rights to *In the Wine Time* by Ed Bullins should be addressed to the author's agent, Helen Merrill, Ltd., 435 West 23rd Street, Suite 1A, New York, NY 10011, USA. No amateur performance of the play may be given without obtaining, in advance, the written permission of Helen Merrill, Ltd.

All inquiries concerning rights (other than production rights) should also be addressed to Helen Merrill, Ltd.

THE PROLOGUE

She passed the corner every evening during my last wine time, wearing a light summer dress with big pockets, in small ballerina slippers, swinging her head back and to the side all special-like, hearing a private melody singing in her head. I waited for her each dusk, and for this she granted me a smile, but on some days her selfish tune would drift out to me in a hum; we shared the smile and sad tune and met for a moment each day but one of that long-ago summer.

The times I would be late she lingered, in the sweating twilight, at the corner in the barber shop doorway, ignoring the leers and coughs from within, until she saw me hurrying along the tenement fronts. On these days her yellow and pinks and whites would flash out from the smoked walls, beckoning me to hurry hurry to see the lights in her eyes before they fleeted away above the single smile, which would turn about and then down the street, hidden by the little pretty head. Then, afterwards, I would stand before the shop refusing to believe the slander from within.

"Ray . . . why do you act so stupid?" Lou asked each day I arose to await the rendezvous.

"I don't know . . . just do, that's all," I always explained.

"Well, if you know you're bein' a fool, why do you go on moonin' out there in the streets for *that?* . . ."

"She's a friend of mine, Lou . . . she's a friend."

August dragged in the wake of July in steaming sequence of sun and then hell and finally sweltering night. The nights found me awake with Cliff and Lou and our bottles of port, all waiting for the sun to rise again and then to sleep in dozes during the miserable hours. And then for me to wake hustling my liquor money and then to wait on the corner for my friend to pass.

"What'd the hell you say to her, Ray?" Cliff asked.

"Nothin'."

"Nothing?"

"Nawh . . . nothin'."

"Do you ever try?"

"Nawh," I said.

"Why? She's probably just waiting for you to . . ."

"Nawh, she's not. We don't need to say anything to each other. We know all we want to find out."

And we would go on like that until we were so loaded our voices would crack and break as fragile as eggs and the subject would escape us, flapping off over the roofs like a fat pigeon.

Summer and Cliff and Lou and me together—all poured from the same brew, all hating each other and loving, and consuming and never forgiving—but not letting go of the circle until the earth swung again into winter, bringing me closer to manhood and the freedom to do all the things that I had done for the past three summers.

We were the group, the gang. Cliff and Lou entangled within their union, soon to have Baby Man, and Henrietta, and Stinky, and Debra, and maybe who knows who by now. Summer and me wrapped in our embrace like lovers, accepting each as an inferior, continually finding faults and my weaknesses, pretending to forgive though never forgetting, always at each other's vitals . . . My coterie and my friend . . .

She with the swinging head and flat-footed stance and the single smile and private song for me. She was missing for a day in the last week of summer.

I waited on the corner until the night boiled up from the pavements and the wine time approached too uncomfortably.

Cliff didn't laugh when learning of my loss; Lou stole a half a glass more than I should have received. The night stewed us as we blocked the stoop fighting for air and more than our shares of the port, while the bandit patrol cruised by as sinister as gods.

She was there waiting next day, not smiling nor humming but waving me near. I approached and saw my very own smile.

"I love you, little boy," she said.

I nodded, trying to comprehend.

"You're my little boy, aren't you?" She took my hand. "I have to go away but I wanted to tell you this before I left." She looked into my eyes and over my shaggy uncut hair. "I must be years older than you, but you look so much older than I. In two more years you won't be able to stop with only wine," she said. "Do you have to do it?"

"I don't know . . . just do, that's all," I explained.

"I'm sorry, my dear," she said. "I must go now."

"Why?"

"I just must."

"Can I go with you?"

She let go of my hand and smiled for the last time.

"No, not now, but you can come find me when you're ready."

"But where?" I asked.

"Out in the world, little boy, out in the world. Remember, when you're ready, all you have to do is leave this place and come to me, I'll be waiting. All you'll need to do is search!"

Her eyes lighted for the last time before hiding behind the pretty head, swinging then away from me, carrying our sorrowful, secret tune.

I stood listening to the barber shop taunts follow her into the darkness, watching her until the wicked city night captured her; then I turned back to meet autumn and Cliff and Lou in our last wine time, meeting the years which had to hurry hurry so I could begin the search that I have not completed.

ACT I

The people in this play are black except for the Krumps and the Policeman.

Scene: *Derby Street. A small side street of a large northern American industrial city, in the early 1950's.*

At left, the houses stand together on one side of the street in unbroken relief, except for a tunnel-like alley which opens between the Krumps' and the Garrisons' houses, forming a low, two-storied canyon, the smoke-stained chimneys the pinnacles of the ridges. Four-letter words, arrowpierced hearts and slangy street-talk, scrawled in haste, smear a wooden fence, painted green, across the narrow street. Tattered posters of political candidates wearing scribbled, smudged mustaches, circuses of seasons passed and fading, golden and orange snuff containers decorate the enclosure. Each building's front is dull red, not brick colored, but a grey- and violent-tinged red, the shade the paint becomes after successive seasons of assault by the city's smoke- and grit-ladened atmosphere. Precise white lines, the older ones yellowing, outline each brick of the walls, and every house has a squat stoop of five white stone steps.

A raised level, upstage right, between the fence and the houses, represents "The Avenue."

From within the Dawsons' house black music of the period—called rhythm 'n blues by disc jockeys at that time—is heard not too loudly, and continues throughout the play, interrupted only seldom by amusing, jive-talking commercials for used cars, televisions, appliances, hair straighteners, and skin lighteners. Some of the recording stars of this season are King Pleasure, Johnnie Otis, Fats Domino, Little Esther, Ray Charles and "The Queen," Miss Dinah Washington. When Miss Minny Garrison raises her window gospel music can be heard.

At Rise: *It is a sultry evening in late August. All the steps are occupied by members of the various Derby Street households.*

At the end of the street, downstage, is a corner lighted by a streetlamp, the gasburning variety found still then in some sections of Philadelphia, Baltimore, New York and Boston.

All lights are down but the corner streetlamp, though dim shadows of the people on the stoops can be seen carrying on their evening activities: talking, gossiping, playing checkers and cards, drinking sodas, wine and beer.

Mr. Krump enters and stands at the streetlamp. He is very drunk.

Lights on the Krumps' doorstoop, the nearer to the corner.

The Krumps' front door opens and Mrs. Krump leans out.

The Radio. And here we are folks . . . on a black juicy, jammin' 'n' groovin' hot August night . . . yeah . . . one of them nights fo' bein' wit' tha one ya loves . . .

Mrs. Krump. *(strident, over the radio)* *Krumpy!* What cha doin' on da corner? Hey, Krumpy! Hey, Krumpy! . . . *Krumpy . . . Get the hell on over here!*

(light on third doorstoop)

Cliff. Heee . . . heee . . . look 'a ole man Krump work out.

(Bunny Gillette and Doris enter Derby Street at the corner and see Mr. Krump.)

Lou. Hush up, Cliff.
Cliff. Sheeet.
Bunny Gillette. Look 'a there, Doris!
Lou. Be quiet, Cliff. Will ya, huh?
Doris. Awww, shit, girl. That's nothin' . . . it just that goddamn Mr. Krump again . . . drunk out of his fucken' mind.
The Radio. It's eighty-two degrees . . . maaan, that's hot-oh-rooney . . . yeah, burnin' up this evenin' . . . red hot! . . . Ouch! . . . But we're cool on the Hep Harrison red-hot, up-tight, out-a-sight weather lookout indicator. That's eighty-two degrees . . . that's eight two out there . . . And here's a cool number that will hit you right where you're at . . . for your listenin' pleasure . . .

(Mrs. Krump has stepped to the center of Derby Street and calls up to her second-floor window as the music begins.)

Mrs. Krump. *(raspy, urban voice)* Hey, Edward . . . Hey, Edward . . . ! Hey, Edward . . . come on down here and get your fa'tha! Hey, Edward . . .
Doris. Hey, lissen ta that cow yell.
Bunny. Ain't it a shame, girl? *(Bunny starts off.)*
Cliff. *(disgust)* God dammit . . . Lou. You always tellin' me to be quiet . . . I don't even make half the noise that some of our *good* neighbors do.
Doris. *(to Bunny)* Where ya goin', broad?
Lou. *(sitting beside Cliff)* Awww . . . she should leave Mr. Krump alone. All he's doin' is peein' aside the pole . . . and then he's goin' in and go ta bed.
Bunny. Up on "The Avenue."
Doris. Where?

(Eddie Krump sticks his head from his upstairs window. He has dirty blond hair and a sharp, red nose. He is about eleven.)

Eddie. Ohhh, Christ, Ma . . . what'cha want?
Bunny. "The Avenue," Doris.
Mrs. Krump. *(furious)* Don't you Christ me, Edward . . . Come down here right away, young man!
Cliff. *(to Lou)* I bet he ain't gonna do it.
Doris. Ain't you gonna see Ray? That's what you come down this way for.
Lou. He might, Cliff. Besides . . . you the one that's always sayin' everybody here on Derby Street only does what they want to do most of the time, anyway.
Bunny. He's up there on the step . . . he could see me if he wanted . . . C'mon, girl . . . let's split.

(They exit.)

Cliff. 'Specially mindin' other people's business.

(Ray sits between Cliff and Lou, one step below them.)

Lou. Wasn't that Bunny, Ray?
Ray. Think I should go and help Mr. Krump out, Cliff?
Cliff. Nawh.

(pause)

Lou. Why, Cliff?
Cliff. You stay yo' ass here where ya belong, Ray.
Lou. Don't you talk like that, Cliff.
Mrs. Krump. *(to Eddie in window)* Eddie . . . are you comin' down here?
Eddie. Nawh.
Cliff. *(incredulous)* Did you hear that?
Lou. Remember . . . we mind our own business.

(From the upstairs window of the Garrisons' house, Miss Minny Garrison pushes her head; she has a bandanna tied about her head, and she is a huge black woman.)

Mrs. Krump. *(starting for her door)* I'm going to come up there and beat the hell out of you, Edward.

*(Eddie ducks his head in the window as his mother enters the door below.
  Sounds of Mrs. Krump's screams, the shouts of Eddie Krump and of running feet.
  Silence.
  Rhythm 'n blues and gospel music mingle softly.
  Red and Bama enter at the corner. They see Mr. Krump and nod to each other, then slowly, stiff-leggedly stalk about the streetlamp, tightening the circle about Mr. Krump on each full swing around.)*

Miss Minny. Ray . . . wha don't you help Mr. Krump git home?

(Ray stands and looks up at her.)

Ray. Yas'sum.
Cliff. *(to Ray)* Wha' . . . you gonna go down there and help? . . .

(Ray hesitates.)

Lou. Awww, Cliff . . . there ain't no harm in it.
Cliff. No harm?
Lou. Ray always does it.
Cliff. Well, it's about time he stopped.
Miss Minny. Go on, Ray. Go on and git Mr. Krump.
Ray. Yas'sum. *(He trots to the corner.)*
Cliff. *(mimics Ray in high falsetto)* Yas'sum.
Lou. *(angry)* Stop that, Cliff!
Cliff. Sheeet!
Red. Hey . . . Ray . . . is this lump ah shit a friend of yours? . . .
Ray. Nawh.
Lou. Why don't you stop that stuff, Cliff? Ain't nothin' bein' hurt because Ray's helpin' out Mr. Krump.
Bama. Maybe they're related.
Red. *(chuckling)* Hey, man, cool it. I know Ray don't play that. Do you, Ray?
Ray. *(trying to support Mr. Krump)* Nawh, Red. Nawh.
Red. *(to Bama)* See, Bama, Ray don't play the dozens. You better be careful.
Bama. Shit.

(Ray and Bama exchange stares. Bama is several years older than Ray.)

Red. You seen Bunny and Doris, Ray?
Ray. Yeah . . . they headed for "The Avenue."
Cliff. Nothin' bein' hurt? Just look at that. Look at that, Lou!

(Ray has slung Mr. Krump across his shoulder. He is husky and carries his load well.
  Standing, shouting.)

> Hey, Ray! Make sure his pants fly is zipped up or you'll be a victim of a horrible calamity!

Lou. You think you so smart, Cliff.
Bama. *(to Ray)* Tote dat bar', boy . . . lift dat bale.
Red. *(booting Ray in the seat of the pants)* Git along, little doggie.

(Cliff is pleased with himself but starts as Red kicks Ray and stands, but Lou

tugs at his trouser leg and he sits back down, chuckling over his wit, though scowling at Red and Bama who turn laughing and exit.

Ray carries his load to the Krumps' door. Cliff lights a cigarette and takes a drink. Lou tries to ignore him.

Mrs. Krump, wearing a perpetual worried expression, at her door.)

Mrs. Krump. Why, thank you, Ray. Just bring him in here and put him on the couch. Thank you, Ray. That Edward is just . . .

(They go in, Mrs. Krump at the rear, peering at Mr. Krump's head that dangles down Ray's back.)

Cliff. That goddamn Miss Minny's always startin' some shit!
Lou. Shusss . . . Cliff. She'll hear you.
Cliff. *(bitter)* I don't care if the big sow does. Always pretendin' her ears are filled with nothin' but holy holy *gospel* music . . . when they're nothin' but brimmin' with Derby Street dirt. *(mutters)* Ole bitch!
Lou. *(uneasy)* Cliff!
Cliff. *(looks up at Miss Minny)* Always startin' some trouble.

(Miss Minny closes her window. Her light goes off.)

Lou. See, she did hear you!
Cliff. I don't give a damn . . . who she thinks she is anyway?
Lou. Cliff, you just tryin' to start some trouble with Mr. Garrison. You wouldn't say those things if Homer were home.
Cliff. *(challenging)* Wouldn't I?
Lou. No, you wouldn't!
Cliff. I would do anything I do now if ole four-eyed Homer was sittin' right over there on that step pickin' his big nose.
Lou. He don't pick his nose no more.
Cliff. How do you know? Is that what Miss Minny told you?
Lou. No, Miss Minny didn't tell me a thing. His sister, Marigold, showed me a picture of him in his sergeant's uniform . . . and I know nobody in the United States Army who makes sergeant still picks their nose.
Cliff. Sheeet!

(silence)

Lou. Cliff?
Cliff. *(angry)* Look what you've done to that boy, Lou. Look what you and his mother . . .
Lou. *(angry)* Now don't you start in talkin' 'bout my dead sister!
Cliff. *(angrier)* Shut up! *(pause and stare)* Don't you see what all of you are tryin' to do . . . Miss Minny . . .
Lou. Who's tryin' to do what, Cliff?

Cliff. *(continues)* Miss Minny . . . you . . . all the so-called high-falutin' pussy on this block . . .
Lou. *(indignant)* Now you watch your mouth . . .
Cliff. Pussy! Cunt! Bitches! Always startin' some trouble.
Lou. *(apologetic)* That was no trouble, Cliff.
Cliff. It was so . . . Who the hell Miss Minny thinks she is anyway tellin' Ray to go down ther an' get ole man Krump? And gettin' kicked by that punk Red . . . Ray's nearly a man . . . he shouldn't . . .
Lou. *(cutting)* She didn't mean nothin' by it.
Cliff. Just like she didn't mean nothin' the time she passed around that petition to have us run off'a Derby Street when we first moved here.
Lou. She didn't know us then . . . we was strangers. Why don't you forget it?
Cliff. *(raising voice)* What's so strange about us, huh? What was so strange about us back then when we moved in? What was so strange? Was we strange because I was goin' ta school on the G.I. Bill and not totin' a lunch pail like all these other asses? . . .
Lou. Shusss . . . Cliff.
Cliff. I will not shusss . . . that's what they are, aren't they? Asses! Mules! Donkeys!
Lou. I'm goin' in if you keep that up, Cliff.
The Radio. . . . and Fat Abe . . . your local honest used car dealer is now offering a custom bargain fo' one of you real swingers out there . . .

(Cliff reaches up and pulls the door shut with a slam, muffling the radio.)

Cliff. You ain't goin' nowhere just because you don't want to hear the truth. *(Silence. Lou sulks.)* Well, they are asses . . . *(ridicule)* Derby Street Donkeys!
Lou. *(apologetic)* Well, I was workin', Cliff. And . . .
Cliff. *(cutting)* And they made a hell of a noise about that, too. Always whisperin' how you work so hard all day in a laundry for no count me who goes around carryin' books. And gets home in the middle of the afternoon and jest lays around like a playboy . . .
Lou. They did see you with them girls all the time, Cliff.
Cliff. I ain't been with no bitches.
Lou. Cliff . . .
Cliff. They're lies! That's all . . . every one a lie . . . and don't you let me hear you tell me them lies again.

(silence)

Lou. Never?
Cliff. Never!
Lou. What should I say when I find lipstick on your shirt . . . shades I don't

use. *(silence)* What should I say when I see you flirtin' with the young girls on the street and with my friends? *(silence)*

Cliff. *(tired)* Light me a cigarette, will ya? *(She does.)*

Lou. This street ain't so bad now.

Cliff. Was we so strange because your nephew Ray stays with us . . . and don't have to work *(bitter)* like an ass or mule or fool . . . like a Derby Street Donkey!

Lou. Cliff!

Cliff. Why was we so strange?

Lou. Nawh, we wasn't . . .

Cliff. Who wasn't?

Lou. We wasn't!

Cliff. Yes, we was!

Lou. Nawh . . . we seemed strange because we always drinkin' this . . . *(raising her glass)*

Cliff. Everybody else drinks somethin' around here . . . ole man Garrison puts at least a pint of white lightnin' away a night . . . pure'dee cooked corn whisky!

Lou. But their ignorant oil don't make them yell and hollar half the night like this wine makes us.

Cliff. *(yells)* Who yells!

Lou. *(amused)* . . . and we sing and laugh and you cuss like a sailor.

Cliff. Who sings and laughs? . . .

Lou. We do!

Cliff. You a liar!

Lou. Nawh, I'm not, Cliff. *(He grabs her arm and twists it behind her back.)*

Cliff. Say you a liar.

Lou. Nawh, Cliff . . . don't do that.

Cliff. *(twists it more)* Who's a liar?

Lou. I am, Cliff.

Cliff. *(a slight jerk)* Who?

Lou. *I am, Cliff. I am!* *(He releases her.)*

Cliff. That's right . . . sing out when I want you to. Ha ha ha . . . *(He tries to caress her.)*

Lou. *(rubs arm and shoves him)* Leave me alone.

Cliff. *(kisses her)* I'm glad you finally confessed . . . It'll do your soul some good.

Lou. *(sulking)* You shouldn't do that, Cliff.

Cliff. Do what?

Lou. You know what.

Cliff. Give you spiritual comfort? . . . Apply some soul ointment?

Lou. *(disgusted)* Awwww . . .

Cliff. I don't know if you never tell me, hon.
Lou. You know alright.
Cliff. That I cuss like a sailor?
Lou. *(remembering)* That's right . . . and . . .
Cliff. *(cutting)* Well, you didn't say that.
Lou. I didn't? *(pause)* I did too, Cliff.
Cliff. What?
Lou. Say that we yell and hollar and sing and laugh and cuss like sailors half the night.
Cliff. *(toasts her)* Ohhh, Lou. To Lou Lou, my Hottentot queen.
Lou. I'm not!
Cliff. My queen?
Lou. Hottentot! . . . My features are more northern . . . more Ethiopian.
Cliff. *(ridicule)* Haaaah! *(pause)* Haaaaah! More northern . . . more Ethiopian! That beak nose of yours comes from that shanty Irishman who screwed your grandmammy down on the plantation.
Lou. Watch your mouth, Cliff.
Cliff. Watch my mouth?
Lou. Yea, watch your mouth. Some things I just won't allow you to say.
Cliff. *(mocking)* "Some things I just won't allow you to say." *(offended)* Watch my mouth? Well, take a look at yours. Yours comes from that Ubangi great grandaddy on your father's side . . . your "northern" nose, well, we've gone through its . . .
Lou. *(warning)* Stop it, Cliff!
Cliff. . . . but your build is pure Hottentot, darling . . . and that's why I shall forever love you . . . however the Derby Street Donkeys bray about me being with other girls . . . younger, prettier girls, mind you . . . But Lou, baby, you are married to an "A" number one ass man . . . and *yours* is one of the Hottentot greats of northern America.
Lou. *(indignant)* Fuck you!
Cliff. *(fake dialect)* Wahl, hon-nee chile . . . I just wanted ta tell yawhl dat yo' husband is one of dem connoisseurs of dem fleshy Hottentot parts which'n yous is so wonderfully invested wit'.
Lou. Fuck you, Cliff! . . . Ohhh, just listen to that. You make me say bad things, man. You think you so smart and know all them big words since you been goin' to school. You still ain't nothin' but a lowdown bastard at heart as far as I'm concerned.

(Silence. Cliff takes a drink. Lou is wary but defiant.)

Cliff. *(smiles)* We do cuss too much, don't we?
Lou. *(smiles)* And we drink too much.

(He pulls her over and fondles her; she kisses him but pushes him away.)

Cliff. Like sailors?
Lou. Yes!
Cliff. *(amused)* I thought we cussed like sailors.
Lou. We do.
Cliff. *(raises voice)* Make up yo' mind, broad. Now what is it . . . do we cuss and drink like sailors or cuss like sailors and drink like . . . like . . . like . . . what?
Lou. Like niggers.

(At the last word lights go up on other stoops, revealing the occupants looking at Cliff and Lou.
 Then lights dim and come up on "The Avenue." The figures of Red, Bama, Doris and Bunny Gillette are seen.)

Bunny Gillette. Go on now, Red . . . stop messin' with me.
Red. Awww . . . woman . . . stop all your bullshit. You know you like me to feel your little ass . . . c'mere.
Doris. Stop fucken with that girl, Red.
Red. What's wrong, Doris? You jealous or somethin'?
Doris. Man . . . if you melted and turned to water and ran down the gutter I wouldn't even step over you.
Red. Why . . . scared I'd look up your dress and see your tonsils?
Bunny Gillette. *(giggling)* Ohhh . . . girl, ain't he bad.
Bama. C'mere, Doris. I wanna talk to you.
Doris. You ain't never wanted to talk to me before, Bama.

(Red has his arm about Bunny Gillette's waist. Bama takes Doris's hand.)

Red. C'mon, Bunny . . . I'll buy you a fish sandwich. *(to Bama)* Hey, Bam ah lam . . . do you think these broads deserve a fish sandwich?
Bama. Nawh, man, they don't deserve shit.
Doris. Hey, Bunny, we really hooked us some sports . . . you better make it back to Ray, girl.

(Lights down on "The Avenue."
 Lights up on Derby Street. Cliff and Lou laugh as Ray comes out of the Krumps'. The radio is muffled in the background.)

Mrs. Krump. *(off)* You sure you don't want another slice of cake and a glass of milk, Raymond?
Ray. Naw, thank you, Mrs. Krump.

(Eddie Krump sticks his head out of his window.)

Eddie. Thanks ah lot, Ray.
Ray. That's okay; why don't you come on down for a while?
Eddie. Nawh . . . I can't . . . I gotta headache.

Cliff. *(to Ray)* Little white Eddie don't want to come down after you carry his pissy pukey drunk daddy in for him, huh?
Lou. Cliff!
Ray. *(embarrassed)* Nawh.
Lou. Cliff . . . no wonder they sent around that petition. Just look how you act.
Cliff. *(angry)* Yeah, just look how I act . . . fuck how I act.
Lou. You got the dirtiest mouth, Cliff.
Cliff. *(angrier)* Fuck how I act . . . fuck it!

(Cliff stands and glares about at his neighbors. They turn their heads and resume their activities.)

Lou. Just like a sailor.
Cliff. *(satisfied)* Yup . . . just like I always said . . . folks on Derby Street sure know how to mind their own business.
Lou. Just like the no-'count sailor I met and married.
Cliff. Well, I am a mathafukken shit-ass sailor. The same you met and married, Lou.
Lou. Not any more.
Cliff. Still! I still am. Once a sailor . . . always a sailor.
Lou. Not any more. Besides . . . you stayed most of your time in the guardhouse.
Cliff. *(to Ray)* Listen to that . . . listen to that, Ray. Guardhouse.
Lou. That was the reason I married you. Felt sorry for you and knew your commanding officer would go light on you if he knew you had been married when you deserted and not put you in the guardhouse for so long.
Cliff. Yeah?
Lou. Yeah!
Cliff. Don't think you did me any favors, baby.
Lou. Well, who else did? I went to your ship and testified . . . I kept you from gettin' a bad discharge. In fact, I'm the one who made a man out of you even though your mother and the whole entire United States Navy failed.
Cliff. *(mutters)* Bitch!
Lou. Do you hear that? Failed . . . to make a man or a sailor of ya.
Cliff. *(ridicule)* Ray. This broad, pardon the expression, this woman named Lou . . . Lou Ellen Margarita Crawford Dawson . . . who calls herself your aunt, by the way . . .
Lou. I am his aunt!
Cliff. This bitch don't know what a sailor is.
Lou. I don't? . . . I don't? Then I guess you know even though you spent most of your navy time in the guardhouse.

Ray. Brig, Lou . . .
Cliff. Thank you, son. Thank you.
Lou. What? . . .
Ray. Brig, Lou . . . not guardhouse.
Cliff. That's right . . . that's fucken "A" right . . .
Lou. *(mutters and takes a drink)* Dirtiest mouth I ever heard.
Cliff. That's a lie . . . your sister has the dirtiest mouth in north, south, west and all of this town. *(to Ray)* That's your play-aunt Doris I'm talkin' about, Ray, not your dear dead mother . . . may she rest in peace . . .
Lou. You two-faced bastard. Listen to you soundin' like one of them white missionaries . . . "May she rest in peace . . ." Dirty-mouthed liar!
Cliff. Liar? About what? My not being in the guardhouse?
Ray. Brig.
Lou. You know that's not what I mean.
Cliff. Pour yourself a drink, Ray. Put some hair on your . . . ding-a-ling. *(begins humming)*
Lou. I pity the day you talked me into allowing Ray to take a drink.
Cliff. Whatta ya mean? He was a lush when he came here. His mother and him both almost drank themselves to death.
Lou. Cliff!
Cliff. *(defensive)* Ain't that right, Ray?
Ray. Sort'a. I did kinda drink along with Mamma for a while until they put her away.
Cliff. Sort'a? Stop jivin' . . . for a youngblood you can really hide some port.
Ray. *(flattered)* Yeah . . . I do my share.
Lou. Now, Ray, I want you to . . .
Cliff. *(loud)* Quiet! You heard him . . . he does his share. Here's a toast to you, youngblood. *(lifts his glass)* To Ray who does his share.

(They drink, except for Lou.)

Ray. Thanks, Cliff.
Cliff. Don't mention it, Ray. Just don't mention it at all. It's your world, son. It's really your world. *(to Lou)* Well, isn't it? *(silence)* You don't feel like toasting Ray? *(silence)* Ray . . . you know, Lou is a lot like your mother used to be. Quiet, except that your mother usually had a glass up to her mouth instead of her mouth clamped tight.
Lou. You shouldn't of said that, Cliff. You're goin'a pay for that.
Cliff. Pay? Ray, it's your world . . . does your ole Uncle Cliff have to pay?
Ray. Well, I don't . . .
Lou. *(cutting)* Stop it, Cliff. Ray, I'm sorry. Cliff gets too much to drink in him . . .

Cliff. *(loud, cutting)* Nice night we havin' out here on our white well-scrubbed steps . . .

(both together)

Lou. . . . and he runs off at the mouth somethin' terrible. I know you wasn't much past twelve when I came an' got you and kept them from puttin' you in a home. And you had already started in drinkin' 'n smokin' and foolin' around with girls . . . and I knew you drank too much for a growin' boy, much less a man. But I couldn't see you in a home—it would have messed you up . . . or sent down South to Cousin Frank's. I don't mean you so young you don't know what you want to do, Ray. I'm only six years older than you . . . but Cliff still shouldn't be givin' you so much wine and teachin' you bad habits. It ain't good for none of us, not even me. I hardly know where I'm at some of the times when I start in drinkin' after I come home from work . . . but it sho' do relaxes me. And your mother is gonna call me to account for it when we meet up in heaven . . . I really know that. The devil's in Cliff, I know that, to do what he's doin' to us . . . and I ain't helpin' things much. Listen to what I say, Ray, and not to the devil. Listen to me, Ray.

Cliff. . . . with all of God's white stars shinin' above your black heads. Ain't that right, Lord? You old shyster. You pour white heat on these niggers, these Derby Street Donkeys, in the daytime and roast and fry them while they shovel shit for nex' to nothin', and steam them at night like big black lobsters . . . ha ha . . . the Krumps are little red lobsters of Yourn . . . and they just drink, an' screw in the dark, and listen to jive talk an' jive music an' jive *holy* music . . . but they still think they have to face You in the mornin'. That's right, face You, You jive-ass sucker! They don't know they got to face Your jive-hot, blazin' face . . . simple niggers . . . but they do 'cause they believe in You and Your lies. Stupid donkeys! They only got to look my god in the face once and forget about You, You jive-time sucker . . . *(remembering an old joke)* . . . ha ha . . . she's black as night and as cool and slick as a king snake . . . *(singing)* . . . Yes, Lord, yes, Lord, yes, Lord, yes, Lord . . .

Lou. Stop it, Cliff! You're drunk 'n' crazy 'n' drivin' me out of my head!

(Silence. Cliff stares at her.)

Ray. *(to both)* It's all right. It's all right.

Lou. Ray, when I get to heaven your mother's gonna have a lot to say to me.
Cliff. *(laughs)* Heaven?
Lou. Yeah, heaven. And you better get some of the fear of the Lord in you, Cliff.
Cliff. *(disgust)* Every night. Every goddamn night when you start in feelin' your juice.
Lou. 'Cause I know better, that's why.
Cliff. Is that why when I get you in bed every night you hollar: *(whining falsetto)* "Yes, Lord. Yes, Lord. Ohhh . . . Jesus . . . one more time."

(Ray giggles.)

Lou. You're bad, Cliff. You're bad. Bad!
Cliff. Sho' I'm bad, hon-nee chile. *(singing)* I'm forty hands across mah chest . . . don't fear nothin' . . . not God nor death . . . I got a tombstone mind an' a graveyard disposition . . . I'm a bad mathafukker an' I don't mind . . . dyin'.
Lou. *(cutting)* You're just a dirty-mouthed . . .
Cliff. *(cutting)* Yeah, I know . . . and I'll have you know that just because I spent one third of my navy time in various brigs, not just one, understand, baby girl, but at least an even dozen between here and Istanbul, that I was still one of the saltiest salt water sailors in the fleet . . . on dry land, in the fleet or in some fucken marine brig!
Lou. You wasn't shit, Cliff . . . You know that, don't you?
Cliff. Sticks 'n' stones, Lou . . . sticks 'n' stones.
Lou. Pour me a drink, Ray . . . and give your no-'count step-uncle one too.

(Ray pours drinks for the three of them.)

Cliff. Step-uncle? Now how in Jesus' name did I get demoted from uncle to step?
Lou. You just did . . . suddenly you just stepped down.
Ray. Do you think I can get into the navy, Cliff?
Cliff. *(grabs Lou's arm)* Sometimes, Lou . . .
Ray. Huh, Cliff?
Cliff. *(recovering)* Navy? . . . Why sure . . . sure, Ray. When you come of age I'll sign the papers myself.
Lou. Steps can't, Cliff. But I can.
Cliff. I can, Lou . . . I should know. *(proudly)* I joined on my sixteenth birthday.
Lou. Steps can't.
Cliff. *(pinches her shoulder)* Bitch!
Lou. *(feigning)* Owww, Cliff. Owww.
Ray. If I'm of age then you won't have to sign, will ya?

Cliff. No, I won't. Not if you're of age, Ray.
Lou. He can't sign anyway.
Cliff. I can too, Ray. You just watch me when the time comes.
Ray. I'll be sixteen next week, Cliff.
Cliff. You will?
Ray. Yeah.
Cliff. Already?
Ray. Yeah.
Cliff. *(to Lou)* He will?
Lou. If that's what he says.
Cliff. Damn . . . so soon.
Lou. Sixteen ain't old enough. You have to be seventeen before they'll even let me sign for you, Ray.
Cliff. I went when I was sixteen . . . my sixteenth birthday.
Lou. *(peeved)* That's because you were down in Virginia in the woods . . . fool! They don't even have birth certificates down there . . . you could of went when you were thirteen if your mother had'a sworn you was old enough.
Cliff. I was too old enough!
Lou. No, you wasn't. And Ray ain't either. He's got to wait until he's seventeen. And then I might sign for him.
Ray. I got to wait? But Uncle Cliff said I could go.
Cliff. Yeah, you can go, Ray. I'll sign the papers myself. You're goin' to the navy and see how real men live.
Lou. *(angry)* He's not goin' . . . he's not old enough . . . and you ain't signin' no papers for him, Cliff. His mother wouldn't . . .
Cliff. I'll sign anything I want fo' him. I'm his guardian . . .
Lou. *(ridicule)* Guardian? How? With what? You ain't never had a job in your life over six months. What you raise him with . . . the few lousy bucks you don't drink up from your government check? You somebody's guardian . . . I . . .

(Cliff slaps her violently.)

Cliff. *(low, menacing)* You talk too much, Lou.
Lou. *(defiant)* It's my responsibility, Cliff. Mine. Mine. My responsibility. I'm not going to sign or let you sign. His mother . . .
Cliff. Damn that! Damn it! I don't care what his dead mother wants. Who the hell cares what the dead want? It's what Ray wants that counts. He's got to get out of here . . . don't you, Ray? . . . Off'a Derby Street and away from here so he can grow up to be his own man.
Lou. *(crying)* Like you?
Cliff. No, not like me . . . not tied down to a half-grown, scared, childish bitch!

Lou. You don't have to be.
Cliff. But I love you.

(Lights down, up on "The Avenue." Red slaps Bunny Gillette.)

Doris. Red . . . you mathafukker . . . Stop that!
Bunny Gillette. *(crying)* Go on now, Red. Leave me alone . . .
Red. Bitch! Who you think you tellin' to kiss your ass? You want me to kiss your nasty ass?
Bama. *(reaching for him)* Hey, lighten up, Red.
Doris. Leave her alone!
Red. *(being held by Bama)* You want me to kiss your . . .
Bunny Gillette. Nawh, Red. Nawh.
Doris. *(a short knife in her hand)* You better not touch her again . . . you better not. You goin'a be sorry for this.

(lights down on "The Avenue" and up on Derby Street)

Ray. I'm sorry, Lou.
Lou. It's alright, Ray. We've fought before . . . I'm just sorry you have to see us act like this.
Cliff. Awww, honey . . . I'll forget it if you do.
Lou. You beat on me and I'm supposed to forget it? In my condition.
Cliff. You got nearly six months before the baby. He can't get hurt by just a little . . .
Lou. You know the doctor told you not to be hittin' on me no mo'. You did it on purpose 'cause you don't want it.
Cliff. I'm sorry, Lou.
Lou. It's a wonder you didn't hit me in the stomach.
Cliff. Well, it's a wonder I didn't.
Lou. See there. You don't want it.
Cliff. Nawh, I don't want a baby I can't take care of . . . do you?
Lou. You can get a job.
Cliff. At a dollar an hour? Dollar-an-hour Dawson, that's me. Nawh, I don't want any kids until I can afford them. That's why I'm goin' ta school.
Lou. You studying business so you can take care of me an' your kids? What kind of job can you get in business? You got money to open you a business?
Cliff. Lou, we've gone over this before. I'll manage.
Lou. Like you have gettin' a job?
Cliff. Well, you want me to get a job in the laundry? Like all your cousins?
Lou. And me!
Cliff. Startin' at a buck an hour. Hell no, I won't work!
Lou. *(scared)* But what are we goin'a do when your checks run out, Cliff?

Cliff. Me? I'll do the best I can. Maybe ship out again.
Lou. No, Cliff!
Cliff. If I can't turn up anything . . . well, you and the kid can get on relief.

(silence)

Lou. Where's your pride? A big strong man like . . .
Cliff. A dollar an hour don't buy that much pride, Lou. There's a big rich world out there . . . I'm goin'a get me part of it or not at all.

(both together)

Lou. You ain't no man. My daddy he worked twenty years with his hands . . . his poor hands are hard and rough with corns and callouses. He was a man . . . he worked and brought us up to take pride in ourselves and to fear God. What did I marry? I thought you was a man, Cliff. I thought because you was loud and was always fightin' and drinkin' and was so big and strong that you was a man . . . but you ain't nothin' but a lowdown and less than nothin'!

Cliff. I'm goin' ta get me part of that world or stare your God in the eye and scream *why*. I am not a beast . . . an animal to be used for the plows of the world. But if I am then I'll act like one, I'll be one and turn this fucken world of dreams and lies and fairy tales into a jungle or a desert. And I don't give much of a happy fuck which. There's a world out there, woman. Just beyond that lamppost . . . just across "The Avenue" and it'll be mine and Ray's.

Lou. *(screams) You're nothin'!*
Cliff. In the navy Ray can travel and see things and learn and meet lots of different . . .
Lou. *No!!!*
Cliff. . . . girls and make somethin' . . .
Lou. *Is that what it did for you?*
Cliff. Yeah, that's what it did for me!
Lou. Well, I don't want him to be like you.
Cliff. How would you want him to be like . . . one of the Derby Street Donkeys? Or one of the ditty boppers or an avenue hype . . . or . . . a drug addict . . . or what?
Lou. *(standing)* He ain't turned out so bad so far. *(determined)* He's not goin', Cliff. *(pause)* Ray, just get it out of your mind. I'm not signin' no navy papers . . . you're too young.

(She enters the house as the lights fade to blackness.)

(Curtain)

ACT II
. . . . . .

Mythic blues plays. Lights up on "The Avenue."
The couples are in embrace.

Bunny Gillette. *(to Red)* I like you a lot . . . really I do . . . but what will Ray say?
Red. Fuck that little punk!
Doris. *(to Red)* What you say 'bout my nephew?
Bama. He wasn't talkin' to you, Doris.
Bunny Gillette. You ain't gonna fight me anymo' . . . are ya, Red?
Doris. I'd cut that nigger's nut off if he had'a hit me like that, Bunny!
Bama. You wouldn'a do nothin', Doris . . . you just . . .
Doris. Yeah, I would . . . and that goes double for any jive nigger who lays a finger on me or mine!
Red. *(places his hands on Bunny's rear)* Why don't all you mathafukkers shut up! Can't you see I'm concentratin'?

(Lights down, up on Derby Street.
Cliff and Ray sit upon their stoop. The remainder of the street is in shadow.
Silence.
From the last stoop up the street Beatrice detaches herself from the shadows and walks toward the corner.
She is a buxom, brown girl and carries herself proudly. She speaks as she passes each shadowy group of forms upon the stoops.)

The Radio. It's seventy-eight degrees . . . that's seven . . . eight . . .
Beatrice. *(passing)* Hello, Mr. Cooper. Miz Cooper.
Shadows. Hello, Beatrice. How you doin' tonight?
Beatrice. *(passing)* Hello, Miss Francis.
Shadows. Why hello, Bea. How ya doin', girl?
Beatrice. *(passing)* Hello, Mr. Roy.
Shadows. Howdy, Beatrice. How's your folks?
Beatrice. Just fine.

(She passes on.
Miss Minny puts her head out her window. Beatrice passes Cliff and Ray without speaking, her pug nose up, her head sighting on something upon the Derby Street fence, on the far side of the street.
Beatrice comes abreast the Garrisons' house and looks up.)

Hello, Miss Minny.
Miss Minny. Hello, Beatrice . . . how y'all?

Beatrice. *(stops)* Just fine, Miss Minny. How's Marigold and Ruth?
Miss Minny. Awww . . . they're fine, Beatrice. They off visitin' mah sister this week.
Beatrice. That's nice, Miss Minny. Tell them I asked about them, will ya?
Miss Minny. All right, dear. Did you know that Homer asked about you in his last letter?
Beatrice. No, I didn't. Is he still in Korea?
Miss Minny. Yeah, he's still over there. They done made him a sergeant.
Beatrice. Yes, I know. Marigold told me. He's doing okay, isn't he?
Miss Minny. Oh, yes, he's just doin' fine and everything. Says he likes it over there.
Beatrice. Tell him I asked about him, will you?
Miss Minny. All right, Beatrice.

(Beatrice continues, and reaching the corner, she exits. Miss Minny withdraws and shuts her window.)

The Radio. . . . And now the genius of the great . . .

(Music plays, softly.)

Cliff. Sheeet.
Ray. What'cha say, Cliff?

*(Silence.
Both together.)*

Cliff. I said that . . .   **Ray.** I wonder if . . .

*(Silence.
Both together.)*

(annoyed) Go on!   *(embarrassed)* Excuse me.

(lengthy silence; both take drinks and drag upon their cigarettes)

Cliff. *(hurriedly)* How old's that broad?
Ray. How old? . . .
Cliff. Yeah.
Ray. Oh, Bea? . . . About my age, I guess.
Cliff. She's certainly a snotty little stuckup heifer, ain't she?
Ray. Yeah, I guess so.

*(Silence.
Both together.)*

Cliff. *(almost leering)* I wonder   **Ray.** *(explaining)* She's
what . . .   always . . .

(Both halt. Cliff stubs out his cigarette.)

Cliff. *(yells over his shoulder)* Hey, Lou! *(no answer; to Ray)* Guess she's out back in the kitchen or the john.
Ray. Yeah.
Cliff. Ray?
Ray. Huh?
Cliff. Did you ever get any ah that?
Ray. Beatrice?
Cliff. Yeah.
Ray. Nawh.
Cliff. What she doin', savin' it for Homer?
Ray. Homer? *(laughing)* She can't stand Homer. Calls him "Ole Country."
Cliff. What'cha waitin' on, boy?
Ray. Nothin'.
Cliff. When I was yo' age I'd ah had every little pussy on Derby Street all to myself.
Ray. You'd have them all sewed up, huh?
Cliff. *(not perceiving Ray's humor)* Yeah, sho' would.
Ray. Ahhhuh.
Cliff. How 'bout Marigold and Ruth?
Ray. What about them?
Cliff. You ain't gettin' none of that either?
Ray. Nawh.
Cliff. Why not, boy? What's the matter with you?
Ray. Nothin'.
Cliff. Nothing?
Ray. Nawh, nothin'.
Cliff. With all this good stuff runnin' 'round here you lettin' the chance of a lifetime slip by . . .
Ray. Yeah, I guess I am.
Cliff. . . . always over there on Thirteenth Street messin' round with li'l Bunny when you should be takin' care of business back home.
Ray. I don't like any of the girls round here.
Cliff. What's wrong with them? A girl's a girl . . . well, most of them are anyway.
Ray. *(embarrassed)* Well, I like Bunny. Me and her's in love.
Cliff. In love? In love? *(cracking the door and over the music)* Hey, Lou Ellen . . . Your nephew's in love! *(no answer; muttering)* Musta' fell in. *(looking at Ray)* Boy . . . you got a lot to learn.
Ray. I can't help it, Cliff. And she loves me too.
Cliff. Ohhh, yeah . . . you really got a lot to learn.
Ray. Cliff . . . I . . .

Cliff. Just because she comes down here with you on the nights that me and Lou are out don't make you be in love. You didn't think I knew, huh? Well, who the hell you think been turnin' those pillows on the couch over an' wipin' them off? Not your Aunt Lou . . . nawh nawh, she'd damn near die if she knew you were doin' what comes naturally.
Ray. I'm sorry, Cliff.
Cliff. Forget it. Oh yeah, now that reminds me. Clean up your own mess from now on. You're big enough.
Ray. Okay.
Cliff. Bunny's the first girl you've had?
Ray. Nawh.
Cliff. How many?
Ray. 'Bout half a dozen.

(silence)

Cliff. Well . . . you ain't exactly backward . . . but still when I was your age . . . but let's forget about that.
Ray. Okay.
Cliff. Now what about Marigold and Ruth, don't they like you?
Ray. All the girls on the street like me, I guess . . . 'cept'n Beatrice 'n' she used to let me kiss her . . .
Cliff. She did, huh? Well, what happened?
Ray. I don't know.
Cliff. Well, why don't you get one of the girls next door? Screw one of Homer's sisters. *(chuckling)* Get some of his stuff while he's away.
Ray. Yeah . . . yeah, Marigold likes me a lot. Homer even wants me to get Marigold so I might have to marry her and he'd have a brother-in-law he'd like, but she don't want it, not like that, and I don't see the sense of goin' with a girl if I can't do it to her.
Cliff. You showin' some sense there, Ray. An' forget about that marriage stuff too.
Ray. Yeah, and Ruth wants to get married too bad. I'm scared as hell of her.

(silence)

Cliff. Yeah, you better stick with fast little Bunny. Gettin' you in the service is gonna be hard enough . . . If your aunt knew that anyone was thinkin' about you and marriage . . . we'd really have a case on our hands. She'd probably lock you up in the cellar.
Ray. *(contemplating)* And Beatrice thinks she's better than anybody else.
Cliff. Yeah. I guess you do know what you're doin' stickin' with Bunny. But you'll be gone in a month anyway.
Ray. In a week.

Cliff. Yeah, that's right . . . in a week . . . And things will be different then for you. *(pause)* Hey, do you know what, Ray?
Ray. *(slowly)* I met a girl the other day.
Cliff. Do you know what, Ray?
Ray. I met a girl the other day, Cliff.
Cliff. You did?
Ray. *(more sure)* Yeah, I met her the other day . . . she's almost a woman.
Cliff. She is?
Ray. A pretty girl.
Cliff. You met her where, Ray?

(Lights down, and up on "The Avenue."

The girl appears and stands under soft light. She has huge eyes and her skin is a soft black.

The couples are fixed in tableau but Red and Bama pull away from Bunny Gillette and Doris and dance about the girl in a seduction dance, until the two girls break their position and dance against the attraction of the girl, in a symbolic castration of the boys.

Lights down to fantasy hues on "The Avenue" and up on Cliff and Ray.)

Ray. I met her over on "The Avenue."
Cliff. Yeah, and she was pretty?
Ray. Yeah.
Cliff. That's good. But you better not get stuck on her.
Ray. Why? Why, Cliff?
Cliff. 'Cause you goin' away in a month. You goin' to the navy, remember?
Ray. But she can wait for me.
Cliff. Well . . . most women are funny. They don't wait around too long. They get anxious . . . you know, nervous that they won't get something that they think belongs to them. Never could understand what that somethin' was, but most of them are on the lookout for it, whinin' for it all the time, demandin' it. And I guess some of them even get it.
Ray. She'll wait.
Cliff. Don't be too sure, son. Most of them don't.
Ray. Lou waited for you, didn't she? *(silence)* Didn't she? *(silence)*
Cliff. Yeah . . . but that was a little different.
Ray. How?
Cliff. It was just different . . . that's all.
Ray. But how would it be different for you and Lou and not for me and my girl?
Cliff. Well, for one, I don't know your girl so I can't say positively just how she'd act . . . And, two, and you better not breathe a word of this to your aunt . . . you hear? *(pause)* Well, Lou Ellen is different because . . . well, because she's got character.

Ray. My girl . . .
Cliff. *(cutting)* And your aunt's got principle and conviction and you have to be awfully special for that.
Ray. But, Cliff . . .
Cliff. *(continuing)* . . . Now don't tell her, your aunt, I said these things, but she's special in that way.
Ray. I won't tell her.
Cliff. For someone to have all of them qualities in these times is close to bein' insane. She's either got to be hopelessly ignorant or have the faith of an angel . . . and she's neither.
Ray. Nawh, I don't guess she is.
Cliff. I don't deserve her, I know.
Ray. You two pretty happy together, aren't you?
Cliff. Ray?
Ray. Yeah.
Cliff. Don't think about her too much.
Ray. Lou?
Cliff. Nawh . . . you know. Your girl.
Ray. Oh.
Cliff. Yeah.
Ray. *(distant)* Yeah, I guess so.
Cliff. Why do you say it like that?
Ray. Awww, I was just thinkin'. Lou says I can't go . . . and . . . and this girl . . . she . . . well, I see her every day now and . . .
Cliff. Have you . . .
Ray. *(upset, cutting)* Nawh! We don't . . . we don't need to do anything. We just look at each other and smile . . . that's all.
Cliff. Smile?
Ray. Yeah.
Cliff. What else?
Ray. That's all. I just wait on the corner for her every afternoon and she comes dancing along with her little funny walk and sometimes she hums or sings to me a while . . . then smiles some more and goes away . . .

(lights down on "The Avenue" and the dancers)

Cliff. Boy, you better git yourself another drink.
Ray. I won't see her no more if I go to the navy, Cliff.
Cliff. There's other things to see. Get her out of your head, Ray. There's a lot more fish in the ocean . . . ha ha . . . and a lot more girls where she came from. Girls all sizes and shapes . . .
Ray. *(protesting)* You don't know where she came from!
Cliff. Why don't I? I just need to take one look at any girl and I know all about her. And with yours . . . well, your just tellin' me about her

makes me know. I know all about her, Ray. And let me give you some advice . . . now you trust me, don't you? *(pause)* Good. I want you to stay away from her. There's all kinds of girls on this stinkin' planet . . . speakin' all kinds of tongues you never would think of, comin' in all kinds of shades and colors and everything. When you become a swabby, the world will open up to you.

Say, maybe you'll go to France . . . to Nice or Marseilles . . . the Riviera. Lie out in the hot sun . . . you won't need a suntan but you can lie out there anyway so those tourists and Frenchmen can see you and envy you. And you'll see all those sexy French broads in their handkerchief bathin' suits. Yeah, I can see you now, Ray, out there in your bright red trunks with sunglasses on peekin' at those girls. Or maybe you'll go to Italy and git you some of that dago stuff. Ha ha ha . . . best damn poon tang in the world, boy. *(He ruffles Ray's woolly head and takes a goodsized drink.)* Ha ha ha . . . put hair on your tonsils. *(pause; laughing)* Yeah, there's nothin' like walkin' down a street in your navy blues. You know . . . you know . . . you should get tailor-made, skin tights, Ray, with buttons up both sides, and have your wallet slung around back of your pants . . . I can see you now. Your wallet will be fat as a Bible. And . . . and the pretty little broads will be callin' out to you. "Hey, Yankee! Hey, sailor! Hey, Joe! Fucky fucky . . . two American dollah!" Ha ha ha ha . . . yeah!

Yeah, that's livin', Ray. That's livin'.

Ray. *(enthused)* Is it, Cliff? Is it?

Cliff. In some ports you can get a quart of the best imported whisky for two bucks and in some ports you can get the best brandy for only a buck or so.

And the nights . . . ahhh . . . the nights at sea, boy. Ain't nothin' like it. To be on watch on a summer night in the South Atlantic or the Mediterranean when the moon is full is enough to give a year of your life for, Ray. The moon comes from away off and is all silvery, slidin' across the rollin' ocean like a path of cold, wet white fire, straight into your eye. Nothin' like it. Nothin' like it to be at sea . . . unless it's to be in port with a good broad and some mellow booze.

Ray. Do you think I can get in, Cliff?

Cliff. Sure you can. Sure. Don't worry none about what your Aunt Lou says . . . I've got her number. I'll fix it up.

Ray. I sure hope you can.

Cliff. Sure I can. As long as I tell your aunt I'm fixin' to ship out she'll sell you, herself, and probably her soul to keep me with her.

Ray. *(frowning)* You goin'a ship out, Cliff?

Cliff. Nawh . . . nawh . . . I had my crack at the world . . . and I've made it worse, if anything . . . you youngbloods own the future . . .

remember that . . . I had my chance. All I can do now is sit back and raise fat babies. It's your world now, boy.

(Tiny rounds the corner.)

Well, here comes Tiny. *(knocks on door behind him with his elbow)* Lou. Lou. Here comes Tiny.

(It has gotten darker and the shadowy figures have disappeared from the other stoops, into the doors of the houses, one after another.)

Lou. *(off)* What'cha want, Cliff? I just washed my hair.
Cliff. It's Tiny . . . she's comin' down the street.

(Tiny is a small, attractive girl in her late teens. As she comes abreast of the alley a large man in wide-brimmed hat jumps out at her and shouts.)

Clark. *Boo!*
Tiny. *Aaaaaiieeeeeee!!!*

(After the scream there is recognition between the two and Clark laughs, nearly hysterically, and begins trotting first in a circle about Tiny, who looks furious enough to cry, then across the street to the fence where he leans and laughs, pounding the boards with his fists.
   Windows go up.)

Mrs. Krump. Is anything wrong?
Miss Minny. What's all dat noise out dere?
Lou. *(at door, her hair disheveled)* Clark, you shouldn't go 'round scarin' people like that!

(The policeman passes the corner and stops and looks over the scene.)

Tiny. *(regains breath)* You ole stupid mathafukker!
Mrs. Krump. Is anyone hurt?
Cliff. *(stands, his arm around Tiny's shoulder)* Nawh, Krumpy . . . the goddamn natives are restless, that's all.
Mrs. Krump. Ohhhh . . . I'm sorry . . . I just wanted to help.

(Her window closes.)

Miss Minny. You and your friends shouldn't all the time be usin' that kinda language, Cliff . . . gives the street a bad name. We got enough bad streets and boys around here without you makin' it worse.
Cliff. If you kept your head in where it belongs you wouldn't hear so much, Miss Minny. Now would you?
Miss Minny. I'm gonna talk to somebody 'bout you, Cliff. Somethin' should be done about you.

(Her window closes.)

The Policeman. Is everything okay, Cliff?
Cliff. Yeah, Officer Murphy. Everything's great.
The Policeman. Well keep it that way. I want it quiet around here, Cliff.

(The policeman turns the corner.)

Ray. His name's not Murphy, Cliff.
Cliff. To me it is . . . If he doesn't know to call my right name I don't know his.
Ray. He said Cliff.
Cliff. Yeah, he said Cliff like he was sayin' boy. He didn't say Mr. Dawson.
Lou. *(ridicule)* Mr. Dawson . . . and his mob.
Tiny. I'm sorry, Cliff. I didn't mean to make all that noise . . . but that stupid ole Clarkie over there . . .
Cliff. That's okay, Tiny. It's not your fault. Old nose for news up there has been after us as long as I can remember. *(to Clark)* Hey, Silly Willy . . . come the hell on over here and stop tryin' to tear down those people's fence . . . besides, it wasn't that funny anyway.
Ray. You sho' can hollar, Tiny.
Tiny. I was afraid, man. Some big old stupid thing like that jumps out at you. Damn, man . . . I'm just a little thing . . . he makes two of me.
Lou. From the way you hollar, sister, I know they'll have to want you really bad to get you.
Tiny. Fucken "A," baby. If they want mah little ass they gonna have to bring ass.
Cliff. With Clark's big bad feet he couldn't catch a cold.
Tiny. I should'a known better than to be walkin' along beside some alley, anyway. If I hadn't seen you folks up here on the steps I would'a been out in the middle of the street with runnin' 'n' hollarin' room all around.
Ray. You still didn't do so bad.

(Clark comes over, snuffling and wheezing. He has a large moon face and is in his early thirties.)

Clark. *(giggles)* I'm sorry, Tiny . . . ha ha ha . . . but I couldn't help myself when I saw you over on Ninth Street turn the corner.
Tiny. *(peeved)* You been following me that long, man?
Clark. *(nearly convulsed)* Heee heee . . . yeah, I ran through the alley and waited . . . and . . . heee heee . . . and when . . . heee heee . . . I heard your walk I jumped out.
Lou. *(angry)* Somebody's goin'a shoot you, you old dumb nut.
Ray. Wow, Tiny, you almost scared me. You sure can hollar.

Tiny. Yeah, man, I really can when somethin's after me.

Lou. C'mon, girl. C'mon in while I fix my hair. *(Lou's hair is long and bushy, just having been washed. It covers her head like a gigantic crown.)*

Tiny. *(steps across Ray)* Okay, girl. Hey, Ray, don't cha look up my dress.

Ray. *(jest)* Why not, Tiny?

Tiny. You must think you're gettin' big, boy.

Ray. *(drawl)* I is.

Lou. Not that big, boy.

Cliff. Why do you keep pesterin' the boy, Lou? If he didn't try and look I'd be wonderin' what's wrong with him.

Lou. Is that what you do, look?

Cliff. What do you think?

(Silence.
   Clark begins snuffling.)

Lou. The only thing that's wrong with Ray is you, Cliff. I know some of those nasty things you been tellin' him.

(Silence. Lou and Cliff stare at each other.)

Tiny. I saw Doris and Bunny, Lou. *(pause)* They said they'd be over. Said they had some business to take care of. *(pause)*

Clark. Doris comin' over?

Tiny. *(to Clark)* Yeah . . . yeah, stupid ass. She said she'd be down. And Ray, Bunny said you'd better keep yo' ass home too. She wants to ask you some questions about that girl you been seein' out on "The Avenue."

Ray. What did she say?

Cliff. *(grinning)* So it's finally got back home.

Lou. *(hostile)* Yeah, it's gotten back. You don't like it?

Tiny. She said you'd better keep yo' black ass home, Ray. That's what she said.

Cliff. *(weary)* Awww . . . Lou . . . please.

Lou. Followin' after you the way he does it's a wonder he ain't always in some trouble.

Cliff. *(caressing her leg)* But, baby . . .

(She pulls her leg back.)

Ray. *(angry)* What she mean I better keep mah black ass home? I'll go where I want . . . with who I want. She better watch it . . . or I won't be lettin' her come down here.

Clark. Hey, listen to Tiger.

Lou. I ain't gonna let you start anything with little Bunny, you hear, Ray? Don't be hittin' on that little girl.

Ray. Awwww . . . sheeet.
Lou. What'd you say?
Cliff. What'd it sound like he said?
Lou. Now you keep out of this, Cliff.
Clark. You women folks are sho somethin' else.
Tiny. You shut your mouth and mind your business, Clark.
Lou. Now listen here, Ray. Don't you talk to me like that, frownin' up your face an' rollin' yo' eyes. You gittin' too mannish 'round here. You hear?

(Ray doesn't answer, but gives a deep sigh.)

Don't you bother that girl.
Cliff. Ray?
Ray. Yeah?
Cliff. If Bunny fucks with you . . . you knock her on her ass, ya hear?
Ray. Yeah, that's what I'm aimin' ta do, Cliff. Right on her ass.

(Lou and Tiny go in.)

Clark. Hey, how 'bout pourin' me some of that wine you hidin' down there?
Ray. We ain't hidin' no wine.
Cliff. Pour your own troubles, garbage gut.
Clark. Why, hell, you ain't got nothin' here 'cept enough for maybe Ray here.
Cliff. Ray, here? What do you mean "Ray here?" Why this youngblood nephew of mine will drink you underneath the table and into the middle of nex' week, ole Silly Willy Clark.
Clark. Sheeet.
Cliff. Can't you, Ray?
Ray. *(proudly)* Sure as hell can.
Clark. Well, we'll see . . . come on, let's go on up to the store and get us a big man.
Ray. A big man?
Clark. That's right . . . a whole gallon.

(Cliff stands and beckons Ray.)

Cliff. Never stand in the way of a man who wants to part with some coins . . . and buy ya a drink at the same time, I say.
Clark. Yeah, c'mon . . . *(as an afterthought)* . . . I'm buyin'.
Cliff. *(humming)* Hummmm hummm hummm . . . don't mind if I do get a little refreshing night air . . . c'mon, Ray, let's take a stroll.
Clark. Well, which liquor store we goin' to? The one up on "The Avenue" or the one down by the bridge?

Cliff. Let's go up on "The Avenue." *(pause)* That's okay with you, Ray?
Ray. Yeah, fine with me.
Clark. Boy, we gonna get pissy pukey fallin' down drunk tonight.
Cliff. If you see your girl up on "The Avenue" you'll point her out to me, Ray, won'tcha?
Ray. Yeah, Cliff. Yeah.

(They exit. The street is clear. Music plays, then a commercial begins. And lights down.)

(Curtain)

ACT III
· · · · · ·

Time: *Forty-five minutes later.*
Scene: *Derby Street. Lou, Tiny, Doris, Bunny Gillette, Red, and Bama sit upon the Dawsons' stoop.*
   A gallon jug of red wine is on the pavement beside the steps, and everyone except Red and Lou has a paper cup in hand.
   Doris is a small girl, not as small as Tiny, and has a full figure. Red looks like a hungry wolf and Bama seems to be mostly elbows and knees.

Lou. I don't see how you folks drink that nasty ole muscatel wine.
Doris. *(demonstrating)* There's nothin' to it, baby sis.
Red. That's about the only goddamn thing we got in common, Lou. I don't drink that fucken hawg wash neither.
Lou. *(primly)* If you must sit on my steps this late at night, Red, I wish you'd respect me and the other girls here by not bein' so foul mouthed.
Red. *(indignant)* Shit, woman, talk to your ole man, Cliff . . . I'm usin' Mr. Dawson's rule book.
Lou. Don't blame Cliff!
Bama *(to Red)* Forget it, huh?
Red. You sometimes forget who your husband is, don't you, woman?
Tiny. Yeah . . . knock it off, you guys.
Red. *(to Tiny)* Fuck you, bitch!
Lou. *(to Red)* I got a good memory, little red nigger.
Red. So use it . . . and don't bug me.
Bunny Gillette. If you fools gonna keep this up all night I'm goin'a go home!
Bama. Bye!
Lou. But I got to live with Cliff, Red . . . not you . . . hear?

Doris. *(in high voice, nearly drunk)* Do y'all want a hot dog? Do y'all want a hot dog?
Tiny. Why don't we all stop arguing? I knew this would happen if you bought more wine, Bama.
Bunny. You been drinkin' much as anybody.
Bama. Ahhh, don't blame me. If I didn't get it somebody else would.
Bunny. They up on "The Avenue" gettin' some more now.
Lou. Cliff and Ray's probably out lookin' for some ole funky bitches.
Tiny. That's the way those punk-ass men are, girl.
Bunny. Sho' is!
Lou. Who you callin' punk-ass?
Tiny. Not anybody . . . well, I don't mean punk . . . it's just that all men are messed up.
Bama. What chou talkin' 'bout, broad?
Red. Hey, Bama, you better straighten your ole lady out before I have to do it.
Doris. Do y'all want a hot dog?
Bunny. Yeah, who's this girl Ray's been seein', Lou?
Lou. Don't ask me, chile. Don't even let him know I said anything.
Red. Tell Ray I want to meet her, Bunny.

(Bunny threatens to pour her wine on him.)

Tiny. When will Cliff be back?
Doris. I said do y'all want a hot dog?
Lou. You waitin' for Cliff now, Tiny?
Tiny. Yeah . . . Doris, I want one . . . but give them time to cook, will . . .
Lou. I asked you a question, Tiny.
Tiny. Nawh . . . nawh . . . can't you see I'm with Bama. Ain't I, Bama?
Red. *(mutters)* Goddamn . . . what a collection of cop-outs.
Bama. Hey, get me a hot dog too.
Doris. The mathafukkers should be done by now.
Tiny. *(nervous laugh)* Woman, stop usin' all that bad language. You know Lou don't like it.
Doris. Shit on you and Lou both, it's my mouth.
Lou. Now I ain't gonna warn none of you no longer . . . Next one says one bad word has got to go home.
Bama. Will you listen to this now?
Red. Hey, Doris, get me one of those fucken hot dogs, will ya?
Lou. That did it, Red . . . Go home!
Red. Okay.
Tiny. Doris, you can't say two words without cussin'. Don't you know any better?
Red. *(stands)* But before I go, Lou, tell me what did I say that was so bad?

Lou. I don't have to repeat it.
Doris. I wouldn't be talkin' bout people so fucken much if I was you, Tiny. Remember I know somethin' . . . now don't I?
Lou. That goes for you too, Doris.
Tiny. *(frightened)* Whatta ya mean, Doris?
Bunny. Uuuhhh uhhh . . . y'all sure do act funny when you start in drinkin' this mess.
Bama. Yeah . . . whatta ya mean, Doris?
Doris. I ain't talkin' ta you, Bama.
Bama. I'm talkin' ta you. *(to Tiny)* What she got on you, Mamma?
Tiny. Whatta ya mean?
Doris. *(drunk)* Whatta ya think I mean?
Bama. That's what I'm tryin' to find out . . . what ya mean.
Red. Shall we go . . . children?
Tiny. That's what I'm askin' ya . . . whatta ya mean?
Lou. Now look. You broads can take that business back where you got it.
Bama. *(amused)* That's tellin' them, Lou.
Tiny. Don't you be callin' me a broad!
Bunny. *(to Red)* Red . . . don't you think . . .
Red. Shut up, woman!
Lou. *(amazed)* Wha' . . . I didn't . . .
Bama. *(joking)* Yeah, you did. I hear you.
Doris. *(jest)* Don't be talkin' to mah baby sister like that.
Tiny. *(scared and belligerent)* What you gonna do 'bout it, bitch! You gonna tell her bout Cliff and me?
Bama. Hey, cool it, baby.
Lou. What did you say?
Bunny. Now Lou . . . don't get mad . . .
Lou. *(disgust)* Okay, let's forget about it. You guys don't have to go home . . . I want you to wait on Cliff.
Red. *(sitting)* Wasn't plannin' on goin', anyway.
Lou. Now looka hare, Red.
Red. *(angry)* Goddammit! Make up your mind!
Doris. *(to Tiny)* You tryin' to be bad, ain't you, you li'l sawed-off heifer?
Tiny. *(rising)* Little heifer!

(Cliff, Ray and Silly Willy Clark turn the corner. They have a gallon jug of wine, half-emptied, which they pass between themselves and take large draughts.

They visibly feel their drinks and stop under the streetlamp and drink and talk.)

Cliff. Ray . . . just learn this one thing in life . . . When the time comes

. . . be a man . . . however you've lived up till then . . . throw it out of your mind . . . Just do what you have to do as a man.
Ray. *(not sober)* Sure, Cliff . . . sure.
Clark. *(still drunker)* That sho is right, Dawson . . . that's right . . . but why can't we be men all the time, Dawson?
Cliff. *(annoyed)* You don't know what I'm talkin' 'bout, silly ass, do you . . . do you now?
Bunny. Here comes Cliff, Ray, and Silly Willy Clark.
Doris. *(moving toward Tiny)* I'm tired of your little ass jumpin' bad around here, Tiny.
Tiny. *(scared but standing her ground)* You are?
Bama. *(between them)* Hey, knock off the bullshit . . . ya hear?
Red. Nawh, Bama . . . let them get it on and see who's the best.
Tiny. *(crying)* Bama, why you always takin' somebody's side against me?
Lou. Shut up, all of you!
Bama. I'm not takin' nobody's side against you, baby.
Doris. You ain't takin' my side, Bama? And what you callin' her baby fo'?
Tiny. *(to Bama)* Y'are!
Bama. I ain't. We all just out to have a good time . . . that's all . . . a good time, huh?

(He pulls Doris down beside him and puts his arm about her.)

Tiny. *(scratching at his face)* You bastard . . . I thought you was comin' down here to see me.

(Doris pulls her small knife.)

Lou. *Doris, stop!*
Doris. What the fuck's wrong with you, bitch!

(Cliff comes up and sees Doris's knife but doesn't appear to notice; she puts it away.)

I'm goin' in an' get a hot dog. *(same high voice)* Y'all want a hot dog?

(No answer. She enters the house.
 Bama, Tiny, and Lou glare at each other. Red and Bunny sit together.)

Red. Well, if it ain't Mr. Dawson and nephew . . . the Derby Street killjoys. And hello, Mr. Silly Willy Clark . . . you simple mathafukker.
Clark. Hey, everybody . . . *(passing them the bottle)* . . . knock yourselves out.
Bama. We got ours.

(Lou silently stands, looks at Cliff and the drunken Ray and enters the house.)

Red. *(hugs Bunny, looks at Ray)* Hey, what'cha mathafukkers doin'? Why don't you all have a sit down?
Clark. Don't mind if I do, Red . . . Hey, Cliff, is it okay if I sit down on your steps?
Cliff. Be my guest . . . you know me, don't you?
Bunny. *(pulls away from Red)* C'mon now, Red . . . stop all that stuff, man.
Red. You like it.

(He feels her breasts as they break.)

Lou. *(looking out the door)* I don't want to hear any more of that nasty shit from your mouth tonight, Red. And watch how you act!
Red. Watch how I act?
Cliff. Yeah, that's what she said . . . watch how you act.
Lou. Yeah, you keep your hands to yourself. I saw that.
Red. Hey, what's wrong with you goddamn people tonight? Is there a full moon or somethin'?
Bama. Hey, Red, let's split.
Red. Mr. and Mrs. Dawson . . . and nephew . . . I'm sorry. Forgive me. Will you please accept my humble-ass apology, huh? Will you Dawsons do that?

(Red places his hand upon Lou's leg; she pulls away.)

Now what have I done?
Bunny. What's wrong with you, Ray?
Doris. *(sticks head out of door)* Do y'all want a hot dog?
Tiny. Ray's gone off somewhere behind that wine . . . look at him slobber spit . . . probably with his . . .
Bunny. With his what?
Tiny. Nothin', hon . . . I was just kiddin' . . . *(shakes Ray)* . . . Wasn't I, Ray?
Ray. Yeah . . . yeah.
Bama. *(mimics Doris)* "Do yawhl wants a hot dawg?"
Tiny. Don't be so mean, Bama.
Doris. Y'all can kiss mah ass.
Lou. *(caricature)* Don't be so mean, Bama.
Bama. *(furious)* Who you tellin' to kiss your ass, woman? I thought you saw what Bunny got tonight up on "The Avenue" for . . .

(Miss Minny's window goes up.)

Tiny. Don't be so noisy, baby.
Red. I thought you was gonna get me one ah those mathafukkin' hot dogs, woman.

Miss Minny. Cliff . . . Cliff . . . I see you out there . . . I'm callin' the police right now about all this disturbance!

(Her window goes down.)

Doris. You better watch your little self, Tiny.
Lou. I told you about your mouth, Red.
Tiny. Watch myself?
Red. My mouth . . . awww . . . Lou. You can't be serious.
Cliff. Well, children, it's time that Daddy got to bed . . . I suggest that everyone goes home to bed or just home. Good night, all.
Lou. Ain't you gonna stay out here and wait for the cops, Cliff?
Cliff. Good night, my love. Don't be too long . . . I think your hair's sexy.

(Lou has her hair in curlers.
  He goes in, followed by Doris.)

Doris. *(off)* Do y'all wants a hot dog, Cliff?
Red. If I hadn't seen Cliff beat so many bad niggers' asses I would think he's a chicken-hearted punk.
Lou. There's more than one way to be a coward.
Bama. You better not let him hear you say that, lady.
Clark. It's been a hard night, heh, Bunny?
Bunny. Honey, these wine times is somethin' else.
Ray. *(mumbling)* Sho is, baby. Sho is.
Doris. *(back again, peering bleary-eyed at each one)* Do y'all want a hot dog? Do y'all want a hot dog? If y'all don't, speak up . . . dese hare hot dogs gonna be all gone cause I'm eatin' them fast as I can.
Red. Shove 'em up your ass . . . you silly bitch.
Lou. Okay, you all have to go now!

(Red rises and is followed by the rest, except Ray, who snores on the step. Lou goes back into the house and her fussing with Cliff about Ray's condition, his friends, and Tiny can be more sensed than heard.)

Bunny. Ray . . . Ray?
Ray. Yeah?
Bunny. I gotta tell you somethin' . . . Ray? . . . Ray? . . . I got somethin' to tell ya.
Bama. Leave him alone, Bunny.
Tiny. Yeah, let him sleep. He'll find out.
Ray. Yeah . . . what is it?
Bunny. I'm Red's girl now.

(Silly Willy Clark gets up and enters the house.)

Did you hear me, Ray? Did you hear me?

(Red faces the building, and urinates in one of the wine bottles.)

Ray. *(groggy)* Yeah . . . I heard you, Bunny. You're Red's girl now.
Bama. *(giggling)* I guess Ray's really got himself a new girl, Bunny.

(Red hands Ray the wine bottle he has just finished with.)

Red. Let's toast to that, Ray.

(Blindly, Ray lifts the jug to his lips, as Bama and Tiny gasp.)

Bunny. *No! . . . No, Raayyy!!!*

(She knocks the jug out of his grasp, smashing it upon the pavement. Ray wakes instantly, perceives her action, and lashes out at her face. He lands a solid punch that knocks her sprawling in the street.

Red rushes Ray and hits him with a haymaker aside the head. Ray grabs him for support and the two fall to the pavement, grappling.

Tiny screams. And Miss Minny's window goes up.

There are shouts and noise of running feet. The fighters roll about the pavement and Bama reaches down and pulls Ray off Red and holds him as the older boy smashes him in the face.

Silly Willy Clark rushes from the house and grabs Bama from behind. Upon his release from Bama, Ray butts Red in the midriff and staggers him to the entrance of the alley. Red pulls a bone-handled switch-blade; Ray grabs his arm and they fight their way into the alley.

Doris comes out of the house holding her small knife.)

Doris. *(to Bunny)* Where's Ray . . . Where's Ray!

(Bunny, dazed, points to the alley. Doris enters the alley as Cliff runs out of the door in only pants in time to see her disappear in the tunnel.

The street is lit; the Krumps' upper windows are open.)

Eddie. *Kill 'em . . . Kill 'em!*
Mrs. Krump. Keep back, Edward . . . there may be stray bullets!

(Silly Willy Clark has choked Bama into surrender.)

Red. *(from the alley, muffled)* All right . . . all right . . .

(As Cliff runs into the alley there is a sharp sigh, then noise of more struggle and a groan.

Lou, Tiny, Bunny, and Derby Street residents crowd around the alley entrance.)

Miss Minny. Oh Lord . . . what's happened . . . what's happened?
Mrs. Krump. Close the window, Edward . . . Close the window!

(The Krumps' window closes.
The policeman turns the corner at a run.)

Resident. *(to another resident)* Did you see what happen, Mr. Roy?

Mr. Roy. Nawh, Miz Cooper . . . but I knew somethin' had to happen with all this goin' on down here.

(Ray emerges from the alley, blood on his shirt. Doris follows him, her dress splotched with blood.)

The Policeman. *(running up with hand on pistol)* What's happened here?

(Cliff steps out of the alley, holding Red's knife.)

Cliff. *(hands knife to policeman and points in alley)* I killed him.

Lou. *(incredulous)* You killed him . . .

(Cliff nods.)

Resident. Did you hear that?
Miss Minny. What happened? What happened, Miss Francis?
Resident. Cliff Dawson's done killed a boy.
Miss Minny. Ohhh . . . my Lord.
Tiny. *(disbelief)* You killed him?
The Policeman. *(leads Cliff to stoop)* Okay, everybody . . . get back and don't nobody leave. By the looks of most of you . . . we'll want to talk to you. Get back . . . Will somebody call an ambulance and wagon?
Miss Minny. I already did.

(Bama has revived; he looks sick and sits beside the alley entrance. Bunny, Clark and Doris support Ray, who looks to be in shock.)

Lou. Cliff . . . Cliff . . . don't do it . . . don't leave me! Tell the truth.

(Cliff caresses her.)

Cliff. It won't be for long . . . I was protectin' my family . . . our family.

(Lou cries, joining Tiny, Bunny and one of the neighbors.
Doris appears resigned to the situation.)

Ray. She's gone . . . she's gone . . .

(A siren is heard.)

Doris. Who's gone, Ray? Who?
Ray. She is . . . my girl . . . my girl on "The Avenue."
Doris. She'll be back.
Ray. No, she's not. She won't be back.
The Policeman. I have to warn you, Mr. Dawson, that anything you say can be used against you.

Cliff. *(genuine)* Yes, sir.

(Beatrice turns the corner.)

Ray. Never . . . she'll never be back.
Cliff. Lou . . . Lou, I want one thing from you . . .

(Lou looks at him, then at Ray.)

Lou. He's all I got left, Cliff . . . He's all the family I got left.

(He looks at her until she places her head upon his chest and sobs uncontrollably.)

Beatrice. *(walking up, to Miss Minny in her window)* What's the trouble, Miss Minny?
Miss Minny. Ohhh, somethin' terrible, girl . . . I can't tell you now.
Cliff. *(handcuffed to the Policeman)* It's your world, Ray . . . It's yours, boy . . . Go on out there and claim it.

(sirens nearer; lights down and music rises)

Miss Minny. Come down tomorrow for tea, Beatrice, dear, and I'll tell you all about it.
Beatrice. All right, Miss Minny. The Lord bless you tonight.
Miss Minny. He will, dear . . . 'cause he works in mysterious ways.
Beatrice. *(starting off)* Amen!

(lights down to blackness and a commercial begins)

(Curtain)

Five on the Black Hand Side (1969)

Charlie L. Russell (b. 1932–)

Born in Monroe, Louisiana, Charlie L. Russell was reared in Oakland, California, where he was a star athlete at Technical High School. After serving in the United States Army, with a tour of sixteen months in Korea, he earned a bachelor's degree in English from the University of San Francisco. Moving later to New York City, he joined the Harlem Writers' Guild, became interested in theatre, and wrote *Five on the Black Hand Side.* Among his recent projects is a novel about a black family that migrates from the South to Oakland during the early fifties.

Russell's *Five on the Black Hand Side,* which was later made into a motion picture, illustrates the manner in which an imaginative writer can adapt Black Arts revolutionary drama to other purposes. Basically, the play follows the formula of Black Arts revolutionary drama. It includes the requisite major characters: a true black revolutionary hero; a young African American woman who must be educated by the revolutionary; a phony militant who talks black but sleeps white; a young black who does not understand the difference between militancy and revolution; and a middle-class, white-thinking black who must be converted or destroyed. But Russell disguises the Black Arts formula by adding the theme of liberation of black wives and by furnishing enough humor that audiences can delight in the entertainment without being fully aware how much they are being educated.

Published Play by Charlie L. Russell

Five on the Black Hand Side. New York: Samuel French, 1969.

• •

Five on the Black Hand Side
A Play in Three Acts

Five on the Black Hand Side was first presented on December 10, 1969, at the American Place Theatre, New York City, Wynn Handman, Director. The playwright was Charlie L. Russell, the director Barbara Ann Teer. Scenery was by Edward Burbridge, costumes by Gertha Brock, lighting by Shirley Prendergast, with special sound by James Reichert.

Place: *Harlem.*
Time: *Present.*

CHARACTERS
(In Order of Appearance)

Mr. Brooks	*L. Errol Jaye*
Mrs. Brooks	*Clarice Taylor*
Gail	*Jonelle Allen*
Booker T.	*Matthew Bernard Johnson, Jr.*
Gideon	*William Adell Stevenson, III*
Stephanie	*Patricia A. Edomy*
Sampson	*Thabo Quinland R. Gordon*
Nia	*Nia Anderson*
Ruby	*Theresa Merritt*
Stormy Monday	*Judyann Elder*
Sweetmeat	*Gerry Black*
Slim	*Ed Bernard*
Fun Loving	*Tchaka Almoravids*
Black Militant	*Eugene Reynolds*
Evangelist	*Marilyn B. Coleman*
Rolls Royce	*Joseph Attles*
First Junkie	*Demond Wilson*
Second Junkie	*Eugene Reynolds*
Marvin	*Lisle Wilson*

ACT I

SCENE 1

Time: *Present.*

Scene: *Morning. An apartment located in Harlem. There is a living room, kitchen. Mrs. Brooks, who has a scarf on her head, is already on stage. She is humming and singing snatches from a mournful spiritual as she prepares the morning breakfast. She also prepares Mr. Brooks' lunch, which she puts into his attaché case.*

Mr. Brooks. *(Enters excitedly with a piece of paper in his hand. He is fully dressed in a suit and a tie.)* Good morning, Mrs. Brooks. I've got it! I've got it! *(Sits down. Mrs. Brooks immediately gives him a cup of coffee.)*

Mrs. Brooks. Good morning, Mr. Brooks.

Mr. Brooks. Booker T. gave me an idea and I wrote it last night. Ha! Brilliant idea! I'm telling you that Booker T. is all right. *(starts reading)*

Mrs. Brooks. Yes, Mr. Brooks.

Mr. Brooks. This will fix his wagon. Defying his own father. Ha, ha. Yes! I don't see why I didn't think of this myself. Hmmmmm. Yes. This will fix that dad-blasted Gideon. You've got to know how to handle these college boys, Mrs. Brooks. I'm appealing to his sense of logic. *(He finishes reading the letter, much pleased with himself.)* There! Yes! I really laid it on him, Mrs. Brooks. Oh, dad blast it! Oh, thank you, Mrs. Brooks. You can give this to your youngest son. It's a list of my demands. Oh, and by the way. You can tell him that my demands are nonnegotiable. Ha! This will really fix him. But between you and me and the deep blue sea, I've taken an extra added precaution. I asked our son, Booker T., to have a little talk with him today. It's what they call a two-pronged attack.

Mrs. Brooks. Yes, Mr. Brooks. *(takes letter and puts it away; places Mr. Brooks' breakfast before him)*

Mr. Brooks. *(starts reading his newspaper)* A hum. Thank you, Mrs. Brooks. Hmmmmmm. I see here that the Plessey Company has made a 648 million dollar tender offer to the Zanzibar Steel Company. Seems it's a move to strengthen their position against international competition. Brilliant idea! Sound business move! Yes! *(checks his watch which hangs across his vest)* Mrs. Brooks, your book, please.

Mrs. Brooks. Yes, Mr. Brooks. *(gives Mr. Brooks her appointment book and waits patiently as he studies it)*

Mr. Brooks. Hmmmmmm. I see here that you have some free time around noon. After you return from the hairdresser I think you should take a walk. Hmmmmm. Yes, you have a good schedule today, Mrs. Brooks.

A very good schedule. I don't have to remind you what the Bible says about an idle mind. Yes. By the way, I strongly suggest that you make sure your blue dress is in good shape. I've decided that you can wear it to your daughter's wedding.

Mrs. Brooks. But you said I could buy a new one.

Mr. Brooks. Well, I've thought about it and with all the money we're spending on Gail's wedding we simply can't afford it.

Mrs. Brooks. Yes, Mr. Brooks. *(sits down at the table, drinking a cup of coffee)*

Mr. Brooks. It's still kind of hard to believe that Gail is getting married on Sunday, eh, Mrs. Brooks? Why, it seems like only yesterday that she was holding onto your dresstail. Little Gail is getting married. . . . We've done our job, Mrs. Brooks. Harlem is a difficult place to raise a family, but we've done our job.

Mrs. Brooks. Yes, Mr. Brooks. *(starts crying)*

Mr. Brooks. *(He is puzzled by his wife's tears, and he gets up to comfort her. He stands behind her, assuming the stance of the great white hunter.)* There, there, Mrs. Brooks, it's all right. I'm not mad anymore because Gail is getting married, although she knew that I had my heart set on her going to college. She just couldn't get through her thick skull what I was trying to tell her. It's not as though she was a man. A woman needs a good education. Never know when they'll have to take care of themselves. There, there. You did the best you could. I'm not blaming you anymore. Although I must admit that you did seem to be on her side a few times, there. Now, now, Mrs. Brooks, you know I'm not the kind of man who carries a grudge for more than a week. *(pats Mrs. Brooks on the shoulders, and gives her his handkerchief)*

Mrs. Brooks. Thank you, Mr. Brooks.

Mr. Brooks. You know, maybe it's just as well that Gail is getting married. Who knows, she might have gone to college, and turned out to be one of them college rebels like Gideon. Always talking about the white power structure this and the white power structure that. If I ever get my hands on him I'll show him something about a black power structure. *(starts pacing the floor)* That's what's wrong with this younger generation. They won't listen to anybody. If you tell them it's raining, and to take an umbrella, they subject to go outside naked as a jaybird. They've got no sense of values, no respect, that's what the trouble is. Got the nerve to go on a strike against his own father. Have you ever heard of such a thing, your own flesh and blood? Oh, I'm telling you it might be a good thing that Gail is not going to college. One wild bunch in the family is enough. You know, Mrs. Brooks, sometimes I think it's a blessing that all of our children are grown. Maybe now you and I can sort of grow old together graceful like.

Mrs. Brooks. Oh, Mr. Brooks.

Mr. Brooks. Don't worry, Mrs. Brooks. Things are going to work out. Why, look at the way Booker T. has turned out, and you know how he and I used to fight all the time. But he's working steady now, trying to get ahead in life. Why, he can even hold a decent conversation with you now without screaming. Yes, yes, that boy is really maturing, really growing up. Mrs. Brooks, you ought to be proud. We stayed up a long time after you went to bed. Just talking. He's a very sensible boy, you know. Very sensible. *(An alarm clock goes off offstage.)* What's Gail getting up so early for?
Mrs. Brooks. They're rehearsing at the church this morning.
Mr. Brooks. Well, Mrs. Brooks, at least our oldest son is becoming a real man. But that dad-blasted Gideon has spent the entire summer up on that roof. Oh, if I could get just one hand on him, Mrs. Brooks. Just one.
Mrs. Brooks. Oh, I wish you two could get along.
Mr. Brooks. But you know I've tried, Mrs. Brooks. I've really tried, but what can you do when the other fellow is stubborn, pig-headed, and ungrateful? I mean even a good man has his limits, Mrs. Brooks.
Mrs. Brooks. Yes, Mr. Brooks. Gail. Gailll! It's time for you to get up. I knew she'd have a hard time getting up this morning. I told her not to stay at that party so late. Gaillll! She'll be mad if I don't wake her up. Gailllll!
Gail. *(from offstage)* All right, Momma, I'm getting up. *(A radio is turned on offstage, playing rhythm and blues music.)*
Mr. Brooks. And cut off that dad-blasted radio. Booker T. is trying to sleep. *(The sound is lowered.)* That's one noisy girl. Well, in two days she'll be Martin's problem.
Mrs. Brooks. Marvin. His name is Marvin, Mr. Brooks.
Mr. Brooks. Yes, of course.
Gail. *(enters happily, dancing into the room)* Hi, Mom. Hi, Pop. *(does a few dance steps)* Hello, world. HellOOO! Wow, I'm so happy!
Mr. Brooks. It seems to me that happiness don't have to be so frisky. Especially so early in the morning, and Booker T. is trying to sleep.
Gail. Oh, Daddy, don't be so square. *(sits down at the table)* You should be singing with me. It's not every day your only daughter gets married. And you didn't even have to get a shotgun.
Mr. Brooks. HmPH!
Mrs. Brooks. Gail!
Gail. Well, it's true. And that's what makes me so happy. Marvin and I are marrying for love. Thanks, Mom. *(Mrs. Brooks gives her a cup of coffee.)* Did I hear you say Booker T. is here?
Mr. Brooks. He came over to get some of his clothes, and we wound up talking half the night. I was just telling Mrs. Brooks how much that boy has matured in the last year. Too bad that that Gideon doesn't pattern himself after him.
Gail. I wish you two would stop fighting. You've been at it all summer. Isn't there some way you can get together before the wedding?

Mr. Brooks. I've worked out a little something. I cannot divulge my plans at this time, but believe me, you can put your trust in your old father. He'll see you through. He's still got a few tricks up his sleeve, eh, Mrs. Brooks? *(stands, preparing to go to work)*

Gail. Oh, Daddy! You're not going to work today, are you?

Mr. Brooks. And why not? Fridays and Saturdays are my volume days. And you know that's where the profits are.

Gail. I'll bet you'd be much nicer about the whole thing if I was marrying somebody besides Marvin.

Mrs. Brooks. Gail, that's your father you're talking to.

Gail. Well, it's true, Momma. Daddy doesn't like Marvin.

Mr. Brooks. Ah, that's not true. I like that boy.

Gail. Then how come you never talk to him? When he tries to talk to you, you just sit there like a regular old blob.

Mr. Brooks. I just don't have much to say.

Gail. You seem to have a lot to say to everybody else.

Mrs. Brooks. Gail, you shouldn't talk like that. You'll hurt your father's feelings.

Gail. Oh, all right. I'm sorry, Dad. *(kisses her father)* There, I didn't mean to hurt your feelings, Dad. It's just that Marvin is so wonderful, and I want you to like him. Come on, Daddy, smile. Try to be happy. I want everybody to be happy. Come on, Daddy, dance with me. *(Gail does a few steps around him.)*

Mr. Brooks. I'm saving all my dancing for the wedding. I might as well warn you all that I'm going to be a tough cookie on the dance floor. Booker T. is giving me private lessons. These dances you kids are doing now-a-days are not anything new. They're as old as baseball. Not that I'm that old myself, but we used to do a dance just like that when I was a kid in Monroe. *(looks at his watch)* Say, it's getting late. I've got to get to work.

Gail. You really going to dance at the wedding, Daddy?

Mr. Brooks. And I'm going to be a toughie. Booker T. says I'm a natural. *(He stands, and Mrs. Brooks gives him his attaché case in a ritual perfected over the years.)* Hmmmmmm. Yes. Thank you, Mrs. Brooks. Yes, and don't forget that little walk; it's going to be a sun-kissed day, and you know the sun gives body to your skin.

Mrs. Brooks. Yes, Mr. Brooks.

Mr. Brooks. I'll see you all. *(walks toward the front door)*

Gail. Goodbye, Dad.

(Mr. Brooks stops just as he is about to exit, and returns to give Mrs. Brooks, who has not moved away from her spot, a light peck of a kiss on the cheek.)

Mr. Brooks. There! *(exits)*

Gail. Daddy is such a phony. I don't see how you've stood it all these years, Momma. You should get a medal. You know, I'll bet that Dad doesn't like himself being so tight, I'll bet that deep inside he wants to unwind, to let himself go. That's why I love Marvin so much. He knows how to touch people, and he lets people touch him. Oh, Momma, he is so beautiful. Not just outside, but inside. In a lot of ways he's tough and hard like Gideon, but he has a softness about him, a warmness . . . Maybe it's because he spent all that time in jail. He just radiates something, Momma, it makes me want to grab him, to hold him, to protect him against the world. Am I making sense, do you know what I mean, Momma?

Mrs. Brooks. Yes, I know, I know what you mean. *(starts crying, but Gail does not notice it)*

Gail. *(starts reading the newspaper)* I sure hope Gideon remembers to tell a few of the kids to come by here this morning. Hmmmm. Oh, by the way, Momma. Whatever you do, don't forget to color the bride and groom black. Booker T. would simply die if we had a white bride and groom on the wedding cake.

Mrs. Brooks. I won't forget.

Gail. Hey, Momma, remember when I was a little girl how I used to worry you to death because I didn't think anyone would marry me when I grew up? Remember? I used to ask you a thousand questions about how I could get the boys to like me? Wow, I almost pushed the panic button when I didn't have a boyfriend by the time I was eleven. Remember that? I just knew I'd be an old maid. And now I have Marvin. The moon finally has her sun. Oh, Momma, sometimes when I think how happy we'll be it's frightening.

Mrs. Brooks. Oh, Gail. I'm so happy for you. You don't know how many years I've prayed for this day to come. You see, I'm not just happy for you. I'm also happy because when you get married that means I can keep a promise I made to myself many years ago. You see, I promised myself that as soon as you . . .

(The phone rings.)

Gail. I'll get it. Hello? Oh, hi, love. Oh, it was okay—just a bunch of girls and you know where I wanted to be. Marvin! Jive! Blow my mind. Scatter it into a thousand pieces.

Booker T. *(enters)* Jesus Christ, this is a crazy house. Alarm clocks going off all around you. Radios blasting away. And now the phone. Getting my own pad sure was a hip move. A very hip move. Now all we need is for Gideon to come sliding from that roof with all his counter-revolutionary nonsense.

Mrs. Brooks. Good morning, son. Juice and coffee?

Booker T. Thanks, Moms. Did Dad leave already?
Mrs. Brooks. You just missed him. Did you want something?
Booker T. No, not really. Just checking. Hmmmmmm. *(starts reading the newspaper)*
Gail. 'Bye, love. *(kisses the phone a few times)* See you at the rehearsal. *(hangs up phone and joins Booker T. at the table)* Hi, Booker T.
Booker T. Don't call me by that slave name. You know everybody calls me Sharrief.
Gail. Sorry about that, I forgot. That was Marvin, Momma. He just wanted to know how I felt after the party the girls gave me last night. See what I mean? See how wonderful he is? Oh, Momma, we're going to be so happy!
Booker T. Oh, Momma, we're going to be so happy. Girl, why don't you get out of that Doris Day bag?
Gail. And he told me to tell you hello, too, Momma.
Booker T. Walking around in them jive mini-skirts.
Gail. But I guess I won't be completely happy until Dad likes Marvin. Daddy is so quick to judge people, and to turn them off. I'm sure he'd like Marvin, but he won't even talk to him.
Booker T. Oh, girl, you know Dad ain't never liked no light-skinned Negroes.
Gail. Oh, that's so silly. That kind of attitude leads to tribalism. Besides, blackness is a state of mind, not the color of your skin.
Booker T. And a jailbird to boot.
Gail. Marvin was a political prisoner. Refusing to fight in that war is not a real crime. And at least Marvin sacrificed three years of his life for something he believed in. At least he stood up for his convictions. You know, sometimes I don't understand you, Booker T., excuse me, Sharrief. Just last week you told Gideon that anyone who hadn't been to jail was jiving, and now you're trying to sound on Marvin because he has been to jail. I wish you'd get yourself together. I'm tired of your criticisms, I want to see some of your activism.
Booker T. You're beginning to sound just like that creep Gideon.
Mrs. Brooks. Booker T.! Gideon is your baby brother.
Booker T. Ah, Momma, Gideon is incorrect. Going around confusing people with all of that talk he's talking. Instead of being up there at that honkie college he ought to be setting a torch to it. The solution to the black man's problem is so simple. But guys like Gideon start talking, and before you know it, they've got things so complicated that nobody can move because they don't know what foot to move first. All that talk, when all we need to do is put a gun to the heads of a few honkies. Power comes from the barrel of a gun. Chairman Mao has already given the word, and anyone not doing the deed is jiving. The

white man is nothing but the devil and everything we do should be geared towards his destruction.

Gail. Well, I don't feel like arguing with you this morning. I've got better things to do than sit around murder-mouthing people. Ah . . .

Mrs. Brooks. Gail—You can listen to this too, if you want to, Booker T. I was just telling your sister how happy I am that she's getting married because now I'm going to keep a promise I made to myself a long, long time ago. You see, I promised myself that as soon as Gail—that is . . .

Gideon. *(entering)* Wow, sleeping on that roof is beginning to get to me. Momma, you're going to have to give me another blanket. It got cold last night, you hear me? Hey, sis, how you doing? *(kisses his sister)* Sure is sweet. Marvin sure is a lucky dude. We should be living in Africa. He'd have to give the family five hundred cattle, a thousand sheep, might even have to throw in a couple of lions, hey, Booker T.

Booker T. Hey, man, you know my real name.

Gideon. Sorry. I'll remember next time, Booker T.

Booker T. Ah, why don't you dig yourself, man.

Mrs. Brooks. I wish you two wouldn't be at each other all the time.

Gail. Gideon, did you remember to tell some of the gang to come by here this morning?

Gideon. Everything is everything, love. *(looks at his watch)* They ought to be here any minute now. Booker T. Washington Brooks, wow! The old man really hung a name on you, didn't he?

Booker T. Look, man, I don't know what kind of trip you're on, but rather than messing with me this morning you'd be better off going on a lion hunt with a toothpick.

Gideon. Whoa, boy. You'd better practice a little revolutionary discipline.

Booker T. You're pressing your luck, little brother. You'd better dig yourself. I'm buying all the wolf tickets you're selling this morning. *(pushes himself away from the table)* I keep trying to tell you that you don't have a sense of humor. If you did, you'd realize that some things are not funny.

Mrs. Brooks. Booker T.! Gideon! We raised you two to love and respect one another.

Booker T. Hey, man, we'd better listen to Momma and cool it.

Gideon. Yea. But if you want a fair one just come up on the roof, and we can work a light show.

Booker T. Ah, man, be serious sometimes. Hey listen, I've got to talk to you sometime today about something.

Gideon. What?

Booker T. In private, man.

Gideon. Hmmm, O.K. I've got to go to the church, then stop by the art supply store. . . . Yea. All right, I'll meet you on the roof in an hour.

Booker T. Cool.
Mrs. Brooks. There. . . . Well, Gideon, before you came in, I was telling Gail, and your brother, Booker T., how happy I was that Gail was getting married because . . .

(Doorbell rings.)

Gideon. I'll get it. That must be the troops.

(Gideon exits then re-enters with Sampson, Nia and Stephanie. Sampson is carrying a portable tape recorder which is playing rhythm and blues music.)

Gail. Sampson, I want you to meet my older brother, Sharrief; Sharrief, Sampson.
Booker T. I see you carrying your music with you.
Sampson. Yea, it helps us swing while we do our thing, baby. If everyone started their day by listening to some boss sides, they wouldn't have to be taking all kinds of pills and things.
Stephanie. Right on. Music is the way we keep in touch with our ancestors. Where we get our spiritual sustenance from.
Sampson. Yea, it's like our life force.
Gail. Oh, and this is Sampson's sister, Stephanie. Stephanie, this is my brother, Sharrief.
Stephanie. I've sure heard a lot of things about you.
Booker T. I don't know if that's good or bad.
Stephanie. Good or bad, it wouldn't matter. I make my own decisions.
Gideon. Nia, my brother, Sharrief.
Booker T. Nice meeting you.
Sampson. Hey, Gail, I know you want to be down for the wedding reception, let me lay this step on you. I picked it up from some brothers in Philly.

(Sampson and Gail begin to dance, Sampson reluctantly teaching her the step. Gideon and Nia join the party, as do Stephanie and Booker T. Rhythm and blues music.)

Gail. Wow! That's dynamite! Whoa. It's getting late. Gideon, show them where the stuff is. I don't want to be late. Marvin is meeting me at the church. *(Gideon exits with Nia, Sampson, and Stephanie.)* Hey, Momma, you want to come with us?
Mrs. Brooks. No, baby, you all go on. I got my work to do. You know I wash every Friday.
Booker T. Hey, sis, I'll walk to the corner with you. And give you a break. People will see you with me, and they'll think you're into something.

(All exit except Mrs. Brooks.)

Mrs. Brooks. *(remembers Mr. Brooks' letter, and runs to the door)* Gideon!

Gideon. Yeah, Momma. I'll catch you in a minute. Hold the last elevator for me. Yea, Momma?

Mrs. Brooks. Mr. Brooks left this for you. I worry about you, son, you're gonna catch a death of cold sleeping up there on the roof. I wish you'd call off your strike and talk to your father again.

Gideon. Hmmmmmmmm. Ah, Momma, you know how Dad is. *(starts reading the letter)*

Mrs. Brooks. Yes, I know how Mr. Brooks is. What does he say?

Gideon. *(reads aloud)* "Dear son Gideon. Since time is making its noble presence felt upon me, I shall be brief, and not attempt to list all of your numerous sins at this time. But I must point out that it is you who is on strike against your own father because he wants you to be a business major when you know that a degree in anthropology does not prepare one to earn money. It is you who is involved in various political activities on the campus, and thereby jeopardizing your entire college career. And finally, it is you who refuses to speak to your loving father. My demands are that you cool it, that all of these various transgressions be rectified immediately. If not sooner. I have tried to be understanding. I realize how difficult it must be for you, in fact for all of my children, to follow in such large illustrious footsteps as mine are. However, in fairness I must admit that your brother, Booker T., does show some promise. Gideon, you disappoint me. Why, this very morning I asked myself if this failure, if this rebel-rouser was really you. You whose test showed an I.Q. of 157. If we were Jewish, I'd have "shivah" set on you. However, I shall be kind, forgiving, and loving as soon as you meet my demands. Gideon, I stand ready to forgive. Gideon, repent so that you can make a mark in the business world like your loving father. Your humble father, Mr. Brooks." He's full of stuff.

Mrs. Brooks. Gideon!

Sampson. Hey, come on, man!

Gideon. Well, he is full of stuff, Momma. Talking about somebody making a mark in the business world like him. You'd think he was running General Motors instead of that little old barbershop.

Mrs. Brooks. Being a barber is honest work.

Gideon. Ah, Momma. I'm not trying to sound on Dad. It's just that I know where he's coming from. Dad is still into that I, me thing. And it's not about that anymore. We have to start looking at the whole idea of education differently. A college education is not something you get so you can get a better job. It's a tool you get to help your people.

Mrs. Brooks. Oh, I'm telling you it's all so confusing. When I hear your father tell his side, it sounds right. And when I hear you tell yours, yours sounds right. It's so hard to make head or tails out of things. And you're sure you don't want to do like your father says?

Sampson. *(from offstage)* Hey, Gideon! Come on, man!
Gideon. All right! I'm coming! Yea, Momma, I'm sure. Dad wants me to play it safe, and be a good upstanding citizen. That's his way not mine. If I did that I would be turning my back on all the things I believe in.
Mrs. Brooks. Gideon.
Gideon. Yea, Momma?
Sampson. Hey, man, you coming!?
Gideon. Ah, man, be cool! I'm coming! Yea, Momma.
Mrs. Brooks. Oh, nothing. You'd better go now, they're waiting for you. What I have to say can wait until another time.
Gideon. Well . . . O.K., Momma. I'll be back in a little while. I have to meet Booker T. on the roof in an hour. *(kisses his mother on the cheek)* See you, Moms. *(exits)*
Mrs. Brooks. See you, son. *(finishes getting her wash together, starts singing, and humming again, putting clothes, washing powder, bleach into a shopping cart, and exits)*

(Curtain)

ACT I

SCENE 2

Time: *One hour later.*
Scene: *The roof. In one corner there are a rolled-up blanket, some books, and an African spear. Booker T. is already on stage.*

Booker T. Hey, man, what happened to you?
Gideon. *(Enters out of breath. He carries a small package and a piece of poster paper.)* Sorry I'm late. I got hung up at the store. How is it going?
Booker T. I'm just here by being careful, man. Just sneaking by.
Gideon. Yea. *(starts making a "Just Married" sign)*
Booker T. Man, I was checking this place out, I haven't been up here in a long time. Remember when I used to have my pigeons, remember that? I used to have my coop right over there. Boy, the hours I used to spend up here.
Gideon. Yea, I remember. You wouldn't let anyone play with you. You didn't even allow me up here.
Booker T. Yea, man, that sure seems like a long time ago. It's funny how the time just slips away from you. *(goes and looks down on the street*

below) Yea. Hey, remember that chick from across the street? That old big-legged girl you brought up here, and got your first piece from? What was her name? Remember how upset you were because during the whole Johnson she never stopped popping her gum? What was her name? Gloria, Gloria Cook, that was her name.

Gideon. Man, didn't you say you wanted to talk to me about something?

Booker T. Yea, man. Well, it's about Dad. We sat up talking a long time last night, and he's really getting upset.

Gideon. Man, I don't want to hear nothing about Dad.

Booker T. How are you going to show, man?

Gideon. Ah, man. That dude is always upset about something.

Booker T. Well, you could at least listen to what I have to say.

Gideon. Sure, big brother, sure.

Booker T. We had a long talk. You know, it's funny how you've always been able to really get to Dad. I mean if it was me up here, it probably wouldn't bother him as much. Anyway it just seems to me that you two ought to be able to work out some kind of compromise.

Gideon. Compromise? What are you talking about, man? Daddy is wrong as two left shoes. What is there for us to work out? How you going to give me some bullshit advice like that? Especially the way you two fought all the time before you moved out.

Booker T. Well, I understand the old man better now. I know not to argue politics or ideology with him. Hey, Dad is really not that bad when you get to know him. He just talks bad. Look, Gideon, I'm not asking you to give in all the way, I'm just asking you to meet the old man halfway, that's all.

Gideon. This is incredible. This is some incredible shit, man. Dad is living in the nineteen thirties, and you're asking me to meet him halfway. Dad is the one who's got to change. Why don't you dig yourself, man? You're always on Dad's side. Like that time I beat him in that race, and both of you claimed he won.

Booker T. Oh that. Well, he did win.

Gideon. You're full of crap. You're always on Daddy's side.

Booker T. Say, why you bringing up all that old stuff? I didn't take anybody's side. It was a close race, and the way it turned out it was good for the old man's ego.

Gideon. I beat him by at least a foot. What about my ego, man? Don't you think it would have been good for me to beat that old windbag? He's always won every game we played. Whist, Monopoly, Pokeno, Bingo, Scrabble. Everything.

Booker T. Ah, man, why you keep harping on the same old crap? The past is past.

Gideon. What kind of jive answer is that? The past is past. Listen, man, the next time you've got some advice just keep it for yourself. And before you start trying to tell other people what to do, you ought to get your own house in order.

Booker T. What do you mean by that, man?

Gideon. I said what I had to say. People who live in glass houses oughta be cool.

Booker T. Look, man, what's bugging you? I've been getting negative vibes from you all morning. If you've got something to say to me, why don't you just come out and say it?

Gideon. O.K. I will—I don't know—Hey, do you have anything against sisters?

Booker T. Do I have anything against sisters? No, I don't have anything against sisters. Why?

Gideon. I just want to know where you're coming from, that's all. I never see you uptown with any chicks. Every time I see you you're alone.

Booker T. So.

Gideon. There's a whole lot of boss sisters out here, can't you find one?

Booker T. You writing a book, or something?

Gideon. If I were, I'd leave that chapter out.

Booker T. What are you talking about, what's the matter with you?

Gideon. I just want to know if you've got anything against sisters, man. That's all!

Booker T. Well, I don't have anything against sisters, I already told you that.

Gideon. Un hun. You know what, I think, I think you're afraid of the sisters man, because you can't deal with them. I bet you're the kind of cat who ends up marrying some white chick. You've probably got some gray chick right now. What do you think about that?

Booker T. I think you're a crazy Nigger. That's what I think. You sound like you've been taking ignorant pills. Or did you run into some dynamite smokes? If you did, turn me on so I can be crazy like you.

Gideon. Do you, man?

Booker T. Do I what?

Gideon. Do you have a white girl friend?

Booker T. Ah, man, what are you talking about? Look, I came up here to try and get you and Dad together again, that's all. I'm really into a peace thing and I don't want to get into no argument with you, man.

Gideon. Stop playing games, man. Be honest. You were seen going into Terry's with a blonde. You've been seen eating at the Boondock with a blonde. What's happening with you, man? Is that why you're moving your clothes, are you moving in with that blonde? Huh?

Booker T. So I see a white chick every now and then. Why are you getting so excited?

Gideon. Why am I getting so excited?

Booker T. Yea, it's not your business who I hang out with. Who I hang out with is a personal matter. I dig a certain quality in a chick, and I haven't found it in any sisters, O.K.

Gideon. It's probably because you don't show the quality yourself.

Booker T. Look, man, I've been through a whole lot of sisters, and I haven't found any that I can really groove with, one that really understands me. That's all.

Gideon. That's because you don't understand yourself. Hey, man, sisters are some beautiful people. Man, we can't afford to get into a negative thing with the sisters. How are we going to survive without strong families?

Booker T. Tell me anything, boy. Pee on my back and tell me it's raining. The next thing you'll be trying to tell me that you're up here on this roof because you're trying to keep the family together.

Gideon. Yea, man, that's why I'm up here; otherwise I would have moved out. I want to keep the family together. The family is the basic unit in a society.

Booker T. The family is the basic unit in a society. Ha, that sounds like something you read in one of your books. If you kept your head out of them books sometimes you'd probably have some sense. That's what's wrong with you, reading all that shit. That is a white concept.

Gideon. Ah, man, you and Dad are just alike. It's amazing. Why don't you deal with the issues? Concepts are not black or white. Concepts don't have anything to do with color. They are either correct or incorrect. This is really a joke, you standing here trying to run down some white concept crap when you're steady hanging out with a white chick. You're really phoney, man, you really are. You're so full of contradictions.

Booker T. Well, I don't have a monopoly on that. Everybody has contradictions. Who I sleep with is my own private affair.

Gideon. Hey, man, do you realize the political significance involved in that statement you just made? Who you sleep with, the first face you see in the morning is very important. That's your reflection, where you get your energy from. That's your mirror, can you dig that, your mirror. Instead of putting down the sisters, you ought to be dealing with your ownself. Going around sleeping with the enemy.

Booker T. Aw, what are you trying to run down on somebody? That chick is nobody's enemy. She's an individual, and a beautiful one at that. But that's not the point, the thing is, man, I'm me. Me! And if you can't understand that, then shame on your black ass. Different strokes for different folks, that's what I say. You do your thing, and I'll damn sure do mine.

Gideon. Hey, what can I do to make you understand, you've got to get out of that I, I bag, man? We can't have everybody running off doing their own thing. Talking black, and sleeping white is like being a part-time soldier. And we can't win with part-time soldiers, man. We've got to be on the case twenty-five hours a day.

Booker T. Man, I don't care what you say. You're crazy as hell if you think I'm going to let you or anyone else start writing a program for me, not in this life, baby. I'm living my life the way I want to.

Gideon. You're really on an ego trip. Everything is I, I, I, I. Why don't you wake up? The whole notion of individualism is nothing but a game that whites are running down so they can continue to oppress us. If individualism is so great why don't they practice it themselves, instead of isolating, and murdering everyone who tries to stand up for what's right? I don't see how you can be stupid enough to swallow all that garbage anyway. You're worse than Dad. Running around, talking, and criticizing all the time. Why don't you check yourself out before it's too late?

Booker T. I think you'd better check your ownself out, baby brother. Why are you really getting so excited and upset about some white girl you don't even know? Will you tell me that, please?

Gideon. Because I don't want to see my brother running around being a hypocrite and a jive ass phony, that's why. I want to see you get yourself together, that's why. If you're into a white thing, stop talking black. You confuse people. And if you must come around people who are fighting for black self-determination, don't try to hide where you're really at. Don't sneak around. Be a man. Do it out in the open. Just declare yourself a part-time member of the struggle.

Booker T. Ah, later for you, man. I don't have to stand here and listen to a whole lot of bullshit. Why don't you dig yourself? *(starts to leave)*

Gideon. And why don't you dig yourself, superspade. How about it, you bringing your girl friend to the wedding? Shall I tell Momma and Daddy? I understand she went to Vassar. I'm sure that they will be highly impressed.

Booker T. All right, Einstein. I know what you want. I haven't dusted you off in a long time.

Gideon. Why you want to get into a physical thing, when all I'm asking you to do is be a man? You can't be into a black and white thing at the same time. It won't work. That's like being a neutral, and neutrality adds up to zero. You've got to choose, man. Fence straddling is a dangerous game.

Booker T. Ah, what do you know?

Gideon. I know that you're a zero. I'll bet I know that.

Booker T. All right, come on, Mr. Know-It-All. I've got something just for you. I'm going to show you what happens to people who always have smart answers. I'm going to rock your skies. *(approaches Gideon, ready to do much battle)*

Gideon. Ain't going to be no more of that, big brother. *(grabs spear and crouches slightly in a position of defense)* Now, all right, come on, baby, you can rock anything you want to. I just want my cut, that's all.
Booker T. Put down that spear, turkey.
Gideon. I'll put it down all right.
Booker T. Just put it down, I dare you. All that talk about being a man. Where is your heart?
Gideon. In my head, where it suppose to be. See? That's where you and I differ, big brother. You get emotional, and then you don't think. Don't you know better than to attack a man on his own turf? You don't know what else I've got up here.
Booker T. Ah, your heart pumps lemonade. What's the matter with you, chump? You chickenshit? Why don't you drop that spear? You afraid of a fair one?
Gideon. Can't you do anything besides talk, phony?
Booker T. Yea. *(feints at Gideon, testing him)*
Gideon. Ha! *(flicks spear expertly in defense of himself)* What's the matter, John Wayne?
Booker T. Put down the spear and I'll teach you a lesson, knock some sense into your head.
Gideon. I'm already teaching you a lesson, you're just not getting it. You see, it's not about a lot of talk, it's about action. Dig it?
Booker T. Ah, later for you. You're crazy, phony. *(turns to leave)* You're not worth the bother.
Gideon. What's the matter, baby? Where is *your* heart?
Booker T. Put down that spear, and I'll show you.
Gideon. Talk is cheap. The only good ideas are the ones that you put into practice.
Booker T. You going to put down that spear?
Gideon. Can a buffalo skate?
Booker T. All right, all right, Che, I'll be seeing you. *(exits)*
Gideon. Yea, maybe I'll drop by Terry's one night.

(Curtain)

ACT I

SCENE 3

Ruby. *(Ruby and Mrs. Brooks enter through the front door.)* Girl, I sure wish I could get my hands on whoever that is keeps pushing every one of them buttons on the elevator before they get off. The old elevator door banging shut on every floor just about drove me out of my mind. I don't see how you can be so good-natured about it, Gladys.

Mrs. Brooks. Sometimes I think that's my trouble, I'm too good-natured about everything.

Ruby. Ah, girl.

Mrs. Brooks. It's true, and you know it. I just let everybody push me around.

Ruby. Don't be so hard on yourself, Gladys.

Mrs. Brooks. But, girl, this morning I made up my mind, I'm leaving Mr. Brooks.

Ruby. Oh, Gladys, it's not that bad, is it? Remember it ain't the easiest thing in the world to leave a man after all these years.

Mrs. Brooks. Humph. I should have told him this morning right after he told me I couldn't buy a new dress for Gail's wedding; that was the last straw. Every time I started to tell him or the children, I got cold feet or something came up.

Ruby. Well, you know the Good Book says that everything happens in life for a reason. Maybe you were not suppose to tell him this morning. I mean, we all know that Mr. Brooks has his problems, but I'm not sure that you've got to leave him. You know, Gladys, there is such a thing as going from the refrigerator into the frying pan.

Mrs. Brooks. Oh, Ruby, be serious.

Ruby. I am just as serious as cancer. I mean, it's not as though the man won't work. Why, everybody knows that Mr. Brooks ain't missed a day's work in the last twenty years. That he ain't known to mess up a piece of money.

Mrs. Brooks. A lot of good it does me. Everything in the house is in his name. My name don't appear on nothing except the income tax deductions.

Ruby. Oh, I sees what yo' mean, girl. But you got to admit that he ain't like my Wilbur. At least he doesn't beat you when he gets into his liquor.

Mrs. Brooks. There's worse things a man can do. At least a fight stops sometimes. But Mr. Brooks just goes on forever with his mess. Oh, and the way that man courted me before we got married! Such sweet names he called me. And the day after we got married he started calling me Mrs. Brooks. I should have put my foot down then. But I didn't know any better. And now he's got me keeping that old appointment book so he'll know what I'm doing every minute of the day. Sometimes, way off in my mind somewhere, I think he makes me keep that old book because he's jealous. And the Lord above is my witness that I've never given him cause. Before I leave I'm going to throw that old book out the window. That's what I'm going to do. The only thing I don't have to put in it is when I cough or go to the bathroom.

Ruby. Ah, child.

Mrs. Brooks. And don't let me even look like I want to disagree with him. He rants and raves up a storm, acting like he's going to thunder and lightning for forty days and forty nights.

Ruby. If ever there was a man who knows how to get mad, it's Mr. Brooks.

Mrs. Brooks. Last week I overspent buying groceries, and talking about a man carrying on! You'd have thought that seventeen cents was going to cause a panic down on Wall Street.

Ruby. Now, Gladys, you know I'm on your side. But I will say this for Mr. Brooks, sometimes he does have good intentions.

Mrs. Brooks. My granny always said that the road to hell is paved with good intentions.

Ruby. My granny always said that there's some good in everybody.

Mrs. Brooks. If there's some good in Mr. Brooks he's done done a Houdini with it, and made it disappear. 'Cause you sure can't see it.

Ruby. All in all, child. I don't know.

Mrs. Brooks. And he wouldn't even let me buy a new dress for my own daughter's wedding. He starts telling me about his mother. What a good woman she was, and how easy us modern women have it, how she worked from sunup to sundown. Listening to him talk about that woman you'd think she was Joan of Arc, the Virgin Mary, and Aretha Franklin all rolled up into one. And don't let me get started on how he had us raise those children. Or the fact that I'm not even getting a new dress for Gail's wedding Sunday.

Ruby. Well, do what you feel you have to, child. But all the girls sure are going to be disappointed if you leave Mr. Brooks. You know how much pride we take in your sticking in there all these years. You know, you're sort of like our hero. Like our North Star.

Mrs. Brooks. Thanks, Ruby. It's always nice to know that the girls are on my side. It's going to be hard leaving after all these years, and I'm going to need all the moral support I can get. But I can't take it no more. I just can't. They all act like I don't have no feelings—like I'm an invisible woman. Nobody, absolutely nobody pays any attention to me. They act like I'm part of the scenery, like an old couch or something. *(starts crying)*

Ruby. Oh, Gladys. *(The doorbell rings.)* I'll bet that's Stormy Monday.

Mrs. Brooks. Oh Lord, I don't want her to catch me crying. Coming! *(moves toward the door, wiping away her tears)* Coming! Come on in, Stormy, how are you doing?

Stormy Monday. I'm doing it to death. I can't stay long. Well, look who's here. How are you doing this morning, Ruby?

Ruby. Fine.

Stormy Monday. And how is Breck, and Gillette, and Jean Nate, and Ajax, and Wildroot?

Ruby. Fine, just fine. Everybody is fine.

Stormy Monday. Oh, I finished making your dress. But I don't know if it still fits. With the way you keep gaining weight. Hey, Gladys I was reading in the papers this morning about this outfit called Weight Watchers. It seems that this lady lost fifty pounds in two months—not that you have that much to lose. Have you ever heard of the Weight Watchers, Gladys?

Ruby. You ever heard of S.I.J.?

Stormy Monday. Naw, what's that?

Ruby. S.I.J. means sock in the jaw. It's good for people who have diarrhea of the mouth. You keep messing with me this morning, and I'm gonna give you a chance to try it.

Stormy Monday. Un huh. I heard that the welfare people were by your apartment last night, and almost caught Wilbur. Got to admit the man's got a whole lot of heart. Hanging out of the window, fifteen stories up, I wish I'd been there, I'd of poured lye on his hands! Rid the world of another one of them creeps.

Mrs. Brooks. Stormy, be nice to Ruby. You shouldn't be so hard on men.

Ruby. Yea.

Stormy Monday. Shoot, after all you two been through with men I don't see why you want to argue with me. Neither one of you can name me one good man. Not one.

Ruby. Adam Clayton Powell.

Stormy Monday. Ruby, how does it feel to be washed up at thirty-seven?

Ruby. I'd rather be a has-been than a never-was!

Stormy Monday. Wow, that was clever. Listen, all you two do is sit around and complain, talking about what you're going to do. You're scared to death of men. If a man came in right now, and said boo, you'd probably fall out flat on the floor. How either one of you can even fix your mouth to say something good about a man is a mystery to me.

Mrs. Brooks. Oh, Stormy, some men are good people. Just because you've been burnt once you act like you've got a patent on being evil.

Stormy Monday. Oh, Gladys, you're always saying that, when you know it's not true. The fact is, you two have been through more changes with men than I have. Gladys, the way you've been fussing I'm surprised that you're still here. But then I know you, Gladys. All you want to do is sit around and complain. You ain't never going nowhere.

Mrs. Brooks. I am too. I made up my mind this morning. I'm leaving.

Stormy Monday. Uh, huh. Hey, Ruby, you think Gladys is really going to leave this time?

Ruby. My name is hess, I'm not in this mess. Yall know I've been against Gladys leaving all along. Gladys been hanging in there all these years she ought to be used to it by now.

Mrs. Brooks. Oh, Ruby! How can you say such a thing when you know what I've had to put up with all these years? You know the only reason I stayed this long is because of the children. But it's different now Gail is getting married. The boys can take care of themselves. That's all I've been waiting for all these years. When that preacher says I pronounce you man and wife, I'm starting me a new life.

Ruby. I'm sorry I said that, Gladys.

Stormy Monday. What's there to be sorry about? Gladys ain't going anywhere. She's just talking. Gladys, you know you ain't going anywhere. I'll bet you don't even have any money. Sitting around talking about what you're going to do. Hey, Ruby, you think Gladys got any money?

Ruby. I'm not in this mess, I told you.

Mrs. Brooks. I do have some money, I just haven't had a chance to save much. I've got twenty-seven dollars and thirty-one cents.

Stormy Monday. Twenty-seven dollars and thirty-one cents! Where are you planning to go, Times Square?

Mrs. Brooks. Oh, Stormy. *(starts crying)*

Stormy Monday. Oh, come on, Gladys, you know I'm your friend. I'm not trying to hurt you. I'm just trying to make a point. Let me put it to you another way. After getting the money end straight, what's the next thing you'd do?

Mrs. Brooks. Oh, I don't know.

Stormy Monday. How about it, Ruby? What would you do? It ought to be easy for you to figure out, girl, Wilbur is always talking about doing it.

Ruby. Pack your bags?

Stormy Monday. Ruby, sometimes you amaze me, give me five on the black hand side. *(gives Ruby five)* That's what I'm talking about! If you was leaving, wouldn't you be packing your bags, instead of sitting around folding clothes? I'll bet you haven't even thought of getting your clothes together, have you, Gladys?

Mrs. Brooks. Well, I was going to get started packing after I take my walk.

Stormy Monday. What kind of old walk?

Mrs. Brooks. Why, Mr. Brooks told me to take a walk after I come back from the hairdresser today. You know the sun gives body to your skin.

Stormy Monday and Ruby. *(in unison with Mrs. Brooks)* You know the sun gives body to your skin.

Stormy Monday. See, that's what I'm talking about, Gladys. See? Mr. Brooks has kept you in the dark so long, honey, it's hard for you to think for yourself. Truthfully, I don't think you're ready to leave Mr. Brooks.

Ruby. Stormy Monday, I guess I had you wrong all these years. You do have some sense. Gladys, you don't have any business leaving Mr. Brooks. Not as long as he keeps a roof over your head, food in your stomach, and clothes on your back.
Stormy Monday. Yea, it's a lousy idea for you to leave Mr. Brooks, Gladys. But I think you should do something. Hmmm, let me think. Say, I'm dry as a potato chip. Gladys, you got anything to drink?
Mrs. Brooks. I think there's some Scotch left. It's down here under the sink.
Ruby. Speaking of potato chips, you got anything to nibble on?
Mrs. Brooks. Potato chips in the cabinet.
Stormy Monday. Ruby, you'll have to take care of your own weakness. I'll have no part of it. *(looks beneath the sink and gets a bottle)* Yea, this ought to do it. How about you all? You want a drink? Ruby, Gladys?
Ruby. I might have a little taste. For medicinal purposes.
Stormy Monday. Oh! that's my girl.
Mrs. Brooks. Well, you two go ahead. You know Mr. Brooks doesn't like for me to drink.
Stormy Monday. See, Gladys. See what I'm talking about?
Mrs. Brooks. Well, O.K. But not too much.
Stormy Monday. There!
Mrs. Brooks. Stormy! That's too much.
Stormy Monday. Sorry about that. Trade with Ruby, hers don't have as much as yours. *(They all drink.)* Cheers. This is good for what ails you. Helps you relax. Hmmmmm. What was I saying?
Ruby. Come on, Stormy Monday, quit stalling. Run down your commercial.
Stormy Monday. Right, right. Gladys, you have to change yourself.
Mrs. Brooks. Change myself?
Stormy Monday. Well, I got this idea from something Gideon was saying the other day. You see, the thing is, why should you leave a home you've helped to build all these years with your toil and sweat? If anybody should leave, it should be you know who. But we know that'll never happen. So what we have to do is change things so that you can live in peace in this house.
Mrs. Brooks. I see. But that's not going to be easy.
Stormy Monday. Gladys, you've got to become more aggressive, more assertive in this house. Yeah! We've got to figure out a way to change your image.
Mrs. Brooks. Change my image?
Stormy Monday. Yep. We have to create a new Gladys.
Ruby. Create a new Gladys? Don't pay any attention to Stormy Monday, Gladys. She ain't got a bit of sense. Talking about creating a new Gladys. How are you going to change somebody's image, and if you do,

what good would it do? We know Mr. Brooks treated the old Gladys bad. He's subject to treat a new one worse than that.
Stormy Monday. Cool it, Ruby, just cool it. Your mouth is going forty miles an hour in a fifteen mile an hour zone. Gladys can change herself. It's like Gideon was saying. Remember when he was talking about how they took over that building, he said that in a people's struggle for liberation you have to change everything about yourselves? The way you think, the way you look, the way you feel. Well, the way I figure it, that's the kind of change that Gladys has to go through.
Mrs. Brooks. Well, I hope you can think of it pretty soon, Stormy Monday. I have an appointment at the hairdresser.
Stormy Monday. *(pours Gladys another drink)* Gladys, instead of getting your hair straightened, why don't you let me fix your hair in a natural?
Ruby. Gladys, I told you not to listen to Stormy Monday. She ain't got a lick of sense. If they put her brains in a bird it would fly backwards. You too old for that kind of nonsense and, besides, everybody uptown knows that Mr. Brooks hates naturals worse than God hates sin.
Stormy Monday. But that's the whole point. Gladys, if you got your hair done in a natural, Mr. Brooks would have to sit up and take notice. He'd see that he was dealing with a new person. Gladys, that's it, you've got to let me do your hair in a natural. That's the only solution.
Mrs. Brooks. Oh, I don't know about all this, Stormy. I think Ruby is right. I am too old and besides I don't think Mr. Brooks would like it.
Ruby. Yea, Stormy Monday, you acting like you don't know Mr. Brooks. Besides, I doubt if Gladys' hair would do like that.
Mrs. Brooks. Yeah, it's so thin maybe it's too curly.
Stormy Monday. Oh, you two make me sick. You don't have any spin. Letting the man push you around all the time. Well, it's none of my business, it's no skin off my nose. But from now on I don't want to hear you two sitting around complaining all the time. And quit talking about what you're going to do all the time. You act like I'm asking you to blow up a bridge or something. When all I'm asking you to do is stand up for your rights. Gladys, you just made a speech about what you've been going through, and now listen to you, you ought to be ashamed of yourself. And, Ruby, you're no better, telling Gladys to take a whole lot of junk. After what you've been through with Wilbur all these years you should be plotting a way to get to him. The trouble is, neither of you like yourselves or have any respect for yourselves, taking all this crap from men, and that's why your men don't respect you. And you know what? I don't blame them. I've lost respect for both of you myself. Sitting around crying all the time when you could be doing something. *(starts to leave)*
Mrs. Brooks. Stormy?

Stormy Monday. Yea.

Mrs. Brooks. Do you think it will work? Are you sure?

Stormy Monday. No, Gladys, I'm not sure. But I'll tell you this. We are responsible for fifty percent of what happens to us. All I'm asking you to do is to take care of your fifty percent.

Mrs. Brooks. Oh, I don't know. Stormy, maybe you're right, but you've gotta understand. I was just a baby when I married Mr. Brooks. Just a baby. And he treated me like one. And I liked it. I liked him fussing over me. I never had someone to love me before. I liked him taking care of me, telling me what to do. I liked staying home taking care of the children, while he went out working, making the money. But you know what? For years now I've wanted to help him. I wanted to go to school and learn how to be a manicurist. I could have done it, but he wouldn't hear it. He just patted me on my head. Well, he stopped me then, but he won't stop me now. All right, Stormy, you got a deal. I'll do it!

Stormy Monday. Good! Oh, Gladys, I'm so proud of you. You're beginning to change already. Come on, we have to wash your hair, so let's go into the bathroom and get started. Oh, wait. *(They all drink.)* You coming, Ruby?

Ruby. Honey, I wouldn't miss this for nothing in God's whole world.

Mrs. Brooks. Let's go change Gladys' image.

(The lights dim to black as they exit. A moment later they dim back on. Stormy Monday, Ruby, and Gladys enter talking.)

Stormy Monday. Come on out here where we have some room, Gladys. *(Stormy Monday seats Gladys in a chair and removes a towel from around her head and begins combing out Gladys' natural.)* Oh, Gladys, there is one other thing I thought of that you have to do.

Mrs. Brooks. What's that, Stormy?

Stormy Monday. It's really a dynamite idea. You know sometimes I think I border on genius. I was just thinking that we ought to do something about you and that barbershop. Why shouldn't you be able to help in there if you want to? Mr. Brooks' not letting women in there never made any sense anyway. Gladys, you've got to go to that barbershop. Hold your head still, Gladys.

Mrs. Brooks. I don't know about going to that barbershop, Stormy.

Ruby. Yea, getting your hair cut is one thing, but going to that barbershop is something else again.

Stormy Monday. You've got to go to that barbershop, that's all there is to it. Say, Gladys, where is that material I gave you?

Mrs. Brooks. Out in the hall closet.

Stormy Monday. Get it for me, Ruby. I want to try something later on. Go on now, Ruby.

Ruby. Well, don't do nothing while I'm gone.

Stormy Monday. See, Gladys, we've got to change everything. Wearing your hair in a natural takes care of your image, but you've also got to change the way you think. That's why you've got to go to that barbershop. See, Gladys, when you change the way you think, you change the way you act, and if you don't do something dramatic Mr. Brooks will just look at you, and after a while he'll say: "Why, that's old Gladys over there with her hair cut in a natural. She had me fooled for a minute, there!" So you have to go into that barbershop! The idea of not letting women in there! Can you imagine something like that in Harlem in this day and age? Oh, wait, you need some earrings. You see, you ought to demand to work in there, Gladys. They need some women in there. Give the place some style, and class. I hear it's nothing but a den of iniquity anyway. What you ought to do is make up a list of demands and present them to Mr. Brooks at his barbershop.

Ruby. *(who has entered during the last sentences)* Do what?!

Stormy Monday. Gladys needs to make up a list of demands and give them to Mr. Brooks at his shop. Just like Gideon and them kids did up to the college.

Ruby. You're crazy, Stormy Monday, and why are you paying so much attention to them kids all the time?

Stormy Monday. Everybody ought to pay attention to them kids, they're making a lot of sense. What do you say, Gladys? It's like the topping on the cake.

Mrs. Brooks. I don't know, Stormy.

Stormy Monday. Gladys, you've come this far.

Mrs. Brooks. Well, if you say so.

Stormy Monday. Now let me cut just a little more off the top.

Ruby. Not too much. Gladys'll look like a man.

Stormy Monday. Yall so backwards. Do I look like a man? There. You ain't going to look like no man.

Ruby. Touch it up on the sides a little, Stormy Monday.

Stormy Monday. Who's doing this, chick? Yes, we've almost got it. Ruby, get my mirror out of my purse, please. All right, Gladys, stand up.

Mrs. Brooks. Let me see, Ruby, let me see. Is this me?

Stormy Monday. Just one more second, Gladys, and then you can check it out.

Ruby. You do look sort of different . . .

Mrs. Brooks. So this is the new me.

Stormy Monday. Not the new you, Gladys, the real you.

Ruby. . . . sort of like—sort of African. That's it, Gladys, that's what you look like. One of them African queens.

Mrs. Brooks. An African queen.

Stormy Monday. Hey, Ruby. Go see if you can find Gideon.

Ruby. What do you want with Gideon?

Stormy Monday. Well, since the wedding is Sunday we don't have much time. He can help us plan our strategy—you know, be our consultant so when Gladys presents her list of demands we have ourselves together. And another thing, Gladys. If you're going to be an African queen, you've got to carry yourself like one. Hold your chin up. Stop stooping your shoulders. You've got to walk proud. Beautiful. Yea! O.K. Let's go.

Mrs. Brooks. O.K., but I've got to do something else first. *(picks up her appointment book and tears the pages from it, throwing the pieces all over the floor)*

Stormy Monday. The Queen is going to pay a visit to the King's barbershop.

(Curtain)

ACT II

Time: *Early afternoon.*

Scene: *Typical Harlem barbershop. There are two barber chairs, a jukebox, and several chairs for customers to sit in while they wait. There is a dryer, and a chair and a sink in the rear where facials are performed. There is also a closet in the rear of the shop. Pictures of famous theater and sports personalities hang on the walls. Slim, Sweetmeat, and Mr. Brooks are on stage. Slim and Mr. Brooks are cleaning and rearranging their barber's tools. Sweetmeat is sweeping the floor. Well-known jazz classic from the early 1950's is playing.*

Voice. Shell steaks, shell steaks, anybody inside want some shell steaks?

Mr. Brooks and Slim. No, thanks.

Sweetmeat. Come tomorrow, man.

Voice. You must be outta your damn mind.

Sweetmeat. So how's the wedding coming, John Henry?

Mr. Brooks. I'm handling all of the important details.

Sweetmeat. That's good. Now I know we won't have to worry about a thing. I'll bet you're glad that Gail's getting married. You know what they say: You have a boy and you have to watch just him, but if you have a girl you have to watch every boy on the whole block.

Mr. Brooks. You know I've never had to worry about my Gail in that respect. Not for one minute.

Sweetmeat. That's true. *(Fun Loving enters.)* Hey, here's my man. My main-man. What's happening, Fun Loving?
Fun Loving. What you want to happen, baby?
Sweetmeat. You got it.
Fun Loving. Oh, yeah? Well, it's green lights all the way, baby. Nothing but green lights all the way. You got time to do my face, my man?
Mr. Brooks. Sure thing, Fun Loving. Right this way. *(leads him to the rear)*
Fun Loving. *(plays a record on the jukebox—rhythm and blues music)* This is my man. *(hums along with the record for a few bars)* You ready? I've got a lot of business to take care of today, and these streets are mean. Not that that worries me. I'm not giving up nothing. I wouldn't give a cripple crab a crutch if I owned a lumber yard. *(sits in chair)*
Sweetmeat. Deep in the heart of the kingdom sticks, the animals had a poolroom but the baboon was slick. 'Til up jumped the monkey from Cocoa-not Grove. He said let me get some of this money before this joint close. The baboon said: Man, you want to shoot some pool? The monkey said, I can't shoot no pool, but if you'll pull up a stump to fit your rump, I'll play you some Coon-can 'til your rear end jumps. How about it, Slim, you want to play a couple of hands of Coon-can before another customer comes in?
Slim. I don't have time right now, but I don't see why you want to play me, Sweetmeat. You know what happened the last time we played. The score was three to three. You lost three and I won three.
Sweetmeat. Ah, everybody gets unlucky now and then. You quit just when I was getting the feeling of the cards. Hey, John Henry, what's happening with Gideon, he still up on the roof?
Mr. Brooks. Sweetmeat, I've asked you not to mention that name to me.
Slim. Gideon sure is one out-of-sight youngster.
Mr. Brooks. I fixed his wagon this morning. He'll come around. Mark my word.
Sweetmeat. You really laid it on him, huh?
Mr. Brooks. Put my foot down.
Slim. He's still on that strike, ain't he?
Mr. Brooks. Yea, but like I said that mess is coming to a squeaking halt, today. Oh, sometimes . . . If I could just get my hands around his neck.
Sweetmeat. Easy now, John Henry, easy now.
Mr. Brooks. You're right, Sweetmeat. I shouldn't be wasting my time on that boy. He'll be a man soon. Yes, soon all the children will be gone, and Mrs. Brooks and I will be left alone to grow old gracefully together.
Slim. I still don't know how come you were lucky enough to get a good woman like Mrs. Brooks.
Mr. Brooks. What do you mean luck? Mrs. Brooks is no accident. I created her with these very hands. You see, the trouble with you, Slim, is that you don't understand women. My motto is be just, but firm.

Slim. Just but firm! Jesus Christ, John Henry, one of these days she's going to get sick and tired of your crap and she's going to turn you around.

Mr. Brooks. The possibility of Mrs. Brooks being able to, as you say, turn me around is about as likely as our going skiing in Purgatory.

Sweetmeat. Who's that?

Black Militant. *(Enters carrying a poster under his arm. The poster is about a rally that is to be held.)* Seize the time. All power to the people. I'd like to speak to the brother who's in charge here.

Mr. Brooks. You're speaking to him.

Black Militant. Do you own this place, brother?

Mr. Brooks. Lock, stock and barrel!

Black Militant. Right on. Right on. Since you are a brother, I know that you'll put up this poster in your window. See. It's for the legal defense of Brother Ali Hassan. The fascist pig power structure is daily becoming more and more sadistic. We are oppressed because we are black and we've got to unite on the basis of our color. The pigs are not jiving, they are ready to move on us all. Thank you. *(gives Mr. Brooks the poster)* All power to the people. Blood to the horse's brow, and woe to those who can't swim, Jim. *(exits)*

Mr. Brooks. Calling people animals. *(throws poster in the trash)* Filthy mouth rascal.

Slim. Ah, what are you talking about, John Henry? Don't get hung up on the man's words, just deal with where he was coming from.

Sweetmeat. I know where they're coming from, running around talking about "Say it loud, I'm black and I'm proud." I'll start listening to them when they change their tune. Yes, say it soft, I'm black and I'm boss.

Slim. You two belong in a museum. You're museum Negroes. Talk about Uncle Toms, you two are Uncle Remuses. You should have given that boy a play, John Henry.

Mr. Brooks. I'm not looking for controversities, I'm looking for business.

Slim. You're always talking about free enterprise. If you really believe in it, you would give that brother a play. And you're supposed to be a man of principles, too.

Mr. Brooks. I am! But sometimes you have to forget about principles and do what's right.

Slim. Well, I'll say one thing for you, you're consistent. You're wrong about women and politics.

(Sampson enters; phone rings.)

Sampson. Gentlemen, gentlemen. How's it going, Mr. Brooks, Sweetmeat? *(sits in chair)* Sorry I'm late. I got hung up.

Sweetmeat. Hey, here comes Rolls Royce. *(Rolls Royce enters.)* How are you doing, Rolls Royce?

Rolls Royce. As the rooster crowed, those who stood before the bar shouted: Open the door! You know what a little time we have to stay. And once departed, we return no more. What number are you investing in today, Mr. John Henry Brooks?
Mr. Brooks. 333.
Rolls Royce. Thank you, sir. *(does not write any numbers down)* Waste not your time in vain pursuit of this and that endeavor. Groove with the Grape! For 'tis better to be happy with the fruitful grape than sadden after none or bitter fruit. Mr. Sweetmeat.
Sweetmeat. 505. And give me a three-way combination on that, please, sir.
Rolls Royce. Bless you, sir. *(addresses Slim, who does not play the numbers)* Ah, make the most of the time that you have. Before you, too, into dust descend. Dust to dust and under dust to lie. Without songs. Without singers. Without wine. Without end! Yes, when I was young I did eagerly visit philosophers and saints. And I heard great arguments about this and that. But every time I came out of the same door that I went in. *(proceeds to Fun Loving)* And if the wine you drink, if the lips you press, end just the way they started, 'tis a small matter. Then think. You are today what you were yesterday. Tomorrow you shall not be less. Yes, Fun Loving?
Fun Loving. 456. And an extra five dollars on the four to lead.
Rolls Royce. *(takes a wine bottle from his hip pocket)* We are no other than a moving row of magic shadow shapes that come and go around and around a sun-shaped lantern held in the night by the master of the show. *(He emerges from the closet, walking fast. He points a finger at each person he passes.)* Fun Loving. 456. With an extra five dollars on the four to lead, right?
Fun Loving. Right!
Rolls Royce. *(stops in front of Slim)* My man! Come fill the cup, and in the fire of spring your winter garment of repentance fling. The bird of time has but a little while to flutter, and the bird is on his flight. *(moves on to Sweetmeat)* Mr. Sweetmeat, 505. And give me a three-way combination, please, sir. Right?
Sweetmeat. Right!
Rolls Royce. And Mr. John Henry Brooks. 333, right?
Mr. Brooks. Right!
Rolls Royce. And lately, by the open door came shining through the dusk an angel shape bearing a huge vessel on her shoulder. And she offered me a taste from it. And it was the Grape! *(exits)*
Sweetmeat. I see him do it every day, but I still don't believe it. How in the world a man can remember all those numbers without writing them down is a real deep, dark mystery to me. Man!
Mr. Brooks. Why, it's simple enough. Rolls Royce has what they call a photogenic memory.

Sweetmeat. Oh, I see. . . .
Mr. Brooks. He doesn't have to write anything down. People with a memory like his can remember whole books at a time.
Sweetmeat. Mmmmm! My, my, my. A mind like that, and he's only a numbers man. Now to me that seems like an awful waste of talent. He ought to be downtown on Wall Street somewhere.
Slim. I don't know what's wrong with you guys today. You know as well as I do that Rolls Royce worked down on Wall Street for years. As an elevator operator.
Sweetmeat. Hey, that's right, I clean forgot about that. Well, I sure hope I hit today. I can use the dust. I got to do some mean chippie chasing. And to do that, you need some heavy greens in your pockets.
Slim. You sure talk bad for a married man.
Sweetmeat. My wife is the one married, not me. And another thing, Slim. The average black woman, no matter what her age is, wants to get married.
Mr. Brooks. Sweetmeat, man your post!
Sweetmeat. *(rushes to the door, preventing the Lady from entering)* Hey, lady! You can't come in here.
Evangelist. The Kingdom of God is not a matter of talk, but of power. *(attempts to push her way past Sweetmeat)* Choose then: Am I to come to you with a rod in my hand or in a sweet and gentle spirit?
Sweetmeat. Shoot your best shot, lady.
Evangelist. Oh, be proud of yourselves! For His part, though He is absent in body, He is present in spirit. And His judgment upon the sinner is already given. Yes, Jesus! Given as if He were indeed present. . . . *(tries to catch Sweetmeat off guard)*
Sweetmeat. I'm sorry, lady. We loves the word just like everybody else, but you've got to work your show from the outside. I ain't let no woman in here in fifteen years, and there ain't no sense in my breaking a record like that, now is there?
Slim. Preach, brother, preach!
Mr. Brooks. Steady there, Sweetmeat. Steady there!
Evangelist. The man who sins is to be consigned to Satan for the destruction of his body. So that his spirit may be saved on the day of our Lord. In the name of the Lord Jesus Jehovah, Amen!
Sweetmeat. Sure, lady, sure. *(Gives Evangelist money and she exits. Sweetmeat starts walking down the stairs.)*
Mr. Brooks. Stop right there, sir. Stop dead in your tracks. Let's have the treatment.
Sweetmeat. Ah, John Henry. *(gets bottle of disinfectant and starts spraying)*
Mr. Brooks. You missed the doorknob, Sweetmeat.
Sweetmeat. Oh, all right. There, that ought to do it.

Mr. Brooks. That's the closest call we've had in years. I do believe you're getting old there, Sweetmeat.
Sweetmeat. John Henry Brooks! Watch your tongue. Nobody's getting old. I played it like that. It's just like my father used to say, a heap see and a few know. You don't realize the complications of a job like mine. It requires a dab of delicacy. 'Tis true, I had to keep that good woman out, but at the same time, I had to let the word of the good Lord in. You see?
Mr. Brooks. Hmmmmmph!
Slim. Boy, them little old ladies sure tickles me. They're all over Harlem. Don't they know Blackie's already got enough religion? It's Whitey who needs to be turned on to God.
Mr. Brooks. Are you blaspheming there, Slim?
Slim. I'm just telling it like it is. Them old ladies ought to be out in the suburbs spreading the word. It's Whitey who needs to be reminded that the Bible says that you got to reap what you sow, and the way I see it, Whitey sure has a lot of dues to pay.
Sweetmeat. I heard that God is a black woman.
Mr. Brooks. Oh, my God!
Sweetmeat. And if that's true, we're all going to have to pay some mighty steep dues. Can't nobody tell me about black women, man. They're evil! Of course, you can get around them if you're smooth. You've got to have style. Am I telling him right, Fun Loving? You got to be smooth with black women, right?
Slim. Ah, man. *(enter First and Second Junkies)*
Sweetmeat. Hey, shine, fellows?
First Junkie. Naw, baby, we're here on business. *(passes out business card)* Yeah. That's right. Aikens and Poole Enterprises, Unlimited. We gives the best deals in town. Hey, man! *(whispers to his partner, who has dropped into a nod)* Yeah, bay-bee, you can do business with us.
Sweetmeat. Say, let me see that camera. Hmmmm. Hey, John Henry, I can use this to take pictures at the wedding. Hmmmm. How much?
First Junkie. Fifteen.
Sweetmeat. Fifteen dollars sure seems like an awful lot of money to me. . . .
First Junkie. It's made by the Japanese, my-man. Some of that Eastern Soul. Check it out. My competitors downtown are selling it for five times as much. But we can sell ours cheaper because we've got a boss connection, dig?
Sweetmeat. Yeah, I see. I'll give you ten for it.
First Junkie. Ah, man, you bad as them white cats up on one-two-five street. *(drops into a nod)* O.K., baby, you got a deal. *(nods on this line)* Everything is everything. Everybody is everybody. *(Sweetmeat pays*

him.) Thank you, my-man. Thank you for doing business with Aikens and Poole Enterprises, Unlimited. And remember, you can always do business with us. Even if you don't have a friend at Chase Manhattan. *(They exit. Sampson gets his coat.)*

Slim. Man, when we get control of our community, that's the first thing we should deal with.

Sampson. Right on.

Sweetmeat. Man, things sure are changing. I'm going to get me some films, and take me up some pictures at that wedding on Sunday. I remember the time when I coulda got a camera like this for eight dollars. Prices are sure going up.

(Sampson leaves, saying good-bye. Slim cleans up.)

Mr. Brooks. It's true that things are going up. But actually we're all better off with prices being higher, since that means the economy has excess capital for investing.

Sweetmeat. That makes sense. *(He is involved with his camera.)*

Mr. Brooks. Oh, I'm telling you, America is the world's richest country. And all because of free enterprise. Yes, that's what it's all about. Free enterprise. Equal competition!

Slim. How are you gonna talk about equal competition when white people control everything?

Mr. Brooks. That's the black man's trouble. He doesn't understand the various concepts of Big Business. And it's so simple. Goods and services! Free enterprise!

Slim. Oh, come on now, John Henry, don't start that stuff this morning. I don't want to get a headache. The way the government subsidizes big business, the only ones who can practice free enterprise in America are poor people. How you can still talk all that nonsense is beyond me. The man talks all that free enterprise to keep you down. Brothers ain't free nowhere else, so how they get to be free in business all of a sudden?

Mr. Brooks. You'll understand these things when you get older, Slim.

Slim. Ah, why don't you wake up, John Henry? The man makes the goods, and as long as we're hung up on material things, we'll always be in a trick. I keep telling you that things have changed. People are skipping off to the moon, and you're still talking that talk. Like I said, you're consistent. You were wrong about women, and politics, and now you're wrong about business.

Sweetmeat. Speaking of business. Somebody better come in here soon and get a shoeshine. The eagle flies on Friday, and Saturday I go out to play. And I need some money. M-O-N-E-Y.

Slim. You give up every little bit you get.

Sweetmeat. Don't you worry about it. You see I've studied black women. And I know if you want to get to them you need some cash.
Mr. Brooks. Hmmmmmmph!
Sweetmeat. Now I agree with you, John Henry, on everything but the subject of women. Being just and firm won't work on the average black woman. Black women like to be entertained. They don't want to go out with you if you can't go first class. I've studied them. I know what I'm talking about. I know 'em.
Mr. Brooks. How's that, Fun Loving? *(gives Fun Loving a mirror)*
Fun Loving. That looks boss, my-man. Real boss.
Sweetmeat. Let me dust your shoes off there, Fun Loving. Then you'll be cleaner than the board of health.
Fun Loving. Why not? I'm free as the breeze, and I do what I please. Besides, everything else about me is neat and clean. And it don't take nothing but money. Here you go, baby. *(pays Mr. Brooks, giving him a liberal tip from his huge bankroll)*
Mr. Brooks. Thank you, Fun Loving, you're a gentleman and a scholar.
Slim. Hey, Sweetmeat.
Sweetmeat. What's that? *(shining Fun Loving's shoes)*
Slim. Women understand us better than we understand them. That's why we have so much trouble with them. 'Cause guys are so busy running down their game that they don't really listen to what their chicks are saying. We should study them more.
Fun Loving. Hmmmmmmph!
Sweetmeat. What's the matter there, Fun Loving?
Fun Loving. In my alley if you're hip to yourself that makes you hip to everybody else. I don't mean to be dipping into your business. Now I've been checking out you dudes talking about women, I'm going to let you peep a little of my game. All you need to get a woman is a strong rap. Hey! What'd I say? Every woman in the streets wants a piece of me. You dig it. They call me sweet Peter Jeter, the womb beater, the baby maker, the cradle shaker. The deer slayer, the buck binder and woman finder. I'm known from the gold coast to the rocky shores of Maine. Dig? Fun Loving is my name, and love is my game. I'm the bed tucker, the cock plucker, the mother fucker. The milk shaker, the record breaker, the population maker. The gun slinger, the baby bringer, the hum dinger, the pussy ringer, the man with the terrible middle finger. I'm Fun Loving the hard hitter, the bull-shitter, the poly-nuci gitter, the beast from the east. The judge, the sludge, the wimmen's pet, the men's fret, the faggot's pin-up boy. Fun Loving the dicker, the ass kicker, the cherry picker, the city slicker, the tiddy licker. I ain't giving up nothing but bubbly gum, and hard times. And I'm fresh out of bubble gum. I'm the man who walked the water and tied a whale's tail

in a knot. I taught the fish how to swim, crossed the burning sand, and shook the devil's hand. I rode around the world on a snail, carrying a sack that said airmail. I walked forty-nine miles of barbed wire and used a cobra snake for a necktie. I took a hammer and a nail and built the world. Yes! I'm hemp the demp, the woman's pimp. I'm a bad dude. Women fight for my delights. Johnny Rip-Saw, the devil's son-in-law. I gave a highway patrolman a speeding ticket, and sold a blind man a flashlight. Oh yes! I roam the world, God knows I wander. Smoking stuff is where I get my thunder. I'm the only man in the world who knows why white milk makes yellow butter. . . . I even know where the lights go when you cut the switch off. Now I might not be the baddest man in the whole world, but I'm in the top two. And my father is getting old.

Sweetmeat. Work your show, Fun Loving. Work your show.
Fun Loving. What can I tell you? With women you either got it or you don't. Here you go. *(gives Sweetmeat money plus tip and plays jukebox—rhythm and blurs music—romantic)*
Booker T. *(rushes in out of breath)* Hey, Dad. Hey day!
Mr. Brooks. What's the matter, son? Calm down, son, calm down. Here, you'd better sit down.
Booker T. No, you'd better sit down, Dad. Momma is coming here.
Sweetmeat. Here! To this barbershop! *(runs to guard the front door)*
Mr. Brooks. Relax there, Sweetmeat, relax. Get me a glass of water, Sweetmeat. I made up Mrs. Brooks' schedule myself, and I know it don't call for her to be coming to my barbershop.
Booker T. But I'm telling you she's on her way here.
Sweetmeat. Sure thing, John Henry. *(goes to the rear for a glass of water)* The sun must have gotten to that boy. Talking about Mrs. Brooks is on her way here.
Mrs. Brooks. *(Enters with Ruby and Stormy Monday. She has a scroll in her hand.)* John Henry!
Mr. Brooks. Sweetmeat! Sweetmeat! We're being invaded. Invaded. The door. Get the door. We've got to keep these women out of here. You can't come in here, you can't.
Sweetmeat. Oh, Lordy. Hey, ladies, you can't come in here. Women can't cross this doorway. *(slips and falls)*
Mrs. Brooks. John Henry Brooks, Jr. This is a new day!
Booker T. It's Momma!
Mr. Brooks. What! Mrs. Brooks!
Slim. Mrs. Brooks!
Sweetmeat. Mrs. Brooks! *(gets up, but falls down again)*
Mrs. Brooks. Mrs. Brooks! And in the name of peace, self-determination, and liberation. I demand that you sign this list of demands.

Mr. Brooks. A list of demands . . .
Fun Loving, Sweetmeat, Slim. A list of demands?
Ruby, Stormy Monday. A list of demands!
Mrs. Brooks. A list of demands. And they're not negotiable.

(Curtain)

ACT III

SCENE 1

Time: *The next day, early morning.*
Scene: *The Brooks' apartment.*

Mr. Brooks. Messing me up like this, and on a Saturday, too. My volume day. Don't you realize what you're doing, Mrs. Brooks? Of course she realizes what she's doing, that's why she's doing it. She's ungrateful . . . Just like her son, Gideon. With both of them up on that roof, if there was any justice in life, it would have rained last night like I prayed it would. Ouch! *(burns finger on frying pan)* Booker T. Booker T.! Are you coming or not?
Booker T. *(from offstage)* Coming, Dad, coming.
Mr. Brooks. Oh, that woman. Up there putting all our business in the streets. Gail better talk some sense into her head. I'll tell you that. Come on in, son. I need some help.
Booker T. *(enters, not quite finished dressing)* Dad, I don't know how to cook. What are you cooking, anyway?
Mr. Brooks. You know I have French toast every Saturday morning. Something told me I was making a mistake sending Gail up there to talk to your mother instead of you. How could you take so long getting dressed when you know that we're in a crisis? Where is the cinnamon? I can't find the cinnamon.
Booker T. Hey, Dad, you know what? You should try to figure out some kind of counterplan.
Mr. Brooks. I've already taken care of that. I sent Gail up there to tell your mother that she can return home this morning without any penalties. I'm a just man, I'm willing to forgive all. Ah, here it is.
Booker T. Dad, I really think we need to come up with some kind of an overall strategy.
Mr. Brooks. Now where is the salt? Where in the world is that salt?
Booker T. Here it is, Dad. Yea, we've got to figure out a long-range plan.

Mr. Brooks. And I'm telling you that's not necessary, your mother is just bluffing. She's come to her senses, don't worry.
Booker T. I'm not worried. I just think we should figure out something in case Momma tells Gail she doesn't want to come home right now.
Mr. Brooks. That'll never happen. One night away from me is about all your mother will be able to stand. You want some French toast?
Booker T. Thanks, Dad, but I'm not hungry right now. Hey, you know, it might not be a bad idea for you to sign a few of Momma's demands, you know that?
Mr. Brooks. It sounds to me like you're mixing up your loyalties there, son.
Booker T. Ah, Dad, you know I'm on your side. But it would be a brilliant move if you signed a few of the unimportant ones. Make it look like you're for what's right. Momma might go for that.
Mr. Brooks. Absolutely not. If that's the kind of strategy you were talking about, you can keep it. Son, you don't understand women. You have to be firm with them. You can't waver. If you give a woman an inch, she'll think she's a ruler.
Booker T. I dig what you're saying, Dad. But what if Momma doesn't?
Mr. Brooks. Relax, son, relax. Put your trust in your father. Class always tells in the end. Remember that. *(looks up—balls up fist)* Are you sure you won't have a piece of French toast? *(tastes toast—it is horrible)* Oh, if I could just get my hands on that woman!
Gail. Momma, Momma, Momma. Oh, Momma, are you all right, did you sleep well?

(End of Scene)

(Dressed in Army fatigues, Mrs. Brooks is up on the roof. Army eating utensils, a first aid kit, and a helmet have been added. Mrs. Brooks, who has a pair of binoculars, is looking out onto the street below.)

Mrs. Brooks. Hmmmmm. Gail, are you down there?
Gail. Did you sleep well, Momma?
Mrs. Brooks. Just like a top. . . . And how is that father of yours this morning? Is he having his French toast?
Gail. I guess so, he was cooking when I left. He told me to tell you that you can come home, without any penalties.
Mrs. Brooks. Did he say anything about my demands? Uh . . . uh . . . uh. . . .
Gail. No, he didn't even mention them.
Mrs. Brooks. Oh, that man is impossible. Now I can come back home, eh? Oh, well, that's mighty big of him. Mighty big. But I'm not going for it.

Gail, you go back down there and tell your father that I'm not taking one step until he signs my demands. All of them. Do you hear me? All of them. Oh, what's the matter, Gail?

Gail. Oh, Momma.

Mrs. Brooks. What's the matter, baby?

Gail. Oh, Momma. I'm so worried. My wedding is tomorrow, and you and Daddy are still fighting. I know I'm being selfish, but I can't help it. Why did you have to choose now to stand up to Dad?

Mrs. Brooks. Baby, I'm sorry, but I didn't choose now. I didn't choose the time. It's more like the times chose me. It just happened. It was time, that's all. Time for me to stand up for my rights.

Gail. I'm really proud of you, Momma. I know I should be happy for you because I think you're right, but I've waited so long for Marvin and I want everything to be right with you and Dad and Gideon.

Mrs. Brooks. Don't worry, everything is going to be fine, Gail, I promise you that. While he's been down there sleeping me and Gideon have been up here organizing. So don't worry, Gail, Mr. Brooks and I will get together before the wedding. Now where is Stormy?

Gail. Does Stormy Monday have very much to do with this?

Mrs. Brooks. Sure, Gideon has gotten everyone involved—Stormy, Ruby, her children, most of Gideon's friends. Oh, I'm telling you that everything is under control. Your father will come to his senses. And he is going to learn a lesson. We've got right on our side, so don't worry, you'll have a lovely wedding.

Gail. All right, if you say so, Momma.

Mrs. Brooks. Good. Now you run along and take this list to Mr.—your father. And tell him that I want him to sign every single one of the items or else, do you hear?

Gail. Or else what, Momma?

Gideon. Hey, sis.

Mrs. Brooks. Hi, son. How is it going at the barbershop?

Gideon. It's going great, Momma. Would you believe everyone showed up on time? Everything went like clockwork. How is it going, sis?

Gail. A family squabble in the middle of your wedding. What can I tell you?

Gideon. Yea, well, like I'm sorry about the timing. But I'm glad to see Momma trying to get herself together.

Gail. Oh, Gideon, what's going on, what's going to happen?

Gideon. I guess it all depends on Dad. He's been a good winner all these years, now we'll see if he can be a good loser.

Gail. Well, what are you two up to anyway?

Gideon. Just a little organizing, that's all.

Gail. Well, it looks to me like you're trying to organize a war or something. What are you all doing?

Mrs. Brooks. Don't ask so many questions, Gail. Just take that list down to your father. And tell him it's his last chance.
Gail. Well, I'll see you all later.
Gideon. O.K., sis, keep the faith.
Mrs. Brooks. Stormy should have been here by now! Gideon. See if you can get her on that set!
Gideon. O.K., Momma. But in the meantime you just relax, everything's going to work out just fine.
Mrs. Brooks. We're already five minutes off schedule. Gideon, tell her to hurry up. She knows that we can't start the next phase without her.
Gideon. Right, Moms. Hmmmmm, H1 to H5, do you read me, H5?
Mr. Brooks. *(enters with several ties in his hand)* Oh, I'm late. I'm late. Which one of these do you think looks the best?
Booker T. *(gets up from the table where he has been having a cup of coffee)* Let me see, Dad.
Mr. Brooks. Leaving me at a time like this. She could have put out my clothes before she left. I'll tell you, son, there is a whole lot of inconsideration going on in the world today.
Booker T. I like this one. Say, Dad, what if Momma decides not to come back until you've signed that list of demands that you haven't even read yet?
Mr. Brooks. Son, you're dipping in my business. Do you think you can tell me something about a woman I've known for over twenty-five years?
Booker T. Ah, come on, Dad. You never thought that Momma would go this far. The whole thing caught you by surprise. I'm telling you, you should be making some plans of your own, just in case Momma is not jiving.
Mr. Brooks. I'm not, as you say, jiving either. I can put my foot down too, you know. *(Gail enters.)* Gail, what did Mrs. Brooks say?
Gail. She wants you to sign this, she said it's your last chance.
Mr. Brooks. I wouldn't touch that piece of paper with a pair of gloves. What is wrong with that woman anyway? The very idea. Well, let me finish dressing so I can get to work. *(goes offstage)*
Gail. But you could at least read it, Daddy.
Mr. Brooks. Never.
Gail. Oh, he's so pig-headed! What am I going to do?

(Chanting, then a commotion is heard down stairs. "Take that chain off your brain, John Henry Brooks.")

Booker T. Hey, what's going on? *(goes over to the window, and looks down)* Say, what's this? Dig this.

("Women want Equality," "Equal rights like you and me.")

Gail. What's happening? *(Phone rings.)* Oh, it would ring at a time like this. Hello, Marvin! Am I glad you called!
Booker T. Hey, it's Ruby and Gideon's friends, they've got picket signs. Hey, they're trying to stop somebody from coming in the building.
Gail. What! Oh, I'm not excited. Momma has just got pickets around the front door, that's all. I don't know. Hey, Booker, what do the picket signs say?
Booker T. Hey, that's Sweetmeat they're trying to keep out.
Mr. Brooks. What's all that racket out there?
Gail. Sweetmeat! Oh, he's one of the men who works in Daddy's barbershop, Marvin.
Booker T. Look at them go at it.
Gail. Look at who go? Hold on, Marvin, I'll be right back. Let me see.
Mr. Brooks. I said what's all that commotion?
Booker T. You missed him, he just ran up the stairs.
Mr. Brooks. What's going on?
Gail. Hey, look at the signs they're carrying. "Male chauvinism must go. What's good for the gander is good for the goose." Wow! "Women want to be free, give them equality."
Mr. Brooks. *(from offstage)* Why, the nerve! Just wait 'til I get my hands on that woman.
Booker T. *(opens front door to Sweetmeat)* Come on in, Sweetmeat.
Sweetmeat. Where's John Henry, where's John Henry? It's a matter of life and death. *(He is out of breath.)* Where's John Henry?
Mr. Brooks. Sweetmeat! I'm right here. *(enters, dressed to go to work)*
Sweetmeat. John Henry, you've got to do something. They've taken over our barbershop!
Mr. Brooks. What!
Gail and Booker T. Taken over the barbershop??!! Who?
Sweetmeat. A bunch of kids with a lot of hair on their heads. When I got to work they was sitting in them chairs just as big as life. They even had the nerve to ask me if I had a pass from Gideon to get in. John Henry, we've got to do something. . . . We've got all of our equipment in there.
Mr. Brooks. Gideon!
Gail. So that's what Gideon was doing.
Mr. Brooks. They can't do that to me.

(Chanting starts again from the streets.)

Sweetmeat. John Henry, everything is crazy. Some fat lady and her kids carrying picket signs tried to stop me from coming in here.
Mr. Brooks. Fat lady? What are you saying? Ruby? *(goes to look out of the window)*

Sweetmeat. Say, John Henry, you in some kind of trouble?

Mr. Brooks. No, of course not. Get away from there! Get away from that door! *(turns away from the window)* You're right, son, we've got to do something. *(closes the window, shutting out the noise)*

Booker T. Right on, Dad. Right on. That's what I've been trying to tell you all along.

Mr. Brooks. Come on, Sweetmeat, let's go clear the front door first and then we'll mop up the barbershop.

Booker T. Wait, Dad. Use your head, that's not the way. How would it look if people in the neighborhood saw you fighting with Ruby in the streets?

Mr. Brooks. I don't have to stand for this. They're trying my patience.

Booker T. I know. But we've got to use our heads. The smart thing to do is try and deal with Momma. Maybe we can get her to call off the pickets, and let you open the barbershop. Then you can talk about the demands. How about it, Dad? Let's make a deal with Momma, if we still can. Let's see if we can work out something before the whole neighborhood gets involved in this thing. What do you say? You don't want to ruin your good name, do you?

Mr. Brooks. Hmmmmm. Well, I'll think about it.

Gail. Oh, Daddy!

Mr. Brooks. All right, I'll think hard about it.

Booker T. O.K. O.K. First I'll go talk to Momma and see what she's got to say. Gail, why don't you read those demands to Dad while I'm gone? That way we'll know what we're dealing with. *(starts to leave)*

Mr. Brooks. Hey, son. *(walks Booker T. to the door)* See if you can get Gideon to talk some sense into your mother's head. Before I have to come up there and drag her down here.

Gail. Here we go, Daddy. *(starts reading from the list of demands)* Hmmmmmmm. I, John Henry Brooks, Jr., being of sound mind and limb, do hereby agree to all of my wrongdoings over the past twenty-some odd years. And I do solemnly swear that I will stop all such further wrongdoings. Therefore, be it known that I agree to the following: I will call my wife Gladys. I will no longer slurp my coffee. I will start putting the top back on the tooth paste. I will not pass gas in the bedroom. I will go to church at least once a month. I will give my wife a weekly allowance and money to buy a new dress. I will no longer require my wife to keep an appointment book.

Mr. Brooks. What? No appointment book?

Gail. I will no longer require my wife to save the trays from the T.V. dinners.

Sweetmeat. Trays from the T.V. dinners.

Gail. I will start cutting naturals in my barbershop. I will send my wife to school so that she can learn how to be a manicurist and work in the barbershop.

Mr. Brooks. Over my dead body! Enough!

Gail. I will no longer . . .

Mr. Brooks. Enough! I've heard enough!

Gail. . . . No longer lose my temper, but maintain control of myself at all times.

Mr. Brooks. *(shouts)* I said that's enough. *(lowers his voice)* I absolutely, positively, resolutely refuse to so much as look at that piece of paper any longer.

Gail. But, Daddy, I'm not even half through yet. You could at least listen to them.

Mr. Brooks. I said that's enough. And what's more, what is that phone doing off the hook?

Gail. Oh, God! Marvin! He hung up. Oh, no. I give up. I'm going to my room.

Mr. Brooks. This is a madhouse. I can't believe all this is really happening to me, Sweetmeat.

Sweetmeat. Well, I've got to admit that it does look like you've got your elbows in the sand.

Mr. Brooks. Ah, things are not that bad. I'll come up with something brilliant. When you're in a tough situation, there is always one thing you have to remember, Sweetmeat. And that's not to panic. Yes, you must maintain your equilibrium at all times. *(Doorbell rings.)* Booker T. back already? Why would Booker T. ring the doorbell? Oh, come in, son. What can we do for you?

Marvin. Is Gail all right? What's going on? Is Gail all right?

Mr. Brooks. Of course she's all right. We're having a little misunderstanding, that's all. Oh, Sweetmeat, this is Martin. Martin is marrying . . .

Gail. Who's that at the door, Daddy? Marvin! Am I glad to see you. Daddy, why don't you give Marvin a cup of coffee?

Mr. Brooks. Hummmph!

Gail. Oh, Marvin, I'm so glad you came. I tried to call you back. You're not mad, are you?

Marvin. No, I'm not mad. I was just worried. What's going on, anyway? Why the pickets?

(Booker T. starts whistling on the roof.)

Gail. I don't know where to start. Booker T. went up on the roof to talk to Momma. Momma and Daddy have a disagreement.

Mr. Brooks. Where is that Booker T.?

Gail. She gave him this list of demands . . .

Booker T. Good morning, everybody. It sure is a pretty day, ain't it? How is everybody?
Mrs. Brooks. Unless you came to tell me that Mr. Brooks has agreed to my demands, the answer is no. Did you come to tell me that?
Booker T. Well, not exactly, Momma. I was just sort of hoping that you two could work out some kind of deal, you know, a compromise.
Mrs. Brooks. I don't have anything more to say unless you've brought that piece of paper signed. *(Booker T. paces, exasperated.)*
Mr. Brooks. *(enters and crosses to the window)* Where is that Booker T.? Booker T.? Booker T.
Gail. Hey, Dad.
Mr. Brooks. *(enters the kitchen)* That Booker T. is getting as bad as that dad-blasted Gideon. *(Sweetmeat enters and crosses to the kitchen window.)* Sweetmeat, why couldn't this have happened on a Monday? Booker T. Booker T. *(exits)*
Gail. Dad, Daddy. *(crosses upstage to where Mr. Brooks exited)*

(Marvin crosses to Gail and sits her at the kitchen table and begins preparing her a glass of hot milk. Sweetmeat crosses to the kitchen window.)

Booker T. Hey, Gideon. Hey, man, look here. Why don't you try and talk to Momma, and get her to cut the old man a little slack.
Gideon. Why don't you dig yourself, Sharrief? Daddy has been dead wrong for years, you know that, and yet you want me to talk to Momma. If you really knew what was happening you'd be for what's right, and not on anybody's side. Excuse me.
Marvin. Wow! I can see where your mother is coming from but I don't *understand* Gideon.
Gail. And they are not coming back in this house until Daddy signs *all* the demands.
Marvin. Picketing, taking over his father's shop, fighting in the streets. He knows you don't deal with the members of your family the same way you deal with your enemy. You can use those cold calculating tactics against outsiders, but with your family you should use another value system. You should practice a different kind of morality, one based on love and respect.
Gail. I know. I agree with you, but try and tell that to somebody in this house. Daddy is so pig-headed.
Mr. Brooks. *(enters with Sweetmeat)* Sweetmeat, I've got an idea. Why don't you go downstairs and . . . *(exits with Sweetmeat)*
Gail. Dad, Daddy.
Marvin. Just relax, Gail, we'll figure something out.
Booker T. *(looking at strategy map)* Hey, Momma, there's no need for all

this. I'm sure you and Dad can make a deal if you'll just call off those pickets and get Gideon's friends out of the barbershop.
Gideon. She's already said no deals, man.
Mrs. Brooks. I can't figure you out, Booker T. Instead of trying to convince me to give in to your father, you should be encouraging me to stand up to him.
Booker T. But, Momma, you and Dad love each other. I mean you've been together all these years.
Mrs. Brooks. Only because I kept my mouth shut all these years.
Stormy Monday. Oh, somebody is coming out of the apartment. A little short fat man! Get him, Ruby, get him. Don't let him get by.
Mrs. Brooks. What's happening? Let me see too, Stormy.
Stormy Monday. Get up, Ruby, get up! Oh, shoot! That's it, Ruby. Here, Gladys. Gideon, what's the report from the barbershop?
Gideon. Everything is cool. *(Stormy Monday climbs down the ladder.)*
Mrs. Brooks. That's it, Ruby, that's it. That's it, Ruby. Get him. Look at Sweetmeat run back up those stairs. Sure must have done something to Ruby, they're having a hard time keeping her from going after him. Let her go, let her go!

(Mr. Brooks enters kitchen at the run, gets a bandaid from a cabinet and exits, on the run.)

Stormy Monday. Come on, Gladys, let's get our planning session started. We're already late. All right, Gideon, will you please report what happened on phase one and two so we can get phase three started.
Gideon. Right. Well, we took over the barbershop. That was phase one. In phase two we set up pickets around the house. Phase three is where you come in, Stormy Monday.
Stormy Monday. Right on. We're ready. *(does a karate kick)*
Gideon. Wow! You've really got your thing together! *(Stormy Monday and Mrs. Brooks climb the ladder to the upper section and Gideon goes back to his planning.)*

(Sweetmeat enters the kitchen.)

Gail. Dad. Dad. *(Mr. Brooks enters.)* Dad, we're going outside for a walk.
Mr. Brooks. What! Deserting me at a time like this. You women always stick together.
Gail. Aw, Daddy, you don't understand anything. You never listen. All we're trying to do is communicate with you. Listen, Dad, Momma is not a robot or a machine. She has feelings, she has needs and you've been taking her for granted all these years. All Momma wants to do is express herself.
Mr. Brooks. Express herself—Hmmmph!

Booker T. Momma, come on, I know the old man is rough at times, but I thought you loved him.

Mrs. Brooks. I do, I love your father. We all love him, but nobody wants to live with him, that's the trouble.

Marvin. Gail, I'm going to try and talk to your father.

Gail. You know that Dad won't listen to you or anybody else for that matter.

Marvin. Well, at least it's worth a try.

Mrs. Brooks. Gail had her mind made up to leave even before she met Marvin. You know that.

Booker T. But, Momma!

Marvin. Mr. Brooks, this whole thing is so simple. Gideon is saying let me go so I can be a man, a real man. He doesn't want to follow in your footprints. He wants to make his own tracks.

Mrs. Brooks. Let's face it. We are not a big happy family.

Marvin. Gideon wants to make his own decisions about life and define his own role as a black man in this screwed-up society.

Mrs. Brooks. We could be if someone could talk some sense into that selfish, self-centered man down there.

Marvin. Mr. Brooks, Gideon is just searching, looking for new answers, that's all. And all he and your wife want you to do is love them as they really are and not in some image that you've created for them.

Gail. Oh, Marvin, it's no use. Let's get out of here.

Sweetmeat. Hey, John Henry, I think I've got the answer. Let's have a drink.

(Gail and Marvin exit.)

Gideon. Hey, man, you'd better go back downstairs and talk to Dad.

Stormy Monday. Yeah, man, you can see the pickets and the takeover are just light action.

Gideon. If Daddy don't give in, we gonna sock it to his case. *(exits)*

Stormy Monday. Right on.

Booker T. You know, Momma, I really thought you and Dad were a beautiful couple.

Mrs. Brooks. You've got a lot to learn about women, son. Just remember this—never make a woman do anything that will make her lose her self-respect.

Booker T. Momma, you're out of sight. I better go talk to Dad. See you all later.

Sweetmeat. Remember how you've always said that a good businessman doesn't limit his market?

Mr. Brooks. That's what I calls a truism, Sweetmeat. Of course I remember. So what?

Sweetmeat. And since everybody is wearing naturals now, we are most definitely limiting our market by not cutting them.

Mr. Brooks. Hmmph!

Sweetmeat. And you've said all along that we needed a manicurist in the shop. The way I figure it, letting Mrs. Brooks do it is a good idea. It'll give the place a little class. And the salary you pay her will remain in the family, if you know what I mean.

Mr. Brooks. Ohhhhhhhh. I seeeeeeee.

Sweetmeat. Now I don't know about all them demands on that list . . .

Stormy Monday. In twenty minutes, Gladys, we start operation Beulah.

Mrs. Brooks. You know what they say, a hard head makes a soft behind.

(Marvin, Gail and Booker T. are heard in the hallway.)

Booker T. You know, we've got a dynamite woman for a mother. I just got turned on to her.

Mr. Brooks. What did your mother say, boy?

Booker T. *(enters)* Dad, you've been had.

Mr. Brooks. Had! Had! Boy, what are you talking about?

Booker T. Momma is stone out of sight. Got a mind like Gillette and a heart as big as a watermelon.

Mr. Brooks. Razor blades. Watermelons. What's come over you, Booker T.? Gail, you talk to him. He's crazy.

Marvin. What's happening, man? What's going on?

Booker T. Why Dad's knee deep in a fight. That's what happening. Here, Dad. You'd better sign this while you're still ahead!

Gail. What's come over you? What's going on?

Booker T. If the picketing and the take-over don't work they plan to picket the bank where you keep your account.

Mr. Brooks. Oh God! No! No! No!

Gail. Wow.

Booker T. She's got her communication thing together, too. She's going to print up some leaflets, sort of like her position paper and have the kids pass them out in the community.

Mr. Brooks. Position papers!

Booker T. And dig this. She's setting up the machinery for a press conference. She's already contacted the *Amsterdam News*. And she's working on a contact at CBS.

Mr. Brooks. CBS! I'll crush her with my very hands!

Booker T. And in case there is any rough stuff, she's got a group of women karate experts waiting. Stormy Monday is the commanding officer.

Sweetmeat. You'd better get you a lawyer, man.

Booker T. Momma's already spoken to three lawyers. And the one who

was on your side told Momma that the least she could get in a settlement was everything in the apartment and all the money.
Mr. Brooks and Sweetmeat. All the money!
Gail. You mean Momma's into all that?
Booker T. Why, she's even considering asking for a Congressional investigation.
Mr. Brooks. Children, what are we going to do?
Booker T. What do you mean "we," baby?
Mr. Brooks. What did you say, Booker T.?
Gail. Dad, I just remembered that I have a couple of things I have to buy at the store. Come on, Marvin.
Mr. Brooks. Gail! Marvin! Come back. Ah, no matter, you're still beside me, Booker T. We'll figure something. There must be some way. . . . Booker T.! What are you doing? Where are you going?
Booker T. I've got to go downstairs and talk to a lady.
Mr. Brooks. A lady?
Booker T. Yea, Dad. A lady. A sister.
Mr. Brooks. A sister? Whose sister? Sharrief, my son. Come back. Oh no! No. Oh no, no! The bad guys are winning.

ACT III
. . . . . .

SCENE 2

Time: *The next day. The wedding, which has taken place at the church, is over. Mrs. Brooks, Ruby and Slim [who drove them in his car, from the wedding] are the first to arrive. While Slim, who is not on stage, is bringing up boxes of presents from his car which is parked downstairs, Mrs. Brooks starts putting glasses on the table. Ruby starts making punch. In the center of the table stands a large wedding cake with a black bride and groom on the top. There is another table in the kitchen where the "hard" liquor is kept. Mrs. Brooks and Ruby, dressed in their Sunday best, enter hurriedly and start working.*

Mrs. Brooks. Come on, Ruby, we've got to hurry. Everybody will be here in a little while.
Ruby. Gladys, you've got to give me time. When you've got as much as me to carry around, you've got to go slow and easy with it.
Mrs. Brooks. I'll start making the punch, and we'll start setting up the table.
Ruby. I still can't believe it, girl. How you got that man to sign that piece

of paper is way beyond me. You ought to be mighty proud of yourself. Un, uh! Just think, you got Mr. Brooks to promise to straighten up after all these years.

Mrs. Brooks. I thought he was going to break down and cry when he was signing it, but afterwards he swore that he would try to live up to every single item.

Ruby. If somebody had told me last week that something like this could happen I would have called them a whole croker sackful of liars to their faces.

Mrs. Brooks. It was easy once I made up my mind to do it, girl.

Ruby. Well, I still got to hand it to you, Gladys, it took a lot of gumption to stand up to Mr. Brooks like you did.

Mrs. Brooks. Well, I had a lot of help. And I want to thank you too, Ruby.

Ruby. Ah, it was nothing, Gladys. I didn't do nothing but carry a picket sign. It was fun. Say, I wonder if something like that would work on my Wilbur?

(The doorbell rings.)

Mrs. Brooks. That must be Slim. Get that, will you, Ruby?

Ruby. Hold on, I'm coming. Just hold your horses. *(Slim enters carrying wedding presents. Ruby follows him in.)* Where do you want him to put these, Gladys?

Mrs. Brooks. Right over there. And, Ruby, why don't you leave the door open? Everybody will start coming pretty soon. Slim, would you like to try some of my punch? Ruby, why don't you offer the gentleman some of my punch?

Ruby. Would you like to try some punch, Mr. Slim?

Slim. Don't mind if I do. *(Ruby adds to Slim's glass of punch from a bottle.)* Thank you. Whoooo! This sure is some mighty potent stuff.

Mrs. Brooks. Thank you. I'm sorry you had to bring all of those presents by yourself, Slim. I don't know where everybody else is. And John Henry really should be here by now. He said he would help. I hope this is not a sign that he's going to start being trifling again. Do you know if he's coming with Sweetmeat?

Slim. I'm not sure. John Henry disappeared right after the wedding. The last time I saw him he was with Gideon. That was a surprise.

Mrs. Brooks. Yes, they made up last night, too. Both of them were so funny, just like two little boys. Both of them had tears in their eyes. Talk about two happy people. John Henry told Gideon he could be anything he wanted to be, as long as he too was the best at it.

Ruby. That sounds like Mr. Brooks, all right.

Sweetmeat. *(enters with camera)* Hold that pose. *(takes a picture of Ruby and Mrs. Brooks)* Beautiful, beautiful. Howdy, Mrs. Brooks. Slim.

Slim. You're early, but you're late.

Mrs. Brooks. Sweetmeat, have you seen John Henry? I thought he was coming with you.

Sweetmeat. He didn't come with me, he told me to go on.

Mrs. Brooks. I wonder where he is. Oh, Sweetmeat, I want you to meet my friend, Ruby. Ruby, this is Sweetmeat.

Sweetmeat. Pleased to meet you, ma'am.

Ruby. Your face looks awfully familiar. Haven't I seen you somewhere before?

Sweetmeat. I don't think so. But I've got that kind of face. Somebody is always trying to give me credit for being somebody else.

Ruby. No, I know I've seen you before.

Mrs. Brooks. You probably saw him at the barbershop, Ruby. He works with John Henry.

Sweetmeat. You don't know me, woman.

Sweetmeat. Say, what are you drinking, Slim?

Slim. Punch. I told you you were early, but you're late.

Mrs. Brooks. Would you like some punch, or would you rather have some Scotch? It's right in there on the table.

Sweetmeat. Well, if I've got a choice. Come on, man. *(takes a bottle and pours himself a drink and gives bottle to Slim)* This is some good stuff. Hey, Slim, you'd better take it easy, there. You know how you country boys are when you get to the big city, you don't know how to act.

Slim. Pass the ice, man.

Sweetmeat. Down home you all don't drink nothing but that white lightning. You ain't used to this good J & B. You stick with me, and I'll make you a big-time operator like me.

Slim. You'd better be careful that you don't end up like my cousin, Elmo.

Sweetmeat. What happened to your cousin, Elmo?

Slim. He drove himself to death.

Sweetmeat. Oh yeah? How did he do that?

Slim. He drove around in his Volkswagen all last summer with the windows up so people would think that he had air-conditioning. And he suffocated.

Sweetmeat. Ah, man! You sure are low. Setting up your man, and sounding on him like that. How are you gonna show?

Slim. What can I tell you? Sometimes it bees that way.

Gideon. Get ready, everybody, get ready! They're coming! *(enters carrying rice)* This is fun. We must have thrown a ton on them already. Here, take some rice, Momma. *(gives rice to Mrs. Brooks, Ruby, Slim and Sweetmeat)*

(Sampson stands by the door pretending to be blowing a trumpet, as Nia and Stephanie file past him.)

Booker T. Da de da de daaaaaaaaaa.

All. *(chanting)* Black is so bad!

Mrs. Brooks. Gail! I'm so happy for you. Congratulations, son. See, I told you everything was going to work out just fine.

Marvin. *(overlaps above)* Thank you, Mrs. Brooks.

Ruby. Nice going, Gail, you sure are a pretty bride.

Sweetmeat. That's it. *(Sweetmeat takes a picture.)* Now let me kiss the bride.

Booker T. Welcome to the family, bro.

Marvin. I'm the luckiest man in the world.

Mrs. Brooks. *(overlaps above)* Gideon, have you seen your father? He should have been here by now.

Gideon. Not since we left the church. Excuse me, Momma. Everybody. I think it's time to propose a toast to our newlywed king and queen.

Sampson. Hey, man, Stormy Monday said she was going to make that toast.

Gideon. Well, where is she?

All. Where is Stormy Monday?

Stormy Monday. *(enters, posing at the entrance-way)* I'm here, I'm here, I'm right here. Now I want you all to know that I was up half the night getting this number together. Now if someone will get me that chair— Thank you. Now I need a drink. Thank you. All right. May your tribe increase. May your feet always point toward Mecca. May happiness hound you like a tax collector. And whether you love wisely or foolishly, may you always love. O.K., let's start dancing before I do something foolish like crying.

Gideon. We'll get that, Stormy. *(Gideon and Nia cross to the record player.)*

Stormy Monday. Gladys, we did it, we did it.

Mrs. Brooks. Thanks to you, Stormy. Stormy, have you seen John Henry?

Stormy Monday. No, Gladys, I haven't seen Mr. Brooks, that is not since the wedding.

Mrs. Brooks. Oh, Stormy, I want you to meet a friend of John Henry's. Slim, this is Stormy Monday. Stormy, this is Slim.

Stormy Monday. Did Mrs. Brooks say you were a friend of John Henry's?

Slim. Well, not exactly, we just work together.

Sweetmeat. Hold that pose. *(takes a picture of Slim and Stormy Monday)* Thank you. What is all this loveliness you have with you, Slim?

Slim. Stormy Monday, this is Sweetmeat. Sweetmeat, this is Stormy Monday.

Stormy Monday. Howdy. Say, what kind of a camera is that you got there?

Sweetmeat. It's Japanese. You know, some of that Nippon Soul!

Stormy Monday. The Germans make a better camera. What kind of a lens does it have, a two point five, or a three point eight?

Sweetmeat. Does it make a difference?

Stormy Monday. And where is your light meter?

Sweetmeat. I don't rightly know, you see I don't live around here, you know. Excuse me, you all. Nice meeting you, Miss Cloudy. Hold that pose, Booker T. *(crosses and takes a picture of Booker T. and Stephanie as Slim and Stormy are talking)*

Slim. That sure is a lucky dress you're wearing.

Stormy Monday. Why?

Slim. It gets a chance to stay so close to you.

(The music begins—rhythm and blues, for dancing fast. As the music begins the younger generation begins to dance. At that moment Fun Loving enters.)

Fun Loving. Hey, look out, let a man come in.

(Fun Loving slaps five with most of the males in the room and then starts everyone dancing by twirling Gail around and dancing with her. Everyone joins the dancing, including Mrs. Brooks under the guidance of Gideon and then Ruby under the guidance of Fun Loving. Sampson starts a line. As the line is moving the record sticks. Mrs. Brooks removes the needle and the younger generation begins a chant of "WE DON'T NEED NO MUSIC" to replace the sound of the record and the dancing continues. Mr. Brooks enters wearing a loud Dashikie and various emblems around his neck, including a necktie.)

Mr. Brooks. Somebody give me five. Give me five—on the black hand side.

(The following six speeches are spoken together.)

Slim. Man! Look at John Henry!

Ruby. They say that wonders will never cease.

Stormy Monday. Get a load of Mr. Brooks strutting around. Got enough stuff around his neck to start a five and ten cent store.

Stephanie. Mr. Brooks is really way out there.

Booker T. Hey, Dad, you are really out of sight.

Gideon. Yea, Dad, you're really a gas.

Mr. Brooks. Don't let me stop you all from dancing. *(turns to Gail)* I told you I was going to dance at your wedding. *(picks her up and twirls her around)*

Sweetmeat. Hold that pose.

Gideon. Wait a minute, man. *(begins to remove Mr. Brooks' necktie, and Sweetmeat snaps the picture)* Oh, Sweetmeat.

Mr. Brooks. Now where is that beautiful, wonderful, ever-loving, sweetheart, gorgeous Gladys Brooks?

Sweetmeat. Hold that pose.

Mr. Brooks. Hold it there, Sweetmeat. Gideon, come over here and join us. I want to hang this picture in the barbershop for good luck.
Sweetmeat. *(takes a picture of the three)* Got to load up again.
Sampson. Mr. Brooks, since you're wearing your bad Dashikie and all, I know you're into something. Will you tell me what is the most helpful book for us to read for our liberation struggle? Wretched of the Earth, Malcolm X's Autobiography, or The Crisis of the Negro Intellectual?
Ruby. All right, break it up now. I'm hungry and I want some cake.

Ruby. Gail, Mr. Marvin, come on over here and cut your cake. We've got to get a picture of this, Mr. Photographer. *(Ruby exits and re-enters with Sweetmeat who takes picture of the cake cutting.)*

Gideon. Nia, Sampson, come here. Stormy. *(They get involved in a discussion which ends with the picture as Gideon speaks.)*

Gideon. Everybody. Momma, we were discussing the way you got everybody to help you this weekend, and we came up with this dynamite idea. Now that the family is back together let's keep the ball rolling and move on to some heavier action. Like community control. The schools, the police.
Mrs. Brooks. Child, I don't know anything about no community control. Remember I'm only a housewife.
Stephanie. What's that got to do with it?
Gideon. Oh, Momma; besides, Momma, it's sort of your obligation.
Mr. Brooks. Obligation?
Nia. That's right. Now that Mrs. Brooks has got her hair cut in a natural, more is expected of her. Being Black means being involved in the struggle.
Sweetmeat. All right, you're getting too serious. Let's get the family together for the big one. It's picture-taking time and I'm steady setting fire to every twig in sight.

(Stormy Monday and Sweetmeat set out directing the family and all concerned into a suitable pose for the big picture. John Henry is the last one in place.)

Sweetmeat. Good job, sister Cloudy. Fine job. Fine as the wine you drink as you dine. Hold it steady, everybody.
Booker T. *(who has been talking to Stephanie)* Hey, Gideon, how's that for a starter?
Gideon. That's beautiful, man. Bea-uti-ful.
Booker T. Right on.
Sweetmeat. Now everybody say cheese.
All. Cheese. *(The younger generation says BLACK IS SO BAD.)*
Stormy Monday. And don't forget your light meter.

(Curtain)

Great Goodness of Life
(A Coon Show) (1970)

Amiri Baraka (LeRoi Jones) (b. 1934–)

A poet, a novelist, and a cultural leader, Amiri Baraka (LeRoi Jones) is the progenitor of black revolutionary drama of the 1960s. Born in Newark, New Jersey, he attended the Newark branch of Rutgers University, then later transferred to Howard University, which he attended for two years before joining the United States Army Air Corps. After serving in the army, Baraka returned to civilian life to be a teacher and a writer.

First known for avant-garde poetry, Baraka earned recognition as a dramatist in 1964 with the initial production of *Dutchman,* which won an Obie (Off Broadway) Award. This success was followed quickly by productions of *The Toilet* and *The Slave,* which intensified national identification of Baraka as a "bitter" dramatist preaching racial hatred in virulent tones. Actually, however, in his earliest dramas, Baraka focused on the dilemma of a young black seeking identity and role. In each of the three plays, the protagonist is a sensitive young black man who has been and is culturally and emotionally/sexually attached to the tastes and standards of the white world in which he has been educated; simultaneously, however, the protagonist perceives that violence is the only means of liberating black people from the domination of that world, which is oppressively sterile and perverted. Ambivalent and vacillating, the protagonist moves from the hope for reconciliation in *The Toilet* to acceptance of his own destruction in *Dutchman* to a nihilistic vision of the total destruction of "civilization" in *The Slave.*

Since then, identifying himself even more closely with the black community within which he has attempted to develop recognition of the importance of cultural nationalism, Baraka, in the two theatres he has founded—the Black Arts Repertory Theatre in Harlem and Spirit House in Newark—has concentrated on that kind of drama which Ed Bullins has identified as "black revolutionary agit-prop." Didactic, moralistic, and frequently allegorical—especially in the writings of Baraka's fellow playwrights—it is designed to educate the black community to awareness of the nature of their oppression and their oppressors. Baraka's most powerful effort in this vein is *Great Goodness of Life (A Coon Show)* in which Court Royal, a Negro postal employee, maintains his unsuspecting role as buffoon or jester for white America by killing his son.

Selected Published Plays by Amiri Baraka (LeRoi Jones)

The Baptism and The Toilet. New York: Grove, 1966.
Dutchman and The Slave. New York: Morrow, 1964.
Four Black Revolutionary Plays. Indianapolis: Bobbs-Merrill, 1970.
>*A Black Mass*
>*The Death of Malcolm X*
>*Experimental Death Unit #1*
>*Great Goodness of Life (A Coon Show)*

"Home on the Range." *The Drama Review,* 12 (Summer 1968), pp. 106–11.
Jello. Detroit: Broadside, 1970.
"Madheart." *Black Fire,* ed. by L. Jones and L. Neal. New York: Morrow, 1968.
The Motion of History and Other Plays. New York: Morrow, 1978.
>*The Motion of History*
>*Slave Ship*
>*S-1*

Selected Plays and Prose of Amiri Baraka/LeRoi Jones. New York: Morrow, 1979.

Great Goodness of Life (A Coon Show)
Directed by Irving Vincent

CHARACTERS

Voice of the White Judge .... *Frank Carey*
Court Royal .... *L. Errol Jaye*
Attorney Breck .... *Jimmy Hayeson*
Young Man .... *Sam Singleton*
Hood 1 & 3 .... *Jimmy Hayeson*
Hood 2 & 4 .... *Paul Rodger-Reid*
Young Woman .... *Anna Maria Horsford*
Leader .... *Carl Boissiere*

The Scene: *An old house, with morning frost letting up a little.*

A Voice. Court.

(A man comes out, gray but still young looking. He is around 50. He walks straight, though he is nervous. He comes uncertainly. Pauses.)

Come on.

(He walks right up to the center of the lights.)

Come on.
Court. I don't quite understand.
Voice. Shut up, nigger.
Court. What? *(meekly, then trying to get some force up)* Now what's going on? I don't see why I should . . .
Voice. I told you to shut up, nigger.
Court. I don't understand. What's going on?
Voice. Black lunatic. I said shut up. I'm not going to tell you again!
Court. But . . . Yes.
Voice. You are Court Royal, are you not?
Court. Yes. I am. But I don't understand.
Voice. You are charged with shielding a wanted criminal. A murderer.
Court. What? Now I know you have the wrong man. I've done no such thing. I work in the Post Office. I'm Court Royal. I've done nothing wrong. I work in the Post Office and have done nothing wrong.
Voice. Shut up.
Court. But I'm Court Royal. Everybody knows me. I've always done everything . . .
Voice. Court Royal, you are charged with harboring a murderer. How do you plead?
Court. Plead? There's a mistake being made. I've never done anything.
Voice. How do you plead?
Court. I'm not a criminal. I've done nothing . . .
Voice. Then you plead "not guilty"?
Court. Of course, I'm not guilty. I work in the Post Office. *(tries to work up a little humor)* You know me, probably. Didn't you ever see me in the Post Office? I'm a supervisor, you know me. I work at the Post Office. I'm no criminal. I've worked at the Post Office for thirty years. I'm a supervisor. There must be some mistake. I've worked at the Post Office for thirty years.
Voice. Do you have an attorney?
Court. Attorney? Look you'd better check you got the right man. You're making a mistake. I'll sue. That's what I'll do. *(The Voice laughs long*

and cruelly.) I'll call my attorney right now. We'll find out just what's going on here.
Voice. If you don't have an attorney, the court will assign you one.
Court. Don't bother. I have an attorney. John Breck's my attorney. He'll be down here in a few minutes—the minute I call.
Voice. The court will assign you an attorney.
Court. But I have an attorney. John Breck. See, it's on this card.
Voice. Will the legal-aid man please step forward.
Court. No. I have an attorney. If you'll just call, or adjourn the case until my attorney gets here.
Voice. We have an attorney for you. Where is the legal-aid man?
Court. But I have an attorney. I want my attorney. I don't need any legal-aid man. I have money, I have an attorney. I work at the Post Office. I'm a supervisor, here look at my badge.

(A bald-headed smiling house slave in a wrinkled dirty tuxedo crawls across the stage; he has a wire attached to his back leading off stage. A huge key in the side of his head. We hear the motors "animating" his body groaning like tremendous weights. He grins, and slobbers, turning his head slowly from side to side. He grins. He makes little quivering sounds.)

Voice. Your attorney.
Court. What kind of foolishness is this? *(He looks at the Man.)* What's going on? What's your name?
Attorney. *(His "voice" begins sometime after the question, the wheels churn out his answer, and the deliberating motors sound throughout the scene.)* Pul . . . lead . . . errrr . . . *(as if the motors are having trouble starting)* Pul—pul— . . . lead . . . er . . . err Guilty! *(Motors get it together and move in proper synchronization.)* Pul—Plead Guilty, it's your only chance. Just plead guilty brother. Just plead guilty. It's your only chance. Your only chance.
Court. Guilty? Of what? What are you talking about? What kind of defense attorney are you? I don't even know what I'm being charged with, and you say plead guilty. What's happening here? *(at Voice)* Can't I even know the charge?
Voice. We told you the charge. Harboring a murderer.
Court. But that's an obvious mistake.
Attorney. There's no mistake. Plead guilty. Get off easy. Otherwise *thrrrrit.* *(makes throat cutting gesture, then chuckles)* Plead guilty, brother, it's your only chance. *(laughs)*
Voice. Plea changed to guilty?
Court. What? No. I'm not pleading guilty. And I want my lawyer.
Voice. You have your lawyer.
Court. No, my lawyer is John Breck.

Attorney. Mr. Royal look at me. *(grabs him by the shoulders)* I am John Breck. *(laughs)* Your attorney, and friend. And I say plead guilty.
Court. John Bre . . . what? *(He looks at Attorney closely.)* Breck. Great God, what's happened to you? Why do you look like this?
Attorney. Why? Haha, I've always looked like this, Mr. Royal. Always.

(Now Another Voice, strong, young, begins to shout in the darkness at Royal.)

Young Voice. Now will you believe me stupid fool? Will you believe what I tell you or your eyes? Even your eyes. You're here with me, with us, all of us, and you can't understand. Plead guilty you are guilty stupid nigger. You'll die they'll kill you and you don't know why, now will you believe me? Believe me, half-white coward. Will you believe reality?
Voice. Get that criminal out of here. Beat him. Shut him up. Get him.

(Now sounds of scuffling come out of darkness. Screams. Of a group of men subduing another man.)

Young Voice. You bastard. And you Court Royal you let them take me. You liar. You weakling. You woman in the face of degenerates. You let me be taken. How can you walk the earttttt . . .

(He is apparently taken away.)

Court. Who's that? *(peers into darkness)* Who's that talking to me?
Voice. Shut up Royal. Fix your plea. Let's get on with it.
Court. That voice sounded very familiar *(caught in thought momentarily)* I almost thought it was . . .
Voice. Since you keep your plea of not guilty you won't need a lawyer. We can proceed without your services counselor.
Attorney. As you wish your honor. Good-bye Mr. Royal. *(He begins to crawl off.)* Good-bye, dead sucker! Hahahaha . . . *(waving hands as he crawls off and laughing)* Hahahaha, ain't I a bitch . . . I mean ain't I? *(exits)*
Court. John, John. You're my attorney, you can't leave me here like this. *(starts after him . . . shouts)* John!

(A siren begins to scream, like in jailbreak pictures . . . "Arrrrrrr." The lights beat off, on, in time with the metallic siren shriek. Court Royal is stopped in his tracks, bent in anticipation, the siren continues. Machine guns begin to bang bang as if very close to him, cell doors slamming, whistles, yells "Break . . . Break," the machine guns shatter, Court Royal stands frozen half bent arms held away from his body balancing him in his terror. As the noise, din, continues, his eyes grow until he is almost going to faint.)

Court. Ahhhhhhhgggg. Please . . . Please . . . don't kill me. Don't shoot me, I didn't do anything. I'm not trying to escape. Please . . . Please . . . PLEEEEEAS . . .

(The Voice begins to shriek almost as loud with laughter, as all the other sounds, and jumping lights stop as Voice starts to laugh. The Voice just laughs and laughs, laughs until you think it will explode or spit up blood; it laughs long and eerily out of the darkness.)

Court. *(Still dazed and staggered. He looks around quickly, trying to get himself together. He speaks now very quietly, and shaken.)* Please. Please.

(The other Voice begins to subside, the laughs coming in sharp cutoff bursts of hysteria.)

Voice. You donkey. *(laughs)* You piece of wood. You shiny shuffling piece of black vomit.

(The laughter quits like the tide rolling softly back to silence. Now there is no sound, except for Court Royal's breathing, and shivering clothes. He whispers . . .)

Court. Please? *(He is completely shaken and defeated, frightened like a small animal, eyes barely rolling.)* Please. I won't escape. *(His words sound corny tinny stupid dropped in such silence.)* Please, I won't try again. Just tell me where I am?

(The silence again. For a while no movement, Court is frozen, stiff, with only eyes sneaking, now they stop, he's frozen, cannot move, staring off into the cold darkness. A chain, slightly, more, now heavier, dragged bent, wiggled slowly, light now heavily in the darkness, from another direction. Chains. They're dragged, like things are pulling them across the earth. The chains. And now low chanting voices, moaning, with incredible pain and despair, the voices press just softly behind the chains, for a few seconds, so very very briefly then gone. And silence. Court does not move. His eyes roll a little back and around. He bends his knees dipping his head bending. He moans . . .)

Court. Just tell me where I am?
Voice. Heaven.

(The Voice is cool and businesslike. Court's eyes, head raise an imperceptible trifle. He begins to pull his arms slowly to his sides, and claps them together. The lights dim, and only Court is seen in dimmer illumination. The Voice again . . .)

Heaven. *(pause)* Welcome.
Court. *(mumbling)* I never understood . . . these things are so confusing.

(His head jerks like he's suddenly heard Albert Ayler. It raises, his whole body jerks around like suddenly animate ragdoll. He does a weird dance like a marionette jiggling and waggling.)

> You'll wonder what the devil-meant. A jiggedy bobbidy fool. You'll wonder what the devil-sent. Diggedy dobbidy cool. Ah man. *(singing)* Ah man, you'll wonder who the devil-sent. And what was heaven heaven heaven.

(This is like a funny joke-dance, with sudden funniness from Court, then suddenly as before he stops frozen again, eyes rolling, no other sound heard. Now a scream, and white hooded Men push a greasy-head nigger lady across in front of Court. They are pulling her hair, and feeling her ass. One whispers from time to time in her ear. She screams and bites occasionally, occasionally kicking.)

Hood 1. *(to the Voice)* She's drunk. *(now to Court)* You want to smell her breath?
Court. *(frightened; also sickened at the sight, embarrassed)* N-no. I don't want to. I smell it from here. She drinks and stinks and brings our whole race down.
Hood 2. Ain't it the truth!
Voice. Grind her into poison jelly. Smear it on her daughter's head.
Hood 1. Right, Your Honor. You got a break, sister. *(They go off.)* Hey, uncle, you sure you don't want to smell her breath?

(Court shivers "No.")

Voice. Royal, you have concealed a murderer, and we have your punishment ready for you. Are you ready?
Court. What? No. I want a trial. Please a trial. I deserve that. I'm a good man.
Voice. Royal, you're not a man!
Court. Please . . . . *(voice breaking)* Your Honor, a trial. A simple one, very quick, nothing fancy . . . I'm very conservative . . . no frills or loud colors, a simple concrete black toilet paper trial.
Voice. And funeral.

(Now two Men in Hoods, white work gloves, and suits, very sporty, come in with a stretcher. A black man is dead on it. There is long very piped applause. "Yea. Yea.")

Hood 1. It's the Prince, Your Honor. We banged him down.
Voice. He's dead?
Hood 2. Yes. A nigger did it for us.
Voice. Conceal the body in a stone. And sink the stone deep under the

ocean. Call the newspapers and give the official history. Make sure his voice is in that stone too, or *(heavy nervous pause)* . . . just go ahead.

Hood 1. Of course Your Honor. *(looks to Court, almost as an afterthought)* You want to smell his breath?

(They go out.)

Court. *(mumbling, still very frightened)* No . . . no . . . I have nothing to do with any of this. I'm a good man. I have a car. A home. *(running down)* A club. *(looks up pleading)* Please there's some mistake. Isn't there? I've done nothing wrong. I have a family. I work in the Post Office, I'm a supervisor. I've worked for thirty years. I've done nothing wrong.

Voice. Shut up whimpering pig. Shut up and get ready for sentencing. It'll be hard on you, you can bet that.

Court. *(A little life; he sees he's faced with danger.)* But tell me what I've done. I can remember no criminal, no murderer I've housed. I work eight hours, then home, and television, dinner, then bowling. I've harbored no murderers. I don't know any. I'm a good man.

Voice. Shut up liar. Do you know this man?

(An image is flashed on the screen behind him. It is a rapidly shifting series of faces. Malcolm. Patrice. Robert Williams. Garvey. Dead nigger kids killed by the police. Medgar Evers.)

Court. What?

Voice. I asked you do you know this man? I'm asking again, for the last time. There's no need to lie.

Court. But this is many men, many faces. They shift so fast I cannot tell who they are . . . or what is meant. It's so confusing.

Voice. Don't lie, Royal. We know all about you. You are guilty. Look at that face. You know this man.

Court. I do? *(in rising terror)* No. No. I don't, I never saw that man, it's so many faces, I've never seen those faces . . . never . . .

Voice. Look closer, Royal. You cannot get away with what you've done. Look more closely. You recognize that face . . . don't you? The face of the murderer you've sheltered all these years. Look, you liar, look at that face.

Court. No, no, no . . . I don't know them. I can't be forced into admitting something I never did. Uhhh . . . I have worked. My God, I've worked. I've meant to do the right thing. I've tried to be a . . .

(The faces shift, a long slow wail, like moan, like secret screaming has underscored the flashing faces . . . now it rises sharply to screaming point thrusts. Court wheels around to face the image on the screen, directly. He begins shouting loud as the voices . . .)

Court. No, I've tried . . . please I never wanted anything but peace . . . please I tried to be a man. I did. I lost my . . . heart . . . please it was so deep, I wanted to do the right thing, just to do the right thing. I wanted . . . everything to be . . . all right. Oh, please . . . please.

Voice. Now tell me, whether you know that murderer's face or not. Tell me before you die!

Court. No, no. I don't know him. I don't. I want to do the right thing. I don't know them. *(raises his hands in his agony)* Oh, son . . . son . . . dear God, my flesh, forgive me . . . *(begins to weep and shake)* my sons. *(He clutches his body shaken throughout by his ugly sobs.)* Dear God . . .

Voice. Just as we thought. You are the one. And you must be sentenced.

Court. I must be sentenced. I am the one. *(almost trancelike)* I must be sentenced. I am the one.

Voice. The murderer is dead. You must be sentenced alone.

Court. *(as first realization)* The murderer . . . is . . . dead?

Voice. And you must be sentenced. Now. Alone.

Court. *(voice rising, in panic, but catching it up short)* The murderer . . . is dead.

Voice. Yes. And your sentence is—

Court. I must be sentenced . . . alone. Where is the murderer? Where is his corpse?

Voice. You will see it presently.

Court. *(head bowed)* God. And I am now to die like the murderer died?

Voice. No. *(long pause)* We have decided to spare you. We admire your spirit. It is a compliment to know you can see the clearness of your fate, and the rightness of it. That you love the beauty of the way of life you've chosen here in the anonymous world. No one beautiful is guilty. So how can you be? All the guilty have been punished. Or are being punished. You are absolved of your crime, at this moment, because of your infinite understanding of the compassionate God Of The Cross. Whose head was cut off for you, to absolve you of your weakness. The murderer is dead. The murderer is dead.

(applause from the darkness)

Court. And I am not guilty now?

Voice. No, you are free. Forever. It is asked only that you give the final instruction.

Court. Final instruction . . . I don't understand . . .

Voice. Heroes! bring the last issue in.

(The last two Hooded Men return with a Young Black Man of about twenty. The boy does not look up. He walks stiff-legged to the center of Court. He

wears a large ankh around his neck. His head comes up slowly. He looks into Court's face.)

Young Man. Peace.

(Court looks at his face; he begins to draw back. The Hooded Man comes and places arms around Court's shoulders.)

Voice. Give him the instruction instrument.

(Hooded Man takes a pistol out of his pocket and gives it with great show to Court.)

Hood 1. The silver bullet is in the chamber. The gun is made of diamonds and gold.
Hood 2. You get to keep it after the ceremony.
Voice. And now, with the rite of instruction, the last bit of guilt falls from you as if it was never there, Court Royal. Now, at last, you can go free. Perform the rite, Court Royal, the final instruction.
Court. What? No. I don't understand.
Voice. The final instruction is the death of the murderer. The murderer is dead and must die, with each gift of our God. This gift is the cleansing of guilt, and the bestowal of freedom.
Court. But you told me the murderer was dead, already.
Voice. It *is* already. The murderer has been sentenced. You have only to carry out the rite.
Court. But you told me the murderer was dead. *(starts to back away)* You told me . . . you said I would be sentenced alone.
Voice. The murderer *is* dead. This is his shadow. This one is not real. This is the myth of the murderer. His last fleeting astral projection. It is the murderer's myth that we ask you to instruct. To bind it forever . . . with death.
Court. I don't . . . Why do . . . you said I was not guilty. That my guilt had fallen away.
Voice. The rite must be finished. This ghost must be lost in cold space. Court Royal, this is your destiny. This act was done by you a million years ago. This is only the memory of it. This is only a rite. You cannot kill a shadow, a fleeting bit of light and memory. This is only a rite, to show that you would be guilty but for the cleansing rite. The shadow is killed in place of the killer. The shadow for reality. So reality can exist beautiful like it is. This is your destiny, and your already lived-out life. Instruct, Court Royal, as the centuries pass, and bring you back to your natural reality. Without guilt. Without shame. Pure and blameless, your soul washed *(pause)* white as snow.
Court. *(falling to his knees, arms extended as in loving prayer, to a bright*

light falling on him, racing around the space) Oh, yes . . . I hear you. And have waited, for this promise to be fulfilled.
Voice. This is the fulfillment. You must, at this moment, enter into the covenant of guiltless silence. Perform the rite, Court Royal.
Court. Oh, yes, yes . . . I want so much to be happy . . . and relaxed.
Voice. Then carry out your destiny . . .
Court. Yes, yes . . . I will . . . I will be happy . . . *(He rises, pointing the gun straight at the Young Boy's face.)* I must be . . . fulfilled . . . I will . . . *(He fires the weapon into Boy's face. One short sound comes from the Boy's mouth.)*
Young Boy. Papa.

(He falls. Court stands looking at the dead Boy with the gun still up. He is motionless.)

Voice. Case dismissed, Court Royal . . . you are free.
Court. *(Now suddenly to life, the lights go up full. He has the gun in his hand. He drops, flings it away from him.)* My soul is as white as snow. *(He wanders up to the body.)* My soul is as white as snow. *(He starts to wander off the stage.)* White as snow. I'm free. I'm free. My life is a beautiful thing. *(He mopes slowly toward the edge of the stage, then suddenly a brighter mood strikes him. Raising his hand as if calling someone.)* Hey, Louise, have you seen my bowling bag? I'm going down to the alley for a minute. *(He is frozen. The lights dim to . . .)*

(Black)

Black Masque: The Passion of Darkie's Bones (1971; rev. 1981)

George Houston Bass (1938–1990)

Born in Murfreesboro, Tennessee, George Houston Bass was the son of a preacher and a teacher. He was one of nine children. In 1959, he received his A.B. (honors in mathematics) from Fisk University and, in 1964, an A.M. from the New York University Film School. Bass attended the Yale School of Drama from 1966 to 1968, and in 1969 produced thirteen original teleplays for Boston's WGBH-TV's program "On Being Black." An appointment at Brown University in the English department followed in 1970, and at the time of his death, Bass was a full professor with a dual appointment in the Theatre and Afro-American Studies departments at Brown. In 1973, he succeeded Arna Bontemps as the executor of the Langston Hughes Estate. Bass had worked as Hughes's secretary from 1959 to 1964, and would help to found the Langston Hughes Society in 1981 and, in 1982, help to launch the *Langston Hughes Review*. Among Bass's numerous citations and fellowships are the Rosenthal Award from the American Society of Cinematologists; the plaque of the Lion of St. Mark from the Venice Film Festival; the John Hay Whitney Fellowship; the John Golden Fellowship; a Harlem Cultural Council Grant; a Howard Foundation Fellowship; and a Fulbright Research Grant to India. Just before his death, Bass edited and revised the text of *Mule Bone,* which premiered at the Ethel Barrymore Theatre on Broadway in 1991.

As poet, playwright, director, and professor, Bass made a contribution to

African American and American theatre that is of singular importance. In 1970 he founded Rites & Reason Theater at Brown and for twenty years created works of epic proportion in and around Providence in an effort to bring back the historical relationship between community and theatre and to restore the imaginative power of poetry in the theatre through the creation of poetic myths. With Rhett Jones, also of Brown, Bass developed a "research to performance" method he envisioned as a way of strengthening the imaginative vision of the playwright by giving him or her access to the wider knowledge of scholars and of the community. In 1976, Bass began developing a mythic cycle, *Blood, Rivers, and Rainbows,* by producing community festival dramas, which he staged in churches, Providence's train station, and other environments. The cycle includes *Providence Festival I: Jamm in the Key of Z,* an eight-day festival (1976), and *The Blacker the Berry,* a forty-day festival (1980). Bass's American myth of re-creation ends with *Regenesis* and *The Tale of a Dragon Fire.*

Bass's other plays includes *Malacoff Blue,* which he regarded as his masterpiece. In all of his plays there is evidence of his concern for poetry and ritual in theatre as means of achieving a heightened sense of humanity. His plays also show his refined knowledge and use of theatricality and spectacle. Bass's orientation is toward performance of poetic utterance and a stage vision excited and enlivened by music and audience participation. In his writing, Bass plays the language for its poetic worth, as in *Black Masque: The Passion of Darkie's Bones,* where the characters whir and blend into a succession of historical imagery.

Selected Published Plays by George H. Bass

"Black Masque." *Callaloo,* Vol. 8 No. 2 (Spring/Summer 1985). Charlottesville: University of Virginia Press.
"Games." *Breakout: In Search of New Theatrical Environments,* by James Schevill. Chicago: Swallow Press, 1973.

Black Masque: The Passion of Darkie's Bones
A Ritual Drama

DEDICATION

*For my mother, Mabel Dixon Bass,
For Rosa Parks, Mother of the Civil Rights Movement, and
For Katherine Dunham, Queen Mother of our Sacred Dance of Life . . .*

Three brave and caring women who have Mothered many persons through darkness in the best tradition of the Great Mammies presented here.

O Negro slaves, dark purple ripened plums,
Squeezed, and bursting in the pine-wood air,
Passing, before they stripped the old tree bare
One plum was saved for me, one seed becomes

An everlasting song, a singing tree,
Caroling softly souls of slavery,
What they were, and what they are to me,
Caroling softly souls of slavery.
—Jean Toomer
"Song of the Son" from *Cane* (1923)

© Copyrighted by the authors. All rights reserved.

Black Masque was the first performance work written and developed for Rites & Reason at Brown University. It was created during the academic year 1970–71, and first performed April 20–22, 1971, with music by Clinton Utterbach. A revised text was produced by Rites & Reason in March 1981, with music by Robert L. Holmes, Jr. (Mr. Utterbach was not available to continue working with the project.) The text presented here is a reshaping that draws together the 1971 and 1981 production experiences. The 1971 production was directed by George Houston Bass. The 1981 production was directed by Mohammed Ghaffari.

All roles are to be played by Afro-American performers as if characters in an Afro-American *Egungun* play of ancestral spirits. The roles of Midknight and Queen Anne Lady should be played by light-skinned Afro-Americans. The use of white performers in playing Euro-American roles would create a reality base that is inappropriate for the aesthetic intentions of this work. White makeup *should not* be used. It, too, would violate the aesthetic intent of the text.

CHARACTERS

Host Attendants (to be played by five of the Members)
First Attendant
Second Attendant
Third Attendant
Fourth Attendant
Fifth Attendant

Ancestral Spirits of an Ancient World
Mammy One
Mammy Two
Mammy Three

Captured People from an Old World
Mann, the King of Embers
Hannah, the Queen of Embers
Members, men and women from the Land of Embers

Wielders of a New World Might
Sir Midknight, self-proclaimed lord and master of the New World
Miss Queen Anne Lady, the chaste wife of Sir Midknight
Darkie, manservant and jester for Sir Midknight

PERFORMANCE CHART FOR
AUDIENCE ENTRANCE
· · · · · ·

When audience members enter the lobby outside the main performance space, they should encounter three signs. The Red Cross emblem is used as a background for the text on each of the signs:

1. BLOOD SAVED LIVES
   BLOOD SAVES LIVES
   BLOODS SAVE LOVE
2. GIVING GETS
   GETTING GIVES
3. RECEIVING LINE FORMS HERE

Five Host Attendants dressed in graded shades of priestly habits (e.g. a range of colors from beige to dark brown) stand in a receiving line to greet each member of the audience as she/he enters the lobby space just outside the theatre. Each of the Host Attendants wears a different color belt on his/her habit—red, black, yellow, white, brown—signifying the five races of people in America. Each holds a specific ritual item and speaks a ritual text as greeting for the arriving audience. The attendants stand before a long piece of fabric designed in the manner of Mali mud cloth (Bobolanfini).

First Attendant wears a red belt with small Native American masks attached to it, and holds a crucifix. Words to be spoken to each member of the audience by the First Attendant are:

Kiss the feet of Jesus.

Each audience member may choose to kiss the feet of the Christ figure on the crucifix. No one should feel forced to perform any of the ritual actions.

Second Attendant wears a black belt with small African masks attached, and holds a marble slab with a bleeding heart of Jesus fixed on it. Words to be spoken to each member of the audience by the Second Attendant are:

Touch the Heart of Jesus.

Third Attendant wears a yellow belt with Asian masks attached to it, and holds a marble slab with the head of Jesus wearing the crown of thorns fixed on it. The spoken words by the Third Attendant are:

Bless the head of Jesus.

Fourth Attendant wears a white belt with Greco-Roman masks attached and holds a painting or drawing of a black man hanging from a tree. The image of the lynched victim should be executed in the mode of liturgical art from the Middle Ages of Western Europe. Words to be spoken by the Fourth Attendant are:

Was Jesus once a nigger, lynched because he was black?

Fifth Attendant wears a brown belt with Mexican (Aztec) masks attached, and holds a compass card designed as a collage showing images of people from a range of centuries, representing all races of people who have participated in the making and remaking of the Americas. (NOTE: The painting of the lynched victim and the compass card collage should be approximately the same size.) The words spoken by the Fifth Attendant are:

Look here. Look here and find your Jesus. *(pause)* Sweet Jesus.

After moving through the receiving line, each audience member should be assisted in finding a seat in the performance space by an usher. The ushers wear ashes on the forehead as worn by some Christians on Ash Wednesday, and two blood red tears near an eye.

Recorded music from the Afro-American folk tradition—Spirituals, Blues, Jazz, Gospel, and Rhythm 'n' Blues—should be played until moments before the entry processions of the performers begin.

This is a performance script. The reader should understand that many of the meanings of the text will be expressed with choreographic gestures, sounds, and rhythms discovered in the rehearsal process. It is important that the work be performed with a great sense of play and a deep appreciation for the rich Afro-American tradition of signifying with style and grace—being dead serious in a mood of outrageous fun. The action of the text explores configurations of collective dream-memory in the American society from an Afro-American perspective. It is also an interpretation of historical transformations occurring within a transition of world values from a Eurocentric reality of Old World beliefs to an American-centered view of democratic vistas. History is seen as a mirror—an instrument for shaping reflections on memory and dreams. Myth is entertained as an instrument of rediscovery and re-creation. The ritual action to be realized in a performance of the script is the death and the rebirth of heritage, history, and hope—a poetic reconstruction of the American creed.

Setting: *A Ceremonial Battleground—an open field of grass about a war monument that could be at a place called Gettysburg. The monument is upstage left. Plastic red roses from a deteriorated memorial wreath are scattered nearby.*
Time: *Here and now, in the present moment.*

Tape music out. House lights are still up. Silence. The voices of the Mammies are heard from offstage entoning a sound, as if the Winds of Change talking. As they almost end the sound, percussive instruments begin to play, then other instruments join as if making an invocation or call to ancestral spirits.

Mammies. *(offstage)*
    Whoo-oo-oa . . . woe, who-ooo-ooo-oo-a.

(Music: Percussive instruments. The Mammies enter from behind the war monument. Mammies Two and Three hold an 1863 United States flag open, using it to carry the unassembled bones of an adult human skeleton and a crown of thorns. Mammy One follows.)

Mammies Two and Three.
    Once, once, once, once upon a time . . . .
Mammy One.
    Once, once, once upon a heritage time in history
    Said, once, once, once upon a time of hope
    Talking time after time when no mo' time
    Had some people crowding
    People upon people all over
    People throughout time.
    Said, once, once, once when the hope of history
    Was our heritage
    That was all he, she, we ever ever wrote

(Mammy One takes the bones and crown of thorns from the flag and places them in a scattered pattern about the field of grass that is the performance space.)

Mammies Two and Three.
    One by one and two by two
    Two by two and four by fo'
    One by one and two by two
    Two by two and four by fo'
    One by one and two by two
    Two by two and four by fo'
    These leaves of grass seed more than mo'
    Two by two and four by fo'

(continue under dialogue)

Mammy One. (spoken over song as she places bones and crown of thorns in performance area) July First, Second and Third, not the Fourth, Eighteen Sixty-Three. Gettysburg. The Blue and The Gray clashing November Nineteenth, Eighteen Sixty-Three. Gettysburg. Old man Abe issuing a balm for fallen bodies and wounded spirit-minds. A union at war begetting a reunion of the dream. Gettysburg begetting Gettysburg and dry bones. Said, Eighteen Sixty-Three, two hundred forty-four years after Jamestown and the shadow of that slave block they made in Virginia one year before the Mayflower made Plymouth Rock. Said, 1863—one hundred years before some man named King dreamed his great dream on the steps of old Abe's monument overlooking Mr. Washington's reflecting sea and the blue-black Potomac. Dry bones walking and talking. Rites of US people making right our New World creed. Said, Abe Lincoln . . . George Washington . . . Dr. Martin Luther King. Heritage . . . History . . . Hope. Dry bones. Said, a new trinity of dry bones rising up to see and be seen anew.

(A procession enters through the audience. It is led by Darkie who carries a full-length mirror on his back. He is followed by Mann, Hannah, Sir Midknight and Miss Queen Anne Lady. They carry a charred, lynched victim on a bier—"The Soul of Man Thrice Crucified"—the form of a Black sharecropper who was lynched then cut down from the tree and burned. The figure should be a ceremonial sculpture, not a realistic rendering. Ten Members from the Land of Embers, five men, five women, follow. Each except Darkie wears a chain about the head. Darkie wears two chains about his neck. Darkie also leads the group in song.)

Darkie.
Mmmmm-hmmmm, ummmmm-hmmmmm.
All.
Looking for the light.
Darkie.
Mmmmm-hmmmm, ummmmm-hmmmmm.
All.
Looking for the light.
Darkie.
Mmmmm-hmmmmm, ummmm-hmmmm.
All.
Looking for the light.
Looking, looking, looking for the light
To light up the night that still claims my soul
Darkie.
Many generations have been here and gone
Darkness is still holding strong

>
> Hard times got me thinking my time ain't long
> And keep me singing old revival songs

All.
> Mmmmm-hmmmm, ummmm-hmmmm.

Darkie.
> Looking for the light

All.
> Mmmmm-hmmmm, ummmm-hmmmm.

Darkie.
> Looking for the light

All.
> Mmmmm-hmmmm, ummmmm-hmmmm.

Darkie.
> Looking for the light

All.
> Looking, looking for the light
> To light up the night
> That still claims my soul.

Darkie.
> Oh, Lord, please help me save my soul.
> Oh, Lord, please help me save my soul.
> Lay your head in the window and hear
> your servant's prayer,
> "Help me save my charred black soul."

All.
> Mmmmm-hmmmm, ummmm-hmmmm. Looking for the light.
> Mmmmm-hmmmm, ummmm-hmmmm. Looking for the light.
> Mmmmm-hmmmm, ummmm-hmmmm. Looking for the light.
> Looking, looking for the light to light up the night
> That still claims my soul.

(Darkie places the mirror to face the audience—it should fold out into three panels and be self-supporting. Both the front and back of the mirror should be reflective surfaces. The ceremonial lynched figure is placed in front of the mirror and members of the procession form a circle about it so that their reflections can be seen by the audience. All bow their heads.

Darkie does not join the circle. He begins collecting the bones and crown of thorns from about the performance space, tying them together like a string of fish. The bones should be of a full human skeleton and capable of being assembled during the performance. Darkie chants as he collects the bones. After gathering all the bones, Darkie ties them to the top of the war monument.)

Darkie. *(an improvised mix of moaning, chanted texts and spoken exclamations in the black folk church tradition)*

We hold these truths . . . *(moan)* . . . Whoa!
Men endowed by their creator . . . *(moan)* . . . Man, oh man!
Self-evident . . . *(moan)* . . . Woe man whoa!
Certain inalienable rights . . . *(moan)* . . .
Of the people . . . by the people . . . My God!
For the people . . . My, my, my!
Liberty . . . life . . . created . . . equal . . . *(moan)*
One nation under God . . . indivisible
Oh, say can you see . . . Who man, whoa!
Oh, say can you see . . . indivisible *(moan)*
In God we trust . . .

(As Darkie gathers bones, performers in the circle discover their reflections in the mirror and see the chains on their heads as chains. They throw off the chains with difficulty, then move to the bier and take hold of red ribbons attached to the chest area of the lynched figure. They move slowly about the figure as if in a maypole dance, creating a tangle of blood.)

Mammy One. This fountain of blood . . .
Mammy Two. This fountain of bleeding memories . . .
Mammy Three. And us—a tangled maypole turned crimson from the heat of old, old angers . . .
Mammies. Aching. Old angers aching.
Mammy One. This fountain bleeding.
Mammy Two. Curses that have no shame
Mammy Three. Hope cradled with despair
Mammy One. And memories of our war.
Mammy Two. Raw memories of bloody bones and old, old angers recalled in the name of many, many thousand.
Mammy Three. The many thousand gone, and the many thousand longing to be gone.
Mammy Two. Then let the roll be called.
Mammy Three. Here and now?
Mammy Two. Here and now.
Mammy One. *(to audience)* When the roll is called . . . when our roles are called . . . When the call is called from yonder . . . will you be there?

(Performers stop moving about bier and face Mammies as their roles are announced.)

Mammy Two. Mann? Hannah? Members from the Land of Embers?
Mammy Three. Sir Midknight? Miss Queen Anne Lady? Darkie?
Mammy One. What manner of man or woman dare rise from these ranks to set our dry bones free?

Mammies. When the roll is called . . . when our roles are called . . . When the call is called from yonder, will you be there?
All. *(except Mammies)*

(singing as they exit)

> Mmmmm-hmmmm, ummmm-hmmmm. Looking for the light.
> Mmmmm-hmmmm, ummmm-hmmmm. Looking for the light.
> Mmmmm-hmmmm, ummmm-hmmmm. Looking for the light.
> Looking, looking for the light to light up the night
> That still claims my soul.

Mammy One. The Sun
Mammy Two. Great Ball of fire
Mammy Three. Old Hannah
Mammy One. Rode the sky
Mammy Two. Knowing all, seeing all
Mammy Three. And saying nothing.
Mammy One. Then one day, some old Black mammy grew so tired she asked the Sun to entertain her younguns while she slept.
Mammy Two. Hear now the story that the Sun told
Mammy Three. While that old Black mammy slept.

(Midknight enters as Mammies drape themselves in one very large, gold cloth as if to become the Sun.)

Sir Midknight. Excuse me. I said, excuse me. This is now my land. You must move on.
Mammy One. But we are the Sun. You'll need us.
Sir Midknight. Maybe, but now it's time for you to move on. This is my land. God has given it to me.
Mammy One. I said, we are the Sun. The S-U-N.
Mammies Two and Three. The Ancient Source of healing waters.
Mammy One. Light of the land.
Sir Midknight. *(draws his sword)* I'm the new center of this universe. Move on.

(Mammies do not move.)

Sir Midknight. Darkie.

(Sir Midknight extends his hand. Darkie enters hurriedly with a gatling gun and places it in Midknight's hand.)

Sir Midknight. Need I say more?

(Mammies withdraw to their watch place with the lynched figure/bier which becomes their station. Midknight grabs hold of the gold cloth they wear as

Shawl of the Sun and puts it about his own shoulders. He claps his hands sharply as giving a command. Darkie rushes off and returns with a platform and chair to set up a throne of power. Miss Queen Anne Lady enters and Sir Midknight leads her to a seat on top of the war monument where he chains her by the ankle. It is as if she is chained to a pedestal in an ivory tower. He picks up scattered plastic roses and gives them to her. Darkie enters with a trunk, struggling with the weight. He places it on the platform near the throne chair. Midknight admires himself in the mirror, then directs Darkie in placing the mirror so that it better helps define his throne as the center of things. Then he stands before the mirror, raises his sword and pronounces his oath. The sword is raised handle up to emphasize the shape of a cross.)

Sir Midknight.
      Sir Midknight those damn lords call me
      Because they say I'm half a knight.
      Sir Midknight they call me, but I'll show them.
      I am the true son of God. My call is divine and real.
      I am the holy knight sent to break death's final seal.
      God's right and might will lead the way.
      I'm not afraid, I will obey, O Lord, God, Jehovah.
      No matter what comes, no matter what falls,
      I've heard your voice crying and I've answered the call—
      The call of your son named Jesus, crying
      In the wilderness. Crying for blind men
      Who refuse to see that we were sent to save all
      Humanity. I'll hold our banner high on this hill
      And all who come this way must kneel to glorify our name
      Or come to know the pain of a just might.
      They call me Sir Midknight. They say I'm a half-ass knight.
      But with your guide I'll turn the tide.
      All praises be to thee and me, Sir Midknight.

(He takes off sun cloth, admires it, then drapes it on his throne seat.)

Sir Midknight. Darkie.
Darkie. Yes, sir?
Sir Midknight. Is everything in order?
Darkie. Yes, sir.
Sir Midknight. Then let us move on.
Darkie. Yes, sir.

(Darkie unpacks the trunk as Midknight strolls about proudly surveying his kingdom. Darkie removes a grail and plate holding the Eucharist, an old Bible, an accounting book, a quill pen, a crucifix, a hand gun, a whip, a box

of war medals and apples. After the items are unpacked and placed about the throne, Midknight sits on his throne and begins eating an apple.)

Sir Midknight. Children of darkness come forth and I will give you light.

(Mann, Hannah and Members enter, singing. The Mammies join the singing. Mann leads the line of march.)
Members.
>We wade in darkness, lost is our night's journey.
>We wade in darkness, exiled from the light.
>We wade in darkness, lost is our night's journey.
>We wade in darkness, exiled from the light.
>
>No sun is shining, no star is glowing.
>The moon has forgotten us—
>Exiled from the light.
>
>All you who hear us, come help us on our journey.
>All you who hear us, help free us from the night.

Solo.
>The night is not friendly
>He closes his hands around our necks
>He closes his mouth on our heads
>Choking our breath and our beauty
>Choking our life.

All.
>We wade in darkness, lost is our night's journey
>We wade in darkness, exiled from the light.

Sir Midknight. Shut up! This is my God's world and he doesn't like that heathen kind of singing.

Mann. We are singing to our own Gods.

Sir Midknight. I'm in control here—me and my God. *(points at the lynched figure)* And that will be your fate if you dare oppose me.

Mann. We have our Gods, too.

Sir Midknight. Then that is your fate, nigger. Nigger . . . I like that . . . Yes, I like that. *(throws sprinkles of water from grail toward them as if to baptize them)* I baptize you *nigger* now and forevermore.

Mann.
>A wild young tree with leaves of blood
>Has chased away the sun
>Darkness, mmmmm-hmmmm, darkness
>Darkness holds midnight at our door.
>Said, a wild young magnolia tree
>Half charred and bleeding still
>Blots out our sun and holds midnight
>Cold, cold midnight at our door.

Mammies and Members.
>Midnight go 'way. Midnight go way from me.
>Midnight go 'way. I want to see the sun.
>Said, Midnight go 'way. Midnight go way from me.
>Midnight go 'way. I got to see the sun.

Hannah.
>Sun left here long time ago.
>Just where she went we don't know.
>But she's not here and that's for sho'
>Cause midnight hangs all 'round our door.

Mammies and Members.
>Midnight go 'way. Midnight go way from me.
>Midnight go 'way. I want to see the sun.

(Midknight fires his hand gun. Members run to take cover. Hannah and Mann hold their positions. Mammies watch.)

Sir Midknight. I was sent to conquer.
Mann. Be still my people, your king is with you.
Midknight. King? You? A king?
Mann. I am called Mann, the King of Embers. This is Hannah, my wife and queen. And these are my people.

(Midknight holds up crucifix.)

Sir Midknight. And this is your new God. Get down on your knees. Get down on your knees and worship the Lord Jesus. Get down on your knees and worship the Prince of Peace. Get down on your knees and worship the King of Kings. Get down on your knees. Get down on your knees and worship me—the chosen one.

(No one moves. Midknight fires his gatling gun. Members all fall to their knees, except Mann and Hannah.)

Mann. Get up! Get up! In the name of our Gods and our fathers, I command you to get up.
Sir Midknight. *(pointing gun)* Stay on your knees, niggers.
Mann. All you who hear us, come help us on our journey.
>All you who hear us, help free us—

(Midknight shoots Mann. Mann falls dead.)

Sir Midknight. Be free, nigger. Be free. Are there anymore heroes ready to volunteer?

(Hannah quietly falls on the body of her husband and cradles him in her arms. She slowly extends arms and legs as she emits a silent scream. The pieta transformed. Midknight pins war medals on his chest.)

Sir Midknight. Don't worry, Hannah, ole girl. I'll fuck you. I'll fuck all of you. Posterity shall know me as Cock-the-Great, the Father of the New World.

(Queen Anne Lady chants prayers in Latin and English, chained atop the war monument. [The text and performance chart for Queen Anne Lady are given in the appendix.] Mammies comfort Hannah as they lead Members in song.)

Mammies.
> Members, members from the land of embers,
> Lean on the Lord, lean on the Lord.

Mammies and Members.
> Members, members from the land of embers
> Lean on the Lord, the blessed Lord.
> He will hear your feeble cry—
> Send an answer bye and bye.
> Members, members from the land of embers
> Lean on the Lord.

Member. *(interrupting song)* No! God has forsaken us.
Another Member. Our Gods have not forsaken us.
Members. *(various voices in conflict)* Our Gods have forsaken us.
> Our Gods have not forsaken us.
> They have.
> They have not.

Sir Midknight. Enough! I am here to meet your every need.

(spoken)
> You'll raise the wheat, I'll give you the corn.
> You'll bake the bread, I'll give you the crust.
> You'll sift the meal, I'll give you the husk.
> You'll peel the meat, I'll give you the skin.
> And that's the way we'll make amends.

(Members grumble sounds of protest.)

> I said that's the way we'll make amends.
> Now sing with me.
> I'll own the wheat

Members.
> You'll give us the corn

Midknight.
> I'll own the bread

Members.
> You'll give us the crust

Midknight.
    I'll own the meal
Members.
    You'll give us the husk
Midknight.
    I'll own the meat
Members.
    You'll give us the skin
Midknight.
    And that's the way
    This saga ends.
You see, I'm your friend. Your Lord, master and friend. You can count on me to supply your needs. Darkie.

Darkie. Yes, sir?
Sir Midknight. Help those niggers bury that boy. I've got work for them to do.
Darkie. Yes, sir. Y'all heard what the man said, so get a move on. Get a move on, now. Y'all better get a move on.

(Members lift Mann and carry him to the bier where he is placed in the lynched figure—the sides should be pulled out to reveal a flat surface, transforming the construction into a ceremonial coffin.)

Members.
    Spirits of our ancestors, spirit of Mann.
    Great spirits of all good things here in this land
    Come to us, be with us.
    Help us keep true to the humane will
    Of our human race. Hear us,
    Great spirits of all good things here in this place,
    Be with us now and always be with us.

(Hannah takes a long, red ribbon from Mann's chest and uses it in a ritual to affirm the bond of community—a blood binding rite in which each Member takes hold of the red ribbon. She entones the story in the haunting style of Nina Simone. Members hold onto the ribbon as they re-enact the shared memory Hannah narrates. It is a dance of historical transformations performed as slowly changing tableaux. A film montage of The Middle Passage should be projected during the dance. The film image should be very, very large and without sound. [When production resources do not permit use of the film sequences indicated in the text, the director may choose to use slides or some other visual convention.])

Hannah.
    Waters were deep and wide in our village
    Little boys swam and played.

Little girls sang and danced.
Women had babies. Men built houses
And compounds for their wives and their babies.
Life was full and joyous most times.
Life was full and joyous.

Then one day strange faces rose from out the deep
Deep waters spitting fire. Our houses burned.
Many people died. Women screamed. Children cried.
Libertade! Liberte! Freedom!

Our little girls danced no more.
Our little boys played drums no more.
Our women had babies for us no more,
But for strange faces. And our men built
New houses in strange places
For those same strange faces.

Fire! Fire! Smoldering fire!
Our souls turned to fire anxious to ignite.
But instead we kneeled. At the cross we kneeled.
Have mercy! Help us Lord.
Instead we kneeled at the cross.
We kneeled to forgive them.

Strange faces that brought us
To whip lash and lynch tree . . .
Strange faces that taught us to no longer be free . . .
Broke our backs and dreams . . .
Chained our flesh and minds
With fears and schemes . . .
Then stacked us in strange places for slaughter.
No more! No more! No more! No more!
No more! No more! No more!

Though chains are now matted to our souls,
Our will to be free must remain
Whole for Mann's sake . . .
And for his son . . .
His unborn son moving within me.

Mammy One. The seed of Mann lives within you?!
Mammies Two and Three. Praises! Praises be!
Members.
Praises he lives! I'm so glad he lives!
He lives! Praises! I'm so glad he lives.

Praises he lives! I'm so glad he lives!
He lives! Praises! I'm so glad he lives.

Thank you father, thank you mother.
Ancestors be praised.
The breath of Mann still is.
I'm so glad he lives.

Praises he lives! I'm so glad he lives!
He lives! Praises! I'm so glad he lives!

(Midknight fires his gatling gun. Members throw down red ribbon and run to take cover. Hannah winds the ribbon into a ball and places it in her bosom. Queen Anne Lady pulls up the string of bones attached to the war monument. From this moment onward, she works to reassemble the human skeleton . . . bone by bone. The chart for the ritual action of her mime show is in the appendix.)

Midknight. Darkie.
Darkie. Yes, sir?
Midknight. Bring Hannah up here to me. My bed needs warming.
Darkie. Yes, sir. Don't just stand there, gal. You heard the man. Get a move on. You better get a move on, now. Hannah? Gal? You hear me, gal? You hear me. 'Scuse me, sir, but you gon have to make her come yourself. She won't have no parts of me.
Sir Midknight. Come here woman. I said come here.

(Hannah does not move. Midknight points his gun at her.)

Members. *(various voices)* Don't go.
   Hush.
   Go on, Queen Hannah.
   Don't go.
   Please go.
   The seed of Mann lives within you.
   You must go.
   No!
   Go on.
   You have to go.
   Don't go!
   Please.
   Your unborn son is our new hope.
   Go.
Sir Midknight. One. Two.

(Hannah begins moving toward Midknight. He lowers his gun.)

Hannah. *(sings)*
>The night is not friendly.
>He closes his hands about my neck.
>He closes his mouth on my head—
>Choking my breath and my beauty—
>Choking my life.

Midknight. Darkie.
Darkie. Yes, sir?
Midknight. *(giving him whip)* Take care of the niggers, I'm busy. Hannah.

(Midknight moves about Hannah, inspecting her, then the Copulation Ritual begins. Hannah lies on the floor downstage center with her knees raised in an open position. Midknight stands upstage at the center of his throne platform directly behind Hannah and performs a slow sexual grind. Hannah does not respond to him. Mammies begin a moan which continues throughout the Copulation Ritual. Members create work tableaux.)

Members.
>The land is his
>The law is his
>And we sweat for his, his, his
>Smile and grin.
>The land is his
>The law is his
>And we sweat for his, his, his
>Smile and grin.

Sir Midknight. Not bad. Not bad at all, though it could be done with more feeling. Run along, now. I have things to do. Run along.

(Hannah moves toward the Members. Midknight goes to the mirror to practice his gyrations then moves about inspecting the ears, eyes and teeth of the Members.)

Members. Did you hear about those Maroons?
>Did you hear about Cinque?
>Did you hear about Gabriel Prosser?
>Did you hear about—
>Lord, ain't they something.
>We could be something, too.

Midknight. *(at his throne)* Darkie.

(Midknight gives Darkie an empty money bag.)

>Hannah.

Members. *(various voices)* Go on.
>Don't go.

    Please go.
    You have to go.
    No. You don't.
    Mann lives within you.
    You must go.
    Don't go. Please.
    Go on.
    Your unborn son is our new hope.

(group)

    Go!

(Hannah takes her position. Mammies moan as the Copulation Ritual is repeated. Members work the fields in a series of somewhat rebellious tableaux. Darkie collects gold coins from them as a magic act—pulling the money out of thin air about them, and from their backs, hair, mouths, behinds, etc. He puts the coins in the money bag.)

Members.
    The land is his
    The law is his
    And we sweat for his, his, his
    Smile and grin.
    The land is his
    The law is his
    And we sweat for his, his, his
    Smile and grin.

Sir Midknight. Run along now, Hannah. Run along. I have things to do.

(Hannah leaves. Midknight sits on his throne eating the bread and drinking the wine of the Eucharist, and reading his Bible. Darkie gives the bag of coins to Midknight. He judges its weight and makes an entry in his account book.)

Members. Did you hear about our folk in Haiti?
    Did you hear about Nat, Harriet and Sojourner?
    Did you hear—
    Did you
    Well, they—

(Members whisper in one another's ear concerning the rumors of escape, revolt and rebellion.)

    Have mercy, Lord.
    Lord, have mercy.
    Well, did you ever . . . ?

Steal away to Jesus.
Hannah. *(singing)*
>The child in my belly is long overdue
>Said, the child in my belly is long overdue
>He knows they hanged his daddy
>And they plan to hang him, too
>He refuses, refuses to be born.

Midknight. Darkie.
Darkie. Yes, sir?

(Film projection of a montage of three events intercut with video noise— (1) scenes from The Middle Passage, (2) shots of Hannah holding Mann's body and silently screaming after he is killed by Midknight; and (3) Miss Queen Anne Lady cradling the skeleton and praying. The images should flow quickly and be no more than twenty seconds. The same film is to be projected each time Midknight hears the noise. The film should be without sound.)

Midknight. What's that noise I hear?
Darkie. Noise, sir?

(Midknight listens until film ends.)

Midknight. Never mind. Hannah.
Members. *(various voices)* I still say no.
>Go on, now.
>You have to go.
>No!
>The seed of Mann is within you.
>Your unborn son is our new hope.
>You've got to go.
>Don't go.
>It's a habit, now.
>Didn't my Lord deliver Daniel?
>Go.
>I'm wasting my breath.

(Hannah takes her position for the Copulation Ritual. Mammies moan. Members create tableaux of social interactions—debating their plight.)

Members.
>The land is his
>The law is his
>And we sweat for his, his, his
>Smile and grin.
>The land is his

The law is his
And we sweat for his, his, his
Smile and grin.

Midknight. Don't go.

(Hannah moves to him. They embrace.)

Member. *(Ellamae)* I don't care what y'all say, that bitch is liking it up there.
Member. Tell 'em girl. Tell 'em.
Member. *(Dee)* Watch your mouth, Ellamae, you talkin 'bout our queen.
Member. *(Ellamae)* Queen? That bitch ain't nothing now but another nigger.
Another Member. A *house* nigger.
Another Member. *(female)* I done told you about that lie. I work in the big house, too.
Member. *(Ellamae)* Yeah. Nigger is nigger and everybody knows it.
Members. *(males)* Sounds like somebody's sounding to me.
Run it on down, now.
Run it on down.
Member. *(Dee)* Ah, girl, you just jealous.
Member. *(Ellamae)* You damn right I'm jealous. Even a fool would rather work in bed 'stead of the damn field.
Member. *(Dee)* I said, watch your mouth, gal.
Member. *(Ellamae)* Last time I looked you was picking cotton just like me.
Member. *(Dee)* You better get out of my face with your mess, 'cause I don't play. No time.
Members. She's right about that, Ellamae.
She sho' is.
Dee don't play.
She never did.
Member. *(male)* Ah, come on now ladies, let's see some action.
Member. *(male)* That's right. If you can't get along, get it on.

(Midknight releases Hannah from the embrace.)

Midknight. I knew you could do it ole girl. I knew you would. Run along now. I have things to do.
Hannah. Run along now, Hannah. Run along. I have things to do. Run along. Run along. Run along.
Midknight. Hannah. Hannah, girl. I love you.
Hannah. You love my ass—that's all you love.
Midknight. And you love what I do to it. *(grabs her forcefully and pulls her to him)* Don't you?

(Hannah breaks Midknight's embrace and runs from him. She is encountered by Members standing watching her.)

Hannah. May I pass, please. May I pass?
Members. May she pass?
   What's she?
   Master's she.
   Did you say sheep or she?
   What?
   Sheep as in grass or she as in ass?
   I said can master's piece of ass get pass.
Hannah. Why do you mock me?
Members. Is that what we doing?
   Is we mocking you?
   Well, hush my mouth. We mocking.
Hannah. Have you forgotten our bond—our blood bond?
Ellamae. The only bond we knows about is bondage.

(Members break into derisive laughter.
Hannah backs away from them. Silence.
Darkie moves toward Members cracking his whip.)

Darkie. Y'all standing 'round here like y'all white folks. Get to them fields. Today ain't no Sunday. Get to them fields. Move. Go. The man done put me in charge. Y'all better move faster than that 'cause I'm in charge and you know I don't play.

(All members move, except one male. Darkie tries to intimidate him with threat of the whip.)

   Bend your back, boy.

(Man catches hold of whip and pulls it—a tug of war. Darkie and the man pull at each other. Darkie hits man with butt of whip, knocking him down.)

   Anymore heroes want to volunteer?

(Members move into formation to sing and mime working the fields. They begin at a very slow tempo.)

Members.
   We planting, chopping, picking, hoeing
   To keep ole master's money growing
Darkie. Wait a minute. I said wait a minute. If you niggers gon sing, sing happy.

(Musicians establish lively tempo and Members sing and dance a happy work song.)

Members.
> Planting, chopping, picking, hoeing
> Keeps old master's money growing
> Keep us tied to the field
> Got to give master a better yield
> Or know what for, or know what for
>
> We raise the wheat, he gives us the corn
> We bake the bread, he gives us the crust
> We sift the meal, he gives us the husk
> We peel the meat, he gives us the skin
> And that's the way, he hems us in.

Ellamae. Stop! Just stop! I'm tired of this mess.
Darkie. What's wrong with you. I didn't say stop.
Ellamae. I'm tired.
Darkie. Niggers ain't allowed to get tired around here.
Ellamae. Be nice to me and I'll be nice to you.
Darkie. Why didn't you say you was thirsty. Go on and get some water. Just don't let it take all day.
Ellamae. *(sensual grin)* Yes, sir. Yes, sir. Yes, sir.

(Hannah has been watching.)

Hannah. Where is your pride?
Ellamae. Out there in the field, honey. Waiting for somebody like you to pick it up.

(Hannah takes ribbons from her bosom.)

Ellamae. I ain't spreading my legs every night for the man who killed him.

(Ellamae switches away from Hannah past Darkie.)

Darkie. Don't water down the sugar, now. I likes it strong and long.

(Hannah looks at Darkie with disgust, then turns away.)

Darkie. Ah, you don't have to get all high-falutin with me. I'm just as good as he is. Maybe a little better.
Hannah. Better at what?
Darkie. Oh, you know. That steady grind.
Hannah. You must be out of your mind.
Darkie. Damn sho' is. But you could help me get back to my right senses. And that would be good for both of us.

(Hannah glares at him in silence.)

Darkie. Tom? Nigger? Lackey. Say it. Damn lackey. I ain't so dumb as you think. I read your eyes. You call me lackey every time you look at me. Been calling me that. Lackey, lackey, lackey! Maybe I am, sort of. But you ought to understand that. Circumstances beyond my control. You also know I ain't as dumb as he thinks, neither. But no need for us to talk about him. I got him figured out good. Real good. What to do. What to say. When and how to say it. Had a whole lot of time to figure him out. But you . . . that's another matter.

Hannah. I am not a traitor.
Darkie. And I ain't no dead hero.
Hannah. Oh?
Darkie. I'm still alive and breathing strong—all man. And I do mean inside and out. I have dreams, too. Why I could be up there on that throne. I could. Can't you see? It could be me up there instead of him. It could.
Hannah. And what if you were up there? Would you do things differently?
Darkie. I ain't been up there yet to know.
Hannah. Yet?
Darkie. Conspire with me and see.
Hannah. I've already seen far too much of you to trust anything you do or say.
Darkie. Well, now, Miss Hannah, I can understand that 'cause it looks to me like we two peas in the same pod. And that's a kind of closeness that don't always breed goodwill. But I'm willing to work good and hard to change all that.

(Darkie pinches Hannah's behind.)

Hannah. How dare you?!
Darkie. Oh, I dare to do all sorts of things. All the time. That's why I am where I am.
>I's a dancing darkie
>Been dancing since I was three years old.
>Said I's a dancing darkie
>Been dancing since I was three years old.
>That's how I do what I do
>And say anything I please
>Down on my knees.
>Do-be, do-be, do-wah, she-wah-aaa
>Do-be, do-be, do-wah, she-aaa

Hannah. Must everything be made a joke, and anything be done for a laugh?
Darkie. Well, now, Miss Hannah, I tell you. I thinks everything and anything is done right now for staying alive. And judging from where you been sleeping and why you claim to be sleeping there, it looks to

me like that's just what you been thinking, too. But I figure we can change all that, if Midknight ain't your sho' enough love.

(Hannah starts to leave. Darkie grabs her by the arm.)

Hannah. Let me go. And don't you ever dare touch me again.
Darkie. But I told you, m'am, I dare do anything to stay alive. I was born that way.
Hannah. I said, let go. *(jerks herself free)*
Darkie. I love black pepper. Let me be your back-door man. Don't you walk away from me, woman. Who the hell do you think you are?
Hannah. I know who I am. The problem is, you don't.
Darkie. So tell me. I'm listening. I said, I'm listening. Cat got your tongue? Well, it ain't got mine. Master told me to find him a new young piece. Said he's tired of old meat. Bored stiff. I'm willing to do a little tenderizing to help you cure him of his boredom. Make you feel young again.
Hannah. You listen to me!
Darkie. No, you listen. We both can be replaced. *(pause)* Now you gon have to 'cuse me. Duh sun's a-settin' an' we still got lots of work to do befo' night falls. An' believe me, duh night will fall.

(Darkie exits laughing, and leaving Hannah alone.)

(The act break should come here when the script is performed with an intermission.)

PART II
. . . . . .

If an intermission is observed, Hannah enters alone and others enter as appropriate to the flow of action in which they participate. If the script is performed without a break, the action flows without interruption.

Hannah. *(sings)*
>The child in my belly is long overdue—
>One hundred fifty years overdue.
>He knows they hanged his daddy
>And they plan to hang him too.
>He refuses, refuses to be born.

(Mammies move to Hannah to comfort her.)

When Midknight calls, I go to him. Fear drives me there. Fear for my unborn son. His hands are heavy. His breath is cold. I lie quiet and still.

He pounds his body against me . . . Desperately. I lie there. Dead still. Struggling to force my mind to some other place. I lie there. With Midknight. His breath . . . his touch become hot with passion . . . and my body submits. Forgetting the hate and anger of my heart. Responding to his desperate act of love . . . I move. My body moves, and Midknight finds his pleasure in me. What should I do? What can I do? *(pause)* Be born, my child. Please be born. You must be born. Mann. Dear husband. Please . . . Help me.

(Mammies embrace Hannah and rock her to sleep. Darkie and Members also fall asleep as the Mammies sing.)

Mammies.
>Sleep, sleep, you know the game
>Of singing songs to ease your pain.
>You are not to bear the blame of whips and chains.
>One plus one make two make four
>Make more strong backs to break the roar
>Of whips that chain and chains that blind,
>Making folk forget their mind.
>Rest, rest until the great day.
>Mind what your mammies say.
>We won't lead you astray.
>Go easy 'til that day, I say.
>Go easy 'til that day.
>Then you'll cast all bonds away.
>Then you'll cast all bonds away.

(After Hannah is asleep, Mammies move to the bier and gently touch Mann. He rises from the bier and moves to Hannah who remains asleep.)

Mann. Hannah, wife, mother of my sons and daughters, I hear you and my heart weeps with you. But how can I help ease your pain and suffering? I am no longer flesh. Sun. Moon. Stars. Spirits of Light. Mothers and Fathers of this great Universe, hear me. I am Mann, King of Embers. I was a good king . . . true to my people. And I gave honor to you . . . Oh, great Ancestors . . . Hear me.

(Mammies become Ancestral Spirits of Light.)

Mammies. *(Ancestral Spirits of Light)* We hear you and we have come.
Mammy One. What will you have us do?
Mann. It is for my wife and children that I come. It is for my people that I am here. They walk the earth cursed and spat upon. Damned long before they leave their mother's womb. Have mercy. Grant them

comfort. Grant them strength. Inspire them with the courage and will to break free.

Mammy One. They live in a world of new horizons . . . of new possibilities.

Mammy Two. We can not work our old powers yet, in this new land.

Mammy Three. Your people must learn to make their own way.

Mammy One. We can not—

Mann. Aaa! What good are you?! If this is the fixed end of life for all my generations, what good are you?!

Mammy One. We can bless them with the patience of love.

Mammy Two. And renew the strength of their undying faith.

Mammy Three. And ease their days with laughter and song.

Mann. They know how to laugh. They know how to sing. What good is faith if they're eternally damned?

Mammy One. Faith kindles the power of dreams . . .

Mammy Three. *(whispered)* Hold fast, hold fast to dreams.

Mammy Two. Lets them see beyond the darkness . . .

Mammy Three. Beyond their suffering and shame.

Mammy One. It will help them look through muddy waters and spy dry land.

Mann. Is that all you have to offer?

Mammy One. Did you ever look through muddy waters and spy dry land?

(Mann does not respond.)

Mammies Two and Three. Then don't knock it.

(Mann laughs.)

Mammies. Let the hand of fate be revealed . . . and let the will of their way be made known to them.

(The Mammies intone, dance and gesture working themselves and Mann into a state of possession which will allow them to enact a vision of their fate. As they dance, they gather the mask and props needed for the enactment and place them before the mirror. Lights establish a dream space which places Members, Hannah, Darkie, Midknight and Queen Anne Lady under the spell of the dream. Mammies raise a veil before Mann then prepare Mann to perform the dream ballet, "Man-God With The Long White Reach." Mann is dressed by the Mammies in the mask of The Great White Father With The Long White Reach. It is a full body mask constructed to stand on its own. The hands can be detached from the arms to allow long white strips of fabric to unfold and wrap about the figures of people and things that become the captured possessions of The Great White Father. The hands keep reaching and claiming until The Great White Father is trapped by the mass of his

earthly possessions of people, places and things entangled in the long white strips of fabric. Three Members are masked by the Mammies to perform in the dream ballet as Helping Hands of Fate. The Mammies tell the story of the ballet with jazz-like rhythms in a freely improvised arrangement of the narrative text.)

Mammies.
>The Great-Father-God With The Long White Reach
>Grows arms that spread like the wild roots of trees.
>Said, The Great Man-God With The Long White Reach
>And hands with very sticky fingers
>Makes cages and prison bars from all things everywhere
>Water and air . . . earth and sky
>Makes cages and bars to shut up people and more people
>As people shut up.
>Then in the silence of those many shut up people
>The Great-Father-God With The Long White Reach
>Steals and kills dream after dream
>Said he steals and kills the dreamers and their dreams
>With his very very very sticky fingers.
>
>And The Great Man-God With The Long White Reach
>Claims more and more and more than before
>Said more and more mostly from the weak and poor
>Until one day as he plots his next great scam . . . wham!!
>Stuck at the end of his long white reach
>Trapped in the tangles of his long white grope
>Snared by the noose of his own choke rope
>He stands exposed by the hand of time
>And the arrogant misdeeds that made him deaf and blind.
>His eminence goes to seed.
>The Great-Father-God With The Long White Reach
>Goes to seed . . . goes to seed . . .
>Stuck in his own misdeeds.

(The dream continues as Mann crawls out from under the entangled mask of the Man-God to perform a soft-shoe song and dance number behind the veil. The Members who helped in the ballet return to their sleeping positions and are unmasked to again become part of the sleeping Members.)

Mann.
>When a man walks like he thinks he's God, let him.
>When a man talks like he thinks he's God, let him.
>When a man schemes like he thinks he's God, let him.
>When a man deems himself as God, let him.

And keep your ass down his throat—
Yes sir him to death.
Keep your ass down his throat—
Help him run clean out of breath.
Then as he gasps to keep among the quick,
He'll know he wasn't the only one God made slick.
For your yes sirs down his throat
Will have done the trick
Cause he'll be dying sick.

(Hannah cries out from her sleep, entering the dream as a character in it.)

Hannah. No! No! I can't. I won't.
Mann. You've got to hold on tight, now, and shout out the pain. I say, hold on with all your might and spit out the shame. Niggers creating a lot of confusion don't ever have to be explained.
Hannah. I can't be like Darkie. I won't be another darkie. I won't.
Mann. Doom is trapped in your soul. Free doom. Doom is trapped in my soul. Free doom. Free doom.

(Mann returns to the bier and his death position. Hannah sits in silence a moment, then returns to her sleeping position.)

Mammies.
Hear the dream. Know the dream.
Speak the dream. Be the dream.
Hear the dream. Know the dream.
Speak the dream. Be the dream.
Be the door to the dream. Be the bearer of the scheme
And scream it. Scream it into the power of your songs.
Then inch by inch reforge some healing rites from
Those cold, old selfish wrongs.

(Queen Anne Lady throws plastic roses as a plea for help. The roses hit Hannah, Darkie and some of the Members. They stir, but continue to sleep—except for Darkie. He gets up as a part of the dream to gather the roses and make a garland which he hangs about his neck. Then he dances before the mirror, recalling Mann's song and dance. The silent film of Midknight's "noise" is projected, giving Midknight an intense headache within the dream.)

Darkie.
"Keep dat nigger running"
Is the name of the game
From the sands of California and Florida
To the rocky coasts of Washington and Maine.

So brighten up your "Yes, Sirs"
Make them think you're playing their game
Niggers running around in circles
Don't have to be explained.

Just keep your ass down their throats—
Yes Sir them to death.
Keep your ass down their throats—
And put your dignity on the shelf.
Then as they gasp to keep among the quick,
Let go a full blow. Explode your dirty trick.
They weren't the only ones God made slick.
Keep your ass down their throats—
Yes Sir them 'til they're dying sick.

(Darkie stops dancing and stares into the mirror as if seeing himself anew. He turns to the audience.)

Doom is trapped down in my soul.
Free doom. Free doom.
Doom is trapped down in your soul.
Free doom.
Said, Doom is trapped down in our soul,
Trying to find a way to get its story told.
Doom is trapped deep in our souls.
Free doom.

(Midknight becomes a character in the dream.)

Midknight. Darkie.

(Darkie stands quietly. He does not answer.)

Midknight. Darkie, my boy.

Darkie. For centuries longer than memory he's called me his boy with never a thought that I do understand that I'm a man. So . . . child play begets child play.

(Darkie dons the mask of the buffoon again, looks back into the mirror.)

(*self-mocking*) Well, I be. You reckon dat was me? He-he-he.

(Darkie hides behind the mask and watches.)

Midknight. Darkie . . . Hannah . . . Somebody.

(Hannah has a sharp labor pain. She sings. Midknight goes to Queen Anne Lady who is awakened in the dream by Hannah's song. She cradles the skeleton and chants prayers, unaware of Midknight's presence.)

Hannah.
> The child in my belly is long overdue—
> Two hundred fifty years overdue.
> He knows they hanged his daddy
> And they plan to hang him, too.
> He refuses, refuses to be born.

Midknight. Queen Anne Lady . . . My Queen Anne Lady . . . listen to me. That lock and chain you wear are not signs of rejection, but devotion. I deny you for your own good. I cannot share with you the terrible things I must endure. This is my fate. God has placed the burden and crown on me. But, don't be afraid. This situation will not always have to be. My choices have been hard and cold to keep me fixed on my great mission as the chosen in God's great Master plan. I was born to conquer and rule. So, I accept my fate and revel in the power that it brings. Be patient. Be happy. Learn to revel in your fate as I do in mine. For I am God's chosen victor, and you are my prize. So brighten your heart and days with the knowledge that it is my destiny to rule all things—in your name, and mine.

Darkie. I, too, can fancy myself the chosen of God. A back handed guarantee that we all will be whole and free, again. And I'm hell bound bent on making it so . . . don't you know? Even if it's not until the day of my dying.

(Darkie and all other characters within the dream return to their sleeping positions. Mammies raise the veil into a canopy under which the remaining action will flow—people living beneath the veil [Du Bois's metaphor]. They speak and intone [as] the veil is raised into place.)

Mammies. Let the dream you all have dreamed become real. Let the dream you all have dreamed become truly real. And let your world be made whole through the transforming power of laughter and song.

(Everyone will wake from their sleep into the unfolding reality beneath the veil.)

Midknight. Darkie. Darkie!
Darkie. Yes, sir.?

(The film is not projected this time.)

Midknight. I hear that damn noise again.
Darkie. Noise, sir? I don't hear no noise.
Midknight. How dare you tell me I don't hear a noise.
Darkie. I didn't say you don't hear a noise, sir. I said, I don't hear no noise.
Midknight. Where are my niggers?

Darkie. Sleeping, sir.
Midknight. Sleeping! It's Saturday night.
Darkie. Yes, sir. But I think they might be feeling tired.
Midknight. Tired!? Tell the niggers to have a little fun. Kick up their heels. Entertain me.
Darkie. Wake up. Wake up, y'all. Wake up. The man said for y'all to wake up. Who you want to see dance, sir?
Midknight. You and Hannah for a start.
Darkie. Sir?
Midknight. You and Hannah for a start.
Darkie. Yes, sir. Don't mind if I do. Show these niggers how to sho' 'nough shuffle. Come on Miss Hannah.
Hannah. Isn't it enough that I warm your bed?
Midknight. Come warm it now. Come on, ole girl. Entertain me.

(Hannah moves slowly to Midknight. Midknight takes a large bottle of wine from his trunk.)

Midknight. Here, Darkie. A little treat to help the merriment. Drink up.
Darkie. You de boss, boss.

(Darkie drinks from the bottle.)

Darkie. Come on, y'all. The man said for us to kick up our heels.
Members. *(various voices)* Told you to kick up your heels. Didn't say nothing 'bout us.
I'm gon rest, myself.
Yeah, me too.
I ain't thinking 'bout that man.
I'm on my own time now.

(in concert)

We're on our own time now.
Mammies. Free doom. Free doom. Free doom.
Darkie. The man sho' put a whipping on y'all. Umph, umph, umph! Y'all is some tired niggers. Sho' 'nough tired niggers. But don't worry 'bout it. Have some wine. Get blind. Ease your mind. Get loose with this joy juice. Fall in the monkey bin. Have some fun.

(Members all crowd about Darkie and pass the bottle of wine. Everyone drinks from the bottle. Darkie initiates a chant which develops into a minstrel show chorus line routine—a real darkie coon show.)

Darkie and Members.
Shoo-be-do. Shoo-be-do.
Shoo-be-shoo-be-shoo-be-do.

Shoo-be-do. Shoo-be-do.
Shoo-be-shoo-be-shoo-be-do.
Shoo-be-shoo-be-shoo-be-shoo-be
Shoo-be-shoo-be-shoo-be-do.
Shoo-be-shoo-be-shoo-be-shoo-be
Shoo-be-shoo-be-shoo-be-do.

(The chant is continued as long as needed for the routine. After routine is established, each Member moves out from line—darkie style—performs a bit then returns to line as next Member comes out to perform a bit. Members ad lib responses.)

Darkie. The chicken and the rooster had a fight. The rooster knocked the chicken out of sight. The chicken told the rooster, that's all right. I'll see you in the gumbo Friday night. Oh, yeah.

Member. *(male)* Woke up this morning with the devil by my side. Yes, I woke up this morning with the devil by my side. Gonna go cut up somebody 'till I'm more than satisfied.

Members.
Shoo-be-shoo-be-shoo-be-shoo-be
Shoo-be-shoo-be-shoo-be-do.

Member. *(female)* I ain't loved but three men in my life. Said, I ain't loved but three men in my life. My father, my brother and the man that wrecked my life.

Members.
Shoo-be-shoo-be-shoo-be-shoo-be
Shoo-be-shoo-be-shoo-be-do.

Member. *(female)* Oh, my soul! My soul! Oh, my sweet soul! Papa Legba! Father Divine! Daddy Grace! Prophet Jones! Jesus! Ogun! Somebody! Anybody! Come save my soul. My sweet, sweet soul!

Members.
Shoo-be-shoo-be-shoo-be-shoo-be
Shoo-be-shoo-be-shoo-be-do.

Member. *(Ellamae)* When a black cat cuts cross your path, that's bad luck I've heard it said. When a black cat cross your path, bad luck I've heard it said. One started cross my path, got halfway and fell dead.

Member. *(male)* She's one bad motor scooter, mean to the bone. I advise everybody to leave her alone.

Members.
Shoo-be-shoo-be-shoo-be-shoo-be
Shoo-be-shoo-be-shoo-be-do.

(Members repeat part of their chorus line darkie routine in very slow

movement [tempo of song does not change] and move downstage to form a frozen tableaux across the front of the acting area.)

Members.
    Shoo-be-do. Shoo-be-do. Shoo-be-shoo-be-shoo-be-do.
    Shoo-be-do. Shoo-be-do. Shoo-be-shoo-be-shoo-be-do.
    Shoo-be-shoo-be-shoo-be-shoo-be
    Shoo-be-shoo-be-shoo-be-do.
    Shoo-be-shoo-be-shoo-be-shoo-be
    Shoo-be-shoo-be-shoo-be-do.

(Hannah moves behind frozen tableaux.)

Hannah. Strange faces still hold us to whip lash and lynch tree. Strange faces will teach us to no longer be free. Break our backs and dreams. Chain our flesh and minds with fears and schemes, then stack us in strange places for slaughter.

(Hannah has labor pains.)

    Be born, please. Please be born.
Midknight. Darkie.

(Darkie breaks from tableaux.)

Darkie. Yes, sir.
Midknight. Is it still Saturday?
Darkie. No, sir.
Midknight. Then why are the niggers laughing at me?
Darkie. Laughing, sir? I don't hear nobody laughing.
Midknight. Are you disputing my word?
Darkie. No, sir. I ain't 'sputing your word. I just don't hear what you hears.

(Sir Midknight takes a needle of heroin and a handful of trinkets [charms on chains] and gives them to Darkie. Midknight makes more entries in his accounting book.)

Midknight. Here.
Darkie. What is it, sir?
Midknight. Something to help you stop the noise.
Darkie. What noise, sir?
Midknight. That nigger noise. Find it.

(Darkie moves about listening for noise then goes to Hannah.)

Mammies. Free doom. Free doom. Free doom.
Darkie. The might of pain, the pain of might can make you feel all uptight.

Turn on to bliss, it's out of sight. Make your dreams sprout wings and take flight. Oh, yeah.

Hannah. Must you forever be a jackass?

Darkie. Don't be a nag hag, turn on to this scag.

Hannah. Get away from me.

Darkie. Mama is sho' 'nough mean this evening. Tell me my name. What's my name, uh? Is my name Shit? I said, is my name Shit?

Midknight. It's yours, Darkie. Forget her.

Darkie. You de boss, boss.

(Darkie puts gold chains with charms about his neck, then shoots up. Members move to form tableaux about Darkie.)

Darkie. Wow! This is some good shit. Tell me what I say. Yea. Yea. Yeah! You know, I believe my name is Shit.

Member. Then don't just stand there, Shit. Share the shit.

Mammies. Free doom. Free doom. Free doom.

(Members break tableaux and take charms from Darkie. They use them like needles to shoot up. Three of the Members do not use the drugs and pull others coat tails trying to stop them. They are not successful. Two then join in the revelry. All but one take delight in the new trinkets which should be charms of wealth and power—car, house, dollar sign, yacht, etc.)

Members. Ride that white lady! Ride that 'hoe! Sweet lady of paradise! Get on that bitch! Ride that white lady! Ride that 'hoe! Sweet lady of paradise! Get on that bitch! Ride that white lady! Ride that 'hoe.

(Members begin moving about slapping five. Congratulating one another on their possessions. Darkie initiates the chant and action.)

Members.
> Mmmmm-hummmmm yea-yea give me five.
> Mmmmm-hummmmm yea-yea give me five.
> Mmmmm-hummmmm yea-yea give me five.
> Mmmmm-hummmmm yea-yea give me five.

(Members move about in the haze of "high" slapping five. All action freezes as each Member speaks his individual line, they resume motion on the chant. The lines are spoken as jazz phrases.)

Member. I'm feeling good. I'm high and free. Done aced the space that wouldn't let me be.

Members.
> Mmmmm-hummmmm yea-yea give me five.
> Mmmmm-hummmmm yea-yea give me five.

Member. Feeling no pain. Bearing no blame. Sharing no shame. Don't need no fame.

Members.
    Mmmmm-hummmmm yea-yea give me five.
    Mmmmm-hummmmm yea-yea give me five.

Member. Feeling, feeling, feeling, feeling, feeling. Feeling, feeling no pain. Unnn-ummmmm, no pain. Them folks ain't gon drive me insane. No pain. No pain, no pain.

Members.
    Mmmmm-hummmmm yea-yea give me five.
    Mmmmm-hummmmm yea-yea give me five.

Member. My head is my head is my head is my head is so nice. So nice. I mean nice. My head is oh so nice so very nice so nice, nice, nice, so nice.

Members.
    Mmmmm-hummmmm yea-yea give me five.
    Mmmmm-hummmmm yea-yea give me five.

Member. Don't need no pain. Don't want no blame. Won't wear no shame. That is my fame.

Member. I'm free. I'm free. I'm free. I'm free. I'm free. I'm free. I'm free as I wanna be.

Members.
    Mmmmm-hummmmm yea-yea give me five.
    Mmmmm-hummmmm yea-yea give me five.

Member. Flying high. Flying high, flying, high-high, flying high. Flying high, flying high, flying, high-high-high, flying high. Flying high.

(Members begin falling out moving through a zombie hang to prone positions.)

Members. Yea. Yea. Yea. Yeah. Yeah.

Members. *(various voices, all lying on floor)*
    Oooo-wee. Ooooo-weee.
    Ooo-wee let me be.
    Ain't I a man suppose to be free.
    Get off my back and let me be.
    Oooo-wee. Oooo-weee.
    Ooooo-weee what's wrong with me.
    Mama. Daddy. White folks. Please.
    Somebody done give me some strange disease.

All Members. Help me. Help me, please.

(Members lie out prostrate in silence—overcome by the drugs. The "noise" film is projected.)

Hannah.
>The child in my belly is long overdue,
>Three hundred fifty years overdue.
>He knows they hanged his daddy
>And they plan to hang him too.
>He refuses, refuses to be born

Midknight. Hannah! Darkie! Stop that noise.

(Darkie sits up with his finger over his lips. He gestures to Hannah. She ignores him. Darkie moves the mirror so that Hannah sees her own reflection and his. Silence. They look in the mirror at one another.)

Hannah. What do you want from me?
Darkie. Satisfaction guaranteed.
Hannah. If you would keep your mind from between my legs—
Darkie. I'm talking about the survival of generations . . . whole and free.
Hannah. *(turning from mirror)* You're hopeless.
Darkie. Hopeless? Hope is one of the two things I'm full of. And inch by inch I mean to get rid of the other.
Hannah. Crawling all the way, no doubt.

(Queen Anne Lady's prayers in Latin and English are mixed up and near shrill. She cradles the full skeleton as she prays. Hannah turns and sees a loose block in the war monument. She removes the stone block, climbs upon the monument and uses it to strike the lock and chain that fetter Queen Anne Lady. The chain is broken from the monument, but remains attached to Queen Ann Lady's ankle. She is free to move from her confinement, but does not. When she notices the chain is broken, picks it up and stares at the end. Midknight leaves his throne looking for Hannah. He is eating an apple.)

Midknight. Hannah? Hannah. Darkie, my boy, where is she?

(Midknight sees her. He offers her his apple.)

Hannah. I wish you were dead.
Midknight. Darkie.
Darkie. Yes, sir?
Midknight. Did I ever show you how to tame a bitch?
Darkie. No, sir.
Midknight. Then bring me my whip.
Darkie. And who, sir?
Midknight. She's already here. Hannah, the Queen.
Darkie. You don't look your best, sir.
Midknight. Don't keep me waiting, boy. The whip.
Darkie. She's carrying a child, sir.

Midknight. The whip.
Darkie. Twins, sir. Or even triplets.
Midknight. Do you want me to get my whip for you?

(The "noise" film is projected.)

Darkie. You really don't look your best, sir.
Midknight. That noise. That noise. Go tell the niggers to make a lot of noise. Drown out that other noise I hear. *(to Hannah)* Get down on your knees. Get down on your knees. I said, get on your knees. Damn you.
Hannah. Get down on your knees. You're the one most in need of prayer.

(Midknight runs to his throne to get the whip.)

Mammies. Free doom. Free doom. Free doom.
Darkie. Y'all better get a move on, now. Come on, get up. We got the man's permission to have a sho' 'nough stomp. Let everything hang all out. Come on. Let's hit it for real.

(After Midknight gets to his throne, he is overcome by the pain of noise in his head and drops the whip. Members, led by Darkie, begin "Black Power" routines in rhythmical march patterns.)

Darkie.
    Beep-beep, bang-bang
Members. *(joining chant)*
    Ummm-gower, take power!
    Beep-beep, bang-bang, ummm-gower, take power!
    Beep-beep, bang-bang, ummm-gower, take power!
    Beep-beep, bang-bang, ummm-gower, take power!
Darkie. Listen my brothers, this is the hour. This is the hour to seize power. We got the courage. We got the cause. It's time for us to stop listening to laws.
Members. We're gonna rise up. Break down bars. Take what's ours, now.
Members. *(various voices)* No more waiting. No more hesitating.
  Take power, now.
  Right on brothers. Down with the mothers.
  Off the pig. I mean, can't you dig. It's power to the people.
All Members. Power to the people! Power to the people! Power to the people!
Darkie. I said, rise up brothers, let's kill the mothers.
Members. *(various voices)* Rise up and fight. End your nigger fright.
  Be a man. Follow our plan.
  Rise up. Rise up, now!

All Members.
>Power to the people! Power to the people! Power to the people! Power to the people! Power to the people! Power to the people!

(Members encircle Darkie and beat him to death. Silence. Ellamae takes the garland of flowers from Darkie's neck and puts it about her own neck.)

Midknight. Why have you stopped your noise?
Member. Darkie's dead, sir.
Midknight. What?
Member. Darkie's dead.
Midknight. Dead? My God. That can't be.
Member. Maybe it ain't suppose to be, but it is, sir.

(Midknight moves to Darkie tries to awaken him.)

Midknight. Darkie . . . Darkie, my boy. Darkie. *(pause)* Get up! Damn you!

(Midknight hears the noise. The film is not projected.)

>Stop that noise. That goddamn noise. I said stop it.

Hannah. They can't.
Midknight. Why not?
Hannah. It's the son of Mann—crying out from the grave you have tried to make of my womb.
Midknight. Then, I'll pull it out, goddamn you. I'll pull it out.

(Hannah moves away from Midknight. He tries to pursue her, but Members block his path and move slowly toward him. He backs away then turns to flee but trips over Darkie and falls. His head collides into the mirror. Blood flows from his mouth. He looks in the mirror and becomes transfixed by the sight of his own blood. Members move behind the mirror to animate it. Other Members animate the Man-God Mask. Midknight backs away. Members begin a soft laughter. The mirror, the mask and Members slowly move around Midknight.)

Midknight. Be quiet. Be still. Stop laughing at me. I'm lord and master. God has willed it so. Obey me. I'm in command. Be still!

(Midknight attacks the mirror, pounding his own image. He sees the mask in the mirror and turns to face it. Midknight stands petrified. Darkie gets up and wraps the long white fabric arms of the mask about Midknight's feet. Midknight falls. All is still.)

Midknight. Darkie.
Darkie. Finish him.

Member. *(Ellamae)* Gladly.
Midknight. No, Darkie. Help me. You were born to help me.
Mammies. Yes, sir. Yes, sir. Yes sir him to death.

(Ellamae takes off her bloomers then lifts her skirts and sits on Midknight's face, smothering him.)

Darkie. Yes, sir. Yes, sir. Yes, sir.

(Darkie pulls down the veil canopy as he slowly falls back into death.)

Solo.
>Sun left here long time ago
>Just where she went we don't know
>But she'll be back here soon shining in our front do'
>Cause we done fixed Midnight, and that's for sho'

Members.
>Midnight, go 'way. Midnight go 'way from me.
>Midnight, go 'way. I want to see the sun.
>Said, Midnight go 'way.

(Hannah has labor pains. Her cry interrupts the song.)

Hannah. He's coming. My son. The son of Mann is coming.

(Female Members gather around Hannah as Mammies attend Hannah in her labor.)

Mammies. Push. Push. Push. My God! Three great spirits rising.
Hannah.
>Day, oh day done broke in-a my soul.
>Day, oh day done broke in-a my soul.
>Said, Midnight has passed away.
>Now the rising sun brings the light of day.
>Day, oh day done broke in-a my soul.

(Hannah sees a vision before her.)

Look there! Three great spirits walking across the sea, and one looks just like me.
Mammy One. She's dead. Hannah is dead.
Ellamae. No. Hannah and Mann live within us all—whole and free. Say it. We must all say it!
Members. *(individual voices, ad lib)* Hannah and Mann live within us all—whole and free.
Mammies. *(whispered)* Free doom. Free doom. Free doom.

(Members, inspired anew, begin affirming their kinship.)

Members. *(individual voices)* Give me your hand, brother.
Give me your hand, sister.
Give me your hand. Give me your hand.

(Members take one another's hands in silence. It is a ritual affirming their kinship bonds.)

Mammies.
Mmmmm-hmmmm. Ummmm-hmmm. Looking for the light.
Mmmmm-hmmmm. Ummmm-hmmm. Looking for the light.

(Mammies continue humming the processional song as Members speak in concert over the hum.)

Members. "We hold these Truths to be self-evident that all people are created equal; that they are endowed by their creator with certain inalienable rights; that among these are Life, Liberty and the Pursuit of Happiness."

(Members and Mammies begin a more spirited arrangement of Hannah's final song. They place Hannah on the bier with Mann, and the Mammies drape them in the Shawl of the Sun from the throne. As they exit singing, Ellamae pauses, then goes to replace the garland of flowers about Darkie's neck. As this all happens, Queen Anne Lady climbs down from the war monument, picks up the stone block and breaks away the chain attached to her leg.)

Members and Mammies.
Day, oh day done broke in-a my soul.
Day, oh day done broke in-a my soul.
Said, Midnight has passed away.
Now the rising sun brings the light of day.
Day, oh day done broke in-a my soul.

(After the Members and Mammies exit, Queen Anne Lady gets the skeleton from the war monument and places it with the body of Midknight. She then moves to Midknight's throne, picks up an apple and holds it at arm's length, contemplating it. Ellamae enters.)

Ellamae. I forgot something.

(She picks up her bloomers. Ellamae and Queen Anne Lady look at one another in silence. Queen Anne Lady throws her an apple. She catches it and leaves polishing it against her sleeve.)

Mammy One.

(offstage)
Once, once, once . . . once upon a time

(Slow fade to black as Queen Anne Lady turns her head to listen to the words of warning.)

    Once, once, once . . . once upon a time

(Blackout. In the darkness a quiet gospel chorale is sung by the cast, from offstage. The audience should be left in total darkness until the end of the song.)

The Cast.
    Lead us Lord.
    Lead us by the light of joy and understanding.
    Lead us Lord.
    Lead us by the sustaining light of our love.
    And let a once divisible nation
    Become an indivisible people
    Led by the light of joy and goodwill.
    Lead us, Lord.
    Lead us by the light.
    Lead us by the light.
    Lead us by the sustaining light of our love.
    Amen. Amen. Amen.

(Lights come up to reveal the Skeleton tangled in the white strips of fabric that are the arms of the Mask. No one else is on stage.
    Members and Mammies enter, singing, to take curtain calls. Queen Anne Lady, Mann, Midknight, Hannah, and Darkie enter after them to join in the singing and curtain calls.)

All.
    Let a new day break in-a your soul.
    Let a new day break in-a my soul.
    Now that Midknight has passed away
    Let's all help the rising sun
    Spread the light of a new day.
    And let it take hold . . .
    Said, let it unfold
    In all our souls.

(The Cast moves into the audience and invites members of the audience to join them in their Song of New Beginnings. They riff . . .)

Cast and Audience Members.
    Joy! . . . Joy! . . . Joy!
    In-a my soul! . . .

In-a your soul! . . .
Joy! . . . Joy! . . . Joy!
In-a our souls! . . .
Joy! Joy!

(The Passion of Darkie's Bones ends with all assembled leaving in song.)

BLACK MASQUE APPENDIX

*Prayer Fragments and Performance Chart
for Miss Queen Anne Lady*

The following prayer fragments are the text which can be used by Miss Queen Anne Lady in playing the moments that mark the unfolding of her personhood from a chained possession of Midknight locked away for safe keeping to a woman ready to claim the authority of her own mind and will. The prayer fragments may be used in any order or substituted with other prayer fragments. The progression of attitudes and gestures that mark the transformation of Self should be unhurried and almost unnoticed. Miss Queen Anne Lady should be accepting of her suffering in the beginning. As she assembles the bones into a reconstructed human form, her awareness of herself and her own personhood is awakened. She begins to accept and explore the depths of her thoughts, dreams, memories and the new possibilities they unlock—bone by bone. The reassembled bones become a human presence of her own living death as well as characters in her dream-memory of things past and yet to come—her son, a brother or friend, a sister or mother . . . her aged father, a wounded enemy of war, a hero or heroine, a lover . . . etc. The mime show is to be developed and performed as an improvisation that is quietly present as a shadowy contrast in most instances, but claims and commands focus at crucial points in the unfolding of Self. It should never be forced but must not be lost or ignored. The fears, angers, hurts, defeats and longings developed by the director and performer must hold emotional recognition for the audience that is unmistakably connected to the meanings of the script. The attitudinal posture of surrender expressed in the spiritual, "Prayer is The Key," is a useful mindset for Miss Queen Anne Lady that mirrors a seemingly passive strategy that was a part of the Afro-American will to be free. Her final moment seated on the throne contemplating the apple is a deliberate question about the choices a victim makes once seemingly free. The moments in Queen Anne Lady's scenario from the beginning to the end should be played to help the audience recognize this important question: *"In the face of all the abuse and hurt I have been through . . . what will I do with my freedom?"*

Prayer Fragments
1. Oh God, our help in ages past, our hope for years to come . . . come by here. Come by here.
2. Ave Maria. Thy Kingdom Come.
3. Kyrie Eleison. Thy will be done . . .
4. Give me searchings of heart to see all that is wrong.
5. Christe Eleison. I am unworthy.
6. Lead me, Lord. Guide me. I am so afraid.
7. Deus Misereatur . . . Be merciful Father. I know it was your blood that saved me. It was your blood.
8. I grieve because I have grieved thee.
9. Hear my prayer, oh Lord. Hear my prayer.
10. Grant me power, most merciful Father, I am unworthy.

11. Enable me to forgive all who have done or wish me evil.
12. Help me in the face of my enemies. Show me the way.
13. Prayer is the key. Prayer is the key. Unlock the heavenly door for me.
14. Lord, help me to be who I truly am.
15. I am. I Am. Who and What I am, I Am. I AM.

Note: The performer can also choose other fragments to help mark the movement toward personhood. But *no long passages should be used* that demand careful attention. The words are emotional sound cues. The clarity of meanings expressed in a moment must not be dependent on the audience hearing every word. The words should be heard as prayerful sounds . . . the selfless drone of a non-person evolving into a confident sound of affirmation, "I Am." One of the objectives is to help the audience recognize the undaunted will and power of change that abide within what appears to be an act of surrender.

A Soldier's Play (1981)

Charles H. Fuller, Jr. (b. 1939–   )

Born and reared in Philadelphia, Charles H. Fuller, Jr., in 1982, became the second African American to win a Pulitzer Prize for drama. After studies at Villanova University and La Salle College and a four-year term in the United States Army, Fuller began to write skits and short plays. He helped found the Afro-American Theatre of Philadelphia before he moved to New York City in 1970. Villanova University has awarded him an honorary doctorate in fine arts. In addition to *A Soldier's Play,* Fuller is best known for his other plays produced by the Negro Ensemble Company—*The Brownsville Raid* (1976), *Zooman and the Sign* (1980), and the *We* plays (1990). *The Brownsville Raid* explores an incident that occurred in Texas in 1906. A regiment of African American soldiers was court-martialed and dishonorably discharged following an accusation that they had raided Brownsville, Texas, in revenge for the racist practices of the townspeople. *Zooman and the Sign* (1980), which earned Obie (Off Broadway) awards for best play and best playwright, is based on a true incident in which a black youth in Philadelphia killed a young black girl. The *We* plays constitute an ambitious project in which, in a series of full-length plays, Fuller examines African American life and experience during the Civil War and Reconstruction.

In 1982, *A Soldier's Play* earned the New York Drama Critics' Best American Play Award, the Outer Circle Critics' Award for Best Play, and a Pulitzer Prize. In 1984, it was adapted into a motion picture, *A Soldier's Story.* On one level, it is a murder mystery placed in the context of the racism in the United States Army during World War II. But, on a deeper, less sensational level, it raises questions about the images of African Americans in a predominantly white society and about the rights of African Americans to determine how other African Americans should conduct themselves. In this latter dimension, the play evokes a sense of timelessness as, without attempting to answer them, Fuller poses questions that were as provocative in the 1890s or the 1960s as they are in the 1990s.

Selected Published Plays by Charles H. Fuller

Zooman and the Sign. New York: Samuel French, 1982.
A Soldier's Play. New York: Hill and Wang, 1982.

A Soldier's Play

A Soldier's Play opened on November 10, 1981, at Theatre Four in New York City. It was presented by the Negro Ensemble Company—Leon B. Denmark, Managing Director, and Douglas Turner Ward, Artistic Director. Direction was by Douglas Turner Ward; scenery by Felix E. Cochren; lighting by Allen Lee Hughes; costumes by Judy Dearing; sound by Regge Life. The cast was as follows:

CHARACTERS

Tech/Sergeant Vernon C. Waters	*Adolph Caesar*
Captain Charles Taylor	*Peter Friedman*
Corporal Bernard Cobb	*Eugene Lee*
Private First Class Melvin Peterson	*Denzel Washington*
Corporal Ellis	*James Pickens, Jr.*
Private Louis Henson	*Samuel L. Jackson*
Private James Wilkie	*Steven A. Jones*
Private Tony Smalls	*Brent Jennings*
Captain Richard Davenport	*Charles Brown*
Private C. J. Memphis	*Larry Riley*
Lieutenant Byrd	*Cotter Smith*
Captain Wilcox	*Stephen Zettler*

Time: *1944.*
Place: *Fort Neal, Louisiana.*
Scene: *The inner shell of the stage is black. On the stage, in a horseshoe-like half circle, are several platforms at varying levels.*

On the left side of this horseshoe is a military office arrangement with a small desk (a nameplate on the desk reads: CAPTAIN CHARLES TAYLOR*), two office-type chairs, one straight-backed, a regimental, and an American flag. A picture of F.D.R. is on the wall.*

On the right side of the horseshoe, and curved toward the rear, is a barracks arrangement, with three bunk beds and footlockers set in typical military fashion. The exit to this barracks is a free-standing doorway on the far right. (This barracks should be changeable—these bunks with little movement can look like a different place.) On the edge of this barracks is a poster, semi-blown up, of Joe Louis in an army uniform, helmet, rifle, and bayonet. It reads: PVT. JOE LOUIS SAYS, "WE'RE GOING TO DO OUR PART— AND WE'LL WIN BECAUSE WE'RE ON GOD'S SIDE."

On the rear of the horseshoe, upstage center, is a bare platform, raised several feet above everything else. It can be anything we want it to be—a limbo if you will.

The entire set should resemble a courtroom. The sets, barracks and office, will both be elevated, so that from anywhere on the horseshoe one may look down onto a space at center stage that is on the stage floor. The levels should have easy access by either stairs or ramps, and the entire set should be raked ever so slightly so that one does not perceive much difference between floor and set, and the bottom edges of the horseshoe. There must also be enough area on both sides of the horseshoe to see exits and entrances.

Lighting will play an integral part in the realization of the play. It should therefore be sharp, so that areas are clearly defined, with as little spill into other areas as possible. Lights must also be capable of suggesting mood, time, and place.

As the play opens, the stage is black. In the background, rising in volume, we hear the song "Don't Sit under the Apple Tree," sung by the Andrews Sisters. Quite suddenly, in a sharp though narrow beam of light, in limbo, Tech/Sergeant Vernon C. Waters, a well-built, light-brown-skinned man in a World War II, winter army uniform, is seen down on all fours. He is stinking drunk, trying to stand and mumbling to himself.

Waters. *(repeating)* They'll still hate you! They still hate you. . . . They still hate you!

(Waters is laughing as suddenly someone steps into the light. [We never see this person.] He is holding a .45 caliber pistol. He lifts it swiftly and ominously toward Waters's head and fires. Waters is knocked over backward. He is dead. The music has stopped and there is a strong silence onstage.)

Voice. Le's go!

(The man with the gun takes a step, then stops. He points the gun at Waters again and fires a second time. There is another silence as limbo is plunged into darkness, and the barracks is just as quickly lit.

We are in the barracks of Company B, 221st Chemical Smoke Generating Company, at Fort Neal. Five black enlisted men stand at "parade rest" with their hands above their heads and submit to a search. They are: Corporal Bernard Cobb, a man in his mid to late twenties, dressed in a T-shirt, dog tags, fatigues, and slippers. Private James Wilkie, a man in his early forties, a career soldier, is dressed in fatigues from which the stripes have been removed, with a baseball cap on, and smoking a cigar. Private Louis Henson, thin, in his late twenties or early thirties, is wearing a baseball T-shirt that reads "Fort Neal" on the front and "#4" on the back, with fatigues and boots on. PFC Melvin Peterson, a man in his late twenties, wearing glasses, looks angelic. His shirt is open but he does not look sloppy; of all the men, his stripe is the most visible, his boots the most highly polished. Private Tony Smalls, a man in his late thirties, a career man, is as small as his name feels. All five men are being searched by Corporal Ellis, a soldier who is simply always "spit and polish." Ellis is also black, and moves from man to man, patting them down in a police-like search. Captain Charles Taylor, a young white man in his mid to late thirties, looks on, a bit disturbed. All the men's uniforms are from World War II.)

Taylor. I'm afraid this kind of thing can't be helped, men—you can put your arms down when Ellis finishes. *(Several men drop their arms. Ellis is searching Pvt. Henson.)* We don't want anyone from Fort Neal going into Tynin looking for red-necks.

Cobb. May I speak, sir? *(Taylor nods.)* Why do this, Captain? They got M.P.'s surrounding us, and hell, the Colonel must know nobody colored killed the man!

Taylor. This is a precaution, Cobb. We can't have revenge killings, so we search for weapons.

Peterson. Where'd they find the Sarge, sir?

Taylor. In the woods out by the Junction—and so we don't have any rumors. Sergeant Waters was shot twice—we don't know that he was lynched! *(pause)* Twice. Once in the chest, and a bullet in the head. *(Ellis finishes with the last man.)* You finished the footlockers?

Ellis. Yes, sir! There aren't any weapons.

Taylor. *(relaxes)* I didn't think there would be. At ease, men! *(The men relax.)* Tech/Sergeant Waters, in my opinion, served the 221st and this platoon in particular with distinction, and I for one shall miss the man. *(slight pause)* But no matter what we think of the Sergeant's death, we will not allow this incident to make us forget our responsibility to this uniform. We are soldiers, and our war is with the Nazis and Japs, not the civilians in Tynin. Any enlisted man found with unauthorized weapons will be immediately subject to summary court-martial. *(softens)* Sergeant Waters's replacement won't be assigned for several weeks. Until that time, you will all report to Sergeant Dorsey of C Company. Corporal Cobb will be barracks N.C.O.—any questions?

Peterson. Who do they think did it, sir?

Taylor. At this time there are no suspects.

Henson. You know the Klan did it, sir.

Taylor. Were you an eyewitness, soldier?

Henson. Who else goes around killin' Negroes in the South?—They lynched Jefferson the week I got here, sir! And that Signal Corps guy, Daniels, two months later!

Taylor. Henson, unless you saw it, keep your opinions to yourself! Is that clear? *(Henson nods.)* And that's an order! It also applies to everybody else!

All. *(almost simultaneously)* Yes, sir!

Taylor. You men who have details this afternoon, report to the orderly room for your assignments. The rest of you are assigned to the Colonel's quarters—clean-up detail. Cobb, I want to see you in my office at 1350 hours.

Cobb. Yes, sir.

Taylor. As of 0600 hours this morning, the town of Tynin was placed off-limits to all military personnel. *(slight groan from the men)* The Friday night dance has also been canceled— *(All the men moan. Taylor is sympathetic.)* O.K., O.K.! Some of the officers are going to the Colonel—I can't promise anything. Right now, it's canceled.

Ellis. Tenn-hut!

(The men snap to. The Captain salutes. Only Cobb salutes him back. The Captain starts out.)

Taylor. As you were!

(The Captain and Ellis exit the barracks. The men move to their bunks or footlockers. Wilkie goes to the rear of the bunks and looks out.)

Cobb. They still out there, Wilkie?

Wilkie. Yeah. Got the whole place surrounded.

Henson. I don't know what the hell they thought we'd go into that town with—mops and dishrags?

Wilkie. Y'all recruits know what Colonel's clean-up detail is, don't you? Shovelin' horseshit in his stables—

Cobb. Ain't no different from what we been doin'. *(He lies down and begins scratching around his groin area.)*

Peterson. *(to Cobb)* Made you the barracks Commander-in-Chief, huh? *(Cobb nods.)* Don't git like ole Stone-ass— What are you doin'?
Cobb. Scratchin'!
Henson. *(overlapping)* Taylor knows the Klan did it—I hope y'all know that!
Smalls. *(sudden)* Then why are the M.P.'s outside with rifles? Why hold us prisoner?
Peterson. They scared we may kill a couple peckerwoods, Smalls. Calm down, man!
Wilkie. *(quickly)* Smalls, you wanna play some coon-can?

(Smalls shakes his head no. He is quiet, staring.)

Cobb. *(examining himself)* Peterson, you know I think Eva gave me the crabs.
Henson. Cobb, the kinda women you find, it's a wonda your nuts ain't fell off—crabs? You probably got lice, ticks, bedbugs, fleas—tapeworms—
Cobb. Shut up, Henson! Pete—I ain't foolin', man! *(He starts to open his pants.)*
Peterson. Get some powder from the PX.
Wilkie. *(almost simultaneously)* Which one of y'all feels like playin' me some cards? *(He looks at Henson.)*
Henson. Me and Peterson's goin' down the mess hall—you still goin', Pete?
Peterson. *(nods)* Wilkie? I thought all you could do was play go-fer?
Henson. *(slyly)* Yeah, Wilkie—whose ass can you kiss, now that your number-one ass is dead?
Cobb. *(laughing)* That sounds like something C.J. would sing! *(looks at himself again)* Ain't this a bitch? *(picks at himself)*
Wilkie. *(overlapping, to Henson)* You know what you can do for me, Henson—you too, Peterson!
Peterson. Naughty, naughty!

(Wilkie moves to his bunk, justifying.)

Wilkie. I'm the one lost three stripes—and I'm the only man in here with kids, so when the man said jump, I jumped!
Henson. *(derisively)* Don't put your wife and kids between you and Waters's ass, man!
Wilkie. I wanted my stripes back!
Cobb. I'm goin' to sick call after chow.
Wilkie. *(continuing)* Y'all ain't neva' had nothin', that's why you can't understand a man like me! There was a time I was a sergeant major, you know!

(Henson waves disdainfully at him, turning his attention to Cobb.)

Henson. Ole V-girl slipped Cobb the crabs! How you gonna explain that to the girl back home, Corporal? How will that fine, big-thighed Moma feel, when the only ribbon you bring home from this war is the Purple Heart for crab bites? *(Henson laughs as Smalls stands suddenly.)*
Smalls. Don't any of you guys give a damn?
Peterson. What's the matta', Smalls?
Smalls. The man's dead! We saw him alive last night!
Cobb. *(quickly)* I saw him, too. At least I know he died good and drunk!
Smalls. *(loud)* What's the matter with y'all?
Henson. The man got hisself lynched! We're in the South, and we can't do a goddamn thing about it—you heard the Captain! But don't start actin' like we guilty of somethin'. *(softens)* I just hope we get lucky enough to get shipped outta this hellhole to the war! *(to himself)* Besides, whoever did it, didn't kill much anyway.
Smalls. He deserved better than that!
Cobb. Look, everybody feels rotten, Smalls. But it won't bring the man back, so let's forget about it!

(Peterson moves to pat Smalls on the back.)

Peterson. Why don't you walk it off, man?

(Smalls moves away to his bunk. Peterson shrugs.)

Henson. Yeah—or go turn on a smoke machine, let the fog make you think you in London!

(Smalls sits down on his bunk and looks at them for a moment, then lays down, his face in the pillow.)

Wilkie. *(overlapping)* Let Cobb bring his Eva over, she'll take his mind off Waters plus give him a bonus of crabs!

(The men laugh, but Smalls doesn't move as the lights begin slowly to fade out.)

Henson. *(counting)* —an' blue-balls. Clap. Syphilis. Pimples! *(Cobb throws a pillow at Henson.)* Piles! Fever blisters. Cock-eyes. Cooties!

(The men are laughing as the lights go out. As they do, a rather wiry black officer wearing glasses, Captain Richard Davenport, walks across the stage from the wings, dressed sharply in an M.P. uniform, his hat cocked to the side and strapped down, the way airmen wear theirs. He is carrying a briefcase, and we are aware of a man who is very confident and self-assured. He is smiling as he faces the audience, cleaning his glasses as he begins to speak.)

Davenport. Call me Davenport—Captain, United States Army, attached to the 343rd Military Police Corps Unit, Fort Neal, Louisiana. I'm a lawyer the segregated Armed Services couldn't find a place for. My job in this war? Policing colored troops. *(slight pause)* One morning, during mid-April 1944, a colored tech/sergeant, Vernon C. Waters, assigned to the 221st Chemical Smoke Generating Company, stationed here before transfer to Europe, was brutally shot to death in a wooded section off the New Post Road and the junction of Highway 51—just two hundred yards from the colored N.C.O. club—by a person or persons unknown. *(pauses a little)* Naturally, the unofficial consensus was the local Ku Klux Klan, and for that reason, I was told at the time, Colonel Barton Nivens ordered the Military Police to surround the enlisted men's quarters—then instructed all his company commanders to initiate a thorough search of all personal property for unauthorized knives, guns—weapons of any kind. *(slight pause)* You see, ninety percent of the Colonel's command—all of the enlisted men stationed here are Negroes, and the Colonel felt—and I suppose justly—that once word of the Sergeant's death spread among his troops, there might be some retaliation against the white citizens of Tynin. *(shrugs)* What he did worked—there was no retaliation, and no racial incidents. *(pause)* The week after the killing took place, several correspondents from the Negro press wrote lead articles about it. But the headlines faded—*(smiles)* The NAACP got me involved in this. Rumor has it, Thurgood Marshall ordered an immediate investigation of the killing, and the army, pressured by Secretary of War Stimson, rather randomly ordered Colonel Nivens to initiate a preliminary inquiry into the Sergeant's death. Now, the Colonel didn't want to rehash the murder, but he complied with the army's order by instructing the Provost Marshal, my C.O., Major Hines, to conduct a *few* question-and-answer sessions among the men of Sergeant Waters's platoon and file a report. The matter was to be given the lowest priority. *(pause)* The case was mine, five minutes later. It was four to five weeks after his death—the month of May. *(He pauses as the light builds in Captain Taylor's office. Taylor is facing Davenport, expressionless. Davenport is a bit puzzled.)* Captain?

Taylor. Forgive me for occasionally staring, Davenport, you're the first colored officer I've ever met. I'd heard you had arrived a month ago, and you're a bit startling. *(quickly)* I mean you no offense. *(starts back to his desk and sits on the edge of it, as Davenport starts into the office a bit cautiously)* We'll be getting some of you as replacements, but we don't expect them until next month. Sit down, Davenport. *(Davenport sits.)* You came out of Fort Benning in '43?

Davenport. Yes.

Taylor. And they assigned a lawyer to the Military Police? I'm Infantry and I've been with the Engineers, Field Artillery, and Signal Corps—this is some army. Where'd you graduate law school?

Davenport. Howard University.

Taylor. Your daddy a rich minister or something? *(Davenport shakes his head no.)* I graduated the Point—*(pause)* We didn't have any Negroes at the Point. I never saw a Negro until I was twelve or thirteen. *(pause)* You like the army, I suppose, huh?

Davenport. Captain, did you see my orders?

Taylor. *(bristling slightly)* I saw them right after Colonel Nivens sent them to Major Hines. I sent my orderly to the barracks and told him to have the men waiting for you.

Davenport. Thank you.

Taylor. I didn't know at the time that Major Hines was assigning a Negro, Davenport. *(Davenport stiffens.)* My preparations were made in the belief that you'd be a white man. I think it only fair to tell you that had I known what Hines intended I would have requested the immediate suspension of the investigation— May I speak freely?

Davenport. You haven't stopped yet, Captain.

Taylor. Look—how far could you get even if you succeed? These local people aren't going to charge a white man in this parish on the strength of an investigation conducted by a Negro!—and Nivens and Hines know that! The Colonel doesn't give a damn about finding the men responsible for this thing! And they're making a fool of you—can't you see that?—and—take off those sunglasses!

Davenport. I intend to carry out my orders—and I like these glasses—they're like MacArthur's.

Taylor. You go near that sheriff's office in Tynin in your uniform—carrying a briefcase, looking and sounding white, and charging local people—and you'll be found just as dead as Sergeant Waters! People around here don't respect the colored!

Davenport. I know that.

Taylor. *(annoyed)* You know how many times I've asked Nivens to look into this killing? Every day, since it happened, Davenport. Major Hines didn't tell you that!

Davenport. Do you suspect someone, Captain?

Taylor. Don't play cat-and-mouse with me, soldier!

Davenport. *(calmly)* Captain, like it or not, I'm all you've got. I've been ordered to look into Sergeant Waters's death, and I intend to do exactly that.

(There is a long pause.)

Taylor. Can I tell you a little story? *(Davenport nods.)* Before you were assigned here? Nivens got us together after dinner one night, and all we did was discuss Negroes in the officer ranks. We all commanded Negro troops, but nobody had ever come face to face with colored officers—

there were a lot of questions that night—for example, your quarters—had to be equal to ours, but we had none—no mess hall for you! *(slight pause)* Anyway, Jed Harris was the only officer who defended it—my own feelings were mixed. The only Negroes I've ever known were subordinates— My father hired the first Negro I ever saw—man named Colfax—to help him fix the shed one summer. Nice man—worked hard—did a good job, too. *(remembering; smiles thoughtfully)* But I never met a Negro with any education until I graduated the Point—hardly an officer of equal rank. So I frankly wasn't sure how I'd feel—until right now—and— *(struggles)* I don't want to offend you, but I just cannot get used to it—the bars, the uniform—being in charge just doesn't look right on Negroes!

Davenport. *(rises)* Captain, are you through?

Taylor. You could ask Hines for another assignment—this case if not for you! By the time you overcome the obstacles to your race, this case would be dead!

Davenport. *(sharply)* I got it. And I *am* in charge! All your orders instruct you to do is cooperate!

(There is a moment of silence.)

Taylor. I won't be made a fool of, Davenport. *(straightens)* Ellis! You're right, there's no need to discuss this any further.

(Ellis appears on the edge of the office.)

Ellis. Yes, sir!

Taylor. Captain Davenport will need assistance with the men—I can't prevent that, Davenport, but I intend to do all I can to have this so-called investigation stopped.

Davenport. Do what you like. If there's nothing else, you'll excuse me, won't you, Captain?

Taylor. *(sardonically)* Glad I met you, Captain.

(Davenport salutes and Taylor returns salute. For an instant the two men trade cold stares, then Davenport gestures to Ellis, and the two of them start out of the office by way of the stage. Davenport follows Ellis out. Behind them, Taylor stares after them as the lights in his office fade out. Davenport removes his glasses.)

Ellis. We heard it was you, sir—you know how the grapevine is. Sad thing—what happened to the Sarge.

Davenport. What's on the grapevine about the killing?

(The two men stop as slowly, almost imperceptibly, on the right the barracks area is lit. In it, a small table and two chairs have been set up. Ellis shrugs.)

Ellis. We figure the Klan. They ain't crazy about us tan yanks in this part of the country.
Davenport. Is there anything on the grapevine about trouble in the town before Sergeant Waters was killed?
Ellis. None that I know of before—after, there were rumors around the post—couple our guys from the Tank Corps wanted to drive them Shermans into Tynin—then I guess you heard that somebody said two officers did it—I figure that's why the Colonel surrounded our barracks.
Davenport. Was the rumor confirmed—I didn't hear that! Did anything ever come of it?
Ellis. Not that I know of, sir.
Davenport. Thanks, Ellis—I'd better start seeing the men. *(They start into the barracks from the stage floor.)* Did you set this up? *(Ellis nods.)* Good— *(He sets his briefcase on the table.)* Are they ready?
Ellis. The Captain instructed everybody in the Sarge's platoon to be here, sir. He told them you'd be starting this morning.

(Davenport smiles.)

Davenport. *(to himself)* Before he found out, huh?
Ellis. *(puzzled)* Sir?
Davenport. Nothing. Call the first man in, Corporal—and stay loose, I might need you.
Ellis. Yes, sir! Sir, may I say something? *(Davenport nods.)* It sure is good to see one of us wearin' them Captain's bars, sir.
Davenport. Thank you.

(Ellis salutes, does a sharp about-face, and starts out.)

Ellis. *(loud)* Private Wilkie!
Wilkie. *(offstage)* Yes, sir! *(Almost immediately, Wilkie appears in the doorway. He is dressed in proper uniform of fatigues, boots, and cap.)*
Ellis. Cap'n wants to see you!
Wilkie. Yes indeedy! *(moves quickly to the table, where he comes to attention and salutes)* Private James Wilkie reporting as ordered, sir.
Davenport. At ease, Private. Have a seat. *(to Ellis as Wilkie sits)* That will be all, Corporal.
Ellis. Yes, sir.

(Ellis salutes and exits. Davenport waits until he leaves before speaking.)

Davenport. Private Wilkie, I am Captain Davenport—
Wilkie. *(interjecting)* Everybody knows that, sir. You all we got down here. *(smiles broadly)* I was on that first detail got your quarters togetha', sir.

(Davenport nods.)

Davenport. *(coldly)* I'm conducting an investigation into the events surrounding Sergeant Waters's death. Everything you say to me will go in my report, but that report is confidential.
Wilkie. I understand, sir.

(Davenport removes pad and pencil from the briefcase.)

Davenport. How long did you know Sergeant Waters?
Wilkie. 'Bout a year, sir. I met him last March—March 5th—I remember the date, I had been a staff sergeant exactly two years the day after he was assigned. This company was basically a baseball team then, sir. See, most of the boys had played for the Negro League, so naturally the army put us all together. *(chuckles at the memory)* We'd be assigned to different companies—Motor Pool—Dump Truck all week long—made us do the dirty work on the post—garbage, clean-up—but on Saturdays we were whippin' the hell out of 'em on the baseball diamond! I was hittin' .352 myself! And we had a boy, C. J. Memphis? He coulda hit a ball from Fort Neal to Berlin, Germany—or Tokyo—if he was battin' right-handed. *(pauses, catches Davenport's impatience)* Well, the army sent Waters to manage the team. He had been in Field Artillery—Gunnery Sergeant. Had a croix de guerre from the First War, too.
Davenport. What kind of man was he?
Wilkie. All spit and polish, sir.

(At that moment, in limbo, a spotlight hits Sergeant Waters. He is dressed in a well-creased uniform, wearing a helmet liner and standing at parade-rest, facing the audience. The light around him, however, is strange—it is blue-gray like the past. The light around Davenport and Wilkie abates somewhat. Dialogue is continuous.)

Davenport. Tell me about him.
Wilkie. He took my stripes! *(smiles)* But I was in the wrong, sir!

(Waters stands at ease. His voice is crisp and sharp, his movements minimal. He is the typical hard-nosed N.C.O.—strict, soldierly.)

Waters. Sergeant Wilkie! You are a noncommissioned officer in the army of a country at war—the penalty for being drunk on duty is severe in peacetime, so don't bring me no po'colored-folks-can't-do-nothin'-unless-they-drunk shit as an excuse! You are supposed to be an example to your men—so, I'm gonna send you to jail for ten days *and* take them goddamn stripes. Teach you a lesson— You in the army! *(derisively)* Colored folks always runnin' off at the mouth 'bout what y'all gonna do if the white man gives you a chance—and you get it, and what do you do with it? You wind up drunk on guard duty—I don't blame the white man—why the hell should he put colored and white together in this war? You can't even be trusted to guard your own quarters—no wonder they treat us like dogs—Get outta' my sight, *Private!*

(Light fades at once on Waters.)

Davenport. What about the other men?
Wilkie. Sometimes the Southern guys caught a little hell—Sarge always said he was from up North somewhere. He was a good soldier, sir. I'm from Detroit myself—born and raised there. Joe Louis started in Detroit—did you know that, sir?
Davenport. What about the Southerners?
Wilkie. Sarge wasn't exactly crazy 'bout 'em—'cept for C.J. Now C.J. was from the South, but with him Sarge was different—probably because C.J. was the best ball player we had. He could sing too! *(slight pause)* Sarge never got too close to nobody—maybe me—but he didn' mess with C.J., you know what I mean? Not like he did with everybody else.

(In limbo the spotlight illuminates C. J. Memphis, a young, handsome black man. He is in a soldier's uniform, cap on the side. He is strumming a guitar. Waters is watching him, smiling. Their light is the strange light of the past. C.J. begins to sing, his voice deep, melodious, and bluesy.)

C.J. It's a low/it's a low, low/lowdown dirty shame! Yeah, it's a low/it's a low, low/lowdown dirty shame!
Wilkie. *(before C.J. finishes)* Big Mississippi boy!

(Wilkie and C.J. simultaneously sing.)

C.J. and Wilkie. They say we fightin' Hitler! But they won't let us in the game!

(C.J. strums and hums as Waters looks on.)

Wilkie. Worked harder and faster than everybody—wasn' a man on the team didn't like him. Sarge took to him the first time he saw him. "Wilkie," he says.
Wilkie and Waters. *(simultaneously)* What have we got here?
Waters. A guitar-playin' man! Boy, you eva' heard of Blind Willie Reynolds? Son House? Henry Sims?

(C.J. nods to everything.)

C.J. You heard them play, Sarge?
Waters. Every one of 'em. I was stationed in Mississippi couple years ago—you from down that way, ain't you?
C.J. Yes, sah!

Waters. Well, they use ta play over at the Bandana Club outside Camp J. J. Reilly.
C.J. I played there once!
Waters. *(smiles)* Ain't that somethin'? I'd go over there from time to time—people use ta come from everywhere! *(to Wilkie)* Place was always dark, Wilkie—smoky. Folks would be dancin'—sweatin'—guitar pickers be strummin', shoutin'—it would be wild in there sometimes. Reminded me of a place I use ta go in France durin' the First War—the women, the whiskey—place called the Café Napoleon.
C.J. You really like the blues, huh?
Waters. No other kind of music—where'd you learn to play so good? I came by here yesterday and heard this pickin'—one of the men tol' me it was you.
C.J. My daddy taught me, Sarge.
Waters. You play pretty good, boy. Wilkie, wasn' that good?
Wilkie. Yes indeed, Sarge.
Wilkie. *(to Davenport)* I mostly agreed with the Sarge, sir. He was a good man. Good to his men. Talked about his wife and kids all the time— *(Waters starts down from the limbo area, as the lights around C.J. fade out. Waters pulls a pipe from his pocket, lights it as he moves to the edge of the Captain's office and sits on the edge of the platform supporting it. He puffs a few times. Wilkie's talk is continuous.)* Use ta write home every day. I don't see why nobody would want to kill the Sarge, sir.

(Waters smiles.)

Waters. Wilkie? *(Wilkie rises and walks into the blue-gray light and the scene with Waters. Davenport will watch.)* You know what I'ma get that boy of mine for his birthday? One of them Schwinn bikes. He'll be twelve—time flies, don't it? Let me show you something?
Wilkie. *(to Davenport)* He was always pullin' out snapshots, sir.

(Waters hands him a snapshot.)

Waters. My wife let a neighbor take this a couple weeks ago—ain't he growin' fast?
Wilkie. He's over your wife's shoulder! *(Hands it back. Waters looks at the photo.)*
Waters. I hope this kid never has to be a soldier.
Wilkie. It was good enough for you.
Waters. I couldn't do any better—and this army was the closest I figured the white man would let me get to any kind of authority. No, the army ain't for this boy. When this war's over, things are going to change, Wilkie—and I want him to be ready for it—my daughter, too! I'm sendin' bot' of 'em to some big white college—let 'em rub elbows with

the whites, learn the white man's language—how he does things. Otherwise, we'll be left behind—you can see it in the army. White man runnin' rings around us.

Wilkie. A lot of us didn't get the chance or the schoolin' the white folks got.

Waters. That ain't no excuse, Wilkie. Most niggahs just don't care—tomorrow don't mean nothin' to 'em. My daddy shoveled coal from the back of a wagon all his life. He couldn't read or write, but he saw to it we did! Not havin' ain't no excuse for not gettin'.

Wilkie. Can't get pee from a rock, Sarge.

(Waters rises abruptly.)

Waters. You just like the rest of 'em, Wilkie—I thought bustin' you would teach you something—we got to challenge this man in his arena—use his weapons, don't you know that? We need lawyers, doctors—generals—senators! Stop thinkin' like a niggah!

Wilkie. All I said—

Waters. Is the equipment ready for tomorrow's game?

Wilkie. Yeah.

Waters. Good. You can go now, Wilkie. *(Wilkie is stunned.)* That's an order!

(Wilkie turns toward Davenport. In the background, the humming of C.J. rises a bit as the light around Waters fades out.)

Wilkie. He could be two people sometimes, sir. Warm one minute—ice the next.

Davenport. How did you feel about him?

Wilkie. Overall—I guess he was all right. You could always borrow a ten-spot off him if you needed it.

Davenport. Did you see the Sergeant any time immediately preceding his death?

Wilkie. I don't know how much before it was, but a couple of us had been over the N.C.O. club that night and Sarge had been juicin' pretty heavy.

Davenport. Did Waters drink a lot?

Wilkie. No more than most— *(pause)* Could I ask you a question, sir? *(Davenport nods.)* Is it true, when they found Sarge all his stripes and insignia were still on his uniform?

Davenport. I don't recall it being mentioned in my preliminary report. Why?

Wilkie. If that's the way they found him, something's wrong, ain't it, sir? Them Klan boys don't like to see us in these uniforms. They usually take the stripes and stuff off, before they lynch us.

(Davenport is quiet, thoughtful for a moment.)

Davenport. Thank you, Private—I might want to call you again, but for now you're excused.

(Wilkie rises.)

Wilkie. Yes, sir! *(sudden mood swing, hesitant)* Sir?
Davenport. Yes?
Wilkie. Can you do anything about allotment checks? My wife didn't get hers last month.
Davenport. There's nothing I can do directly—did you see the finance officer? *(Wilkie nods.)* Well—I'll—I'll mention it to Captain Taylor.
Wilkie. Thank you, sir. You want me to send the next man in?

(Davenport nods. Wilkie salutes, does an about-face, and exits. Davenport returns the salute, then leans back in his chair thoughtfully. In the background, the humming of C.J. rises again as the next man, PFC Melvin Peterson, enters. Dressed in fatigues, he is the model soldier. He walks quickly to the table, stands at attention, and salutes. The humming fades out as Davenport returns the salute.)

Peterson. Private First Class Melvin Peterson reporting as ordered, sir!
Davenport. Sit down, Private. *(Peterson sits.)* Do you know why I'm here?
Peterson. Yes, sir.
Davenport. Fine. Now, everything you tell me is confidential, so I want you to speak as freely as possible. *(Peterson nods.)* Where are you from?
Peterson. Hollywood, California—by way of Alabama, sir. I enlisted in '42—thought we'd get a chance to fight.
Davenport. *(ignores the comment)* Did you know Sergeant Waters well?
Peterson. No, sir. He was already with the company when I got assigned here. And us common G.I.'s don't mix well with N.C.O.'s.
Davenport. Were you on the baseball team?
Peterson. Yes, sir—I played shortstop.
Davenport. Did you like the Sergeant?
Peterson. No, sir.

(Before Davenport can speak, Ellis enters.)

Ellis. Beg your pardon, sir. Captain Taylor would like to see you in his office at once.
Davenport. Did he say why?
Ellis. No, sir—just that you should report to him immediately.
Davenport. *(annoyed)* Tell the men to stick around. When I finish with the Captain, I'll be back.
Ellis. Yes, sir!

(Ellis exits.)

Davenport. *(to Peterson)* Feel like walking, Private? We can continue this on the way. *(begins to put his things in his briefcase)* Why didn't you like the Sergeant?

(Davenport and Peterson start out as the light begins to fade in the barracks. They go through doorway, exit, and reenter the stage in full view.)

Peterson. It goes back to the team, sir. I got here in—baseball season had started, so it had to be June—June of last year. The team had won maybe nine—ten games in a row, there was a rumor that they would even get a chance to play the Yankees in exhibition. So when I got assigned to a team like that, sir—I mean, I felt good. Anyway, ole Stone-ass—
Davenport. Stone-ass?
Peterson. I'm the only one called him that—Sergeant Waters, sir.

(As the two of them pass in front of the barracks area, the light begins to rise very slowly, but it is the blue-gray light of the past. The chairs and tables are gone, and the room looks different.)

Davenport. Respect his rank, with me, Private.
Peterson. I didn't mean no offense, sir. *(slight pause)* Well, the Sergeant and that brown-nosin' Wilkie? They ran the team—and like it was a chain gang, sir. A chain gang!

(The two men exit the stage. As they do, C.J. Memphis, Henson, Cobb, and Smalls enter in their baseball uniforms. T-shirts with "Fort Neal" stamped on the fronts, and numbers on the back, and baseball caps. They are carrying equipment—bats, gloves. C.J. is carrying his guitar. Smalls enters tossing a baseball into the air and catching it. They almost all enter at once, with the exuberance of young men. Their talk is locker-room loud, and filled with bursts of laughter.)

Henson. You see the look on that umpire's face when C.J. hit that home run? I thought he was gonna die on the spot, he turned so pale!

(They move to their respective bunks.)

Smalls. Serves the fat bastard right! Some of them pitches he called strikes were well ova' my head!

(C.J. strums his guitar. Cobb begins to brush off his boots.)

Cobb. C.J.? Who was that fine, river-hip thing you was talkin' to, homey?

(C.J. shrugs and smiles.)

Henson. Speakin' of women, I got to write my Lady a letter. *(He begins to dig for his writing things.)*

Cobb. She looked mighty good to me, C.J.

Smalls. *(overlapping)* Y'all hear Henson? Henson, you ain't had a woman since a woman had you!

(Henson makes an obscene geture.)

C.J. *(overlapping Smalls)* Now, all she did was ask me for my autograph.

Cobb. Look like she was askin' you fo' mor'n that. *(to Smalls)* You see him, Smalls? Leanin' against the fence, all in the woman's face, breathin' heavy—

Henson. If Smalls couldn't see enough to catch a ground ball right in his glove, how the hell could he see C.J. ova' by the fence?

Smalls. That ball got caught in the sun!

Henson. On the ground?

Cobb. *(at once)* We beat 'em nine to one! Y'all be quiet, I'm askin' this man 'bout a woman he was with had tits like two helmets!

C.J. If I had'a give that gal what she asked fo'—she'da give me somethin' I didn't want! Them V-gals git you a bad case a' clap. 'Sides, she wasn' but sixteen.

Smalls. You shoulda introduced her to Henson—sixteen's about his speed.

(Henson makes a farting sound in retaliation.)

C.J. Aroun' home? There's a fella folks use ta call, Lil' Jimmy One Leg—on account of his thing was so big? Two years ago—ole young pretty thing laid clap on Jimmy so bad, he los' the one good leg he had! Now folks jes' call him Little!

(laughter)

C.J. That young thing talkin' to me ain' look so clean.

Henson. Dirty or clean, she had them white boys lookin'.

Cobb. Eyes popin' out they sockets, wasn' they? Remind me of that pitcher las' week! The one from 35th Ordnance? The one everybody claimed was so good? Afta' twelve straight hits, he looked the same way!

(Peterson enters, carrying two baseball bats.)

Smalls. It might be funny ta y'all, but when me and Pete had duty in the Ordnance mess hall, that same white pitcher was the first one started the name-callin'—

Henson. Forget them dudes in Ordnance—lissen to this! *(Henson begins to read from a short letter.)* "Dear, Louis"—y'all hear that? The name is Louis—

Cobb. Read the damn letter!

Henson. *(makes obscene gesture)* "Dear, Louis. You and the boys keep up the good work. All of us here at home are praying for you and inspired in this great cause by you. We know that the Nazis and the Japs can't be stopped unless we all work together, so tell your buddies to press forward and win this war. All our hopes for the future go with you, Louis. Love Mattie." I think I'm in love with the sepia Winston Churchill—what kina' letter do you write a nut like this?
Cobb. Send her a round of ammunition and a bayonet, *Louis!*

(Henson waves disdainfully.)

Peterson. Y'all oughta listen to what Smalls said. Every time we beat them at baseball, they get back at us every way they can.
Cobb. It's worth it to me just to wipe those superior smiles off they faces.
Peterson. I don't know—seems like it makes it that much harder for us.
C.J. They tell me, coupla them big-time Negroes is on the verge a' gittin' all of us togetha'—colored and white—say they want one army.
Peterson. Forget that, C.J.! White folks'll neva' integrate no army!
C.J. *(strums)* If they do—I'ma be ready for 'em! *(sing)* Well, I got me a bright red zoot suit / And a pair a' patent-leatha' shoes / And my woman she sittin' waitin' / Fo' the day we hea' the news! Lawd, lawd, lawd, lawd, / Lawd, lawd, lawd, lawd!

(Sergeant Waters, followed by Wilkie, enters, immediately crossing to the center of the barracks, his strident voice abruptly cutting off C.J.'s singing and playing.)

Waters. Listen up! *(to C.J.)* We don't need that guitar playin'-sittin'-round-the-shack music today, C.J.! *(smiles)* I want all you men out of those baseball uniforms and into work clothes! You will all report to me at 1300 hours in front of the Officers Club. We've got a work detail. We're painting the lobby of the club.

(collective groan)

Smalls. The officers can't paint their own club?
Cobb. Hell no, Smalls! Let the great-colored-clean-up company do it! Our motto is: Anything you don't want to do, the colored troops will do for you!
Henson. *(like a cheer)* Anything you don't want to do, the colored troops will do for you! *(He starts to lead the others.)*
Others. Anything you don't—
Waters. That's enough!

(The men are instantly silent.)

Henson. When do we get a rest? We just played nine innings of baseball, Sarge!
Smalls. We can't go in the place, why the hell should we paint it?
Cobb. Amen, brother!

(There is a moment of quiet before Waters speaks.)

Waters. Let me tell you fancy-assed ball-playin' Negroes somethin'! The *reasons* for any orders given by a superior officer is none of y'all's business! You obey them! This country is at war, and you niggahs are soldiers—nothin' else! So baseball teams—win or lose—get no special privileges! They need to work some of you niggahs till your legs fall off! *(intense)* And something else—from now on, when I tell you to do something, I want it done—is that clear? *(The men are quiet.)* Now, Wilkie's gonna' take all them funky shirts you got on over to the laundry. I could smell you suckers before I hit the field!
Peterson. What kinda colored man are you?
Waters. I'm a soldier, Peterson! First, last, and always! I'm the kinda colored man that don't like lazy, shiftless Negroes!
Peterson. You ain't got to come in here and call us names!
Waters. The Nazis call you schvatza! You gonna tell them they hurt your little feelings?
C.J. Don't look like to me we could do too much to them Nazis wit' paint brushes, Sarge.

(The men laugh. The moment is gone, and though Waters is angry, his tone becomes overly solicitous, smiling.)

Waters. You tryin' to mock me, C.J.?
C.J. No, sah, Sarge.
Waters. Good, because whatever an ignorant, low-class geechy like you has to say isn't worth paying attention to, is it? *(pause)* Is it?
C.J. I reckon not, Sarge.
Peterson. You' a creep, Waters!
Waters. Boy, you are something—ain't been in the company a month, Wilkie, and already everybody's champion!
C.J. *(interjecting)* Sarge was just jokin', Pete—he don't mean no harm!
Peterson. He does! We take enough from the white boys!
Waters. Yes, you do—and if it wasn' for you Southern niggahs, yessahin', bowin' and scrapin', scratchin' your heads, white folks wouldn' think we were all fools!
Peterson. Where you from, England?

(Men snicker.)

Henson. *(at once)* Peterson!

Waters. *(immediately)* You got somethin' to say, Henson?
Henson. Nothin', Sarge.

(Henson shakes his head as Waters turns back to Peterson.)

Waters. Peterson, you got a real comic streak in you. Wilkie, looks like we got us a wise-ass Alabama boy here! *(He moves toward Peterson.)* Yes, sir— *(He snatches Peterson in the collar.)* Don't get smart, niggah!

(Peterson yanks away.)

Peterson. Get your fuckin' hands off me!

(Waters smiles, leans forward.)

Waters. You wanna hit ole Sergeant Waters, boy? *(whispers)* Come on! Please! Come on, niggah!

(Captain Taylor enters the barracks quite suddenly, unaware of what is going on.)

Henson. Tenn-hut!

(All the men snap to.)

Taylor. At ease! *(He moves toward Waters, feeling the tension.)* What's going on here, Sergeant?
Waters. Nothin', sir—I was going over the *Manual of Arms*. Is there something in particular you wanted, sir? Something I can do?
Taylor. *(relaxed somewhat)* Nothing— *(to the men)* Men, I congratulate you on the game you won today. We've only got seven more to play, and if we win them, we'll be the first team in Fort Neal history to play the Yanks in exhibition. Everyone in the regiment is counting on you. In times like these, morale is important—and winning can help a lot of things. *(pause)* Sergeant, as far as I'm concerned, they've got the rest of the day off.

(The men are pleased.)

Waters. Begging your pardon, sir, but these men need all the work they can get. They don't need time off—our fellas aren't getting time off in North Africa—besides, we've got orders to report to the Officers Club for a paint detail at 1300 hours.
Taylor. Who issued that order?
Waters. Major Harris, sir.
Taylor. I'll speak to the Major.
Waters. Sir, I don't think it's such a good idea to get a colored N.C.O. mixed up in the middle of you officers, sir.
Taylor. I said, I'd speak to him, Sergeant.

Waters. Yes, sir!
Taylor. I respect the men's duty to service, but they need time off.
Waters. Yes, sir.

(pause)

Taylor. You men played a great game of baseball out there today—that catch you made in center field, Memphis—how the hell'd you get up so high?
C.J. *(shrugs, smiles)* They say I got "Bird" in mah blood, sir.

(Taylor is startled by the statement, his smile is an uncomfortable one. Waters is standing on "eggs.")

Taylor. American eagle, I hope. *(laughs a little)*
C.J. No, sah, crow— *(Waters starts to move, but C.J. stops him by continuing. Several of the men are beginning to get uncomfortable.)* Man tol' my daddy the day I was born, the shadow of a crow's wings—
Taylor. *(cutting him off)* Fine—men, I'll say it again—you played superbly. *(turns to Waters)* Sergeant. *(He starts out abruptly.)*
Waters. Tenn-hut!

(Waters salutes as the men snap to.)

Taylor. *(exiting)* As you were.

(Taylor salutes as he goes. There is an instant of quiet. The men relax a little, but their focus is C.J.)

Waters. *(laughing)* Ain't these geechies somethin'? How long a story was you gonna tell the man, C.J.? My God! *(The men join him, but as he turns toward Peterson, he stiffens.)* Peterson! Oh, I didn't forget you, boy. *(The room quiets.)* It's time to teach you a lesson!
Peterson. Why don't you drop dead, Sarge?
Waters. Nooo! I'ma drop you, boy! Out behind the barracks—Wilkie, you go out and make sure it's all set up.
Wilkie. You want all the N.C.O.'s?

(Waters nods. Wilkie goes out smiling.)

Waters. I'm going outside and wait for you, geechy! And when you come out, I'm gonna whip your black Southern ass—let the whole company watch it, too! *(points)* You need to learn respect, boy—how to talk to your betters. *(starts toward the door)* Fight hard, hea'? I'ma try to bust your fuckin' head open—the rest of you get those goddamn shirts off like I said!

(He exits. The barracks is quiet for a moment.)

Cobb. You gonna fight him?
Henson. *(overlapping)* I tried to warn you!
Peterson. You ain't do nothin'!
Smalls. He'll fight you dirty, Pete—don't do it!

(Peterson goes to his bunk and throws his cap off angrily.)

Cobb. You don't want to do it?
Peterson. You wanna fight in my place, Cobb? *(He sits.)* Shit!

(Slight pause. Henson pulls off his shirt.)

C.J. I got some Farmers Dust—jes' a pinch'll make you strong as a bull—they say it comes from the city of Zar. *(removes a pouch from his neck)* I seen a man use this stuff and pull a mule outta a sinkhole by hisself!
Peterson. Get the hell outta here with that backwater crap—can't you speak up for yourself—let that bastard treat you like a dog!
C.J. 'Long as his han's ain't on me—he ain't done me no harm, Pete. Callin' names ain't nothin', I know what I is. *(softens)* Sarge ain't so bad—been good to me.
Peterson. The man despises you!
C.J. Sarge? You wrong, Pete—plus I feel kinda sorry for him myself. Any man ain't sure where he belongs must be in a whole lotta pain.
Peterson. Don't y'all care?
Henson. Don't nobody like it, Pete—but when you here a little longer—I mean, what can you do? This hea's the army and Sarge got all the stripes.

(Peterson rises, disgusted, and starts out. Smalls moves at once.)

Smalls. Peterson, look, if you want me to, I'll get the Captain. You don't have to go out there and get your head beat in!
Peterson. Somebody's got to fight him.

(He exits. There is quiet as Smalls walks back to his bunk.)

C.J. *(singing)* It's a low / it's a low, low / lowdown dirty shame! It's a low / it's a low, low / lowdown dirty shame! Been playin' in this hea' army / an ain't even learned the game! Lawd, lawd, lawd, lawd—

(C.J. begins to hum as the lights slowly fade out over the barracks. As they do, the lights come up simultaneously in the Captain's office. It is empty. Peterson [in proper uniform] and Davenport enter from off-stage. They stop outside the Captain's office.)

Peterson. He beat me pretty bad that day, sir. The man was crazy!
Davenport. Was the incident ever reported?

Peterson. I never reported it, sir—I know I should have, but he left me alone after that. *(shrugs)* I just played ball.
Waters. Did you see Waters the night he died?
Peterson. No, sir—me and Smalls had guard duty.
Davenport. Thank you, Private. That'll be all for now. *(Peterson comes to attention.)* By the way, did the team ever get to play the Yankees?
Peterson. No, sir. We lost the last game to a Sanitation Company.

(He salutes. Davenport returns salute. Peterson does a crisp about-face and exits. Slowly Davenport starts into the Captain's office, surprised that no one is about.)

Davenport. Captain? *(There is no response. For a moment or two, Davenport looks around. He is somewhat annoyed.)* Captain?

(He starts out. Taylor enters. He crosses the room to his desk, where he sits.)

Taylor. I asked you back here because I wanted you to see the request I've sent to Colonel Nivens to have your investigation terminated. *(He picks up several sheets of paper on his desk and hands them to Davenport, who ignores them.)*
Davenport. What?
Taylor. I wanted you to see that my reasons have nothing to do with you personally—my request will not hurt your army record in any way! *(pause)* There are other things to consider in this case!
Davenport. Only the color of my skin, Captain.
Taylor. *(sharply)* I want the people responsible for killing one of my men found and jailed, Davenport!
Davenport. So do I!
Taylor. Then give this up! *(rises)* Whites down here won't see their duty—or justice. They'll see *you!* And once they do, the law—due process—it all goes! And what is the point of continuing an investigation that can't possibly get at the truth?
Davenport. Captain, my orders are very specific, so unless you want charges brought against you for interfering in a criminal investigation, stay the hell out of my way and leave me and my investigation alone!
Taylor. *(almost sneering)* Don't take yourself too seriously, Davenport. You couldn't find an officer within five hundred miles who would convey charges to a court-martial board against me for something like that, and you know it!
Davenport. Maybe not, but I'd—I'd see to it that your name, rank, and duty station got into the Negro press! Yeah, let a few colored newspapers call you a Negro-hater! Make you an embarrassment to the United States Army, Captain—like Major Albright at Fort Jefferson,

and you'd never command troops again—or wear more than those captain's bars on that uniform, Mr. West Point!

Taylor. I'll never be more than a captain, Davenport, because I won't let them get away with dismissing things like Waters's death. I've been the commanding officer of three outfits! I raised hell in all of them, so threatening me won't change my request. Let the Negro press print that I don't like being made a fool of with phony investigations!

Davenport. *(studies Taylor for a moment)* There are two white officers involved in this, Captain—aren't there?

Taylor. I want them in jail—out of the army! And there is no way *you* can get them charged, or court-martialed, or put away! The white officers on this post won't let you—they won't let me!

Davenport. Why wasn't there any mention of them in your preliminary report? I checked my own summary on the way over here, Captain—nothing! You think I'ma let you get away with this? *(There is a long silence. Taylor walks back to his desk as Davenport watches him. Taylor sits.)* Why?

Taylor. I couldn't prove the men in question had anything to do with it.

Davenport. Why didn't you report it?

Taylor. I was ordered not to. *(pause)* Nivens and Hines. The doctors took two .45 caliber bullets out of Waters—army issue. But remember what it was like that morning? If these men had thought a white officer killed Waters, there would have been a slaughter! *(pause)* Cobb reported the incident innocently the night before—then suddenly it was all over the Fort.

Davenport. Who were they, Captain? I want their names!

Taylor. Byrd and Wilcox. Byrd's in Ordnance—Wilcox's with the 12th Hospital Group. I was Captain of the Guard the night Waters was killed. About 2100 hours, Cobb came into my office and told me he'd just seen Waters and two white officers fighting outside the colored N.C.O. club. I called *your* office, and when I couldn't get two M.P.'s, I started over myself to break it up. When I got there—no Waters, no officers. I checked the officers' billet and found Byrd and Wilcox in bed. Several officers verified they'd come in around 2130. I then told Cobb to go back to the barracks and forget it.

Davenport. What made you do that?

Taylor. At the time there was no reason to believe anything was wrong! Waters wasn't found until the following morning. I told the Colonel what had happened the previous night, and about the doctor's report, and I was told, since the situation at the Fort was potentially dangerous, to keep my mouth shut until it blew over. He agreed to let me question Byrd and Wilcox, but I've asked him for a follow-up investigation every day since it happened. *(slight pause)* When I saw you, I exploded—it was like he was laughing at me.

Davenport. Then you never believed the Klan was involved?
Taylor. No. Now, can you see why this thing needs—someone else?
Davenport. What did they tell you, Captain? Byrd and Wilcox?
Taylor. They're not going to let you charge those two men!
Davenport. *(snaps)* Tell me what they told you!

(Taylor is quiet for a moment. At this time, on center stage in limbo, Sergeant Waters is staggering. He is dressed as we first saw him. Behind him a blinking light reads: 221st N.C.O. Club. As he staggers toward the stairs leading to center stage, two white officers, Lieutenant Byrd, a spit-and-polish soldier in his twenties, and Captain Wilcox, a medical officer, walk on-stage. Both are in full combat gear—rifles, pistol belts, packs—and both are tired. Taylor looks out as if he can see them.)

Taylor. They were coming off bivouac.

(The two men see Waters. In the background is the faint hum of C.J.'s music.)

Taylor. They saw him outside the club.

(He rises, as Waters sees Byrd and Wilcox, and smiles.)

Waters. Well, if it ain't the white boys!

(Waters straightens and begins to march in a mock circle and then down in their direction. He is mumbling, barely audibly: "One, two, three, four! Hup, hup, three, four! Hup, hup, three, four!" Byrd's speech overlaps Waters's.)

Byrd. And it wasn't like we were looking for trouble, Captain—were we, Wilcox?

(Wilcox shakes his head no, but he is astonished by Waters's behavior and stares at him, disbelieving.)

Waters. White boys! All starched and stiff! Wanted everybody to learn all that symphony shit! That's what you were saying in France—and you know, I listened to you? Am I all right now? Am I?
Byrd. Boy, you'd better straighten up and salute when you see an officer, or you'll find yourself without those stripes! *(to Wilcox as Waters nears them, smiling the "coon" smile and doing a juba)* Will you look at this niggah? *(loud)* Come to attention, Sergeant! That's an order!
Waters. No, sah! I ain't straightenin' up for y'all no more! I ain't doin' nothin' white folks say do, no more! *(sudden change of mood, smiles, sings)* No more, no more / no more, no more, noooo! No more, no more / no more, no more, noooooo!

(Byrd faces Taylor as Waters continues to sing.)

Byrd. *(overlapping)* Sir, I thought the man was crazy!
Taylor. And what did you think, Wilcox?

(Byrd moves toward Waters, and Waters, still singing low, drunk and staggering, moves back and begins to circle Byrd, stalk him, shaking his head no as he sings. Wilcox watches apprehensively.)

Wilcox. *(at once)* He did appear to be intoxicated, sir—out of his mind almost! *(He turns to Byrd.)* Byrd, listen—

(Byrd ignores him.)

Davenport. *(suddenly)* Did they see anyone else in the area?
Taylor. No. *(to Byrd)* I asked them what they did next.
Byrd. I told that niggah to shut up!
Waters. *(sharply)* No! *(change of mood)* Followin' behind y'all? Look what it's done to me!—I hate myself!
Byrd. Don't blame us, boy! God made you black, not me!
Waters. *(smiles)* My daddy use ta say—
Wilcox. Sergeant, get hold of yourself!
Waters. *(points)* Listen!

(Byrd steps toward him and shoves him in the face.)

Byrd. I gave you an order, niggah!

(Wilcox grabs Byrd, and stops him from advancing, as Waters begins to cry.)

Waters. My daddy said, "Don't talk like dis'—talk like that!" "Don't live hea'—live there!" *(to them)* I've killed for you! *(to himself; incredulous)* And nothin' changed!

(Byrd pulls free of Wilcox and charges Waters.)

Byrd. He needs to be taught a lesson!

(He shoves Waters onto the ground, where he begins to beat and kick the man, until he is forcibly restrained by Wilcox. Waters moans.)

Wilcox. Let him be! You'll kill the man! He's sick—leave him alone!

(Byrd pulls away; he is flushed. Waters tries to get up.)

Waters. Nothin' changed—see? And I've tried everything! Everything!
Byrd. I'm gonna bust his black ass to buck private!—I should blow his coward's head off! *(shouts)* There are good men killing for you, niggah! Gettin' their guts all blown to hell for you!

(Wilcox pulls him away. He pulls Byrd off-stage as the light around Waters

and that section of the stage begins to fade out. As it does, a trace of C.J.'s music is left on the air. Waters is on his knees, groveling, as the lights go out around him.)

Davenport. Did they shove Waters again?
Taylor. No. But Byrd's got a history of scrapes with Negroes. They told me they left Waters at 2110—and everyone in the officers' billet verifies they were both in by 2130. And neither man left—Byrd had duty the next morning, and Wilcox was scheduled at the hospital at 0500 hours—both men reported for duty.
Davenport. I don't believe it.
Taylor. I couldn't shake their stories—
Davenport. That's nothing more than officers lying to protect two of their own and you know it! I'm going to arrest and charge both of them, Captain—and you may consider yourself confined to your quarters pending my charges against *you!*
Taylor. What charges?
Davenport. It was *your* duty to go over Nivens's head if you had to!
Taylor. Will you arrest Colonel Nivens too, Davenport? Because he's part of their alibi—he was there when they came in—played poker—from 2100 to 0300 hours the following morning, the Colonel—your Major Hines, "Shack" Callahan—Major Callahan, and Jed Harris—and Jed wouldn't lie for either of them!
Davenport. They're all lying!
Taylor. Prove it, hotshot—I told you all I know, now you go out and prove it!
Davenport. I will, Captain! You can bet your sweet ass on that! I will!

(Davenport starts out as the lights begin to fade, and Taylor looks after him and shakes his head. In the background, the sound of "Don't Sit under the Apple Tree" comes up again and continues to play as the lights fade to black.)

ACT II
. . . . .

Scene: *As before.*
Light rises slowly over limbo. We hear a snippet of "Don't Sit under the Apple Tree" as Davenport, seated on the edge of a bunk, finishes dressing. He is putting on a shirt, tie, bars, etc., and addresses the audience as he does so.

Davenport. During May of '44, the Allies were making final preparations for the invasion of Europe. Invasion! Even the sound of it made

Negroes think we'd be in it—be swept into Europe in the waves of men and equipment—I know I felt it. *(thoughtfully)* We hadn't seen a lot of action except in North Africa—or Sicily. But the rumor in orderly rooms that spring was, pretty soon most of us would be in combat—somebody said Ike wanted to find out if the colored boys could fight—shiiit, we'd been fighting all along—right here, in these small Southern towns—*(intense)* I don't have the authority to arrest a white *private* without a white officer present! *(slight pause)* Then I get a case like this? There was no way I wouldn't see this through to its end. *(smiles)* And after my first twenty-four hours, I wasn't doing too badly. I had two prime suspects—a motive, and opportunity! *(pause)* I went to Colonel Nivens and convinced him that word of Byrd's and Wilcox's involvement couldn't be kept secret any longer. However, before anyone in the press could accuse him of complicity—I would silence all suspicions by pursuing the investigation openly—on his orders—*(mimics himself)* "Yes, sir, Colonel, you can even send along a white officer—not Captain Taylor, though—I think he's a little too close to the case, sir." Colonel Nivens gave me permission to question Byrd and Wilcox, and having succeeded sooo easily, I decided to spend some time finding out more about Waters and Memphis. Somehow the real drama seemed to be there, and my curiosity wouldn't allow me to ignore it.

(Davenport is dressed and ready to go as a spotlight in the barracks area opens on Private Henson. He is seated on a footlocker. He rises as Davenport descends to the stage. He will not enter the barracks, but will almost handle this like a courtroom investigation. He returns Henson's salute.)

Davenport. Sit down, Private. Your name is Louis Henson, is that right?
Henson. Yes, sir.

(Henson sits, as Davenport paces.)

Davenport. Tell me what you know about Sergeant Waters and C. J. Memphis. *(Henson looks at him strangely.)* Is there something wrong?
Henson. No, sir—I was just surprised you knew about it.
Davenport. Why?
Henson. You're an officer.
Davenport. *(quickly)* And?
Henson. *(hesitantly)* Well—officers are up here, sir—and us enlisted men—down here. *(slight pause)* C.J. and Waters—that was just between enlisted men, sir. But I guess ain't nothin' a secret around colored folks—not that it was a secret. *(shrugs)* There ain't that much to tell—sir. Sarge ain't like C.J. When I got to the company in May of las' year, the first person I saw Sarge chew out was C.J.! *(He is quiet.)*
Davenport. Go on.

(Henson's expression is pained.)

Henson. Is that an order, sir?
Davenport. Does it have to be?
Henson. I don't like tattle-talin', sir—an' I don't mean no offense, but I ain't crazy 'bout talkin' to officers—colored or white.
Davenport. It's an order, Henson!

(Henson nods.)

Henson. C.J. wasn' movin' fast enough for *him*. Said C.J. didn' have enough *fire-under-his-behind* out on the field.
Davenport. You were on the team?
Henson. Pitcher. *(Pause. Davenport urges with a look.)* He jus' *stayed* on C.J. all the time—every little thing, it seemed like to me—then the shootin' went down, and C.J. caught all the hell.
Davenport. What shooting?
Henson. The shootin' at Williams's Golden Palace, sir—here, las' year!—way before you got here. Toward the end of baseball season.
(Davenport nods his recognition.) The night it happened, a whole lotta gunshots went off near the barracks. I had gotten drunk over at the enlisted men's club, so when I got to the barracks I just sat down in a stupor!

(Suddenly shots are heard in the distance and grow ever closer as the eerie blue-gray light rises in the barracks over the sleeping figures of men in their bunks. Henson is seated, staring at the ground. He looks up once as the gunshots go off, and as he does, someone—we cannot be sure who—sneaks into the barracks as the men begin to shift and awaken. This person puts something under C.J.'s bed and rushes out. Henson watches—surprised at first, rising, then disbelieving. He shakes his head, then sits back down as several men wake up. Davenport recedes to one side of the barracks, watching.)

Cobb. What the hell's goin' on? Don't they know a man needs his sleep?
(He is quickly back to sleep.)
Smalls. *(simultaneously)* Huh? Who is it? *(looks around, then falls back to sleep)*
Davenport. Are you sure you saw someone?
Henson. Well—I saw something, sir.
Davenport. What did you do?

(The shooting suddenly stops and the men settle down.)

Henson. I sat, sir—I was juiced— *(shrugs)* The gunshots weren't any of my business—plus I wasn't sure what I had seen in the first place, then out of nowhere Sergeant Waters, he came in.

(Waters enters the barracks suddenly, followed by Wilkie. Henson stands immediately, staggering a bit.)

Waters. All right, all right! Everybody up! Wake them, Wilkie!

(Wilkie moves around the bunks, shaking the men.)

Wilkie. Let's go! Up! Let's go, you guys!

(Cobb shoves Wilkie's hand aside angrily as the others awaken slowly.)

Waters. Un-ass them bunks! Tenn-hut! *(Most of the men snap to. Smalls is the last one, and Waters moves menacingly toward him.)* There's been a shooting! One of ours bucked the line at Williams's pay phone and three soldiers are dead! Two colored and one white M.P. *(pauses)* Now, the man who bucked the line, he killed the M.P., and the white boys started shootin' everybody—that's how our two got shot. And this lowdown niggah we lookin' for got chased down here—and was almost caught, 'til somebody in these barracks started shootin' at the men chasin' him. So, we got us a vicious, murderin' piece of black trash in here somewhere—and a few people who helped him. If any of you are in this, I want you to step forward. *(No one moves.)* All you baseball niggahs are innocent, huh? Wilkie, make the search. *(Peterson turns around as Wilkie begins.)* Eyes front!

Peterson. I don't want that creep in my stuff!

Waters. You don't talk at attention!

(Wilkie will search three bunks, top and bottom, along with footlockers. Under C.J.'s bed he will find what he is looking for.)

Waters. I almost hope it is some of you geechies—get rid of you Southern niggahs! *(to Wilkie)* Anything yet?

Wilkie. Nawwww!

Waters. Memphis, are you in this?

C.J. No, sah, Sarge.

Waters. How many of you were out tonight?

Smalls. I was over at Williams's around seven—got me some Lucky Strikes—I didn't try to call home, though.

Cobb. I was there, this mornin'!

Waters. Didn't I say *tonight*—uncle?

Wilkie. Got somethin'!

(Wilkie is holding up a .45 caliber automatic pistol, army issue. Everyone's attention focuses on it. The men are surprised, puzzled.)

Waters. Where'd you find it?

(Wilkie points to C.J., who recoils at the idea.)

C.J. Naaaawww, man!
Waters. C.J.? This yours?
C.J. You know it ain't mine, Sarge!
Waters. It's still warm—how come it's under your bunk?
C.J. Anybody coulda' put it thea', Sarge!
Waters. Who? Or maybe this .45 crawled in through an open window—looked around the whole room—passed Cobb's bunk, and decided to snuggle up under yours? Must be voodoo, right, boy? Or some of that Farmers Dust round that neck of yours, huh?
C.J. That pistol ain't mine!
Waters. Liar!
C.J. No, Sarge—I hate guns! Make me feel bad jes' to see a gun!
Waters. You're under arrest—Wilkie, escort this man to the stockade!

(Peterson steps forward.)

Peterson. C.J. couldn't hurt a fly, Waters, you know that!
Waters. I found a gun, soldier—now get out of the way!
Peterson. Goddammit, Waters, you know it ain't him!
Waters. How do I know?
Henson. Right before you came in, I thought I saw somebody sneak in.
Waters. You were drunk when you left the club—I saw you myself!
Wilkie. Besides, how you know it wasn't C.J.?
Cobb. I was here all night. C.J. didn't go out.

(Waters looks at them, intense.)

Waters. We got the right man. *(points at C.J., impassioned)* You think he's innocent, don't you? C. J. Memphis, playin' cottonpicker singin' the blues, bowin' and scrapin'—smilin' in everybody's face—this man undermined us! You and me! The description of the man who did the shooting fits C.J.! *(to Henson)* You saw C.J. sneak in here! *(points)* Don't be fooled—that yassah boss is hidin' something—niggahs ain't like that today! This is 1943—he shot that white boy!

(C.J. is stunned, then suddenly the enormity of his predicament hits him and he breaks free of Wilkie and hits Waters in the chest. The blow knocks Waters down, and C.J. is immediately grabbed by the other men in the barracks. Cobb goes to Waters and helps him up slowly. The blow hurt Waters, but he forces a smile at C.J., who has suddenly gone immobile, surprised by what he has done.)

Waters. What did you go and do now, boy? Hit a noncommissioned officer.
Cobb. Sarge, he didn't mean it!
Waters. Shut up! *(straightens)* Take him out, Wilkie.

(Wilkie grabs C.J. by the arm and leads him out. C.J. goes calmly, almost

passively. Waters looks at all the men quietly for a moment, then walks out without saying a word. There is a momentary silence in the barracks.)

Smalls. Niggah like that can't have a mother.
Henson. I know I saw something!
Peterson. C.J. was sleepin' when I came in! It's Waters—can't y'all see that? I've seen him before—we had 'em in Alabama! White man gives them a little ass job as a servant—close to the big house, and when the boss ain't lookin', old copycat niggahs act like they the new owner! They take to soundin' like the boss—shoutin', orderin' people aroun'—and when it comes to you and me—they sell us to continue favor. They think the high-jailers like that. Arrestin' C.J.—that'll get Waters another stripe! Next it'll be you—or you. He can't look good unless he's standin' on you! Cobb tol' him C.J. was in all evening—Waters didn't even listen! Turning somebody in *(mimics)*: "Look what I done, Captain Boss!" They let him in the army 'cause they know he'll do anything they tell him to—I've seen his kind of fool before. Someone's going to kill him.
Smalls. I heard they killed a sergeant at Fort Robinson—recruit did it—
Cobb. It'll just be our luck, Sarge'll come through the whole war without a scratch.
Peterson. Maybe—but I'm goin' over to the stockade—tell the M.P.'s what I know—C.J. was here all evening. *(He starts dressing.)*
Smalls. I'll go with you!
Cobb. Me too, I guess.

(They all begin to dress as the light fades slowly in the barracks area. Henson rises and starts toward Davenport. In the background, C.J.'s music comes up a bit.)

Davenport. Could the person you thought you saw have stayed in the barracks—did you actually see someone go out?
Henson. Yes, sir!
Davenport. Was Wilkie the only man out of his bunk that night?
Henson. Guess so—he came in with Sarge.
Davenport. And Peterson—he did most of the talking?
Henson. As I recall. It's been a while ago—an' I was juiced!

(Davenport rises.)

Davenport. Ellis!

(Ellis appears at the door.)

Ellis. Sir!
Davenport. I want Private Wilkie and PFC Peterson to report to me at once.

Ellis. They're probably on work detail, sir.
Davenport. Find them.
Ellis. Yes, sir!

(Ellis exits quickly and Davenport lapses into a quiet thoughtfulness.)

Henson. Is there anything else?—Sir?
Davenport. *(vexed)* No! That will be all—send in the next man.

(Henson comes to attention and salutes. Davenport returns salute as Henson exits through the barracks. C.J.'s music plays in background. There is a silence. Davenport rises, mumbling something to himself. Cobb appears suddenly at the doorway. He watches Davenport for a moment.)

Cobb. Sir? *(Davenport faces him.)* Corporal Cobb reporting as ordered, sir. *(He salutes.)*
Davenport. Have a seat, Corporal. *(Cobb crosses the room and sits.)* And let's get something straight from the beginning—I don't care whether you like officers or not—is that clear?

(Cobb looks at him strangely.)

Cobb. Sir?

(Pause. Davenport calms down somewhat.)

Davenport. I'm sorry— Did you know Sergeant Waters well?
Cobb. As well as the next man, sir—I was already with the team when he took over. Me and C.J., we made the team the same time.
Davenport. Were you close to C.J.?
Cobb. Me and him were "homeys," sir! Both came from Mississippi. C.J. from Carmella—me, I'm from up 'roun' Jutlerville, what they call snake county. Plus, we both played for the Negro League before the war.
Davenport. How did you feel about his arrest?
Cobb. Terrible—C.J. didn't kill nobody, sir.
Davenport. He struck Sergeant Waters—
Cobb. Waters made him, sir! He called that boy things he had never heard of before—C.J., he was so confused he didn't know what else to do— *(pause)* An' when they put him in the stockade, he jus' seemed to go to pieces. *(Lowly in the background, C.J.'s music comes up.)* See, we both lived on farms—and even though C.J.'s daddy played music, C.J., he liked the wide-open spaces. *(shakes his head)* That cell? It started closin' in on him right away. *(Blue-gray light rises in limbo, where C.J. is sitting on the edge of a bunk. A shadow of bars cuts across the space. His guitar is on the bunk beside him.)* I went to see him, the second day he was in there. He looked pale and ashy, sir—like something dead.

(C.J. faces Cobb.)

C.J. It's hard to breathe in these little spaces, Cobb—man wasn' made for this hea'—nothin' was! I don't think I'll eva' see a' animal in a cage agin' and not feel sorry for it. *(to himself)* I'd rather be on the chain gang.

(Cobb looks up at him.)

Cobb. Come on, homey! *(He rises, moves toward C.J.)*
C.J. I don't think I'm comin' outta here, Cobb—feels like I'm goin' crazy. Can't walk in hea'—can't see the sun! I tried singin', Cobb, but nothin' won't come out. I sure don't wanna die in this jail!
Cobb. *(moving closer)* Ain't nobody gonna die, C.J.!
C.J. Yesterday I broke a guitar string—lost my Dust! I got no protection—nothin' to keep the dog from tearin' at my bones!
Cobb. Stop talkin' crazy!

(C.J. is quiet for a moment. He starts forward. Slowly, in center stage, Waters emerges. He faces the audience.)

C.J. You know, he come up hea' las' night? Sergeant Waters?

(Waters smiles, pulls out his pipe, lights it.)

Waters. *(calmly)* You should learn never to hit sergeants, boy—man can get in a lot of trouble doin' that kinda thing durin' wartime—they talkin' 'bout givin' you five years—they call what you did mutiny in the navy. Mutiny, boy.
C.J. That gun ain't mine!
Waters. Oh, we know that, C.J. *(C.J. is surprised.)* That gun belonged to the niggah did the shootin' over at Williams's place—me and Wilkie caught him hidin' in the Motor Pool, and he confessed his head off. You're in here for striking a superior officer, boy. And I got a whole barracks full of your friends to prove it! *(smiles broadly, as C.J. shakes his head)*
Davenport. *(to Cobb, at once)* Memphis wasn't charged with the shooting?
Cobb. No, sir—
Waters. Don't feel too bad, boy. It's not your fault entirely—it has to be this way. The First War, it didn't change much for us, boy—but this one—it's gonna change a lot of things. Them Nazis ain't all crazy—a whole lot of people just can't fit into where things seem to be goin'—like you, C.J. The black race can't afford you no more. There use ta be a time when we'd see somebody like you, singin', clownin'—yas-sah-bossin'—and we wouldn't do anything. *(smiles)* Folks liked that—you were good—homey kinda' niggah—they needed somebody to

mistreat—call a name, they paraded you, reminded them of the old days—corn-bread bakin', greens and ham cookin'—Daddy out pickin' cotton, Grandmammy sit on the front porch smokin' a pipe. *(slight pause)* Not no more. The day of the geechy is gone, boy—the only thing that can move the race is power. It's all the white respects—and people like you just make us seem like fools. And we can't let nobody go on believin' we all like you! You bring us down—make people think the whole race is unfit! *(quietly pleased)* I waited a long time for you, boy, but I gotcha! And I try to git rid of you wherever I go. I put two geechies in jail at Fort Campbell, Kentucky—three at Fort Huachuca. Now I got you—one less fool for the race to be ashamed of! *(points)* And I'ma git that ole boy Cobb next! *(Light begins to fade around Waters.)*

Davenport. *(at once)* You?
Cobb. Yes, sir. *(slight pause)*
Davenport. Go on.
C.J. You imagin' anybody sayin' that? I know I'm not gittin' outta' hea', Cobb! *(quiets)* You remember I tol' you 'bout a place I use ta go outside Carmella? When I was a little ole tiny thing? Place out behind O'Connell's Farm? Place would be stinkin' of plums, Cobb. Shaded— that ripe smell be weavin' through the cotton fields and clear on in ta town on a warm day. First time I had Evelyn? I had her unda' them plum trees. I wrote a song for her—*(talks, sings)* My ginger-colored Moma—she had thighs the size of hams! *(chuckles)* And when you spread them, Momaaaa! / *(talks)* You let me have my jelly roll and jam! *(pause, mood swing)* O'Connell, he had a dog—meanes' dog I *eva'* did see! An' the only way you could enjoy them plum trees was to outsmart that dog. Waters is like that ole dog, Cobb—you gotta run circles roun' ole Windy—that was his name. They say he tore a man's arm off once, and got to likin' it. So, you had to cheat that dog outta' bitin' you every time. Every time. *(Slowly the light begins to fade around C.J.)*
Cobb. He didn't make sense, sir. I tried talkin' about the team—the war— ain't nothin' work—seem like he jes' got worse.
Davenport. What happened to him?

(Cobb looks at him incredulously.)

Cobb. The next day—afta' the day I saw him? C.J., he hung hisself, sir! Suicide—jes' couldn't stand it. M.P.'s found him hung from the bars.

(Davenport is silent for a moment.)

Davenport. What happened after that?
Cobb. We lost our last game—we jes' threw it—we did it for C.J.—

Captain, he was mad 'cause we ain't git to play the Yankees. Peterson was right on that one—somebody needed to protest that man!

Davenport. What did Waters do?

Cobb. Well, afta' we lost, the commanding officer, he broke up the team, and we all got reassigned to this Smoke Company. Waters, he started actin' funny, sir—stayed drunk—talked to hisself all the time.

Davenport. Did you think you were next?

Cobb. I ain't sure I eva' believed Waters said that, sir—C.J. had to be outta' his head or he wouldna' killed hisself—Sarge, he neva' came near me afta' C.J. died.

Davenport. What time did you get back the night Waters was killed?

Cobb. I'd say between 2120 and 9:30.

Davenport. And you didn't go out again?

Cobb. No, sir—me and Henson sat and listened to the radio till Abbott and Lou Costello went off, then I played checkers with Wilkie for 'notha' hour, then everybody went to bed. What C.J. said about Waters? It ain't botha' me, sir.

(Davenport is silent.)

Davenport. Who were the last ones in that night?

Cobb. Smalls and Peterson—they had guard duty.

(Taylor enters the barracks area and stops just inside the door when he sees Davenport isn't quite finished.)

Davenport. Thank you, Corporal.

(Cobb rises at attention and salutes. Davenport returns salute and Cobb starts out. He nods to Taylor, who advances toward Davenport.)

Taylor. *(smiling)* You surprise me, Davenport—I just left Colonel Nivens. He's given you permission to question Byrd and Wilcox? *(Davenport nods.)* How'd you manage that? You threatened him with an article in the Chicago *Defenders,* I suppose.

Davenport. I convinced the Colonel it was in his best interests to allow it.

Taylor. Really? Did he tell you I would assist you?

Davenport. I told him I especially didn't want you.

Taylor. That's precisely why he sent me—he didn't want you to think you could get your away entirely—not with him. Then neither Byrd or Wilcox would submit to it without a white officer present. That's how it is. *(There is a rather long silence.)* But there's something else, Davenport. The Colonel began talking about the affidavits he and the others signed—and the discrepancies in their statements that night. *(mimics)* He wants me with you because he doesn't want Byrd and

Wilcox giving you the wrong impression—he never elaborated on what he meant by the wrong impression. I want to be there!

Davenport. So you're not on *that* side anymore—you're on *my* side now, right?

Taylor. *(bristles)* I want whoever killed my sergeant, Davenport!

Davenport. Bullshit! Yesterday you were daring me to try! And today we're allies? Besides, you don't give that much of a damn about your men! I've been around you a full day and you haven't uttered a word that would tell me you had any more than a minor acquaintance with Waters! He managed your baseball team—was an N.C.O. in your company, and you haven't offered *any* opinion of the man as a soldier—sergeant—platoon leader! Who the hell was he?

Taylor. He was one of my men! On my roster—a man these bars make me responsible for! And no, I don't know a helluva lot about him—or a lot of their names or where they come from, but I'm still their commanding officer and in a little while I may have to trust them with my life! And I want them to know they can trust me with theirs—here and now! *(pause)* I have Byrd and Wilcox in my office. *(Davenport stares at him for a long moment, then rises and starts out toward center stage.)* Why didn't you tell Nivens that you'd placed me under arrest?

(Davenport stops.)

Davenport. I didn't find it necessary.

(They stare at one another. Taylor is noticeably strained.)

Davenport. *(starts away)* What do you know about C. J. Memphis?

(Taylor follows.)

Taylor. *(shrugs)* He was a big man as I recall—more a boy than a man, though. Played the guitar sometimes at the Officers Club—there was something embarrassing about him. Committed suicide in the stockade. Pretty good center fielder—

(Davenport stops.)

Davenport. Did you investigate his arrest—the charges against him?

Taylor. He was charged with assaulting a noncommissioned officer—I questioned him—he didn't say much. He admitted he struck Waters—I started questioning several of the men in the platoon and he killed himself before I could finish—open-and-shut case.

Davenport. I think Waters tricked C.J. into assaulting him.

Taylor. Waters wasn't that kind of a man! He admitted he might have provoked the boy—he accused him of that Golden Palace shooting—

(Behind them, the Captain's office is lit. In two chairs facing Taylor's desk are Lieutenant Byrd and Captain Wilcox, both in dress uniform.)

Taylor. Listen, Waters didn't have a fifth-grade education—he wasn't a schemer! And colored soldiers aren't devious like that.
Davenport. What do you mean we aren't devious?
Taylor. *(sharply)* You're not as devious—! *(Davenport stares as Taylor waves disdainfully and starts into the office.)* Anyway, what has that to do with this? *(He is distracted by Byrd and Wilcox before Davenport can answer. Taylor speaks as he moves to his desk.)* This is *Captain* Davenport—you've both been briefed by Colonel Nivens to give the Captain your full cooperation.

(Davenport puts on his glasses. Taylor notices and almost smiles.)

Byrd. *(to Davenport)* They tell me you a lawyer, huh?
Davenport. I am not here to answer your questions, Lieutenant. And I am Captain Davenport, is that clear?
Byrd. *(to Taylor)* Captain, is he crazy?
Taylor. You got your orders.
Byrd. Sir, I vigorously protest as an officer—
Taylor. *(cuts him off)* You answer him the way he wants you to, Byrd, or I'll have your ass in a sling so tight you won't be able to pee, soldier!

(Byrd backs off slightly.)

Davenport. When did you last see Sergeant Waters?
Byrd. The night he was killed, but I didn' kill him—I should have blown his head off, the way he spoke to me and Captain Wilcox here.
Davenport. How did he speak to you, Captain?
Wilcox. Well, he was very drunk—and he said a lot of things he shouldn't have. I told the Lieutenant here not to make the situation worse and he agreed, and we left the Sergeant on his knees, wallowing in self-pity. *(shrugs)*
Davenport. What exactly did he say?
Wilcox. Some pretty stupid things about us—I mean white people, sir.

(Byrd reacts to the term "sir.")

Davenport. What kind of things?
Byrd. *(annoyed)* He said he wasn't going to obey no white man's orders! And that me and Wilcox here were to blame for him being black, and not able to sleep or keep his food down! And I didn't even know the man! Never even spoke to him before that night!
Davenport. Anything else?
Wilcox. Well—he said he'd killed somebody.

Davenport. Did he call a name—or say who?
Wilcox. Not that I recall, sir.

(Davenport looks at Byrd.)

Byrd. No— *(sudden and sharp)* Look—the goddamn Negro was disrespectful! He wouldn't salute! Wouldn't come to attention! And where I come from, colored don't talk the way he spoke to us—not to white people they don't!
Davenport. Is that the reason you killed him?
Byrd. I killed nobody! I said "where I come from," didn't I? You'd be dead yourself, where I come from! But I didn't kill the—the *Negro!*
Davenport. But you hit him, didn't you?
Byrd. I knocked him down!
Davenport. *(quickens pace)* And when you went to look at him, he was dead, wasn't he?
Byrd. He was alive when we left!
Davenport. You're a liar! You beat Waters up—you went back and you shot him!
Byrd. No! *(rises)* But you better get outta my face before I kill you!

(Davenport stands firm.)

Davenport. Like you killed Waters?
Byrd. No! *(He almost raises a hand to Davenport.)*
Taylor. *(at once)* Soldier!
Byrd. He's trying to put it on me!
Taylor. Answer his questions, Lieutenant.
Davenport. You were both coming off bivouac, right?
Wilcox. Yes.
Davenport. So you both had weapons?
Byrd. So what? We didn't fire them!
Davenport. Were the weapons turned in immediately?
Wilcox. Yes, sir—Colonel Nivens took our .45's to Major Hines. It was all kept quiet because the Colonel didn't want the colored boys to know that anyone white from the Fort was involved in any way—ballistics cleared them.
Davenport. We can check.
Byrd. Go ahead.
Taylor. I don't believe it—why wasn't I told?
Wilcox. The weapons had cleared—and the Colonel felt if he involved you further, you'd take the matter to Washington and there'd be a scandal about colored and white soldiers—as it turned out, he thinks you went to Washington anyway. *(to Davenport)* I'd like to say, Captain, that neither Lieutenant Byrd or myself had anything whatsoever to do with

Sergeant Waters's death—I swear that as an officer and a gentleman. He was on the ground when we left him, but very much alive.

Taylor. Consider yourselves under arrest, *gentlemen!*
Byrd. On what charge?
Taylor. Murder! You think I believe that crap—
Davenport. Let them go, Captain.
Taylor. You've got motive—a witness to their being at the scene—
Davenport. Let them go! This is still my investigation—you two are dismissed!

(Byrd rises quickly. Wilcox follows his lead.)

Wilcox. Are we being charged, sir?
Davenport. Not by me.
Wilcox. Thank you.

(Wilcox comes to attention, joined by a reluctant Byrd. They both salute. Davenport returns salute.)

Byrd. I expected more from a white man, Captain.
Taylor. Get out of here, before I have you cashiered out of the army, Byrd!

(Both men exit quietly, and for a moment Taylor and Davenport are quiet.)

Taylor. What the hell is the matter with you? You could have charged both of them—Byrd for insubordination—Wilcox, tampering with evidence.
Davenport. Neither charge is murder—you think Wilcox would tell a story like that if he didn't have Hines and Nivens to back it up? *(slightly tired)* They've got a report.
Taylor. So what do you do now?
Davenport. Finish the investigation.
Taylor. They're lying, dammit! So is the Colonel! You were ordered to investigate and charge the people responsible—charge them! I'll back you up!
Davenport. I'm not satisfied yet, Captain.
Taylor. I am! Dammit!—I wish they'd sent somebody else! I do—you—you're afraid! You thought you'd accuse the Klan, didn't you?—and that would be the end of it, right? Another story of midnight riders for your Negro press! And now it's officers—white men in the army. It's too much for you—what will happen when Captain Davenport comes up for promotion to major if he accuses white officers, right?
Davenport. I'm not afraid of white men, Captain.
Taylor. Then why the hell won't you arrest them?
Davenport. Because I do what the facts tell me, Captain—not you!
Taylor. You don't know what a fact is, Davenport!

(Ellis enters suddenly and salutes.)

Ellis. Begging your pardon, sir.

Taylor. What is it, Corporal?

Ellis. Ah—it's for Captain Davenport— *(to Davenport)* We found Private Wilkie, sir. We haven't located PFC Peterson yet. Seems him and Private Smalls went out on detail together, and neither one of 'em showed up—but I got a few men from the company lookin' for 'em around the N.C.O. club and in the PX, sir.

Davenport. Where's Wilkie?

Ellis. He's waiting for you in the barracks, Captain.

(Davenport nods, and Ellis goes out after saluting. The lights come up around Wilkie, who is seated in a chair in the barracks reading a Negro newspaper. Davenport is thoughtful for a moment.)

Taylor. Didn't you question Wilkie and Peterson yesterday? *(Davenport starts out.)* Davenport? *(Davenport does not answer.)* Don't you ignore me!

Davenport. Get off my back! What I do—how I do it—who I interrogate is my business, Captain! This investigation is mine! *(holds out the back of his hand, showing Taylor the color of his skin)* Mine!

Taylor. Don't treat me with that kind of contempt—I'm not some red-neck cracker!

Davenport. And I'm not your yessirin' colored boy either!

Taylor. I asked you a question!

Davenport. I don't have to answer it!

(There is a long silence. The two men glare at one another—Taylor in another time, disturbed.)

Taylor. Indeed you don't—*Captain*.

(pause)

Davenport. Now, *Captain*—what if Byrd and Wilcox are telling the truth?

Taylor. Neither one of us believes that.

Davenport. What if they are?

Taylor. Then who killed the goddamn man?

Davenport. I don't know yet. *(slight pause)* Is there anything else?

(Taylor shakes his head no as Davenport starts toward center stage, headed toward Wilkie.)

Taylor. No, hotshot. Nothing.

(Davenport enters the barracks area. Wilkie quickly puts his paper aside and snaps to attention and salutes. Davenport returns salute but remains silent, going right to the desk and removing his pad and pencil. The light around the office fades out.)

Davenport. *(snapping at Wilkie)* When did you lose your stripes? *(He is standing over Wilkie.)*
Wilkie. Couple months before they broke up the team—right after Sergeant Waters got assigned to us, sir.
Davenport. Nervous, Wilkie?
Wilkie. *(smiles haltingly)* I couldn't figure out why you called me back, sir? *(laughs nervously)*
Davenport. You lost your stripes for being drunk on duty, is that correct?
Wilkie. Yes, sir.
Davenport. You said Waters busted you, didn't you?
Wilkie. He got me busted—he's the one reported me to the Captain.
Davenport. How did you feel? Must have been awful— *(Davenport paces.)* Weren't you and the Sergeant good friends? Didn't you tell me he was all right? A nice guy?
Wilkie. Yes, sir.
Davenport. Would a nice guy have gotten a friend busted?
Wilkie. No, sir.
Davenport. So you lied when you said he was a nice guy, right?
Wilkie. No, sir—I mean—
Davenport. Speak up! Speak up! Was the Sergeant a nice guy or not?
Wilkie. No, sir.
Davenport. Why not? Answer me!
Wilkie. Well, you wouldn't turn somebody in over something like that!
Davenport. Not a good friend, right?
Wilkie. Right, sir—I mean, a friend would give you extra duty—I would have—or even call you a whole buncha' names—you'd expect that, sir—but damn! Three stripes? They took ten years to get in this army, sir! Ten years! I started out with the 24th Infantry—I—
Davenport. Made you mad, didn't it?
Wilkie. Yeah, it made me mad—all the things I did for him!
Davenport. *(quickly)* That's right! You were his assistant, weren't you? Took care of the team— *(Wilkie nods.)* Ran all his errands, looked at his family snapshots *(Wilkie nods again),* policed his quarters, put the gun under C.J.'s bed—

(Wilkie looks up suddenly.)

Wilkie. No!
Davenport. *(quickly)* It was you Henson saw, wasn't it, Wilkie?
Wilkie. No, sir!
Davenport. Liar! You lied about Waters, and you're lying now! You were the only person out of the barracks that night, and the only one who knew the layout well enough to go straight to C.J.'s bunk! Not even Waters knew the place that well! Henson didn't see who it was, but he

saw what the person did—he was positive about that—only you knew the barracks in the dark!

Wilkie. *(pleadingly)* It was the Sarge, Captain—he ordered me to do it—he said I'd get my stripes back—he wanted to scare that boy C.J.! Let him stew in jail! Then C.J. hit him—and he had the boy right where he wanted him— *(confused)* But it backfired—C.J. killed hisself—Sarge didn't figure on that.

Davenport. Why did he pick Memphis?

Wilkie. He despised him, Captain—he'd hide it, 'cause everybody in the company liked that boy so much. But underneath—it was a crazy hate, sir—he'd go cold when he talked about C.J. You could feel it.

(In limbo, the blue-gray light rises on C.J. and Waters. C.J. is humming a blues song and Waters is standing smiling, smoking a pipe as he was in Act I. Waters turns away from C.J. His speech takes place over C.J.'s humming.)

Waters. He's the kinda boy seems innocent, Wilkie. Got everybody around the post thinking he's a strong, black buck! Hits home runs—white boys envy his strength—his speed, the power in his swing. Then this colored champion lets those same white boys call him Shine—or Sambo at the Officers Club. They laugh at his blues songs, and he just smiles—can't talk, barely read or write his own name—and don't care! He'll tell you they like him—or that colored folks ain't supposed to have but so much sense. *(intense)* Do you know the damage one ignorant *Negro* can do? *(remembering)* We were in France during the First War, Wilkie. We had won decorations, but the white boys had told all the French gals we had tails. And they found this ignorant colored soldier. Paid him to tie a tail to his ass and parade around naked making monkey sounds. *(shakes his head)* They sat him on a big, round table in the Café Napoleon, put a reed in his hand, a crown on his head, a blanket on his shoulders, and made him eat bananas in front of them Frenchies. And ohhh, the white boys danced that night—passed out leaflets with that boy's picture on them—called him Moonshine, King of the Monkeys. And when we slit his throat, you know that fool asked us what he had done wrong? *(pause)* My daddy told me, we got to turn our backs on his kind, Wilkie. Close our ranks to the chittlin's, the collard greens—the cornbread style. We are men—soldiers, and I don't intend to have our race cheated out of its place of honor and respect in *this* war because of fools like C.J.! You watch everything he does—*everything!*)

(Light fades slowly around Waters and C.J., and as it does, C.J. stops humming.)

Wilkie. And I watched him, sir—but Waters—he couldn't wait! He wouldn't talk about nothin' else—it was C.J. this—C.J. all the time!

Davenport. *(troubled)* Why didn't he pick Peterson—they fought.
Wilkie. They fought all the time, sir—but the Sarge, he likes Peterson. *(nods)* Peterson fought back, and Waters admired that. He promoted Pete! Imagine that—he thought Peterson would make a fine soldier!
Davenport. What was Peterson's reaction—when C.J. died?
Wilkie. Like everybody else, he was sad—he put together that protest that broke up the team, but afta' that he didn't say much. And he usually runs off at the mouth. Kept to himself—or with Smalls.

(slight pause)

Davenport. The night Waters was killed, what time did you get in?
Wilkie. Around nine forty-five—couple of us came from the club and listened to the radio awhile—I played some checkers, then I went to bed. Sir? I didn't mean to do what I did—it wasn't my fault—he promised me my stripes!

(Suddenly, out of nowhere, in the near distance, is the sound of gunfire, a bugle blaring, something like a cannon going off. The noise is continuous through scene. Davenport rises, startled.)
Davenport. I'm placing you under arrest, Private!

(Ellis bursts into the room.)

Ellis. Did you hear, sir? *(Davenport, surprised, shakes his head no.)* Our orders! They came down from Washington, Captain! We're shippin' out! They finally gonna let us Negroes fight!

(Davenport is immediately elated, and almost forgets Wilkie as he shakes Ellis's hand.)

Davenport. Axis ain't got a chance!
Ellis. Surrrre—we'll win this mother in six months now! Afta' what Jesse Owens did to them people? Joe Louis?

(Henson bursts in.)

Henson. Did y'all hear it? Forty-eight-hour standby alert? We goin' into combat! *(loud)* Look out, Hitler, the niggahs is comin' to git your ass through the fog!
Ellis. With real rifles—it's really O.K., you know?
Henson. They tell me them girls in England—woooow!

(Davenport faces Wilkie as Cobb enters, yelling.)

Cobb. They gonna let us git in it! We may lay so much smoke the Germans may never get to see what a colored soldier looks like 'til the war's over! *(to Henson)* I wrote my woman jes' the otha' day that we'd be goin' soon!

Ellis. Go on!

Henson. *(overlapping)* Man, you ain't nothin'!

(Davenport begins to move Wilkie toward Ellis.)

Henson. If the army said we was all discharged, you'd claim you wrote that! *(He quiets, watching Davenport.)*

Cobb. *(quickly)* You hea' this fool, sir?

Henson. Shhhhh!

Davenport. *(to Ellis)* Corporal, escort Private Wilkie to the stockade.

Ellis. *(surprised)* Yes, sir!

(Ellis starts Wilkie out, even though he is bewildered by it. They exit.)

Henson. Wilkie's under arrest, sir? *(Davenport nods.)* How come? I apologize, sir—I didn't mean that.

Davenport. Do either of you know where Smalls and Peterson can be located?

(Henson shrugs.)

Cobb. Your men got Smalls in the stockade, sir!

Davenport. When?

Cobb. I saw two colored M.P.'s takin' him through the main gate. Jes' a while ago—I was on my way ova' hea'!

(Davenport goes to the desk and picks up his things and starts out.)

Cobb. Tenn-hut.

(Davenport stops and salutes.)

Davenport. As you were. By the way—congratulations!

(Davenport exits the barracks through the doorway.)

Henson. Look out, Hitler!
Cobb. The niggahs is coming to get yo' ass.
Henson and Cobb. Through the fog.

(The lights in the barracks go down at once. Simultaneously, they rise in limbo, where Smalls is pacing back and forth. He is smoking a cigarette. There is a bunk, and the shadow of a screen over his cell. In the background, the sounds of celebration continue. Davenport emerges from the right, and begins to speak immediately as the noises of celebration fade.)

Davenport. Why'd you go AWOL, soldier?

(Smalls faces him, unable to see Davenport at first. When he sees him, he snaps to attention and salutes.)

Smalls. Private Anthony Smalls, sir!
Davenport. At ease—answer my question!
Smalls. I didn't go AWOL, sir—I—I got drunk in Tynin and fell asleep in the bus depot—it was the only public place I could find to sleep it off.
Davenport. Where'd you get drunk? Where in Tynin?
Smalls. Jake's—Jake's and Lilly's Golden Slipper—on Melville Street—
Davenport. Weren't you and Peterson supposed to be on detail? *(Smalls nods.)* Where was Peterson? Speak up!
Smalls. I don't know, sir!
Davenport. You're lying! You just walked off your detail and Peterson did nothing?
Smalls. No, sir—he warned me, sir—"Listen, Smalls!" he said—
Davenport. *(cutting him off)* You trying to make a fool of me, Smalls? Huh? *(loud)* Are you?
Smalls. No, sir!
Davenport. The two of you went A-W-O-L together, didn't you? *(Smalls is quiet.)* Answer me!
Smalls. Yes!
Davenport. You left together because Peterson knew I would find out the two of you killed Waters, didn' you? *(Smalls suddenly bursts into quiet tears, shaking his head.)* What? I can't hear you! *(Smalls is sobbing.)* You killed Waters, didn't you? I want an answer!
Smalls. I can't sleep—I can't sleep!
Davenport. Did you kill Sergeant Waters?
Smalls. It was Peterson, sir! *(as if he can see it)* I watched! It wasn't me!

(The blue-gray light builds in center stage. As it does, Sergeant Waters staggers forward and falls on his knees. He can't get up, he is so drunk. He has been beaten, and looks the way we saw him in the opening of Act I).

Smalls. We were changing the guard.
Waters. Can't be trusted—no matter what we do, there are no guarantees—and your mind won't let you forget it. *(shakes his head repeatedly)* No, no, no!
Smalls. *(overlapping)* On our way back to the Captain's office—and Sarge, he was on the road. We just walked into him! He was ranting, and acting crazy, sir!

(Peterson emerges from the right. He is dressed in a long coat, pistol belt and pistol, rifle, helmet, his pants bloused over his boots. He sees Waters and smiles. Waters continues to babble.)

Peterson. Smalls, look who's drunk on his ass, boy! *(He begins to circle Waters.)*
Smalls. *(to Davenport)* I told him to forget Waters!

Peterson. Noooo! I'm gonna' enjoy this, Smalls—big, bad Sergeant Waters down on his knees? No, sah—I'm gonna' love this! *(leans over Waters)* Hey, Sarge—need some help? *(Waters looks up; almost smiles. He reaches for Peterson, who pushes him back down.)* That's the kinda help I'll give yah, boy! Let me help you again—all right? *(kicks Waters)* Like that, Sarge? Huh? Like that, dog?
Smalls. *(shouts)* Peterson!
Peterson. No! *(almost pleading)* Smalls—some people, man— If this was a German, would you kill it? If it was Hitler—or that fuckin' Tojo? Would you kill him? *(kicks Waters again)*
Waters. *(mumbling throughout)* There's a trick to it, Peterson—it's the only way you can win—C.J. could never make it—he was a clown! *(grabs at Peterson)* A clown in blackface! A niggah!

(Peterson steps out of reach. He is suddenly expressionless as he easily removes his pistol from his holster.)

Waters. You got to be like them! And I was! I was—but the rules are fixed. *(whispers)* Shhhh! Listen. It's C.J.— *(laughs)* I made him do it, but it doesn't make any difference! They still hate you! *(looks at Peterson, who has moved closer to him)* They still hate you! *(Waters laughs.)*
Peterson. *(to Smalls)* Justice, Smalls. *(He raises the pistol.)*
Davenport. *(suddenly, harshly)* That isn't justice!

(Smalls almost recoils.)

Peterson. *(simultaneously, continuing)* For C.J.! Everybody!

(Peterson fires the gun at Waters's chest, and the shot stops everything. The celebration noise stops. Even Davenport in his way seems to hear it. Peterson fires again. There is a moment of quiet on stage. Davenport is angered and troubled.)

Davenport. You call that justice?
Smalls. No, sir.
Davenport. *(enraged)* Then why the fuck didn't you do something?
Smalls. I'm scared of Peterson—just scared of him!

(Peterson has been looking at Waters's body throughout. He now begins to lift Waters as best he can, and pull him offstage. It is done with some difficulty.)

Smalls. I tried to get him to go, sir, but he wanted to drag the Sergeant's body back into the woods—

(Light fades quickly around Peterson, as Davenport paces.)

Smalls. Said everybody would think white people did it.

Davenport. *(somewhat drained)* Then what happened?
Smalls. I got sick, sir—and Peterson, when he got done, he helped me back to the barracks and told me to keep quiet. *(slight pause)* I'm sorry, sir.

(There is a long pause, during which Davenport stares at Smalls with disgust, then abruptly starts out without saluting. He almost flees. Smalls rises quickly.)

Smalls. Sir?

(Davenport turns around. Smalls comes to attention and salutes. Davenport returns salute and starts out of the cell and down toward center stage. He is thoughtful as the light fades around Smalls. Davenport removes his glasses and begins to clean them as he speaks.)

Davenport. Peterson was apprehended a week later in Alabama. Colonel Nivens called it "just another black mess of cuttin', slashin', and shootin'!" He was delighted there were no white officers mixed up in it, and his report to Washington characterized the events surrounding Waters's murder as "the usual, common violence any commander faces in Negro Military units." It was the kind of "mess" that turns up on page 3 in the colored papers—the Cain and Abel story of the week— the headline we Negroes can't quite read in comfort. *(shakes head and paces)* For me? Two colored soldiers are dead—two on their way to prison. Four less men to fight with—and none of their reasons—nothing anyone *said,* or *did,* would have been worth a life to men with larger hearts—men less split by the madness of race in America. *(pause)* The case got little attention. The details were filed in my report and I was quickly and rather unceremoniously ordered back to my M.P. unit. *(smiles)* A style of guitar pickin' and a dance called the C.J. caught on for a while in Tynin saloons during 1945. *(slight pause)* In northern New Jersey, through a military foul-up, Sergeant Waters's family was informed that he had been killed in action. The Sergeant was, therefore, thought and unofficially rumored to have been the first colored casualty of the war from that county and under the circumstances was declared a hero. Nothing could be done officially, but his picture was hung on a Wall of Honor in the Dorie Miller VFW Post #978. *(pause)* The men of the 221st Chemical Smoke Generating Company? The entire outfit— officers and enlisted men—was wiped out in the Ruhr Valley during a German advance. *(He turns toward Taylor, who enters quietly.)* Captain?

Taylor. Davenport—I see you got your man.
Davenport. I got him—what is it, Captain?
Taylor. Will you accept my saying, you did a splendid job?

Davenport. I'll take the praise—but how did I manage it?

Taylor. Dammit, Davenport—I didn't come here to be made fun of— *(slight pause)* The men—the regiment—we all ship out for Europe tomorrow, and *(hesitates)* I was wrong, Davenport—about the bars—the uniform—about Negroes being in charge. *(slight pause)* I guess I'll *have* to get used to it.

Davenport. Oh, you'll get used to it—you can bet your ass on that. Captain—you will get used to it.

(Lights begin to fade slowly as the music "Don't Sit under the Apple Tree" rises in the background, and the house goes to black.)

Ma Rainey's Black Bottom (1984)

August Wilson (b. 1945–)

Born in Pittsburgh, Pennsylvania, where he later cofounded Black Horizons Theatre, August Wilson has won Pulitzer Prizes in drama for *Fences* (1987) and *The Piano Lesson* (1990). Among his various fellowships are Rockefeller and Guggenheim Foundation fellowships for playwriting. In addition to the Pulitzer Prizes, he has earned a Tony "Best Play" award (for *Fences*) and a New York Drama Critics' Award for each of his first four professional dramas.

Set in Chicago in 1927, *Ma Rainey's Black Bottom* examines the problems of African American musicians during that exciting but schizophrenic decade known as the "Jazz Age" and the "Harlem Renaissance." History recalls the glamor of the "New Negro." Broadway audiences thrilled to *Shuffle Along* (1921) and other black musicals. Singer Florence Mills captured hearts in the United States and abroad. Duke Ellington was developing his first orchestra, and young Louis Armstrong was playing his horn in Chicago at a club controlled by racketeers. But August Wilson recreates the "sob of the jazz band" as he portrays a world that evokes memories of Langston Hughes's piano player in "The Weary Blues." Like Wilson's other professional plays, *Ma Rainey's Black Bottom* was developed at the Eugene O'Neill Theatre Center's National Conference and premiered at the Yale Repertory Theater.

Selected Plays by August Wilson

Ma Rainey's Black Bottom (1984).
Fences (1987).
Joe Turner's Come and Gone (1988).
The Piano Lesson (1990).

Ma Rainey's Black Bottom
A Play in Two Acts

For My Mother

CHARACTERS

Ma Rainey
Sturdyvant
Irwin
Cutler
Slow Drag
Toledo
Levee
Dussie Mae
Sylvester
Policeman

THE SETTING

There are two playing areas: what is called the "band room," and the recording studio. The band room is at stage left and is in the basement of the building. It is entered through a door up left. There are benches and chairs scattered about, a piano, a row of lockers, and miscellaneous paraphernalia stacked in a corner and long since forgotten. A mirror hangs on a wall with various posters.

The studio is upstairs at stage right, and resembles a recording studio of the late 1920's. The entrance is from a hall on the right wall. A small control booth is at the rear and its access is gained by means of a spiral staircase. Against one wall there is a line of chairs, and a horn through which the control room communicates with the performers. A door in the rear wall allows access to the band room.

THE PLAY

It is early March in Chicago, 1927. There is a bit of a chill in the air. Winter has broken but the wind coming off the lake does not carry the promise of spring. The people of the city are bundled and brisk in their defense against such misfortunes as the weather, and the business of the city proceeds largely undisturbed.

Chicago in 1927 is a rough city, a bruising city, a city of millionaires and derelicts, gangsters and roughhouse dandies, whores and Irish grandmothers who move through its streets fingering long black rosaries. Somewhere a man is wrestling with the taste of a woman in his cheek. Somewhere a dog is barking. Somewhere the moon has fallen through a window and broken into thirty pieces of silver.

It is one o'clock in the afternoon. Secretaries are returning from their lunch, the noon Mass at St. Anthony's is over, and the priest is mumbling over his vestments while the altar boys practice their Latin. The procession of cattle cars through the stockyards continues unabated. The busboys in Mac's Place are cleaning away the last of the corned beef and cabbage, and on the city's Southside, sleepy-eyed negroes move lazily toward their small cold-water flats and rented rooms to await the onslaught of night, which will find them crowded in the bars and juke joints both dazed and dazzling in their rapport with life. It is with these negroes that our concern lies most heavily: their values, their attitudes, and particularly their music.

It is hard to define this music. Suffice it to say that it is music that breathes and touches. That connects. That is in itself a way of being, separate and distinct from any other. This music is called blues. Whether this music came from Alabama or Mississippi or other parts of the South doesn't matter anymore. The men and women who make this music have learned it from the narrow crooked streets of East St. Louis, or the streets of the city's Southside, and the Alabama or Mississippi roots have been strangled by the northern manners and customs of free men of definite and sincere worth, men for whom this music often lies at the forefront of their conscience and concerns. Thus they are laid open to be consumed by it; its warmth and redress, its braggadocio and roughly poignant comments, its vision and prayer, which would instruct and allow them to reconnect, to reassemble and gird up for the next battle in which they would be both victim and the ten thousand slain.

ACT I

The lights come up in the studio. Irvin enters, carrying a microphone. He is a tall, fleshy man who prides himself on his knowledge of blacks and his ability to deal with them. He hooks up the microphone, blows into it, taps it, etc. He crosses over to the piano, opens it, and fingers a few keys. Sturdyvant is visible in the control booth. Preoccupied with money, he is insensitive to black performers and prefers to deal with them at arm's length. He puts on a pair of earphones.

Sturdyvant. *(over speaker)* Irv . . . let's crack that mike, huh? Let's do a check on it.

Irvin. *(crosses to mike, speaks into it)* Testing . . . one . . . two . . . three . . . *(There is a loud feedback. Sturdyvant fiddles with the dials.)* Testing . . . one . . . two . . . three . . . testing. How's that, Mel? *(Sturdyvant doesn't respond.)* Testing . . . one . . . two . . .

Sturdyvant. *(taking off earphones)* Okay . . . that checks. We got a good reading. *(pause)* You got that list, Irv?

Irvin. Yeah . . . yeah, I got it. Don't worry about nothing.

Sturdyvant. Listen, Irv . . . you keep her in line, okay? I'm holding you responsible for her . . . If she starts any of her . . .

Irvin. Mel, what's with the goddamn horn? You wanna talk to me . . . okay! I can't talk to you over the goddamn horn . . . Christ!

Sturdyvant. I'm not putting up with any shenanigans. You hear, Irv? *(Irvin crosses over to the piano and mindlessly runs his fingers over the keys.)* I'm just not gonna stand for it. I want you to keep her in line. Irv? *(Sturdyvant enters from the control booth.)* Listen, Irv . . . you're her manager . . . she's your responsibility . . .

Irvin. Okay, okay, Mel . . . let me handle it.

Sturdyvant. She's your responsibility. I'm not putting up with any Royal Highness . . . Queen of the Blues bullshit!

Irvin. Mother of the Blues, Mel. Mother of the Blues.

Sturdyvant. I don't care what she calls herself. I'm not putting up with it. I just want to get her in here . . . record those songs on that list . . . and get her out. Just like clockwork, huh?

Irvin. Like clockwork, Mel. You just stay out of the way and let me handle it.

Sturdyvant. Yeah . . . yeah . . . you handled it last time. Remember? She marches in here like she owns the damn place . . . doesn't like the songs we picked out . . . says her throat is sore . . . doesn't want to do more than one take . . .

Irvin. Okay . . . okay . . . I was here! I know all about it.

Sturdyvant. Complains about the building being cold . . . and then . . . trips over the mike wire and threatens to sue me. That's taking care of it?

Irvin. I've got it all worked out this time. I talked with her last night. Her throat is fine . . . We went over the songs together . . . I got everything straight, Mel.

Sturdyvant. Irv, that horn player . . . the one who gave me those songs . . . is he gonna be here today? Good. I want to hear more of that sound. Times are changing. This is a tricky business now. We've got to jazz it up . . . put in something different. You know, something wild . . . with a lot of rhythm. *(pause)* You know what we put out last time, Irv? We put out garbage last time. It was garbage. I don't even know why I bother with this anymore.

Irvin. You did all right last time, Mel. Not as good as you did before, but you did all right.

Sturdyvant. You know how many records we sold in New York? You wanna see the sheet? And you know what's in New York, Irv? Harlem. Harlem's in New York, Irv.

Irvin. Okay, so they didn't sell in New York. But look at Memphis . . . Birmingham . . . Atlanta. Christ, you made a bundle.

Sturdyvant. It's not the money, Irv. You know I couldn't sleep last night? This business is bad for my nerves. My wife is after me to slow down and take a vacation. Two more years and I'm gonna get out . . . get into something respectable. Textiles. That's a respectable business. You know what you could do with a shipload of textiles from Ireland?

(A buzzer is heard offstage.)

Irvin. Why don't you go upstairs and let me handle it, Mel?

Sturdyvant. Remember . . . you're responsible for her.

(Sturdyvant exits to the control booth. Irvin crosses to get the door. Cutler, Slow Drag, and Toledo enter. Cutler is in his mid-fifties, as are most of the others. He plays guitar and trombone and is the leader of the group, possibly because he is the most sensible. His playing is solid and almost totally unembellished. His understanding of his music is limited to the chord he is playing at the time he is playing it. He has all the qualities of a loner except the introspection. Slow Drag, the bass player, is perhaps the one most bored by life. He resembles Cutler, but lacks Cutler's energy. He is deceptively intelligent, though, as his name implies, he appears to be slow. He is a rather large man with a wicked smile. Innate African rhythms underlie everything he plays, and he plays with an ease that is at times startling. Toledo is the piano player. In control of his instrument, he understands and recognizes that its limitations are an extension of himself. He is the only one in the

group who can read. He is self-taught but misunderstands and misapplies his knowledge, though he is quick to penetrate to the core of a situation and his insights are thought-provoking. All of the men are dressed in a style of clothing befitting the members of a successful band of the era.)

Irvin. How you boys doing, Cutler? Come on in. *(pause)* Where's Ma? Is she with you?

Cutler. I don't know, Mr. Irvin. She told us to be here at one o'clock. That's all I know.

Irvin. Where's . . . huh . . . the horn player? Is he coming with Ma?

Cutler. Levee's supposed to be here same as we is. I reckon he'll be here in a minute. I can't rightly say.

Irvin. Well, come on . . . I'll show you to the band room, let you get set up and rehearsed. You boys hungry? I'll call over to the deli and get some sandwiches. Get you fed and ready to make some music. Cutler . . . here's the list of songs we're gonna record.

Sturdyvant. *(over speaker)* Irvin, what's happening? Where's Ma?

Irvin. Everything under control, Mel. I got it under control.

Sturdyvant. Where's Ma? How come she isn't with the band?

Irvin. She'll be here in a minute, Mel. Let me get these fellows down to the band room, huh? *(They exit the studio. The lights go down in the studio and up in the band room. Irvin opens the door and allows them to pass as they enter.)* You boys go ahead and rehearse. I'll let you know when Ma comes. *(Irvin exits. Cutler hands Toledo the list of songs.)*

Cutler. What we got here, Toledo?

Toledo. *(reading)* We got . . . "Prove It on Me" . . . "Hear Me Talking to You" . . . "Ma Rainey's Black Bottom" . . . and "Moonshine Blues."

Cutler. Where Mr. Irvin go? Them ain't the songs Ma told me.

Slow Drag. I wouldn't worry about if it I were you, Cutler. They'll get it straightened out. Ma will get it straightened out.

Cutler. I just don't want no trouble about these songs, that's all. Ma ain't told me them songs. She told me something else.

Slow Drag. What she tell you?

Cutler. This "Moonshine Blues" wasn't in it. That's one of Bessie's songs.

Toledo. Slow Drag's right . . . I wouldn't worry about it. Let them straighten it up.

Cutler. Levee know what time he supposed to be here?

Slow Drag. Levee gone out to spend your four dollars. He left the hotel this morning talking about he was gonna go buy some shoes. Say it's the first time he ever beat you shooting craps.

Cutler. Do he know what time he supposed to be here? That's what I wanna know. I ain't thinking about no four dollars.

Slow Drag. Levee sure was thinking about it. That four dollars liked to burn a hole in his pocket.

Cutler. Well, he's supposed to be here at one o'clock. That's what time Ma said. That nigger get out in the streets with that four dollars and ain't no telling when he's liable to show. You ought to have seen him at the club last night, Toledo. Trying to talk to some gal Ma had with her.
Toledo. You ain't got to tell me. I know how Levee do.

(Buzzer is heard offstage.)

Slow Drag. Levee tried to talk to that gal and got his feelings hurt. She didn't want no part of him. She told Levee he'd have to turn his money green before he could talk with her.
Cutler. She out for what she can get. Anybody could see that.
Slow Drag. That's why Levee run out to buy some shoes. He's looking to make an impression on that gal.
Cutler. What the hell she gonna do with his shoes? She can't do nothing with the nigger's shoes.

(Slow Drag takes out a pint bottle and drinks.)

Toledo. Let me hit that, Slow Drag.
Slow Drag. *(handing him the bottle)* This some of that good Chicago bourbon!

(The door opens and Levee enters, carrying a shoe box. In his early thirties, Levee is younger than the other men. His flamboyance is sometimes subtle and sneaks up on you. His temper is rakish and bright. He lacks fuel for himself and is somewhat of a buffoon. But it is an intelligent buffoonery, clearly calculated to shift control of the situation to where he can grasp it. He plays trumpet. His voice is strident and totally dependent on his manipulation of breath. He plays wrong notes frequently. He often gets his skill and talent confused with each other.)

Cutler. Levee . . . where Mr. Irvin go?
Levee. Hell, I don't know. I ain't none of his keeper.
Slow Drag. What you got there, Levee?
Levee. Look here, Cutler . . . I got me some shoes!
Cutler. Nigger, I ain't studying you.

(Levee takes the shoes out of the box and starts to put them on.)

Toledo. How much you pay for something like that, Levee?
Levee. Eleven dollars. Four dollars of it belong to Cutler.
Slow Drag. Levee say if it wasn't for Cutler . . . he wouldn't have no new shoes.
Cutler. I ain't thinking about Levee or his shoes. Come on . . . let's get ready to rehearse.
Slow Drag. I'm with you on that score, Cutler. I wanna get out of here. I

don't want to be around here all night. When it comes time to go up there and record them songs . . . I just wanna go up there and do it. Last time it took us all day and half the night.

Toledo. Ain't but four songs on the list. Last time we recorded six songs.

Slow Drag. It felt like it was sixteen!

Levee. *(finishes with his shoes)* Yeah! Now I'm ready! I can play some good music now! *(He goes to put up his old shoes and looks around the room.)* Damn! They done changed things around. Don't never leave well enough alone.

Toledo. Everything changing all the time. Even the air you breathing change. You got, monoxide, hydrogen . . . changing all the time. Skin changing . . . different molecules and everything.

Levee. Nigger, what is you talking about? I'm talking about the room. I ain't talking about no skin and air. I'm talking about something I can see! Last time the band room was upstairs. This time it's downstairs. Next time it be over there. I'm talking about what I can see. I ain't talking about no molecules or nothing.

Toledo. Hell, I know what you talking about. I just said everything changin'. I know what you talking about, but you don't know what I'm talking about.

Levee. That door! Nigger, you see that door? That's what I'm talking about. That door wasn't there before.

Cutler. Levee, you wouldn't know your right from your left. This is where they used to keep the recording horns and things . . . and damn if that door wasn't there. How in hell else you gonna get in here? Now, if you talking about they done switched rooms, you right. But don't go telling me that damn door wasn't there!

Slow Drag. Damn the door and let's get set up. I wanna get out of here.

Levee. Toledo started all that about the door. I'm just saying that things change.

Toledo. What the hell you think I was saying? Things change. The air and everything. Now you gonna say you was saying it. You gonna fit two propositions on the same track . . . run them into each other, and because they crash, you gonna say it's the same train.

Levee. Now this nigger talking about trains! We done went from the air to the skin to the door . . . and now trains. Toledo, I'd just like to be inside your head for five minutes. Just to see how you think. You done got more shit piled up and mixed up in there than the devil got sinners. You been reading too many goddamn books.

Toledo. What you care about how much I read? I'm gonna ignore you 'cause you ignorant.

(Levee takes off his coat and hangs it in the locker.)

Slow Drag. Come on, let's rehearse the music.
Levee. You ain't gotta rehearse that . . . ain't nothing but old jug-band music. They need one of them jug bands for this.
Slow Drag. Don't make me no difference. Long as we get paid.
Levee. That ain't what I'm talking about, nigger. I'm talking about art!
Slow Drag. What's drawing got to do with it?
Levee. Where you get this nigger from, Cutler? He sound like one of them Alabama niggers.
Cutler. Slow Drag's all right. It's you talking all that weird shit about art. Just play the piece, nigger. You wanna be one of them . . . what you call . . . virtuoso or something, you in the wrong place. You ain't no Buddy Bolden or King Oliver . . . you just an old trumpet player come a dime a dozen. Talking about art.
Levee. What is you? I don't see your name in lights.
Cutler. I just play the piece. Whatever they want. I don't go talking about art and criticizing other people's music.
Levee. I ain't like you, Cutler. I got talent! Me and this horn . . . we's tight. If my daddy knowed I was gonna turn out like this, he would've named me Gabriel. I'm gonna get me a band and make me some records. I done give Mr. Sturdyvant some of my songs I wrote and he says he's gonna let me record them when I get my band together. *(takes some papers out of his pocket)* I just gotta finish the last part of this song. And Mr. Sturdyvant wants me to write another part to this song.
Slow Drag. How you learn to write music, Levee?
Levee. I just picked it up . . . like you pick up anything. Miss Eula used to play the piano . . . she learned me a lot. I knows how to play *real* music . . . not this old jug-band shit. I got style!
Toledo. Everybody got style. Style ain't nothing but keeping the same idea from beginning to end. Everybody got it.
Levee. But everybody can't play like I do. Everybody can't have their own band.
Cutler. Well, until you get your own band where you can play what you want, you just play the piece and stop complaining. I told you when you came on here, this ain't none of them hot bands. This is an accompaniment band. You play Ma's music when you here.
Levee. I got sense enough to know that. Hell, I can look at you all and see what kind of band it is. I can look at Toledo and see what kind of band it is.
Toledo. Toledo ain't said nothing to you now. Don't let Toledo get started. You can't even spell music, much less play it.
Levee. What you talking about? I can spell music. I got a dollar say I can spell it! Put your dollar up. Where your dollar? *(Toledo waves him away.)* Now come on. Put your dollar up. Talking about I can't spell

music. *(Levee peels a dollar off his roll and slams it down on the bench beside Toledo.)*

Toledo. All right, I'm gonna show you. Cutler. Slow Drag. You hear this? The nigger betting me a dollar he can spell music. I don't want no shit now! *(Toledo lays a dollar down beside Levee's.)* All right. Go ahead. Spell it.

Levee. It's a bet then. Talking about I can't spell music.

Toledo. Go ahead, then. Spell it. Music. Spell it.

Levee. I can spell it, nigger! M-U-S-I-K. There! *(He reaches for the money.)*

Toledo. Naw! Naw! Leave that money alone! You ain't spelled it.

Levee. What you mean I ain't spelled it? I said M-U-S-I-K!

Toledo. That ain't how you spell it! That ain't how you spell it! It's M-U-S-I-*C*! C, nigger. Not K! C! M-U-S-I-C!

Levee. What you mean, C? Who says it's C?

Toledo. Cutler. Slow Drag. Tell this fool. *(They look at each other and then away.)* Well, I'll be a monkey's uncle! *(Toledo picks up the money and hands Levee his dollar back.)* Here's your dollar back, Levee. I done won it, you understand. I done won the dollar. But if don't nobody know but me, how am I gonna prove it to you?

Levee. You just mad 'cause I spelled it.

Toledo. Spelled what! M-U-S-I-K don't spell nothing. I just wish there was some way I could show you the right and wrong of it. How you gonna know something if the other fellow don't know if you're right or not? Now I can't even be sure that I'm spelling it right.

Levee. That's what I'm talking about. You don't know it. Talking about C. You ought to give me that dollar I won from you.

Toledo. All right. All right. I'm gonna show you how ridiculous you sound. You know the Lord's Prayer?

Levee. Why? You wanna bet a dollar on that?

Toledo. Just answer the question. Do you know the Lord's Prayer or don't you?

Levee. Yeah, I know it. What of it?

Toledo. Cutler?

Cutler. What you Cutlering me for? I ain't got nothing to do with it.

Toledo. I just want to show the man how ridiculous he is.

Cutler. Both of you all sound like damn fools. Arguing about something silly. Yeah. I know the Lord's Prayer. My daddy was a deacon in the church. Come asking me if I know the Lord's Prayer. Yeah, I know it.

Toledo. Slow Drag?

Slow Drag. Yeah.

Toledo. All right. Now I'm gonna tell you a story to show just how ridiculous he sound. There was these two fellows, see. So, the one of them go up to this church and commence to taking up the church learning. The other fellow see him out on the road and he say, "I done heard you taking up the church learning," say, "Is you learning anything up there?" The other one say, "Yeah, I done take up the church learning and I's learning all kinds of things about the Bible and what it say and all. Why you be asking?" The other one say, "Well, do you know the Lord's Prayer?" And he say, "Why, sure I know the Lord's Prayer, I'm taking up learning at the church ain't I? I know the Lord's Prayer backwards and forwards." And the other fellow says, "I bet you five dollars you don't know the Lord's Prayer, 'cause I don't think you knows it. I think you be going up to the church 'cause the Widow Jenkins be going up there and you just wanna be sitting in the same room with her when she cross them big, fine, pretty legs she got." And the other one say, "Well, I'm gonna prove you wrong and I'm gonna bet you that five dollars." So he say, "Well, go on and say it then." So he commenced to saying the Lord's Prayer. He say, "Now I lay me down to sleep, I pray the Lord my soul to keep." The other one say, "Here's your five dollars. I didn't think you knew it." *(They all laugh.)* Now, that's just how ridiculous Levee sound. Only 'cause I knowed how to spell music, I still got my dollar.

Levee. That don't prove nothing. What's that supposed to prove?

(Toledo takes a newspaper out of his back pocket and begins to read.)

Toledo. I'm through with it.
Slow Drag. Is you all gonna rehearse this music or ain't you?

(Cutler takes out some papers and starts to roll a reefer.)

Levee. How many times you done played them songs? What you gotta rehearse for?
Slow Drag. This is a recording session. I wanna get it right the first time and get on out of here.
Cutler. Slow Drag's right. Let's go on and rehearse and get it over with.
Levee. You all go and rehearse, then. I got to finish this song for Mr. Sturdyvant.
Cutler. Come on, Levee . . . I don't want no shit now. You rehearse like everybody else. You in the band like everybody else. Mr. Sturdyvant just gonna have to wait. You got to do that on your own time. This is the band's time.
Levee. Well, what is you doing? You sitting there rolling a reefer talking about let's rehearse. Toledo reading a newspaper. Hell, I'm ready if you wanna rehearse. I just say there ain't no point in it. Ma ain't here. What's the point in it?
Cutler. Nigger, why you gotta complain all the time?

Toledo. Levee would complain if a gal ain't laid across his bed just right.
Cutler. That's what I know. That's why I try to tell him just play the music and forget about it. It ain't no big thing.
Toledo. Levee ain't got an eye for that. He wants to tie on to some abstract component and sit down on the elemental.
Levee. This is get-on-Levee time, huh? Levee ain't said nothing except this some old jug-band music.
Toledo. Under the right circumstances you'd play anything. If you know music, then you play it. Straight on or off to the side. Ain't nothing abstract about it.
Levee. Toledo, you sound like you got a mouth full of marbles. You the only cracker-talking nigger I know.
Toledo. You ought to have learned yourself to read . . . then you'd understand the basic understanding of everything.
Slow Drag. Both of you all gonna drive me crazy with that philosophy bullshit. Cutler, give me a reefer.
Cutler. Ain't you got some reefer? Where's your reefer? Why you all the time asking me?
Slow Drag. Cutler, how long I done known you? How long we been together? Twenty-two years. We been doing this together for twenty-two years. All up and down the back roads, the side roads, the front roads . . . We done played the juke joints, the whorehouses, the barn dances, and city sit-downs . . . I done lied for you and lied with you . . . We done laughed together, fought together, slept in the same bed together, done sucked on the same titty . . . and now you don't wanna give me no reefer.
Cutler. You see this nigger trying to talk me out of my reefer, Toledo? Running all that about how long he done knowed me and how we done sucked on the same titty. Nigger, you *still* ain't getting none of my reefer!
Toledo. That's African.
Slow Drag. What? What are you talking about? What's African?
Levee. I know he ain't talking about me. You don't see me running around in no jungle with no bone between my nose.
Toledo. Levee, you worse than ignorant. You ignorant without a premise. *(pauses)* Now, what I was saying is what Slow Drag was doing is African. That's what you call an African conceptualization. That's when you name the gods or call on the ancestors to achieve whatever your desires are.
Slow Drag. Nigger, I ain't no African! I ain't doing no African nothing!
Toledo. Naming all those things you and Cutler done together is like trying to solicit some reefer based on a bond of kinship. That's African. An ancestral retention. Only you forgot the name of the gods.

Slow Drag. I ain't forgot nothing. I was telling the nigger how cheap he is. Don't come talking that African nonsense to me.

Toledo. You just like Levee. No eye for taking an abstract and fixing it to a specific. There's so much that goes on around you and you can't even see it.

Cutler. Wait a minute . . . wait a minute. Toledo, now when this nigger . . . when an African do all them things you say and name all the gods and whatnot . . . then what happens?

Toledo. Depends on if the gods is sympathetic with his cause for which he is calling them with the right names. Then his success comes with the right proportion of his naming. That's the way that go.

Cutler. *(taking out a reefer)* Here, Slow Drag. Here's a reefer. You done talked yourself up on that one.

Slow Drag. Thank you. You ought to have done that in the first place and saved me all the aggravation.

Cutler. What I wants to know is . . . what's the same titty we done sucked on. That's what I want to know.

Slow Drag. Oh, I just threw that in there to make it sound good.

(They all laugh.)

Cutler. Nigger, you ain't right.

Slow Drag. I knows it.

Cutler. Well, come on . . . let's get it rehearsed. Time's wasting. *(The musicians pick up their instruments.)* Let's do it. "Ma Rainey's Black Bottom." One . . . two . . . You know what to do.

(They begin to play. Levee is playing something different. He stops.)

Levee. Naw! Naw! We ain't doing it that way. *(Toledo stops playing, then Slow Drag.)* We doing my version. It say so right there on that piece of paper you got. Ask Toledo. That's what Mr. Irvin told me . . . say it's on the list he gave you.

Cutler. Let me worry about what's on the list and what ain't on the list. How you gonna tell me what's on the list?

Levee. 'Cause I know what Mr. Irvin told me! Ask Toledo!

Cutler. Let me worry about what's on the list. You just play the song I say.

Levee. What kind of sense it make to rehearse the wrong version of the song? That's what I wanna know. Why you wanna rehearse that version.

Slow Drag. You supposed to rehearse what you gonna play. That's the way they taught me. Now, *whatever* version we gonna play . . . let's go on and rehearse it.

Levee. That's what I'm trying to tell the man.

Cutler. You trying to tell me what we is and ain't gonna play. And that ain't none of your business. Your business is to play what I say.

Levee. Oh, I see now. You done got jealous cause Mr. Irvin using my version. You done got jealous cause I proved I know something about music.

Cutler. What the hell . . . nigger, you talk like a fool! What the hell I got to be jealous of you about? The day I get jealous of you I may as well lay down and die.

Toledo. Levee started all that 'cause he too lazy to rehearse. *(to Levee)* You ought to just go on and play the song . . . What difference does it make?

Levee. Where's the paper? Look at the paper! Get the paper and look at it! See what it say. Gonna tell me I'm too lazy to rehearse.

Cutler. We ain't talking about the paper. We talking about you understanding where you fit in when you around here. You just play what I say.

Levee. Look . . . I don't care what you play! All right? It don't matter to me. Mr. Irvin gonna straighten it up! I don't care what you play.

Cutler. Thank you. *(pauses)* Let's play this "Hear Me Talking to You" till we find out what's happening with the "Black Bottom." Slow Drag, you sing Ma's part. *(pauses)* "Hear Me Talking to You." Let's do it. One . . . Two . . . You know what to do.

(They play.)

Slow Drag. *(singing)*
>Rambling man makes no change in me
>I'm gonna ramble back to my used-to-be
>Ah, you hear me talking to you
>I don't bite my tongue
>You wants to be my man
>You got to fetch it with you when you come.
>
>Eve and Adam in the garden taking a chance
>Adam didn't take time to get his pants
>Ah, you hear me talking to you
>I don't bite my tongue
>You wants to be my man
>You got to fetch it with you when you come.
>
>Our old cat swallowed a ball of yarn
>When the kittens were born they had sweaters on
>Ah, you hear me talking to you
>I don't bite my tongue
>You wants to be my man
>You got to fetch it with you when you come.

(Irvin enters. The musicians stop playing.)

Irvin. Any of you boys know what's keeping Ma?
Cutler. Can't say, Mr. Irvin. She'll be along directly, I reckon. I talked to her this morning, she say she'll be here in time to rehearse.
Irvin. Well, you boys go ahead.

(He starts to exit.)

Cutler. Mr. Irvin, about these songs . . . Levee say . . .
Irvin. Whatever's on the list, Cutler. You got that list I gave you?
Cutler. Yessir, I got it right here.
Irvin. Whatever's on there. Whatever that says.
Cutler. I'm asking about this "Black Bottom" piece . . . Levee say . . .
Irvin. Oh, it's on the list. "Ma Rainey's Black Bottom" on the list.
Cutler. I know it's on the list. I wanna know what version. We got two versions of that song.
Irvin. Oh. Levee's arrangement. We're using Levee's arrangement.
Cutler. Ok. I got that straight. Now, this "Moonshine Blues" . . .
Irvin. We'll work it out with Ma, Cutler. Just rehearse whatever's on the list and use Levee's arrangement on that "Black Bottom" piece.

(He exits.)

Levee. See. I told you! It don't mean nothing when I say it. You got to wait for Mr. Irvin to say it. Well, I told you the way it is.
Cutler. Levee, the sooner you understand it ain't what you say, or what Mr. Irvin say . . . it's what Ma say that counts.
Slow Drag. Don't nobody say when it come to Ma. She's gonna do what she wants to do. Ma says what happens with her.
Levee. Hell, the man's the one putting out the record! He's gonna put out what he wanna put out!
Slow Drag. He's gonna put out what Ma want him to put out.
Levee. You heard what the man told you . . . "Ma Rainey's Black Bottom," Levee's arrangement. There you go! That's what he told you.
Slow Drag. What you gonna do, Cutler?
Cutler. Ma ain't told me what version. Let's go on and play it Levee's way.
Toledo. See, now . . . I'll tell you something. As long as the colored man look to white folks to put the crown on what he say . . . as long as he looks to white folks for approval . . . then he ain't never gonna find out who he is and what he's about. He's just gonna be about what white folks want him to be about. That's one sure thing.
Levee. I'm just trying to show Cutler where he's wrong.
Cutler. Cutler don't need you to show him nothing.
Slow Drag. *(irritated)* Come on, let's get this shit rehearsed! You all can bicker afterward!

Cutler. Levee's confused about who the boss is. He don't know Ma's the boss.
Levee. Ma's the boss on the road! We at a recording session. Mr. Sturdyvant and Mr. Irvin say what's gonna be here! We's in Chicago, we ain't in Memphis! I don't know why you all wanna pick me about it, shit! I'm with Slow Drag . . . Let's go on and get it rehearsed.
Cutler. All right. All right. I know how to solve this. "Ma Rainey's Black Bottom." Levee's version. Let's do it. Come on.
Toledo. How that first part go again, Levee?
Levee. It go like this. *(He plays.)* That's to get the people's attention to the song. That's when you and Slow Drag come in with the rhythm part. Me and Cutler play on the breaks. *(becoming animated)* Now we gonna dance it . . . but we ain't gonna countrify it. This ain't no barn dance. We gonna play it like . . .
Cutler. The man ask you how the first part go. He don't wanna hear all that. Just tell him how the piece go.
Toledo. I got it. I got it. Let's go. I know how to do it.
Cutler. "Ma Rainey's Black Bottom." One . . . two . . . You know what to do.

(They begin to play. Levee stops.)

Levee. You all got to keep up now. You playing in the wrong time. Ma come in over the top. She got to find her own way in.
Cutler. Nigger, will you let us play this song? When you get your own band . . . then you tell them that nonsense. We know how to play the piece. I was playing music before you was born. Gonna tell me how to play . . . All right. Let's try it again.
Slow Drag. Cutler, wait till I fix this. This string started to unravel. *(playfully)* And you know I want to play Levee's music right.
Levee. If you was any kind of musician, you'd take care of your instrument. Keep it in tip-top order. If you was any kind of musician, I'd let you be in my band.
Slow Drag. Shhheeeeet!

(He crosses to get his string and steps on Levee's shoes.)

Levee. Damn, Slow Drag! Watch them big-ass shoes you got.
Slow Drag. Boy, ain't nobody done nothing to you.
Levee. You done stepped on my shoes.
Slow Drag. Move them the hell out the way, then. You was in my way . . . I wasn't in your way. *(Cutler lights up another reefer. Slow Drag rummages around in his belongings for a string. Levee takes out a rag and begins to shine his shoes.)* You can shine these when you get done, Levee.

Cutler. If I had them shoes Levee got, I could buy me a whole suit of clothes.

Levee. What kind of difference it make what kind of shoes I got? Ain't nothing wrong with having nice shoes. I ain't said nothing about your shoes. Why you wanna talk about me and my Florsheims?

Cutler. Any man who takes a whole week's pay and puts it on some shoes—you understand what I mean, what you walk around on the ground with—is a fool! And I don't mind telling you.

Levee. *(irritated)* What difference it make to you, Cutler?

Slow Drag. The man ain't said nothing about your shoes. Ain't nothing wrong with having nice shoes. Look at Toledo.

Toledo. What about Toledo?

Slow Drag. I said ain't nothing wrong with having nice shoes.

Levee. Nigger got them clodhoppers! Old brogans! He ain't nothing but a sharecropper.

Toledo. You can make all the fun you want. It don't mean nothing. I'm satisfied with them and that's what counts.

Levee. Nigger, why don't you get some decent shoes? Got nerve to put on a suit and tie with them farming boots.

Cutler. What you just tell me? It don't make no difference about the man's shoes. That's what you told me.

Levee. Aw, hell, I don't care what the nigger wear. I'll be honest with you. I don't care if he went barefoot. *(Slow Drag has put his string on the bass and is tuning it.)* Play something for me, Slow Drag. *(Slow Drag plays.)* A man got to have some shoes to dance like this! You can't dance like this with them clodhoppers Toledo got. *(Levee sings.)*

   Hello Central give me Doctor Jazz
   He's got just what I need I'll say he has
   When the world goes wrong and I have got the blues
   He's the man who makes me get on my dancing shoes.

Toledo. That's the trouble with colored folks . . . always wanna have a good time. Good times done got more niggers killed than God got ways to count. What the hell having a good time mean? That's what I wanna know.

Levee. Hell, nigger . . . it don't need explaining. Ain't you never had no good time before?

Toledo. The more niggers get killed having a good time, the more good times niggers wanna have. *(Slow Drag stops playing.)* There's more to life than having a good time. If there ain't, then this is a piss-poor life we're having . . . if that's all there is to be got out of it.

Slow Drag. Toledo, just 'cause you like to read them books and study and whatnot . . . that's your good time. People get other things they likes to do to have a good time. Ain't no need you picking them about it.

Cutler. Niggers been having a good time before you was born, and they gonna keep having a good time after you gone.
Toledo. Yeah, but what else they gonna do? Ain't nobody talking about making the lot of the colored man better for him here in America.
Levee. Now you gonna be Booker T. Washington.
Toledo. Everybody worried about having a good time. Ain't nobody thinking about what kind of world they gonna leave their youngens. "Just give me the good time, that's all I want." It just makes me sick.
Slow Drag. Well, the colored man's gonna be all right. He got through slavery, and he'll get through whatever else the white man put on him. I ain't worried about that. Good times is what makes life worth living. Now, you take the white man . . . The white man don't know how to have a good time. That's why he's troubled all the time. He don't know how to have a good time. He don't know how to laugh at life.
Levee. That's what the problem is with Toledo . . . reading all them books and things. He done got to the point where he forgot how to laugh and have a good time. Just like the white man.
Toledo. I know how to have a good time as well as the next man. I said, there's got to be more to life than having a good time. I said the colored man ought to be doing more than just trying to have a good time all the time.
Levee. Well, what is you doing, nigger? Talking all them highfalutin ideas about making a better world for the colored man. What is you doing to make it better? You playing the music and looking for your next piece of pussy same as we is. What is you doing? That's what I wanna know. Tell him, Cutler.
Cutler. You all leave Cutler out of this. Cutler ain't got nothing to do with it.
Toledo. Levee, you just about the most ignorant nigger I know. Sometimes I wonder why I ever bother to try and talk with you.
Levee. Well, what is you doing? Talking that shit to me about I'm ignorant! What is you doing? You just a whole lot of mouth. A great big windbag. Thinking you smarter than everybody else. What is you doing, huh?
Toledo. It ain't just me, fool! It's everybody! What you think . . . I'm gonna solve the colored man's problems by myself? I said, we. You understand that? We. That's every living colored man in the world got to do his share. Got to do his part. I ain't talking about what I'm gonna do . . . or what you or Cutler or Slow Drag or anybody else. I'm talking about all of us together. What all of us is gonna do. That's what I'm talking about, nigger!
Levee. Well, why didn't you say that, then?
Cutler. Toledo, I don't know why you waste your time on this fool.

Toledo. That's what I'm trying to figure out.

Levee. Now there go Cutler with his shit. Calling me a fool. You wasn't even in the conversation. Now you gonna take sides and call me a fool.

Cutler. Hell, I was listening to the man. I got sense enough to know what he was saying. I could tell it straight back to you.

Levee. Well, you go on with it. But I'll tell you this . . . I ain't gonna be too many more of your fools. I'll tell you that. Now you put that in your pipe and smoke it.

Cutler. Boy, ain't nobody studying you. Telling me what to put in my pipe. Who's you to tell me what to do?

Levee. All right, I ain't nobody. Don't pay me no mind. I ain't nobody.

Toledo. Levee, you ain't nothing but the devil.

Levee. There you go! That's who I am. I'm the devil. I ain't nothing but the devil.

Cutler. I can see that. That's something you know about. You know all about the devil.

Levee. I ain't saying what I know. I know plenty. What you know about the devil? Telling me what I know. What you know?

Slow Drag. I know a man sold his soul to the devil.

Levee. There you go! That's the only thing I ask about the devil . . . to see him coming so I can sell him this one I got. 'Cause if there's a god up there, he done went to sleep.

Slow Drag. Sold his soul to the devil himself. Name of Eliza Cotter. Lived in Tuscaloosa County, Alabama. The devil came by and he done upped and sold him his soul.

Cutler. How you know the man done sold his soul to the devil, nigger? You talking that old-woman foolishness.

Slow Drag. Everybody know. It wasn't no secret. He went around working for the devil and everybody knowed it. Carried him a bag . . . one of them carpetbags. Folks say he carried the devil's papers and whatnot where he put your fingerprint on the paper with blood.

Levee. Where he at now? That's what I want to know. He can put my whole handprint if he want to!

Cutler. That's the damnedest thing I ever heard! Folks kill me with that talk.

Toledo. Oh, that's real enough, all right. Some folks go arm in arm with the devil, shoulder to shoulder, and talk to him all the time. That's real, ain't nothing wrong in believing that.

Slow Drag. That's what I'm saying. Eliza Cotter is one of them. All right. The man living up in an old shack on Ben Foster's place, shoeing mules and horses, making them charms and things in secret. He done hooked up with the devil, showed up one day all fancied out with just the finest clothes you ever seen on a colored man . . . dressed just like one of them crackers . . . and carrying this bag with them papers and things. All right. Had a pocketful of money, just living the life of a rich man. Ain't done no more work or nothing. Just had him a string of women he run around with and throw his money away on. Bought him a big fine house . . . Well, it wasn't all that big, but it did have one of them white picket fences around it. Used to hire a man once a week just to paint that fence. Messed around there and one of the fellows of them gals he was messing with got fixed on him wrong and Eliza killed him. And he laughed about it. Sheriff come and arrest him, and then let him go. And he went around in that town laughing about killing this fellow. Trial come up, and the judge cut him loose. He must have been in converse with the devil too . . . 'cause he cut him loose and give him a bottle of whiskey! Folks ask what done happened to make him change, and he'd tell them straight out he done sold his soul to the devil and ask them if they wanted to sell theirs 'cause he could arrange it for them. Preacher see him coming, used to cross on the other side of the road. He'd just stand there and laugh at the preacher and call him a fool to his face.

Cutler. Well, whatever happened to this fellow? What come of him? A man who, as you say, done sold his soul to the devil is bound to come to a bad end.

Toledo. I don't know about that. The devil's strong. The devil ain't no pushover.

Slow Drag. Oh, the devil had him under his wing, all right. Took good care of him. He ain't wanted for nothing.

Cutler. What happened to him? That's what I want to know.

Slow Drag. Last I heard, he headed north with that bag of his, handing out hundred-dollar bills on the spot to whoever wanted to sign on with the devil. That's what I hear tell of him.

Cutler. That's a bunch of fool talk. I don't know how you fix your mouth to tell that story. I don't believe that.

Slow Drag. I ain't asking you to believe it. I'm just telling you the facts of it.

Levee. I sure wish I knew where he went. He wouldn't have to convince me long. Hell, I'd even help him sign people up.

Cutler. Nigger, God's gonna strike you down with that blasphemy you talking.

Levee. Oh, shit! God don't mean nothing to me. Let him strike me! Here I am, standing right here. What you talking about he's gonna strike me? Here I am! Let him strike me! I ain't scared of him. Talking that stuff to me.

Cutler. All right. You gonna be sorry. You gonna fix yourself to have bad luck. Ain't nothing gonna work for you.

(Buzzer sounds offstage.)

Levee. Bad luck? What I care about some bad luck? You talking simple. I ain't knowed nothing but bad luck all my life. Couldn't get no worse. What the hell I care about some bad luck? Hell, I eat it everyday for breakfast! You dumber than I thought you was . . . talking about bad luck.

Cutler. All right, nigger, you'll see! Can't tell a fool nothing. You'll see!

Irvin. *(Irvin enters the studio, checks his watch, and calls down the stairs.)* Cutler . . . you boys' sandwiches are up here . . . Cutler?

Cutler. Yessir, Mr. Irvin . . . be right there.

Toledo. I'll walk up there and get them.

(Toledo exits. The lights go down in the band room and up in the studio. Irvin paces back and forth in an agitated manner. Sturdyvant enters.)

Sturdyvant. Irv, what's happening? Is she here yet? Was that her?

Irvin. It's the sandwiches, Mel. I told you . . . I'll let you know when she comes, huh?

Sturdyvant. What's keeping her? Do you know what time it is? Have you looked at the clock? You told me she'd be here. You told me you'd take care of it.

Irvin. Mel, for Chrissakes! What do you want from me? What do you want me to do?

Sturdyvant. Look what time it is, Irv. You told me she'd be here.

Irvin. She'll be here, okay? I don't know what's keeping her. You know they're always late, Mel.

Sturdyvant. You should have went by the hotel and made sure she was on time. You should have taken care of this. That's what you told me, huh? "I'll take care of it."

Irvin. Okay! Okay! I didn't go by the hotel! What do you want me to do? She'll be here, okay? The band's here . . . she'll be here.

Sturdyvant. Okay, Irv. I'll take your word. But if she doesn't come . . . if she doesn't come . . .

(Sturdyvant exits to the control booth as Toledo enters.)

Toledo. Mr. Irvin . . . I come up to get the sandwiches.

Irvin. Say . . . uh . . . look . . . one o'clock, right? She said one o'clock.

Toledo. That's what time she told us. Say be here at one o'clock.

Irvin. Do you know what's keeping her? Do you know why she ain't here?

Toledo. I can't say, Mr. Irvin. Told us one o'clock.

(The buzzer sounds. Irvin goes to the door. There is a flurry of commotion as Ma Rainey enters, followed closely by the Policeman, Dussie Mae, and Sylvester. Ma Rainey is a short, heavy woman. She is dressed in a full-length

fur coat with matching hat, an emerald-green dress, and several strands of pearls of varying lengths. Her hair is secured by a headband that matches her dress. Her manner is simple and direct, and she carries herself in a royal fashion. Dussie Mae is a young, dark-skinned woman whose greatest asset is the sensual energy which seems to flow from her. She is dressed in a fur jacket and a tight-fitting canary-yellow dress. Sylvester is an Arkansas country boy, the size of a fullback. He wears a new suit and coat, in which he is obviously uncomfortable. Most of the time, he stutters when he speaks.)

Ma Rainey. Irvin . . . you better tell this man who I am! You better get him straight!
Irvin. Ma, do you know what time it is? Do you have any idea? We've been waiting . . .
Dussie Mae. *(to Sylvester)* If you was watching where you was going . . .
Sylvester. I was watching . . . What you mean?
Irvin. *(notices Policeman)* What's going on here? Officer, what's the matter?
Ma Rainey. Tell the man who he's messing with!
Policeman. Do you know this lady?
Ma Rainey. Just tell the man who I am! That's all you gotta do.
Policeman. Lady, will you let me talk, huh?
Ma Rainey. Tell the man who I am!
Irvin. Wait a minute . . . wait a minute! Let me handle it. Ma, will you let me handle it?
Ma Rainey. Tell him who he's messing with!
Irvin. Okay! Okay! Give me a chance! Officer, this is one of our recording artists . . . Ma Rainey.
Ma Rainey. Madame Rainey! Get it straight! Madame Rainey! Talking about taking me to jail!
Irvin. Look, Ma . . . give me a chance, okay? Here . . . sit down. I'll take care of it. Officer, what's the problem?
Dussie Mae. *(to Sylvester)* It's all your fault.
Sylvester. I ain't done nothing . . . Ask Ma.
Policeman. Well . . . when I walked up on the incident . . .
Dussie Mae. Sylvester wrecked Ma's car.
Sylvester. I d-d-did not! The m-m-man ran into me!
Policeman. *(to Irvin)* Look, buddy . . . if you want it in a nutshell, we got her charged with assault and battery.
Ma Rainey. Assault and what for what!
Dussie Mae. See . . . we was trying to get a cab . . . and so Ma . . .
Ma Rainey. Wait a minute! I'll tell you if you wanna know what happened. *(She points to Sylvester.)* Now, that's Sylvester. That's my nephew. He was driving my car . . .

Policeman. Lady, we don't know whose car he was driving.
Ma Rainey. That's my car!
Dussie Mae and Sylvester. That's Ma's car!
Ma Rainey. What you mean you don't know whose car it is? I bought and paid for that car.
Policeman. That's what you say, lady . . . We still gotta check. *(to Irvin)* They hit a car on Market Street. The guy said the kid ran a stoplight.
Sylvester. What you mean? The man c-c-come around the corner and hit m-m-me!
Policeman. While I was calling a paddy wagon to haul them to the station, they try to hop into a parked cab. The cabbie said he was waiting on a fare . . .
Ma Rainey. The man was just sitting there. Wasn't waiting for nobody. I don't know why he wanna tell that lie.
Policeman. Look, lady . . . will you let me tell the story?
Ma Rainey. Go ahead and tell it then. But tell it right!
Policeman. Like I say . . . she tries to get in this cab. The cabbie's waiting on a fare. She starts creating a disturbance. The cabbie gets out to try and explain the situation to her . . . and she knocks him down.
Dussie Mae. She ain't hit him! He just fell!
Sylvester. He just s-s-s-slipped!
Policeman. He claims she knocked him down. We got her charged with assault and battery.
Ma Rainey. If that don't beat all to hell. I ain't touched the man! The man was trying to reach around me to keep his car door closed. I opened the door and it hit him and he fell down. I ain't touched the man!
Irvin. Okay. Okay . . . I got it straight now, Ma. You didn't touch him. All right? Officer, can I see you for a minute?
Dussie Mae. Ma was just trying to open the door.
Sylvester. He j-j-just got in t-t-the way!
Ma Rainey. Said he wasn't gonna haul no colored folks . . . if you want to know the truth of it.
Irvin. Okay, Ma . . . I got it straight now. Officer?

(Irvin pulls the Policeman off to the side.)

Ma Rainey. *(noticing Toledo)* Toledo, Cutler and everybody here?
Toledo. Yeah, they down in the band room. What happened to your car?
Sturdyvant. *(entering)* Irv, what's the problem? What's going on? Officer . . .
Irvin. Mel, let me take care of it. I can handle it.
Sturdyvant. What's happening? What the hell's going on?
Irvin. Let me handle it, Mel, huh?

(Sturdyvant crosses over to Ma Rainey.)

Sturdyvant. What's going on, Ma? What'd you do?
Ma Rainey. Sturdyvant, get on away from me! That's the last thing I need . . . to go through some of your shit!
Irvin. Mel, I'll take care of it. I'll explain it all to you. Let me handle it, huh?

(Sturdyvant reluctantly returns to the control booth.)

Policeman. Look, buddy, like I say . . . we got her charged with assault and battery . . . and the kid with threatening the cabbie.
Sylvester. I ain't done n-n-nothing!
Ma Rainey. You leave the boy out of it. He ain't done nothing. What's he supposed to have done?
Policeman. He threatened the cabbie, lady! You just can't go around threatening people.
Sylvester. I ain't done nothing to him! He's the one talking about he g-g-gonna get a b-b-baseball bat on me! I just told him what I'd do with it. But I ain't done nothing 'cause he didn't get the b-b-bat!
Irvin. *(pulling the Policeman aside)* Officer . . . look here . . .
Policeman. We was on our way down to the precinct . . . but I figured I'd do you a favor and bring her by here. I mean, if she's as important as she says she is . . .
Irvin. *(slides a bill from his pocket)* Look, Officer . . . I'm Madame Rainey's manager . . . It's good to meet you. *(He shakes the Policeman's hand and passes him the bill.)* As soon as we're finished with the recording session, I'll personally stop by the precinct house and straighten up this misunderstanding.
Policeman. Well . . . I guess that's all right. As long as someone is responsible for them. *(He pockets the bill and winks at Irvin.)* No need to come down . . . I'll take care of it myself. Of course, we wouldn't want nothing like this to happen again.
Irvin. Don't worry, Officer . . . I'll take care of everything. Thanks for your help. *(Irvin escorts the Policeman to the door and returns. He crosses over to Ma Rainey.)* Here, Ma . . . let me take your coat. *(to Sylvester)* I don't believe I know you.
Ma Rainey. That's my nephew, Sylvester.
Irvin. I'm very pleased to meet you. Here . . . you can give me your coat.
Ma Rainey. That there is Dussie Mae.
Irvin. Hello . . . *(Dussie Mae hands Irvin her coat.)* Listen, Ma, just sit there and relax. The boys are in the band room rehearsing. You just sit and relax a minute.

Ma Rainey. I ain't for no sitting. I ain't never heard of such. Talking about taking me to jail. Irvin, call down there and see about my car.
Irvin. Okay, Ma . . . I'll take care of it. You just relax.

(Irvin exits with the coats.)

Ma Rainey. Why you all keep it so cold in here? Sturdyvant try and pinch every penny he can. You all wanna make some records, you better put some heat on in here or give me back my coat.
Irvin. *(entering)* We got the heat turned up, Ma. It's warming up. It'll be warm in a minute.
Dussie Mae. *(whispering to Ma Rainey)* Where's the bathroom?
Ma Rainey. It's in the back. Down the hall next to Sturdyvant's office. Come on, I'll show you where it is. Irvin, call down there and see about my car. I want my car fixed today.
Irvin. I'll take care of everything, Ma. *(He notices Toledo.)* Say . . . uh . . . uh . . .
Toledo. Toledo.
Irvin. Yeah . . . Toledo. I got the sandwiches, you can take down to the rest of the boys. We'll be ready to go in a minute. Give you boys a chance to eat and then we'll be ready to go.

(Irvin and Toledo exit. The lights go down in the studio and come up in the band room.)

Levee. Slow Drag, you ever been to New Orleans?
Slow Drag. What's in New Orleans that I want?
Levee. How you call yourself a musician and ain't never been to New Orleans.
Slow Drag. You ever been to Fat Back, Arkansas? *(pauses)* All right, then. Ain't never been nothing in New Orleans that I couldn't get in Fat Back.
Levee. That's why you backwards. You just an old country boy talking about Fat Back, Arkansas, and New Orleans in the same breath.
Cutler. I been to New Orleans. What about it?
Levee. You ever been to Lula White's?
Cutler. Lula White's? I ain't never heard of it.
Levee. Man, they got some gals in there just won't wait! I seen a man get killed in there once. Got drunk and grabbed one of the gals wrong . . . I don't know what the matter of it was. But he grabbed her and she stuck a knife in him all the way up to the hilt. He ain't even fell. He just stood there and choked on his own blood. I was just asking Slow Drag 'cause I was gonna take him to Lula White's when we get down to New Orleans and show him a good time. Introduce him to one of them gals I know down there.

Cutler. Slow Drag don't need you to find him no pussy. He can take care of his own self. Fact is . . . you better watch your gal when Slow Drag's around. They don't call him Slow Drag for nothing. *(He laughs.)* Tell him how you got your name Slow Drag.

Slow Drag. I ain't thinking about Levee.

Cutler. Slow Drag break a woman's back when he dance. They had this contest one time in this little town called Bolingbroke about a hundred miles outside of Macon. We was playing for this dance and they was giving twenty dollars to the best slow draggers. Slow Drag looked over the competition, got down off the bandstand, grabbed hold of one of them gals, and stuck to her like a fly to jelly. Like wood to glue. Man had that gal whooping and hollering so . . . everybody stopped to watch. This fellow come in . . . this gal's fellow . . . and pulled a knife a foot long on Slow Drag. 'Member that, Slow Drag?

Slow Drag. Boy that mama was hot! The front of her dress was wet as a dishrag!

Levee. So what happened? What the man do?

Cutler. Slow Drag ain't missed a stroke. The gal, she just look at her man with that sweet dizzy look in her eye. She ain't about to stop! Folks was clearing out, ducking and hiding under tables, figuring there's gonna be a fight. Slow Drag just looked over the gal's shoulder at the man and said, "Mister, if you'd quit hollering and wait a minute . . . you'll see I'm doing you a favor. I'm helping this gal win ten dollars so she can buy you a gold watch." The man just stood there and looked at him, all the while stroking that knife. Told Slow Drag, say, "All right, then, nigger. You just better make damn sure you win." That's when folks started calling him Slow Drag. The women got to hanging around him so bad after that, them fellows in that town ran us out of there.

(Toledo enters, carrying a small cardboard box with the sandwiches.)

Levee. Yeah . . . well, them gals in Lula White's will put a harness on his ass.

Toledo. Ma's up there. Some kind of commotion with the police.

Cutler. Police? What the police up there for?

Toledo. I couldn't get it straight. Something about her car. They gone now . . . she's all right. Mr. Irvin sent some sandwiches.

(Levee springs across the room.)

Levee. Yeah, all right. What we got here?

(He takes two sandwiches out of the box.)

Toledo. What you doing grabbing two? There ain't but five in there . . . How you figure you get two?

Levee. 'Cause I grabbed them first. There's enough for everybody . . . What you talking about? It ain't like I'm taking food out of nobody's mouth.
Cutler. That's all right. He can have mine too. I don't want none.

(Levee starts toward the box to get another sandwich.)

Toledo. Nigger, you better get out of here. Slow Drag, you want this?
Slow Drag. Naw, you can have it.
Toledo. With Levee around, you don't have to worry about no leftovers. I can see that.
Levee. What's the matter with you? Ain't you eating two sandwiches? Then why you wanna talk about me? Talking about there won't be no leftovers with Levee around. Look at your own self before you look at me.
Toledo. That's what you is. That's what we all is. A leftover from history. You see now, I'll show you.
Levee. Aw, shit . . . I done got the nigger started now.
Toledo. Now, I'm gonna show you how this goes . . . where you just a leftover from history. Everybody come from different places in Africa, right? Come from different tribes and things. Soonawhile they began to make one big stew. You had the carrots, the peas, and potatoes and whatnot over here. And over there you had the meat, the nuts, the okra, corn . . . and then you mix it up and let it cook right through to get the flavors flowing together . . . then you got one thing. You got a stew.

Now you take and eat the stew. You take and make your history with that stew. All right. Now it's over. Your history's over and you done ate the stew. But you look around and you see some carrots over here, some potatoes over there. That stew's still there. You done made your history and it's still there. You can't eat it all. So what you got? You got some leftovers. That's what it is. You got leftovers and you can't do nothing with it. You already making you another history . . . cooking you another meal, and you don't need them leftovers no more. What to do?

See, we's the leftovers. The colored man is the leftovers. Now, what's the colored man gonna do with himself? That's what we waiting to find out. But first we gotta know we the leftovers. Now, who knows that? You find me a nigger that knows that and I'll turn any whichaway you want me to. I'll bend over for you. You ain't gonna find that. And that's what the problem is. The problem ain't with the white man. The white man knows you just a leftover. 'Cause he the one who done the eating and he know what he done ate. But we don't know that we been took and made history out of. Done went and filled the white man's belly and now he's full and tired and wants you to get out the way and let him be by himself. Now, I know what I'm talking about. And if you wanna find out, you just ask Mr. Irvin what he had for supper yesterday. And if he's an honest white man . . . which is asking for a whole heap of a lot . . . he'll tell you he done ate your black ass and if you please I'm full up with you . . . so go on and get off the plate and let me eat something else.

Slow Drag. What that mean? What's eating got to do with how the white man treat you? He don't treat you no different according to what he ate.

Toledo. I ain't said it had nothing to do with how he treat you.

Cutler. The man's trying to tell you something, fool!

Slow Drag. What he trying to tell me? Ain't you here? Why you say he was trying to tell *me* something? Wasn't he trying to tell you too?

Levee. He was trying all right. He was trying a whole heap. I'll say that for him. But trying ain't worth a damn. I got lost right there trying to figure out who puts nuts in their stew.

Slow Drag. I knowed that before. My grandpappy used to put nuts in his stew. He and my grandmama both. That ain't nothing new.

Toledo. They put nuts in their stew all over Africa. But the stew they eat, and the stew your grandpappy made, and all the stew that you and me eat, and the stew Mr. Irvin eats . . . ain't in no way the same stew. That's the way that go. I'm through with it. That's the last you know me to ever try and explain something to you.

Cutler. *(after a pause)* Well, time's getting along . . . Come on, let's finish rehearsing.

Levee. *(stretching out on a bench)* I don't feel like rehearsing. I ain't nothing but a leftover. You go and rehearse with Toledo . . . He's gonna teach you how to make a stew.

Slow Drag. Cutler, what you gonna do? I don't want to be around here all day.

Levee. I know my part. You all go on and rehearse your part. You all need some rehearsal.

Cutler. Come on, Levee, get up off your ass and rehearse the songs.

Levee. I already know them songs . . . What I wanna rehearse them for?

Slow Drag. You in the band, ain't you? You supposed to rehearse when the band rehearse.

Toledo. Levee think he the king of the barnyard. He thinks he's the only rooster know how to crow.

Levee. All right! All right! Come on, I'm gonna show you I know them songs. Come on, let's rehearse. I bet you the first one mess be Toledo. Come on . . . I wanna see if he know how to crow.

Cutler. "Ma Rainey's Black Bottom." Levee's version. Let's do it.

(They begin to rehearse. The lights go down in the band room and up in the studio. Ma Rainey sits and takes off her shoe, rubs her feet. Dussie Mae wanders about looking at the studio. Sylvester is over by the piano.)

Ma Rainey. *(singing to herself)*
    Oh, Lord, these dogs of mine
    They sure do worry me all the time
    The reason why I don't know
    Lord, I beg to be excused
    I can't wear me no sharp-toed shoes.
    I went for a walk
    I stopped to talk
    Oh, how my corns did bark.

Dussie Mae. It feels kinda spooky in here. I ain't never been in no recording studio before. Where's the band at?

Ma Rainey. They off somewhere rehearsing. I don't know where Irvin went to. All this hurry up and he goes off back there with Sturdyvant. I know he better come on 'cause Ma ain't gonna be waiting. Come here . . . let me see that dress. *(Dussie Mae crosses over. Ma Rainey tugs at the dress around the waist, appraising the fit.)* That dress looks nice. I'm gonna take you tomorrow and get you some more things before I take you down to Memphis. They got clothes up here you can't get in Memphis. I want you to look nice for me. If you gonna travel with the show you got to look nice.

Dussie Mae. I need me some more shoes. These hurt my feet.

Ma Rainey. You get you some shoes that fit your feet. Don't you be messing around with no shoes that pinch your feet. Ma know something about bad feet. Hand me my slippers out my bag over yonder.

(Dussie Mae brings the slippers.)

Dussie Mae. I just want to get a pair of them yellow ones. About a half-size larger.

Ma Rainey. We'll get you whatever you need. Sylvester, too . . . I'm gonna get him some more clothes. Sylvester, tuck your clothes in. Straighten them up and look nice. Look like a gentleman.

Dussie Mae. Look at Sylvester with that hat on.

Ma Rainey. Sylvester, take your hat off inside. Act like your mama taught you something. I know she taught you better than that. *(Sylvester bangs on the piano.)* Come on over here and leave that piano alone.

Sylvester. I ain't d-d-doing nothing to the p-p-piano. I'm just l-l-looking at it.

Ma Rainey. Well. Come on over here and sit down. As soon as Mr. Irvin comes back, I'll have him take you down and introduce you to the band. *(Sylvester comes over.)* He's gonna take you down there and introduce you in a minute . . . have Cutler show you how your part go. And when you get your money, you gonna send some of it home to your mama. Let her know you doing all right. Make her feel good to know you doing all right in the world.

(Dussie Mae wanders about the studio and opens the door leading to the band room. The strains of Levee's version of "Ma Rainey's Black Bottom" can be heard. Irvin enters.)

Irvin. Ma, I called down to the garage and checked on your car. It's just a scratch. They'll have it ready for you this afternoon. They're gonna send it over with one of their fellows.

Ma Rainey. They better have my car fixed right too. I ain't going for that. Brand-new car . . . they better fix it like new.

Irvin. It was just a scratch on the fender, Ma . . . They'll take care of it . . . don't worry . . . they'll have it like new.

Ma Rainey. Irvin, what is that I hear? What is that the band's rehearsing? I know they ain't rehearsing Levee's "Black Bottom." I know I ain't hearing that?

Irvin. Ma, listen . . . that's what I wanted to talk to you about. Levee's version of that song . . . it's got a nice arrangement . . . a nice horn intro . . . It really picks it up . . .

Ma Rainey. I ain't studying Levee nothing. I know what he done to that song and I don't like to sing it that way. I'm doing it the old way. That's why I brought my nephew to do the voice intro.

Irvin. Ma, that's what the people want now. They want something they can dance to. Times are changing. Levee's arrangement gives the people what they want. It gets them excited . . . makes them forget about their troubles.

Ma Rainey. I don't care what you say, Irvin. Levee ain't messing up my song. If he got what the people want, let him take it somewhere else. I'm singing Ma Rainey's song. I ain't singing Levee's song. Now that's all there is to it. Carry my nephew on down there and introduce him to the band. I promised my sister I'd look out for him and he's gonna do the voice intro on the song my way.

Irvin. Ma, we just figured that . . .

Ma Rainey. Who's this "we"? What you mean "we"? I ain't studying Levee nothing. Come talking this "we" stuff. Who's "we"?

Irvin. Me and Sturdyvant. We decided that it would . . .

Ma Rainey. You decided, huh? I'm just a bump on the log. I'm gonna go which ever way the river drift. Is that it? You and Sturdyvant decided.

Irvin. Ma, it was just that we thought it would be better.
Ma Rainey. I ain't got good sense. I don't know nothing about music. I don't know what's a good song and what ain't. You know more about my fans than I do.
Irvin. It's not that, Ma. It would just be easier to do. It's more what the people want.
Ma Rainey. I'm gonna tell you something, Irvin . . . and you go on up there and tell Sturdyvant. What you all say don't count with me. You understand? Ma listens to her heart. Ma listens to the voice inside her. That's what counts with Ma. Now, you carry my nephew on down there . . . tell Cutler he's gonna do the voice intro on that "Black Bottom" song and that Levee ain't messing up my song with none of his music shit. Now, if that don't set right with you and Sturdyvant . . . then I can carry my black bottom on back down South to my tour, 'cause I don't like it up here no ways.
Irvin. Okay, Ma . . . I don't care. I just thought . . .
Ma Rainey. Damn what you thought! What you look like telling me how to sing my song? This Levee and Sturdyvant nonsense . . . I ain't going for it! Sylvester, go on down there and introduce yourself. I'm through playing with Irvin.
Sylvester. Which way you go? Where they at?
Ma Rainey. Here . . . I'll carry you down there myself.
Dussie Mae. Can I go? I wanna see the band.
Ma Rainey. You stay your behind up here. Ain't no cause in you being down there. Come on, Sylvester.
Irvin. Okay, Ma. Have it your way. We'll be ready to go in fifteen minutes.
Ma Rainey. We'll be ready to go when Madame says we're ready. That's the way it goes around here. *(Ma Rainey and Sylvester exit. The lights go down in the studio and up in the band room. Ma Rainey enters with Sylvester.)* Cutler, this here is my nephew Sylvester. He's gonna do that voice intro on the "Black Bottom" song using the old version.
Levee. What you talking about? Mr. Irvin say he's using my version. What you talking about?
Ma Rainey. Levee, I ain't studying you or Mr. Irvin. Cutler, get him straightened out on how to do his part. I ain't thinking about Levee. These folks done messed with the wrong person this day. Sylvester, Cutler gonna teach you your part. You go ahead and get it straight. Don't worry about what nobody else say.

(Ma Rainey exits.)

Cutler. Well, come on in, boy. I'm Cutler. You got Slow Drag . . . Levee . . . and that's Toledo over there. Sylvester, huh?
Sylvester. Sylvester Brown.

Levee. I done wrote a version of that song what picks it up and sets it down in the people's lap! Now she come talking this! You don't need that old circus bullshit! I know what I'm talking about. You gonna mess up the song Cutler and you know it.

Cutler. I ain't gonna mess up nothing. Ma say . . .

Levee. I don't care what Ma say! I'm talking about what the intro gonna do to the song. The peoples in the North ain't gonna buy all that tent-show nonsense. They wanna hear some music!

Cutler. Nigger, I done told you time and again . . . you just in the band. You plays the piece . . . whatever they want! Ma says what to play! Not you! You ain't here to be doing no creating. Your job is to play whatever Ma says!

Levee. I might not play nothing! I might quit!

Cutler. Nigger, don't nobody care if you quit. Whose heart you gonna break?

Toledo. Levee ain't gonna quit. He got to make some money to keep him in shoe polish.

Levee. I done told you all . . . you all don't know me. You don't know what I'll do.

Cutler. I don't think nobody too much give a damn! Sylvester, here's the way your part go. The band plays the intro . . . I'll tell you where to come in. The band plays the intro and then you say, "All right, boys, you done seen the rest . . . Now I'm gonna show you the best. Ma Rainey's gonna show you her black bottom." You got that? *(Sylvester nods.)* Let me hear you say it one time.

Sylvester. "All right, boys, you done s-s-seen the rest n-n-now I'm gonna show you the best. M-m-m-m-m-m-ma Rainey's gonna s-s-show you her black b-b-bottom."

Levee. What kind of . . . All right, Cutler! Let me see you fix that! You straighten that out! You hear that shit, Slow Drag? How in the hell the boy gonna do the part and he can't even talk!

Sylvester. W-w-w-who's you to tell me what to do, nigger! This ain't your band! Ma tell me to d-d-d-do it and I'm gonna do it. You can go to hell, n-n-n-nigger!

Levee. B-b-b-boy, ain't nobody studying you. You go on and fix that one, Cutler. You fix that one and I'll . . . I'll shine your shoes for you. You go on and fix that one!

Toledo. You say you Ma's nephew, huh?

Sylvester. Yeah. So w-w-what that mean?

Toledo. Oh, I ain't meant nothing . . . I was just asking.

Slow Drag. Well, come on and let's rehearse so the boy can get it right.

Levee. I ain't rehearsing nothing! You just wait till I get my band. I'm gonna record that song and show you how it supposed to go!

Cutler. We can do it without Levee. Let him sit on over there. Sylvester, you remember your part?
Sylvester. I remember it pretty g-g-g-good.
Cutler. Well, come on, let's do it, then.

(The band begins to play. Levee sits and pouts. Sturdyvant enters the band room.)

Sturdyvant. Good . . . you boys are rehearsing, I see.
Levee. *(jumping up)* Yessir! We rehearsing. We know them songs real good.
Sturdyvant. Good! Say, Levee, did you finish that song?
Levee. Yessir, Mr. Sturdyvant. I got it right here. I wrote that other part just like you say. I go like:
> You can shake it, you can break it
> You can dance at any hall
> You can slide across the floor
> You'll never have to stall
> My jelly, my roll,
> Sweet Mama, don't you let it fall.

Then I put that part in there for the people to dance, like you say, for them to forget about their troubles.
Sturdyvant. Good! Good! I'll just take this. I wanna see you about your songs as soon as I get the chance.
Levee. Yessir! As soon as you get the chance, Mr. Sturdyvant.

(Sturdyvant exits.)

Cutler. You hear, Levee? You hear this nigger? "Yessuh, we's rehearsing, boss."
Slow Drag. I heard him. Seen him too. Shuffling them feet.
Toledo. Aw, Levee can't help it none. He's like all of us. Spooked up with the white men.
Levee. I'm spooked up with him, all right. You let one of them crackers fix on me wrong. I'll show you how spooked up I am with him.
Toledo. That's the trouble of it. You wouldn't know if he was fixed on you wrong or not. You so spooked up by him you ain't had the time to study him.
Levee. I studies the white man. I got him studied good. The first time one fixes on me wrong, I'm gonna let him know just how much I studied. Come telling me I'm spooked up with the white man. You let one of them mess with me, I'll show you how spooked up I am.
Cutler. You talking out your hat. The man come in here, call you a boy, tell you to get up off your ass and rehearse, and you ain't had nothing to say to him, except "Yessir!"

Levee. I can say "yessir" to whoever I please. What you got to do with it? I know how to handle white folks. I been handling them for thirty-two years, and now you gonna tell me how to do it. Just 'cause I say "yessir" don't mean I'm spooked up with him. I know what I'm doing. Let me handle him my way.

Cutler. Well, go on and handle it, then.

Levee. Toledo, you always messing with somebody! Always agitating somebody with that old philosophy bullshit you be talking. You stay out of my way about what I do and say. I'm my own person. Just let me alone.

Toledo. You right, Levee. I apologize. It ain't none of my business that you spooked up by the white man.

Levee. All right! See! That's the shit I'm talking about. You all back up and leave Levee alone.

Slow Drag. Aw, Levee, we was all just having fun. Toledo ain't said nothing about you he ain't said about me. You just taking it all wrong.

Toledo. I ain't meant nothing by it Levee. *(pauses)* Cutler, you ready to rehearse?

Levee. Levee got to be Levee! And he don't need nobody messing with him about the white man—cause you don't know nothing about me. You don't know Levee. You don't know nothing about what kind of blood I got! What kind of heart I got beating here! *(He pounds his chest.)* I was eight years old when I watched a gang of white mens come into my daddy's house and have to do with my mama any way they wanted. *(pauses)* We was living in Jefferson County, about eighty miles outside of Natchez. My daddy's name was Memphis . . . Memphis Lee Green . . . had him near fifty acres of good farming land. I'm talking about good land! Grow anything you want! He done gone off of shares and bought this land from Mr. Hallie's widow woman after he done passed on. Folks called him an uppity nigger 'cause he done saved and borrowed to where he could buy this land and be independent. *(pauses)* It was coming on planting time and my daddy went into Natchez to get him some seed and fertilizer. Called me, say, "Levee you the man of the house now. Take care of your mama while I'm gone." I wasn't but a little boy, eight years old. *(pauses)* My mama was frying up some chicken when them mens come in that house. Must have been eight or nine of them. She standing there frying that chicken and them mens come and took hold of her just like you take hold of a mule and make him do what you want. *(pauses)* There was my mama with a gang of white mens. She tried to fight them off, but I could see where it wasn't gonna do her any good. I didn't know what they were doing to her . . . but I figured whatever it was they may as well do to me too. My daddy had a knife that he kept around there for hunting and working and whatnot. I knew where he kept it and I went and got it.

I'm gonna show you how spooked up I was by the white man. I tried my damndest to cut one of them's throat! I hit him on the shoulder with it. He reached back and grabbed hold of that knife and whacked me across the chest with it. *(Levee raises his shirt to show a long ugly scar.)* That's what made them stop. They was scared I was gonna bleed to death. My mama wrapped a sheet around me and carried me two miles down to the Furlow place and they drove me up to Doc Albans. He was waiting on a calf to be born, and say he ain't had time to see me. They carried me up to Miss Etta, the midwife, and she fixed me up.

My daddy came back and acted like he done accepted the facts of what happened. But he got the names of them mens from mama. He found out who they was and then we announced we was moving out of that county. Said good-bye to everybody . . . all the neighbors. My daddy went and smiled in the face of one of them crackers who had been with my mama. Smiled in his face and sold him our land. We moved over with relations in Caldwell. He got us settled in and then he took off one day. I ain't never seen him since. He sneaked back, hiding up in the woods, laying to get them eight or nine men. *(pauses)* He got four of them before they got him. They tracked him down in the woods. Caught up with him and hung him and set him afire. *(pauses)* My daddy wasn't spooked up by the white man. Nosir! And that taught me how to handle them. I seen my daddy go up and grin in this cracker's face . . . smile in his face and sell him his land. All the while he's planning how he's gonna get him and what he's gonna do to him. That taught me how to handle them. So you all just back up and leave Levee alone about the white man. I can smile and say yessir to whoever I please. I got time coming to me. You all just leave Levee alone about the white man.

(There is a long pause. Slow Drag begins playing on the bass and sings.)

Slow Drag. *(singing)*
>If I had my way
>If I had my way
>If I had my way
>I would tear this old building down.

ACT II

The lights come up in the studio. The musicians are setting up their instruments. Ma Rainey walks about shoeless, singing softly to herself. Levee stands near Dussie Mae, who hikes up her dress and crosses her leg. Cutler speaks to Irvin off to the side.

Cutler. Mr. Irvin, I don't know what you gonna do. I ain't got nothing to do with it, but the boy can't do the part. He stutters. He can't get it right. He stutters right through it every time.

Irvin. Christ! Okay. We'll . . . Shit! We'll just do it like we planned. We'll do Levee's version. I'll handle it, Cutler. Come on, let's go. I'll think of something.

(He exits to the control booth.)

Ma Rainey. *(calling Cutler over)* Levee's got his eyes in the wrong place. You better school him, Cutler.
Cutler. Come on, Levee . . . let's get ready to play! Get your mind on your work!
Irvin. *(over speaker)* Okay, boys, we're gonna do "Moonshine Blues" first. "Moonshine Blues," Ma.
Ma Rainey. I ain't doing no "Moonshine" nothing. I'm doing the "Black Bottom" first. Come on, Sylvester. *(to Irvin)* Where's Sylvester's mike? You need a mike for Sylvester. Irvin . . . get him a mike.
Irvin. Uh . . . Ma, the boys say he can't do it. We'll have to do Levee's version.
Ma Rainey. What you mean he can't do it? Who say he can't do it? What boys say he can't do it?
Irvin. The band, Ma . . . the boys in the band.
Ma Rainey. What band? The band work for me! I say what goes! Cutler, what's he talking about? Levee, this some of your shit?
Irvin. He stutters, Ma. They say he stutters.
Ma Rainey. I don't care if he do. I promised the boy he could do the part . . . and he's gonna do it! That's all there is to it. He don't stutter all the time. Get a microphone down here for him.
Irvin. Ma, we don't have time. We can't . . .
Ma Rainey. If you wanna make a record, you gonna find time. I ain't playing with you, Irvin. I can walk out of here and go back to my tour. I got plenty fans. I don't need to go through all of this. Just go and get the boy a microphone.

(Irvin and Sturdyvant consult in the booth. Irvin exits.)

Sturdyvant. All right, Ma . . . we'll get him a microphone. But if he messes up . . . He's only getting one chance . . . The cost . . .
Ma Rainey. Damn the cost. You always talking about the cost. I make more money for this outfit than anybody else you got put together. If he messes up he'll just do it till he gets it right. Levee, I know you had something to do with this. You better watch yourself.
Levee. It was Cutler!
Sylvester. It was you! You the only one m-m-mad about it.

Levee. The boy stutter. He can't do the part. Everybody see that. I don't know why you want the boy to do the part no ways.
Ma Rainey. Well, can or can't . . . he's gonna do it! You ain't got nothing to do with it!
Levee. I don't care what you do! He can sing the whole goddamned song for all I care!
Ma Rainey. Well, all right. Thank you.

(Irvin enters with a microphone and hooks it up. He exits to the control booth.)

Ma Rainey. Come on, Sylvester. You just stand here and hold your hands like I told you. Just remember the words and say them . . . That's all there is to it. Don't worry about messing up. If you mess up, we'll do it again. Now, let me hear you say it. Play for him, Cutler.
Cutler. One . . . two . . . you know what to do.

(The band begins to play and Sylvester curls his fingers and clasps his hands together in front of his chest, pulling in opposite directions as he says his lines.)

Sylvester. "All right, boys, you d-d-d-done s-s-s-seen the best . . . *(Levee stops playing.)* Now I'm g-g-g-gonna show you the rest . . . Ma R-r-rainey's gonna show you her b-b-b-black b-b-b-bottom."

(The rest of the band stops playing.)

Ma Rainey. That's all right. That's real good. You take your time, you'll get it right.
Sturdyvant. *(over speaker)* Listen, Ma . . . now, when you come in, don't wait so long to come in. Don't take so long on the intro, huh?
Ma Rainey. Sturdyvant, don't you go trying to tell me how to sing. You just take care of that up there and let me take care of this down here. Where's my Coke?
Irvin. Okay, Ma. We're all set up to go up here. "Ma Rainey's Black Bottom," boys.
Ma Rainey. Where's my Coke? I need a Coke. You ain't got no Coke down here? Where's my Coke?
Irvin. What's the matter, Ma? What's . . .
Ma Rainey. Where's my Coke? I need a Coca-Cola.
Irvin. Uh . . . Ma, look, I forgot the Coke, huh? Let's do it without it, huh? Just this one song. What say, boys?
Ma Rainey. Damn what the band say! You know I don't sing nothing without my Coca-Cola!
Sturdyvant. We don't have any, Ma. There's no Coca-Cola here. We're all set up and we'll just go ahead and . . .

Ma Rainey. You supposed to have Coca-Cola. Irvin knew that. I ain't singing nothing without my Coca-Cola!

(She walks away from the mike, singing to herself. Sturdyvant enters from the control booth.)

Sturdyvant. Now, just a minute here, Ma. You come in an hour late . . . we're way behind schedule as it is . . . the band is set up and ready to go . . . I'm burning my lights . . . I've turned up the heat . . . We're ready to make a record and what? You decide you want a Coca-Cola?

Ma Rainey. Sturdyvant, get out of my face. *(Irvin enters.)* Irvin . . . I told you to keep him away from me.

Irvin. Mel, I'll handle it.

Sturdyvant. I'm tired of her nonsense, Irv. I'm not gonna put up with this!

Irvin. Let me handle it, Mel. I know how to handle her. *(Irvin to Ma Rainey)* Look, Ma . . . I'll call down to the deli and get you a Coke. But let's get started, huh? Sylvester's standing there ready to go . . . the band's set up . . . let's do this one song, huh?

Ma Rainey. If you too cheap to buy me a Coke, I'll buy my own. Slow Drag! Sylvester, go with Slow Drag and get me a Coca-Cola. *(Slow Drag comes over.)* Slow Drag, walk down to that store on the corner and get me three bottles of Coca-Cola. Get out of my face, Irvin. You all just wait until I get my Coke. It ain't gonna kill you.

Irvin. Okay, Ma. Get your Coke, for Chrissakes! Get your Coke!

(Irvin and Sturdyvant exit into the hallway followed by Slow Drag and Sylvester. Toledo, Cutler and Levee head for the band room.)

Ma Rainey. Cutler, come here a minute. I want to talk to you. *(Cutler crosses over somewhat reluctantly.)* What's all this about "the boys in the band say"? I tells you what to do. I says what the matter is with the band. I say who can and can't do what.

Cutler. We just say 'cause the boy stutter . . .

Ma Rainey. I know he stutters. Don't you think I know he stutters. This is what's gonna help him.

Cutler. Well, how can he do the part if he stutters? You want him to stutter through it? We just thought it be easier to go on and let Levee do it like we planned.

Ma Rainey. I don't care if he stutters or not! He's doing the part and I don't wanna hear any more of this shit about what the band says. And I want you to find somebody to replace Levee when we get to Memphis. Levee ain't nothing but trouble.

Cutler. Levee's all right. He plays good music when he puts his mind to it. He knows how to write music too.

Ma Rainey. I don't care what he know. He ain't nothing but bad news.

Find somebody else. I know it was his idea about who to say who can do what. *(Dussie Mae wanders over to where they are sitting.)* Dussie Mae, go sit your behind down somewhere and quit flaunting yourself around.

Dussie Mae. I ain't doing nothing.

Ma Rainey. Well, just go on somewhere and stay out of the way.

Cutler. I been meaning to ask you, Ma . . . about these songs. This "Moonshine Blues" . . . that's one of them songs Bessie Smith sang, I believes.

Ma Rainey. Bessie what? Ain't nobody thinking about Bessie. I taught Bessie. She ain't doing nothing but imitating me. What I care about Bessie? I don't care if she sell a million records. She got her people and I got mine. I don't care what nobody else do. Ma was the *first* and don't you forget it!

Cutler. Ain't nobody said nothing about that. I just said that's the same song she sang.

Ma Rainey. I been doing this a long time. Ever since I was a little girl. I don't care what nobody else do. That's what gets me so mad with Irvin. White folks try to be put out with you all the time. Too cheap to buy me a Coca-Cola. I lets them know it, though. Ma don't stand for no shit. Wanna take my voice and trap it in them fancy boxes with all them buttons and dials . . . and then too cheap to buy me a Coca-Cola. And it don't cost but a nickel a bottle.

Cutler. I knows what you mean about that.

Ma Rainey. They don't care nothing about me. All they want is my voice. Well, I done learned that, and they gonna treat me like I want to be treated no matter how much it hurt them. They back there now calling me all kinds of names . . . calling me everything but a child of God. But they can't do nothing else. They ain't got what they wanted yet. As soon as they get my voice down on them recording machines, then it's just like if I'd be some whore and they roll over and put their pants on. Ain't got no use for me then. I know what I'm talking about. You watch Irvin right there with the rest of them. He don't care nothing about me either. He's been my manager for six years, always talking about sticking together, and the only time he had me in his house was to sing for some of his friends.

Cutler. I know how they do.

Ma Rainey. If you colored and can make them some money, then you all right with them. Otherwise, you just a dog in the alley. I done made this company more money from my records than all the other recording artists they got put together. And they wanna balk about how much this session is costing them.

Cutler. I don't see where it's costing them all what they say.

Ma Rainey. It ain't! I don't pay that kind of talk no mind.

(The lights go down on the studio and come up on the band room. Toledo sits reading a newspaper. Levee sings and hums his song.)

Levee. *(singing)*
>You can shake it, you can break it
>You can dance at any hall
>You can slide across the floor
>You'll never have to stall
>My jelly, my roll,
>Sweet Mama, don't you let it fall.

Wait till Sturdyvant hear me play that! I'm talking about some real music, Toledo! I'm talking about *real* music! *(The door opens and Dussie Mae enters.)* Hey, mama! Come on in.

Dussie Mae. Oh, hi! I just wanted to see what it looks like down here.

Levee. Well, come on in . . . I don't bite.

Dussie Mae. I didn't know you could really write music. I thought you was just jiving me at the club last night.

Levee. Naw, baby . . . I knows how to write music. I done give Mr. Sturdyvant some of my songs and he says he's gonna let me record them. Ask Toledo. I'm gonna have my own band! Toledo, ain't I give Mr. Sturdyvant some of my songs I wrote?

Toledo. Don't get Toledo mixed up in nothing.

(He exits.)

Dussie Mae. You gonna get your own band sure enough?

Levee. That's right! Levee Green and his Footstompers.

Dussie Mae. That's real nice.

Levee. That's what I was trying to tell you last night. A man what's gonna get his own band need to have a woman like you.

Dussie Mae. A woman like me wants somebody to bring it and put it in my hand. I don't need nobody wanna get something for nothing and leave me standing in my door.

Levee. That ain't Levee's style, sugar. I got more style than that. I knows how to treat a woman. Buy her presents and things . . . treat her like she wants to be treated.

Dussie Mae. That's what they all say . . . till it come time to be buying the presents.

Levee. When we get down to Memphis, I'm gonna show you what I'm talking about. I'm gonna take you out and show you a good time. Show you Levee knows how to treat a woman.

Dussie Mae. When you getting your own band?

Levee. *(moves closer to slip his arm around her)* Soon as Mr. Sturdyvant say. I done got my fellows already picked out. Getting me some good fellows know how to play real sweet music.

Dussie Mae. *(moves away)* Go on now, I don't go for all that pawing and stuff. When you get your own band, maybe we can see about this stuff you talking.

Levee. *(moving toward her)* I just wanna show you I know what the women like. They don't call me Sweet Lemonade for nothing.

(Levee takes her in his arms and attempts to kiss her.)

Dussie Mae. Stop it now. Somebody's gonna come in here.

Levee. Naw they ain't. Look here, sugar . . . what I wanna know is . . . can I introduce my red rooster to your brown hen?

Dussie Mae. You get your band, then we'll see if that rooster know how to crow.

(He grinds up against her and feels her buttocks.)

Levee. Now I know why my grandpappy sat on the back porch with his straight razor when grandma hung out the wash.

Dussie Mae. Nigger, you crazy!

Levee. I bet you sound like the midnight train from Alabama when it crosses the Mason-Dixon line.

Dussie Mae. How's you get so crazy?

Levee. It's women like you . . . drives me that way.

(He moves to kiss her as the lights go down in the band room and up in the studio. Ma Rainey sits with Cutler and Toledo.)

Ma Rainey. It sure done got quiet in here. I never could stand no silence. I always got to have some music going on in my head somewhere. It keeps things balanced. Music will do that. It fills things up. The more music you got in the world, the fuller it is.

Cutler. I can agree with that. I got to have my music too.

Ma Rainey. White folks don't understand about the blues. They hear it come out, but they don't know how it got there. They don't understand that's life's way of talking. You don't sing to feel better. You sing 'cause that's a way of understanding life.

Cutler. That's right. You get that understanding and you done got a grip on life to where you can hold your head up and go on to see what else life got to offer.

Ma Rainey. The blues help you get out of bed in the morning. You get up knowing you ain't alone. There's something else in the world. Something's been added by that song. This be an empty world without the blues. I take that emptiness and try to fill it up with something.

Toledo. You fill it up with something the people can't be without, Ma.

That's why they call you the Mother of the Blues. You fill up that emptiness in a way ain't nobody ever thought of doing before. And now they can't be without it.

Ma Rainey. I ain't started the blues way of singing. The blues always been here.

Cutler. In the church sometimes you find that way of singing. They got blues in the church.

Ma Rainey. They say I started it . . . but I didn't. I just helped it out. Filled up that empty space a little bit. That's all. But if they wanna call me the Mother of the Blues, that's all right with me. It don't hurt none. *(Slow Drag and Sylvester enter with the Cokes.)* It sure took you long enough. That store ain't but on the corner.

Slow Drag. That one was closed. We had to find another one.

Ma Rainey. Sylvester, go and find Mr. Irvin and tell him we ready to go.

(Sylvester exits. The lights in the band room come up while the lights in the studio stay on. Levee and Dussie Mae are kissing. Slow Drag enters. They break their embrace. Dussie Mae straightens up her clothes.)

Slow Drag. Cold out. I just wanted to warm up with a little sip. *(He goes to his locker, takes out his bottle and drinks.)* Ma got her Coke, Levee. We about ready to start.

(Slow Drag exits. Levee attempts to kiss Dussie Mae again.)

Dussie Mae. No . . . Come on! I got to go. You gonna get me in trouble.

(She pulls away and exits up the stairs. Levee watches after her.)

Levee. Good God! Happy birthday to the lady with the cakes!

(The lights go down in the band room and come up in the studio. Ma Rainey drinks her Coke. Levee enters from the band room. The musicians take their places. Sylvester stands by his mike. Irvin and Sturdyvant look on from the control booth.)

Irvin. We're all set up here, Ma. We're all set to go. You ready down there?

Ma Rainey. Sylvester you just remember your part and say it. That's all there is to it. *(to Irvin)* Yeah, we ready.

Irvin. Okay, boys. "Ma Rainey's Black Bottom." Take one.

Cutler. One . . . two . . . You know what to do.

(The band plays.)

Sylvester. All right boys, you d-d-d-done s-s-seen the rest. . . .

Irvin. Hold it! *(The band stops. Sturdyvant changes the recording disk and nods to Irvin.)* Okay, take two.

Cutler. One . . . two . . . You know what to do.

(The band plays.)

Sylvester. All right, boys, you done seen the rest . . . now I'm gonna show you the best. Ma Rainey's g-g-g-gonna s-s-show you her b-b-black bottom.
Irvin. Hold it! Hold it! *(The band stops. Sturdyvant changes the recording disk.)* Okay. Take Three. Ma, let's do it without the intro, huh? No voice intro . . . you just come in singing.
Ma Rainey. Irvin, I done told you . . . the boy's gonna do the part. He don't stutter all the time. Just give him a chance. Sylvester, hold your hands like I told you and just relax. Just relax and concentrate.
Irvin. All right. Take three.
Cutler. One . . . Two . . . You know what to do.

(The band plays.)

Sylvester. All right, boys, you done seen the rest . . . now, I'm gonna show you the best. Ma Rainey's gonna show you her black bottom.
Ma Rainey. *(singing)*

    Way down south in Alabamy
    I got a friend they call dancing Sammy
    Who's crazy about all the latest dances
    Black Bottom stomping, two babies prancing

    The other night at a swell affair
    As soon as the boys found out that I was there
    They said, come on, Ma, let's go to the cabaret.
    When I got there, you ought to hear them say,

    I want to see the dance you call the black bottom
    I want to learn that dance
    I want to see the dance you call your big black bottom
    It'll put you in a trance.

    All the boys in the neighborhood
    They say your black bottom is really good
    Come on and show me your black bottom
    I want to learn that dance

    I want to see the dance you call the black bottom
    I want to learn that dance
    Come on and show the dance you call your big black bottom
    It puts you in a trance.

    Early last morning about the break of day
    Grandpa told my grandma, I heard him say,

>   Get up and show your old man your black bottom
>   I want to learn that dance.

(instrumental break)

>   I done showed you all my black bottom
>   You ought to learn that dance.

Irvin. Okay, that's good, Ma. That sounded great! Good job, boys!
Ma Rainey. *(to Sylvester)* See! I told you. I knew you could do it. You just have to put your mind to it. Didn't he do good, Cutler? Sound real good. I told him he could do it.
Cutler. He sure did. He did better than I thought he was gonna do.
Irvin. *(entering to remove Sylvester's mike)* Okay, boys . . . Ma . . . let's do "Moonshine Blues" next, huh? "Moonshine Blues," boys.
Sturdyvant. *(over speaker)* Irv! Something's wrong down there. We don't have it right.
Irvin. What? What's the matter Mel . . .
Sturdyvant. We don't have it right. Something happened. We don't have the goddamn song recorded!
Irvin. What's the matter? Mel, what happened? You sure you don't have nothing?
Sturdyvant. Check that mike, huh, Irv. It's the kid's mike. Something's wrong with the mike. We've got everything all screwed up here.
Irvin. Christ almighty! Ma, we got to do it again. We don't have it. We didn't record the song.
Ma Rainey. What you mean you didn't record it? What was you and Sturdyvant doing up there?
Irvin. *(following the mike wire)* Here . . . Levee must have kicked the plug out.
Levee. I ain't done nothing; I ain't kicked nothing!
Slow Drag. If Levee had his mind on what he's doing . . .
Ma Rainey. Levee, if it ain't one thing, it's another. You better straighten yourself up!
Levee. Hell . . . it ain't my fault. I ain't done nothing!
Sturdyvant. What's the matter with that mike, Irv? What's the problem?
Irvin. It's the cord, Mel. The cord's all chewed up. We need another cord.
Ma Rainey. This is the most disorganized . . . Irvin, I'm going home! Come on. Come on, Dussie.

(Ma Rainey walks past Sturdyvant as he enters from the control booth. She exits offstage to get her coat.)

Sturdyvant. *(to Irvin)* Where's she going?
Irvin. She said she's going home.

Sturdyvant. Irvin, you get her! If she walks out of here . . .

(Ma Rainey enters carrying her and Dussie Mae's coats.)

Ma Rainey. Come on, Sylvester.
Irvin. *(helping her with her coat)* Ma . . . Ma . . . listen. Fifteen minutes? All I ask is fifteen minutes!
Ma Rainey. Come on, Sylvester, get your coat.
Sturdyvant. Ma, if you walk out of this studio . . .
Irvin. Fifteen minutes, Ma!
Sturdyvant. You'll be through . . . washed up! If you walk out on me . . .
Irvin. Mel, for Chrissakes, shut up and let me handle it! *(He goes after Ma Rainey, who has started for the door.)* Ma, listen! These records are gonna be hits! They're gonna sell like crazy! Hell, even Sylvester will be a star. Fifteen minutes. That's all, I'm asking! Fifteen minutes.
Ma Rainey. *(crosses to a chair and sits with her coat on)* Fifteen minutes! You hear me, Irvin? Fifteen minutes . . . and then I'm gonna take my black bottom on back down to Georgia. Fifteen minutes. Then Madame Rainey is leaving!
Irvin. *(kisses her)* All right, Ma . . . fifteen minutes. I promise. *(to the band)* You boys go ahead and take a break. Fifteen minutes and we'll be ready to go.
Cutler. Slow Drag, you got any of that bourbon left?
Slow Drag. Yeah, there's some down there.
Cutler. I could use a little nip.

(Cutler and Slow Drag exit to the band room, followed by Levee and Toledo. The lights go down in the studio and up in the band room.)

Slow Drag. Don't make me no difference if she leave or not. I was kinda hoping she would leave.
Cutler. I'm like Mr. Irvin . . . After all this time we done put in here, it's best to go ahead and get something out of it.
Toledo. Ma gonna do what she wanna do, that's for sure. If I was Mr. Irvin, I'd best go and get them cords and things hooked up right. And I wouldn't take no longer than fifteen minutes doing it.
Cutler. If Levee had his mind on his work, we wouldn't be in this fix. We'd be up there finishing up. Now we got to go back and see if that boy get that part right. Ain't no telling if he ever get that right again in his life.
Levee. Hey, Levee ain't done nothing!
Slow Drag. Levee up there got one eye on the gal and the other on his trumpet.
Cutler. Nigger, don't you know that's Ma's gal?
Levee. I don't care whose gal it is. I ain't done nothing to her. I just talk to her like I talk to anybody else.

Cutler. Well, that being Ma's gal, and that being that boy's gal, is one and two different things. The boy is liable to kill you . . . but you' ass gonna be out there scraping the concrete looking for a job if you messing with Ma's gal.

Levee. How am I messing with her? I ain't done nothing to the gal. I just asked her her name. Now, if you telling me I can't do that, then Ma will just have to go to hell.

Cutler. All I can do is warn you.

Slow Drag. Let him hang himself, Cutler. Let him string his neck out.

Levee. I ain't done nothing to the gal! You all talk like I done went and done something to her. Leave me go with my business.

Cutler. I'm through with it. Try and talk to a fool . . .

Toledo. Some mens got it worse than others . . . this foolishness I'm talking about. Some mens is excited to be fools. That excitement is something else. I know about it. I done experienced it. It makes you feel good to be a fool. But it don't last long. It's over in a minute. Then you got to tend with the consequences. You got to tend with what comes after. That's when you wish you had learned something about it.

Levee. That's the best sense you made all day. Talking about being a fool. That's the only sensible thing you said today. Admitting you was a fool.

Toledo. I admits it, all right. Ain't nothing wrong with it. I done been a little bit of everything.

Levee. Now you're talking. You's as big a fool as they make.

Toledo. Gonna be a bit more things before I'm finished with it. Gonna be foolish again. But I ain't never been the same fool twice. I might be a different kind of fool, but I ain't gonna be the same fool twice. That's where we parts ways.

Slow Drag. Toledo, you done been a fool about a woman?

Toledo. Sure. Sure I have. Same as everybody.

Slow Drag. Hell, I ain't never seen you mess with no woman. I thought them books was your woman.

Toledo. Sure I messed with them. Done messed with a whole heap of them. And gonna mess with some more. But I ain't gonna be no fool about them. What you think? I done come in the world full-grown, with my head in a book? I done been young. Married. Got kids. I done been around and I done loved women to where you shake in your shoes just at the sight of them. Feel it all up and down your spine.

Slow Drag. I didn't know you was married.

Toledo. Sure. Legally. I been married legally. Got the papers and all. I done been through life. Made my marks. Followed some signs on the road. Ignored some others. I done been all through it. I touched and been touched by it. But I ain't never been the same fool twice. That's what I can say.

Levee. But you been a fool. That's what counts. Talking about I'm a fool for asking the gal her name and here you is one yourself.

Toledo. Now, I married a woman. A good woman. To this day I can't say she wasn't a good woman. I can't say nothing bad about her. I married that woman with all the good graces and intentions of being hooked up and bound to her for the rest of my life. I was looking for her to put me in my grave. But, you see . . . it ain't all the time what you' intentions and wishes are. She went out and joined the church. All right. There ain't nothing wrong with that. A good Christian woman going to church and wanna do right by her god. There ain't nothing wrong with that. But she got up there, got to seeing them good Christian mens and wondering why I ain't like that. Soon she figure she got a heathen on her hands. She figured she couldn't live like that. The church was more important than I was. So she left. Packed up one day and moved out. To this day I ain't never said another word to her. Come home one day and my house was empty! And I sat down and figured out that I was a fool not to see that she needed something that I wasn't giving her. Else she wouldn't have been up there at the church in the first place. I ain't blaming her. I just said it wasn't gonna happen to me again. So, yeah, Toledo been a fool about a woman. That's part of making life.

Cutler. Well, yeah, I been a fool too. Everybody done been a fool once or twice. But, you see, Toledo, what you call a fool and what I call a fool is two different things. I can't see where you was being a fool for that. You ain't done nothing foolish. You can't help what happened, and I wouldn't call you a fool for it. A fool is responsible for what happens to him. A fool cause it to happen. Like Levee . . . if he keeps messing with Ma's gal and his feet be out there scraping the ground. That's a fool.

Levee. Ain't nothing gonna happen to Levee. Levee ain't gonna let nothing happen to him. Now. I'm gonna say it again. I asked the gal her name. That's all I done. And if that's being a fool, then you looking at the biggest fool in the world . . . 'cause I sure as hell asked her.

Slow Drag. You just better not let Ma see you ask her. That's what the man's trying to tell you.

Levee. I don't need nobody to tell me nothing.

Cutler. Well, Toledo, all I gots to say is that from the looks of it . . . from your story . . . I don't think life did you fair.

Toledo. Oh, life is fair. It's just in the taking what it gives you.

Levee. Life ain't shit. You can put it in a paper bag and carry it around with you. It ain't got no balls. Now, death . . . death got some style! Death will kick your ass and make you wish you never been born! That's how bad death is! But you can rule over life. Life ain't nothing.

Toledo. Cutler, how's your brother doing?

Cutler. Who, Nevada? Oh, he's doing all right. Staying in St. Louis. Got a bunch of kids, last I heard.

Toledo. Me and him was all right with each other. Done a lot of farming together down in Plattsville.

Cutler. Yeah, I know you all was tight. He in St. Louis now. Running an elevator, last I hear about it.

Slow Drag. That's better than stepping in muleshit.

Toledo. Oh, I don't know now. I liked farming. Get out there in the sun . . . smell that dirt. Be out there by yourself . . . nice and peaceful. Yeah, farming was all right by me. Sometimes I think I'd like to get me a little old place . . . but I done got too old to be following behind one of them balky mules now.

Levee. Nigger talking about life is fair. And ain't got a pot to piss in.

Toledo. See, now, I'm gonna tell you something. A nigger gonna be dissatisfied no matter what. Give a nigger some bread and butter . . . and he'll cry 'cause he ain't got no jelly. Give him some jelly, and he'll cry 'cause he ain't got no knife to put it on with. If there's one thing I done learned in this life, it's that you can't satisfy a nigger no matter what you do. A nigger's gonna make his own dissatisfaction.

Levee. Niggers got a right to be dissatisfied. Is you gonna be satisfied with a bone somebody done throwed you when you see them eating the whole hog?

Toledo. You lucky they let you be an entertainer. They ain't got to accept your way of entertaining. You lucky and don't even know it. You's entertaining and the rest of the people is hauling wood. That's the only kind of job for the colored man.

Slow Drag. Ain't nothing wrong with hauling wood. I done hauled plenty wood. My daddy used to haul wood. Ain't nothing wrong with that. That's honest work.

Levee. That ain't what I'm talking about. I ain't talking about hauling no wood. I'm talking about being satisfied with a bone somebody done throwed you. That's what's the matter with you all. You satisfied sitting in one place. You got to move on down the road from where you sitting . . . and all the time you got to keep an eye out for that devil who's looking to buy up souls. And hope you get lucky and find him!

Cutler. I done told you about that blasphemy. Talking about selling your soul to the devil.

Toledo. We done the same thing, Cutler. There ain't no difference. We done sold Africa for the price of tomatoes. We done sold ourselves to the white man in order to be like him. Look at the way you dressed . . . That ain't African. That's the white man. We trying to be just like him. We done sold who we are in order to become someone else. We's imitation white men.

Cutler. What else we gonna be, living over here?

Levee. I'm Levee. Just me. I ain't no imitation nothing!

Slow Drag. You can't change who you are by how you dress. That's what I got to say.

Toledo. It ain't all how you dress. It's how you act, how you see the world. It's how you follow life.

Levee. It don't matter what you talking about. I ain't no imitation white man. And I don't want to be no white man. As soon as I get my band together and make them records like Mr. Sturdyvant done told me I can make, I'm gonna be like Ma and tell the white man just what he can do. Ma tell Mr. Irvin she gonna leave . . . and Mr. Irvin get down on his knees and beg her to stay! That's the way I'm gonna be! Make the white man respect me!

Cutler. The white man don't care nothing about Ma. The colored folks made Ma a star. White folks don't care nothing about who she is . . . what kind of music she make.

Slow Drag. That's the truth about that. You let her go down to one of them white-folks hotels and see how big she is.

Cutler. Hell, she ain't got to do that. She can't even get a cab up here in the North. I'm gonna tell you something. Reverend Gates . . . you know Reverend Gates? . . . Slow Drag know who I'm talking about. Reverend Gates . . . now I'm gonna show you how this go where the white man don't care a thing about who you is. Reverend Gates was coming from Tallahassee to Atlanta, going to see his sister, who was sick at that time with the consumption. The train come up through Thomasville, then past Moultrie, and stopped in this little town called Sigsbee . . .

Levee. You can stop telling that right there! That train don't stop in Sigsbee. I know what train you talking about. That train got four stops before it reach Macon to go on to Atlanta. One in Thomasville, one in Moultrie, one in Cordele . . . and it stop in Centerville.

Cutler. Nigger, I know what I'm talking about. You gonna tell me where the train stop?

Levee. Hell, yeah, if you talking about it stop in Sigsbee. I'm gonna tell you the truth.

Cutler. I'm talking about *this* train! I don't know what train you been riding. I'm talking about *this* train!

Levee. Ain't but one train. Ain't but one train come out of Tallahassee heading north to Atlanta, and it don't stop at Sigsbee. Tell him, Toledo . . . that train don't stop at Sigsbee. The only train that stops at Sigsbee is the Yazoo Delta, and you have to transfer at Moultrie to get it!

Cutler. Well, hell, maybe that what he done! I don't know. I'm just telling you the man got off the train at Sigsbee . . .

Levee. All right . . . you telling it. Tell it your way. Just make up anything.
Slow Drag. Levee, leave the man alone and let him finish.
Cutler. I ain't paying Levee no never mind.
Levee. Go on and tell it your way.
Cutler. Anyway . . . Reverend Gates got off this train in Sigsbee. The train done stopped there and he figured he'd get off and check the schedule to be sure he arrive in time for somebody to pick him up. All right. While he's there checking the schedule, it come upon him that he had to go to the bathroom. Now, they ain't had no colored rest rooms at the station. The only colored rest room is an outhouse they got sitting way back two hundred yards or so from the station. All right. He in the outhouse and the train go off and leave him there. He don't know nothing about this town. Ain't never been there before—in fact, ain't never even heard of it before.
Levee. I heard of it! I know just where it's at . . . and he ain't got off no train coming out of Tallahassee in Sigsbee!
Cutler. The man standing there, trying to figure out what he's gonna do . . . where this train done left him in this strange town. It started getting dark. He see where the sun's getting low in the sky and he's trying to figure out what he's gonna do, when he noticed a couple of white fellows standing across the street from this station. Just standing there, watching him. And then two or three more come up and joined the other one. He look around; ain't seen no colored folks nowhere. He didn't know what was getting in these here fellows' minds, so he commence to walking. He ain't knowed where he was going. He just walking down the railroad tracks when he hear them call him. "Hey, nigger!" See, just like that, "Hey, nigger!" He kept on walking. They called him some more and he just keep walking. Just going down the tracks. And then he heard a gunshot where somebody done fired a gun in the air. He stopped then, you know.
Toledo. You don't even have to tell me no more. I know the facts of it. I done heard the same story a hundred times. It happened to me too. Same thing.
Cutler. Naw, I'm gonna show you how the white folks don't care nothing about who or what you is. They crowded around him. These gang of mens made a circle around him. Now, he's standing there, you understand . . . got his cross around his neck like them preachers wear. Had his little Bible with him what he carry all the time. So they crowd on around him and one of them ask who he is. He told them he was Reverend Gates and that he was going to see his sister who was sick and the train left without him. And they said, "Yeah, nigger . . . but can you dance?" He looked at them and commenced to dancing. One of them reached up and tore his cross off his neck. Said he was committing

heresy by dancing with a cross and Bible. Took his Bible and tore it up and had him dancing till they got tired of watching him.

Slow Drag. White folks ain't never had no respect for the colored minister.

Cutler. That's the only way he got out of there alive . . . was to dance. Ain't even had no respect for a man of God! Wanna make him into a clown. Reverend Gates sat right in my house and told me that story from his own mouth. So . . . the white folks don't care nothing about Ma Rainey. She's just another nigger who they can use to make some money.

Levee. What I wants to know is . . . if he's a man of God, then where the hell was God when all of this was going on? Why wasn't God looking out for him? Why didn't God strike down them crackers with some of this lightning you talk about to me?

Cutler. Levee, you gonna burn in hell.

Levee. What I care about burning in hell? You talk like a fool . . . burning in hell. Why didn't God strike some of them crackers down? Tell me that! That's the question! Don't come telling me this burning-in-hell shit! He a man of God . . . why didn't God strike some of them crackers down? I'll tell you why! I'll tell you the truth! It's sitting out there as plain as day! 'Cause he a white man's God. That's why! God ain't never listened to no nigger's prayers. God take a nigger's prayers and throw them in the garbage. God don't pay niggers no mind. In fact . . . God hate niggers! Hate them with all the fury in his heart. Jesus don't love you, nigger! Jesus hate your black ass! Come talking that shit to me. Talking about burning in hell! God can kiss my ass.

(Cutler can stand no more. He jumps up and punches Levee in the mouth. The force of the blow knocks Levee down and Cutler jumps on him.)

Cutler. You worthless . . . That's my God! That's my God! That's my God! You wanna blaspheme my God!

(Toledo and Slow Drag grab Cutler and try to pull him off Levee.)

Slow Drag. Come on, Cutler . . . let it go! It don't mean nothing!

(Cutler has Levee down on the floor and pounds on him with a fury.)

Cutler. Wanna blaspheme my God! You worthless . . . talking about my God!

(Toledo and Slow Drag succeed in pulling Cutler off Levee, who is bleeding at the nose and mouth.)

Levee. Naw, let him go! Let him go! *(He pulls out a knife.)* That's your God, huh? That's your God, huh? Is that right? Your God, huh? All right. I'm gonna give your God a chance. I'm gonna give your God a chance. I'm gonna give him a chance to save your black ass.

(Levee circles Cutler with the knife. Cutler picks up a chair to protect himself.)

Toledo. Come on, Levee . . . put the knife up!
Levee. Stay out of this, Toledo!
Toledo. That ain't no way to solve nothing.

(Levee alternately swipes at Cutler during the following.)

Levee. I'm calling Cutler's God! I'm talking to Cutler's God! You hear me? Cutler's God! I'm calling Cutler's God. Come on and save this nigger! Strike me down before I cut his throat!
Slow Drag. Watch him, Cutler! Put that knife up, Levee!
Levee. *(to Cutler)* I'm calling your God! I'm gonna give him a chance to save you! I'm calling your God! We gonna find out whose God he is!
Cutler. You gonna burn in hell, nigger!
Levee. Cutler's God! Come on and save this nigger! Come on and save him like you did my mama! Save him like you did my mama! I heard her when she called you! I heard her when she said, "Lord, have mercy! Jesus, help me! Please, God, have mercy on me, Lord Jesus, help me!" And did you turn your back? Did you turn your back, motherfucker? Did you turn your back? *(Levee becomes so caught up in his dialogue with God that he forgets about Cutler and begins to stab upward in the air, trying to reach God.)* Come on! Come on and turn your back on me! Turn your back on me! Come on! Where is you? Come on and turn your back on me! Turn your back on me, motherfucker! I'll cut your heart out! Come on, turn your back on me! Come on! What's the matter? Where is you? Come on and turn your back on me! Come on, what you scared of? Turn your back on me! Come on! Coward, motherfucker! *(Levee folds his knife and stands triumphantly.)* Your God ain't shit, Cutler.

(The lights fade to black.)

Ma Rainey. *(singing)*
> Ah, you hear me talking to you
> I don't bite my tongue
> You wants to be my man
> You got to fetch it with you when you come.

(Lights come up in the studio. The last bars of the last song of the session are dying out.)

Irvin. *(over speaker)* Good! Wonderful! We have that, boys. Good session. That's great, Ma. We've got ourselves some winners.
Toledo. Well, I'm glad that's over.
Ma Rainey. Slow Drag, where you learn to play the bass at? You had it singing! I heard you! Had that bass jumping all over the place.
Slow Drag. I was following Toledo. Nigger got them long fingers striding all over the piano. I was trying to keep up with him.
Toledo. That's what you supposed to do, ain't it? Play the music. Ain't nothing abstract about it.
Ma Rainey. Cutler, you hear Slow Drag on that bass? He make it do what he want it to do! Spank it just like you spank a baby.
Cutler. Don't be telling him that. Nigger's head get so big his hat won't fit him.
Slow Drag. If Cutler tune that guitar up, we would really have something!
Cutler. You wouldn't know what a tuned-up guitar sounded like if you heard one.
Toledo. Cutler was talking. I heard him moaning. He was all up in it.
Ma Rainey. Levee . . . what is that you doing? Why you playing all them notes? You play ten notes for every one you supposed to play. It don't call for that.
Levee. You supposed to improvise on the theme. That's what I was doing.
Ma Rainey. You supposed to play the song the way I sing it. The way everybody else play it. You ain't supposed to go off by yourself and play what you want.
Levee. I was playing the song. I was playing it the way I felt it.
Ma Rainey. I couldn't keep up with what was going on. I'm trying to sing the song and you up there messing up my ear. That's what you was doing. Call yourself playing music.
Levee. Hey . . . I know what I'm doing. I know what I'm doing, all right. I know how to play music. You all back up and leave me alone about my music.
Cutler. I done told you . . . it ain't about *your* music. It's about *Ma's* music.
Ma Rainey. That's all right, Cutler. I done told you what to do.
Levee. I don't care what you do. You supposed to improvise on the theme. Not play note for note the same thing over and over again.
Ma Rainey. You just better watch yourself. You hear me?
Levee. What I care what you or Cutler do? Come telling me to watch myself. What's that supposed to mean?
Ma Rainey. All right . . . you gonna find out what it means.
Levee. Go ahead and fire me. I don't care. I'm gonna get my own band anyway.
Ma Rainey. You keep messing with me.

Levee. Ain't nobody studying you. You ain't gonna do nothing to me. Ain't nobody gonna do nothing to Levee.
Ma Rainey. All right, nigger . . . you fired!
Levee. You think I care about being fired? I don't care nothing about that. You doing me a favor.
Ma Rainey. Cutler, Levee's out! He don't play in my band no more.
Levee. I'm fired . . . Good! Best thing that ever happened to me. I don't need this shit!

(Levee exits to the band room. Irvin enters from the control booth.)

Ma Rainey. Cutler, I'll see you back at the hotel.
Irvin. Okay, boys . . . you can pack up. I'll get your money for you.
Cutler. That's cash money, Mr. Irvin. I don't want no check.
Irvin. I'll see what I can do. I can't promise you nothing.
Cutler. As long as it ain't no check. I ain't got no use for a check.
Irvin. I'll see what I can do, Cutler. *(Cutler, Toledo, and Slow Drag exit to the band room.)* Oh, Ma, listen . . . I talked to Sturdyvant, and he said . . . Now, I tried to talk him out of it . . . He said the best he can do is to take twenty-five dollars of your money and give it to Sylvester.
Ma Rainey. Take what and do what? If I wanted the boy to have twenty-five dollars of my money, I'd give it to him. He supposed to get his own money. He supposed to get paid like everybody else.
Irvin. Ma, I talked to him . . . He said . . .
Ma Rainey. Go talk to him again! Tell him if he don't pay that boy, he'll never make another record of mine again. Tell him that. You supposed to be my manager. All this talk about sticking together. Start sticking! Go on up there and get that boy his money!
Irvin. Okay, Ma . . . I'll talk to him again. I'll see what I can do.
Ma Rainey. Ain't no see about it! You bring that boy's money back here!

(Irvin exits. The lights stay on in the studio and come up in the band room. The men have their instruments packed and sit waiting for Irvin to come and pay them. Slow Drag has a pack of cards.)

Slow Drag. Come on, Levee, let me show you a card trick.
Levee. I don't want to see no card trick. What you wanna show me for? Why you wanna bother me with that?
Slow Drag. I was just trying to be nice.
Levee. I don't need you to be nice to me. What I need you to be nice to me for? I ain't gonna be nice to you. I ain't even gonna let you be in my band no more.
Slow Drag. Toledo, let me show you a card trick.
Cutler. I just hope Mr. Irvin don't bring no check down here. What the hell I'm gonna do with a check?

Slow Drag. All right now . . . pick a card. Any card . . . go on . . . take any of them. I'm gonna show you something.
Toledo. I agrees with you, Cutler. I don't want no check either.
Cutler. It don't make no sense to give a nigger a check.
Slow Drag. Okay, now. Remember your card. Remember which one you got. Now . . . put it back in the deck. Anywhere you want. I'm gonna show you something. *(Toledo puts the card in the deck.)* You remember your card? All right. Now I'm gonna shuffle the deck. Now . . . I'm gonna show you what card you picked. Don't say nothing now. I'm gonna tell you what card you picked.
Cutler. Slow Drag, that trick is as old as my mama.
Slow Drag. Naw, naw . . . wait a minute! I'm gonna show him his card . . . There it go! The six of diamonds. Ain't that your card? Ain't that it?
Toledo. Yeah, that's it . . . the six of diamonds.
Slow Drag. Told you! Told you I'd show him what it was!

(The lights fade in the band room and come up full on the studio. Sturdyvant enters with Irvin.)

Sturdyvant. Ma, is there something wrong? Is there a problem?
Ma Rainey. Sturdyvant, I want you to pay that boy his money.
Sturdyvant. Sure, Ma. I got it right here. Two hundred for you and twenty-five for the kid, right? *(Sturdyvant hands the money to Irvin, who hands it to Ma Rainey and Sylvester.)* Irvin misunderstood me. It was all a mistake. Irv made a mistake.
Ma Rainey. A mistake, huh?
Irvin. Sure, Ma. I made a mistake. He's paid, right? I straightened it out.
Ma Rainey. The only mistake was when you found out I hadn't signed the release forms. That was the mistake. Come on, Sylvester.

(She starts to exit.)

Sturdyvant. Hey, Ma . . . come on, sign the forms, huh?
Irvin. Ma . . . come on now.
Ma Rainey. Get your coat, Sylvester. Irvin, where's my car?
Irvin. It's right out front, Ma. Here . . . I got the keys right here. Come on, sign the forms, huh?
Ma Rainey. Irvin, give me my car keys!
Irvin. Sure, Ma . . . just sign the forms, huh?

(He gives her the keys, expecting a trade-off.)

Ma Rainey. Send them to my address and I'll get around to them.
Irvin. Come on, Ma . . . I took care of everything, right? I straightened everything out.
Ma Rainey. Give me the pen, Irvin. *(She signs the forms.)* You tell

Sturdyvant . . . one more mistake like that and I can make my records someplace else. *(She turns to exit.)* Sylvester, straighten up your clothes. Come on, Dussie Mae.

(She exits, followed by Dussie Mae and Sylvester. The lights go down in the studio and come up on the band room.)

Cutler. I know what's keeping him so long. He up there writing out checks. You watch. I ain't gonna stand for it. He ain't gonna bring me no check down here. If he do, he's gonna take it right back upstairs and get some cash.

Toledo. Don't get yourself all worked up about it. Wait and see. Think positive.

Cutler. I am thinking positive. He positively gonna give me some cash. Man give me a check last time . . . you remember . . . we went all over Chicago trying to get it cashed. See a nigger with a check, the first thing they think is he done stole it someplace.

Levee. I ain't had no trouble cashing mine.

Cutler. I don't visit no whorehouses.

Levee. You don't know about my business. So don't start nothing. I'm tired of you as it is. I ain't but two seconds off your ass no way.

Toledo. Don't you all start nothing now.

Cutler. What the hell I care what you tired of. I wasn't even talking to you. I was talking to this man right here.

(Irvin and Sturdyvant enter.)

Irvin. Okay, boys. Mr. Sturdyvant has your pay.

Cutler. As long as it's cash money, Mr. Sturdyvant. 'Cause I have too much trouble trying to cash a check.

Sturdyvant. Oh, yes . . . I'm aware of that. Mr. Irvin told me you boys prefer cash, and that's what I have for you. *(He starts handing out the money.)* That was a good session you boys put in . . . That's twenty-five for you. Yessir, you boys really know your business and we are going to . . . Twenty-five for you . . . We are going to get you back in here real soon . . . twenty-five . . . and have another session so you can make some more money . . . and twenty-five for you. Okay, thank you, boys. You can get your things together and Mr. Irvin will make sure you find your way out.

Irvin. I'll be out front when you get your things together, Cutler.

(Irvin exits. Sturdyvant starts to follow.)

Levee. Mr. Sturdyvant, sir. About them songs I give you? . . .

Sturdyvant. Oh, yes, . . . uh . . . Levee. About them songs you gave me.

I've thought about it and I just don't think the people will buy them. They're not the type of songs we're looking for.

Levee. Mr. Sturdyvant, sir . . . I done got my band picked out and they's real good fellows. They knows how to play real good. I know if the peoples hear the music, they'll buy it.

Sturdyvant. Well, Levee. I'll be fair with you . . . but they're just not the right songs.

Levee. Mr. Sturdyvant, you got to understand about that music. That music is what the people is looking for. They's tired of jug-band music. They wants something that excites them. Something with some fire to it.

Sturdyvant. Okay, Levee. I'll tell you what I'll do. I'll give you five dollars apiece for them. Now that's the best I can do.

Levee. I don't want no five dollars, Mr. Sturdyvant. I wants to record them songs, like you say.

Sturdyvant. Well, Levee, like I say . . . they just aren't the kind of songs we're looking for.

Levee. Mr. Sturdyvant, you asked me to write them songs. Now, why didn't you tell me that before when I first give them to you? You told me you was gonna let me record them. What's the difference between then and now?

Sturdyvant. Well, look . . . I'll pay you for your trouble . . .

Levee. What's the difference, Mr. Sturdyvant? That's what I wanna know.

Sturdyvant. I had my fellows play your songs, and when I heard them, they just didn't sound like the kind of songs I'm looking for right now.

Levee. You got to hear *me* play them, Mr. Sturdyvant! You ain't heard *me* play them. That's what's gonna make them sound right.

Sturdyvant. Well, Levee, I don't doubt that really. It's just that . . . well, I don't think they'd sell like Ma's records. But I'll take them off your hands for you.

Levee. The people's tired of jug-band music, Mr. Sturdyvant. They wants something that's gonna excite them! They wants something with some fire! I don't know what fellows you had playing them songs . . . but if I could play them! I'd set them down in the people's lap! Now you told me I could record them songs!

Sturdyvant. Well, there's nothing I can do about that. Like I say, it's five dollars apiece. That's what I'll give you. I'm doing you a favor. Now, if you write any more, I'll help you out and take them off your hands. The price is five dollars apiece. Just like now.

(*He attempts to hand Levee the money, finally shoves it in Levee's coat pocket and is gone in a flash. Levee follows him to the door and it slams in his face. He takes the money from his pocket, balls it up and throws it on the floor. The other musicians silently gather up their belongings. Toledo walks past Levee and steps on his shoe.*)

Levee. Hey! Watch it . . . Shit Toledo! You stepped on my shoe!
Toledo. Excuse me there, Levee.
Levee. Look at that! Look at that! Nigger, you stepped on my shoe. What you do that for?
Toledo. I said I'm sorry.
Levee. Nigger gonna step on my goddamn shoe! You done fucked up my shoe! Look at that! Look at what you done to my shoe, nigger! I ain't stepped on your shoe! What you wanna step on my shoe for?
Cutler. The man said he's sorry.
Levee. Sorry! How the hell he gonna be sorry after he gone ruint my shoe? Come talking about sorry! *(turns his attention back to Toledo)* Nigger, you stepped on my shoe! You know that! *(Levee snatches his shoe off his foot and holds it up for Toledo to see.)* See what you done done?
Toledo. What you want me to do about it? It's done now. I said excuse me.
Levee. Wanna go and fuck up my shoe like that. I ain't done nothing to your shoe. Look at this!

(Toledo turns and continues to gather up his things. Levee spins him around by his shoulder.)

Levee. Naw . . . naw . . . look what you done! *(He shoves the shoe in Toledo's face.)* Look at that! That's my shoe! Look at that! You did it! You did it! You fucked up my shoe! You stepped on my shoe with them raggedy-ass clodhoppers!
Toledo. Nigger, ain't nobody studying you and your shoe! I said excuse me. If you can't accept that, then the hell with it. What you want me to do?

(Levee is in a near rage, breathing hard. He is trying to get a grip on himself, as even he senses, or perhaps only he senses, he is about to lose control. He looks around, uncertain of what to do. Toledo has gone back to packing, as have Cutler and Slow Drag. They purposefully avoid looking at Levee in hopes he'll calm down if he doesn't have an audience. All the weight in the world suddenly falls on Levee and he rushes at Toledo with his knife in his hand.)

Levee. Nigger, you stepped on my shoe! *(He plunges the knife into Toledo's back up to the hilt. Toledo lets out a sound of surprise and agony. Cutler and Slow Drag freeze. Toledo falls backward with Levee, his hand still on the knife, holding him up. Levee is suddenly faced with the realization of what he has done. He shoves Toledo forward and takes a step back. Toledo slumps to the floor.)* He . . . he stepped on my shoe. He did. Honest, Cutler, he stepped on my shoe. What he do that for? Toledo, what you do that for? Cutler, help me. He stepped on my shoe, Cutler. *(He turns his attention to Toledo.)* Toledo! Toledo, get up. *(He crosses to Toledo and tries to pick him up.)* It's okay, Toledo. Come on . . . I'll help you. Come on, stand up now. Levee'll help you. *(Toledo is limp and heavy and awkward. He slumps back to the floor. Levee gets mad at him.)* Don't look at me like that! Toledo! Nigger, don't look at me like that! I'm warning you, nigger! Close your eyes! Don't you look at me like that! *(He turns to Cutler.)* Tell him to close his eyes, Cutler. Tell him don't look at me like that.

Cutler. Slow Drag, get Mr. Irvin down here.

(The sound of a trumpet is heard, Levee's trumpet, a muted trumpet struggling for the highest of possibilities and blowing pain and warning.)

(Black out)

Miss Honey's Young'uns (1966 as The Mau Mau Room; rev. 1989)

J. e Franklin (b. 1937–   )

Born in Houston, Texas, J. e Franklin earned a bachelor of arts degree from the University of Texas (Austin) in 1964 and has studied further at Union Theological Seminary. A lecturer at Herbert Lehman College of the City University of New York from 1969 to 1975, she has served as a resident director at Skidmore College; as a playwright-in-residence at the Phoenix Theatre and the Rites & Reason Theatre of Brown University; and as a visiting professor of playwriting and dramatic literature at the University of Iowa. Recipient of a Rockefeller Fellowship, two Creative Artists grants from the New York State Council on the Arts, and fellowships from both the National Endowment for the Arts and the New York Foundation for the Arts, Ms. Franklin earned her first major attention as a playwright with *Black Girl* (1971), which earned her a 1972 New York Drama Desk Award. *Black Girl* was later made into a motion picture. Ms. Franklin has published a nonfiction book, *Black Girl: From Genesis to Revelations,* about the development of that drama from video to stage and screen. Ms. Franklin is the 1992–93 winner of The John F. Kennedy Center's New American Play Award, a joint project of The American Express Company and The President's Committee on the Arts and the Humanities.

Set in the 1960s, *Miss Honey's Young'uns* tells the story of a young undergraduate's spiritual struggle with the racially charged ideologies that inform the desegregation process at a southern university. In this play, Ms. Franklin explores the values held by the African American elder and the role these values play in determining responses to oppression.

Selected Plays by J. e Franklin

Christchild (1981; rev. 1989).
Grey Panthers (two decatets, 1989, 1990, 1991, 1992).
The Hand-Me Downs (1979; rev. 1992).
The In-Crowd (1965; rev. 1977).
Liars Die (1978).
Miss Honey's Young'uns (1966 as *The Mau Mau Room*; rev. 1989).
Whistling Girls and Crowing Hens (1983).
Miss N'Victas (1977 as *Another Morning Rising*; rev. 1981, 1985).

Miss Honey's Young'uns
A Drama in Seven Rituals

CHARACTERS
(Cast in Order of Appearance)

Miss Honey
Evelyn
Berna Mae
Janice
Veena
Cordell
Falvie
Winston
Jimmy
Mavis

RITUAL I
· · · · · ·

The setting is an old plantation house, no longer elegant.

The furniture dates back to the Civil War. The couch and armchair sag, their stuffings exposed. Doilies have been placed on the arms and backs in an attempt to "decorate" the place.

The wallpaper is buckling, the rug tattered and worn. Thick, faded draperies hang from windows on either side of the space, which consists of a sitting room, a small lobby, and a flight of stairs leading from the lobby to the second floor. Near the stairway is an antique table, just large enough for letters or small packages.

Somewhere between the sitting room and the lobby is a door which leads to the kitchen.

On the wall in the sitting room is an old tapestry of St. George, on his horse triumphant, his terrible-swift-sword dripping blood, a dragon figure with severed head at the feet of the horse.

When the play opens, Miss Honey is adjusting the doilies, running the dust rag over the place, giving it the last few licks. We can tell by her hurried movements that she is expecting someone.

The sound of a car door slamming can be heard off-stage. Miss Honey is startled by the sound, hurries to one of the windows to look, and her face lights up.

Miss Honey. Yon' they come! God bless they hearts!

(Miss Honey is a slight, energetic woman in her late fifties or early sixties. Her uniform is grey with a white collar . . . just pressed, not ironed . . . and with no apron. Even when she wears her wig, the hair is always held in place by a black hair net.

Honey gives the furniture one more, quick lick before hurrying to the door.)

Miss Honey. God bless y'awl's hearts! I been just a-waiting and a-waiting for ya'! Come on in! And don't y'awl look nice! I just finished airing the place out for you! Where's the rest of you? Is this all?! H'it's plenty rooms. I tell you I'm a happy soul today! Just set your things down there and let me show you down here first, then y'awl can see upstairs. I reckon y'awl can pick your own room. Did they tell you which ones you gonna be in?

Evelyn. Mam?!

(The girls cannot believe their ears . . . or their eyes, as they each react to the place, and to the news that this is where they will be living.)

Janice. Pick what room?!
Berna Mae. That's what I wanna know!
Evelyn. This where we gonna be staying?!
Janice. Can't be!
Honey. Why, yeah, honey . . .
Evelyn. This ain't no dormitory!
Janice. It shore ain't!
Evelyn. And it stinks in here.

(Berna Mae elbows Evelyn to silence her.)

Honey. . . . H'it'll air out soon.
Berna Mae. I knew I should-a stayed at Mother Walter's!
Janice. Did the cab leave?!

(She hurries to the door to check.)

Evelyn. He's gone.
Janice. Can't we call him back?
Berna Mae. Forget it, Janice . . .
Veena. It's too crowded over at Mother Walter's.
Evelyn. I don't care.
Honey. Oh, Lord . . .
Janice. I rather go back over to Mother Walter's, too.
Veena. We said we wanted to come over here.
Janice. I thought it was gonna be pretty.
Evelyn. Me, too.
Veena. I knew something wasn't right when the cab passed on by them brick buildings.
Janice. I'm going back over to Mother Walter's.
Honey. Now, wait, y'awl . . .
Janice. I'm not staying here!
Evelyn. Me, neither.
Veena. I'm not dragging that big trunk back 'cross-town. I ain't got no mo' money for no cab-fare, nohow.
Bernie. I ain't got none, either . . . and it's four to a room over there.
Evelyn. I don't care . . . I ain't staying here.
Janice. I'm calling my parents!
Honey. Oh, don't y'awl be this way! They done gived you your own place . . . !
Evelyn. This ain't nothing to give nobody.
Honey. When I was coming up, we'd say thank you, whatever was gived to us, then give it somebody else if we didn't want it.
Janice. Somebody else can have it!
Honey. Aw, don't y'awl take this from Miss Honey. You don't know what

h'it'll give me to be able to run over here every day and see y'awl. Don't y'awl run off . . . Miss Honey'll help you fix it up.

Veena. I ain't goin' nowhere, me.

Honey. Bless your heart!

Evelyn. Are any white girls gonna be living here?

Berna Mae. What you think, Evelyn?

Honey. That's what you come here for, to live with white girls?

Evelyn. N'ome, not live with 'em . . . just live in nice places like they live in. They got grass and flowers in their yard . . .

Janice. And water fountains with birds flying all around . . .

Evelyn. How come we can't live over there?

Berna Mae. Don't ask dumb questions . . . you know why.

Honey. Do white and Colored live together where you come from? I ain't never heard tell of it 'round these parts.

Evelyn. If they don't want us for roommates, we'll be our own roommates. If they just have one room, we can all fit in it . . .

Honey. Oh, honey, don't do this to yourself . . .

Evelyn. They do have vacancy, don't they? That big'old place! It can't be all full! I can see by your face they got room.

Honey. They ain't gonna let you over there and that's all there is to it! Let Miss Honey show you the rooms upstairs . . . I done cleaned 'em and aired 'em out.

Veena. Aw, let's just go'on see what they look like.

(Veena heads toward the kitchen.)

Honey. That's right, honey . . . you got good sense!

Janice. I started to go to Fisk or Howard . . . let my teachers talk me into this mess!

Berna Mae. Didn't we all?! We been bragging to our friends about we gonna be living in a pretty dorm!

Veena. H'it's a kitchen in here, y'awl!

Honey. H'it's a brand new stove coming next week!

Janice. I didn't come here to do no cooking.

Berna Mae. I came to college to get out the kitchen . . .

Evelyn. So this is it? Ain't no room in the inn . . . we got our own private stable, so we should be grateful?

Honey. Better a stable with peace than a mansion with strife.

(Veena returns from the kitchen and heads upstairs.)

Veena. Y'awl coming or ain't you? 'Cause I can't go back home. I done spent all the money my church done took up for me . . .

Berna Mae. I know if I go back, the first thing old Miss Phillips gonna say is I got up here and got scared I couldn't make it . . . and, Evelyn, you

know what she gonna say about you 'cause she didn't want you to get that scholarship, in the first place.
Veena. They all prophesied I wouldn't make it, but I'm gonna make it!
Honey. Bless your heart! Shore you gonna make it! Miss Honey gonna be on her knees every night for her young'uns . . . you all gonna make it!
Evelyn. I just wanted to have fun in college . . .
Honey. You can't have no fun less'en you living with white girls?
Veena. I know I can! Come on, y'awl, let's go'on see the rooms.
Honey. Now, that child got sense!
Berna Mae. Come on, Evelyn . . . you see this is all we gonna get.
Evelyn. I know what I'm gonna do.
Berna Mae. Do what? You ain't gonna do nothing, Evelyn, but get your behind on up them stairs . . .
Evelyn. Watch and see don't I picket.
Veena. Picket?!
Honey. Chile, what kind-a girl is you?!
Berna Mae. A fool!
Evelyn. Back to you! And don't be calling me out-a my name.
Veena. I ain't doing no picketing!
Berna Mae. Ain't nobody doing no picketing . . . and we all staying.
Honey. You talking good sense, honey!
Evelyn. Watch and see don't I picket.
Veena. By yourself!?
Berna Mae. I know you crazy enough to, Evelyn . . . and Miss Harris told you not to come up here starting that mess.
Veena. I didn't come up here to tote no picket sign.
Berna Mae. Evelyn bet'not either if she know what's good for her.
Honey. That's right, honey . . . give her a good talking to.
Janice. But I kind-a agree with Evelyn that we ought-a do something . . . maybe not picket, but something! Why do we always have to take the ugly? They probably think this is all we used to, and I have them know I come from way better than this!
Berna Mae. Well, Evelyn ain't come from no better, so why she acting all nice'nasty . . .
Evelyn. *(stung by the betrayal)* Why'n't you shut your big mouth, Bernie?! You po', too!
Berna Mae. I didn't say I wasn't. You think I don't want something nice? But, let's face it . . . this is it! Now, it's either this, Mother Walter's or go back home!
Veena. It's gonna take more'n a nasty house to run me back home.
Honey. Now you talking!
Veena. I'm a Home Economics major . . . watch me decorate this joint. I can make curtains and slip covers if somebody buy the material.

Honey. I shore will talk to Dean Crouse about that. Anything I ask'es her for, I gets it. The white girls leaves all kind-a things in they rooms when school's over and Dean Crouse told the housemothers to let me have 'em . . . brand new clothes ain't never been wore! I takes and gives 'em to people. Miss Honey can get you all the material you need . . . you just leave it to Miss Honey.
Bernie. Can you get 'em to paint the outside and plant some flowers?
Honey. I shore can!
Veena. I don't care bout no flowers. They put me in the mind-a a graveyard and I be dreaming-a haints and spirits.
Janice. Will they let us take a picture in front of that fountain?
Honey. Shore, honey! Y'awl can go over there and take all the pictures you want!
Veena. They might run us away from over there.
Honey. Naw, they won't! You just let Miss Honey handle this mess. 'Tween me and God we gonna take this whole burden off-a His black chill'uns.
Bernie. My pastor's wife gave me a good camera for graduation!
Janice. I got one, too.
Veena. Mine a Kodak!
Bernie. Let's go put our things up and take some pictures at the fountain.
Janice. I wanna go over there right now.

(Veena, Janice and Bernie head up the stairs with their bags. Evelyn does not move.)

Honey. That's what Miss Honey wanna see!
Bernie. Evelyn, you coming?
Honey. Shore, she's coming . . . ain't you, sugar?
Bernie. You know you can't go back home.
Evelyn. Just go'on leave me here.
Bernie. I didn't mean no harm by what I said. I admit I'm po', too.
Honey. We all is po' in the eyes-a God. What is these little treasures we store up down here on this earth? We all comes into the world n'eked and leaves here n'eked. Didn't The Master have swaddling clothes the day he was born, and nothing but the rags on his back when they dragged up that hill and nailed him to a tree? We can't eat but one meal at a time or sleep in but one bed at a time, that's rich and po' alike. Let Miss Honey help you tote your bag . . .

(When Honey reaches for the bag, Evelyn sobers and comes to herself.)

Evelyn. No-mam, that's all right . . . I can take it!
Veena. *(offstage)* Ooo, y'awl, these rooms is big!
Janice. *(offstage)* First-come, first-served!
Bernie. Y'awl bet'not be taking the best ones!

(Bernie struggles up the stairs with her bags.)

Honey. Hurry up, honey! Don't let 'em get the best rooms!

(Resignedly, Evelyn heads up the stairs.)

Bernie. We still gonna be roommates, ain't we, Evelyn?

(Evelyn is still smarting over Bernie's betrayal and does not respond. Bernie leaves her suitcase on the stairs and comes to help Evelyn. Honey looks on proudly as the girls head up the stairs.)

Honey. Bless y'awl's hearts! H'it's gonna be all right . . . you just watch and see.

(Alone on the stage, Honey takes a good look at the room, seeing it through the eyes of the girls now.
She mutters to herself as she tries to stretch the doilies over the flaws.)

Honey. Bless they hearts! I'm gonna see 'bout this. Bless they hearts!

(The lights dim on the scene as Honey tries to do the impossible.)

(End of Ritual I)

RITUAL II

The next day. Same place, same set.
  Evelyn enters in low spirits. She is dressed in typical first-day clothing for freshman girls—penny loafers with white socks, a skirt with blouse and sweater.
  She puts her books down and, after a beat, goes to the window to look out with longing and envy.
  Honey calls out, then heads down the stairs.

Honey. Hey, down there . . . that one-a y'awl!
Evelyn. *(leaving the window)* Yes-mam, Miss Honey, it's me, Evelyn.
Honey. Bless your heart! How'd the first day go?
Evelyn. Fine.
Honey. Any more Colored in your classes with you or you in there by yourself?
Evelyn. I'm the only Colored in the ones I had today . . .
Honey. Bless your heart! You just hold your head up . . . hold it high!
Evelyn. Yes-mam.
Honey. *(confidentially)* I heard Dean Crouse telling one-a the other deans h'it's a Colored girl out to the law school, what's living crosstown . . .

they gonna ask her to come live here . . . y'awl'll have somebody to look after ya'.

(Honey chatters on, insensitive to Evelyn's mood.)

Honey. . . . I 'magine she be a bit older than y'awl . . . I didn't know they still had Colored over there in that law school. Years back the "coats" made 'em let that Colored fellow in b'name-a Sweatt. I 'members his name just as good 'cause folks joked about it so much, said when the white folks get holt of him, he shore will sweat. I heard tell he had to be put away, they done him so bad . . .

(Honey is suddenly aware of Evelyn.)

Honey. Lord, I'm just runnin' my mouth . . . ! What's the matter, sugar?
Evelyn. Nothing.
Honey. Miss Honey know when the heart is troubled. You can tell Honey anything . . . the white girls comes to me. Did they mistreat you?
Evelyn. They don't serve Colored in them places around the corner.
Honey. You didn't go in none of 'em, did you?
Evelyn. I thought they was integrated.
Honey. Why'n't y'awl just eat in the school cafeteria and leave them places alone, honey? They so low-down! Old Man Harper done bragged 'bout he got ax handles for whatever Colored come in his place. Miss Honey'll show you where the cafeteria is, what they calls The Commons . . .
Evelyn. I know where it is.
Honey. White and Colored can eat there . . . that belongst to the University.
Evelyn. They didn't have to call me no nigger and be pushing me all in my back . . . they saw I was leaving.
Honey. Oh, Miss Honey's so sorry they hurt your feelings!

(Honey comforts the weeping Evelyn.)

Honey. Now, now! H'it's gonna be all right. Don't you worry . . . you gonna set at that welcome table one-a these days. The Book gonna be fulfilled. H'it say the last gonna be first and the first gonna be last. God is a time-God. Just leave it to Him. Po' little thing! They don't know no better. Dry your eyes, now, and come look at these books Miss Honey done brought. See can you use any of 'em . . . the white girls just throws 'em away . . .

(Evelyn looks through the books, sees some she needs and sobers up.)

Evelyn. Can I have these two, Miss Honey?
Honey. Shore, honey! Take all you need.
Evelyn. These are the ones I need in history.

Honey. See there?

Evelyn. I would-a had to spend a lot-a money, even for used one! Thank you, Miss Honey.

Honey. Oh, you welcome, sugar. You just let Miss Honey know which ones you need. 'Shore wish I could read them books, I wouldn't never put 'em down. But that's all right, my young'uns gonna git that book-learning for me.

Evelyn. You can't read, Miss Honey?

Honey. *(realizing she has revealed it)* Lord, me and my big mouth!

Evelyn. I won't tell nobody, Miss Honey. My father can't read.

Honey. I writes my name, though . . . and counts my money. People think I can read. I tells 'em I leaves my glasses home so I won't lose 'em.

Evelyn. Miss Honey, I'll teach you how to read. I won't tell nobody what we doing.

Honey. Bless your heart! Naw, Miss Honey too old now . . .

Evelyn. Naw you ain't, Miss Honey. That's the same thing my daddy keep saying and won't let nobody teach him.

Honey. Pride, honey . . . that's all it is. But don't worry bout us. Just get that learning. Y'awl is the hope. H'it's too late for us. Some of us wanted that learnin back then but we had to work in the fields, don't we wouldn't eat . . .

(Bernie and Janice enter, coming from classes. They are dispirited.)

Honey. Yon' come some more-a my young'uns . . . !

(Janice and Bernie ad lib: "Hi'ya', Miss Honey.")

Honey. Bless y'awl's hearts! How was things for y'awl today?

Bernie. *(noncommittally)* Fine.

Honey. Did any of 'em speak to you?

Bernie. They wouldn't even sit by us. We sit by them, they move.

Janice. I don't care if they don't speak to me. I didn't come here to make friends.

Honey. They'll get tired-a acting a fool some day. Y'awl just hold your heads up. The same heat what melts the butter harden the egg.

Evelyn. Miss Honey brought us some books! I got both-a my history books.

(Janice does not respond.)

Bernie. They got me taking trigonometry and I gotta buy a big ol' book!

Evelyn. Here's a trigonometry book. Ain't it, Miss Honey?

(Evelyn holds it up for Miss Honey to pretend to read the title.)

Honey. *(emphatically)* H'it shore is!

Bernie. Ooo! That's the one I need!

Honey. Hot-dog! Miss Honey gonna see if she can get some more.
Bernie. Can you see if they got any chemistry books, Miss Honey?
Honey. I shore will! Let me run on over there now 'fore they be looking for me. Miss Honey gonna try to get back over here 'fore I catch that old slow bus.
Bernie. Thank you for the book.
Honey. You welcome, sugar. Y'awl be sweet, now.

(The girls ad lib responses and Honey hurries out.)

Janice. Why do y'awl keep talking to her when she come over here? That's why she can't half clean this place.
Bernie. 'Long as she find these books so I won't have to buy 'em, I don't care if she don't never clean up.
Janice. I don't want no books them crackers had their hands all on. That's all we got all through school, every raggedy-ass book they didn't want no more . . . their names all in 'em.
Bernie. Me and Evelyn ain't got no rich parents to buy us brand-new books, and, from what Veena told us, she ain't neither.

(Evelyn has not forgotten the earlier betrayal and eyes Bernie suspiciously.)

Janice. Where's my roommate, anyhow? What time is it . . . ?
Evelyn. They're making her take basic English.
Bernie. Git on back!
Evelyn. She went to get 'em to change it.
Janice. Ooo, I know my roommate is mad!
Bernie. I'm in regular!
Janice. Me, too! But just between us, though . . . Veena's my roommate, but she could use a little basic English.
Bernie. I didn't wanna say it . . .
Janice. Can't she take a ax to some verbs?! As country as they come! She nice, though.
Evelyn. Guess who goes here now!
Bernie. Who?
Evelyn. Guess.
Bernie. I'm leaving the room when you do that 'cause I ain't in no mood.

(Bernie gets up to go.)

Evelyn. O.K. Scrap goes here.
Bernie. Cordell?! You lying!
Evelyn. I cross my heart.
Janice. What he doing here?
Evelyn. The same thing we doing here.
Janice. I thought he was at Yale.

Evelyn. He transferred.
Bernie. Did you give him our address?
Janice. I hope not.
Evelyn. I did. He's coming. He said it's about six Colored fellows here. They put 'em 'way cross campus in some army barracks.
Bernie. I saw some of 'em . . . they was fine!
Janice. Why'n't yaw'l invite some-a them over here? Naw, leave it to Evelyn to dig up some trash! I'm surprised it ain't one-a them garbage men you was waving at this morning. And I shore wish you would stop that mess before they think they can come over here and date us.
Evelyn. We can't speak to nobody Colored unless they go to school here?
Janice. You wasn't just speaking, you was "Hey, brother!" Like you ain't seen nobody Colored in years.
Evelyn. Don't run it in the ground.
Bernie. What time did Cordell say he was coming?
Janice. Who cares?
Evelyn. Janice, don't you think two years is a long time to be mad at somebody for such a small thing?
Bernie. That's right!
Janice. What small thing?! That's the fool that ran the wrong way with the damn football and made us lose the championship! Then come joining the basketball team and put the ball in the other team's basket!
Evelyn. So what?!
Bernie. That's right. That's all in the past.
Janice. Just leave me out of it.
Bernie. You got it.
Evelyn. One thing about it, Cordell know how to help us get our rights.
Janice. He gonna stop these crackers from kicking us all on the back-a our seats, pushing us out-a lines and calling us "nigger"? All on buildings, NIGGER, GO BACK TO AFFICA . . . ain't even spelled Africa right . . . even the blackboards. These damn professors won't even erase it . . .
Bernie. Miss Walls asked us were we strong enough to take it.
Janice. Strong ain't got nothing to do with it. They act like they didn't even know we were coming here . . . their heads be all doing double-takes and their mouths dropping open . . . watching us like a hound eyeing a rabbit . . .
Evelyn. Cordell shore ain't gonna stand for the fact that we can't go in none-a those places around the corner.
Janice. Says who?
Bernie. Those movies and restaurants and places?!
Evelyn. I went in one-a the restaurants.
Bernie. They made you leave?

Evelyn. First they asked me was I white or Colored . . . then they come shoving on me . . .
Janice. Asked you was you white or Colored?!
Bernie. They really asked you that?!
Janice. I guess you must-a told 'em you were Colored!
Bernie. What else could she say?!
Janice. Let one of 'em ask me that . . . I'll show you what to say.
Bernie. I know one thing, somebody better let me in that movie where *Rebel Without a Cause* is playing 'cause I gotta write a theme about it for English.
Janice. Tell the professor they won't let you in, then you won't have to write the paper.
Bernie. I shore won't, will I?! But, shoot, I wanna see that movie. I heard it was good!

(A car door slams offstage. Evelyn goes to the window to check.)

Evelyn. Come see, y'awl! It's Scrap! He driving a car!

(Bernie and Janice run to the window.)

Bernie. It's Cordell?!   **Janice.** A car?! What kind?!
Evelyn. A Triumph!
Janice. Ooo, Daddy Warbucks?!

(Everyone breaks for the door. Bernie blocks Janice's way.)

Bernie. Oh, naw you don't, Janice! You didn't even wanna see Cordell.
Janice. I'm just going to look at the car, Bernie.
Bernie. Car, my ass! This is Berna Mae Wilson you talking to. Remember me? I'm the girl Cordell used to like before you come cutting in.
Janice. It never was what you thought it was, Bernie. Scrap still go for you, and you can have him.
Bernie. You think you slick.

(Cordell enters with Evelyn swinging on his arm. Cordell/Scrap is tall, good-looking and fair-skinned enough to pass for white. Janice runs to him.)

Janice. Cordell! Sugar, I'm so glad to see you!
Cordell. Are you, baby? You ain't mad at me no more?
Janice. That little old game!? That's all in the past.

(Bernie and Evelyn give each other a look, then together they react: "Ooo, Janice!")

Janice. It's over, sugar . . . scout's honor.
Cordell. That's good enough for me . . . I was kind-a scared to come over here . . . baby, you just made me so happy! . . .

(He notices Bernie, love-struck and standing aside, waiting for a sign.)

Cordell. Bernie . . . !
Bernie. Hi, Cordell.
Cordell. Well . . . ? Where's my hug?
Bernie. Do I owe you one?
Cordell. Aw, come on, Bernie. We're all back together now. All we got is us . . . we gonna need each other more than we know.

(Bernie struggles to keep her feelings from showing.)

Bernie. I guess you right about that.

(Cordell goes to Bernie and she responds with a sisterly hug but it is not enough to overcome the great pain between them.)

Cordell. After Miss Walls told me y'awl was coming up here to pave the way, she just kept at me 'bout what a shame it was that y'awl was coming to face this by y'awlselves . . . kept on about somebody with some sense need to come up here with y'awl. Ain't that a blip!? After all the things I messed up, she still had faith in me. How could I say no? So I lose a few credits by transferring . . . so what?
Janice. You see what they put us in.
Cordell. I shore do smell it. This ain't even separate-but-equal.
Bernie. They promised to fix it up.
Janice. Yeah, promise! The Dean of Women promised to come over here yesterday. If she came the pope came.
Evelyn. I wanted to picket.
Cordell. Picket or something! And strike while the iron is hot.
Evelyn. I told y'awl that!
Janice. You ain't had to tell me . . . I wanted to protest.
Bernie. Cordell, I know you mean well, but you don't understand. You're saying just what Evelyn wanna hear and she's gonna use that as the excuse to pull something like she did on the senior trip.
Cordell. What did she do?
Bernie. You didn't hear about it?
Evelyn. I don't care if you tell it. We went to Louisiana on the senior trip and I moved the "Colored" sign from the back of the bus all the way to the front of the bus so we could sit down.
Cordell. Good for you, Evelyn!
Bernie. Good? Even if she had-a got killed or got some-a us killed?
Cordell. Somebody gotta die. This cracker ain't never conceded nothing unless we pay him with our blood, and he ain't about to change. Do they still make Colored come through the front door and pay the fare, then get off and board through the back door?

Evelyn. That's how it was.
Janice. And gotta sit behind the Colored sign.
Evelyn. It was all the way back to the last seat, Cordell, and plenty empty seats were on the white side, so I moved it.
Cordell. That's my girl! I'm glad somebody stood up for something!
Bernie. She wasn't standing up for nothing . . . she was just showing off.
Evelyn. That's what you call it.
Bernie. So why did you turn the Colored side toward the white people and the white side toward us?

(Cordell and Janice have a good laugh.)

Cordell. Give 'em hell, Evelyn!
Bernie. Y'awl think it's funny, but if Mr. Sanders hadn't made her walk backward out the front door and come in the back door backward to make an example of her, that bus driver might-a stomped her brains out.
Cordell. Who was gonna stand by and let him do it?
Evelyn. That's what I wanna know!
Bernie. But we didn't go there for that.
Evelyn. What did we come here for, Bernie?
Bernie. I came here to be a student.
Cordell. You can be a student anywhere, Bernie. Naw, baby, our teachers asked us to come here to let this state know it can't take our parents' tax money and treat us like they want us to go back to picking cotton.
Janice. Here-here!
Evelyn. They won't let us in those places around the corner, Cordell.
Cordell. What places? On that big strip they call The Drag?
Evelyn. The restaurants and places . . .
Janice. . . . and Bernie gotta write a paper on a movie . . .
Cordell. I saw an African eating in one-a the restaurants.
Evelyn. They let Africans in 'em?
Janice. They told Evelyn they don't serve Colored.
Cordell. Oh, so that's the game they wanna play! They'll serve Africans but not us.
Evelyn. But ain't Africans Colored, too?
Cordell. The one I saw was quite Colored! He had his robe and turban on and the crackers were back in the kitchen whispering but they served him . . . after they decided he wasn't made in the USA.
Evelyn. I don't understand.
Janice. They asked Evelyn was she white or Colored.
Cordell. Git-on-back! I know you told 'em you were white.
Janice. I told her that's what she should-a said.
Evelyn. How could I?

Cordell. They were giving you a choice . . . maybe that African told 'em he was white.
Evelyn. I don't understand.
Janice. Don't nobody understand it.
Cordell. *That's* what we're here for. To understand this white man's shit! And do something about it.
Bernie. Do what, Cordell?! How're we gonna fight all these crackers?
Cordell. You think it can't be done? Numbers ain't nothing.
Evelyn. If all of us go sit in at one-a the places . . .
Cordell. Aw, to hell with that!
Evelyn. But, Cordell, that's what we're doing all over the South and . . .
Cordell. To hell with that! You wanna sit at a lunch counter and let 'em put lighted cigarettes down your back?
Bernie. I know I don't.

(Evelyn is silenced by the horror of the act. Veena enters in a state of agitation.)

Janice. Veena, where you been? What happened?!
Veena. Look on the back-a me, roomin'mate. What you see?
Janice. Ooo! Somebody spit on you!

(Everyone reacts as Veena hurriedly gets out of the sweater.)

Veena. Old low-down-dirty dogs! I heard 'em!
Cordell. Did you spit back?!
Veena. It was a whole bunch of 'em!
Cordell. When did it happen? They still out there?

(Cordell moves impulsively toward the door.)

Veena. While'ago.
Cordell. Nasty bastards! I wish I had-a seen 'em . . . the no-dick cowards!
Veena. We need the marshalls down here 'cause they got big'old cannons!
Janice. Cannons?!
Veena. They 'way over yonder 'cause I got lost.
Janice. Where, Veena?!
Cordell. Damn! You were in Confederate Square! They shoot those cannons off every year to celebrate some Confederate victory.
Bernie. What victory?! They lost!
Cordell. Let'em go'on knock themselves out! They can fight the Civil War over again as many times as they want to as long as they lose.
Bernie. I wish I had-a went to Howard or Fisk!
Veena. This was my good sweater!
Janice. If I was you, roommate, I wouldn't wear it no more.
Cordell. Bernie, you still think we can just "be a student" here?

Bernie. I didn't say it was possible, Cordell. I just said that's all I came here for.

Janice. Did you get your program straight, roommate?

Veena. They wouldn't change it, and this just ain't right 'cause I made all A's and B's in English all through high school.

Cordell. They put you in the wrong English class? What did you score on proficiency?

Veena. What 'ficiency?

(The others try to avoid revealing their attitudes, but they slip each other looks.)

Cordell. That battery of tests you had to take.

Veena. I don't 'member . . . they was all bunched up together.

Cordell. One of 'em was an English proficiency exam.

Janice. All of us had to take it, Veena.

Veena. I ain't saying I didn't take it . . . I just don't 'member . . . it was months ago . . .

Cordell. They placed you according to how you scored on the proficiency.

Veena. I couldn't-a did that bad! I mean, I don't profess to be no whiz in the shit, but I know I knows me some kind-a English!

(Janice flinches discreetly.)

Cordell. I think we have a crisis here. Take the class, home-girl.

(Veena notices the reactions of the others.)

Veena. Y'awl think I need it, don't you?

Cordell. Put it this way. When we're in our own element, relaxing and shooting the bull, we all break a few rules of grammar. After all, English is a foreign tongue to us. But most of us, if we have to, can speak the Queen's English.

Evelyn. Veena, we'll help you.

Veena. I just can't go to that class. I'm not going. All them people gonna be laughing at me.

Janice. All what people?

Bernie. That's what I wanna know.

Veena. All them white people.

Cordell. Naw, naw . . . where's that bulletin? Come here, home'girl . . .

(Someone hands Cordell the bulletin and he runs through it with Veena.)

Cordell. Look at this! You see how many sections of Basic English they got in here? You think they're all for you? They had these courses in here long before we got here.

(The others ad lib responses: "That's right.")

Janice. See there, roommate? They dumb, too. Oops! I didn't mean it like it sounds.

Evelyn. Look . . . if all of us study together . . . if the strong help the weak, we'll all make it.

(Everyone ad libs responses.
   Honey enters with a platter of food wrapped neatly. If Cordell is seated, he will rise and ad lib greetings: "How you today?")

Honey. Oh, hey'dere! You goes to school here, too?

(ad libs of "Yes, mam.")

Honey. Bless your hearts! Honey just so proud of ya'! I brung y'awl something t'eat . . . I didn't know y'awl had company, 'did I'd-a brung more.

Evelyn. That's all right, Miss Honey . . . thank you for this . . . we'll stretch it.

Honey. What's that good sweater doing on the floor? Y'awl take care-a your things.

Janice. It's spit on it . . . those crackers spit on Veena.

Honey. Oh, did they do that?! Miss Honey's so sorry! They don't know no better.

Cordell. They know better.

Honey. Naw they don't . . . Honey done tended to 'em and waited on 'em and wiped they boodie all my life and they just gonna spit and pee-pee on you don't care what you try to teach 'em.

Cordell. Then something's wrong with the lesson we're trying to teach 'em . . . or with the way we're teaching it. We've been marching and singing and praying and trying to reason with 'em when the only thing they understand is bloodshed.

(Honey studies Cordell for a quick moment then lays down her principles.)

Honey. Well-now, I don't know 'bout that. Y'awl just git this book-larning. That's something they can't take away from you.

Cordell. They can take away our right and our opportunity to use it.

Honey. Naw they can't! You just know what you knows and be three times good'er in it than them and can't nothing keep a good man down. If I wasn't runnin' to catch this bus and these corns wasn't killing me . . . but I'll get my chance to tell y'awl plenty 'bout these white folks. Gimme that good sweater so I can take and wash it out.

Janice. You gonna touch it!?

Honey. Soap and water clean anything. If we throw 'way everything white folks done did they dirt on we wouldn't have nothing left.

Janice. Miss Honey, we've been meaning to tell you, it's some roaches in that refrigerator.
Honey. What you want me to do, c'ary 'em home with me?

(Honey stuffs the sweater into a bag and heads out.)

Honey. I'll ask Dean Crouse will she send the roach man. Y'awl eat that food 'fore it git cold . . . and don't forget curfew.

(The Women ad lib responses, and Honey exits.)

Janice. Everytime we say something to her, she got some smart remark. She don't even act like no maid. All she do is hit this place a lick and a promise.
Cordell. Look like y'awl get more promise than licking.
Janice. She ain't nothing but a old "uncle tom . . ." She gonna "ask" the dean to send the roach man!
Evelyn. If the dean don't come over here and hear our grievances, we ought-a make a list of the things we want and take it over there to her.
Cordell. We need to have a little pow-wow before we make any kind-a move. I'm gonna get some-a the brothers over here.
Janice. Well, all right!

*(Cordell prepares to leave.
Evelyn and Bernie comfort Veena.)*

Evelyn. Veena, you gonna make me start crying.
Janice. Don't cry, roommate.
Bernie. Let her cry it out . . . it'll make her feel better.
Veena. If they just hadn't-a spit on my good sweater . . .
Cordell. Don't worry . . . every dog'll have his day, and a good dog'll have two days.
Evelyn. Miss Honey found us some-a the books we need. You wanna look through 'em and see if you can use any of 'em?

(Veena sobers a bit.)

Cordell. I'll be back.

*(Evelyn is about to get the books and Cordell is on his way out, when shots ring out and the sound of a car can be heard speeding off.
Cordell hits the floor.)*

Evelyn. What was that . . . ?!
Cordell. HIT THE FLOOR! IT'S GUNSHOTS! HIT THE LIGHTS! STAY LOW! THEY SHOOTING AT THE HOUSE!
The Women. OH, GOD! I'M SCARED! THEY TRYING TO KILL US!

Cordell. THEY CIRCLING THE BLOCK! WHERE'S THE PHONE!
The Women. WE AIN'T GOT NO PHONE!
Cordell. GET ME A WHITE SHEET, SOMEBODY!
Evelyn. I'LL GET IT!

(Evelyn dashes up the stairs.)

Cordell. KEEP LOW, EVELYN! AND HURRY UP!
Veena. PLEASE, GOD! LORD-GOD-JEHOVAH, DON'T LET US DIE!
Janice. I'M GONNA TELL MY DADDY! YOU JUST WATCH AND SEE!
Cordell. Y'awl gotta pipe down some! Just stay down low . . . the bullets can't find you!

(Cordell crawls over to the window to see what he can see. The women ad lib their fear: "Mama! I want my mama!")

Bernie. Cordell, please be careful!
Cordell. I started to bring something with me!

(Offstage, we can see the flickering of a flame.)

Cordell. Where's another exit?!
The Women. Back through the kitchen!
  Something's burning!
  They setting the house on fire!?
  We gotta get out-a here!
Cordell. BE STILL! THEY BURNING A CROSS! JUST STAY PUT! HURRY UP WITH THAT SHEET, EVELYN!
Evelyn. I got it!

(Evelyn hurries down the stairs.)

Cordell. Bend down, dammit!

(Cordell begins to fashion the sheet like a Ku Klux Klan robe.)

The Women. Somebody gotta get the sheriff!
Cordell. Shit, it might be the sheriff doing the shooting!
Janice. Cordell, where you going?! Don't leave us!
Cordell. I'll be back . . . just stay put! I mean don't move a hair! Do y'awl understand that?!

(The women ad lib "yes.")

Bernie. Cordell, if you go out there, they'll shoot you!
Cordell. Not with this sheet on they won't! Do like I say and stay still!

(Cordell hurries out the back way, leaving the women cringing on the floor.)

Evelyn. Be careful, Cordell!
Bernie. I could kick myself in the ass for coming here!
Janice. I'm gonna tell my parents to come and get me!
Evelyn. Please, Janice! We made a pact. We all agreed no one would leave 'cause if one leaves, everybody's gonna wanna go.
Janice. I don't care . . . I ain't staying here for nobody's target practice.
Bernie. Let's just do what Cordell said and be still till he gets back.

(Veena continues uninterrupted with her prayer: "Please, God! Lord-God-Jehovah! Please, God! Save us, Lord!")

Evelyn. I ain't running. I ain't running. . . .

(The lights dim, then go to sudden black.)

(End of Ritual II)

RITUAL III

The next day.

The set is the same. The Men have arrived, and they include Falvie, slight and wearing glasses; and Winston, more muscular than the other men, and more taciturn. He wears his slide rule on his hip like a pistol.

Cordell is at the window, counting the number of guards stationed outside. Everyone else is bunched around Falvie as he reads from the newspaper which is spread out on the table.

Cordell. Including the one on the roof across the street, I count seven.
Veena. I think they should-a sent the whole army down here.
Falvie. Listen to this y'awl! "Last night a carload of unidentified men fired several shots into The Old Jefferson Davis House . . ."
Cordell. Unidentified! I gave a full description of them and the car and they're still unidentified!
Falvie. Hold it, hold it! Dig this . . . ". . . where four Negroes are being housed" . . . oh, that's what y'awl are! You're Negroes!
Winston. Come on, Falvie-man! Read the thing if you gonna do it.
Falvie. "Firemen were called to the Main Campus to put out a fire in what appeared to have been a related incident . . ."

(There are reactions of disbelief at the deliberate omissions.)

Cordell. That's right, it was a fire. It wasn't a cross-burning.
Janice. And we're the ones who set the fire, right?
Falvie. ". . . The University is investigating the two incidents. Meanwhile,

guards have been placed outside the House, once the home of General Jefferson Davis, President of the Confederacy."

Veena. So this is what this damn place is!
Bernie. I know he must be turning over in his grave!
Evelyn. What did the Colored papers say about it?
Cordell. They wouldn't let them even come on the campus.

(Everyone ad libs reactions.)

Cordell. Don't worry, I got the license number of the car. We gonna meet again. They ain't the only ones know how to burn crosses and shoot guns. We can learn that, can't we fellows?
Winston. Damn straight!
Falvie. That's what they trying to teach us.
Cordell. We can burn a bigger cross with a hotter fire. Get us some sheets, too. Dye 'em black. Wash 'em in Ivory Soap just like them . . .
Bernie. Cordell, don't y'awl start nothing . . .
Cordell. Don't y'awl? What y'awl? They're the ones started something. And we're gonna finish it.
Bernie. With all those guns they got?
Cordell. They ain't got all the guns.
Winston. They shore got mine.
Cordell. That can be fixed.
Winston. So what's stopping us?
Falvie. Twenty thousand crackers is stopping me!
Janice. Is it really that many crackers here?!
Winston. You scared, Falvie?
Falvie. Scared ain't got nothing to do with it. Although I'd rather it be said "there he runs" than "there he lays." I'm just being realistic . . . like Bernie. Maybe they ain't got all the guns, but they got most of 'em . . . and most-a the bullets.
Winston. Bullets can't turn corners.
Falvie. But they can beat us to the corner.
Cordell. Can bullets shoot out a fire?

(A beat as Falvie has no come-back. The Women listen with interest.)

Cordell. They didn't shoot out the one in Chicago when Mrs. O'Leary's cow kicked that lantern over.
Falvie. That cow had four legs. I ain't got but two.
Winston. Look, Falvie-man, if you ain't with us, just stay here with the babes.
Cordell. This ain't no time for jive, Falvie. Just 'cause those guards are out there don't mean nothing. Nazi boots are still gonna march tonight. Why you think those swastikas are all over the place?

Winston. 'Cause they wanna play Nazi, that's why . . . and I ain't gonna play Jew.
Falvie. All right, man, I give.
Bernie. What are y'awl thinking about doing?
Winston. When it's done, it'll have our mark on it.
Evelyn. I think we should go to President Wolfgang.
Cordell. And tell him what, Evelyn?
Janice. *(mockingly)* . . . Mr. President Wolfgang, your people shot at us last night and burned a cross under our window.
Evelyn. We can tell him we don't wanna be over here like sitting ducks. We can tell him to keep those guards out there indefinitely. And maybe he don't know we can't go in those places on The Drag or join no clubs or play no sports that involve body-contact with white students . . .
Falvie. It's not just body-contact sports. We can't run track, either. You ain't gotta touch nobody in track.
Janice. Y'awl tried out for the track team?
Cordell. Falvie did.
Falvie. No niggers. Period. In those very words.
Winston. Don't worry, we'll get our revenge. Soon, too. They gotta play Syracuse in the Cotton Bowl, and a bad-brother named Ernie Davis is gonna buss'ass without even touching them creampuffs.

(Reactions are ad libbed.)

Cordell. How many of us wanna go to Wolfgang's office, like Evelyn is suggesting?

(No one votes.)

Winston. First thing he gonna do is start calling us "boy" and that shit goes all through me!
Janice. I shore don't want him calling me no "gal" . . .

(Everyone ad libs agreement.)

Bernie. If Wolfgang don't ask to meet with us, I don't think we should ask to meet with him. We're not part of no organization with no kind-a power . . . but, Evelyn, if nobody else will go with you, I'll go just to keep you from going by yourself.
Janice. . . . but how else would you present him with our list of the things we want? He gonna say he didn't get it if we just leave it . . .
Cordell. A list? Is that what you wanna go over there for? He's just gonna throw that in the wastebasket after you leave, anyhow.
Janice. So why the hell did we spend all that time making up the list? I see what Evelyn is saying . . .
Cordell. I don't know why you made the list.

Janice. We made the list to let these crackers know what we want, but I thought we were gonna give it to the Dean if she ever get her ass over here.
Cordell. Y'awl think they're that damn dumb that they don't know what we want?!
Janice. I do!
Cordell. Then tell 'em to make a list of everything they'd want their sons and daughters to have and sign our names.

(Ad libbed responses from the men.)

Veena. If they just keep them guards out there and leave us alone, I'm satisfied.
Janice. How long will those guards be out there? I agree with Evelyn that we should demand those guards stay, otherwise it's gonna be just like it was when Hayes pulled the troops out-a the South. These crackers gonna start going for our blood all over again.
Winston. I'm all for making that demand, but why do we have to go to somebody's office? That's one demand we should nail out in the open where the whole campus can see it . . .
Evelyn. Yeah! Like Martin Luther did his 95-Theses . . . or else a open letter to *The Longhorn*.
Bernie. I like the open letter idea. Will everybody sign it?
Evelyn. I will.

(no other volunteers)

Falvie. Two signatures.
Evelyn. I don't understand this . . . ! All over the South we're standing up for our rights . . .
Cordell. Look, Evelyn, I know what you wanna do . . . you wanna march and sing and picket. Well, go ahead . . . go to Wolfgang if you want to. To each his own. I know what I'm gonna do.
Veena. I ain't signing my name to nothing. These professors see my name, they can fail me.
Bernie. Can't we just sign it "From The *Negro* Students"? That might be better, anyway . . . that way they won't know whether it's seven of us or seventy.
Winston. What else is on that list?
Evelyn. A school boycott of The Drag, until they open their doors to us.
Cordell. Those are private merchants. The school ain't got nothing to do with 'em.
Falvie. I'm boycotting their ass, anyway.
Evelyn. That ain't no boycott . . . you ain't got no choice.
Falvie. How'some'ever you call it, they ain't getting my money.

Evelyn. You buy your books around there.
Falvie. Where else I'm gonna buy 'em?
Evelyn. That's the point. They're deciding what place you can spend your money in.

(Winston hears someone outside and goes to the window to check.)

Winston. Somebody's coming up on the porch.
Honey. *(offstage)* Hey in there . . .
Janice. That's old Miss Honey . . . I don't wanna hear her mouth.

(Janice heads upstairs. Bernie gathers up her things and starts for class.)

Janice. I'll see y'awl later.
Bernie. I gotta go, too.

(Honey enters. Greetings are ad libbed.)

Honey. Is y'awl all right? Bless y'awl's hearts! Miss Honey heard what happened . . . and y'awl got plenty protection! Praise God! Everybody's talking 'bout it! Ain't it a shame! Y'awl just go'on to your classes like ain't nothing happened.
Veena. Whatever these white folks tell me to do, I'm doing it. If they say sit, I'm gonna sit . . . if they say stand, I'm gonna stand.
Honey. That's right, honey. Kill a dog with kindness. Talk to 'em real soft . . . they likes that.
Cordell. I'm gonna talk soft, too, but I'm gonna carry a big stick.
Honey. And shake it at who? Just leave these white folks to God. H'it's something in store for 'em, something terrible! Just you watch!
Cordell. Leave 'em to God, huh?
Honey. That's right! You can't separate a fool from his foolishness.
Cordell. God done had 'em longer than us, and He don't seem to be able to do nothing with 'em, either.
Honey. That's what Ol'Pharaoh thought. And didn't God drown his whole army? Didn't He deliver them three Hebrew boys from that fire'y furnace what was sebenty-seb'n times hotter'n hell . . . ?
Cordell. He must not see these crackers down here mucking with everybody in the world. Where's the hell for them? When is He gonna throw them in a fiery furnace?
Honey. Don't you worry . . . these old hellhounds is headed for hell, and the ones like Old Man Harper gonna c'ar'y they fire wid 'em.
Cordell. Well, God better make haste before we end up out there in that museum with the dinosaur bones. They already got the Indians in there.
Veena. Excuse me, y'awl. I got a class.
Honey. That's right, honey! Git that book-learnin'! If y'awl can't do it, then h'it just can't be done.

Veena. Yes-mam.
Falvie. Hold up, Veena . . . we're going your way.
Cordell. See you later, Evelyn.
Evelyn. Y'awl coming back this evening?

(The men ad lib responses, then exit. Honey goes to work while Evelyn falls into a mood.)

Honey. Humph! I tell you, the words of a fool is a dime a dozen! You chill'un is young and needs to look and listen more. Y'awl wasn't even born yet when them Colored soldiers come through here, had just come from 'cross the water . . . these white folks hung ever'last one of 'em with Uncle Sam's uniforms still on 'em! Y'awl can't fight these devils with no slingshots. Chile, don't start me to tellin' what I done seen-a these heathens, 'cause I'll tell everything I know!

Evelyn. But, Miss Honey, are we supposed to just leave things the way we found them? How're we gonna stay here four years and don't do nothing but go to class and come back? We feel caged in . . .

Honey. I know h'it ain't gonna be easy, but just hold on, honey. The same heat what melt the butter harden the egg. You ain't missin' nothing b'not going everywhere the white folks go . . . they ain't having the fun you think they havin'.

Evelyn. How come they ain't having no fun? Ain't nobody spitting on them and calling them "nigger" or shooting at 'em and burning crosses and stuff. They must be having fun doing it to us.

(a beat)

Honey. All of 'em don't 'gree with this foolishness. Some of 'em say they be glad when this mess is over . . . they been talkin' 'bout boycottin' Harper's and n'em till they treat y'awl equal . . .

Evelyn. They really said that?!

Honey. Don't say nothin' yet . . . some-a the girls at Waggoner Hall was talkin'.

Evelyn. Miss Honey, if they do that . . . !

Honey. Don't say nothin, now! They don't know I heard 'em but they be talkin'.

Evelyn. I won't say nothing, Miss Honey . . . Miss Honey, can I come over there one day while you're there? I just wanna see what it look like inside! I won't stay long and I'll help you finish up.

Honey. Bless your heart! Shore you can come, honey. But never you mind helping me work . . . you just hit them books and make them A's. You just tell the housemother you one-a Miss Honey's young'uns and they'll show you where to find me.

Evelyn. Yes-mam! Thank you, Miss Honey!

Honey. Let me git on over there 'fore they be lookin' for me. Miss Honey gonna put up a prayer for all her young'uns.

(Honey goes on out singing.)

Evelyn. Yes-mam.

(Evelyn holds for a beat her new hope.
The lights dim on her hopeful face and her suppressed excitement.)

(End of Ritual III)

RITUAL IV
. . . . . .

A few days later. Same set.
    There is a desperate banging coming from the back of the house. After a few moments, Bernie comes downstairs with her hair half-combed.
    First she thinks the sound is coming from the front door . . . then she discovers its source and goes toward the kitchen.

Veena. *(offstage)* Open the door, somebody! Somebody open this door!
Bernie. I'm coming! Who is it? Where you at?!
Veena. *(offstage)* I'm at the back door! Come on, open it . . . it's me, Veena. Hurry up!
Bernie. I'm coming! Just wait!

(Bernie disappears, and after a few moments she and Veena hurry into the room.)

Bernie. What you coming through the back door for?!
Veena. It's a black cat out there!
Bernie. What black cat?!
Veena. On the front porch! With a whole lot-a white stuff in the yard! Somebody trying to work something on us!

(Bernie goes toward the front door.)

Veena. Don't open that door!
Bernie. God, Veena! You making me nervous! All right, I'll just look out the window.

(Bernie goes to the window.)

Veena. Cross your fingers, Bernie!
Bernie. I don't see no cat.
Veena. He must-a ran under the house.

Bernie. I don't even believe in that stuff.
Veena. That stuff is real! Somebody worked some roots on me one time and all my hair fell out and I had a nervous breakdown . . . I ain't letting that thing cross my path.

(The men are heard approaching. Bernie dashes upstairs.)

Bernie. That's the fellows! Let 'em in, Veena! If it's Winston, tell him don't leave!

(Winston and Falvie enter. Falvie is carrying a small package.)

Veena. Y'awl scared me!
Winston. What you scared of? Y'awl still got two guards out there.
Veena. That dev'lish cat is out there, too.
Winston. A cat?
Veena. A black one!
Falvie. I didn't see no cat.
Veena. I know what I saw.
Winston. Maybe it belong to somebody.
Veena. It shore don't belong to me.
Winston. Did Cordell come by here and bring some guy?
Veena. I just now got here . . . and Bernie say don't leave 'cause she wanna see you, Winston . . .

(Veena notices Falvie sniffing at the box.)

Falvie. *(reading)* "To Occupants."
Veena. Who box is that?
Falvie. Smell like it got cookies in it.
Veena. It was on the porch? That's ours . . . don't be shaking it.

(Veena tries to take the box.)

Falvie. Stop grabbing!
Veena. They ours.
Falvie. You left 'em out there. How come y'awl get sent all the goodies? They burned a cross under our window, too . . . broke in our rooms and peed on our homework. We always dodging bullets. Ain't that right, Winston?
Winston. That's right.
Veena. So tell somebody to send y'awl some cookies . . .

(Falvie lets down his guard, and Veena grabs the box and dashes upstairs.)

Falvie. Hey! Come on, now, Veena . . . I saw it first!

(Falvie runs up the stairs after Veena.)

Winston. Get her, Falvie!
Veena. You better get back down there . . . boys can't come up here!

(Falvie stops, hesitates.)

Winston. Ain't no boys down here.
Falvie. That's right.

(Falvie takes another step.)

Veena. You know what I mean. I'm gonna holler.
Falvie. Holler to who? Y'awl ain't got no housemother up there.
Veena. How you know?
Falvie. She would-a been down here by now.
Veena. I ain't playing, Falvie.
Falvie. Throw the cookies down.
Veena. They ain't your'n.
Falvie. . . . Y'awl just wanna eat 'em all by y'awl'self.
Winston. Let her have'em, Fal. We'll get our satisfaction another way. 'Bout time we had us a little panty-raid, anyhow.

(Falvie warms to the idea.)

Veena. A what?
Falvie. Yeah . . .

(Falvie leaves a confused Veena at the head of the stairs and goes into the kitchen.)

Winston. I rather have chocolate-covered cherries.
Veena. I know what y'awl talking about.
Winston. Good! Then we won't have-ta explain it to you.

(At the sound of someone approaching on the porch, Veena takes this opportunity to disappear.
 Winston scrambles anxiously for a seat and pretends to be studying.
 Cordell enters with Jimmy, a virile, muscular older student wearing army green and carrying a briefcase.
 The Men all ad lib greetings.)

Cordell. This is Jim.
Winston. Right on time.
Cordell. Where the women at?
Winston. Upstairs.

(Falvie comes out of the kitchen with a small plate of food. He speaks between chews.)

Cordell. I knew you'd be eating.

Falvie. Uhn-uhn . . . how you doing, man?
Cordell. This is the brother I told you about who was in Korea.
Jimmy. Y'awl ever used a gun before?
Winston. I know how to use a rifle.

(Jimmy takes a large gun from the briefcase.)

Jimmy. Ever shot one-a these . . .
The Men. OH, SHIT, MAN! WHERE YOU GET THAT?! LEMME SEE! IS IT REAL?! THIS YOUR SERVICE GUN, MAN?!
Cordell. Damn straight it's real.

(Winston runs to check at the windows, then runs back to the action.)

Winston. Oh, God, man! Let me make sure ain't nobody coming!
Falvie. Damn, man! You said you was gonna get us something!

(Falvie tries to twirl it Wyatt Earp-style.)

Cordell. Watch it, man . . . don't be twirling it like that!
Falvie. It's loaded!?
Jimmy. Hell-yeah it's loaded!
Winston. Lemme hold it, man!
Falvie. Wait a minute . . . I just wanna try one more thing!

(Falvie tries some trick he saw in the movies or on television.)

Winston. Hurry up, man! Come on, now Falvie-man . . . you had it long enough!
Falvie. O.K., man.

(Winston gets the gun from Falvie and strokes it respectfully, then aims, points it at the tapestry on the wall and imitates the sound of gunfire.)

Winston. Let 'em burn another cross! . . . sic this dragon on 'em!
Cordell. Let 'em shoot at the babes one more time!
Winston. POW! POW! Got me a dragon!
Cordell. Now you see why these peckerwoods act so bad? Cause they got these bad-boys!
Winston. Is this for us?
Jimmy. It's up to you.
Winston. You know I want me one!
Falvie. I'm ready!
Cordell. This is the final solution to the "white problem."
Jimmy. Listen up. Serious business. Y'awl gonna have to come to some meetings 'crosstown . . . if y'awl ain't never had no military training or shot one-a these, you gotta be trained.
Cordell. I had R.O.T.C.

Jimmy. That's better than nothing. Cordell, you gonna have to stay away from over here ... and you brothers cool out being seen with him for a while. We need him to go on a mission and he's gotta pass for white. Can y'awl handle that?
Cordell. All this white blood in me ought-a be worth *some*thing!
Jimmy. Just remember, a loose lip'll sink a ship so y'awl can't be running your mouths. This ain't no game and these guns ain't no toys. If you aim it at somebody, make sure you ready to shoot.
Winston. You ain't gotta show me how to handle this booga but once!

(The Men boast of their warrior abilities.)

Cordell. I'm gonna get me some power if it's the last thing I do!
Falvie. Umm-gowa! Black power! St. George gonna kill some dragons!
Cordell. White blood! Ten for one, right fellows? If they kill one-a us, we gonna take off ten of them. Right fellows?

*(The Men ad lib in the affirmative.
Bernie calls out from the top of the stairs.)*

Bernie. *(offstage)* Winston, that's you? Don't leave yet ... I'm coming down!

(The Men hurry to conceal the guns.)

Winston. Yeah, all right ...
Cordell. I'm gonna split before she get down here ... later, y'awl.
Jimmy. I don't need to be seen here, either.

(Cordell exits.)

Falvie. Hold up, I'm coming with you.
Jimmy. We'll go out the back.
Falvie. Winston, you coming?
Winston. *(calling up to Bernie)* Bernie, I gotta go!

*(Jimmy and Falvie exit.
Bernie bounds down the stairs, book and homework in hand.)*

Bernie. Wait a minute! You told me you was gonna help me with trig.
Winston. I know ... and I will, but not now, baby. Cordell n'em are waiting for me ... it's very important.
Bernie. Well, damn! Jump in the bayou when Cordell n'em ask you to!
Winston. I know I promised you ...
Bernie. The professor gave a pop quiz today and all I could do was just stare at the paper.

(She chokes up with tears of frustration. Winston comforts her.)

Winston. Heyyy . . . ! Cut that out, now! Everything's gonna be all right. I ain't going nowhere. Come on, now . . . they'll leave without me. See? I'm still here. Let Winston dry your eyes for you.

(Winston takes out his handkerchief, dabs at Bernie's tears.)

Winston. Stop worrying . . . let Winston see the quiz.

(Bernie opens the textbook and the quiz paper.)

Bernie. I'm so scared I'm gonna get on sco pro and lose my scholarship.
Winston. It is gonna be all right . . . just trust us.
Bernie. I didn't even turn the paper in.
Winston. Turn to your function table . . . you know what your function table is, don't you?
Bernie. I know what it is . . . I just don't know what to do with it.
Winston. In all these problems you gotta find the angle first . . . now, just stay on this line after you find the angle . . . here's your angle.
Bernie. Oh, this is my angle!
Winston. That's it . . . and here's your tangent.
Bernie. Oh . . . so this would be .4316.
Winston. That's to the nearest ten-thousandth . . .
Bernie. That's all I have to do?
Winston. That's all you have to do with these few . . . they get harder and harder.
Bernie. Winston, if you keep helping me . . . I'll give you something.
Winston. You got it.
Bernie. I'm not gonna forget you for this.

(Bernie goes back to working the problems. She is not aware that Winston has changed moods.)

Winston. I hope not. Matter of fact, I wish you could remember me now . . . I'm really hard up, so to speak.
Bernie. Oh, you need something . . . oh, sure. How much you want?
Winston. How much? Baby, I want the whole hog. But I'll just take a little "slice."
Bernie. Aww . . . I know what you talking about. You crazy, Winston!
Winston. I know you go for Cordell.
Bernie. I don't wanna talk about it, Winston, O.K.?
Winston. He's all wrong for you. That's all I wanna say about Mr. Scrap, as y'awl call him . . . 'cause you know I go for you, Bernie . . . and I don't run the wrong way with the ball. I know what basket to put my ball in . . . and I can make it good to you, baby . . .

(Bernie gets up to leave.)

Bernie. I have a class.

Winston. Baby, this is an emergency! I helped you with the trig, didn't I? You said you was gonna give me something.

Bernie. I thought you meant money, Winston.

Winston. Money? Well . . . as Shakespeare always said, "Man can't live by money alone."

Bernie. Shakespeare said that?

Winston. Somebody said it.

Bernie. I'll talk to you later.

Winston. You want me to end up in that insane asylum they got out there?

Bernie. How could you even think of something like that with these crackers shooting at us and burning crosses and stuff . . . ?

Winston. Baby, I can't brain-wash my "johnson."

(Bernie tries to leave again.)

Bernie. I gotta go.

Winston. Baby, don't go yet . . . just let me get the head in . . . !

(Bernie pulls herself away and goes upstairs.
After a few seconds, Winston heads up, too.
Honey enters with Mavis, a tall and shapely woman in her twenties or early thirties. She is dressed in a light suit, her hair in an Afro, and she is carrying a small footlocker.)

Honey. Just set your trunk right over here and let me show you the downstairs first. They sent the mens over here just yes'tiddy to do something to this kitchen . . . I reckon they worked on it . . .

(Honey and Mavis disappear into the kitchen. Suddenly, from upstairs, the girls' screams cut across the ceiling: MAN ON THE HALL! MAN ON THE HALL!
Honey and Mavis run from the kitchen.)

Honey. *(skillet in her hands)* What's the trouble! Who dat up there . . . !? What's the matter?!

(As Winston passes Honey on the stairs, she brings the skillet down on his head.)

Honey. What is this?! What business you got up there?!

Winston. Yes-mam! Yes-mam . . . !

(Veena and Bernie come to the top of the stairs.)

Veena. He come up here for that panty-raid thing, Miss Honey, 'cause they was down there talking about it!

Honey. Say he come up here for what?!

(Mavis tries to block Winston's path.)

Mavis. Don't let him get away! Do y'awl know him?!
Veena. Yes-mam, we know him . . . he come for that thing the white folks do where the men come get the women's drawers!
Honey. Ain't nothing like that up here, son!
Winston. Yes-mam . . . I'm sorry, Miss Honey!
Honey. Now, you stay 'way from up here. These girls could-a been up here n'eked or something!
Winston. Yes-mam, Miss Honey!

(Winston grabs his books and flees for his life.)

Honey. I'm glad your housemother is here now so y'awl won't have'ta put up with this kind-a foolishness no mo'.
Veena. That's our housemother, Miss Honey!
Honey. 'Name Miss Simpson.
Mavis. Mavis.
Honey. Miss Mavis.

(The girls ad lib greetings.)

Honey. Come on up, Miss Mavis . . . let me show you up here. Take this down to the kitchen for me, honey.
Veena. Yes-mam.

(Honey hands Veena the skillet. She heads downstairs as Mavis heads up.)

Bernie. Get the hot plate while you down there, Veena . . . I need you to give my hair a little bump.
Veena. All right.
Mavis. Getting ready to go under the heat, huh?
Bernie. Yes-mam.
Mavis. 'Last time I went under the heat, I was eight years old and my teacher had picked me to wrap the Maypole. My mother, bless her heart, wanted it "fixed" for the occasion. She took me to my auntie, a so-called beautician . . . took one look at my hair, and in front of a shop full of people, said "I've been doing hair for over 30 years, and this is the worse hair I've ever seen!" I haven't set foot in a so-called beauty parlor since.

(The women are too intimidated to respond.)

Mavis. Well . . . that's my hair lecture for today.
Veena. You gonna wear it to class like that, Miss Mavis?
Mavis. Can you give me a good reason why I shouldn't?
Veena. N'ome.

(Mavis goes on her way. Bernie and Veena exchange glances until Mavis disappears.)

Bernie. Fool, you asked her that!
Veena. I just wanted to know. You still want your'n pressed?
Bernie. Hell-yeah! Get your ass in that kitchen and get that hot-plate!
Veena. Tell me something!

(Veena goes into the kitchen as Bernie starts setting up for the hair event. A few seconds later, a livid Veena sounds an alarm.)

Veena. *(offstage)* Oooo! WHERE MY FOOD!? WHO TOOK MY FOOD!
Bernie. What?! What's the matter, Veena . . . ?!

(Veena storms in.)

Veena. WHAT HAPPEN TO ALL THAT FOOD I HAD IN THERE?!
Bernie. I don't know, Veena . . it's not in there?!
Veena. NAW IT AIN'T IN THERE! SOMEBODY DONE ATE IT ALL UP!
Bernie. It wasn't me, Veena . . .
Honey. *(offstage)* What's the trouble now?!

(Mavis and Honey appear at the top of the stairs.)

Mavis. What happened?
Veena. Miss Honey, all that food you brought over here yes'tiddy, I was trying to save mine and somebody ate it all up!
Honey. Now, ain't that a shame?! They ought not to done that! They had theirs, they should-a left your'n alone.
Veena. Ain't nobody did it but old greedy-gut Falvie! Why y'awl let them nigguhs in that kitchen? Everytime they come here they begging for something . . .
Bernie. If I had-a seen 'em, you know I would-a stopped them, Veena.
Honey. Honey'll bring you some more tomorrow. Just let it go. They must-a been awfully hungry to do something like that.
Veena. Done picked all out of it! I don't know where they hands been.
Bernie. I don't know nothing about it, Veena . . .
Veena. I know what I'm gonna do! I'm gonna put some lye in it, and whoever die, I'll know they the one ate it.
Mavis. They're not supposed to go no further than that living room when they come over here.
Bernie. We tell 'em that.
Veena. I have to make my food last 'cause my daddy can't send me no money til' next week.
Honey. Just stop frettin', now. The part they ate off, just take and give it to the cat. Miss Honey'll get you some more.

Veena. I ain't feeding that old cat! It's black!
Bernie. Miss Honey, whose cat is that?
Honey. That's my cat! What's the matter with it being black? Ain't a black sheep still God's lamb? King Solomon say I'm black and I'm comely. Y'awl needs to come to my church and hear my pastor preach. He turning this thing 'round. Y'awl just leave my cat 'lone. I'll feed him if y'awl won't.
Bernie. Miss Honey, I'll feed him. I just wanted to know whose cat it was.
Honey. Bless your heart! Miss Honey didn't go to scare y'awl. My cat and that other "work" is out there to keep these white folks 'way from here. H'it won't hurt the righteous.
Bernie. Yes-mam.

(Veena keeps a good distance, with her fingers crossed. After Mavis and Honey leave, Veena blurts out fearfully.)

Veena. She one-a them "working women"! She do hoo-doo!
Bernie. *(exasperated)* Veena, will you please come on do my hair for me? I don't even believe in that stuff.
Veena. You just don't know! I ain't eating nothing she bring here! I'm glad Falvie n'em ate it.

(Bernie plugs in the hot-plate.)

Bernie. Miss Honey wouldn't do nothing to hurt us.

(Evelyn rushes in, highly excited.)

Evelyn. BOYCOTT! A BOYCOTT! THE WHITE STUDENTS GONNA BOYCOTT THE DRAG! BOYCOTT! THEY GONNA BOYCOTT!!!

(Veena and Bernie are stunned as Evelyn runs through the house like Paul Revere.)

(End of Ritual IV)

RITUAL V

Same set. A week or so later.

Bernie, Veena and Janice are present. Veena is trying to memorize a verse from a book, while Bernie, dipping into a jar of Dixie Peach Hair grease, is putting Janice's hair on rollers.

Veena. Aw, shit! I thought I had that thing.
Janice. Try it one more time, roommate.

Veena.
"Tomorrow and tomorrow and tomorrow
Creeps in this petty pace from day to day
To the last syllable of recorded time;
And all our yesterdays have lighted fools
The way to dusty death . . ."

(Mavis enters, very agitated. She is carrying large law books, which she rests somewhere in the room before heaving an exasperated sigh.
The women ad lib greetings: "Hi, Miss Mavis.")

Bernie. Is something wrong, Miss Mavis?
Mavis. Will somebody tell me why a nigger would sit her black ass up in a big, white cafeteria, at a table full-a crackers, and eat watermelon?!
Janice. We shore ain't gotta ask you who it is.
Mavis. And half a watermelon?! Come on, people!
Bernie. A half?!
Mavis. Damn near!
Janice. I told Bernie she should talk to her roommate.
Bernie. Don't try to be cute, Janice . . . you know her name.
Mavis. You mean she's done this before?!
Janice. She do it all the time . . . eat it down to the "rime." I'm surprised it ain't a whole one.

(Veena tries to muffle her giggle.
Bernie is embarrassed. She, too, giggles nervously.)

Mavis. This just won't do! Don't y'awl care?! Don't you say anything to her about it . . . ?!
Janice. I've said something to her. It don't do no good. She tells me "White people eat watermelon, too . . . they didn't buy all this watermelon just for us."
Mavis. Naw, but they enjoy watching niggers like her eat it.
Janice. They probably bought it for her.
Mavis. Bernie, can't you talk to her?
Bernie. Miss Mavis, I'm sick-a hearing about Evelyn . . . even before we came up here, all my teachers "Keep a eye on Evelyn . . . keep a eye on Evelyn . . ." I washed my hands of that fool a long time ago. She hard-headed and got a mind of her own.
Mavis. She don't act like she got no mind.
Veena. She shore making them A's and B's 'round here. I wish I could make 'em.
Bernie. That's just book-sense, that ain't no common sense.
Janice. She won't even mind you, Miss Mavis . . . you know she won't listen to us.

Mavis. Where I come from, we'd just throw a croaker-sack over her head and beat her ass, and I ain't but two inches away from doing it.
Bernie. Throw the book at her, Miss Mavis . . . I don't care.

(Veena is examining Mavis' law books, tests them curiously to feel their weight.)

Veena. These law books shore is heavy! I see what they mean by the judge throw the book at you . . . one-a these big-boogas hit you, the mercy-a the court won't do you no good.
Mavis. Stop speaking to her. Everybody. I mean not a mumbling word. Not even good-morning or good-evening. Anybody got a problem with that?
Janice. I shore don't!

(This is more than Veena and Bernie bargained for.)

Veena. She helping me with this theme I gotta write.
Janice. I'll help you with the theme, roommate . . . she ain't the only one know how to write a theme.
Veena. But you been busy, roomin'mate . . .
Mavis. Don't worry about it . . . we'll make sure the theme gets done.
Bernie. But I'm in the same room with her, Miss Mavis . . .
Mavis. Move out. Move in with me. How close are you to finishing up with the hair?
Bernie. This is the last one.
Mavis. As soon as you finish, come on up and start moving your things. I'll make room right now.

(Mavis heads upstairs, leaving the girls exchanging looks. Veena gathers up her books. She wants no part of this.)

Veena. I got a class.
Janice. You gonna do it, Bernie?

(Bernie does not answer. Veena catches the look on Bernie's face and heads out, reciting her homework.)

Veena. ". . . tomorrow and tomorrow and tomorrow . . ." Y'awl done made me forget my speech!

(The lights go quickly to black.)

(End of Ritual V)

RITUAL VI

One week later.
  Bernie enters, coming from class. She puts her books down, sits and reflects.
  Honey appears at the top of the stairs.

Honey. Is that my Little Rosa Parks down there?
Bernie. It's me, Miss Honey . . . Bernie.
Honey. Oh, hey'dere . . . thought that was my girl. I be down there d'rectly to clean.
Bernie. Yes-mam.

(Honey disappears.
  Veena enters from the kitchen with the hot plate. Bernie pretends to read.)

Veena. Bernie, you busy now? You got time to bump my hair a little bit for me?
Bernie. It don't matter.

(Honey comes downstairs. Veena sets up the hot plate . . . yells upstairs to Janice.)

Veena. Janice, bring me the hair grease, please! Oh, hi'ya, Miss Honey.
Honey. I reckon my Little Rosa Parks still over to Waggoner. She be over there all the time, tellin' the white girls how it is and they listens. She been to my church! What church y'awl goes to?
Veena. Colored can't go to these churches 'round here.
Honey. Then come to my church, honey! We haves a good time! Be plenty food there. And we eats!

(Janice comes down with the grease, overhears the conversation.)

Veena. It's so far crosstown, Miss Honey . . . we gotta take two buses.
Honey. Little Rosa take 'em. She come early so me and her can sit and read the Bible together. Why'n't y'awl come on go wid her?
Janice. I'm Catholic.

(Honey lets this sink in, then eyes Janice suspiciously.)

Honey. Oh. I don't think they got nothing like that here for the Colored. Do they believe in Jesus?
Janice. Yes-mam!
Honey. Oh, then I guess they all right.
Veena. Do they have a holiness church here?

Honey. Oh, yeah, got plenty-a them. But you wanna hear good preaching and singing and testifying, come to the Baptist church, honey . . . I mean my pastor can preach! Ask little Rosa.

Veena. I'm gonna come, Miss Honey.

Honey. Bless your heart! Bring them others with you . . . I done told 'em 'bout all my young'uns. Well, let me run finish my work.

(After Honey leaves, Janice breaks into an imitation of Honey's cleaning . . . flicking the dustrag over the furniture.)

Janice. All finished! Time to go to the white dorms!

Bernie. Be still and hold your ear, Veena!

Veena. Stop it, roommate . . . I can't be laughing . . . I might get burned.

Janice. *(near the window)* Oh, Lord, here come the fellows.

Veena. Oh, shit! Hide my food, roommate! Hurry up, 'fore that old greedy-gut Falvie go in there and find it!

Bernie. Hide mine, too!

Janice. I will!

(Janice hurries to the kitchen.
Winston and Falvie enter. They have a newspaper in their hands, and act upset.)

Falvie. I want y'awl to see something!

Bernie. What is it?

Falvie. Look at this picture of Evelyn in here . . .

Winston. They got two whole pages of stuff she's saying . . . telling 'em everything!

Bernie. What did she say?

Falvie. Just read it . . . you'll see.

(Janice reenters from the kitchen.)

Winston. And we just saw her in The Common with a bunch-a crackers.

Janice. Who? Evelyn?

Falvie. How did you guess?

(Bernie remains silent, identifying strongly with the attack on Evelyn.)

Winston. Read what she saying about y'awl.

Janice. Lemme see! What? She bet'not be saying nothing about me.

Falvie. She ain't called none of our names, but we know who she talking about.

(Bernie reads, then goes back to Veena's hair . . . an unsettled look on her face.)

Winston. The crackers putting her up to saying all that shit.

Janice. Ooo! Wait till Miss Mavis see this!
Falvie. Show it to her.
Veena. What did she say?
Bernie. Everybody got a right to their opinion.
Winston. Then express her opinion for her own'self . . . don't be expressing it for us. Who appointed her to be our spokesman?
Janice. The crackers did.
Winston. Well, since they picked her, why don't they let her speak for them?
Falvie. She's our spokesman now.
Janice. She don't speak for me.
Falvie. Boy, they done really turned her head!
Janice. Miss Honey is her shepherd . . .
Falvie. Somebody gonna have to bring that runaway slave back to the plantation.
Janice. Ooo! She saying we wanna live with white girls! Hell, I don't wanna live with no white girls!

(Bernie stops pressing Veena's hair, unable to contain herself any longer.)

Bernie. *(irritated)* You did say you wanted to live in the white dorms . . . all of us did.
Janice. Living in the dorm doesn't mean living with them, Bernie . . . I meant we could live in a separate wing to ourselves. She making it sound like we wanna mix all in with them . . .
Winston. How come she's talking to 'em and giving them all this information in the first place?
Bernie. What damn information? Ain't even no information to give.
Falvie. It's information to give about what we've been doing.
Bernie. What have y'awl been doing besides running back and forth over here begging us for things? If it ain't food and money, it's pussy.

(Janice runs upstairs.)

Janice. I'm telling Miss Mavis!
Falvie. I ain't asked you for no "yeah-I'll-excuse-your-French . . ."
Winston. *(rising to leave)* Let's go, man.
Janice. Don't y'awl leave . . . I'm coming back down!
Falvie. We leaving 'til we get our respect.
Winston. That's right . . . done even crossed they legs on us!

(When Cordell enters, Janice runs back down.)

Cordell. Where y'awl going? Hold up.
Winston. You better get these babes straight, man. They all up in our faces with some shit.

Bernie. I didn't get up in your face, Winston.
Falvie. You was shooting off your mouth about what we ain't doing. You don't know what we doing . . . just because we don't tell you. We have to deal with hand grenades outside our door and tar babies hanging in trees with our names on 'em. We can't study like y'awl can . . .
Cordell. Lighten up, Falvie. Everybody lighten up! What's the matter with y'awl?
Janice. Evelyn started it, Cordell . . . giving interviews in the paper and meeting with Wolfgang. Miss Mavis told her to stop talking to these crackers.
Cordell. How come she can't talk to 'em?
Bernie. That's what I wanna know.
Janice. You know why, Bernie. Miss Simpson told us she was filing a case in the courts and we should watch what we're saying.
Cordell. Talking to the whites can't stop no court case. Hell, I talk to 'em.
Winston. But we know why you doing it.
Cordell. This Miss Simpson don't know why. She gonna tell me to stop, too? Who the hell is she, anyway? If she ain't the Miss Simpson that made King Edward give up the throne, she can't make nobody do nothing.

(Mavis appears at the top of the stairs. Veena notices her.)

Veena. Oh, hi, Miss Mavis.
Mavis. Naw, you don't know me, and I don't know you. But you're still on the same plantation I'm on, so that makes us both slaves.
Cordell. I ain't no slave, and I don't care who Evelyn meet with. It won't stop my plans.
Falvie. You better read what she's saying in this paper first.
Cordell. She got my name in there?
Falvie. She saying the merchants on The Drag don't know it but Colored students are already eating in the restaurants and going to the movies and nobody knows they're Colored. Who she talking about if she ain't talking about you? You know what Jim said you have to do before you get found out.
Winston. Hey, Falvie's right, man. Next think you know, she'll be pointing you out to the wrong person.

(Cordell consults the newspaper and we see him grow uneasy by what he reads.)

Bernie. What are y'awl talking about? Point you out to who?
Falvie. That's for us to know and you to find out, and then I wanna see you say we ain't doing nothing.
Mavis. Well, I don't know what you're planning. I just know she's dangerous. No one should meet unilaterally with these crackers.

Janice. That's old Miss Honey got her doing that mess, 'cause she's a white-folks-nigger her own'self.
Cordell. *(coming to a decision)* When she gets here, let me deal with her . . . in my way! And whoever takes it out-a the house, I'm gonna punch 'em in the mouth!
Bernie. You ain't punching me in no mouth, Cordell.
Cordell. Come on, Bernie, don't start no war between us.
Mavis. I didn't hear him call no name. Why'd you jump, Bernie. Are you planning on taking something out-a the house?
Bernie. I didn't say I was gonna take nothing out-a the house . . . he come looking at me . . .
Cordell. I just turned my head in that general direction, Bernie.
Bernie. Y'awl ain't even asked nobody what they think about this . . . everybody is just yeah-yeah, do this, do that . . .
Mavis. Are you telling me that you have not had sufficient time to deal with your roommate, Bernie?
Cordell. Y'awl tried to talk to her before now?
Janice. How many times?
Mavis. I told the sisters to stop speaking to her. That didn't work. I asked Bernie to move out-a the room and leave her in there by herself . . . what do we have to do to stop her?
Janice. She's hard-headed, Cordell . . . you know that.
Cordell. Then it's settled. Everybody in favor of me dealing with her my way, raise your hand.

(Veena and Bernie do not vote. Veena, of course, does not dare.)

Falvie. Case closed.
Cordell. I know how much you love Evelyn, Bernie, but what she's doing is affecting all of us. She's not in this by herself.
Bernie. It's working some, me moving out-a the room. She don't wanna let on it's hurting, but I know her.
Janice. She ain't acting like it. 'Cause you keep speaking to her on the sly.
Bernie. So everybody can't just pass by somebody like they don't exist. So bully for you if you can.
Cordell. Forget it, Bernie. We voted on it already. That's democracy.
Mavis. If somebody holds her, I'll pull her drawers down and beat her ass.
Cordell. I'll try to reason with her first . . .

(Veena cringes from the hot-comb's heat.)

Veena. Watch what you doing, Berna Mae.
Bernie. *(lashing out at her)* Who the hell you talking to?!
Veena. I was just . . . ! I felt the heat close to my scalp . . .

Bernie. That's cause the goddamn straightening comb is hot! That's how nappy hair get straight, heiffer! You want it straight or not?!
Veena. Gol-lee, Berna Mae! I ain't even did nothing to you!
Cordell. Cool it, Bernie. Don't be taking it out on Veena. I know what you mad about, but you gonna have to let Evelyn go. She ain't your baby.
Bernie. I didn't say she was.
Cordell. You always putting her between me and you. Let me see you deny that. You know why you and I couldn't make it.
Janice. Why you getting all hancty, Bernie? You talk about her more than anybody.
Bernie. Anything I said about Evelyn, I've already told her to her face, so you ain't exposing nobody.
Janice. Let's see you tell her to her face that it was you wrote Miss Harding that letter about her up here disgracing the race.
Winston. Cool it, y'awl.

(Evelyn enters. Bernie averts her guilty eyes.)

Evelyn. Hi, everybody . . . even the ones who ain't speaking to me.
Cordell. Hey, baby. We saw your interview in *The Longhorn*. I see y'awl are calling yourselves The John Brown Alliance. Y'awl getting ready to raid Harper's?
Evelyn. Harpers is gonna be the first to fall. But we gonna meet with President Wolfgang to give the school a chance to handle it. If we don't hear from him by next Friday, the boycott is on.
Mavis. You shore picked the right name to go to . . . "a gang of wolves."
Cordell. You fixing to mess up something, baby.
Evelyn. Mess up what?
Cordell. Nevermind what. Just stay out-a this thing, Evelyn. The whites didn't need us when they closed the doors to us, so why do they need us to open 'em?
Evelyn. I told my friends I would be with them. All we're gonna do is kneel in front-a Harpers with a few signs, and just read from our Bibles . . . some of us'll be wearing our crosses in plain view.
Mavis. Fool! Those pecks will rip that cross off your neck and hang you on it!
Falvie. And take out their joints and pee on your Bible.
Winston. While-ago in The Commons, Evelyn . . . that white babe next to you with the hair down to here . . .

(Winston indicates the length.)

Winston. . . . is she gonna be marching with y'awl?
Evelyn. She's one of the leaders.

Winston. I know that babe ain't gonna pee on nobody's Bible.
Janice. How you know, Winston?
Winston. Shee-it . . . good as she look, she can pee on anything I got!
Veena. Ooo! Now, see there, Miss Mavis?!
Winston. Well, hell-mell! Y'awl ain't getting up off-a nothing! My bar-a soap look like a Dentler Maid Potato Chip!
Falvie. Better your bar-a soap look like that than your "johnson" if you get caught with her.
Janice. Don't tell him nothing!
Winston. They had their day with Colored babes. Look at Cordell. The way I see it, somebody owe me a whole lot-a white babes!
Cordell. Knock it off, Winston-man!
Mavis. That's why we can't have revolution. Black rams got their minds on white ewes.
Winston. You talking to me? Yeah, I admit, I dig me some white babes.
Mavis. Then maybe you should join Evelyn.

(Winston does not take the challenge.)

Evelyn. Bernie, you said you would be with us. You keeping your word?
Bernie. I said I wouldn't let you face Wolfgang by yourself. I never said I'd join with a bunch-a white people I don't even know.
Evelyn. I know them.
Mavis. You think you know them. If you really knew them, you wouldn't go nowhere near them.
Cordell. When the sheriff and his men come to break it up, Evelyn, whose ass you think they gonna kick first?
Falvie. She must wanna see what them boot-licks feel like.
Cordell. And as quiet as it's kept, those places on The Drag ain't all they're trumped up to be. Yeah, I passed for white and ate that tasteless food . . . and the movies ain't nothing . . . they ain't gonna liberate us from this shit . . . so for my part . . .
Falvie. I already told y'awl I boycotted their ass a long time ago. I didn't want 'em to have my money.
Mavis. People can say what they want about the Jews, but when those pecks won't let them in a place, they get their money together and come back and buy the joint . . . we go get a picket sign so we can give the sucker our money and make him rich. Where did we come from?!
Falvie. We descended from the moth. That's true! We fly toward the flame.

(Evelyn heads upstairs.)

Cordell. Where you going, Evelyn?
Evelyn. I don't wanna hear no more-a this.

Cordell. I bet you don't walk out when them whiteys is trying to talk to you. Go 'head on, then . . . go . . . Don't keep your friends waiting.
Evelyn. I thought I was with friends here.
Janice. Who told you you had any friends here?
Evelyn. *(looking to Bernie)* I thought I had one.
Cordell. I guess you thought like "Lit." Now, I was willing to let you go'on do your thing, but you're starting to sound like one-a those mad prophets that go around mumbling to his'self . . . talking about you don't hate these crackers! Why not? They hate you.
Mavis. As soon as she gets in Wolfgang's office, he's gonna single her out and question her about us, about what we do in this house.
Cordell. Stay out of his office, Evelyn.
Evelyn. Why don't y'awl come and hear what's being said.
Mavis. We'll meet with "the wolf-gang" in due time, and that decision is not yours to make unilaterally.
Evelyn. Don't nobody tell me what to do.

(Evelyn heads out. Cordell blocks her way.)

Janice. See there? Ever since Miss Mavis came she been disrespecting her. I bet if she was a white housemother, she'd mind her . . .
Cordell. Don't walk away from us when we're talking to you, Evelyn.
Mavis. We ain't doing nothing but playing with her . . . she thinks this is a game.

(Cordell seizes her by the arm.)

Evelyn. You just mad 'cause I won't bow down to you, Miss Mavis! If all-a y'awl are so bad, why'n't you go 'round to Harpers and grab them ax handles?!
Cordell. Get back here . . .
Evelyn. Turn me loose, Cordell! All you old armchair warriors can kiss my behind!

(There is immediate reaction to the insult.)

Janice. Ooo, did you hear that?!
Winston. What kind-a warriors?!
Falvie. Naw, I don't excuse your French!
Mavis. Who're you telling to kiss your funky behind? You're just beside yourself!
Cordell. I wanna know who you calling a armchair warrior?!
Evelyn. You, for one, Mr. Scrap! Mr. Wrong-Way-With-The-Ball Scrap . . . !

(Cordell slaps Evelyn across the face, and there is a chain reaction:

Bernie instinctively tears into Cordell, Falvie tries to restrain Bernie, Winston intervenes on Bernie's behalf.)

Cordell. Shut up! You big-mouth Aunt Jemima! I'll bust your eye-balls out!
Bernie. You leave her alone! Damn you, Cordell!
Evelyn. Scrap! Wrong-Way-With-The-Ball Scrap . . . ! You white nigger . . . !
Bernie. Get off me!

(Cordell produces the gun and places it against Evelyn's head. Everyone freezes.)

Cordell. You call me that one more time, I'll blow you to Kingdom-Come! I swear on my mama's grave, Evelyn! I dare you . . . I dare you, Evelyn . . . !
Mavis. *(cautiously)* Take it easy, now . . . !
Falvie. Oh, God . . . put the safety on that thing, man! Come on, Cordell!

(Meanwhile, at the very sight of the gun, Veena is frightened to near trauma.)

Winston. Come on, Cordell, man . . . ! She ain't worth all that . . . !
Evelyn. I ain't even did nothing to y'awl . . .
Cordell. Shut up, I said! I dare you to even grunt! These crackers around here kicking our ass and you licking theirs.

(Veena mumbles over and over: "Jehova God . . . please, Jehovah God.")

Bernie. Please, Cordell . . . ! She ain't did nothing to you . . .
Cordell. She gonna give me my respect!
Falvie. Just put the safety on, Cordell, please, man . . . !
Winston. Come on, Cordell-man . . . forget it . . . let's get out-a here. Let the women handle that ig'nant "tom."

(Cordell shoves Evelyn to the floor.
Jimmy enters. Everyone is startled by his appearance. Cordell hurriedly tucks the gun under his clothes.
Evelyn is sobbing on the floor.)

Jimmy. What is this?!
Falvie. Oh, hey, man! Ain't nothing happening!
Jimmy. The hell it ain't! Y'awl was making so damn much noise, you didn't even hear me come up on the porch. If them guards had-a still been out there, they'd-a burst in here shooting first and asking questions last.
Cordell. Ain't nobody did nothing to her.
Mavis. You fellows can discuss this outside.

(The men head toward the door.)

Jimmy. Tell me what happened.
Mavis. Nothing happened . . . she's all right. Run get a wet towel for her to wipe her face, Janice . . . I'll handle this. And it's time for curfew, anyway . . . all you fellows have to leave now.

(Janice goes for the towel. Jimmy presses on.)

Jimmy. Ain't nobody gonna do nothing to you . . . just tell me what they did.
Mavis. Excuse me, I said it's curfew and you fellows have to leave . . .
Jimmy. You can tell me . . . they ain't gonna bother you . . .

(The other men hover near the door to see what will happen.)

Mavis. Listen, you better get out-a here . . .
Jimmy. After I find out what happened. She's the only one crying, so the rest-a y'awl must-a did something to her . . .
Cordell. Don't lie, now, heiffer!
Evelyn. Cordell slapped me and . . .
Cordell. You bet'not lie!
Bernie. She's not lying! You did slap her . . . and you got a gun and you was holding it to her head!
Jimmy. What the hell you call yourself doing, Cordell? You ain't even supposed to be coming over here with that gun.
Cordell. Don't nobody tell me where I can't go.
Jimmy. Gimme the damn gun if that's what you gonna do with it.
Cordell. I ain't giving you nothing.

(Jimmy starts walking toward Cordell.)

Cordell. Back off me, man! I ain't playing!

(Cordell draws the gun.)

Winston. Come on, y'awl . . . take it easy!

(Everyone shrinks away from the men.)

Jimmy. You draw a gun on me, man, I'm gonna make you use it!
Falvie. Hey, y'awl cut this out! Come on, man, I'm on scholarship!

(Janice returns, freezes on seeing the gun.)

Mavis. Cut this out! Get out-a here with this!

(Cordell takes the safety off the gun.)

Cordell. The safety's off now, motherfucker! Come on take this gun from me!
Winston. Come on, Cordell, man . . . !

Bernie. Y'awl stop this . . . !

(Jimmy lunges at Cordell, and during the struggle over the gun, it fires: BANG! Jimmy is hit. He does not fall. He holds the wounded place. Cordell is stunned. Everyone falls back in surprise.

And then there is screaming and running. Veena screams continuously in uncontrollable terror.

Strobe lights capture the frenzy and horror of the tragedy.

Veena begins babbling: SAVE US, LORD, SAVE US . . . SAVE YOUR CHILDREN, JESUS . . . SAVE US LORD . . . SAVE US, LORD . . . ! JEHOVAH GOD! HOLY GOD JEHOVAH!

While Veena is having her breakdown, Honey enters, sees the blood and goes to Jimmy.)

Honey. Lord-Lord! Mercy, Jesus! What is this?! Somebody go call the Colored ambulance! Lord-Lord . . . !

(The stage goes to black as into the darkness we hear crying, Honey's and Veena's voices, and the voices of the men: "God, what've we done?!")

(End of Ritual VI)

RITUAL VII

The same place.

Honey is onstage, wearing mourning clothes under her apron. She is moving slowly about the room, putting papers in a wastebasket.

Evelyn and Berna Mae start down the stairs. When they get to the bottom, Honey enfolds one, then the other, with her arms.

Honey. I'm so sorry!

(The girls begin to weep.)

Evelyn. Bye, Miss Honey.
Honey. Miss Honey's so sorry . . . ! Is they sending the others home, too?
Bernie. *(wiping her tears)* Yes-mam. Veena's daddy's coming for her day after tomorrow.
Honey. Po' little thing! I hope they don't have to have her put away. I'm gonna keep on praying for her. Honey gonna pray for all of you . . .
Evelyn. Yes-mam. Thank you, Miss Honey . . . Thank you for everything.
Honey. Chile, you near'bout had me readin . . . !

(Evelyn tears herself away and hurries out. Honey stands looking at the space where the girls disappeared, and then she weeps.

When she composes herself, she goes back to her work putting paper in the wastebasket. She finds one sheet of paper and painstakingly reads what is on it.)

Honey. A . . . tale . . . told . . . by . . . a . . . .

(This word stumps her, and she throws the paper away.)

Honey. Such big words!

(She gives the furniture a few licks with her dustrag and then the lights go out when she leaves the stage.)

(End of Ritual VII)
CURTAIN

Flyin' West (1992)

Pearl Cleage (b. 1948–   )

Pearl Cleage's full-length drama *Flyin' West* has launched her as one of the most exciting and dynamic playwrights of the 1990s. With the aid of a major AT&T grant, *Flyin' West* premiered at the Alliance Theatre in Atlanta in 1992. Since its opening, the play has been produced at various regional theatres such as Indiana Repertory, Alabama Repertory, and St. Louis Black Repertory. This powerful and captivating historical play focuses on the lives of four African American women who, like many African Americans during the late 1800s, fled the racist South and headed for the western frontier in search of prosperity, security, and autonomy as a result of the 1860 Homestead Act. The play also examines how these women struggle to keep their land in the all-black town of Nicodemus, Kansas. *Flyin' West* weaves story-telling about slavery, the conditions of blacks in the South, spousal abuse, and women who take control of their lives. Like many of Cleage's works, *Flyin' West* "creates black women characters at the center of the world" (Tomika DePriest, "Multi-Talented Writer Pearl Cleage is Flyin'," *RPM Magazine* [1993], 14–15).

A prolific poet, playwright, essayist, and performance artist, Cleage was born in Springfield, Massachusetts, but was reared in Detroit. She attended Howard University from 1966 to 1969, where she studied under Owen Dodson, Ted Shine, and Paul Carter Harrison. Her first play, *Duet for Three Voices,* was produced at Howard in 1968. From 1970 to 1971 she attended

Spelman College, where she studied under Baldwin Burroughs and Carlton Molette, and received her B.A. degree in drama. She has been the recipient of numerous grants and awards, including the 1983 AUDELCO Award for her Off Broadway play *Hospice,* which also was performed in its first international production in 1990 by the MAMU Players in South Africa. Other grant support for her writings has come from such varied organizations as the National Endowment for the Arts, the Georgia Council on the Arts, the Coca-Cola Company, and the Whitter-Bynner Foundation for Poetry. Some of her other plays include *Puppetplay*, *Hymn for the Rebels*, *Good News*, *Essentials*, *Porch Songs*, *Banana Bread*, and *Come and Get These Memories*. Her plays have been performed at theatres and colleges throughout the country. Her two newest one-act plays, *Chain* and *Late Bus to Mecca,* premiered Off Broadway, coproduced in 1991 by the Women's Project and Productions and the New Federal Theatre. The Atlanta-based writer is Playwright-in-Residence at Spelman College and also the artistic director of Just Us Theatre Company.

Cleage's nondramatic works include the best-selling book *Mad at Miles: A Blackwoman's Guide to Truth* (1990) and *Deals with the Devil and Other Reasons to Riot* (1993), a collection of 37 essays. In addition to these two volumes, she has published a book of poetry titled *We Don't Need No Music* (1972), and her first book of short fiction, *The Brass Bed and Other Stories,* was published in 1991. She is the editor of *Catalyst* magazine, and she writes regularly for *Essence* magazine and other periodicals, and contributes a column to the *Atlanta Tribune.*

Much of Cleage's work examines domestic violence. Not only does she explore this issue in *Flyin' West* but she also deals with it in much of her recent writings. According to Cleage, ". . . I am writing because five women a day are murdered by men who say they love them. . . . I am writing to expose and explore the point where racism and sexism meet. . . . I am writing to find solutions and pass them on . . ." (Pearl Cleage, *Deals with the Devil and Other Reasons to Riot* [New York: Ballantine/One World, 1993], 7).

Selected Published Plays by Pearl Cleage

Chain. In *Playwriting Women: 7 Plays from the Women's Project,* ed. Julia Miles. Portsmouth, NH: Heinemann, 1993.
Hospice. In *New Plays for the Black Theatre,* ed. Woodie King, Jr. Chicago: Third World Press, 1989.
Late Bus To Mecca. In *Playwriting Women: 7 Plays from the Women's Project,* ed. Julia Miles. Portsmouth, NH: Heinemann, 1993.

Flyin' West
A Play in Two Acts

CHARACTERS

Sophie Washington, a black woman, born into slavery, age 36
Miss Leah, a black woman, born into slavery, age 73
Fannie Dove, a black woman, age 32
Wil Parrish, a black man, born into slavery, age 40
Minnie Dove Charles, a black woman, age 21
Frank Charles, a very light skinned black man, born into slavery, age 36

SCENES

Time: Fall 1898.
Place: Outside the all-black town of Nicodemus, Kansas.
Setting: The play takes place in and around the house shared by Sophie, Fan and, more recently, Miss Leah. The women are wheat farmers and the house sits in the midst of the vastness of the Kansas prairie. Activity will take place mainly in the house's kitchen/dining/living room, which has a table, chairs, a small desk, a wood burning stove, etc. In the back and upstairs are other bedrooms, one of which will also be the scene of action during the play. Other activity takes place in the area outside the front door, including wood gathering and chopping, hanging of clothes to dry, etc. There is also a brief arrival scene at the nearby train station, which need only be suggested.

ACT I

Scene 1: A fall evening.
Scene 2: Two days later; early afternoon.
Scene 3: The same day; evening.
Scene 4: The next morning.
Scene 5: Late that night.

ACT II

Scene 1: Early the next morning.
Scene 2: The next Sunday; early morning.
Scene 3: Sunday afternoon.
Scene 4: Sunday evening.
Scene 5: Monday morning.
Scene 6: Seven months later; April 1899.

AUTHOR'S PROGRAM NOTES

The Homestead Act of 1860 offered 320 acres of "free" land, stolen from the dwindling populations of Native Americans, to U.S. citizens who were willing to settle in the western states. Although many settlers lived in traditional family groups, by 1890, a quarter of a million unmarried or widowed women were running their own farms and ranches. The farm work was hard and constant, but many of these women were able to survive due to their own physical stamina, determination and the help of their neighbors.

Large groups of African American homesteaders left the South following the Civil War to settle all black towns. The so-called "Exodus of 1879" saw twenty to forty thousand African American men, women and children—"Exodusters"—reach Kansas under the guidance of a charismatic leader, Benjamin "Pap" Singleton, who escaped from slavery and claimed later "I am the whole cause of the Kansas migration!"

Crusading black journalist Ida B. Wells's call to her readers to leave Memphis, Tennessee, after an 1892 lynching and riot, was heeded by over 7,000 black residents of the city who packed up as many of their belongings as they could carry and headed west in search of a life free from racist violence. Unfortunately, their dreams were shattered as many western states enacted Jim Crow laws as cruel as any in the old Confederacy and effectively destroyed most of the black settlements by the early 1900s.

This is a story of some of the black people who went west.

ACT I

SCENE 1

A fall evening.

Sophie enters rapidly. Her heavy coat is unbuttoned and her scarf flies out around her neck. It is chilly, but the cold has exhilarated her. She has just returned from a trip into town. She has a large bag of flour slung over her shoulder and a canvas shoulder bag full of groceries. She is carrying a shotgun, which she places by the door. She slings the bag of flour carelessly on the table and, coat still on, puts the other bag on a chair. She fumbles through her pockets, first withdrawing a letter, which she holds for a moment thoughtfully, then sticks in the growing pile on the overflowing desk. She fumbles through her pockets again and withdraws some long strips of black licorice. She takes a bite, sighs, chews appreciatively. She pulls a chair over to the window, opens it wide and sits down, propping her booted feet up on the window sill. She looks out the window with great contentment, takes another bite of licorice and chews slowly, completely satisfied with the candy's sweetness, the chill in the air and the privacy of the moment.

Miss Leah enters haltingly. She walks unsteadily but has no cane to steady herself so she holds on to the furniture as she walks slowly in to the room. She is looking for something and her manner is exasperated. Sophie does not notice her entering. Miss Leah looks at Sophie, immediately notices the open window and her irritation increases.

Miss Leah. Well, ain't you somethin'!

Sophie. I didn't know you were up, Miss Leah. Want a piece? *(Sophie gets up and closes the window, stokes the fire, etc.)*

Miss Leah. I hate licorice. *(Miss Leah stumbles a little. Sophie moves to steady her and is stopped by a "don't you dare" look from Miss Leah.)*

Sophie. You miss your cane?

Miss Leah. I don't need no cane! I told you that before. You can lay it next to my bed or prop it against my chair like it walked out there on its own. It still ain't gonna make me no never mind. I don't want no cane and I don't need no cane.

Sophie. Suit yourself. *(Takes another bite of licorice as she hangs her coat. Miss Leah's shawl is hanging there in plain view. Sophie starts to reach for it, stops, ignores it and begins putting things away. Miss Leah finally speaks with cold dignity.)*

Miss Leah. I am looking for my shawl, if you must know.

Sophie. It's right . . .

Miss Leah. Don't tell me! If you start tellin' me, you'll just keep at it 'til I won't be able to remember a darn thing on my own.

Sophie. I'll make some coffee.
Miss Leah. I don't know why. Can't nobody drink that stuff but you.
Sophie. It'll warm you up.
Miss Leah. It'll kill me.
Sophie. Well, then, you haven't got much time to put your affairs in order.
Miss Leah. My affairs are already in order, thank you. *(pulls her chair as far from the window as possible and sits with effort)* It's too cold for first October. *(shivering)* Where's my shawl? Don't tell me!
Sophie. I brought you some tobacco.
Miss Leah. What kind?
Sophie. The kind you like.
Miss Leah. *(pleased in spite of herself)* Well, thank you, Sister Sophie. Maybe a good pipe can cut the taste of that mess you cookin' up in Fan's good coffee pot. *(She proceeds to make a pipe while Sophie makes coffee.)* What are we celebrating?
Sophie. We are celebrating my ability not to let these Nicodemus Negroes worry me, no matter how hard they try.
Miss Leah. Then we ought to be drinking corn whiskey. *(Miss Leah lights the pipe and draws on it contentedly.)* Are you still worrying about the vote?
Sophie. I just told you. I'm celebrating an end to worrying. *(a beat)* I rode in by way of the south ridge this morning. Smells like snow up there already.
Miss Leah. What were you doing way over there?
Sophie. Just looking . . .
Miss Leah. Ain't you got enough land to worry about?
Sophie. I'll have enough when I can step outside my door and spin around with my eyes closed and wherever I stop, as far as I can see, there'll be nothing but land that belongs to me and my sisters.
Miss Leah. Well, I'll try not to let the smoke from my chimney drift out over your sky.
Sophie. That's very neighborly of you. Now drink some of this.
Miss Leah. *(drinks and grimaces)* Every other wagon pull in here nowadays got a bunch of colored women on it call themselves homesteadin' and can't even make a decent cup of coffee, much less bring a crop in! When I got here, it wadn't nobody to do nothin' for me but me . . .
Sophie and Miss Leah. *(together)* . . . and I did everything there was to be done and then some . . .
Miss Leah. That's right! Because I was not prepared to put up with a whole lotta mouth. Colored men always tryin' to tell you how to do somethin' even if you been doin' it longer than they been peein' standin' up. *(a beat)* They got that in common with you.
Sophie. I don't pee standing up.

Miss Leah. You would if you could! *(sips coffee and grimaces again)*
Sophie. Put some milk in it, Miss Leah.
Miss Leah. When I want milk, I drink milk. When I want coffee, I want Fan's coffee!
Sophie. Suit yourself. *(a beat)* People were asking about Baker at the land office.
Miss Leah. What people?
Sophie. White people. Asked me if I had heard anything from him.
Miss Leah. Ain't no white folks looking to settle in no Nicodemus, Kansas.
Sophie. It's some of the best land around here. You said it yourself.
Miss Leah. Ain't nothin' good to no white folks once a bunch of colored folks get set up on it!
Sophie. There's already a new family over by the Gaddy's and a widower with four sons between here and the Jordan place. They've probably been looking at your place, too.
Miss Leah. Who said so?
Sophie. Nobody said anything. I just mean since you've been staying with us for awhile.
Miss Leah. Well, I ain't no wet behind the ears homesteader. I own my land. Free and clear. My name the only name on the deed to it. Anybody lookin' at my land is countin' they chickens. I made twenty winters on that land and I intend to make twenty more.

(While Miss Leah fusses, Sophie quietly goes and gets her shawl and gently drops it around her shoulders.)

Sophie. And then what?
Miss Leah. Then maybe I'll let you have it.
Sophie. You gonna make me wait until I'm old as you are to get my hands on your orchard?
Miss Leah. That'll be time enough. If I tell you you can have it any sooner, my life won't be worth two cents!
Sophie. You don't really think I'd murder you for your land, do you?

(Miss Leah looks at Sophie for a beat before drawing deeply on her pipe.)

Miss Leah. I like Baker. And Miz Baker sweet as she can be. They just tryin' to stay in the city long enough for her to get her strength back and build that baby up a little.
Sophie. She'll never make it out here and you know it.
Miss Leah. Losing three babies in three years take it out of you, girl!
Sophie. They wouldn't have made it through the first winter if Wil Parrish hadn't been here to help them.
Miss Leah. You had a lot of help your first coupla winters, if I remember it right.
Sophie. And I'm grateful for it.

Miss Leah. Some of us were here when you got here. Don't forget it!
Sophie. All I'm trying to say is the Bakers have been gone almost two years and he hasn't even filed an extension. It's against the rules.
Miss Leah. Against whose rules? Don't nobody but colored folks know they been gone that long no way. Them white folks never come out here to even check and see if we're dead or alive. You know that good as the next person. *(a beat)* Sometimes I suspect you think you the only one love this land, Sister, but you not.
Sophie. What are you getting at?
Miss Leah. Just the way you were speechifyin' and carryin' on in town meetin' last week like you the only one got a opinion that matter.
Sophie. Why didn't the others speak up if they had so much to say?
Miss Leah. Can't get a word in edgewise with you goin' on and on about who ain't doin' this and that like they 'spose to.
Sophie. But you know I'm right!
Miss Leah. Bein' right ain't always the only thing you got to think about. The thing you gotta remember about colored folks is all the stuff they don't say when they want to, they just gonna say it double time later. That's why you gonna lose that vote if you ain't careful.
Sophie. It doesn't make sense. A lot of the colored settlements have already passed rules saying nobody can sell to outsiders unless everybody agrees.
Miss Leah. Ain't nobody gonna give you the right to tell them when and how to sell their land. No point in ownin' it if you can't do what you want to with it.
Sophie. But half of them will sell to the speculators! You know they will!
Miss Leah. Then that's what they gonna have to do.
Sophie. We could have so much here if these colored folks would just step lively. We could own this whole prairie. Nothing but colored folks farms and colored folks wheat fields and colored folks cattle everywhere you look. Nothing but colored folks! But they can't see it. They look at Nicodemus and all they can see is a bunch of scuffling people trying to get ready for the winter instead of something free and fine and all our own. Most of them don't even know what we're doing here!
Miss Leah. That's cause some of them come cause they ain't never had nothin' that belonged to 'em. Some of them come cause they can't stand the smell of the city. Some of them just tired of evil white folks. Some of 'em killed somebody or wanted to. All everybody got in common is they plunked down twelve dollars for a piece of good land and now they tryin' to live on it long enough to claim it.
Sophie. Everybody isn't even doing that.
Miss Leah. Everybody doin' the best they can, Sister Sophie.
Sophie. And what happens when that isn't good enough?

Miss Leah. Then they have to drink your coffee!

(Sophie laughs as Wil and Fannie enter outside. We can still see the activity in the house, but we no longer hear it. Miss Leah is smoking her pipe and Sophie is working on her ledgers at the messy desk. She pushes Fan's papers aside carelessly, completely focused.
   Wil is dressed in work clothes. Fannie is dressed in boots, long skirt, shawl. They are strolling companionably and chatting with the ease of old and trusted friends.)

Wil. I guess I'd have to say the weather more than anything. I miss that Mexican sunshine. Makes everything warm. You know how cold these creeks are when you want to take a swim? Well, I like to swim, bein' from Florida and all, so I close my eyes and jump in real quick! But that water would neigh'bout kill a Mexican. They don't know nothin' 'bout no cold. They even eat their food hot!

(Fan laughing stops to pick a flower to add to her already overflowing basket.)

Fan. Look! *(holding it up for Wil's inspection)* That'll be the last of these until spring.
Wil. I imagine it will be. I ate a Mexican hot pepper one time. It looked just like a Louisiana hot pepper, but when I bit into it, it neigh 'bout lifted the top of my head off. Them Mexicans were laughing so hard they couldn't even bring me no water. I like to died!
Fan. You really miss it, don't you?
Wil. Miss Fannie, sometimes I surely do. But I know Baker needs somebody to keep an eye on things for him until he gets back. And now I got Miss Leah's place to look in on too.
Fan. Do you think they'll be back this spring?
Wil. He swears they will.
Fan. Sophie doesn't think they're strong enough for this life.
Wil. Sometimes people are a lot stronger then you can tell by just lookin' at 'em.
Fan. Did he say anything about the baby?
Wil. Said he's fat and healthy and looks just like him, poor little thing!
Fan. *(laughing)* Shame on you! *(a beat)* Has Miss Leah said anything to you about going home?
Wil. No. Not lately.
Fan. Good! We're trying to convince her to stay the winter with us.
Wil. She's not tryin' to go back to her place alone, is she?
Fan. She really wants to, but she's just gotten so frail. Sophie says it was just a matter of time before she fell and broke something.
Wil. *(a beat)* You know what else I like? I mean about Mexico?

Fan. What?
Wil. I like Mexicans.
Fan. Well, that works out nice, I guess.
Wil. Everybody livin' in Mexico don't like Mexicans, Miss Fannie. They separate out the people from the stuff they do like and go on about their business like they ain't even there.
Fan. I never met any Mexicans.
Wil. Nicest people you ever wanna see. Friendly, but know how to keep to they self, too. Didn't no Mexicans ever say nothin' out of the way to me as long as I was livin' down there. They a lot like them Seminoles I grew up around in Florida. When I run away, them Indians took me in and raised me up like I was one of their own. They most all gone now. Ain't got enough land left to spit on, if you'll forgive me sayin' it that way.
Fan. Do you think you'll go back? To Mexico, I mean.
Wil. I used to think so, but I spent seven years down there. As long as I spent on anybody's plantation, so I guess I'm back even. *(a beat)* I might even be a little ahead. *(He hands her a flower that has fallen out of her basket.)*
Fan. *(embarrassed)* My mother loved flowers. Roses were her favorites. My father used to say, "colored women ain't got no time to be foolin' with no roses" and my mother would say, as long as colored men had time to worry about how colored women spent their time, she guessed she had time enough to grow some roses.
Wil. I like sunflowers. They got sunflowers in Mexico big as a plate.
Fan. Sophie likes sunflowers, too, but they're too big to put inside the house. They belong outside. *(a beat)* It's lonely out here without flowers. Sophie laughed the first time everything I planted around the house came into bloom. She said I had planted so many flowers there wasn't any room for the beans and tomatoes.
Wil. That's where your sister's wrong. There's room for everything to grow out here. If there ain't nothin' else out here, there's plenty of room.

(They stand together, looking at the beauty of the sunset. Wil turns after a moment and looks at her, quietly removing his hat and holding it nervously in his hands.)

Fan. You think it's going to be a long winter, Wil?
Wil. They're all long winters, Miss Fannie. This one will be about the same.
Fan. Sophie found her laugh out here. I don't remember ever hearing her laugh the whole time we were in Memphis. But everything in Kansas was funny to her. Sometimes when we first got here, she'd laugh so hard she'd start crying, but she didn't care. One time, she was laughing so

hard I was afraid she was going to have a stroke. She scared me to death. When she calmed down, I asked her, well, why didn't you ever laugh like that in Memphis? And she said her laugh was too free to come out in a place where a colored woman's life wasn't worth two cents on the dollar. What kind of fool would find that funny, she asked me. She was right, too. Sophie's always right. *(While she speaks, Wil reaches out very slowly and almost puts his arm around her waist. She does not see him and he stops before touching her, suddenly terrified she would not appreciate the gesture. She picks up the flowers and hesitates.)* We're friends, aren't we?

Wil. Yes, Miss Fannie. I would say we are.

Fan. Then I wish you'd just call me Fannie. You don't have to call me Miss Fannie.

Wil. *(embarrassed)* I didn't mean to offend you, Miss . . . I just sort of like to call you that because it reminds me that a colored woman is a precious jewel deserving of my respect, my love and my protection.

Fan. *(taken aback and delighted)* Why, Wil! What a sweet thing to say!

Wil. My mother taught it to me. She used to make me say it at night like other folks said prayers. There were some other things she said, too, but I can't remember them anymore. When I first run off after they sold her, I tried to close my eyes and remember her voice sayin' 'em, but all them new Indian words was lookin' for a place in my head, too. So I lost 'em all but that one I just told you. She used to say if a colored man could just remember that one thing, life would be a whole lot easier on the colored woman.

Fan. Can I put it in the book?

Wil. With Miss Leah's stories?

Fan. It's not just Miss Leah's stories anymore, Wil. It's sort of about all of us.

Wil. I would call it an honor to be included.

Fan. Well, good! *(Suddenly embarrassed, she adjusts her shawl and prepares to go inside.)*

Wil. Walkin' with you has been the pleasure of my day.

Fan. Would you like some coffee before you start back?

Wil. No, thanks. I want to catch the last of the light. Give my best to your sister.

Fan. I will.

Wil. And Miss Leah.

Fan. Yes, I will.

Wil. Tell her . . . Miss Leah . . . maybe I'll stop in . . . tomorrow?

Fan. We'll look for you.

Wil. Well, good evening then.

Fan. Good evening.

(He starts off. Miss Leah comes to the window and watches the parting.)

Fan. Wil . . . *(He turns back hopefully. Fan walks to him and puts a flower in his button hole.)* Take this for company on your way back.
Wil. Why, thank you! I do thank you.
Fan. Good evening, Wil.
Wil. And to you . . . Miss Fannie.

(He tips his hat and walks off, adjusting the flower in his button hole. Fan watches him until he is gone, then walks slowly to the house. Miss Leah returns to her seat and begins humming "Amazing Grace." Sophie looks at her. She continues humming loudly and rocking with a smug look on her face.)

Sophie. What is it?
Miss Leah. I ain't said a word to you.
Sophie. You're humming at me!
Miss Leah. I ain't hummin' at nobody. I am just hummin'.

(Fan enters with flowers.)

Fan. I'm sorry to be so late!
Miss Leah. Sophie made coffee.
Sophie. She's been humming at me ever since.

(Fan kisses Sophie's cheek and pats Miss Leah.)

Fan. Everything is fine at your place, Miss Leah.

(She puts the flowers in water and arranges them quickly around the room.)

Miss Leah. Everythin's fine but me.
Fan. Aren't you feeling good?
Miss Leah. I'm too old to feel good. How's Wil Parrish feelin'?
Fan. He's just fine, thank you.
Sophie. Did he walk back with you? Why didn't he come in?
Fan. He'll be by tomorrow.
Sophie. You should have invited Wil Parrish in for a cup of coffee.
Fan. I did. He wanted to catch the last light.
Miss Leah. Well, that sure was a friendly flower you stuck in his button hole a few minutes ago! But it's none of my business. *(starts humming again)*
Fan. I ran into him watering his horse near the creek and he walked back with me. That's all.
Sophie. Has he heard from Baker?
Fan. He had a letter last week. Mother and baby are both doing fine.
Sophie. There's some people interested in that land.

Fan. Who?
Sophie. Families. White families.
Fan. In Nicodemus?
Miss Leah. Just what I said!
Fan. I don't believe it. All the settlements they've got, why would they want to file a claim over here with us?
Sophie. Why don't you ask some of those land speculators holed up at the boarding house?

(The food is laid out and they seat themselves. Sophie moves to help Miss Leah who waves her away and will only accept help from Fan.)

Fan. Well, it's neither here nor there. They'll be back on that land themselves by spring.
Sophie. I hope so. I don't need a whole bunch of strange white folks living that close to me!

(They are seated and Fan lights a candle in the center of the table. The three join hands.)

Fan. Bless this food, oh, Lord, we are about to receive for the nourishment of our bodies, through Jesus Christ our Lord, Amen.
Miss Leah. Jesus wept!
Sophie. Amen!
Fan. Baker's a good man to take his wife back east to have her baby. I don't think she could have survived losing another one out here.
Miss Leah. These young women wouldn't have lasted a minute before the war. Overseer make you squat right down beside the field and drop your baby out like an animal. All ten of my sons was born after sundown 'cause that was the only way to be sure I could lay down to have 'em.
Fan. How did your babies know it was nighttime?
Miss Leah. I knew it! If I felt 'em tryin' to come early, I'd hold 'em up in there and wouldn't let 'em. Bad enough bein' born a slave without that peckerwood overseer watchin' 'em take the first breath of life before their daddy done seen if they a boy or a girlchild.
Fan. I think Miz Baker will be all right. I think she was just scared and lonesome for her mother. She can't be more than twenty.
Miss Leah. I wadn't but fourteen when I had my first one! Got up the next morning and strapped him on my back and went back out to the field. Overseer didn't notice him 'til the day half over. What you got there, nigger? He say to me. This here my son, I say. I callin' him Samson like in the bible 'cause he gonna be strong! Overseer laugh and say, good! Colonel Harrison always lookin' for strong niggers to pick his cotton. I want to tell him that not what I got in mind for my Samson, but I kept my mouth shut like I had some sense. I ain't never been no fool.

Fan. Wil said he didn't think there would be snow for another couple of weeks at least.
Sophie. If he's got that much time to chit chat, maybe I can get him to help me repair that stretch of fence out beyond the north pasture.
Fan. He already did.
Sophie. He did? When?
Fan. Yesterday. He told me to tell you not to worry about it.
Miss Leah. *(enjoying Sophie's surprise)* Now that Wil Parrish is a good man and a good neighbor. You can't ask for better than that. Don't you think so, Fan?
Fan. Yes. I do think so.
Sophie. Are you sweet on Wil Parrish?
Fan. We're friends, Sister.
Miss Leah. You could do a lot worse. And he likes you. I can tell it sure as you sittin' here. Look at her blush! We gonna have a weddin' come spring!
Sophie. I already lost one sister. Don't give Fan away too!
Miss Leah. Shoot, you ought to be glad. Once Fan gets out of the way, you might find somebody fool enough to take a look at you.
Sophie. Two things I'm sure of. I don't want no white folks tellin' me what to do all day, and no man tellin' me what to do all night.
Miss Leah. I'll say amen to that!
Fan. *(clearing up dishes)* Do you want to work on your stories some tonight?

(Sophie takes out her shotgun and begins to clean and oil it. She breaks it down quickly and efficiently. She has done this a thousand times.)

Miss Leah. I'm too tired.
Fan. *(coaxing)* Let's just finish the one we were working on Sunday night.
Miss Leah. I keep tellin' you these ain't writin' stories. These are tellin' stories.
Fan. Then tell them to me!
Miss Leah. So you can write 'em!
Fan. So we can remember them.
Miss Leah. Colored folks can't forget the plantation any more than they can forget their own names. If we forget that, we ain't got no history past last week.
Sophie. But you won't always be around to tell it.
Miss Leah. Long enough, Sister Sophie. Long enough. *(She gets up unsteadily.)* Good night, Fan.
Fan. Good night, Miss Leah.

(Miss Leah looks at Sophie who speaks without looking up.)

Sophie. You're not going to be mad at me all winter, are you?
Miss Leah. Good night, Sister Sophie.
Sophie. Good night, Miss Leah.

(Miss Leah exits.)

Fan. Why do you agitate her?
Sophie. She'll live longer if she's doing it to irritate me. *(a beat)* I need a new hoop for that back wheel and it won't be in by Friday. Do you think Wil Parrish has got plans for his wagon on Friday?
Fan. You can ask him. He's going to stop by tomorrow . . . to see Miss Leah.
Sophie. Good . . . I'm sure Miss Leah will be pleased to see him.
Fan. I wish you wouldn't work at my desk. Look at this mess! What's this?
Sophie. It's from Miss Lewiston.
Fan. She's still coming isn't she? *(anxiously reading the letter)*
Sophie. She "regrets she will be unable to fulfill the position of instructor at the Nicodemus School and wishes us the best of luck in finding someone else to assume this important responsibility."
Fan. She's getting married.
Sophie. And her husband's scared of life on the frontier. What kind of colored men are they raising in the city these days anyway?
Fan. She didn't say he was scared.
Sophie. She said he was nervous about moving to a place where there were still gangs of wild Indians at large.
Fan. People are scared of different things.
Sophie. No they're not. They're either scared or they're not.
Fan. *(folding up the letter; resigned to it)* Do you ever regret it? Coming west like we did.
Sophie. I never regret anything.
Fan. I miss the conversation more than anything, I think.
Sophie. Don't Miss Leah and I keep you amused?
Fan. That wouldn't be the word I'd use. No! Of course you do. That's not what I mean . . . I mean, the literary societies and the Sunday socials and the forums. Mama and Daddy's house was always full of people talking at the top of their lungs about the best way to save the race. And then somebody would start thumping away on Mama's old piano and begging her to sing something. I used to hide at the top of the steps and watch them until I'd fall asleep right there.
Sophie. Well, Minnie ought to be able to fill you in on the latest in that kind of life.
Fan. London, Sister. It may as well be on another planet. I can't believe she'll really be here. It seems like she's been gone forever.
Sophie. Almost a year and a half.

Fan. Fifteen months, three weeks and five days.
Sophie. But who's counting?
Fan. I miss her so! If I try to talk her into staying longer, don't let me!
Sophie. Why?
Fan. You know how Frank feels about the frontier.
Sophie. How can I stop you?
Fan. Kick me under the table or something! At least she'll be here for her birthday. She said Frank thinks it will take a couple of weeks to get the will settled. I hope everything turns out all right. Frank is counting so much on this inheritance.
Sophie. Frank better figure out how to work for a living! I picked up the new deeds today. One for you, one for me and one for Baby Sister. That ought to make her feel grown.
Fan. She's not going to believe it.
Sophie. Why? I always told her she'd have her share officially when she got old enough.
Fan. Knowing you, I think she thought you meant about sixty-five! Sometimes I try to imagine what Baby Sister's life is like over there. How it feels. It must be exciting. Museums and theaters all over the place. She said Frank did a public recital from his book and there were fifty people there.
Sophie. How many colored people were there?
Fan. She didn't say.
Sophie. None! No! Two! Her and Frank. Who ever heard of a colored poet moving someplace where there aren't any colored people?
Fan. Where do you expect him to live? Nicodemus?
Sophie. Why not? I'm giving her the deed to one third of the land we're standing on and she's married to a man who'd rather take a tour of Piccadilly Circus!
Fan. Some people are not raised for this kind of life.
Sophie. Did we raise Min for the life she's living halfway around the world?
Fan. Of course, we did. We always exposed her to the finest things.
Sophie. But why do all those fine things have to be so far away from Negroes?
Fan. I think our baby sister is having so much fun out there in the world, coming back here is probably the last thing on her mind.
Sophie. Do you know how much land they could be buying with all that money they're running through living so high on the hog?
Fan. They've got plenty of time to buy land.
Sophie. All that money and the best he can think of to do with it is move to England and print up some books of bad poetry.
Fan. They weren't that bad.

Sophie. They were terrible! "Odes to Spring." You couldn't even tell a Negro wrote them.
Fan. What's so bad about that? We don't have to see spring differently just because we're Negroes, do we?
Sophie. We have to see everything differently because we're Negroes, Fan. I think Frank is going to find that out when they finish with this business about his father's will.
Fan. Min says Frank has hired a lawyer. You don't think they'll cut him out of the will, do you?
Sophie. How many white gentlemen do you know who want to share their inheritance with a bastard?
Fan. That's not fair.
Sophie. He's the one who kept talking about his father this and his father that and the man wouldn't even come to the wedding!
Fan. Well, I just try to give him the benefit of the doubt. Mama said every colored man deserved at least that much from a colored woman.
Sophie. Suit yourself. All I know is, we're going to have a school by spring if I have to teach in it myself!
Fan. Poor children would be crazy before they had a chance to learn their ABC's!
Sophie. *(suddenly)* Sh-h-h-h-h! *(She motions toward the candle and Fan blows it out immediately. Sophie clicks the gun quickly into place and loads two shells into place. She goes quickly to the window and peers out. Fan stands motionless, watching her. Sophie breathes a sigh of relief.)* Deer! Three of them! Come look.

(Sophie sits down the gun and the two stand looking at the deer in the moonlight.)

Sophie. I'll be nice to Frank. For Min's sake. Butter won't melt in my mouth.
Fan. Promise?
Sophie. I promise. *(They embrace warmly. Fan relights the candle and Sophie fixes the fire in the stove for the night.)* Did you talk Miss Leah out of going to the station with us?
Fan. I think so.
Sophie. You did? How?
Fan. I told her you didn't think it was a good idea.
Sophie. No wonder she's mad at me!
Fan. She's always mad at you!
Sophie. Well, good. Maybe she'll live to be a hundred!

(They exit for bed.)

(Black)

SCENE 2

Two days later; early afternoon.

Sophie, Fan and Wil are at the train station to meet Min and Frank. We hear the blast of the train whistle as the lights come up on the platform. Sophie and Wil are waiting patiently. Fan is very excited.

Fan. It's so hard to wait once you see it, isn't it? Why is it taking so long? It doesn't even look like it's moving very fast anymore, does it?
Sophie. They're right on time.
Wil. And that's real lucky for you. This train don't never run on time.
Fan. But it's on time today, isn't it? And that's what counts!
Wil. Yes, it is, Miss Fannie. That's what counts!
Fan. Is it still moving? Can you tell? I can't tell! I'm going to find the station manager. *(She exits.)*
Sophie. Fan told me you took care of my fence.
Wil. Yes.
Sophie. That was very neighborly of you. I'm much obliged.
Wil. You're welcome.
Sophie. Would you like to have dinner with us this evening?
Wil. You don't have to . . .
Sophie. I want you to come. And I'm sure Fan would enjoy having you.
Wil. Well, thank you. It'd be my . . .

(Fan enters, excitedly.)

Fan. It's pulling in! Oh, Sophie, I'm so excited. Do you see them yet? Can you see them, Wil?
Sophie. I don't see any . . . there she is!
Fan. Where? Where? I still don't . . . Minnie! Min! Here! We're here!

(Minnie enters on the run. She is wearing a fur trimmed coat and carrying a fur muff. Her hat dips fashionably low over her face.)

Minnie. Fannie! Oh, Fannie! *(They embrace.)* Oh, Sister! I missed you both so much!
Fan. Look at you in that outfit!
Sophie. How about that hat? Who are you hiding from?
Minnie. *(tugging it lower)* They're all the rage in London!
Sophie. Where are your bags?
Minnie. Frank has them. He stopped to send a telegram. He was talking to a man he met on the train . . . a white man. Maybe I better . . .
Wil. I'll give him a hand.

Minnie. Thank you . . . .
Fan. Wil Parrish, meet my baby sister, Minnie.
Wil. Pleased to meet you.
Minnie. Pleased to be met.

(Wil exits.)

Fan. We borrowed Wil's wagon to pick you up.
Sophie. And Wil came with it to make sure Miss Fannie got to town and back safely.
Minnie. Is he your sweetheart? Is he?
Fan. Don't pay Sophie a bit of mind.
Sophie. He's coming to dinner tonight. You can ask him yourself.
Fan. You better not say a word!

(Frank has entered and stands watching them. Frank is immaculately dressed in fine clothes from head to toe. Coat, hat, suit, gloves, shirt—everything of the finest quality and very tasteful. The sheer richness of the clothing is obvious in every piece.)

Frank. Secrets already?
Minnie. Darling! *(She runs to him and takes his arm protectively. Frank allows himself to be led toward her sisters.)*
Fan. *(warmly)* Frank. It's lovely to have you both!

(Frank puts down the small bag he's carrying and takes off one soft leather glove to extend his hand. Fannie kisses his cheek instead.)

Frank. It's good to see you, too.
Fan. I was so sorry to hear about your father.
Frank. Thank you.
Fan. Well, I know it was a long trip, but you're here at last!
Frank. Nothing would do but Minnie had to come and see her sisters, isn't that right, darling?
Fan. You don't mind sharing her with us once in awhile, do you?
Frank. Of course not. And I've got some other things to share with you as well.
Fan. *(teasing and happy)* Just how many riches do you think a poor frontier woman can stand at one time?
Frank. I thought you might enjoy having an autographed copy of Mr. Dunbar's latest volume. *(He hands her a small book of poetry.)*
Fan. Autographed? I've been trying to get my hands on any copy for months!
Minnie. Frank walked me all over New Orleans to find it.
Fan. How can I ever thank you?
Frank. It's my pleasure. *(a beat)* Hello, Sophie.

Sophie. *(nods formally)* Frank . . .
Frank. We'll try not to overstay our welcome.
Fan. Stay as long as you like. You're family.
Minnie. That's just what I told him. We're family! This isn't like coming for a visit. This is coming home.
Frank. But we have a home, don't we, darling?
Minnie. Yes, of course we do. We have a lovely home.
Fan. And you're going to tell me all about . . .
Frank. *(interrupts her)* And where is our home, Minnie?
Minnie. Frank . . . *(He stares at her coldly.)* It's in London.
Frank. So this is really a visit, just like I said, isn't it?
Minnie. *(softly)* Yes, Frank.
Frank. *(false heartiness)* Of course it is! And it's going to be a great visit. I'm sure of it. Well, how long does it take to get from here to there, anyway? I could do with a hot bath.
Fan. Of course you could. Wil's probably got the wagon loaded. Come on! Come on! Miss Leah's at the house and I know she's pacing up and down at the window right now.

(Fan hooks Minnie's arm and draws her away from Frank. Minnie looks back anxiously at Frank who stares at her impassively. He turns to find Sophie looking at him.)

Sophie. Welcome to Nicodemus, Frank.

(Frank tips his hat and bows slightly. He exits, pulling on his gloves and leaving his small suitcase behind. Sophie looks after him, looks at the bag, shifts the shotgun easily to the crook of her arm, picks up the bag and exits.)

(Black)

SCENE 3

The same day; evening.

Fan is taking out plates, laying out food, etc. Miss Leah is tottering around impatiently, making it difficult for Fan to accomplish her task without tripping over Miss Leah.

As we hear Miss Leah talking to Fan, in the bedroom we see Min at the mirror trying to convince herself that her bruised face isn't that noticeable. Frank is taking off his jacket, unbuttoning his shirt, etc. He catches a glimpse of Minnie looking in the mirror. He goes to her, stands behind her. She puts her hand down. He turns her slowly to face him. He gently, tenderly touches her bruised face. She flinches. He kisses her gently. She relaxes and he kisses her more passionately. She breaks away playfully. She looks in the mirror with resignation, grabs up her hat and pulls it back on. One last look at Frank who still watches her. She throws him a kiss and goes out. He lays down on the bed, takes out a book and begins to read.

Miss Leah. I don't see why she has to help him get settled right this minute. He's a grown man. He can unpack a suitcase, can't he?
Fan. I'm sure he can. I think Min just wants to make him feel at home here.
Miss Leah. Why wouldn't he feel at home here?

(Minnie enters quickly. She is nervous because she still wears her hat.)

Fan. Thank goodness. Miss Leah was about to send me back there to rescue you.
Minnie. Did you miss me?
Miss Leah. Lord, chile, I thought that man had tied you to the bed post back there. Take off that hat, honey, and let me look at you.
Fan. Aren't the flowers wonderful? I've got all your favorites . . .

(As Minnie slowly removes her hat, Fan sees the large bruise above Minnie's left eye.)

Fan. Minnie! My God!
Minnie. *(laughing nervously)* It doesn't look that bad, does it?
Miss Leah. What happened to your face, chile?
Minnie. It's so silly.

(They wait in silence.)

Minnie. I bought a new dress for the trip . . . and I . . . I wanted to show it to Frank . . . and I . . . the train . . . I stumbled in the train compartment. You know how clumsy I am. I bumped my head so hard I saw stars! And this is what I've got to show for it. Frank made me promise to be more careful. He worries so about me.

(An awkward pause. They don't believe her.)

Minnie. I told him I used to be much worse. Remember that time I almost fell off the roof? I would have killed myself if it hadn't been for Sophie.
Fan. Yes, I remember . . .
Minnie. Don't look so worried. I'll be careful. It was just an accident.
Fan. All right, Baby Sister.

(Sophie enters with wood in her arms.)

Miss Leah. Close that door!
Sophie. Let me get in it first. Your turn to chop tomorrow, Minnie. Being a

world traveller doesn't excuse you from your chores! *(sees the bruise on Minnie's face for the first time)* What happened to your face?
Minnie. I took a tumble, that's all. It looks a lot worse than it is.
Sophie. A tumble?
Fan. Minnie was showing off for her handsome husband and lost her balance on the train.
Minnie. I know it looks awful. Here! I'll put my beautiful hat back on to hide it!
Fan. No! Anything but that!
Minnie. Then let's not talk about it anymore.

(Sophie looks at Min and Fan and takes off her coat, etc.)

Sophie. Suit yourself.
Miss Leah. How does living in . . .
Minnie. London, Miss Leah. It's in England.
Miss Leah. How does it agree with you?
Minnie. Well, it was kind of scary to me at first. So many people and colored just right in there with everybody else.
Miss Leah. No Jim Crow?
Minnie. None.
Miss Leah. I can't imagine such a thing.
Minnie. That's why you have to come visit me. So you can see for yourself.
Miss Leah. I don't need to see nothin' else new. I done seen enough new to last me. I don't know why anybody wants to be all up next to a bunch of strange white folks anyway.
Sophie. Because somebody told them they weren't supposed to!
Minnie. Oh, they're not so bad. Frank and I even have some white . . . friends.
Miss Leah. Lord, deliver us! What is this chile talking about?
Minnie. Frank says he doesn't see why he only has to be with Negroes since he has as much white blood in him as colored.
Sophie. Frank is talking crazy.
Minnie. It's true. His father was . . .
Sophie. A slaveowner! Just like mine.
Minnie. Frank said his father wanted to marry his mother. They were . . . in love.
Sophie. Did he free her?
Minnie. No . . .
Sophie. Then don't talk to me about love.
Fan. *(quickly)* Let's have some supper before you two start fighting. Min, go tell Frank to come to the table.

(Minnie exits to the bedroom as Wil approaches outside with flowers. Frank

has gotten dressed up for dinner. When Min opens the door, he turns to her and strikes a pose for her approval. She kisses him and they go out arm in arm.)

Miss Leah. There's Wil Parrish at the door.

(Fan opens the door as he raises his hand to knock.)

Fan. You're just in time.
Wil. I stopped for . . . these are for you.
Fan. They're lovely.
Miss Leah. Just what we need.
Wil. Evenin', Miss Leah. How're you feelin'?
Miss Leah. I'd feel a whole lot better if people stopped lettin' that cold air in on me.

(Frank and Minnie enter arm in arm.)

Frank. I'm starved!
Fan. Good! Why don't you sit here next to Min? Wil, you sit here by . . . Sophie. Miss Leah . . .
Wil. You're the first colored poet I ever saw.
Frank. How many white ones have you seen?
Wil. None that I can recall . . .
Frank. Then that makes me the first poet you've ever seen, doesn't it?
Minnie. Frank . . .

(They settle into their places and join hands.)

Fan. Sister, will you bless the table?
Sophie. Thank you for this food we are about to receive and for the safe journey of our beloved sister. *(a beat)* And Frank. Amen.
All. Amen.

(As they talk, the meal is served, consumed and cleared away.)

Fan. Did you have a good rest?
Frank. Enough to hold me, I guess. *(to Sophie)* Min tells me you're a mulatto. *(Sophie is startled.)* Oh, excuse me! I didn't mean to be so personal. It's just that I'm a mulatto myself and I was interested to know if there are many of us this far west. You know you can't always tell by looking!
Sophie. There are just a few.
Frank. I can understand why. This is a lot closer to the field than most of us ever want to get! *(laughs)*
Minnie. *(quickly to Wil)* This is my husband's first visit to the frontier.
Wil. How do you like it so far?

Frank. So far, so good. But to tell the truth, I've always been more of a city person.
Sophie. And what kind of person is that?
Frank. Oh, I think one who enjoys a little more . . . ease than is possible way out here. Although I must admit your home is lovely. This table wouldn't be out of place in the finest dining rooms.
Fan. Why thank you, Frank!
Sophie. Tomorrow we'll go back to eating around the campfire like we usually do.
Minnie. Don't listen to Sister! Fan is famous for setting the prettiest table in Nicodemus.
Frank. I admire the ability to adapt to trying circumstances without a lowering of standards. I wouldn't have expected to see such delicate china way out here.
Fan. These were my mother's things. Sophie stopped speaking to me for a week when I told her I wasn't leaving Memphis without them, but I was determined.
Sophie. I should have left you and them standing in the middle of Main Street. Whoever heard of carrying a set of plates . . .
Minnie. Mama's china!
Fan. Mama's good china!
Sophie. A set of plates halfway across the country when we hardly had room for Min.
Minnie. You weren't going to leave me in the middle of Main Street, too, were you?
Fan. She couldn't have left us. Who would she have had to boss around?
Minnie. I'd like to go back to Memphis sometime. Just to visit. Wouldn't you?
Sophie. Not me! Colored folks lives aren't worth two cents in that town.
Fan. But everybody says things have gotten a lot better.
Frank. Well, that may be true in Memphis, but we were in New Orleans to see my lawyers just before we came here and it's still pretty much the same as it's always been, if you ask me. They had just had a lynching the week before we got there. *(laughs)* Just my luck!
Minnie. After they hung the poor man they threw his body down in the street right in the middle of the colored section of town.
Miss Leah. Don't any of those New Orleans Negroes know how to use a shotgun?
Frank. He pretty much brought it on himself from what I heard down at the bank. He was involved in some . . .
Sophie. *(cuts him off)* I don't care what he was involved in.
Frank. Doesn't it matter?
Sophie. No. Whatever it was, he didn't deserve to die like that.

Frank. Well, I stand corrected. And I do apologize for introducing such inappropriate dinner table conversation.

Miss Leah. I don't know why those Negroes stay down there!

Sophie. Because they haven't got the gumption to try something new. The day our group left Memphis, there were at least two hundred other Negroes standing around, rolling their eyes and trying to tell us we didn't know what it was going to be like way out here in the wilderness. I kept trying to tell them it doesn't matter what it's like. Any place is better than here!

Frank. Well, that's something we agree on!

Wil. I'll say "amen" to that, too! If I never set foot in the Confederacy again, it's too soon for me.

Fan. Oh, no! You two can't start thinking like Sister! One Sophie is enough.

Miss Leah. Too many if you ask me.

Minnie. Has her coffee gotten any better?

Miss Leah. Worse! And her disposition neither. I don't know how I'm gonna make it through the winter with her.

Minnie. She's not so bad. You just have to remember to put cotton in your ears.

Frank. I wish I'd thought of that on the train. Min was so excited she was talking a mile a minute the whole way out here. Weren't you, darling? She hardly took a deep breath.

Minnie. I wasn't that bad, was I?

Frank. I didn't want to hurt your feelings, darling, but you must have told me the same stories ten times!

Minnie. I didn't mean to . . .

Sophie. *(cuts her off)* Which one was your favorite?

Frank. Oh, I think probably the one about you coming to the door asking to do the laundry and then moving right in. I guess you knew a good thing when you saw one!

Minnie. Frank!

Frank. What is it, darling? That is the way the story goes, isn't it?

Fan. I don't know what a good thing we were. Mama and Daddy both gone with the fever. So many people dying there weren't enough left well to take care of the sick ones. I was only twelve and Min still a baby.

Minnie. So when Sophie came asking about doing the laundry, Fan asked her when she could start and Sophie said I can start right now. I'm free as a bird! And once she came, it was like she'd always been there.

Fan. I loved the way she said it. I was scared to death and here was this one talking about free as a bird.

Wil. Are you gonna put that in the book?

Minnie. What book?

Fan. I'm writing a book about Nicodemus. I'm going to call it The True History and Life Stories of Nicodemus, Kansas: A Negro Town.
Minnie. That sounds wonderful. Now we'll have two writers in the family.
Fan. Oh, I'm not really a writer. I'm more of a collector.
Minnie. You could have a whole book with just Miss Leah's stories!
Fan. Well, some people don't think their stories are important enough to put in a book.
Miss Leah. I'm not studyin' you, Fannie May Dove.
Minnie. Why? I don't remember a time we went to your house when I didn't come back with a story.
Miss Leah. Everybody knows them stories I got. Colored folks ain't been free long enough to have forgot what it's like to be a slave.
Minnie. But you didn't always talk about slavery. You talked about how blue the sky would be in the summertime and about how you and the other children would sneak off from prayer meeting to play because you didn't want to work all week and pray all Sunday.
Miss Leah. And got beat for it just as regular as a clock.
Minnie. You used to tell me about how all your babies had such fat legs, remember?
Miss Leah. And where are they now? All them babies. And them grandbabies? Gone! Every last one of 'em!
Minnie. But you loved them, Miss Leah. Who's going to know how much you loved them?
Frank. Min's got a story, don't you darling?
Minnie. I thought you'd heard enough of my stories on the train.
Frank. But you haven't told our story, darling.
Minnie. I don't think this is . . .
Fan. Please? It's such a lovely story. With a happy ending.
Frank. Go ahead, now. Don't be silly.
Minnie. I was at school . . .
Fan. The conservatory . . . go on!
Minnie. It was . . . it was spring. The campus was lovely then. Flowers were everywhere. But all anybody kept talking about was the handsome stranger who was here visiting for a couple of weeks.
Fan. That was Frank, all the way from England!
Sophie. Fannie! Let her tell it, or you tell it!
Fan. Go on! Sorry!
Minnie. Pretty soon, everybody but me had met him, or at least seen him. And then one afternoon, I was out walking and I thought I was alone, so I started singing and Frank was out walking too and he heard me.
Frank. I really scared her!
Minnie. I hadn't heard him behind me.
Frank. I was tracking her like a wild Indian!

(Wil looks up sharply, but lets it pass.)

Minnie. And then he said . . .
Frank. I had been away from England for almost a month and I hadn't heard a note of Puccini in all that time. So I told her she sang like an angel and invited her to have dinner with me.
Minnie. And I said my sisters hadn't raised me to have dinner with a strange gentleman who I met on a walk in the woods.
Sophie. You shouldn't have been walking in the woods alone in the first place.
Fan. But then it wouldn't be a love story! Go on, Min.
Minnie. So I walked away and left him standing there.
Fan. And the next day a friend of hers invited her to attend an evening of Negro poetry at the Chitauqua Literary Society . . .
Minnie. And I looked behind the podium and there was Frank!
Frank. I recognized her right away . . .
Minnie. And he nodded to me like we were old friends.
Fan. And then he dedicated a poem to her.
Minnie. "A Song" by Mr. Paul Laurence Dunbar.
Frank.
> "Thou art the soul of a summer's day,
> Thou art the breath of the rose.
> But the summer is fled
> And the rose is dead.
> Where are they gone, who knows, who knows?"

Miss Leah. A Negro wrote that?
Fan. And me and Sister dashed down to New Orleans in time enough for the wedding and to see them set sail back to England.
Frank. We'd only known each other a few weeks, but I knew Minnie was the girl for me. And she still is.

(He kisses her gently and she blushes.)

Fan. Beautiful! Now you tell one, Sister!
Sophie. I don't want to bore Frank with stories he's heard before.
Minnie. Tell about the ritual. Tell about the day we left Memphis and came west to be free women.
Sophie. Fan's the one always thinking up ceremonies. Let her tell it.
Fan. Not this one! This came straight from you!
Sophie. When we got ready to leave Memphis . . .
Minnie. When you two got ready. I was too little to get a vote.
Sophie. Well, I knew it was the right thing to do. Memphis was full of crazy white men acting like when it came to colored people, they didn't have to be bound by law or common decency. Dragging people off in

the middle of the night. Doing whatever they felt like doing. Colored women not safe in their own houses. Then I heard there were Negroes going west.

Miss Leah. Been done gone!

Sophie. Then that crazy Pap Singleton came to the church looking for people to sign up to go to Kansas. That man had eyes like hot coals. He said he was like Moses leading the children of Israel out of bondage in Egypt.

Fan. Sister didn't even let the man finish talking before she ran down the aisle to sign up! I think Reverend Thomas thought she had finally gotten the spirit!

Sophie. Pap said there'd be all colored towns, full of colored people only! That sounded more like heaven than anything else I'd heard in church.

Minnie. Why does that make you smile?

Wil. That's what landed me in Nicodemus, too. Looking for some neighbors that looked like me.

Frank. At home, we go for weeks and never see another colored face. A few Indians once in awhile—the Eastern kind—but that's not really the same thing, is it?

Miss Leah. Don't you get lonesome for colored people?

Frank. To tell you the truth, I've seen about all the Negroes I need to see in this life. *(laughs)*

Minnie. *(quickly)* Finish about the ritual, Sister!

Sophie. Another time.

Minnie. Please!

Frank. Don't whine, darling. Maybe Sophie is tired of talking.

Miss Leah. Well, if she is, or if she ain't, I'm tired of listenin'!

Minnie. You're not leaving us already, are you?

Miss Leah. Knowing how long winded some of the people at this table can be you all will probably be sittin' here when I get up tomorrow mornin'. *(She gets up unsteadily.)*

Minnie. Let me help you.

Miss Leah. One thing a woman my age should have the good sense to do alone is go to bed. Good night.

Minnie, Wil, Fan, Sophie. Good night, Miss Leah.

(Fan and Minnie begin clearing off the dishes. Wil unobtrusively helps them. Frank pours himself another glass of wine.)

Frank. They don't make you do the woman's work around here too, do they, Parrish?

Wil. Makes it go quicker when everybody does a part.

Fan. I couldn't have said it better myself!

(Sophie puts on her coat.)

Minnie. Where are you off to?
Sophie. To bring in a little more of that wood I spent all week chopping in your honor.
Minnie. Then the least I can do is help you carry it!
Fan. I'll help, too!

(They throw on their shawls and almost rush out the door.)

Frank. You know the night air doesn't agree with you, Minnie!
Fan. We'll keep her warm, I promise. *(Pulls shawl over Min's head and pulls her out the door. Moonlight illuminates the yard. Wood is cut in a stack near the house.)*
Sophie. What's he talking about? You're healthy as a horse.
Minnie. He just worries about me sometimes, that's all. I haven't been so strong lately . . .
Fan. But you're home now. I've got a whole week to toughen you up again!
Minnie. I'm counting on it. *(a beat)* Sister?
Sophie. Yes?
Minnie. Don't mind what Frank said about you coming to the door looking to do the laundry.
Sophie. Didn't I come to your door?
Minnie. Yes . . .
Sophie. And didn't you need somebody to do the laundry?
Minnie. Yes, but, sometimes Frank says things in a way that . . . that doesn't sound like how I know he means them.
Sophie. I'm not ashamed of anything I've ever done and if I was, taking in laundry to make an honest living wouldn't be the thing I'd pick. *(a beat)* You don't have to apologize to me for your husband, Min. If he's good to you, he's good enough for me. Is he good to you, Min?
Minnie. Yes, he's good to me.
Sophie. Then he's all right with me.
Fan. Well, since you two are getting along so well, let's do it before you start fussing again!
Minnie. Do what?
Fan. The ritual. Let's do it now!
Minnie. Oh, yes, please! Can we?

(Wil can be seen sharpening a small knife on a stone. Frank takes out a cigar, prepares it, smokes. The women stand in a circle, holding hands.)

Sophie. Because we are free Negro women . . .
Fan and Minnie. Because we are free Negro women . . .
Sophie. Born of free Negro women . . .

Both. Born of free Negro women . . .
All. Back as far as time begins . . .
Sophie. We choose this day to leave a place where our lives, our honor and our very souls are not our own.
Fan. Say it, Sister!
Sophie. We choose this day to declare our lives to be our own and no one else's. And we promise to always remember the day we left Memphis and went west together to be free women as a sacred bond between us with all our trust.
Both. With all our trust . . .
Sophie. And all our strength . . .
Both. And all our strength . . .

(As they talk, Frank walks over to the window, smoking. He looks at the women holding hands in the moonlight.)

Sophie. And all our courage . . .
Both. And all our courage . . .
Sophie. And all our love.
Both. And all our love.

(a beat)

Sophie. Welcome home, Baby Sister.

(The three embrace, laughing happily. Frank still watches from the window.)

(Black)

SCENE 4

The next morning.
Miss Leah is on the stage alone. She is mending something. Min kisses the sleeping Frank in the bedroom and goes quietly out, closing the door behind her. She is brushing her hair. She looks much younger than she did with her fancy hat and sophisticated hairdo.

Minnie. You're up early.
Miss Leah. Habit, chile. I don't know how to sleep past sun up.
Minnie. Where are Fan and Sister?
Miss Leah. Fan's already up washing and Sophie's probably off somewhere driving some other poor soul crazy. Come sit by me, chile. I couldn't hardly get a word in at dinner last night.

Minnie. You always hold your own.

Miss Leah. If you don't hold it, who gone hold it? Let me look at you. *(a beat)* You look more like yourself this morning.

Minnie. I'm going to braid my hair with ribbons like you used to do it, remember?

Miss Leah. I remember. *(Minnie messes up a braid.)* But don't look like you do. Sit down here, girl, and let me fix that head. *(Minnie sits with her head between Miss Leah's knees.)*

Minnie. Don't you think Frank is fine looking?

Miss Leah. He'll do.

Minnie. I want all my babies to look just like him!

Miss Leah. He ain't that pretty.

Minnie. Do you think I'll be a good mother?

Miss Leah. You better be. Fan gone be too old for many babies by the time her and Wil stop dancin' around each other and Sophie's too mean for anybody to marry. So I'm countin' on you, Baby Sister. None of this makes any sense without the children.

Minnie. It would be hard to have a child way out here.

Miss Leah. There's a lot worse places than this to have a baby. I'd of given anything to a had my babies in my own little house on my own piece of land with James pacing outside and the midwife knowin' what to do to ease you through it. Is that too tight?

Minnie. It's perfect!

(Frank gets up and begins dressing in the bedroom. He is wearing more expensive city clothes. He takes great care with his cuff links, tie, etc. He is especially pleased with his hair.)

Miss Leah. *(resumes her braiding)* I was only thirteen when I got my first one. They wanted me to start early cause I was big and strong. Soon as my womanhood came on me, they took me out in the barn and put James on me. He was older than me and big. He already had children by half the women on the place. My James . . . *(a beat)* But that first time, he was hurting me so bad and I was screamin' and carryin' on somethin' awful and that old overseer just watchin' and laughin' to make sure James really doin' it. He watch us every night for a week and after the third one I hear James tryin' to whisper somethin' to me real quiet while he doin' it. I was so surprised I stopped cryin' for a minute and I hear James sayin' "Leah, Leah, Leah . . ." He just kept sayin' my name over and over. *(a beat)* At the end of the week, I had got my first son. Do you have another ribbon? *(Min hands her one from her pocket.)* Fan's gonna skin you about her ribbons, Missy!

Minnie. Did you love James?

Miss Leah. I always thought I would've if they'd a let me find him for myself. The way it was, we stayed together after the war cause we was closer to each other than to anybody that wadn't dead or sold off and because James said we had ten babies that they sold away from us. We ought to have ten more we could raise free. Done! *(finishes the braiding)*
Minnie. I love my hair in braids.
Miss Leah. Braid it or shave it off, I say. All the rest takes too much fussin' with. Don't leave a woman no time to think.
Minnie. Why won't you let Fannie write down your stories?
Miss Leah. Everything can't be wrote down. No matter what Fannie tell you, some things gotta be said out loud to keep the life in 'em.
Minnie. Do you think James would have liked Kansas?
Miss Leah. I think he would of if he could have walked his mind this far from Tennessee. It takes some doin' to be able to see a place in your mind where you never been before.
Minnie. Frank's been so many places. London. Paris. Rome. Sometimes it seems like he's been everywhere and seen everything.
Miss Leah. Well, I know that ain't true.
Minnie. Why?
Miss Leah. 'Cause this is his first time in Nicodemus.
Minnie. I kept hoping he would like it here. I miss it so much. I tried to describe it to him, and sometimes I'd read him Fannie's letters, but . . .
Miss Leah. Well, some people truly are city people. They like all that noise and confusion. It gives them somethin' to hide behind. Can't do that out here. First winter teach you that. Out here, nothin' stands between you and your soul.
Minnie. It's more than that for Frank. He doesn't just hate the South and the frontier. He hates the whole country.
Miss Leah. Well, maybe the boy's got more sense than I thought he did.
Minnie. He said the first time he went to Europe he begged his father to leave him behind when it was time to go back to New Orleans. But he was only fourteen so his father refused.
Miss Leah. Fourteen can be a grown man if you let it.
Minnie. But he said he knew right then that as soon as he could, he was going to get on a boat for England and never look back. And he did, too.
Miss Leah. *(a beat)* Baby?
Minnie. Yes?
Miss Leah. Do you ever miss colored people?
Minnie. I miss colored people so much sometime I don't know what to do!
Miss Leah. Well, that's good to hear. I thought you might be getting as tired of Negroes as Frank seems to be.

Minnie. Frank doesn't mean any harm. He just doesn't feel like we do about Negroes. He might miss a friend or two, but when I ask him if he doesn't ever just miss being in a big group of Negroes, knowing that we are all going to laugh at the same time and cry at the same time just because we're all there being colored, he just shakes his head. I don't think he's ever felt it, so he can't miss it.
Miss Leah. How can a Negro get that grown and not know how it feels to be around his own people?
Minnie. He isn't used to being treated like other colored people. He gets so angry when we have to get on the Jim Crow car. When we can't go in the restaurants. I think if Frank had to live here, he might go mad.
Miss Leah. Well, Negroes are supposed to get mad, so that's a good sign.
Minnie. Not get mad, Miss Leah. Go mad.
Miss Leah. Six of one. Half a dozen of the other.

(Frank enters from the bedroom.)

Frank. Good morning! Darling! I didn't hear you get up.
Minnie. *(jumps up to hug him quickly)* I didn't want to wake you.
Frank. What have you done to your hair?
Minnie. Miss Leah braided it for me like she used to. Do you like it?
Frank. I've never seen you with your hair in plaits.
Minnie. Yes you have. I was wearing braids when you met me.
Frank. *(being charming for the benefit of Miss Leah)* You looked like such a little country girl then. When I first took Minnie to London, I made sure to take her shopping before I introduced her to my friends. But I always knew she had potential. Anybody could see that. And that's why I married her. Because Minnie deserves the best. Doesn't she?
Miss Leah. She is the best.
Frank. Yes, she is! I'm going to step out for a smoke, if you two will excuse me.
Minnie. I'll come, too. Do you want me to make you some breakfast before we go out? My coffee isn't as bad as Sister's.
Miss Leah. Fan left me a fresh pot. Go ahead, chile. I'll be fine. I've been up long enough to be lookin' for a nap soon.

(Frank and Minnie exit to the yard.)

Frank. *(angrily)* I want you to put your hair back the way it was.
Minnie. I always wore my . . .
Frank. You look like a damn pickaninny! We haven't been here twenty-four hours and look at you!
Minnie. I'm sorry . . .
Frank. You're always sorry, aren't you? Of course you are, but if you

weren't so busy being sorry, you'd know there are some interesting things going on in Nicodemus these days.
Minnie. What do you mean?
Frank. Nothing. I'm going into town to check at the telegraph office and . . . take a look around.
Minnie. Don't be too late, will you?

(He exits. Minnie sits down on the porch wearily and draws her knees to her chest, rocking back and forth wearily. In the kitchen, Fan and Sophie are oblivious.)

(Black)

SCENE 5

Late that night.
  It is late that evening. Sophie and Fan and Minnie are up. Fan is sewing something. Sophie is pulling some papers from her desk. Some of these are rolled maps or plans, etc. These are Sophie's plans for the development of the town. Minnie is standing at the window. Fan takes off her glasses, rubs her eyes sleepily. Minnie goes over to the fire and stirs it up, puts another log on.

Fan. Well, I think I'm going to leave the rest of you night owls! Don't worry. Nicodemus isn't big enough for Frank to get into trouble. Even if he's looking for it.
Minnie. Good night.
Fan. I'll be up early.
Minnie. Me, too.

(They embrace. Fan takes her sewing and exits, patting Sophie affectionately as she passes.)

Fan. Good night, Sister.
Sophie. Check on Miss Leah?
Fan. Always.

(She exits. Sophie pours herself a cup of coffee.)

Minnie. You don't have to wait up with me.
Sophie. I won't be sleeping much between now and the vote next week.
Minnie. What are you doing?
Sophie. I'm writing my speech for Sunday. I'm going to singlehandedly convince these Negroes they have the right to protect their land from speculators and save Nicodemus!

Minnie. Save it from what?

Sophie. From being just one more place where colored people couldn't figure out how to be free.

Minnie. Are politics so important?

Sophie. *(a beat)* Come look at this. *(Sophie has spread out the plans on the table.)* These are the plans for Nicodemus. Here's the store and the post office. In the same places, but bigger. And open every day, not just two days a week. And here's the blacksmith and the school . . .

Minnie. Who did this?

Sophie. I did. We want the school open by spring but the teacher we hired just wrote to say she won't come because she's getting married and her fool husband . . .

(Sophie stops herself abruptly, not wanting to seem critical of Frank.)

Minnie. Doesn't like the frontier, huh?

Sophie. I guess not.

Minnie. This is wonderful.

Sophie. Fan drew the buildings. I was just going to write down what was going where, but Fan said, how about all the people in Nicodemus who can't read? *(a beat)* So the school goes here. The church stays where it is, but bigger. We've got fifty now in the Baptist pews alone! Then the doctor and the dentist will be here together so folks won't have to get their nerve up but once to go inside since it's different offices, but the same building. And see right here?

Minnie. Yes.

Sophie. That's Fan's newspaper office and book publishing company.

Minnie. Look! She put a little face waving out the window!

Sophie. That's her. Fan puts us all on it. Here I am at the feed store. And here's Wil at the blacksmith. Here you are at the train station. Miss Leah's on here some place . . .

Minnie. She forgot to draw Frank.

Sophie. I guess she did.

Minnie. You know I'd come back if I could, don't you?

Sophie. I think you would if you wanted to.

Minnie. It's not that simple.

Sophie. Why isn't it?

Minnie. Does anybody really know what they want? Do you?

Sophie. Of course I do! I want this town to be a place where a colored woman can be free to live her life like a human being. I want this town to be a place where a colored man can work as hard for himself as we used to work for white folks. I want a town where a colored child can go to anybody's door and be treated like they belong there.

Minnie. When you start talking about this place, you make it sound like paradise for colored people.
Sophie. It's not paradise yet, but it can be beautiful. The century is going to change in two years! This can be a great time for colored people. We can really be free instead of spending our lives working for the same people that used to own us. How are we ever going to be free if we have to spend all of our time doing somebody else's laundry?
Minnie. You used to do laundry.
Sophie. There's nothing wrong with doing laundry until you start thinking that's all you can do. That's why the vote is so important. We have to help each other stay strong. The rule doesn't say they can't sell their land. It says they can't sell it unless they are prepared to look the rest of us in the eye and say who they are selling it to and why. As long as they have to face each other, nobody will have nerve enough to sell to speculators, no matter what they're offering.
Minnie. But it wouldn't matter as long as most of the people here are colored, would it?
Sophie. If we start selling to speculators, everything will change. We may as well move back to Memphis. And before I do that, I'll get Wil Parrish to teach me how to speak Spanish and move us all to Mexico!

(She starts gathering up her maps, etc.)

Minnie. Wait, before you put it away. I was thinking maybe you could show it to Frank. So he could see how nice everything is going to be.
Sophie. Mr. Frank Charles ain't no more interested in an all-colored town than the man in the moon.
Minnie. Frank's not so bad, Sister.
Sophie. Suit yourself.
Minnie. Why don't you like him?
Sophie. I don't have to like him.
Minnie. I know. But why don't you?
Sophie. I think Frank hates being colored. I don't understand Negroes like that. They make me nervous.
Minnie. *(stung)* You make me nervous.
Sophie. I didn't used to.
Minnie. No. I guess you didn't.

(Sophie picks up the gun, puts on her coat.)

Sophie. I'm going to check the horses.

(She exits. Minnie goes over to stoke the fire, hears a noise. Frank crosses the yard quickly and enters. Min turns, thinking it is Sophie. She freezes.)

Frank. What are you still doing up? It's late.

(He staggers over, sits and drinks a long pull from a silver flask without taking his eyes off of her.)

Minnie. I was waiting for you.
Frank. Why? Haven't I had enough bad luck for a nigger?
Minnie. Are you all right?
Frank. Do I look like I'm all right?
Minnie. Let me get you some coffee . . .
Frank. You don't need to get me a damn thing. Just sit still! Can you just sit still for once?
Minnie. Yes, Frank.
Frank. You know what happened tonight, don't you? I don't even have to bother telling you anything about it, do I?
Minnie. What is it? What happened?
Frank. I was gambling. A gentleman's game of poker with some of my friends from the train. Ran into them in town. And you know what? I lost. I lost everything. What there was left of it.
Minnie. You were gambling with white men?
Frank. White gentlemen, Min. And I lost every dime. And I want to thank you for that. Things were going fine until one of them asked me about the nigger woman who kept following me around the train. I laughed it off, but my luck changed after that so I know they suspected something. *(He stands behind her, touching her shoulders lightly.)* But I should have known better than to depend on you for luck. You're too black to bring me any good luck. All you got to give is misery. Pure D misery and little black pickaninnies just like you. *(He rubs her arms, stops, keeping his hands lightly on her shoulders. She moves away in fear.)*
Minnie. Frank, were you . . .
Frank. Shut up!

(She looks around for help in a panic.)

Frank. But the game wasn't a total loss. I found out something interesting. Do you know what I found out?
Minnie. No, Frank.
Frank. Your sisters are sitting on a fortune. That white man on the train? He said speculators are paying top dollar for these farms around here.
Minnie. Sister would never sell this land!
Frank. Of course she wouldn't because she's just like all the other Negroes around here. She's content to live her life like a pack mule out in some backwater town . . . I never should have let you talk me into bringing you out here. We damn well could have waited in New Orleans like I wanted to. Taking that damn train all the way across the damn prairie.

You know what they call your precious town? "Niggerdemus"! Niggerdemus, Kansas. Don't you think that's funny, Min?

Minnie. Were you passing?

Frank. I was letting people draw their own conclusions.

Minnie. Who did you tell them I was?

Frank. I told you to shut up!

(He pushes her roughly and she stumbles and falls to the floor at the moment that Sophie enters from the porch. Fan follows almost immediately, awakened by the noise.)

Fan. Minnie! My, God!

Sophie. What do you think you're doing?

Frank. I'm talking to my wife. This is none of your affair.

Minnie. It's all right! It was an accident. I just slipped, didn't I, Frank? I just slipped!

Sophie. Get out.

Frank. You're pretty high and mighty for a nigger woman, aren't you?

Minnie. Shut up, Frank! He's drunk! Don't listen to him!

Frank. What did you say?

(He starts to move toward Minnie in a threatening manner. Sophie raises the shotgun and cocks it.)

Minnie. No, Sister! Don't! Please don't! I'm going to have a baby!

(All stop.)

(Black)

ACT II

SCENE 1

Early the next morning.

Sophie is standing at the window with her gun at her side. Frank is skulking around in the yard, coatless and cold. Fan is getting a tea kettle off the stove. Miss Leah is taking some herbs from small jars laid out before her and preparing them for the tea. Min is wrapped in a blanket, propped up in a chair. She looks fragile and frightened.

Minnie. He doesn't even have his coat with him.

Sophie. Good! Maybe he'll freeze to death.

Fan. Don't say that. You'll just upset her again.

Sophie. Upset her? Don't you think she ought to be upset? Don't you think we all ought to be upset?
Miss Leah. Let her drink this tea and catch her breath before you start fussin' again.

(Frank exits the yard.)

Miss Leah. *(hands cup to Minnie)* Drink all of it. It'll help you hold onto that baby.
Minnie. This is such a hard time for Frank . . .
Sophie. For Frank?
Minnie. He's my husband!
Fan. Of course he is. Be still, now.
Minnie. He's so afraid they will try to trick him out of his inheritance.
Sophie. Of course they will!
Fan. Sister, please!
Minnie. His brothers hate him.
Sophie. His brothers used to own him!
Minnie. That's not his fault too, is it?
Sophie. No. It's his fault for thinking that means they owe him something and if he doesn't get it, he has the right to put his hands on you.
Minnie. I love him.
Sophie. That's not love.
Minnie. *(a beat)* How would you know?

(Sophie looks at Minnie, picks up the shotgun and goes to sit on the porch steps. Miss Leah looks at Minnie then goes to get a pipe and prepares it slowly.)

Fan. You know, Sister only wants what is best for you.
Minnie. I know.
Fan. Sometimes I think if I'd known you were going to stay so long, I'd of thought longer about letting you go.
Minnie. Me, too. *(a beat)* Everything has changed. Everything. When Frank and I went to London, it was like a fairy tale. I felt so free! I could do anything, go anywhere, buy anything. And Frank was always there to show me something I had never seen before or tell me something I'd been waiting to hear all my life . . . and I loved to look at him. But then he changed. . . . He was mad all the time.
Fan. Mad at who?
Minnie. At everybody. But mostly me, I guess.
Miss Leah. Why was he mad at you?
Minnie. I don't know why! I think he just started hating colored people. We'd be walking down the street and he'd say: "Look at those niggers.

No wonder nobody wants to be around them." When his father died and his brothers stopped sending money, it just got worse and worse. It was almost like he couldn't stand to look at me . . .

Fan. Hush, now. It's all right. Me and Miss Leah will take care of you now. There's not a baby in the world that can come before Miss Leah says it's time to.

Minnie. . . . Sometimes I used to think it must be a dream and that I'd wake up one day and Frank would be the way he used to be.

Miss Leah. Grown people don't change except to get more like what they already are.

Fan. Frank is going through a bad time that's all, but he's still Frank. He's still that man that swept you off your feet. The man you want to be the father of your children, isn't he?

Minnie. He scares me sometimes. He gets so angry.

Fan. You know who else had a terrible temper?

Minnie. Who?

Fan. Daddy. You were too young to remember it, but he did. And Daddy was a good man, but he had that temper and sometimes it would get the better of him. Just like your Frank. Sometimes he used to . . . not all the time, but . . . one time they woke me up, fussing about something, and Mama didn't hear me call her, so I went to the top of the stairs where I could see them without them seeing me. I always sat there . . . Daddy was sitting by the fireplace and Mama was talking a mile a minute. I could tell he didn't like what she was saying, and then he got up real fast and grabbed her arm and he just shook her and shook her . . . I was so scared I ran back to bed, but I could still hear everything . . . Sometimes we have to be stronger than they are, Baby Sister. We have to understand and be patient.

Minnie. What did Mama do?

Fan. Mama always said she was biding her time until we could get these white folks off our backs so she could get colored men straightened out on a thing or two a little bit closer to home, but until then, she said she'd give him the benefit of the doubt.

Minnie. I've been trying to do that, too.

Fan. You love Frank, don't you?

Minnie. I used to love him so much . . .

Fan. You still love him. I can see it on your face. You two can work it out. I know you can. For better or for worse, remember?

Minnie. I'll try. I'll really try.

(Frank enters the yard and Minnie sees him from the window.)

Minnie. Frank!

(She rushes past Sophie on the porch and into his arms. He embraces her and grins evilly at Sophie.)

(Black)

SCENE 2

The next Sunday; early morning.
   Fan and Miss Leah are up and ready for church. Sophie is finishing breakfast at the table alone. Frank and Min are in their room getting ready to go.

Fan. How was everything?
Sophie. Fine. Thank you.
Fan. Is your speech ready?
Sophie. As ready as it's going to be. I'm not going to worry about it. I'll say what I have to say and then we'll see which way it goes.
Fan. It'll go your way. You've hardly been home at all this week, out convincing everybody.
Miss Leah. That's not why she hasn't been around here this week. Is it?
Sophie. I don't know what you mean.

(Sophie clears up her plate while Miss Leah watches her.)

Miss Leah. You are the most stubborn colored woman I've ever seen in my life.
Sophie. I'll take that as a compliment coming from you.
Fan. Please don't get her started! I want us to ride to church and back in peace.
Sophie. I can't tell her who to marry, but I won't sit at a table with a man who called me an uppity nigger woman in my own damn house!
Fan. She's forgiven him. Can't you?
Sophie. He doesn't want my forgiveness. And she doesn't need it. She hasn't done anything wrong.
Fan. He made a mistake. He's sorry. I know he is. You haven't spoken a word to either one of them in a week. London is so far away and she'll be gone soon. Don't let her go without a word.
Miss Leah. Colored women ain't got enough sisters to be cutting each other off so easy, I'd say.
Sophie. Easy? I pointed a gun at the man's head and wanted to use it!
Fan. And he's prepared to sit at the table with you!
Miss Leah. Which shows he ain't as smart as he thinks he is!

(Suddenly, Sophie laughs.)

Sophie. All right, you win!
Fan. Thank goodness! Now we can celebrate this birthday right!
Sophie. Don't get carried away. I said I'd be here. I didn't say I'd talk.
Fan. You know how special this birthday is. For all of us. How can you give her the deed if you won't even talk to her?
Sophie. You give it to her. *(puts the envelope with the deed in front of Fan)*
Fan. I can't. Not without you. It has to be all three of us or it doesn't mean anything. "With all our trust. And all our strength. And all our courage. And all our love." Remember?

(Min and Frank enter from the back, ready for church. They both stop when they see Sophie is still there.)

Minnie. Good morning.
Sophie. Happy Birthday, Min. *(hands her the envelope)* This is for you.
Minnie. A present? This early in the day? Can I open it?
Sophie. Ask Fan.
Fan. Go ahead.
Minnie. *(reading, but confused)* But what does it mean?
Frank. It's a deed.
Sophie. It's the deed to your part of this land. You're twenty-one now.
Miss Leah. Every colored woman ought to have a piece of land she can claim as her own.
Frank. Do you know how much that land is worth?
Sophie. We're interested in buying more land, not selling what we've got.
Frank. Well, from what that white fella told me on the train, not everybody around here feels that way. I heard some of your neighbors are considering some pretty generous offers.
Miss Leah. Speculators!
Frank. They're offering $500 an acre.
Miss Leah. I can't believe it.
Frank. Doesn't that at least make you more open to the idea? You could be a very rich woman.
Sophie. And I'd be standing in the middle of Kansas without any place to call home. You can't grow wheat on an acre of money.
Frank. There's plenty of other land around from what I could see. What's the difference?
Sophie. The difference is we own this land. Whether they like it or not, and anybody who tries to say different is going to find himself buried on it.
Frank. You wouldn't really kill somebody over a piece of ground out in the middle of nowhere, would you?

Sophie. This land is the center of the world to me as long as we're standing on it.
Frank. And how do you think the rest of the world feels about sharing their center with a town full of colored people?
Sophie. I have no idea.
Minnie. None of that matters! Can't you see that none of that matters? This is the land that makes us free women, Frank. We can never sell it! Not ever!

(Wil Parrish enters and comes to the door. Fan opens it for him.)

Fan. We thought you'd changed your mind about coming to church with us.
Wil. On the day of Miss Sophie's speech? Not me! I'm sorry I'm late. I stopped by the telegraph office yesterday and there was a wire for Frank. *(searches his pockets for it)* It was too late to bring it over yesterday and this morning I forgot it, so I went back. I thought it was probably the news you been waitin' for.
Frank. I knew it! Didn't I tell you? I knew it! I felt our ship pulling up to the dock. Come on, Parrish! Where is the damn thing?
Wil. Here it is?

(Frank rips it open and reads. His face hardens.)

Frank. What the hell?
Minnie. What is it?

(Frank drops the telegram on the table and walks to the bedroom, slams the door. Fan picks up the telegram.)

Minnie. Read it, Fan.
Fan. *(reading)* "Paternity denied. Stop. All claims to money, property, land and other assets of Mr. John Charles, late of New Orleans, Louisiana, denied. No legal recourse available."
Minnie. You all go on without me. I need to . . . Frank needs me here, I think.
Fan. All right, Baby Sister. Be strong.
Minnie. Yes, I will.

(They exit. Minnie goes down the hall to Frank, who is sitting on the bed drinking from a silver flask.)

Minnie. I'm so sorry!
Frank. Are you? Sorry for what? Marrying a bastard?
Minnie. Don't say that!
Frank. Do you know what this means? This means I've got nothing. Not a dime. Nothing.
Minnie. You can sell your books.

Frank. Don't be so stupid. *(pacing)* They think they can make me an ordinary Negro. That's what they think. They think they're going to have a chance to treat me colored and keep me here where every ignorant white man who walks the street can make me step off to let him pass. They think they can pretend I'm nothing and—presto!—I'll be nothing.

Minnie. You won't let them do that.

Frank. Let them? They've done it! We don't even have passage back to London. We're stuck here being niggers. Common, ordinary, niggers!

Minnie. It'll be all right. We don't have a lot of money, but we've got a place to live. Not forever, but just until we get on our feet. Just until the baby comes! We do have a place.

Frank. What are you talking about?

Minnie. We can stay here. On our own land. Right here. Until you have a chance to figure things out.

Frank. Do you really think I could live here?

Minnie. Sophie has plans. You'll see. It's going to be beautiful. A paradise for colored people.

Frank. A paradise for colored people . . .

Minnie. This is our land, Frank. Nobody can take it from us. You don't have to have your father's money. We have land!

Frank. You're right. We have land . . . *(a beat)* I'm sorry I snapped at you, darling. It's just that when I think about all the things I want to give you, it drives me crazy.

Minnie. I love you. That's all I need.

Frank. But you deserve so much more, Min. You're so beautiful. *(He kisses her. Touches her stomach gently.)* Did you explain to my son that his daddy has a bad temper sometimes?

Minnie. Please try, Frank. Just try . . .

Frank. *(his mood changes abruptly)* Don't you think I'm trying? I'm trying to be a good husband to you. And I want to be a good father. But you have to help me.

Minnie. I need to be able to trust you again.

Frank. You can, darling. You can trust me. I swear it. I know the last few months haven't been easy, but I'll make it up to you. Do you believe me?

Minnie. Yes, Frank . . .

Frank. It'll be just like it used to be. We'll find another place, just like the one we had before, right on the square. You liked that place, didn't you, darling?

Minnie. It was lovely, but it costs too much money to live that way. To live abroad . . .

Frank. Your share of this land is worth over $50,000. Do you know what we can do with that kind of money in London? We'll have the best of everything and so will our baby.

Minnie. Sophie would never sell this land to speculators. Not for a million dollars.

Frank. It wouldn't be all of it. Just your fair share. The town is full of people looking to buy some of this land before your sister gets that damn rule passed. This is the chance we've been waiting for. A chance for me to get back on my feet. To show my brothers I don't need their money.

Minnie. They're not your brothers. They don't even claim you!

Frank. They don't have to claim me. I look just like them!

Minnie. No, Frank. I can't ask Sister to split up this land.

Frank. I'm your husband. Don't you ever tell me no!

Minnie. Don't, Frank! *(moving quickly out of reach)* I don't care what you do to me, but I won't let you hurt our baby!

Frank. *(He grabs her arm and brings her up against him sharply.)* Don't you ever threaten me as long as you live, do you understand me? Do you? *(She nods silently.)* I'll kill you right now, Min. I'll break your damn neck before your precious sisters can hear you holler. I'll kill everybody in this house, don't you understand that? You want to know who I told those white men you were, Min? You really want to know? *(She struggles again, but he holds her.)* I told them you were a black whore I won in a card game. *(He laughs and presses his mouth to hers roughly.)*

(Black)

SCENE 3

Sunday afternoon.

Frank enters the main room, pulling on hat and gloves, clearly preparing to go out. Miss Leah and Fan enter the yard. Fan is helping Miss Leah.

Fan. I thought Sister's speech went well this morning, didn't you Miss Leah?

Miss Leah. Speechifyin' and carryin' on. She ought to run for president.

(They open the door as Frank arrives at it.)

Fan. Frank! You startled me.

Frank. I'm sorry. I didn't hear you coming.

Fan. Are you going out?

Frank. I won't be long. I have some business to attend to in town.

Miss Leah. On Sunday afternoon?

Fan. I'm sorry about the will. I want you to know you always have a place here with us.
Frank. Yes. Thank you. We'll figure out something.
Fan. Is Min going in with you?
Frank. No, she's resting. She'll be out in a few minutes. I won't be long.

(exits quickly)

Fan. I believe he is sorry about what happened, don't you?
Miss Leah. A man that hit a woman once will hit her again.

(Sophie enters and meets Frank in the yard.)

Frank. How was church?
Sophie. You should have been there. *(She crosses to the porch.)*
Frank. You're going to have to stop being so high and mighty. It doesn't become you.

(She turns to him from the porch steps.)

Sophie. I'm sorry for your troubles, because they're Min's troubles, too. But I think you should get on where you're going now and I'll go on inside.
Frank. Well, suit yourself, as you always say, but I think I've got some news you might find interesting. *(Reaches in his pocket; Sophie shifts the gun.)* Take it easy! I'm unarmed . . . as always! *(He pulls out the deed.)* I just thought you'd like to know that we're officially neighbors now. For the moment, anyway.
Sophie. What are you talking about?
Frank. My wife wants me to share in her good fortune, so she's added my name to her deed.
Sophie. I don't believe you.
Frank. I'd let you see it up close, but that probably isn't such a good idea. Hot-tempered woman like you . . .
Sophie. Get off my land. You make me sick.
Frank. I'll get off your land. I'll get so far off it the post office won't even be able to find me.
Sophie. That suits me fine.
Frank. Well, maybe you'll like your new neighbors better. Ask Min about them. She met them on the train. Well, she didn't really meet them. I didn't introduce her, of course, but she saw us talking. White gentlemen. She'll remember them. She wants to tell you, but she's a little nervous about it.
Sophie. Tell me what?
Frank. You can see why. You've raised her to think this place is practically

holy ground. She didn't even want to talk about selling it at first, but she came around.

Sophie. Minnie would never sell this land. You're lying.

Frank. Well, you let her tell you. I figured under the circumstances, I would spend the night in town. I'm sure I'll have our share sold before tomorrow. Hope the sale doesn't hurt your chances in the vote next week. *(laughs)* You know you're getting off easy when you think about it, Sister Sophie. I could stick around here and take over your precious town if I wanted to. You ever see a group of colored people who didn't put the lightest one in charge?

(As Frank and Sophie talk, we see Fan and Miss Leah making coffee, starting the evening meal, etc. In the rear bedroom, Min raises up slowly. She is obviously in great pain and has been badly beaten. She almost cannot stand. She staggers to the door and down the hall. As Frank exits laughing, Min stumbles into the room where Miss Leah and Fan are working.)

Miss Leah. Lord, chile!
Fan. Sister! Sister! Come quick!

(Sophie rushes into the house and runs to help.)

(Black)

SCENE 4

Sunday evening.
  Fan and Wil are sitting on the porch. Wil has a shotgun.

Wil. I don't understand how a colored man can hit a colored woman, Miss Fannie. We been through too much together.
Fan. Maybe there's just too many memories between us.
Wil. I don't think you can have too many memories. I know I wouldn't take nothin' for none of mine.
Fan. Not even the bad ones?
Wil. Nope. The bad ones always make the good ones just that much sweeter. *(a beat)* Does that paper really mean Frank can sell to speculators?
Fan. Well, if Baby Sister really signed it.
Wil. I never met a colored man like Frank before. Seem like he don't care 'bout colored people no different from white folks. Miss Leah says it's because mulattos got a war in them. And sometimes it makes 'em

stronger but sometimes it just makes 'em crazy. Makes 'em think they got a choice about if they gonna be colored or not.

Fan. Sister's a mulatto and she never seems to be confused.

Wil. Well, you're right there. *(a beat)* Miss Fannie, I want you to know . . . I can take care of it.

Fan. Take care of what?

Wil. I mean, he's a colored man and I'm a colored man. We can settle it that way. Man to man.

Fan. I couldn't ask you to hurt anybody.

Wil. You can ask me to kill somebody, Miss Fannie. If I can't protect you and your sisters from a Negro who has lost his mind, what kind of man does that make me?

Fan. Have you ever killed a man?

Wil. Not a colored man, but I guess they ain't that much different from any other kind of man when you get down to it.

(We see Miss Leah and Minnie in the back. Miss Leah is holding Min's hand and talking directly to her.)

Miss Leah. When they sold my first baby boy offa the place, I felt like I couldn't breathe for three days. After that, I could breathe a little better, but my breasts were so full of milk they'd soak the front of my dress. Overseer kept telling me he was gonna have to see if nigger milk was really chocolate like they said it was, so I had to stay away from him 'til my milk stopped runnin'. And one day I saw James and I told him they had sold the baby, but he already knew it. He had twenty sold offa our place by that time. Never saw any of 'em.

When he told me that, I decided he was gonna at least lay eyes on at least one of his babies came through me. So next time they put us together, I told him that I was gonna be sure this time he got to see his chile before Colonel Harrison sold it. But I couldn't. Not that one or the one after or the one after the ones after that. James never saw their faces. Until we got free and had our five free babies. Then he couldn't look at 'em long enough. That was a man who loved his children. Hug 'em and kiss 'em and take 'em everywhere he go.

I think when he saw the fever take all five of them, one by one like that . . . racin' each other to heaven . . . it just broke him down. He'd waited so long to have his sons and now he was losing them all again. He was like a crazy man just before he died. So I buried him next to his children and I closed the door on that little piece of house we had and I started walkin' west. If I'd had wings, I'd a set out flyin' west. I needed to be some place big enough for all my sons and all my ghost grandbabies to roam around. Big enough for me to think about all that sweetness they had stole from me and James and just holler about it as loud as I want to holler.

Minnie. I didn't want to sign it. I was just so scared. I didn't want him to hurt the baby. I can't make him stop . . . hitting me. I just . . . want him . . . to stop . . . hitting me.

Miss Leah. They broke the chain, Baby Sister. But we have to build it back. And build it back strong so the next time nobody can break it. Not from the outside and not from the inside. We can't let nobody take our babies. We've given up all the babies we can afford to lose. *(a beat)* Do you understand what I'm sayin' to you?

Minnie. *(whispers)* Yes, ma'am.

Miss Leah. *(kisses her)* Good. Go to sleep now. That baby needs a nap!

(Miss Leah goes out to Wil and Fan.)

Fan. Is she . . .

Miss Leah. She's sleeping. She held onto that baby, too. I told you she was stronger than you think.

Fan. Thank God!

Miss Leah. Where is Sister?

Wil. She wanted to be sure Frank was headed toward town and not back this way. She told me to bring you the things you wanted from the house for Miss Minnie.

(He hands her a small packet which she takes and opens carefully.)

Miss Leah. I hope she didn't forget anything.

Wil. She had it written down.

(Sophie enters on the move.)

Sophie. He's on his way in, but he's moving slow. Is everything there you need?

Miss Leah. It's here. It's here . . .

Sophie. Min?

Fan. Sleeping. She's going to be okay.

Sophie. *(taking charge)* All right, here's what we're going to do. Wil, I need you to ride out and catch up with Frank. Tell him Min sent you to tell him she loves him more than anything and . . . everything is going to be okay. Tell him she wants him to come here tomorrow afternoon because I'll be in town to try and stop the deal. Tell him she wants to go with him to the land office so they won't have any trouble no matter what I do.

Wil. What if he doesn't believe me? He might think it's a trick.

Sophie. Tell him colored men have to stick together. He'll believe you. Tell him . . . tell him . . . the message is from Fan. That she's on their side now. That should make him feel safe.

Fan. What are you going to do when he gets here?

Sophie. *(a beat)* You and Miss Leah go in the back with Min.

Fan. But what are you going to do?

Sophie. A colored man who will beat a colored woman doesn't deserve to live.

Fan. Just like that?

Sophie. No. Just when he tries to kill my sister and her baby before it's even born yet!

Fan. Stop it! That's just what I was afraid of!

Sophie. What you were afraid of? Me?

Fan. Of what you might do.

Sophie. What I might do? Why aren't you afraid of what he is already doing?

Fan. He's her husband, Sister!

Sophie. If he wasn't her husband would you care what I did to him for beating her half to death?

Fan. That's different.

Sophie. You know as well as I do there are no laws that protect a woman from her husband. Josh beat Belle for years and we all knew it. And because the sheriff didn't do anything, none of us did anything either. It wasn't a crime until he killed her! I'm not going to let that happen to Min. I'm going to watch him prance across this yard and then I'm going to step out on my front porch and blow his brains out.

Fan. And then we'll be savages just like he is!

Sophie. No! Then we'll be doing what free people always have to do if they're going to stay free.

Fan. *(a beat)* Isn't there any other way, Sister?

Sophie. This morning, while I was standing in that church painting a picture of the future of this town, he beat her and did God knows what else to her in this house. Where she's always been safe. We can't let him do that, Fan. All the dreams we have for Nicodemus, all the churches and schools and libraries we can build don't mean a thing if a colored woman isn't safe in her own house.

(Fan turns away.)

Wil. *(quickly)* You don't have to do this. I already told Miss Fannie. All you have to do is say the word.

Sophie. What are you talking about?

Wil. I can take care of it. You can wait here with your sisters and I'll take care of everything.

Sophie. I appreciate the offer, but the day I need somebody else to defend

my land and my family is the day that somebody's name will be on the deed. I need you to help me do what needs to be done. Not do it for me.
Wil. You can count on me.
Sophie. Good! Go on now. I don't want him to get too far ahead of you.
Wil. I'll catch him. *(exits)*
Miss Leah. I can't let you do this.
Sophie. I'm not asking you. This is something I have to do.
Miss Leah. And why is that? Because he hit your baby sister or because he wants to sell your land to some white folks?
Sophie. Aren't those reasons good enough for you?
Miss Leah. Where's the pie tin? *(She gets up and starts laying out utensils, ingredients, etc. to make a pie. This activity goes on throughout the following dialogue.)*
Sophie. What?
Miss Leah. The pie tin.
Fan. It's in the cupboard. What are you doing?
Miss Leah. We're going to make an apple pie.
Sophie. An apple pie?
Miss Leah. In case you forgot, this is still the state of Kansas, a part of the United States of America. Men beat their wives every day of the week, includin' Sunday, and white folks cheat colored folks every time they get a mind to.
Sophie. I know all that.
Miss Leah. Good. I remember when y'all first got here. Green as you could be. Even you, Sister Sophie, way back then. Your group was as raggedy as any we'd seen. All of y'all lookin' like somethin' the cat dragged in. And then here come Min, bouncin' off the back of your wagon, hair all over her head, big ol' eyes and just the sweetest lil' face I ever saw. Didn't even know enough to be scared. *(a beat)* Hand me the sugar.
Fan. Are you feeling all right?
Miss Leah. Am I feelin' all right? If I was you, I'd be worried about folks talkin' 'bout shootin' somebody. That's who I'd be worryin' about. It's a messy business, shootin' folks. It ain't like killin' a hog, you know. Sheriff has to come. White folks have to come. All that come with shootin' somebody.

But folks die all kinds of ways. Sometimes they be goin' along just as nice as you please and they heart just give out. Just like that. Don't nobody know why. Things just happen. *(a beat)* One day a little bit before I left the plantation, Colonel Harrison brought him a new cook. Ella. She was a big strong woman. She didn't make no trouble either. Just worked hard and kept to herself. Ella knew a lot about herbs.

What to put in to make it taste good. Colonel Harrison just love the way she cook. He used to let her roam all over the plantation pickin' wild herbs to put in her soups and stews. And she wouldn't tell nobody what she use. Said it was secrets from Africa. White folks didn't need to know. Colonel Harrison just laugh. He was eatin' good and didn't care 'bout where it come from no way.

But after awhile, that overseer started messin' around her. Tryin' to get Colonel Harrison to let him have his way with her, but Colonel Harrison said no and told him to stay from around her. She belonged in the kitchen. But that ol' overseer still wanted her and everybody knew next time he had a chance, he was gonna get her.

So one day, Colonel Harrison went to town. Gonna be gone all day. So that overseer put some poor colored man in charge of our misery and walked on up to the house like he was the master now cause Colonel Harrison gone off for the day. And when he walk up on the back porch, he had one thing on his mind, but Ella had been up early, too, and the first thing he saw before he even saw her was a fresh apple pie coolin' in the window. And it smelled so good, he almost forgot what he come for. And Ella opened the screen door and smile like he the person she wanna see most in this world and she ask him if he'd like a glass of cold milk and a piece of her hot apple pie. Of course he did! What man wouldn't? And he sat down there and she cut him a big ol' piece and she told him it was hot and to be careful not to burn hisself . . . And do you know what happened? Well, he didn't even get to finish that piece of pie Ella cut for him so pretty. Heart just stopped right in the middle of a great big bite. By the time the master got back, they had him laid out in the barn and Ella was long gone. *(a beat)* But she did do one last thing before she left.

Fannie. And what was that?
Miss Leah. She gave me her recipe for apple pie.

(Black)

SCENE 5

Monday morning.
Miss Leah is in the back sitting with Min who is lying down. Sophie and Wil are hiding outside. Fan is alone in the kitchen where she checks the time and then goes to the oven and takes out a perfect pie.

Frank enters the yard furtively. Fan sees him and watches him from the window. She takes off her apron and goes to the door. She opens it before he knocks. He steps back, startled.

Fan. Come in, Frank.

(Frank hesitates.)

Fan. Sister's gone to town and Miss Leah's in the back with Min. Please. Come in.
Frank. Parrish said you were going to come into the land office with me. Are you ready?
Fan. It's all right. Sister isn't angry anymore. She wants to make you an offer.
Frank. What kind of offer?
Fan. Please. Come inside so we can talk.
Frank. I don't want any trouble.
Fan. We're prepared to make you an offer for your land.
Frank. You can't afford what they're paying in town.
Fan. We're prepared to pay exactly what they're paying in town.
Frank. You don't have that kind of money. Minnie said so.
Fan. Sister and I didn't involve Min in all the details of our household finances. I'll go into town with you now and we can make all the arrangements. Do you have the deed?

(Frank shows it and puts it back in his pocket.)

Fan. Good!
Frank. That's fine by me. I don't care where the money comes from as long as it ends up in my pocket so I can get the hell out of this place! *(extends his hand)* Can we seal the deal, Fannie? Just the two of us?
Fan. Done.
Frank. You know, I'm sorry it had to go this far in the first place. I love Minnie . . . How is she?
Fan. She's asleep right now. Miss Leah's with her.
Frank. Good, good.
Fan. She wanted me to wake her up as soon as you got here, but I told her to get a few more minutes rest and I'd give you a piece of homemade apple pie to keep you busy in the meantime.
Frank. You're not angry with me? About Min, I mean. You know how aggravating she can be some time. She's such a child.
Fan. I understand. She has to understand that a wife's first allegiance is to her husband.
Frank. Well, you're a very understanding person and I appreciate that, but I would just as soon we get on our way. I don't think your sister would be too happy to come home and find me sitting at her table eating up all her . . .
Fan. *(holding out a piece to him)* . . . apple pie. My specialty. Sister won't

be home for hours yet. Besides, now that we know we'll be able to keep the land in the family, Sister's not one to hold a grudge.

Frank. I don't know about that. She didn't seem to mind swinging that shotgun in my direction.

Fan. We've got to put all that behind us now. For Min's sake and for the sake of your baby. I know Sister's prepared to let bygones be bygones. In fact, when she saw me rolling out the crust for this pie, she told me to make sure you got a piece of it.

Frank. She did? Well, it takes a better man than I am to refuse an invitation for a piece of your famous apple pie! *(He sits and begins to eat heartily.)* Delicious! Well, you tell Sophie she's not going to have to worry about Frank Charles hanging around getting in her hair. Not me! *(laughs, coughs a little)* Soon as we get everything signed and proper, good-by Niggerdemus! Hello London! They treat me like a human being over there. You wouldn't believe it. Half the people we know don't even know I'm colored. I told Min if she was just a couple of shades lighter, we could travel first class all over the world. Nobody would suspect a thing. *(laughs, coughs a little, loosens his tie)* Don't get me wrong. I don't outright pass. I just let people draw their own conclusions. *(coughs harder as Fan watches impassively)* Can you get me a glass of water, please? I feel a little . . . strange.

Fan. No, Frank. I can't do that.

Frank. Please! I . . . water . . . my throat's on fire! *(He suddenly realizes.)* What have you done? My God, help me! Please help me!

(She watches him as he tries to stand, but can't. He looks at her in a panic, then slumps over: dead. Fan shudders slightly: it's over. She composes herself, goes to the door and waves a signal to Sophie and Wil, who come immediately. Wil checks the body to be sure Frank is dead. He nods to Sophie and they begin gathering Frank's things to remove the body. Minnie and Miss Leah, hearing the activity, enter from the back. Minnie moves slowly from her injuries and from her reluctance to see the result of their collective action. They see that Frank is dead. Miss Leah watches Minnie who moves toward the body then stops, looking at Frank with a mixture of regret and relief. She approaches the body slowly, her anger and fear battling her bittersweet memories of the love she once felt for Frank. She reaches out and touches him tentatively, realizing the enormity of what they have done. She draws back, but reaches out again, almost involuntarily, to touch his arm, his hand, his shoulder. We see her move through a complex set of emotions, ending with her knowledge of the monster Frank had become. Her face now shows her resolve and even her body seems to gain strength. She steels herself and reaches into Frank's pocket to withdraw the deed. She clutches it in her hand then looks to Sophie, who stands watching her.

Minnie takes a step toward Sophie and extends the deed to her in anticipation of Sophie demanding the return of the deed. Instead, Sophie recloses Minnie's hand around the deed and gently pushes Minnie's hand with the deed back to her. Minnie, grateful and relieved, and finally safe, clutches the deed to her chest with both hands.

(Black)

SCENE 6

Seven months later; April, 1899.

Miss Leah is sleeping in her chair at the table. The cradle is on the table and one of her hands touches it protectively. Minnie enters from the back, dressed for the dance in town. She stops and looks at Miss Leah and her baby. She does not go to them, but looks for a minute and then around the room, slowly. She walks past the side board, touching it absently. She walks to the door and stands looking out at the full moon. She absently touches the broach at her throat. Her hair is braided with ribbons and she wears bright clothes. She looks calm and healthy. She feels Miss Leah's eyes on her and turns. They share a look. Both smile slowly.

Minnie. It's as bright as noon out there.
Miss Leah. That's a good luck moon. It's gonna be a good day tomorrow.
Minnie. Do you think so?
Miss Leah. It's gonna be a good day every day.
Minnie. How do I look?
Miss Leah. You look beautiful, Baby Sister.
Minnie. Is she sleeping? Look! Her eyes are wide open! Hello, darling!
Miss Leah. She's thinkin'.
Minnie. *(crooning to the baby)* What can my sweet baby be thinking, huh? What are you thinking about?
Miss Leah. Leave the chile in peace now! Everybody's got a right to their own thoughts.
Minnie. Do you think she's warm enough?
Miss Leah. You're gonna smother the child if you're not careful. It's spring! Time to let some air get to her.
Minnie. I know. I even took my shawl off while I was hanging clothes out today.
Miss Leah. You better stop that foolishness! This is still pneumonia weather!
Minnie. You just said winter was over, Miss Leah.
Miss Leah. Well, it'll be back before you know it.

(Fan and Sophie enter from the back. Fan is dressed up and Sophie has on a severe dark blue dress.)

Fan. How do we look? *(She twirls around happily.)*
Minnie. You look wonderful! Wil Parrish will be beside himself to have such a beautiful fiancée!
Sophie. If colored people paid as much attention to saving the race as they do to their dancing, we'd be free by now.
Fan. Oh, hush! It's been so peaceful around here since you pushed that vote on through and the speculators went home, it's time to do a little dancing!
Minnie. You're too plain, Sister.
Sophie. Too plain! This is my best dress!
Minnie. It needs . . . something. Here! *(She takes the broach from her own bodice, kisses it, and pins it on Sophie.)* It's Mama's! Don't lose it!
Sophie. I'll guard it with my life!

(Wil enters the yard. He carries flowers.)

Fan. Good evening, Wil.
Wil. And to you, Fannie. These are for you. Hello, Miss Leah. Everybody.
Miss Leah. Please get these women out of here. They are drivin' my granddaughter crazy with all their chatterin'!
Minnie. We're going! We're going! Are you sure she'll be okay? I can stay here with . . .
Miss Leah. I'm not so old I can't handle one little baby! Go on and leave us some peace.
Wil. Baker and his Mrs. passed me on their way!
Sophie. They didn't have that bad baby with them, did they?
Miss Leah. You know that girl don't go no place without carryin' that big head boy with 'em.
Fan. He's not that bad!
Sophie. Bad enough! *(fussing with the pin)* Go on! Go on! I'm coming.
All. Good night, etc.

(They exit.)

Sophie. Too plain! That girl will have me looking like a Christmas tree if I'm not careful.
Miss Leah. You look fine.
Sophie. Thank you.
Miss Leah. Now don't you go makin' any speeches tonight! This is a dance.
Sophie. I won't, Miss Leah. Not tonight.
Miss Leah. Go on, now!

Sophie. *(putting the gun beside Miss Leah's chair)* We won't be too late.

(Sophie exits to the yard. As Miss Leah talks, Sophie walks into the middle of the yard and looks up at the full moon. She extends her arms and slowly turns around to encompass her land, her freedom, the moon, her life and the life of her sisters. She is completely at peace.

Miss Leah reaches into the cradle and gently lifts the well wrapped baby out and looks into her face.)

Miss Leah. Yes, my granddaughter. We got plenty to talk about, me and you. I'm going to tell you about your Mama and her Mama and her gran'Mama before that one. All those strong colored women makin' a way for little ol' you. Yes, they did! Cause they knew you were comin'. And wadn't nobody gonna keep you from us. Not my granddaughter! Yes, yes, yes! All those fine colored women, makin' a place for you. And I'm gonna tell you all about 'em. Yes, I sure am. I surely am . . .

(As Miss Leah rocks the baby, crooning softly to her, Sophie continues to spin slowly in the moonlight as the lights fade to

(Black)

Selected Bibliography

A. Anthologies of Dramas by African Americans

Branch, William, ed. *Black Thunder.* New York: Penguin, 1992.
———. *Crosswinds.* Bloomington, Ind.: Indiana University Press, 1993.
Brasmer, William, and Dominick Consolo, eds. *Black Drama: An Anthology.* Columbus, Ohio: Charles E. Merrill, 1970.
Bullins, Ed, ed. *New Black Playwrights: An Anthology.* New York: Bantam, 1969.
———. *New Plays from the Black Theatre.* New York: Bantam, 1969.
———. *The New Lafayette Theatre Presents the Complete Plays and Aesthetic Comments by Six Black Playwrights.* Garden City, N.J.: Doubleday, 1974.
Couch, William, ed. *New Black Playwrights: An Anthology.* Baton Rouge, La.: Louisiana State University Press, 1968.
Hamalian, Leo, and James V. Hatch. *Roots of Black Drama.* Detroit: Wayne State University Press, 1989.
Hatch, James V., and Ted Shine, eds. *Black Theater USA: Forty-Five Plays by Black-Americans, 1847–1974.* New York: The Free Press, 1974.
Locke, Alain, and Montgomery Gregory, eds. *Plays of Negro Life: A Source-Book of Native American Drama.* New York: Harper, 1927.
Ostrow, Eileen J., ed. *Center Stage: An Anthology of 21 Contemporary Black American Plays.* Oakland, Calif.: Sea Urchin Press, 1981.
Patterson, Lindsay, ed. *Black Theater.* New York: New American Library, 1971.
Perkins, Kathy A. *Black Female Playwrights: An Anthology of Plays Before 1950.* Bloomington, Ind.: Indiana University Press, 1989.

Richardson, Willis, ed. *Plays and Pageants from the Life of the Negro.* Washington, D.C.: Associated Publishers, 1930.

Richardson, Willis, and May Miller, eds. *Negro History in Thirteen Plays.* Washington, D.C.: Associated Publishers, 1935.

Turner, Darwin T., ed. *Black Drama in America: An Anthology.* New York: Fawcett, 1971.

Wilkerson, Margaret B. *9 Plays by Black Women.* New York: Mentor/New American Library, 1986.

B. Selected List of Anthologies Including Plays by African Americans

Alhamisi, Ahmed, and Harun K. Wangara, eds. *Black Arts: An Anthology of Black Creations.* Detroit: Black Arts Publication, 1969.

Brown, Sterling A., Arthur Davis, and Ulysses Lee, eds. *The Negro Caravan.* New York: Dryden, 1941.

Davis, Arthur P., J. Saunders Redding, and Joyce Ann Joyce, eds. *The New Cavalcade: African American Writing from 1760 to the Present, Volume I.* Washington, D.C.: Howard University Press, 1991.

———. *The New Cavalcade: African American Writing from 1760 to the Present, Volume II.* Washington, D.C.: Howard University Press, 1992.

Hoffman, Ted, ed. *Famous American Plays of the 1970s.* New York: Dell, 1981.

Jones, LeRoi, and Larry Neal, eds. *Black Fire.* New York: Morrow, 1968.

Patterson, Lindsay, ed. *Anthology of the American Negro in the Theater.* International Library of Negro Life and History. Washington, D.C.: Associated Publishers, 1967.

Turner, Darwin T., ed. *Black American Literature: Combined Edition.* Columbus, Ohio: Charles E. Merrill, 1970.

Watkins, Sylvester C., ed. *Anthology of American Negro Literature.* New York: Random, 1944.

C. Published Collections and Separately Published Plays

Baldwin, James. *The Amen Corner.* New York: Dial, 1968.

———. *Blues for Mr. Charlie.* New York: Dell, 1964.

Baraka, Amiri (LeRoi Jones). *The Baptism* and *The Toilet.* New York: Grove, 1966.

———. *Dutchman* and *The Slave.* New York: Morrow, 1964.

———. *Four Black Revolutionary Plays.* Indianapolis, Ind.: Bobbs-Merrill, 1969.

———. "Home on the Range." *The Drama Review* XII (Summer 1968): 106–11.

———. *Jello.* Chicago: Third World Press, 1970.

———. *The Motion of History and Other Plays.* New York: Morrow, 1978.

———. *Selected Plays and Prose of Amiri Baraka/LeRoi Jones.* New York: Morrow, 1979.

Bass, George H. "Black Masque." *Callaloo* 8 no. 2 (Spring/Summer 1985). Charlottesville, Va.: University of Virginia Press.

———. "Games." *Breakout: In Search of New Theatrical Environments,* James Schevill, ed. Chicago: Swallow Press, 1973.
Brown, William Wells. *The Escape; or, A Leap for Freedom.* Boston: Wallcut, 1858.
Bullins, Ed. *A Black Quartet: Four New Black Plays.* New York: New American Library, 1970.
———. *The Duplex: A Black Love Fable.* New York: Morrow, 1970.
———. *Five Plays by Ed Bullins.* Indianapolis, Ind.: Bobbs-Merrill, 1969.
———. *Four Dynamite Plays.* New York: Morrow, 1972.
———. *How Do You Do: A Nonsense Drama.* Mill Valley, Calif.: Illuminations Press, 1965.
———. *The Theme Is Blackness: The Corner and Other Plays.* New York: Morrow, 1973.
Childress, Alice. *Let's Hear it for the Queen.* New York: Coward, McCann, & Geoghegan, 1976.
———. *Mojo and String: Two Plays.* New York: Dramatists Play Service, 1971.
———. *Wedding Band: A Love/Hate Story in Black and White.* New York: French, 1973.
———. *When the Rattlesnake Sounds.* New York: Coward, McCann & Geoghegan, 1975.
———. *Wine in the Wilderness: A Comedy-Drama.* New York: Dramatists Play Service, 1969.
Cleage, Pearl. "Late Bus to Mecca" and "Chain." *7 Plays from the Women's Project,* Julia Miles, ed. Portsmouth, N.H.: Heinemann Press, 1993.
———. "Hospice." *Callaloo* 10 no. 1 (Winter 1987). Charlottesville, Va.: University of Virginia Press.
Cotter, Joseph S. Caleb. *The Degenerate: A Study of the Types, Customs and Needs of the American Negro.* Louisville, Ky.: Bradley and Gilbert, 1903.
Davis, Ossie. *Purlie Victorious.* New York: French, 1961.
Edmonds, Randolph. *The Land of Cotton and Other Plays.* Washington, D.C.: Associated Publishers, 1942.
———. *Shades and Shadows.* Boston: Meador, 1930. (Reprinted, Ann Arbor, Mich.: University Microfilms, 1970.)
———. *Six Plays for a Negro Theater.* Boston: Baker, 1934. (Reprinted, Ann Arbor, Mich.: University Microfilms, 1970.)
Elder, Lonne. *Ceremonies in Dark Old Men.* New York: Farrar, Straus, and Giroux, 1969.
Franklin, J. e. *Black Girl.* Washington, D.C.: Howard University Press, 1977.
Fuller, Charles H. *A Soldier's Play.* New York: Hill and Wang, 1982.
———. *Zooman and the Sign.* New York: Samuel French, 1982.
Gordone, Charles. *No Place to Be Somebody.* Indianapolis, Ind.: Bobbs-Merrill, 1969.
Grimke, Angelina. *Rachel, a Play in Three Acts.* Boston: Cornhill, 1920.
Hansberry, Lorraine. *A Raisin in the Sun* and *The Sign in Sidney Brustein's Window.* New York: Signet, 1966.
Hughes, Langston. *Five Plays by Langston Hughes.* Webster Smalley, ed. Bloomington, Ind.: Indiana University Press, 1963.

———. *Scottsboro Limited: Four Poems and a Play in Verse.* New York: Golden Stair, 1932.
Huntley, Elizabeth M. *What Ye Sow.* New York: Court, 1955.
Madden, Will Anthony. *Two and One.* New York: Exposition, 1961.
Mitchell, Loften. *A Land Beyond the River.* Cody, Wyo.: Pioneer Drama Service, 1963.
Peterson, Louis. *Take a Giant Step.* New York: French, 1954.
Richardson, Willis. *The King's Dilemma and Other Plays for Children.* New York: Exposition, 1956.
Russell, Charlie L. *Five on the Black Hand Side.* New York: Samuel French, 1969.
Ward, Douglas Turner. *Happy Ending* and *Day of Absence.* New York: Dramatists Play Service, 1966.
White, Edgar. *Underground: Four Plays.* New York: Morrow, 1970.
Wilson, August. *August Wilson: Three Plays.* Pittsburgh, Penn.: Pittsburgh University Press, 1991.
———. *Fences.* New York: New American Library, 1987.
———. "The Janitor." *Short Pieces from the New Dramatists,* Stan Chervin, ed. New York: Broadway Play Publishing, 1985.
———. *Joe Turner's Come and Gone.* New York: New American Library, 1988.
———. *Ma Rainey's Black Bottom.* New York: New American Library, 1981.
———. *The Piano Lesson.* New York: Plume, 1990.
———. "Testimonies." *Antaeus* 66 (Spring 1991): 474–479.
———. "Two Trains Running." *Theater* 22 (Fall/Winter 1990–1991): 41–71.
Wright, Richard, and Paul Green. *Native Son, a Biography of a Young American.* New York: Harper and Brothers, 1961.

D. Books on the History and Criticism of African American Drama: A Selected List

Abramson, Doris E. *Negro Playwrights in the American Theatre, 1925–1959.* New York: Columbia University Press, 1969.
Andrews, E. W. D. "American Black Activist Drama of the 1960s." *DAI* 37, no. 3 (1977): 3187C.
Austin, Addell Patricia. "Pioneering Black Authored Dramas: 1924–27." *DAI* 47, no. 7 (1987): 2375A.
Bond, Frederick W. *The Negro and the Drama: The Direct and Indirect Contribution Which the American Negro Has Made to Drama and the Legitimate Stage.* Washington, D.C.: Associated Publishers, 1940.
Brown, Elizabeth. "Six Female Black Playwrights: Images of Blacks in Plays by Lorraine Hansberry, Alice Childress, Sonia Sanchez, Barbara Molette, Martie Charles and Ntozake Shange." *DAI* 41, no. 7 (1981): 3104A.
Brown-Guillory, Elizabeth. *Their Place on the Stage: Black Women Playwrights in America.* Westport, Conn.: Greenwood Press, 1988.
———. *Wines in the Wilderness: Plays by African American Women from the Harlem Renaissance to the Present.* New York: Praeger, 1990.

Brown, Sterling A. *Negro Poetry and Drama*. Washington, D.C.: Associates in Negro Folk Education, 1937.
Couch, William, Jr., ed. *New Black Playwrights*. Baton Rouge, La.: Louisiana State University Press, 1969.
Craig, E. Quita. *Black Drama of the Federal Theatre Era: Beyond the Formal Horizons*. Amherst: University of Massachusetts Press, 1980.
Davis, Ronald O. "A Rhetorical Study of Four Critically Acclaimed Black Dramatic Plays Produced on and off Broadway between 1969 and 1981." *DAI* 46, no. 9 (1986): 2486A.
Davis, Thadious M., and Trudier Harris, eds. *Afro-American Writers After 1955: Dramatists and Prose Writers. Dictionary of Literary Biography*. Detroit: Gale Research Company, 1985.
Dent, Thomas C., Richard Schechner, and Gilbert Moses, eds. *The Free Southern Theater by the Free Southern Theater: A Documentary of the South's Radical Black Theater, with Journals, Letters, Poetry, Essays and a Play Written by Those Who Built It*. Indianapolis, Ind.: Bobbs-Merrill, 1969.
Elam, Harry Justin, Jr. "Theater for Social Change: The Artistic and Social Vision in Revolutionary Theater in America, 1930–1970." *DAI* 45, no. 9 (1985): 2695A–2696A.
Evans, Mari. *Black Women Writers (1950–1980): A Critical Evaluation*. New York: Anchor Books, 1984.
Fabre, Genevieve. *Drumbeats, Masks, and Metaphor: Contemporary Afro-American Theatre*. Trans. Melvin Dixon. Cambridge, Mass.: Harvard University Press, 1983.
Flynn, Joyce, and Joyce Occomy Stricklin, eds. *Frye Street and Environs: The Collected Works of Marita Bonner*. Boston: Beacon Press, 1987.
Fox, Ted. *Showtime at the Apollo*. New York: Da Capo Press, 1993.
Harris, Trudier, and Thadious M. Davis, eds. *Afro-American Poets Since 1955: Dictionary of Literary Biography*. Detroit: Gale Research Company, 1985.
———, ed. *Afro-American Writers from the Harlem Renaissance to 1940: Dictionary of Literary Biography*. Detroit: Gale Research Company, 1987.
Haskins, James. *Black Theater in America*. New York: Crowell, 1982.
Hayes, Donald. "An Analysis of Dramatic Themes Used by Selected Black American Playwrights from 1950–1976 with a Backgrounder: The State of the Art of Contemporary Black Theater and Black Playwriting, Volumes I and II." *DAI* 45, no. 12 (1985): 3483A.
Hill, Errol, ed. *The Theater of Black Americans: A Collection of Critical Essays I: Roots and Rituals. The Search for Identity; The Image Makers: Plays and Playwrights*. Englewood Cliffs, N.J.: Prentice-Hall, 1980.
———, ed. *The Theater of Black Americans, II: The Presenters: Companies of Players; The Participators: Audiences and Critics*. Englewood Cliffs, N.J.: Prentice-Hall, 1980.
Hughes, Langston, and Milton Meltzer. *Black Magic: A Pictorial History of the Negro in American Entertainment*. New York: Prentice-Hall, 1967.
Hull, Gloria T. *Color, Sex, and Poetry: Three Women Writers of the Harlem Renaissance*. Bloomington, Ind.: Indiana University Press, 1987.

Issacs, Edith. *The Negro in American Theatre.* New York: Theatre Arts, 1947.
Johnson, James Weldon. *Black Manhattan.* New York: Knopf, 1930.
Kellner, Bruce. *The Harlem Renaissance: A Historical Dictionary for the Era.* Westport, Conn.: Greenwood Press, 1984.
Keyssar-Franke, Helene. "Strategies in Black Drama." *DAI* 35, no. 12 (1975): 7909A–7910A.
King, Woodie, Jr. *Black Theatre Present Condition.* New York: Publishing Center for Cultural Resources, 1981.
Marre, Diana Katherine. "Traditions and Departures: Lorraine Hansberry and Black Americans in Theatre." *DAI* 48, no. 9 (1988): 2196A.
Mitchell, Loften. *Black Drama: The Story of the American Negro in the Theater.* New York: Hawthorne, 1967.
Molette, Carlton W., and Barbara J. Molette. *Black Theatre: Premise and Presentation.* Bristol, Idaho: Wyndham Hall Press, 1986.
Norflett, Linda K. "The Theatre Career of Rosetta LeNoire." *DAI* 44, no. 9 (1984): 2626A–2627A.
O'Connor, John, and Lorraine Brown, eds. *Free, Adult, Uncensored: The Living History of the Federal Theatre Project.* Washington, D.C.: New Republic, 1978.
Ogunbiyi, Vemi. "New Black Playwrights in America (1960–1970): Essays in Theatrical Criticism." *DAI* 37, no. 3 (1976): 1299A.
Patterson, Lindsay, ed. *Anthology of the American Negro in the Theater.* International Library of Negro Life and History. Washington, D.C.: Associated Publishers, 1967.
Sanders, Leslie Catherine. *The Development of Black Theater in America: From Shadows to Selves.* Baton Rouge, La.: Louisiana State University Press, 1988.
Southgate, Robert L. *Black Plots and Black Characters: A Handbook for Afro-American Literature.* Syracuse, N.Y.: Gaylord, 1978.
Tate, Claudia, ed. *Black Women Writers at Work.* New York: Continuum, 1983.
Williams, Mance. *Black Theater in the 1960s and 1970s: A Historical-Critical Analysis of the Movement.* Westport, Conn.: Greenwood Press, 1985.
Young, Patricia Alzatia. "Female Pioneers in Afro-American Drama: Angelina Weld Grimke, Georgia Douglass Johnson, Alice Dunbar-Nelson, and Mary Powell Burrill." *DAI* 47, no. 8 (1987): 3043A.

E. Articles on the History and Criticism of African American Drama: A Selected List

Abramson, Doris E. "Angelina Weld Grimke, Mary P. Burrill, Georgia Douglass Johnson, and Marita O. Bonner. An Analysis of Their Plays." *Sage* 2, no. 1 (1985): 9–13.
———. "Negro Playwrights in America." *Colorado Quarterly* 12, no. 1 (1969): 11–17.
Adams, George R. "Black Militant Drama." *American Imago* 28 (1971): 107–28.
Ako, Edward O. "Leslie Pinckney Hill's *Toussaint L'Ouverture.*" *Phylon* 48, no. 3 (1987): 190–195.
"American Negro Novelists." *Studies in the Novel* 3, no. 2 (1971): 135–236.

Armstead-Johnson, Helen. "Themes and Values in Afro-American Librettos and Book Musicals, 1898–1930." *Musical Theatre in America*. Ed. Glenn Loney. Westport, Conn.: Greenwood Press, 1984: 133–142.

Austin, Addell. "The Present State of Black Theatre." *The Drama Review* 32, no. 3 (1988): 85–100.

Bailey, A. Peter. "A Look at the Contemporary Black Theatre Movement." *Black American Literature Forum* 17, no. 1 (1983): 19–21.

———, et al. "Annual Round-up: Black Theater in America." *Black World* 20, no. 4 (1971): 4–26, 45–96.

———, et al. "Annual Round-up: Black Theater in America." *Black World* 21, no. 4 (1972): 31–48.

———, et al. "Black Theater in America: A Report." *Negro Digest* 19, no. 4 (1970): 25–37, 42, 85, 98.

Baraka, Amiri. "Black Theater in the Sixties." *Belief vs. Theory in Black American Literary Criticism*. Eds. Joe Weixlmann and Chester J. Fontenot. Greenwood, Fl.: Penkevill, 1986: 225–237.

———. "The Descent of Charlie Fuller into Pulitzerland and the Need for Afro-American Institutions." *Black American Literature Forum* 17, no. 2 (1983): 51–54.

Bass, George Houston. "Theatre and the Afro-American Rite of Being." *Black American Literature Forum* 17, no. 2 (1983): 60–64.

Bass, Ramona, and George Bass. "The Afro-American Experience and the Making of New World Theatre: A Dialogue." *Black Scholar* 10, no. 10 (1979): 21–27.

Benston, Kimberly W. "The Aesthetic of Modern Black Drama: From *Mimesis* to *Methexis*." *The Theater of Black Americans: A Collection of Critical Essays*, I. Ed. Errol Hill. Englewood Cliffs, N.J.: Prentice-Hall, 1980: 61–78.

Boston, Taquiena, and Vera J. Katz. "Witnesses to a Possibility: The Black Theatre Movement in Washington, D.C., 1968–1976." *Black American Literature Forum* 17, no. 1 (1983): 22–26.

Brady, Owen E. "Theodore Ward's *Our Lan'*: From the Slavery of Melodrama to the Freedom of Tragedy." *Callaloo* 7, no. 2[21] (1984): 40–56.

Brooks, Mary E. "Reactionary Trends in Recent Black Drama." *Literature and Ideology* 10 (1971): 41–48.

Brown, Abena Joan. "Politics and/of Black Theatre." *Nummo* (1977): 28–36.

Brown, Lloyd W. "The Cultural Revolution in Black Theatre." *Negro American Literature Forum* 8, no. 1 (1974–75): 159–64.

Brown, Lorraine. "A Story Yet To Be Told: The Federal Theatre Research Project." *Black Scholar* 10, no. 10 (1979): 70–78.

———. "Federal Theatre: Melodrama, Social Protest, and Genius." *Quarterly Journal of the Library of Congress* 36 (1979): 19–37.

Brown-Guillory, Elizabeth. "Black Women Playwrights: Exorcising Myths." *Phylon* 48, no. 3 (1987): 229–239.

———. "Lorraine Hansberry: The Politics of the Politics Surrounding *The Drinking Gourd*." *Griot* 4, no. 1–2 (1985): 18–28.

Conroy, Neil, and James V. Hatch. "An Index of Proper Nouns for 'The Place of the Negro in the Evolution of the American Theatre, 1767 to 1940,' A

Dissertation by Fannin Saffore Belcher, Jr. (Yale University, 1945)." *Black American Literature Forum* 17, no. 1 (1983): 38–48.

Cornish, Roger N. "Black Alley: Theatre in Search of an Identity." *Minority Voices* 1, no. 2 (1977): 63–72.

Couch, William, Jr. "Notes on the Black Theatre." *The Journal of Regional Culture* 19, no. 3 (1985): 95–102.

Cruse, Harold. "The Creative and Performing Arts and the Struggle for Identity and Credibility." *Negotiating the Mainstream: A Survey of the Afro-American Experience*. Ed. Harry A. Johnson. Chicago: American Library Association, 1978: 47–102.

Curb, Rosemary K. "Going through Changes: Mother-Daughter Confrontations in Three Recent Plays by Young Black Women." *Kentucky Folklore Record* 25 (1979): 96–102.

Demastes, William W. "Charles Fuller and *A Soldier's Play*: Attacking Prejudice, Challenging Form." *Studies in American Drama, 1945–Present* 2 (1987): 43–56.

Dewberry, Jonathan. "The African Grove Theater and Company." *Black American Literature Forum* 16, no. 4 (1982): 128–131.

Dixon, Melvin. "Black Theater: The Aesthetics." *Negro Digest* 18, no. 9 (1969): 41–44.

Dodson, Owen. "Who Has Seen the Wind? Playwrights and Black Experience." *Black American Literature Forum* 11, no. 4 (1977): 108–116.

Edmonds, Randolph. "The Negro Little Theatre Movement." *The Negro History Bulletin* (January 1949): 84.

Elder, Arlene A. "Ed Bullins: Black Theatre as Ritual." *Connections: Essays on Black Literature*. Ed. Emmanuel S. Nelson. Canberra: Aboriginal Studies (1988): 101–109.

———. "Paul Carter Harrison and Amos Tutuola: The Vitality of the African Continuum." *World Literature Written in English* 28, no. 2 (1988): 171–178.

Fabre, Genevieve. "The Free Southern Theatre, 1963–1979." *Black American Literature Forum* 17, no. 2 (1983): 55–59.

———. "The New Black Theatre: Achievements and Problems." *Caliban* 15 (1978): 121–129.

Fletcher, Winona L. "A Slender Thread of Hope: The Kennedy Center Black Theatre Project." *Black American Literature Forum* 17, no. 2 (1983): 65–68.

———. "Consider the Possibilities: An Overview of Black Drama in the 1970's." *Essays on Contemporary American Drama*. Eds. Hedwig Bock and Albert Wertheim. Munich: Max Hueber Verlag W. Germany, 1961: 141–160.

Foreman, Ellen. "The Negro Ensemble Company: A Transcendent Vision." *The Theater of Black Americans, II: The Presenters: Companies of Players; The Participators: Audiences and Critics*. Ed. Errol Hill. Englewood Cliffs, N.J.: Prentice-Hall, 1980: 72–84.

Gaffney, Floyd. "Black Drama and Revolutionary Consciousness: What a Difference a Difference Makes." *Theatre Annual* 41 (1986): 1–19.

———. "Black Theatre in the University." *Black Scholar* 10, no. 10 (1979): 16–17.

Garnett, Bernard. "Black Drama Moves Upstage." *Black Times* 2, no. 3 (1972): 16–17.

Gill, Glenda. "Leonard de Paur and WPA Theatre." *Freedomways* 23 (1983): 240–242.
Gilliam, Ted. "Black Theatre in New Orleans, 1978–79: A Report." *Callaloo* 1, no. 4 (1978): 165–169.
Glover, Margaret E. "Two Notes on August Wilson: The Songs of a Marked Man." *Theater* 19, no. 3 (1988): 69–70.
Hansberry, Lorraine. "Original Prospectus for the John Brown Memorial Theatre of Harlem." *Black Scholar* 10, no. 10 (1979): 14–15.
Harrison, Paul C. "Black Theater and the African Continuum." *Black World* 21, no. 4 (1972): 42–48.
Haskins, Jim, and Hugh F. Butts. "America's Debt to the Language of Black Americans." *The Theater of Black Americans: A Collection of Critical Essays.* Ed. Errol Hill. New York: Applause, 1987: 79–88.
Hatch, James V., and Andrzej Ceynowa. "Black Theatre." *Black American Literature Forum* 16, no. 4 (1982): 127.
Hatch, James V. "Sittin' at the Banquet, Talkin' with Ourselves: An Open Letter to Theatre Scholars and Historians on the Status of Black Theatre Research and Publications." *Black American Literature Forum* 16, no. 4 (1982): 168–169.
———. "Some African Influences on the Afro-American Theater." *The Theater of Black Americans: A Collection of Critical Essays.* Ed. Errol Hill. Englewood Cliffs, N.J.: Prentice-Hall, 1980: 13–29.
Hay, Samuel A. "African-American Drama, 1950–1970." *Negro History Bulletin* 36 (1973): 5–8.
Hurd, Myles Raymond. "Bullins' *The Gentleman Caller*: Source and Satire." *Notes on Contemporary Literature* 14, no. 4 (1984): 11–12.
Johnson, Helen A. "Playwrights, Audiences and Critics: Black Theatre." *Negro Digest* 19, no. 4 (1970): 17–24.
Jones, Rhett. "Community and Commentators: Black Theatre and Its Critics." *Black American Literature Forum* 14, no. 2 (1980): 69–76.
———. "Finding the People's Ideology: Black Theatre at Brown University." *Black Scholar* 10, no. 10 (1979): 17–20.
King, Woodie, Jr. "The Dilemma of Black Theater." *Negro Digest* 19, no. 4 (1970): 10–15, 86–87.
———. "Educational Theatre and the Black Community." *Black World* 21, no. 4 (1972): 25–29.
Levin, Tobe, and Gwendolyn Flowers. "Black Feminism in *For Colored Girls Who Have Considered Suicide/When the Rainbow Is Enuf.*" *History and Tradition in Afro-American Culture.* Ed. Günter H. Lenz. Frankfurt: Campus, 1984: 181–193.
McKay, Nellie. "'What Were They Saying?' Black Women Playwrights of the Harlem Renaissance." *The Harlem Renaissance Re-Examined.* Ed. Victor A. Kramer. New York: AMS Pr., 1987: 129–146.
Miller, Jeanne-Marie A. "Black Women Playwrights from Grimké to Shange: Selected Synopses of Their Works." *All the Women Are White, All the Blacks Are Men, But Some of Us Are Brave: Black Women's Studies.* Eds. Gloria T. Hull, Patricia Bell Scott, and Barbara Smith. Old Westbury, NY: Feminist Press, 1982: 280–296.

———. "Images of Black Women in Plays by Black Playwrights." *CLA Journal* 20 (1977): 494–507.

———. "Successful Federal Theatre Dramas by Black Playwrights." *Black Scholar* 10, no. 10 (1979): 79–85.

Mitchell, Carolyn. "'A Laying on of Hands': Transcending the City in Ntozake Shange's *For Colored Girls Who Have Considered Suicide/When the Rainbow Is Enuf*." *Women Writers and the City: Essays in Feminist Literary Criticism.* Ed. Susan Merrill Squier. Knoxville: University of Tennessee Press, 1984: 230–248.

Molette, Barbara. "They Speak. Who Listens? Black Women Playwrights." *Black World* 25, no. 4 (1976): 28–34.

Molette, Carlton W., III. "Afro-American Ritual Drama." *Black World* 22, no. 4 (1973): 4–12.

———. "The First Afro-American Theatre." *Negro Digest* 19, no. 4 (1970): 4–9.

Murray, Timothy. "Screening the Camera's Eye: Black and White Confrontations of Technological Representation." *Modern Drama* 28, no. 1 (1985): 110–124.

Newson, Adele S. "'The Fiery Chariot': A One-Act Play by Zora Neale Hurston." *The Zora Neale Hurston Forum* 1, no. 1 (1986): 32–37.

Norflett, Linda K. "Rosetta LeNoire: The Lady and Her Theatre." *Black American Literature Forum* 17, no. 2 (1983): 69–72.

Norris, William S. "Additional Light on S. Morgan Smith." *Black American Literature Forum* 20, no. 1–2 (1986): 75–79.

O'Neal, John. "The Free Southern Theatre: Living in the Danger Zone." *Black Scholar* 10, no. 10 (1979): 11–13.

Pasquier, Marie-Claire. "Women in the Theatre of Men: What Price Freedom?" *Women in Culture and Politics: A Century of Change.* Eds. Judith Friedlander, Alice Kessler-Harris, Carroll Smith-Rosenberg, and Blanche Wiesen Cook. Bloomington: Indiana University Press, 1986: 194–206.

Peavy, Charles D. "Satire and Contemporary Black Drama." *Satire Newsletter* 7 (1969): 40–49.

Peterson, Bernard L. "Willis Richardson: A Pioneer Playwright." *The Theater of Black Americans: A Collection of Critical Essays.* Ed. Errol Hill. New York: Applause, 1987: 113–125.

Radford-Hill, Sheila. "The Role of Drama Criticism." *First World* 1, no. 3 (1977): 48–49.

Rahman, Aishah. "To Be Black, Female and a Playwright." *Freedomways* 19 (1979): 256–260.

Riach, William A. D. "Telling It Like It Is: An Examination of Black Theatre as Rhetoric." *Quarterly Journal of Speech* 56 (1970): 177–86.

Richards, Sandra L. "Conflicting Impulses in the Plays of Ntozake Shange." *Black American Literature Forum* 17, no. 2 (1983): 73–78.

Riley, Clayton. "The Death Horse Rides Our Harlems." *Black World* 20, no. 4 (1971): 37–38.

Robinson, Edward A. "The Pekin: The Genesis of American Black Theater." *Black American Literature Forum* 16, no. 4 (1982): 136–138.

Robinson, Vivian. "The First Ten Years of Audelco." *Black American Literature Forum* 17, no. 2 (1983): 79–81.

Sanders, Leslie. " 'Dialect Determinism': Ed Bullins' Critique of the Rhetoric of the Black Power Movement." *Belief vs. Theory in Black American Literary Criticism.* Eds. Joe Weixlmann and Chester J. Fontenot. Greenwood, Fl.: Penkevill, 1986: 161–175.
Scott, Freida L. "Black Drama and the Harlem Renaissance." *Theatre Journal* 37, no. 4 (1985): 426–439.
Scott, John S. "Teaching Black Drama." *Players* 47 (1972): 130–131.
Shange, Ntozake. "Unrecovered Losses: Black Theatre Traditions." *Black Scholar* 10, no. 10 (1979): 7–9.
Shaughnessy, Edward Philip. "Eugene O'Neill: The Development of Negro Portraiture." *MELUS* 11, no. 3 (1984): 87–91.
Sherr, Paul C. "Change Your Lock: A Negro Satirizes White America." *Phylon* 32 (1971): 281–289.
Smith, Edward G. "Black Theatre." *Ethnic Theatre in the United States.* Ed. Maxine Schwartz Seller. Westport: Greenwood, 1983: 37–66.
Taylor, Willene Pulliam. "The Reversal of the Tainted Blood Theme in the Works of Writers of the Black Revolutionary Theater." *Negro American Literature Forum* 10, no. 3 (1976): 88–92.
Thompson, Robert Farris. "An Aesthetic of the Cool: West African Dance." *The Theater of Black Americans: A Collection of Critical Essays,* I. Ed. Errol Hill. Englewood Cliffs, N.J.: Prentice-Hall, 1980: 99–111.
Walter, Ethel Pitts. "The American Black Theatre." *The Theater of Black Americans, II: The Presenters: Companies of Players; The Participators: Audiences and Critics.* Ed. Errol Hill. Englewood Cliffs, N.J.: Prentice-Hall, 1980: 49–62.
Washington, J. Charles. "*A Raisin in the Sun* Revisited." *Black American Literature Forum* 22, no. 1 (1988): 109–124.
Wilkerson, Margaret B. "Critics, Standards and Black Theatre." *The Theater of Black Americans: A Collection of Critical Essays,* I. Ed. Errol Hill. Englewood Cliffs, N.J.: Prentice-Hall, 1980: 318–326.
———. "The Sighted Eyes and Feeling Heart of Lorraine Hansberry." *Black American Literature Forum* 17, no. 1 (1983): 8–13.

F. Selected Bibliographies

A List of Negro Plays. Washington, D.C.: WPA Federal Theater Project, 1938.
Arata, Esther Spring. *More Black American Playwrights: A Bibliography.* Metuchen, N.J.: Scarecrow Press, 1970.
Ceynowa, Andrzej. "Black Theaters and Theater Organizations in America, 1961–1982: A Research List." *Black American Literature Forum* 17, no. 2 (1983): 84–93.
Fabre, Genevieve E. "A Check List of Original Plays, Pageants, Rituals, and Musicals by Afro-American Authors Performed in the United States from 1960 to 1973." *Black World* 23, no. 4 (1974): 81–97.
———. "Afro-American Theatre: A Bibliographical Survey." *American Quarterly* 30 (1978): 358–373.

Gray, John. *Black Theatre and Performance: A Pan-African Bibliography.* Westport, Conn.: Greenwood Press, 1990.

Hatch, James V., and Omanii Adullah. *Black Playwrights, 1823–1977: An Annotated Bibliography of Plays.* New York: R. R. Bowker Company, 1977.

Keyssay-Franke, Helene. "Afro-American Drama and its Criticism, 1960–1972: An Annotated Checklist with Appendices." *Bulletin of the New York Public Library* 78 (1975): 276–346.

Lawson, Hilda J. "The Negro in American Drama (Bibliography of Contemporary Negro Drama)," *Bulletin of Bibliography,* XVII (1940), 7–8, 27–30.

Peterson, Bernard L. *Contemporary Black American Playwrights and Their Plays: A Biographical Dictionary and Dramatic Index.* New York: Greenwood Press, 1990.

———. *Early Black American Playwrights and Dramatic Writers: A Biographical Directory and Catalog of Plays, Films, and Broadcasting Scripts.* New York: Greenwood Press, 1990.

Schatt, Stanley. "Contemporary Afro-American Drama: An Annotated Checklist of Primary and Secondary Sources, 1950–1972." *West Coast Review* 8, no. 2 (1973): 41–44.

Sumpter, Clyde G. "The Negro in Twentieth Century American Drama: A Bibliography." *Theatre Documentation* 3, no. 1–2 (1970–71): 3–27.

Turner, Darwin T. *Afro-American Writers.* Goldentree Bibliographies. New York: Appleton-Century-Crofts, 1970.

Willis, Richard A., and Hilda McElroy, comps. "Published Words of Black Playwrights in the United States, 1960–1970." *Black World* 21, no. 4 (1972): 92–98.

Woll, Allen, comp. *Dictionary of the Black Theatre: Broadway, Off-Broadway, and Selected Harlem Theatre.* Westport, Conn.: Greenwood Press, 1983.